EQUALITY

EQUALITY

SELECTED READINGS

Louis P. Pojman
Robert Westmoreland

Editors

New York   Oxford
Oxford University Press
1997

Oxford University Press

Oxford   New York
Athens   Auckland   Bangkok   Bogota   Bombay
Buenos Aires   Calcutta   Cape Town   Dar es Salaam
Delhi   Florence   Hong Kong   Istanbul   Karachi
Kuala Lumpur   Madras   Madrid   Melbourne
Mexico City   Nairobi   Paris   Singapore   Taipei
Tokyo   Toronto

and associated companies in
Berlin   Ibadan

Published by Oxford University Press, Inc.
198 Madison Avenue, New York, New York 10016

Oxford is a registered trademark of Oxford University Press

Library of Congress-in-Publication Data

Equality: selected readings/edited by Louis P. Pojman, Robert
Westmoreland.
p.   cm.
Includes bibliographical references and index.
ISBN 0-19-510249-5 (cloth : acid-free paper). —ISBN
0-19-510250-9 (acid-free paper)
1. Equality.   I. Pojman, Louis P.   II. Westmoreland, Robert.
HM146.E66   1996
305—dc20   95-20886
                                                             CIP

Printing (last digit): 1   3   5   7   9   8   6   4   2
Printed in the United States of America

Dedicated to our wives, Trudy and Joan

Preface

Although equality is a paramount concept in contemporary political philosophy, there has never been a comprehensive anthology on the subject. The last small anthologies were Roland Pennock and John Chapman's *Nomos IX: Equality* (1967) and Hugo Bedau's *Justice and Equality* (1971). These useful volumes were compiled before John Rawls's *Theory of Justice* and the debate over which is the most cogent version of egalitarianism that followed from Rawls' work.

In attempting to be comprehensive we have divided our work into five overlapping parts, including both classic (Part I) and contemporary discussions of equality (the rest of the work, but especially Part V). We have endeavored to examine the logic of the concept of equality, first with Aristotle's analysis and with three readings in Part II. In Part III we include six influential readings on equality that were written during the period from 1950 to the early 1970s. These articles involve the *external* debate between egalitarianism and inegalitarianism. Part IV includes four important readings on Equal Opportunity, a concept widely embraced by contemporary society, but typically not carefully explained. In Part V we take up the contemporary discussion that began with the publication of Rawls's *Theory of Justice* (1971), involving both the external debate over whether Equality is an important moral notion and the internal debate between egalitarians as to which version of egalitarian distributive justice is the most adequate. Although this is a philosophical work and not one in literature, we think that Kurt Vonnegut's satirical short story "Harrison Bergeron" is worthy of inclusion. It illustrates the fears many people have with extreme forms of egalitarianism and should provoke serious discussion of egalitarian policy.

We have sought to be fair to the various sides of the argument, but inevitably some ideas get more and some less attention than the reader may desire. The problem of selection is difficult. We have included most of the articles, plus a number that did not make it into the final cut, from a seminar in Political Philosophy on Equality at the University of Mississippi during the spring semester of 1995. Discussing the articles with the students in that course greatly enabled us to sort out the articles according to their cogency, accessibility and ability to stimulate discussion. Richard Arneson, Sterling Harwood and Larry Temkin provided good advice along the way. We hope that we have at least provided representations of the salient arguments in the current debate and that this work will stimulate more research and analysis of the competing theories. If that cause is advanced, we will be gratified.

Louis P. Pojman, United States Military Academy
Robert Westmoreland, University of Mississippi
June 28, 1995

Contents

Introduction: The Nature and Value of Equality, 1

PART I   CLASSICAL READINGS

1. Aristotle:
   Justice as Equality, 17
2. Thomas Hobbes:
   Equality in the State of Nature, 26
3. Jean-Jacques Rousseau:
   The Discourse On the Origins of Inequality, 36
4. David Hume:
   Justice and Equality, 46
5. Francois-Noel Babeuf and Sylvain Marechal:
   The Manifesto of Equality, 49

PART II   ON THE CONCEPT OF EQUALITY ITSELF

6. Felix E. Oppenheim:
   Egalitarianism as a Descriptive Concept, 55
7. Dennis McKerlie:
   Equality and Time, 65
8. Larry S. Temkin:
   Inequality, 75

PART III   GENERAL CONSIDERATIONS ON THE IDEAL OF EQUALITY

9. Bernard A. O. Williams:
   The Idea of Equality, 91
10. Robert Nozick:
    Justice Does Not Imply Equality, 102
11. J. R. Lucas:
    Against Equality, 104
12. Stanley I. Benn:
    Egalitarianism and the Equal Consideration of Interests, 112
13. Gregory Vlastos:
    Justice and Equality, 120

PART IV   EQUAL OPPORTUNITY

14. John H. Schaar:
    Equality of Opportunity, and Beyond, 137
15. James S. Fishkin:
    Liberty versus Equal Opportunity, 148
16 Peter Westen:
    The Concept of Equal Opportunity, 158
17. Robert Nozick:
    Life Is Not a Race, 167
18. William Galston:
    A Liberal Defense of Equality of Opportunity, 170

PART V   THE CONTEMPORARY DEBATE ON THE NATURE AND
            VALUE OF EQUALITY

19. John Rawls:
    Justice and Equality, 183
20. Wallace Matson: Justice:
    A Funeral Oration, 191
21. Kai Nielsen:
    Radical Welfare Egalitarianism, 204
22. R. M. Hare:
    Justice and Equality, 218
23. Richard J. Arneson:
    Equality and Equal Opportunity for Welfare, 229
24. Eric Rakowski:
    A Critique of Welfare Egalitarianism, 242
25. Thomas Nagel:
    Equality and Partiality, 250
26. Harry Frankfurt:
    Equality as a Moral Ideal, 261
27. Eric Rakowski:
    A Defense of Resource Equality, 274
28. Louis Pojman:
    On Equal Human Worth: A Critique of Contemporary Egalitarianism, 282
29. Michael Walzer:
    Complex Equality, 299

Appendix

30. Kurt Vonnegut, Jr.:
    Harrison Bergeron, 315

Bibliography, 319

Index, 323

Introduction: The Nature and Value of Equality

It is an empirical fact that human beings are unequal in almost every way. They are of different shapes, sizes, and sexes, different genetic endowments, and different abilities. From the earliest age, some children manifest gregariousness, others pugnacity, some pleasant dispositions, others dullness and apathy. Take any characteristic you like: whether it be health, longevity, strength, athletic prowess, sense of humor, ear for music, intelligence, social sensitivity, ability to deliberate or do abstract thinking, sense of responsibility, self-discipline or hormonal endowment (e.g., levels of testosterone and endorphins) and you will find vast differences between humans, ranging from very high amounts of these traits to very low amounts.

Yet it is one of the basic tenets of almost all contemporary moral and political theories that humans are essentially equal, of equal worth, and should have this ideal reflected in the economic, social, and political structures of society. "We hold these truths to be self-evident that all men are created equal and are endowed by their Creator with certain inalienable rights, and among these the rights of life, liberty and the pursuit of happiness," to quote Thomas Jefferson in the *Declaration of Independence*. As Will Kymlicka has recently said, "Every plausible political theory has the same ultimate value, which is equality. They are all 'egalitarian theories'. . . . Some theories, like Nazism deny that each person matters equally, but such theories do not merit serious consideration."[1] According to Ronald Dworkin we have reached an "abstract egalitarian plateau" on which all political discussion must now take place.[2] In the minds of many, equality has come to be identified with *justice*; inequality with *injustice*.[3] Why is this? And how can these opposing theses, empirical inequality and egalitarianism, be reconciled? And exactly what is "equality" in the first place?

The readings in this book address these questions.

Equality may have replaced liberty as the central topic of contemporary political discourse. Egalitarian theories abound. Almost every month a new book or article appears defending some version of the thesis that justice consists in treating people equally. Articles on civil rights, affirmative action, and human rights proceed from egalitarian assumptions. Welfare rights, civil rights, voting rights, and affirmative action policies; national health care proposals, legislation aimed at limiting inheritance, liberal immigration policies, and protests against capital punishment; the dismantling of apartheid in South Africa are typically based on egalitarian interpretations of justice. University letterheads typically announce that they are "an equal opportunity/affirmative action" institution. The notion of equality spills over onto other areas of life. In a recent issue of *Bicycling*, the lead article was entitled "Egalitarian Bicycling" and much of the motivation behind politically correct language is based on the principle that everyone should feel equally good about oneself. Such is the pervasiveness of the concept in contemporary society. People announce, "I am an egalitarian," in a manner and tone that once characterized testimonies to religious or national allegiances, to being a Catholic, a Presbyterian, an American, or an Englishman.

Yet when one inquires *what* exactly should be "equalized" and what are the arguments that ground various egalitarian claims, one may be bewildered by a plethora of competing conceptions and arguments. Among the competing items to be equalized are welfare, preference satisfaction, primary goods, economic resources, social status, political power, capacity for personal fulfillment, opportunity for welfare, and opportunity for scarce resources and social positions. One is sometimes tempted to apply Hume's conclusion on competing theologies to competing egalitarian arguments: when they attack their rivals, they seem completely successful, the result being a mutual self-destruction.[4]

The internal debate between egalitarians as to which version of egalitarianism is the correct one is in full bloom and the issue has not been decided. But there is an even more fundamental debate: the external debate between egalitarians and nonegalitarians, those who argue that equality has little or no moral significance. Despite Kymlicka's insistence to the contrary, there are two sides to this issue, both of which should be heard if we are to make progress in moral and political theory. In this volume we have included readings that engage both the internal and the external debate.

What is the idea of equality? Essentially it involves a triadic relationship. Except with abstract ideas, such as numbers, there is no such thing as pure equality, equality per se. Two objects are always different in some way or other—even two Ping-Pong balls are made up of different pieces of plastic and exist in different places. Two things A and B, if they are equal, are equal with respect to some specific property or properties. Two trees are of equal height, two baseball players have equal batting averages, two workers produce widgets at the same rate. So statements of equality always must answer the question: Equal What? When the concept has a normative dimension, the relationship is quadratic: If A and B are equal with respect to the normative (merit ascribing) property P, then A and B deserve equal amounts of desert D.

We can divide egalitarian theories into two types: *formal* and *substantive*. Formal equality states a formula or policy but includes no specific content. Substantive equality identifies a concrete criterion or metric by which distribution policies are to be assessed. An illustration of formal equality is Aristotle's notion of formal justice (see the first reading) that equals are to be treated equally and unequals unequally. "Injustice arises when equals are treated unequally and also when unequals are treated equally." If two things are equal in some respect, then if we treat one of them one way in virtue of that respect, the other must be treated in the same way. When applied to distributive justice, the formula of formal equality enjoins giving equals equal shares and unequals unequal shares, but it does not specify the criterion. The theory may be represented as an equality of ratios. Let A and B be two individuals, let X and Y be degrees of some value-producing property P, and let Q be some good. Then:

$$\frac{A \text{ has } X \text{ degree of } P}{B \text{ has } Y \text{ degree of } P} = \frac{A \text{ should have } X \text{ degree of } Q}{B \text{ should have } Y \text{ degree of } Q}$$

A's having P to degree X is to B's having P to degree Y as A's deserving Q to degree X is to B's deserving Q to degree Y. For example, if A has twice B's widget-making ability (P), A should receive twice the reward (Q) appropriate to degree Y.

This formal notion of equality doesn't tell us anything substantive. It doesn't tell us what to put in the place of P. It could be need, desire, work, resources, strength, good genes, intelligence, effort, contribution to society, human nature, sense of humor, or any number of things. And, of course, it also leaves Q unspecified. Almost anything can be made into a law and fit the requirements of formal equality. For example, a Connecticut law of 1650 reads: "If any man after legal conviction shall have or worship any other God but the Lord God, he shall be put to death."[5] From the Puritans' perspective, this law is perfectly egalitarian. Everyone has a right to the same true worship and will be judged by the same standard: worship of the Christian God. If a person fails to do his rightful duty, he thereby forfeits his right to life. Of course, the atheist, agnostic, Jew, Muslim, and other nonchristians will probably think this kind of equality not worth much, but it is still a type of equality.

No substantive conclusions seem to follow from purely formal equations, yet it seems that philosophers have sometimes missed this point and tried to derive substantive conclusions from purely formal ideas. Such has been the charge against those egalitarians who argue that equality involves "equal consideration of interests." For the formula itself does not tell us how to rank competing interests or whether the scope of interests should include animals and even plants. More fundamentally, it is not obvious that interest-satisfaction is the appropriate good to be distributed (Williams, Lucas, and Benn in the readings take opposing positions on these matters). The same charge has been brought against the thesis defended in Isaiah Berlin's essay in this volume that there is always a presumption in favor of treating people equally unless and until some relevant difference has been found. Unless we know what metric we are applying, this is an empty notion. Likewise, the idea of equality before the law may be said to be purely formal, because it merely tells us that we all (or those with the specified properties) should be judged by the same laws. It does not tell us what those laws are or ought to be.[6]

Formal equality is simply the principle of consistency. It applies to all serious discourse. If I call the color of the piece of paper on which I am writing "white," then, on pain of contradiction, I must call anything that is the same color "white." Aristotle, who discovered the formula, himself was an inegalitarian who thought the desert determining criterion was personal merit, so that people should be rewarded according to their differing merits. All rational prescriptions, including all rules, entail this principle: Act consistently. Do not act capriciously.

The other type of egalitarianism is *substantive* equality. As Aristotle put it: "Now justice is recognized universally as some sort of equality. Justice involves an assignment of things to persons. Equals are entitled to equal things. But here we are met by the important question: Equals and unequals *in what*? This a difficult problem."[7] This type of egalitarianism identifies some metric and argues that all relevant parties should receive equal amounts of the quality in question. As already noted, people are unequal in many ways. The first question we want to ask is: Which ways are morally indefensible? A second question is: Given that a type of inequality is morally indefensible, what, if anything, should the state do about it? Regarding the second question, socialists and liberals tend to be interventionists, calling for the state to redistribute resources where a moral case can be made for mitigating the effects of inequality. Conservatives and libertarians tend to limit the state's role here, leaving the matter to voluntary action. With regard to the first question, a few idealists, such as the French revolutionists, Gracchus Babeuf and Sylvan Marechal, have called for the abolition of virtually all distinctions between persons.

We declare that we can no longer suffer that the great majority of men shall labor and sweat to serve and pamper the extreme minority. . . . Let there be at length an end to this enormous scandal, which posterity will scarcely credit. Away for ever with the revolting distinctions of rich and poor, of great and little, of masters and servants, of *governors* and *governed*. Let there be no other differences between people than that of age or sex. Since all have the same needs and the same faculties, let them henceforth have the same education and the same diet. They are content with the same sun and the same air for all; why should not the same portion and the same quality of nourishment suffice for each of them?[8]

Their "Manifesto of Equality" (see reading 5) suggested even the elimination of the arts, since they hinder "that real equality" that they would promote. The arts, of course, would reveal the difference between a Rembrandt or Michelangelo and the rest of us. Sports and academic grades would have to be abolished for the same reason.

Though not going to Babeuf's extremes, John Rawls and Kai Nielsen (see readings 19 and 21) seem to think that our intelligence, temperament, and even our industriousness should be disregarded in matters of distribution, for they are outcomes of the natural lottery. Since we do not deserve our native endowments or our better family backgrounds, we do not deserve the results of what we do with these endowments.

However, most egalitarians acknowledge that some inequalities are morally permissible. Differences in ethnicity, interests, aptitudes, intelligence, and conceptions of the good may be innocent. Unlike Rawls and Nielsen most egalitarians (e.g., Dworkin, Rakowski, and Arneson in our readings) would save a place for desert. People are entitled to the fruits of their labor and should be punished for their bad acts. The question becomes on what basis one distinguishes the morally innocent from the immoral differences between people. Criteria for such distinctions have not been worked out as well as one would like, but generally they emerge from the comprehensive theory in question.

Let us then return to our earlier question: What sort of inequalities are morally wrong and should be corrected by a more equal distribution? Candidates for such qualities identified in our readings include primary goods, resources, economic benefits (wealth), power, prestige, class, welfare, satisfaction of desire, satisfaction of interest, need, and opportunity, among others. Some egalitarians emphasize great differences in wealth as the morally repugnant item. In most countries a small percentage of the population (the rich) own a disproportionate amount of the wealth, whereas a large percentage (the poor) own a small percentage of the wealth. Why should the poor suffer while the rich live in luxury? Other egalitarians emphasize political power as the item that should be equalized. Traditionally such egalitarians have fought for universal enfranchisement, extending the vote to women (1919) and in the South to blacks during the Civil Rights Movement of the 1960s. The egalitarian principle opposes the American electoral college system, which enables a minority to elect a president over the votes of the majority. The principle would seem to favor local autonomy, where each voice counts more, over centralization. Yet local autonomy in the United States is supported more by conservatives than liberals, the traditional standard-bearers of equality. Marxist and socialist egalitarians, among others, argue that the franchise is insufficient for political equality. One needs such auxiliary traits as wealth, education, and leisure to participate effectively in the political process. Marx and Engels saw that so long as a state existed, political equality was impossible, since the rulers would always control the direction and speed of power more than the individual worker-citizen. In post-capitalist society the worker owning the means of production in his or her local factory would have equal input with every other worker. Engels wrote:

> We are now rapidly approaching a stage in the development of production at which the existence of these classes has not only ceased to be necessary, but becomes a positive hindrance to production. They will fall as inevitably as they once arose. The State inevitably falls with them. The society which organizes production anew on the basis of free and equal association of the producers will put the whole State machinery where it will then belong—into the museum of antiquities, next to the spinning wheel and the bronze axe.[9]

The question is: How is complete political equality possible, so long as there is the division between ruler and ruled—even if the rule be benevolent, enlightened, and voluntarily accepted by the governed? Government by its very nature seems to entail hierarchical chains of command, coercion, and authority of the governors over the governed. Rousseau recognized this point and so argued that political groups should be confined to small numbers wherein everyone had an equal input. Few egalitarians (including in our readings Kai Nielsen, who is a Marxist) espouse the kind of anarchy required for political equality, so they would seem to opt for severely constrained political equality.

Still other egalitarians (see Nielsen, Hare, and Norman in our readings) have identified equal welfare (or equal opportunity for welfare; see Arneson in our readings) as the goal of egalitarians. Justice requires that social institutions be so arranged that everyone would be as deeply fulfilled or happy as possible. Parts III–V will address these matters.

One important question that has often been sloughed over by participants in the debate over equality is whether or not equality of whatever substance is an intrinsic or simply an instrumental good. Thomas Nagel expresses the notion of equality being an intrinsic value when he writes, "The defense of economic equality on the ground that it is needed to protect political, legal, and social equality [is not] a defense of equality per se—equality in the possession of benefits in general. Yet the latter is a further moral idea of great importance. Its validity would provide an independent reason to favor economic equality as a good in its own right."[10] Even more strongly,

Christopher Jencks, in his famous report on American education *Inequality*, writes, "Most educators and laymen evidently feel that an individual's genes are his, and that they entitle him to whatever advantage he can get from them. . . . for a thoroughgoing egalitarian, however, inequality that derives from biology ought to be as *repulsive* as inequality that derives from early socialization."[11] And Richard Watson argues that equality of resources is such a transcendent value, at least for many purposes, that if equal distribution of food were to result in no one getting enough to eat, we should nevertheless choose this annihilation of the human race rather than an unequal distribution.[12]

Watson's prescription illustrates the problem of treating equality as an intrinsic value, especially as an overriding one, for there are three ways in which we can achieve equality between people. We can bring the worst off and everyone in between up to the level of the best off. We can bring the best off and everyone in between down to the level of the worst off. And we can bring the worse off up and the better off down so that they meet somewhere in between. No doubt egalitarians would like to raise everyone up to the highest level, but with regard to many qualities this seems impossible. Given the present technology there is no way we can raise imbeciles to the level of Einsteins or valetudinarians to the level of optimal health or the blind to the ability level of the sighted, so that the "thoroughgoing egalitarian," if equality is a transcendent value, as Jencks would have it, would have to dumb down the brilliant, infuse the healthy with disease, and blind the sighted. For an instructive thought experiment on this point, we have included Kurt Vonnegut's short story "Harrison Bergeron" at the end of the text. Few egalitarians want to go this far. Equality may be an intrinsic good, but it is not the only good. Others, both egalitarians and inegalitarians, view equality as an instrumental good, relevant to achieving high welfare or justice. But the question remains: What is the basis of the intuition that equality is intrinsically a good thing? Is it a natural intuition constitutive of the human condition, so that those who lack it are fundamentally deficient? Is it product of a religious system which holds that all humans are made in the image of God with infinite value? Is it an aesthetic principle—similar to a sense of symmetry or unity? If for a secularist it is bad that humans are unequal in ability, why is it not bad that humans and apes or dogs or mice are of unequal ability?

There is no doubt but that the ideal of equality has inspired millions to protest undemocratic forms of government, monarchies, oligarchies, despotisms, and even republicanism. The sense that each individual is of equal worth has been the basis for rights claims from the English Civil War (1642–1648) to the Civil Rights Movement in the United States and South Africa. Who is not moved by the appeal of Major William Rainborough, of Cromwell's Parliamentary Army, petitioning for political equality: "I think that the poorest he that is in England hath a life to live, as the greatest he; and therefore truly, sir, I think it's clear, that every man that is to live under a government ought first by his own consent to put himself under that government; and I do think that the poorest man in England is not at all bound in a strict sense to that government that he hath not had a voice to put himself under."[13] But the ideal of equality has dangers, too. The French aristocrat, Alexis de Tocqueville, during his visit to the United States in the 1830s, was amazed at the passion and preoccupation of Americans for equality. He saw in it both the promise of the future and a great danger.

> There is indeed a manly and legitimate passion for equality which rouses in all men a desire to be strong and respected. This passion tends to elevate the little man to the rank of the great. But the human heart also nourishes a debased taste for equality, which leads the weak to want to drag the strong down to their level and which induces men to prefer equality in servitude to inequality in freedom.[14]

R. M. Hare argues that we ought to promote equality of condition in order to stave off envy at great differences between people, but long before Hare, Tocqueville warned that equality actually promoted envy.

One must not blind himself to the fact that *democratic institutions develop to a very high degree the sentiment of envy* in the human heart. This is not because they provide the means for everybody to rise to the level of everybody else but because these means are constantly proving inadequate in the hands of those using them. Democratic institutions awaken and flatter the passion for equality without ever being able to satisfy it entirely. This complete equality is always slipping through the people's fingers at the moment when they believe it attained. The people grow heated in search of this blessing, all the more precious because it is near enough to be seen but too far off to be tasted. They are excited by the chance and irritated by the uncertainty of success: the excitement is followed by weariness and then by bitterness. In that state anything which in any way transcends the people seems an obstacle to their desires, and they are tired by the sight of any superiority, however legitimate. . . . When inequality is the general rule in society, the greatest inequalities attract no attention. *When everything is more or less level, the slightest variation is noticed. Hence the more equal men are, the more insatiable will be their longing for equality.*[15]

Perhaps it is the multifacetedness of the ideal of equality that causes so much perplexity. On the one hand, it seems to be the means of many morally desirable goods (not to deny that it may be an intrinsic good in its own right). On the other hand, it seems to compete with other values such as liberty, efficiency, fraternity, and merit. Making progress toward sorting these values out is one of the primary goals of this anthology.

This anthology is divided into unequal parts. Part I consists of four classical texts—Aristotle's notion of formal equality; Hobbes' idea of practical human equality; Hume's idea of justice as a utilitarian convention and equal distribution as impractical; Rousseau's idea of the origins of inequality as humans renounced their primitive ways of life and claimed property rights—and the Babeuf/Marechal "Manifesto of Equality." Other classical texts could have been utilized, also, but space constraints demanded difficult choices. Because these readings have been taken from larger works and have historical contexts, we have prefaced them with brief introductions.

Part II addresses problems with defining or dealing with the concept of equality and its complement, inequality. Unless we have a clear notion of what we are discussing, we are not likely to produce a clear assessment of the significance of the notion. *Equality* is a word used to stand for many different ideas, and people call themselves egalitarians even though their notion of equality is limited to formal equality or the principle of consistency. Noting that *equality* is often used rhetorically without any clear denotative meaning, Felix Oppenheim seeks to provide adequate descriptive criteria of equality. He first distinguishes three types of equality: that pertaining to personal characteristics, to treatment, and to distribution. It is equality of distribution that mainly concerns him. After providing critical analyses of eight prominent theories of distributive equality, he offers his own proposal, *percentage equality*, having to do with whether the distribution increases or decreases the percentage difference between the holdings of the parties in question. Dennis McKerlie discusses the problems related to assessing equal distribution of welfare as it relates to temporal states—in parts and wholes—of people's lives. Should egalitarians aim at equal averages or totalities of happiness over a life-time? Should they seek to equalize the goods in question over people's complete lifetimes or should they seek to ensure that the various segments of individual lives are as equally well-off as possible (so we design social policies that emphasize well-being in youth and minimize it in old age)? McKerlie's article is especially important for its treatment of the relationship of equality to personal identity. Larry Temkin argues that understanding the idea of "inequality" is fundamental for grasping the idea of equality. He examines the idea of "when is one situation *worse* than another with respect to inequality" and shows that depending on which procedural principle one adopts, contradictory answers are forthcoming. Inequality, it turns out, is a complex and multifaceted concept. Temkin's conclusion is that "Few moral ideals have been more widely discussed, yet less well understood, than the notion of inequality."

Part III is a general survey of the meaning of the ideal of equality. These readings, from the 1960s, set the stage for those written later, which are included in Part V. Assuming we have an adequate idea of what equality is, does it cohere with our other values? Can it be morally justified? What is its value? Bernard Williams, in his seminal paper "The Idea of Equality" (1962), concedes that much of our discussion of equality is vague and rhetorical, but shows that there are important moral concerns implicit in the notion. It serves to remind us of our common humanity. We all suffer and feel affection for close relations. We have common needs. This common core of humanity is just enough to advance a principle that we should treat people as equals unless we have a relevant reason for treating them differently. Williams examines three candidates for equal treatment—those based on need, merit, and equal opportunity—concluding that the ideal of our common humanity can provide guidance in these matters, but that these candidates conflict with each other, leaving the issue problematic but not hopeless. Robert Nozick, in a selection from *Anarchy, State and Utopia*, "Justice Does Not Imply Equality," argues that Williams fails to establish his thesis that it is irrational to satisfy A but to fail to satisfy B with the same need. Nozick, a libertarian, holds that one must not simply examine the needs for goods people have but where the allocations come from. He goes on to illustrate his thesis that freedom is prior to and in conflict with equal distributions. In his essay "Against Equality" (1965) J. R. Lucas, while admitting that formal equality, equal respect for humans, and equality before the law are important ideals, says they fail to support the essential egalitarian goals of equal distribution of goods such as power, prestige, and wealth. The value of Equality has had exaggerated importance in liberal thought. It is not a vacuous value but must be constrained by other more important values such as merit, fraternity, and liberty. Stanley Benn, in "Egalitarianism and the Equal Consideration of Interests" (1967), attempts to meet Lucas's challenge by showing that Lucas's principle of equal respect results in equal consideration of interests, which in turn can provide a basis for a substantive egalitarian policy. Finally, the late distinguished Plato scholar Gregory Vlastos, in "Justice and Equality" (1962), takes Aristotle's statement that "justice is equality, as all men believe it to be, quite apart from any argument," and argues that the two ideas are related in a way Aristotle never intended. Examining various candidates for distributive justice, need, worth, merit, work, and agreement, Vlastos argues that merit and agreement are inadequate principles and that equal human worth is the basis for just distributions and that it leads to an emphasis on allocation according to need. The worth of all persons is equal, however unequal may be their merit. This is because worth is of "infinite value," and human merit is of finite value, so the intrinsic worth always overrides merit.

Part IV deals with the principle of equal opportunity. There are at least two different notions of equal opportunity: (1) Weak Equal Opportunity (sometimes called "formal equal opportunity"), which holds that offices should be open to talent. This was classically set forth in post-revolutionary France by Napoleon Bonaparte, who chose officers not by social class but by ability, announcing that "carriers must be open to talent." It is meritocratic equal opportunity, but does not address the advantages people have due to natural or family resources. It leaves the matter of initial starting points untouched. (2) Strong Equal Opportunity (sometimes called "substantive equal opportunity"), which holds that individuals ought to have equal life chances to fulfill themselves or reach the same heights. It calls for compensation for those who have had less fortune early in life to bring them to the level of those who had advantages. This kind of equal opportunity would support affirmative action programs and other compensatory policies. At the extreme end, as advocated by Onora O'Neill, this sort of equal opportunity would have to result in groups succeeding in obtaining coveted positions in proportion to their representation in the population.[16] Equal opportunity would be equivalent to equal outcomes. Perhaps we should call this "Super Strong Equal Opportunity." We have already noted the initial discussions of equal opportunity in the selections from Williams and Lucas, which you may want to review.

In a seminal article, "Equality of Opportunity and Beyond," John Schaar notes that the ideal of equal opportunity is the most popular of all the various conceptions of equality. "The formula has few enemies—politicians, businessmen, social theorists, and freedom marchers all approve it—and it is rarely subjected to intellectual challenge." With so much popularity by the status quo, we should suspect something is wrong, and Schaar argues that there is. Equality of opportunity is not egalitarian at all, but a deeply cruel conservative "debasement of a genuinely democratic understanding of equality." It actually militates against the ideals of equal worth because it promotes meritocratic hierarchies wherein a person is valued not for his or her humanity but according to how well he or she competes on the social playing field. Thoroughgoing equal opportunity would actually end up increasing inequalities between people.

> In previous ages, when opportunities were restricted to those of the right birth and station, it is highly probable, given the fact that nature seems to delight in distributing many traits in the pattern of a normal distribution, and given the phenomenon of regression toward the mean, that many of those who enjoyed abundant opportunities to develop their talents actually lacked the native ability to benefit from their advantages. . . . Under the regime of equal opportunity, however, only those who genuinely are superior in the desired attributes will enjoy rich opportunities to develop their qualities. This would produce, within a few generations, a social system where the members of the elites really were immensely superior in ability and attainment to the masses.

Yet Schaar concedes that the ideal is not wholly pernicious: it does have a place when speaking of equality before the law and the fullest participation of individuals in the political life.

James Fishkin, in "Liberty versus Equal Opportunity," points out a *trilemma* between strong equal opportunity (equal life chances), family values, and meritocracy. We can combine any two of these, but not all three, into viable social policy. We can have equal life chances and the family if we give up a commitment to excellence. We can preserve equal life chances and meritocracy if we give up our notion of the family and raise children in a Platonic commune or something that will ensure an equal starting point for all. And we can preserve the family and merit if we give up the principle of equal life chances. The problem is not that we are not committed to significant moral values, but that these values compete with one another. We have one value too many.

Peter Westen offers a systematic analysis of the concept "equal opportunity" and argues that the idea of equal opportunity is a complex notion, fraught with problems. Despite its rhetorical appeal, it is not a wholly positive concept because it involves removing obstacles from one group, which in turn may impose obstacles on others. For example, to remove the obstacle of gender regarding admittance to a previously all-male military academy, places a new obstacle on males competing for admittance (some who would have otherwise been admitted will now be excluded). Or a policy to give all children an equal opportunity to have the same type of education places an obstacle before those who would offer their children a special education. The issue is not simply one of advancing equal opportunity, but which particular opportunities.

Next, Robert Nozick argues that the notion of equal opportunity, especially of the "strong" variety, is founded on the metaphor that life is a race in which everyone should start at the same place. That metaphor is inappropriate, he thinks, because life is not a race. Finally, William Galston sets forth what he considers a liberal defense of equal opportunity, which, along the way, responds to the criticisms of Schaar, Fishkin, and Nozick.

Part V represents the contemporary debate on egalitarianism beginning with John Rawls's *Theory of Justice* (1971). No twentieth-century work in moral and political philosophy has had greater influence on our generation than this comprehensive treatment of justice and equality.

In *A Theory of Justice*, from which reading 19 is taken, Rawls sets forth a hypothetical contract theory in which the bargainers go behind a *veil of ignorance* in order to devise a set of fundamental agreements that will govern society. Behind the metaphorical veil no one knows his place in society, class, gender, race, religion, social status, fortune in the distribution of natural assets and abilities, or even intelligence. Parties to the contract are to act as rationally self-interested agents, and choose the basic principles that will govern their society. Rawls thinks that these conditions ensure objectivity and impartiality of judgment. He calls his system "Justice As Fairness" because he seeks a contract on whose fairness all parties will agree. In effect, the parties to the contract should choose the kind of principles they could live with if their enemies were assigning them positions in society. Rawls argues that they would choose the following two principles:

1. Everyone will have an equal right to the most extensive basic liberties compatible with similar liberty for others.
2. Social and economic inequalities must satisfy two conditions:
    (a) They are to the greatest benefit of the least advantaged ("the difference principle").
    (b) They are attached to positions open to all under conditions of fair equality of opportunity.

There are several ways in which Rawls's theory claims to be egalitarian (not including his idea of equal opportunity). First, the difference principle tends toward equalizing holdings. Second, the idea of participating in the original position presupposes that the parties have political equality, as equal participants in the process of choosing the principles by which they would be governed. Third, Rawls holds that all desert must be institutionally defined, depending on the goals of the society. No one deserves his or her talents or family structure—even the ability to make an effort is a product of the natural lottery and so is undeserved. He rejects meritocracy wherein justice consists in giving people what they deserve. Instead of the classic notion that justice gives us what we deserve, for Rawls desert consists of getting what justice demands—with justice consisting of the *equal* distribution of "all social primary goods—liberty and opportunity, income and wealth, and the bases of self-respect." Finally, Rawls holds to a natural basis for equal human worth based on minimal capacity to have a conception of the good and give justice. As Rawls puts it, those who can give justice are owed justice. Most of the articles in this section take as their point of departure—at least to some extent—Rawls's theories.

Wallace Matson, in "Justice: A Funeral Oration," offers a Lockean thought experiment of individuals on separate islands who eventually encounter each other, establish a social contract, and interpret justice as abiding by the rules of the contract, so that each person receives his due. He calls this construction "bottom-up justice" and contrasts it with liberal theories, such as Rawls's, wherein justice is a "top-down" construction, with the state as the dispenser of equal goods to each party. Such an interpretation of "justice as equality" has nothing to do with justice as it arises in natural relationships. It is, in fact, the death of justice, for justice has to do with giving people what they deserve, not the state superimposing egalitarian structures. Matson illustrates this coercive paternalism with the institution of affirmative action.

Contemporary egalitarians divide on whether it is *resources* or *welfare* that is the good to be equally distributed. Resource egalitarians such as Rawls, Ronald Dworkin, and Eric Rakowski hold that in societies of abundance, such as ours, human beings are entitled to equally valuable shares of the resources (the wealth and other primary goods). Welfare egalitarians such as Kai Nielsen and R. M. Hare, go further and maintain that in such societies people should receive equal welfare—interpreted in terms of fulfillment or preference satisfaction. A typical expression of welfare egalitarianism is that of Kai Nielsen:

> Morality requires that we attempt to distribute happiness as evenly as possible. We must be fair: each person is to count for one and none is to count for more than one. Whether we like a person or not, whether he is useful to his society or not, his interests, and what will make him happy, must also be considered in any final decision as to what ought to be done. The requirements of justice make it necessary that each person be given equal consideration.[17]

Criticisms of resource egalitarianism have focused on two central problems: (1) the problem of differential needs and (2) the problem of "slavery of the talented." The first criticism goes like this. According to Rawls and others we are to aim at an equal division of resources, but some people have need for much greater resources than others. Tiny Tim, who needs a wheelchair, may have to spend a large measure of his allotment just to live a minimally good life, whereas the average person will be able to use the same size allotment to satisfy nonbasic needs. This does not seem fair, so we should give additional resources to Tiny Tim in order to bring him up to the same welfare level as the average person. The second criticism, the "slavery of the talented" problem, is this: if we are to have equal shares in all the resources of society, then, since talents are among those resources, we should be able to command the uses of the talents of the gifted. But then persons of great talent will be disadvantaged, for others will want to make use of their talents. They will have to bid away great sums of their other resources to preserve the use of these talents, whereas the lesser talents (upon whom no such great demands are made) will be free to use their resources for their own welfare. But this seems unfair, so resource egalitarianism is implausible. Naturally, the resource egalitarian has responses to these objections. They are found in the writings of Dworkin and Rakowski in our readings.

But welfare egalitarianism has problems also, among which are the following: (1) the problem of external preferences. Happiness depends on many things. Some of them may be external preferences, desires concerning the welfare of others, individuals or groups, than oneself. The racist's happiness may partly consist of the desire that his race flourish at the expense of other races, and the sexist may desire that people of her gender flourish at the expense of the other gender. The racist and sexist would have these preferences even if they knew that they would not profit from them personally, perhaps even if these outcomes would cost them their lives. But all this seems grossly unfair. Why should we grant the racist or sexist's preferences any weight at all—even if this results in lower preference satisfaction?

An application of this problem is that of *double counting*, where one person's preference gets counted twice and so outweighs another person's preference. For example, suppose Sam and Mary both desire to get a prestigious job. However, John, Mary's friend, prefers that she get the job. So Mary's preference gets counted twice and thus gets two units of welfare-preference to Sam's one unit. This seems unfair to Sam.

(2) The second problem of welfare egalitarianism is that of *expensive tastes*. Suppose I have a taste for designer clothes, luxury cars, gourmet food, mansions, and expensive jewelry—and let us suppose these are deeply fixed in my subconscious so that I cannot rid myself of them without significant withdrawal symptoms. Welfarism would enjoin us to take from the modest resources of the contented person and redistribute them to those with expensive tastes. This seems counterintuitive. Similarly, to take an example of Thomas Scanlon, just because someone "would be willing to forego a decent diet in order to build a monument to his god" does not put a strong claim on others to aid in his project[18]—even if it is the only way to bring his welfare quotient up to normal. Of course, welfare egalitarians have responses to these counterexamples.

In addition, both resource and welfare egalitarianism seem to have a problem of down-scaling. Suppose that a necessary condition for making everyone roughly equal is for us to make the supremely happy or talented (i.e., resourceful) less so. To make the blind equal in resources with those now sighted, would we have to reduce everyone to blindness or transplant one eye from the sighted? Again this seems abhorrent, and most egalitarians refuse to carry their egalitarianism that far, asserting that there are other values besides equality. Nevertheless, the problem of down-scaling seems to impose restrictions on egalitarian strategies.

With these problems identified let us continue our description of the readings.

Kai Nielsen, adopting a Marxist stance, which goes beyond Rawls's stance in prioritizing equality, holds that equality is both a fundamental (intrinsic) human good and a universal right. Legal, political, and social equality, which egalitarians—and many inegalitarians—advocate, depend on economic equality. Nielsen's goal, however, is not just equal wealth, but equal *welfare*: people are to have their genuine needs and preferences satisfied, are to be enabled to be equally satisfied or fulfilled. He maintains that the difference between egalitarians and inegalitarians is not a rational difference but one of different intuitions and commitment ("Here commitment rather than reason is king."). Both parties may be rational, but make different leaps of faith.

R. M. Hare offers a utilitarian-welfarist defense of equality. Utilitarian equality is based on Bentham's idea "that each is to count for one, no one for more than one," and applies to all sentient creatures, including animals. Each sentient being has an equal claim on happiness. Utilitarian equality, as Hare emphasizes, is primarily based on the economic principle of *diminishing marginal utility*, the idea that, all things being equal, an additional unit of income, say one dollar, helps the pauper more than it does a rich person, so that we maximize aggregate utility by transferring resources from the rich to the poor. Hare also argues that reducing inequalities creates utility by diminishing envy.

Thomas Nagel argues that our moral and political decisions find themselves in tension between two opposing but legitimate points of view: the personal and the impersonal. The personal provides love and personal fulfillment, but the impersonal, or impartial, "view from nowhere," provides the basis for egalitarian policy. Because everyone's life matters equally to him or her, we must recognize that from an impartial perspective no one's interests should count as superior or inferior to anyone else's.

Richard Arneson's article, "Equality and Equal Opportunity for Welfare," is significant because it identifies problems with both resource and welfare egalitarianism. Nevertheless, he argues that welfare is the correct goal of egalitarians—only it is the *equal opportunity* for welfare that egalitarians should opt for. Two people have equal opportunity for welfare when their chances over the course of their lives for satisfying their ideally considered preferences are such that, if both people take maximal advantage of these opportunities to satisfy their preferences (at each stage in their lives), their welfare level would be identical. Arneson concedes that it would be impractical, to say the least, for the state to try to institutionalize his theory, but it can be used in rough-and-ready fashion in many situations and identifies the correct goal of egalitarianism.

Eric Rakowski's essay offers a critique of welfare egalitarianism, including Arneson's equal opportunity for welfare. He then offers a revised defense of resource egalitarianism. Both Rakowski and Dworkin hold, against welfare egalitarians, that we cannot guarantee people well-being, let alone equal well-being, but we can offer them equal resources and make sure that they are compensated for brute bad luck and do not profit from brute good luck. These concepts will become clearer as you read their essays.

Harry Frankfurt opposes egalitarian theories, arguing that what morality requires is not equal distribution of resources but sufficiency. In an affluent society we have a duty to provide for people's minimal needs, but nothing further. Frankfurt's essay contains an interesting critique of the principle of diminishing marginal utility.

Louis Pojman examines the way the notion of equal human worth is held by contemporary egalitarians and points out problems in each theory. He suggests that the idea of equal positive worth derives from our religious heritage and that without this the concept makes little sense.

Michael Walzer rejects notions of "simple equality," and states that there is one metric by which to measure whether we have fulfilled our moral/political duty by equalizing it. Our social conventions do not allow all goods to be distributed by the same principle. Rather, they consign different types of goods to different spheres of justice, each of which is subject to a different principle of justice. This "complex equality" recognizes the separateness and plurality of the spheres of justice (e.g., you may have more political power, my friend has more social status as a successful brain surgeon, but I have more wealth). The spheres are not allowed to spill over and dominate one another. People can experience roughly equal fulfillment but in different ways. The ballet dancer's road to equal life prospects is different from the carpenter's and both are different from the forest ranger's and the salesperson's, but society should be so arranged that each can reach a roughly equal and significantly high potential.

In the Appendix we have included Kurt Vonnegut's satire on equality, the short story "Harrison Bergeron." A bibliography on equality concludes this work.

Finally we have listed some of the questions that preoccupied us while putting this anthology together. We suggest you consider them as you read the articles in this volume.

1. What is equality? Is it one thing or many? We have already touched on this point, but it will be interesting to see just how many different concepts we can identify while reading the articles in this book, not to mention current literature in moral and political theory.

2. If there are many concepts of equality how are they related to one another? Are they compatible or complementary or competing?

3. Is equality an intrinsic good or just an instrumental good to some other end or is it neither—neutral—or is it actually a bad thing?

4. What is the relationship between equality and merit (or desert). Are they at odds? Is to treat people according to their merit an inegalitarian notion, so that merit and egalitarianism are at odds? Is Rawls correct when he (apparently) denies any natural desert for a notion of institutional desert (whereas the classical notion of justice was to give people what they deserved, the Rawlsian notion is that desert is determined by what justice dictates)?

5. What is the relationship between equality and respect? One form of egalitarianism calls on us to respect every person equally. Is this morally required? Rawls claims that self-respect is the fundamental primary good that society should help guarantee. Is it possible to give people the bases of self-respect?

6. If people are not equal in any one property, can we follow Walzer's program and divide up resources in different ways so that the sum of goods each person has is really equal to everyone else's sum?

7. What is the relationship between equality and responsibility? Are people to be held equally responsible? Are people really equally responsible in their actions? Or is responsibility fundamentally unequal?

8. What is the relationship between equality and freedom? Many egalitarians hold that these are compatible and mutually supportive concepts. Inegalitarians disagree—the more we allow people to be free, the less they will be equal and vice versa.

9. There are sometimes said to be two fundamental and antagonistic types of substantive equality: equal opportunity and equal outcomes. Are these antagonistic? Is equal opportunity really possible? What values would have to be sacrificed to achieve strong equal opportunity? What is the appeal of equal outcomes?

10. Related to this question is the matter of affirmative action (e.g., race and gender norming, reverse discrimination). Are these policies morally permissible? If so, under what circumstances and to what extent, if any?

11. Are all humans of equal (and positive) value? If so, what are the arguments for this claim? Does equal human worth (and with it equal human rights) rest on a theological or metaphysical doctrine, so that lacking those doctrines, the thesis is groundless? In what sense can a secularist justify the conclusion that all people are of positive equal worth? (Kant and Vlastos)

12. What is the relationship of property to equality? Rousseau held that holding property was the beginning of inequality and Marx held that the state should own all property and each person receive according to his need and give according to his ability.

13. Most important, we want to see how equality is related to justice itself. As we will soon see, Aristotle thought the two concepts were related—nearly everyone does—both egalitarians and inegalitarians. We want to see how equality relates to justice. Can we distinguish *formal* from *substantive* equality? What are the theoretical implications of such a separation? Perhaps this is the most important part of the book. Is justice fundamentally egalitarian?

14. Many egalitarians (e.g., Dworkin, Rakowski, and Arneson) propose that we should compensate people only for the results of brute bad luck, but not for optional bad luck. They would hold people responsible for their bad choices. If Jones, a lazy good-for-nothing, will not work, neither shall he eat. But the question may be raised, what about innocent third parties? Suppose Jones begets three children. If left to Jones's resources, the children will not be treated equally with Smith's children, who are the product of a loving, industrious home where a strong self-image is produced. Should Smith, who is struggling to support his own three children, be taxed to feed and educate Jones's children? Should Jones be forced to work in order to support them? Or should the state require people to prove that they are able to support children

before it issues them a license to propagate?

15. Finally, is equality in any *substantive* sense a morally necessary notion? Could all legitimate "equality-talk" be translated into nonegalitarian discourse? That is, is the idea of "equality" merely an *emotive* expression (a positively charged "hurrah" word)? Or is there something fundamentally correct about egalitarianism, which cannot be translated without loss into other forms of discourse?

NOTES

1. Will Kymlicka, *Contemporary Political Philosophy* (Oxford University Press, 1990), p. 4; and *Liberalism, Community and Culture* (Oxford University Press, 1989), p. 40.
2. Ronald Dworkin, "In Defence of Equality," in *Social Philosophy and Policy*, 1983, p. 24.
3. For example, Joseph P. DeMarco and Samuel A. Richmond state "Justice requires legislation and policy that reduces the extent to which differences in inherited wealth, gender, caste, language, religion, or social status of parents determines every other inequality." "Is Equality a Measure of Justice?" delivered at the Central Division Meeting of the American Philosophical Association, April 27, 1995.
4. Hume wrote:

   All religious systems, it is confessed, are subject to great and insuperable difficulties. Each disputant triumphs in his turn; while he carries on an offensive war, and exposes the absurdities, barbarities, and pernicious tenets of his antagonist. But all of them, on the whole, prepare a complete triumph for the Sceptic; who tells them, that no system ought ever to be embraced with regard to such subjects: for this plain reason, that no absurdity ought ever to be assented to with regard to any subject. A total suspense of judgment is here our only reasonable resource. And if every attack, as is commonly observed, and no defence, among Theologians, is successful; how complete must be his victory, who remains always, with all mankind, on the offensive, and has himself no fixed station or abiding city, which he is ever, on any occasion, obliged to defend? (*Dialogues Concerning Natural Religion* [Bobbs-Merrill, 1947], p. 186f.)
5. Alexis de Tocqueville, *Democracy in America* (HarperCollins, 1988), p. 41.
6. This is not to deny that practically speaking wealth can influence one's chances of profiting from the laws. The rich can hire the best lawyers to take advantage of the laws, whether they involve tax loopholes or criminal charges. Harold Laski has written that "wealth is a decisive factor in the power to take advantage of the opportunities the law affords its citizens to protect their rights. . . . Broadly, there is equality before the law only when the price of admission to its opportunities can be equally paid." *The State in Theory and Practice* (London: Allen and Unwin, 1935), p. 175.
7. Aristotle, *Politics*, Book V.
8. Gracchus Babeuf quoted in Steven Lukes, "Socialism and Equality" *Dissent* 22 (1975), p. 155.
9. Friedrich Engels, *Origin of the Family, Private Property and the State* (Lawrence and Wishart, 1940), p. 194.
10. Thomas Nagel, "Equality," in his book *Mortal Questions* (Cambridge University Press, 1979).
11. Christopher Jencks, *Inequality: A Reassessment of the Effect of the Family and Schooling in America* (Basic Books, 1972), p. 73.
    Similar expressions of equality as an intrinsic value are the following:

    "Other things equal, it is bad if some people are worse off than others through no voluntary choice or fault of their own." (Richard Arneson, "Equality and Equal Opportunity for Welfare" [see below]).

    "In my view, a large part of the fundamental egalitarian aim is to extinguish the influence of brute luck on distribution. . . . Brute luck is an enemy of just equality" (G. A. Cohen, "On the Currency of Egalitarian Justice," *Ethics* 99 [July 1989], p. 931).

    "All inequalities resulting from variable brute luck ought to be eliminated, except to the extent that a victim of bad brute luck waived or waives his right to compensation, or someone who enjoyed good brute luck is or was allowed to retain the benefits he received by those who have or would have had a claim to some part of them" (Eric Rakowski, *Equal Justice* [Clarendon Press, 1992], p. 74).
12. Richard Watson, "World Hunger and Equality," in *World Hunger and Moral Obligation*, John Arthur and Hugh LaFollette, eds. (Prentice-Hall, 1978).

13. Quoted in George Abernethy, ed., *The Idea of Equality* (Richmond: John Knox Press, 1959), p. 101.
14. Alexis de Tocqueville, *Democracy in America*, George Lawrence, trans. (Garden City, N.Y.: Doubleday, 1969), p. 57.
15. Op. cit., pp. 198, 673. Italics mine. I have slightly revised the translation.
16. Onora O'Neill, "How Do We Know When Opportunities Are Equal?" in *Feminism and Philosophy*, Mary Vetterling-Braggin, Frederick Elliston, and Jane English, eds. (Littlefield, Adams, & Co., 1977).
17. Kai Nielsen, "Ethics Without Religion," *The Ohio University Review* 6 (1964).
18. Thomas Scanlon, "Preference and Urgency," *Journal of Philosophy* 72, no. 19, November 6, 1975, p. 659.

PART I
CLASSICAL READINGS

Justice as Equality
ARISTOTLE

Aristotle (384–322 B.C.) was born in Stagira in Macedon, the son of a physician. He was a student of Plato at the Academy in Athens and the tutor of Alexander the Great. Aristotle saw ethics as the branch of political science concerned with a good and worthy life. It is thus a *practical* rather than a purely theoretical science. Unlike contemporary sociology and anthropology, Aristotelian ethics does not attempt a morally neutral investigation of moral phenomena. Rather, it assumes and elaborates an objective Good that is desirable even if, due to corruptness of character, it is not actually desired. The worthy life is not the one that yields more of what we happen to want than alternatives. Rather, it is the life in which the virtuous person (the *spoudaios*) desires and realizes true and authentic goods. Because Aristotelian ethics is practical, it cannot achieve the exactness of theoretical science like metaphysics and physics. A moral rulebook that provides a guide to a good life is impossible. Yet ethics is no subjective "matter of opinion": the virtuous person grasps what should be done in the particular case, despite the absence of any method.

In the selection from the *Nicomachean Ethics* included below Aristotle identifies justice as the greatest moral virtue and asserts that justice is a sort of equality. In general it involves treating like cases alike. Aristotle analyzes two different kinds of justice in what he considers equalitarian terms: (chapter 3) *distributive* justice, which concerns distribution of social benefits and burdens proportionate to the worth or merit of the recipients, and (chapter 4) *rectificatory* or *corrective* justice as applicable to litigants. In our second selection from *Politics*, Book III, Aristotle elaborates on his concept of justice, as requiring equal treatment for equals and unequal treatment for unequals.

We have included the translator W. D. Ross's notes in the text to enable you to interpret this difficult material.

1

With regard to justice and injustice we must consider (1) what kind of actions they are concerned with, (2) what sort of mean justice is, and (3) between what extremes the just act is intermediate.

We see that all men mean by justice that kind of state of character which makes people disposed to do what is just and makes them act justly and wish for what is just; and similarly by injustice that state which makes them act unjustly and wish for what is unjust. Let us too, then, lay this down as a general basis. For the same is not true of the sciences and the faculties as of states of character. A faculty or a science which is one and the same is held to relate to contrary objects, but a state of character which is one of two contraries does *not* produce the contrary results; for example as a result of health we do not do what is the opposite of healthy, but only what is healthy; for we say a man walks healthily, when he walks as a healthy man would.

Now often one contrary state is recognized from its contrary, and often states are recognized from the subjects that exhibit them; for (a) if good condition is known, bad condition

Reprinted from *The Nicomachean Ethics*, trans. W. D. Ross (1925) by permission of Oxford University Press.

also becomes known, and (b) good condition is known from the things that are in good condition, and they from it. If good condition is firmness of flesh, it is necessary both that bad condition should be flabbiness of flesh and that the wholesome should be that which causes firmness in flesh. And it follows for the most part that if one contrary is ambiguous the other also will be ambiguous; for example if "just" is so, that "unjust" will be so too.

Now "justice" and "injustice" seem to be ambiguous, but because their different meanings approach near to one another the ambiguity escapes notice and is not obvious as it is, comparatively, when the meanings are far apart, for example (for here the difference in outward form is great) as the ambiguity in the use of *kleis* for the collarbone of an animal and for that with which we lock a door. Let us take as a starting-point, then, the various meanings of "an unjust man." Both the lawless man and the grasping and unfair man are thought to be unjust, so that evidently both the law-abiding and the fair man will be just. The just, then, is the lawful and the fair, the unjust the unlawful and the unfair.

Since the unjust man is grasping, he must be concerned with goods—not all goods, but those with which prosperity and adversity have to do, which taken absolutely are always good, but for a particular person are not always good. Now men pray for and pursue these things; but they should not, but should pray that the things that are good absolutely may also be good for them, and should choose the things that *are* good for them. The unjust man does not always choose the greater, but also the less—in the case of things bad absolutely; but because the lesser evil is itself thought to be in a sense good, and graspingness is directed at the good, therefore he is thought to be grasping. And he is unfair; for this contains and is common to both.

Since the lawless man was seen to be unjust and the law-abiding man just, evidently all lawful acts are in a sense just acts; for the acts laid down by the legislative art are lawful, and each of these, we say, is just. Now the laws in their enactments on all subjects aim at the common advantage either of all or of the best or of those who hold power, or something of the sort; so that in one sense we call those acts just that tend to produce and preserve happiness and its components for the political society. And the law bids

us do both the acts of a brave man (*e.g.* not to desert our post nor take to flight nor throw away our arms), and those of a temperate man (*e.g.* not to commit adultery nor to gratify one's lust), and those of a good-tempered man (*e.g.* not to strike another nor to speak evil), and similarly with regard to the other virtues and forms of wickedness, commanding some acts and forbidding others; and the rightly-framed law does this rightly, and the hastily conceived one less well.

This form of justice, then, is complete virtue, but not absolutely, but in relation to our neighbour. And therefore justice is often thought to be the greatest of virtues, and "neither evening nor morning star" is so wonderful; and proverbially "in justice is every virtue comprehended." And it is complete virtue in its fullest sense, because it is the actual exercise of complete virtue. It is complete because he who possesses it can exercise his virtue not only in himself but towards his neighbour also; for many men can exercise virtue in their own affairs, but not in their relations to their neighbour. This is why the saying of Bias is thought to be true, that "rule will show the man;" for a ruler is necessarily in relation to other men and a member of a society. For this same reason justice, alone of the virtues, is thought to be "another's good," because it is related to our neighbour; for it does what is advantageous to another, either a ruler or a copartner. Now the worst man is he who exercises his wickedness both towards himself and towards his friends, and the best man is not he who exercises his virtue towards himself but he who exercises it towards another; for this is a difficult task. Justice in this sense, then, is not part of virtue but virtue entire, nor is the contrary injustice a part of vice but vice entire. What the difference is between virtue and justice in this sense is plain from what we have said; they are the same but their essence is not the same; what, as a relation to one's neighbour, is justice is, as a certain kind of state without qualification virtue.

2

But at all events what we are investigating is the justice which is a *part* of virtue; for there is a justice of this kind, as we maintain. Similarly it is with injustice in the particular sense that we are concerned.

That there is such a thing is indicated by the fact that while the man who exhibits in action the other forms of wickedness acts wrongly indeed, but not graspingly (*e.g.* the man who throws away his shield through cowardice or speaks harshly through bad temper or fails to help a friend with money through meanness), when a man acts graspingly he often exhibits none of these vices—no, nor all together, but certainly wickedness of some kind (for we blame him) and injustice. There is, then, another kind of injustice which is a part of injustice in the wide sense, and a use of the word "unjust" which answers to a part of what is unjust in the wide sense of "contrary to the law." Again, if one man commits adultery for the sake of gain and makes money by it, while another does so at the bidding of appetite though he loses money and is penalized for it, the latter would be held to be self-indulgent rather than grasping, but the former is unjust, but not self-indulgent; evidently, therefore, he is unjust by reason of his making gain by his act. Again, all other unjust acts are ascribed invariably to some particular kind of wickedness, for example adultery to self-indulgence, the desertion of a comrade in battle to cowardice, physical violence to anger; but if a man makes gain, his action is ascribed to no form of wickedness but injustice. Evidently, therefore, there is apart from injustice in the wide sense another, "particular," injustice which shares the name and nature of the first, because its definition falls within the same genus; for the significance of both consists in a relation to one's neighbour, but the one is concerned with honour or money or safety—or that which includes all these, if we had a single name for it—and its motive is the pleasure that arises from gain; while the other is concerned with all the objects with which the good man is concerned.

It is clear, then, that there is more than one kind of justice, and that there is one which is distinct from virtue entire; we must try to grasp its genus and differentia.

The unjust has been divided into the unlawful and the unfair, and the just into the lawful and the fair. To the unlawful answers the aforementioned sense of injustice. But since the unfair and the unlawful are not the same, but are different as a part is from its whole (for all that is unfair is unlawful, but not all that is unlawful is unfair), the unjust and injustice in the sense of the unfair are not the same as but different from the former kind, as part from whole; for injustice in this sense is a part of injustice in the wide sense, and similarly justice in the one sense of justice in the other. Therefore we must speak also about particular justice and particular injustice, and similarly about the just and the unjust. The justice, then, which answers to the whole of virtue, and the corresponding injustice, one being the exercise of virtue as a whole, and the other that of vice as a whole, towards one's neighbour, we may leave on one side. And how the meanings of "just" and "unjust" which answer to these are to be distinguished is evident; for practically the majority of the acts commanded by the law are those which are prescribed from the point of view of virtue taken as a whole; for the law bids us practise every virtue and forbids us to practise any vice. And the things that tend to produce virtue taken as a whole are those of the acts prescribed by the law which have been prescribed with a view to education for the common good. But with regard to the education of the individual as such, which makes him without qualification a good man, we must determine later whether this is the function of the political art or of another; for perhaps it is not the same to be a good man and a good citizen of any state taken at random.

Of particular justice and that which is just in the corresponding sense, (A) one kind is that which is manifested in distributions of honour or money or the other things that fall to be divided among those who have a share in the constitution (for in these it is possible for one man to have a share either unequal or equal to that of another), and (B) one is that which plays a rectifying part in transactions between man and man. Of this there are two divisions; of transactions (1) some are voluntary and (2) others involuntary—voluntary such transactions as sale, purchase, loan for consumption, pledging, loan for use, depositing, letting (they are called voluntary because the origin of these transactions is voluntary), while of the involuntary (a) some are clandestine, such as theft, adultery, poisoning, procuring, enticement of slaves, assassination, false witness, and (b) others are violent, such as assault, imprisonment, murder, robbery with violence, mutilation, abuse, insult.

3

(A) We have shown that both the unjust man and the unjust act are unfair or unequal; now it is clear that there is also an intermediate between the two unequals involved in either case. And this is the equal; for in any kind of action in which there is a more and a less there is also what is equal. If, then, the unjust is unequal, the just is equal, as all men suppose it to be, even apart from argument. And since the equal is intermediate, the just will be an intermediate. Now equality implies at least two things. The just, then, must be both intermediate and equal and relative (*i.e.* for certain persons). And *qua* intermediate it must be between certain things (which are respectively greater and less); *qua* equal, it involves *two* things; *qua* just, it is for certain people. The just, therefore, involves at least four terms; for the persons for whom it is in fact just are two, and the things in which it is manifested, the objects distributed, are two. And the same equality will exist between the persons and between the things concerned; for as the latter—the things concerned—are related, so are the former; if they are not equal, they will not have what is equal, but this is the origin of quarrels and complaints—when either equals have and are awarded unequal shares, or unequals equal shares. Further, this is plain from the fact that awards should be "according to merit;" for all men agree that what is just in distribution must be according to merit in some sense, though they do not all specify the same sort of merit, but democrats identify it with the status of freeman, supporters of oligarchy with wealth (or with noble birth), and supporters of aristocracy with excellence.

The just, then, is a species of the proportionate (proportion being not a property only of the kind of number which consists of abstract units, but of number in general). For proportion is equality of ratios, and involves four terms at least (that discrete proportion involves four terms is plain, but so does continuous proportion, for it uses one term as two and mentions

it twice; for example "as the line A is to the line B, so is the line B to the line C;" the line B, then, has been mentioned twice, so that if the line B be assumed twice, the proportional terms will be four); and the just, too, involves at least four terms, and the ratio between one pair is the same as that between the other pair; for there is a similar distinction between the persons and between the things. As the term A, then, is to B, so will C be to D, and therefore, alternando, as A is to C, B will be to D. Therefore also the whole is in the same ratio to the whole;[1] and this coupling the distribution effects and, if the terms are so combined, effects justly. The conjunction, then, of the term A with C and of B with D is what is just in distribution,[2] and this species of the just is intermediate, and the unjust is what violates the proportion; for the proportional is intermediate, and the just is proportional. (Mathematicians call this kind of proportion geometrical; for it is in geometrical proportion that it follows that the whole is to the whole as either part is to the corresponding part.) This proportion is not continuous; for we cannot get a single term standing for a person and a thing.

This, then, is what the just is—the proportional; the unjust is what violates the proportion. Hence one term becomes too great, the other too small, as indeed happens in practice; for the man who acts unjustly has too much, and the man who is unjustly treated too little, of what is good. In the case of evil the reverse is true; for the lesser evil is reckoned a good in comparison with the greater evil, since the lesser evil is rather to be chosen than the greater, and what is worthy of choice is good, and what is worthier of choice a greater good.

This, then, is one species of the just.

4

(B) The remaining one is the rectificatory, which arises in connexion with transactions both voluntary and involuntary. This form of the just has a different specific character from the former. For the justice which distributes common possessions is always in accordance with the kind of proportion mentioned above (for in the case also in which the distribution is made from the common funds of a partnership it will be according to the same ratio which the funds put into the business by the partners bear to one another); and the injustice opposed to this kind of justice is that which violates the proportion. But the justice in transactions between man and man is a sort of equality indeed, and the injustice a sort of inequality; not according to that kind of proportion, however, but according to arithmetical proportion.[3] For it makes no difference whether a good man has defrauded a bad man or a bad man a good one, nor whether it is a good or a bad man that has committed adultery; the law looks only to the distinctive character of the injury, and treats the parties as equal, if one is in the wrong and the other is being wronged, and if one inflicted injury and the other has received it. Therefore, this kind of injustice being an inequality, the judge tries to equalize it; for in the case also in which one has received and the other has inflicted a wound, or one has slain and the other been slain, the suffering and the action have been unequally distributed; but the judge tries to equalize things by means of the penalty, taking away from the gain of the assailant. For the term "gain" is applied generally to such cases, even if it be not a term appropriate to certain cases, for example to the person who inflicts a wound—and "loss" to the sufferer; at all events when the suffering has been estimated, the one is called loss and the other gain. Therefore the equal is intermediate between the greater and the less, but the gain and the loss are respectively greater and less in contrary ways; more of the good and less of the evil are gain, and the contrary is loss; intermediate between them is, as we saw, the equal, which we say is just; therefore corrective justice will be the intermediate between loss and gain. This is why, when people dispute, they take refuge in the judge; and to go to the judge is to go to justice; for the nature of the judge is to be a sort of animate justice; and they seek the judge as an intermediate, and in some states they call judges mediators, on the assumption that if they get what is intermediate they will get what is just. The just, then, is an intermediate, since the judge is so. Now the judge restores equality; it is as though there were a line divided into unequal parts, and he took away that by which the greater segment exceeds the half, and added it to the smaller segment. And when the whole has been equally divided, then they say they have "their own" that is, when they have got what is equal. The equal is intermediate between the greater and the lesser line according to arithmetical proportion. It is for this reason also that it is called just (*dikaion*), because it is a division into two equal parts (*dicha*), just as if one were to call it (*dichaion*); and the judge (*dicastes*) is one who bisects (*dichastes*). For when something is subtracted from one of two equals and added to the other, the other is in excess by these two; since if what was taken from the one had not been added to the other, the latter would have been in excess by one only. It therefore exceeds the intermediate by one, and the intermediate exceeds by one that from which something was taken. By this, then, we shall recognize both what we must subtract from that which has more, and what we must add to that which has less; we must add to the latter that by which the intermediate exceeds it, and subtract from the greatest that by which it exceeds the intermediate. Let the lines AA' BB', CC' be equal to one another; from the line AA' let the segment AE have been subtracted, and to the line CC' let the segment CD [*sc,* equal to AE] have been added, so that the whole line DCC' exceeds the line EA' by the segment CD and the segment CF; therefore it exceeds the line BB' by the segment CD.

These names, both loss and gain, have come from voluntary exchange; for to have more than one's own is called gaining, and to have less than one's original share is called losing, for example in buying and selling and in all other matters in which the law has left people free to make their own terms; but when they get neither more nor less but just what belongs to themselves, they say that they have their own and that they neither lose nor gain.

Therefore the just is intermediate between a sort of gain and a sort of loss, namely those which are involuntary [*i.e.* for the loser]; it consists in having an equal amount before and after the transaction.

5

Some think that *reciprocity* is without qualification just, as the Pythagoreans said; for they defined justice without qualification as reciprocity. Now "reciprocity" fits neither distributive nor rectificatory justice—yet people *want* even the justice of Rhadamanthus to mean this:

Should a man suffer what he did, right justice would be done

—for in many cases reciprocity and rectificatory justice are not in accord, for example (1) if an official has inflicted a wound, he should not be wounded in return, and if some one has wounded an official, he ought not to be wounded only but punished in addition. Further (2) there is a great difference between a voluntary and an involuntary act. But in associations for exchange this sort of justice does hold men together—reciprocity in accordance with a proportion and not on the basis of precisely equal return. For it is by proportionate requital that the city holds together. Men seek to return either evil for evil—and if they cannot do so, think their position mere slavery—or good for good—and if they cannot do so there is no exchange, but it is by exchange that they hold together. This is why they give a prominent place to the temple of the Graces—to promote the requital of services; for this is characteristic of grace—we should serve in return one who has shown grace to us, and should another time take the initiative in showing it.

Now proportionate return is secured by cross-conjunction.[4] Let A be a builder, B a shoemaker, C a house, D a shoe. The builder, then, must get from the shoemaker the latter's work, and must himself give him in return his own. If, then, first there is proportionate equality of goods, and then reciprocal action takes place, the result we mention will be effected. If not, the bargain is not equal, and does not hold;

for there is nothing to prevent the work of the one being better than that of the other; they must therefore be equated. (And this is true of the other arts also; for they would have been destroyed if what the patient suffered had not been just what the agent did, and of the same amount and kind.[5]) For it is not two doctors that associate for exchange, but a doctor and a farmer, or in general people who are different and unequal; but these must be equated. This is why all things that are exchanged must be somehow comparable. It is for this end that money has been introduced, and it becomes in a sense an intermediate; for it measures all things—how many shoes are equal to a house or to a given amount of food. The number of shoes exchanged for a house [or for a given amount of food] must therefore correspond to the ratio of builder to shoemaker. For if this be not so, there will be no exchange and no intercourse. And this proportion will not be effected unless the goods are somehow equal. All goods must therefore be measured by some one thing, as we said before.[6] Now this unit is in truth demand, which holds all things together (for if men did not need one another's goods at all, or did not need them equally, there would be either no exchange or not the same exchange); but money has become by convention a sort of representative of demand; and this is why it has the name "money" (*nomisma*)—because it exists not by nature but by law (*nomos*) and it is in our power to change it and make it useless. There will, then, be reciprocity when the terms have been equated so that as farmer is to shoemaker, the amount of the shoemaker's work is to that of the farmer's work for which it exchanges. But we must not bring them into a figure of proportion when they have already exchanged (otherwise one extreme will have both excesses), but when they still have their own goods. Thus they are equals and associates just because this equality can be effected in their case. Let A be a farmer, C food, B a shoemaker, D his product equated to C. If it had not been possible for reciprocity to be thus effected, there would have been no association of the parties. That demand holds things together as a single unit is shown by the fact that when men do not need one another, that is when neither needs the other or one does not need the other, they do not exchange, as we do when some one wants what one has oneself, for example when people permit the exportation of corn in exchange for wine. This equation therefore must be established. And for the future exchange—that if we do not need a thing now we shall have it if ever we do need it—money is as it were our surety; for it must be possible for us to get what we want by bringing the money. Now the same thing happens to money itself as to goods—it is not always worth the same; yet it tends to be steadier. This is why all goods must have a price set on them; for then there will always be exchange, and if so, association of man with man. Money, then, acting as a measure, makes goods commensurate and equates them; for neither would there have been association if there were not exchange, nor exchange if there were not equality, nor equality if there were not commensurability. Now in truth it is impossible that things differing so much should become commensurate, but with reference to demand they may become so sufficiently. There must, then, be a unit, and that fixed by agreement (for which reason it is called money); for it is this that makes all things commensurate, since all things are measured by money. Let A be a house, B ten minae, C a bed. A is half of B, if the house is worth five minae or equal to them; the bed, C, is a tenth of B; it is plain, then, how many beds are equal to a house, namely five. That exchange took place thus before there was money is plain; for it makes no difference whether it is five beds that exchange for a house, or the money value of five beds.

We have now defined the unjust and the just. These having been marked off from each other, it is plain that just action is intermediate between acting unjustly and being unjustly treated; for the one is to have too much and the other to have too little. Justice is a kind of mean, but not in the same way as the other virtues, but because it relates to an intermediate amount, while injustice relates to the extremes. And justice is that in virtue of which the just man is said to be a doer, by choice, of that which is just, and one who will distribute either between himself and another or between two others not so as to give more of what is desirable to himself and less to his neighbour (and conversely with what is harmful), but so as to give what is equal in accordance with proportion; and similarly in distributing between two other persons. Injustice on the other hand is similarly related to the unjust, which is excess and defect, contrary to proportion, of the useful or hurtful. For which reason injustice is excess and defect, namely because it is productive of excess and defect—in one's own case excess of what is in its own nature useful and defect of what is hurtful, while in the case of others it is as a whole like what it is in one's own case, but proportion may be violated in either direction. In the unjust act to have too little is to be unjustly treated; to have too much is to act unjustly.

Let this be taken as our account of the nature of justice and injustice, and similarly of the just and the unjust in general.

6

Since acting unjustly does not necessarily imply being unjust, we must ask what sort of unjust acts imply that the doer is unjust with respect to each type of injustice, for example a thief, an adulterer, or a brigand. Surely the answer does not turn on the difference between these types. For a man might even lie with a woman knowing who she was, but the origin of his act might be not deliberate choice but passion. He acts unjustly, then, but is not unjust; for example a man is not a thief, yet he stole, nor an adulterer, yet he committed adultery; and similarly in all other cases.

Now we have previously stated how the reciprocal is related to the just; but we must not forget that what we are looking for is not only what is just without qualification but also political justice. This is found among men who share their life with a view to self-sufficiency, men who are free and either proportionately or arithmetically equal, so that between those who do not fulfil this condition there is no political justice but justice in a special sense and by analogy. For justice exists only between men whose mutual relations are governed by law; and law exists for men between whom there is injustice; for legal justice is the discrimination of the just and the unjust. And between men between whom there is injustice there is also unjust action (though there is not injustice between all between whom there is unjust action), and this is assigning too much to oneself of things good in themselves and too little of things evil in themselves. This is why we do not allow a *man* to rule, but *rational principle,* because a man behaves thus in his own interests and becomes a tyrant. The magistrate on the other hand is the guardian of justice, and, if of justice, then of equality also. And since he is assumed to have no more than his share, if he is just (for he does not assign to himself more of what is good in itself, unless such a share is proportional to his merits—so that it is for others that he labours, and it is for this reason that men, as we stated previously, say that justice is "another's good"), therefore a reward must be given him, and this is honour and privilege; but those for whom such things are not enough become tyrants.

The justice of a master and that of a father are not the same as the justice of citizens, though they are like it; for there can be no injustice in the unqualified sense towards things that are one's own, but a man's chattel, and his child until it reaches a certain age and sets up for itself, are as it were part of himself, and no one chooses to hurt himself (for which reason there can be no injustice towards oneself). Therefore the justice or injustice of citizens is not manifested in these relations; for it was as we saw according to law, and between people naturally subject to law, and these as we saw are people who have an equal share in ruling and being ruled. Hence justice can more truly be manifested towards a wife than towards children and chattels, for the former is household justice; but even this is different from political justice. . . .

FROM *POLITICS* BOOK III

Let us begin by considering the common definitions of oligarchy and democracy, and what is justice oligarchical and democratical. For all men cling to justice of some kind, but their conceptions are imperfect and they do not express the whole idea. For example, justice is thought by them to be, and is, equality, not, however, for all, but only for equals. And inequality is thought to be, and is, justice; neither is this for all, but only for unequals. When the persons are omitted, then men judge erroneously. The reason is that they are passing judgment on themselves, and most people are bad judges in their own case. And whereas justice implies a relation to persons as well as to things, and a just distribution, as I have already said in the Ethics, embraces alike persons and things, they acknowledge the equality of the things, but dispute about the merit of the persons, chiefly for the reason which I have just given,—because they are bad judges in their own affairs; and secondly, because both the parties to the argument are speaking of a limited and partial justice, but imagine themselves to be speaking of absolute justice. For those who are unequal in one respect, for example wealth, consider themselves to be unequal in all; and any who are equal in one respect, for example freedom, consider themselves to be equal in all. But they leave out the capital point. For if men met and associated out of regard to wealth only, their share in the state would be proportioned to their property, and the oligarchical doctrine would then seem to carry the day. It would not be just that he who paid one mina should have the same share of a hundred minae, whether of the principal or of the profits, as he who paid the remaining ninety-nine. But a state exists for the sake of a good life, and not for the sake of life only: if life only were the object, slaves and brute-animals might form a state, but they cannot, for they have no share in happiness or in a life of free choice. Nor does a state exist for the sake of alliance and security from injustice, nor yet for the sake of exchange and mutual intercourse; for then the Tyrrhenians and the Carthaginians, and all who have commercial treaties with one another, would be the citizens of one state. True, they have agreements about imports, and engagements that they will do no wrong to one another, and written articles of alliance. But there are no magistracies common to the contracting parties who will enforce their engagements; different states have each their own magistracies. Nor does one state take care that the citizens of the other are such as they ought to be, nor see that those who come under the terms of the treaty do no wrong or wickedness at all, but only that they do no injustice to one another. Whereas, those who care for good government take into consideration [the larger question of] virtue and vice in states. Whence it may be further inferred that virtue must be the serious care of a state which truly deserves the name: for [without this ethical end] the community becomes a mere alliance which differs only in place from alliances of which the members live apart; and law is only a convention, 'a surety to one another of justice,' as the sophist Lycophron says, and has no real power to make the citizens good and just.

In all sciences and arts the end is a good, and the greatest good and in the highest degree a good in the most authoritative of all—this is the political science of which the good is justice, in other words, the common interest. All men think justice to be a sort of equality; and to a certain extent they agree with what we have said in our philosophical works about ethics. For they say that what is just is just *for* someone and that it should be equal for equals. But there still remains a question: equality or inequality of what? Here is a difficulty which calls for political speculation. For very likely some persons will say that offices of state ought to be unequally distributed according to superior excellence, in whatever respect, of the citizen, although there is no other difference between him and the rest of the community; for those who differ in any one respect have different rights and claims. But, surely, if this is true, the complexion or height of a man, or any other advantage, will be a reason for his obtaining a greater share of political rights. The error here lies upon the surface, and may be illustrated from the other arts and sciences. When a number of flute-players are equal in their art, there is no reason why those of them who are better born should have better flutes given to them; for they will not play any better on the flute, and the superior instrument should be reserved for him who is the superior artist. If what I am saying is still obscure, it will be made clearer as we proceed. For if there were a superior flute-player who was far inferior in birth and beauty, although either of these may be a greater good than the art of flute-playing and may excel flute-playing in a greater ratio than he excels the others in his art, still he ought to have the best flutes given to him, unless the advantages of wealth and birth contribute to excellence in flute-playing, which they do not. Moreover, upon this principle any good may be compared with any other. For if a given height may be measured against wealth and against freedom, height in general may be so measured. Thus if A excels in height more than B in excellence, even if excellence in general excels height still more, all goods will be comparable; for if a certain amount is better than some other, it is clear that some other will be equal. But since no such comparison can be made, it is evident that there is good reason why in politics men do not ground their claim to office on every sort of inequality. For if some be slow, and others swift, that is no reason why the one should have little and the others much; it is in gymnastic contests that such excellence is rewarded. Whereas the rival claims of candidates for office can only be based on the possession of elements which enter into the composition of a state. And therefore the well-born, or free-born, or rich, may with good reason claim office; for holders of offices must be freemen and tax-payers: a state can be no more composed entirely of poor men than entirely of slaves. But if wealth and freedom are necessary elements, justice and valour are equally so; for without the former qualities a state cannot exist at all, without the latter not well.

NOTES

1. Person A + thing C to person B + thing D.
2. The problem of distributive justice is to divide the distributable honour or reward into parts which are to one another as are the merits of the persons who are to participate. If A (first person) : B (second person) :: C (first portion) : D (second portion) then (*alternando*) A : C :: B : D, and therefore (*componendo*) A + C : B + D :: A : B. In other words the position established answers to the relative merits of the parties.
3. The problem of "rectificatory justice" has nothing to do with punishment proper but is only that of rectifying a wrong that has been done, by awarding damages; *i.e.* rectificatory justice is that of the civil, not that of the criminal courts. The parties are treated by the court as equal (since a law court is not a court of morals), and the wrongful act is reckoned as having brought equal gain to the

wrong-doer and loss to his victim; it brings A to the position A + C, and B to the position B − C. The judge's task is to find the arithmetical mean between these, and this he does by transferring C from A to B. Thus (A being treated as = B) we get the arithmetical "proportion"

$$(A + C) - (A + C - C)$$
$$= (A + C - C) - (B - C)$$

or

$$(A + C) - (B - C + C)$$
$$= (B - C + C) - (B - C).$$

4. The working of proportionate reciprocity is not very clearly described by Aristotle, but seems to be as follows. A and B are workers in different trades, and will normally be of different degrees of worth. Their products, therefore, will also have unequal worth, *i.e.* (though Aristotle does not expressly reduce the question to one of time) if A = nB (what A makes, say, in an hour) will be worth n times as much as D (what B makes in an hour). A fair exchange will then take place if A gets nD and B gets 1 C; *i.e.*, if A gives what it takes him an hour to make, in exchange for what it takes B n hours to make.

5. This sentence conveys a natural enough thought, and echoes closely the language of Plato, *Gorgias*,

476 B–D. But it seems to have no relevance to the context, and probably we have here the unsuccessful attempt of an early editor to find a suitable place for an isolated note of Aristotle's.

6. Aristotle's meaning, which has caused much difficulty, seems to be explained by a reference to *Nichomachean Ethics*, Book IX, chap. 1. That chapter concludes with the observation that ". . . the receiver should assess a thing not at what it seems worth when he has it, but at what he assessed it at before he had it." The reasoning in that chapter shows that Aristotle's meaning here must be that people must not exchange goods in random amounts and *then* bring themselves into a "figure of proportion." For each will then set an unduly high value on the goods he has parted with and an unduly low value on those he has received; and any adjustment that is made will be decided by their respective powers of bluff. One party will have both excesses over the other, since what he gets will exceed the mean and what the other man gets will fall short of it (*cf.* the end of chap. 4, *supra*). The only fair method is for each to set a value on his own and on the other's goods *before* they exchange, and for them to come to an agreement if they can.

Equality in the State of Nature
THOMAS HOBBES

Thomas Hobbes (1588–1679) anticipated many of the major trends of modern philosophy. *Leviathan*, his best-known work, reflects the great impression left by his belated introduction to geometry. Hobbes became an opponent of Aristotelianism, and debunked the reverence for authority and prescription that animated much English political thought, including what he considered the random, connect-the-dots common law tradition. He took the idea of political *science* utterly seriously, though in quite a different sense from Aristotle. Hobbes attempted a deduction of political theorems from axioms of human nature. His axioms manifest a materialistic and mechanistic conception of human beings: though Hobbes wavers on this point, he suggests that the human sciences are deducible from basic principles of motion. *Leviathan* is a deduction of the state from first principles, not an historical account of the genesis of government. It begins with an excursion into psychology. Sense experience is but a series of internal motions; thoughts are tremors within the skull, which sometimes issue in observable movements toward pleasurable things, and away from painful ones. There is no objective Good; good and evil are simply names for objects of desire and aversion, which are continually pursued until death. We naturally desire precedence—

to outdo others, and to be *known* to outdo others. This, along with the competition for scarce resources, occasions ceaseless and self-defeating strife, which induces us, by means of a contract each with all, to cede our freedom to an absolute sovereign in exchange for security. The worth of a person resides solely in his market value, his ability to satisfy the desires of others. Nevertheless, people possess a common practical equality in virtue of the fact that even the weakest, in concert with others, is able to bring down the stronger, so that pretensions to superiority or nobility are baseless. The only objective measure of right is the command of the sovereign, whose threats alone are sufficient to prevent the collision of ambitious bodies that puts an end to those vital motions we call life.

ON HUMAN WORTH

The *value* or WORTH of a man is, as of all other things, his price—that is to say, so much as would be given for the use of his power—and therefore is not absolute but a thing dependent on the need and judgment of another. An able conductor of soldiers is of great price in time of war present or imminent, but in peace not so. A learned and uncorrupt judge is much worth in time of peace, but not so much in war. And as in other things so in men, not the seller but the buyer determines the price. For let a man, as most men do, rate themselves at the highest value they can, yet their true value is no more than it is esteemed by others.

The manifestation of the value we set on one another is that which is commonly called honoring and dishonoring. To value a man at a high rate is to *honor* him, at a low rate is to *dishonor* him. But high and low, in this case, is to be understood by comparison to the rate that each man sets on himself.

The public worth of a man, which is the value set on him by the commonwealth, is that which men commonly call DIGNITY. And this value of him by the commonwealth is understood by offices of command, judicature, public employment, or by names and titles introduced for distinction of such value. . . .

OF THE DIFFERENCE OF MANNERS

What is here meant by manners. By MANNERS I mean not here decency of behavior—as how one should salute another, or how a man should wash his mouth or pick his teeth before company, and such other points of the *small morals*—but those qualities of mankind that concern their living together in peace and unity. To which end we are to consider that the felicity of this life consists not in the repose of a mind satisfied. For there is no such finis ultimus, utmost aim nor summun bonum, greatest good, as is spoken of in the books of the old moral philosophers. Nor can a man any more live whose desires are at an end than he whose senses and imaginations are at a stand. Felicity is a continual progress of the desire from one object to another, the attaining of the former being still but the way to the latter. The cause whereof is that the object of man's desire is not to enjoy once only and for one instant of time, but to assure forever the way of his future desire. And therefore the voluntary actions and inclinations of all men tend, not only to the procuring, but also to the assuring of a contented life; and differ only in the way, which arises partly from the diversity of passions in divers men, and partly from the difference of the knowledge or opinion each one has of the causes which produce the effect desired.

A restless desire of power in all men. So that, in the first place, I put for a general inclination of all mankind a perpetual and restless desire of power after power that ceases only in death. And the cause of this is not always that a man hopes for a more intensive delight than he has already attained to, or that he cannot be content with a moderate power, but because he cannot assure the power and means to live well which he has present without the acquisition of more. And from hence it is that kings, whose power is greatest, turn their endeavors to the assuring it at home by laws or abroad by wars; and when that is done, there succeeds a new desire—in some, of fame from new conquest; in others, of ease and sensual pleasure; in others, of admiration or being flattered for excellence in some art or other ability of the mind.

Love of contention from competition. Competition of riches, honor, command, or other power inclines to contention, enmity, and war, because the way of one competitor to the attaining of his desire is to kill, subdue, supplant, or repel the other. Particularly, competition of praise inclines to a reverence of antiquity. For men contend with the living, not with the dead—to these ascribing more than due, that they may obscure the glory of the other.

Civil obedience from love of ease.

From fear of death or wounds. Desire of ease and sensual delight disposes men to obey a common power, because by such desires a man does abandon the protection that might be hoped for from his own industry and labor. Fear of death and wounds disposes to the same, and for the same reason. On the contrary, needy men and hardy, not contented with their present condition, as also all men that are ambitious of military command, are inclined to continue the causes of war, and to stir up trouble and sedition; for there is no honor military but by war, nor any such hope to mend an ill game as by causing a new shuffle.

And from love of arts. Desire of knowledge and arts of peace inclines men to obey a common power, for such desire contains a desire of leisure, and consequently protection from some other power than their own.

Love of virtue from love of praise. Desire of praise disposes to laudable actions, such as please them whose judgment they value; for of those men whom we contemn, we contemn also the praises. Desire of fame after death does the same. And though after death there be no sense of the praise given us on earth, as being joys that are either swallowed up in the unspeakable joys of heaven or extinguished in the extreme torments of hell, yet is not such fame vain; because men have a present delight therein from the foresight of it and of the benefit that may redound thereby to their posterity, which, though they now see not, yet they imagine; and anything that is pleasure

to the sense, the same also is pleasure in the imagination.

Hate, from difficulty of requiting great benefits. To have received from one to whom we think ourselves equal greater benefits than there is hope to requite disposes to counterfeit love, but really secret hatred; and puts a man into the estate of a desperate debtor that, in declining the sight of his creditor, tacitly wishes him there where he might never see him more. For benefits oblige, and obligation is thralldom, and unrequitable obligation perpetual thralldom—which is to one's equal hateful. But to have received benefits from one whom we acknowledge for superior inclines to love, because the obligation is no new depression, and cheerful acceptance, which men call *gratitude*, is such an honor done to the obliger as is taken generally for retribution. Also to receive benefits, though from an equal or inferior, as long as there is hope of requital, disposes to love; for in the intention of the receiver, the obligation is of aid and service mutual; from whence proceeds an emulation of who shall exceed in benefiting—the most noble and profitable contention possible, wherein the victor is pleased with his victory and the other revenged by confessing it.

And from conscience of deserving to be hated. To have done more hurt to a man than he can or is willing to expiate inclines the doer to hate the sufferer. For he must expect revenge or forgiveness, both which are hateful.

Promptness to hurt, from fear.

And from distrust of their own wit. Fear of oppression disposes a man to anticipate or to seek aid by society, for there is no other way by which a man can secure his life and liberty. Men that distrust their own subtlety are, in tumult and sedition, better disposed for victory than they that suppose themselves wise or crafty. For these love to consult, the other, fearing to be circumvented, to strike first. And in sedition, men being always in the precincts of battle, to hold together and use all advantages of force is a better stratagem than any that can proceed from subtlety of wit.

Vain undertaking from vainglory. Vainglorious men such as, without being conscious to themselves of great sufficiency, delight in supposing themselves gallant men are inclined only to ostentation but not to attempt, because when danger or difficulty appears they look for nothing but to have their insufficiency discovered.

Vainglorious men such as estimate their sufficiency by the flattery of other men or the fortune of some precedent action, without assured ground of hope from the true knowledge of themselves, are inclined to rash engaging; and in the approach of danger or difficulty to retire if they can, because, not seeing the way of safety, they will rather hazard their honor, which may be salved with an excuse, than their lives, for which no salve is sufficient. Men that have a strong opinion of their own wisdom in matter of government are disposed to ambition. Because without public employment in council or magistracy the honor of their wisdom is lost. And therefore eloquent speakers are inclined to ambition, for eloquence seems wisdom, both to themselves and others.

Ambition, from opinion of sufficiency.

Irresolution, from too great valuing of small matters.

Pusillanimity disposes men to irresolution, and consequently to lose the occasions and fittest opportunities of action. For after men have been in deliberation till the time of action approach, if it be not then manifest what is best to be done, it is a sign the difference of motives, the one way and the other, are not great; therefore not to resolve them is to lose the occasion by weighing of trifles, which is pusillanimity.

Frugality, though in poor men a virtue, makes a man unapt to achieve such actions as require the strength of many men at once; for it weakens their endeavor, which is to be nourished and kept in vigor by reward.

Confidence in others, from ignorance of the marks of wisdom and kindness.

Eloquence, with flattery, disposes men to confide in them that have it; because the former is seeming wisdom, the latter seeming kindness. Add to them military reputation, and it disposes men to adhere and subject themselves to those men that have them. The two former having given them caution against danger from him, the latter gives them caution against danger from others. . . .

And from ignorance of natural causes.

Adherence to custom, from ignorance of the nature of right and wrong.

Ignorance of the causes and original constitution of right, equity, law, and justice disposes a man to make custom and example the rule of his actions; in such manner as to think that unjust which it has been the custom to punish, and that just of the impunity and approbation whereof they can produce an example or, as the lawyers which only use this false measure of justice barbarously call it, a precedent; like little children that have no other rule of good and evil manners but the correction they receive from their parents and masters, save that children are constant to their rule, whereas men are not so; because, grown old and stubborn, they appeal from custom to reason and from reason to custom as it serves their turn, receding from custom when their interest requires it and setting themselves against reason as oft as reason is against them; which is the cause that the doctrine of right and wrong is perpetually disputed, both by the pen and the sword, whereas the doctrine of lines and figures is not so; because men care not, in that subject, what be truth, as a thing that crosses no man's ambition, profit, or lust. For I doubt not but if it had been a thing contrary to any man's right of dominion, or to the interest of men that have dominion, *that the three angles of a triangle should be equal to two angles of a square*, that doctrine should have been, if not disputed, yet, by the burning of all books of geometry, suppressed, as far as he whom it concerned was able.

Adherence to private men, from ignorance of the causes of peace.

Ignorance of remote causes disposes men to attribute all events to the causes immediate and instrumental, for these are all the causes they perceive. And hence it comes to pass that in all places men that are grieved with payments to the public discharge their anger upon the publicans—that is to say, farmers, collectors, and other officers of the public revenue—and adhere to such as find fault with the public government, and thereby, when they have engaged themselves beyond hope of justification, fall also upon the supreme authority for fear of punishment or shame of receiving pardon.

OF THE NATURAL CONDITION OF MANKIND AS CONCERNING THEIR FELICITY, AND MISERY

Men by Nature Are Equal

Nature hath made men so equal, in the faculties of the body, and mind; so that though there be found one man sometimes manifestly stronger in body, or of quicker mind than another; yet when all is reckoned together, the difference between man, and man, is not so considerable, as that one man can thereupon claim to himself any benefit, to which another may not pretend, as well as he. For as to the strength of body, the weakest has strength enough to kill the strongest, either by secret machination, or by confederacy with others, that are in the same danger with himself.

And as to the faculties of the mind, setting aside the arts grounded upon words, and especially that skill of proceeding upon general, and infallible rules, called science; which very few have, and but in few things; as being not a native faculty, born with us; nor attained, as prudence, while we look after somewhat else, I find yet a greater equality amongst men, than that of strength. For prudence, is but experience; which equal time, equally bestows on all men, in those things they equally apply themselves unto. That which may perhaps make such equality incredible, is but a vain conceit of one's own wisdom, which almost all men think they have in a greater degree, than the vulgar; that is, than all men but themselves, and a few others, whom by fame, or for concurring with themselves, they approve. For such is the nature of men, that howsoever they may acknowledge many others to be more witty, or more eloquent, or more learned; yet they will hardly believe there be many so wise as themselves; for they see their own wit at hand, and other men's at a distance. But this proveth rather that men are in that point equal, than unequal. For there is not ordinarily a greater sign of the equal distribution of any thing, than that every man is contented with his share.

From Equality Proceeds Fear

From this equality of ability, arises equality of hope in the attaining of our ends. And therefore if any two men desire the same thing, which nevertheless they cannot both enjoy, they become enemies; and in the way to their end, which is principally their own preservation, and sometimes their enjoyment only, endeavour to destroy, or subdue one another. And from hence it comes to pass, that where an invader hath no more to fear, than another man's single power; if one plant, sow, build, or possess a convenient seat, others may probably be expected to come prepared with forces united, to dispossess, and deprive him, not only of the fruit of his labour, but also of his life, or liberty. And the invader again is in the like danger of another.

From Fear Proceeds War

And from this fear of one another, there is no way for any man to secure himself, so reasonable, as anticipation; that is, by force, or wiles, to master the persons of all men he can, so long, till he see no other power great enough to endanger him: and this is no more than his own preservation requireth, and is generally allowed. Also because there be some, that taking pleasure in contemplating their own power in the acts of conquest, which they pursue farther than their security requires; if others, that otherwise would be glad to be at ease within modest bounds, should not by invasion increase their power, they would not be able, long time, by standing only on their defence, to subsist. And by consequence, such increase of dominion over men being necessary to a man's preservation, it ought to be allowed him.

Again, men have no pleasure, but on the contrary a great deal of grief, in keeping company, where there is no power able to over-awe them all. For every man desires that his companion should value him, at the same rate he sets upon himself: and upon all signs of contempt, or undervaluing, naturally endeavours, as far as he dares, (which amongst them that have no common power to keep them in quiet, is far enough to make them destroy each other), to extort a greater value from his contemners, by damage; and from others, by the example.

So that in the nature of man, we find three principal causes of quarrel. First, competition; secondly, fear; thirdly, glory.

The first, maketh men invade for gain; the second, for safety; and the third, for reputation. The first use violence, to make themselves masters of other men's persons, wives, children, and cattle; the second, to defend them; the third, for trifles, as a word, a smile, a different option, and any other sign of undervalue, either direct in their persons, or by reflection in their kindred, their friends, their nation, their profession, or their name.

Out of Civil States There Is Always War of Everyone Against Everyone

Hereby it is manifest, that during the time men live without a common power to keep them all in awe, they are in that condition which is called war; and such a war, as is of every man, against every man. For war consists not in battle only or the act of fighting; but in a tract of time, wherein the will to contend by battle is sufficiently known: and therefore the notion of *time*, is to be considered in the nature of war; as it is in the nature of weather. For as the nature of foul weather, lies not in the shower or two of rain; but in an inclination thereto of many days together: so the nature of war, consists not in actual fighting; but in the known disposition thereto, during all the time there is no assurance to the contrary. All other time is PEACE.

The Problems and Inconvenience of Such a War

Whatsoever therefore occurs in a time of war, where every man is enemy to every man; the same occurs in the time, wherein men live without other security, than what their own strength, and their own invention shall furnish them withal. In such condition, there is no place for industry; because the fruit thereof is uncertain: and consequently no culture of the earth; no navigation, nor use of the commodities that may be imported by sea; no commodious building; no instruments of moving, and removing, such things as require much force; no knowledge of the face of the earth; no account of time; no arts; no letters; no society; and which is worst of all, continual fear, and danger of violent death; and the life of man, solitary, poor, nasty, brutish, and short.

It may seem strange to some man, that has not well weighed these things; that nature should thus dissociate, and render men apt to invade, and destroy one another: and he may therefore, not trusting to this inference, made from the passions, desire perhaps to have the same confirmed by experience. Let him therefore consider with himself, when taking a journey, he arms himself, and seeks to go well accompanied; when going to sleep, he locks his doors; when even in his house he locks his chests; and this when he knows there be laws, and public officers, armed, to revenge all injuries done him; what opinion he has of his fellow subjects, when he rides armed; of his fellow citizens, when he locks his doors; and of his children, and servants, when he locks his chests. Does he not there as much accuse mankind by his actions, as I do by my words? But neither of us accuse man's nature in it. The desires, and other passions of man, are in themselves no sin. No more are the actions, that proceed from those passions, till they know a law that forbids them: which till laws be made they cannot know: nor can any law be made, till they have agreed upon the person that shall make it.

It may perhaps be thought, there was never such a time, nor condition of war as this; and I believe it was never generally so, over all the world: but there are many places, where they live so now. For the savage people in many places of America, except the government of small families, the concord whereof depends on natural lust, have no government at all; and live at this day in that brutish manner, as I said before. Howsoever, it may be perceived what manner of life there would be, where there were no common power to fear, by the manner of life, which men that have formerly lived under a peaceful government, use to degenerate into, in a civil war.

But though there had never been any time, wherein particular men were in a condition of war one against another; yet in all times, kings, and persons of sovereign authority, because of their independency, are in continual jealousies, and in the state and posture of gladiators; having their weapons pointing, and their eyes fixed on one another; that is, their forts, garrisons, and guns upon the frontiers of their kingdoms; and continual spies upon their neighbours;

which is a posture of war. But because they up-hold thereby, the industry of their subjects; there does not follow from it, that misery, which accompanies the liberty of particular men.

In This State of War Nothing Is Unjust

To this war of every man, against every man, this also is a result; that nothing can be unjust. The notions of right and wrong, justice and in-justice have there no place. Where there is no common power, there is no law: where no law, no injustice. Force, and fraud, are in war the two cardinal virtues. Justice, and injustice are none of the faculties neither of the body, nor mind. If they were, they might be in a man that were alone in the world, as well as his senses, and passions. They are qualities, that relate to men in society, not in solitude. It is consequent also to the same condition, that there be no property, no ownership, no *mine* and *thine* dis-tinct; but only that to be every man's, that he can get; and for so long, as he can keep it. And thus much for the ill condition, which man by mere nature is actually placed in; though with a possibility to come out of it, consisting partly in the passions, partly in his reason.

The Passions Which Incline Men to Peace

The passions that incline men to peace, are fear of death; desire of such things as are necessary to commodious living; and a hope by their in-dustry to obtain them. And reason suggests con-venient articles of peace, upon which men may be drawn to agreement. These articles, are they, which otherwise are called the Laws of Nature: whereof I shall speak more particularly, in the two following chapters.

OF THE FIRST AND SECOND NATURAL LAWS, AND OF CONTRACTS

The Right of Nature

The right of nature, which writers commonly call *jus naturale*, is the liberty each man hath, to use his own power, as he will himself, for the preservation of his own nature; that is to

say, of his own life; and consequently, of do-ing any thing, which in his own judgment, and reason, he shall conceive to be the best means thereunto.

Liberty

By LIBERTY, is understood, according to the proper signification of the word, the absence of external impediments: which impediments, may oft take away part of a man's power to do what he would; but cannot hinder him from us-ing the power left him, according as his judg-ment, and reason shall dictate to him.

A Law of Nature

A LAW OF NATURE, *lex naturalis*, is a precept or general rule, found out by reason, by which a man is forbidden to do that, which is destruc-tive of his life, or taketh away the means of pre-serving the same; and to omit that, by which he thinketh it may be best preserved. For though they that speak of this subject, use to confound *jus*, and *lex*, *right* and *law*: yet they ought to be distinguished; because right, consisteth in lib-erty to do, or to forbear; whereas law, deter-mines, and binds to one of them: so that law, and right, differ as much, as obligation and lib-erty; which in one and the same matter are in-consistent.

In the State of Nature Every Man Has a Right to Everything

And because the condition of man, as has been shown in the precedent chapter, is a condition of war of every one against every one; in which case every one is governed by his own reason; and there is nothing he can make use of, that may not be a help unto him, in preserving his life against his enemies; it followeth, that in such a condition, every man has a right to every thing; even to one another's body. And there-fore, as long as this natural right of every man to every thing endures, there can be no security to any man, how strong or wise soever he be, of living out the time, which nature ordinarily alloweth men to live. And consequently it is a precept, or general rule of reason, *that every man, ought to endeavour peace, as far as he has hope of obtaining it; and when he cannot obtain it, that he may seek, and use, all helps, and advantages, of war.* The first branch of which rule, contains the first, and fundamental law of nature; which is, *to seek peace,* and *follow it.* The second, the sum of the right of nature; which is, *by all means we can, to defend ourselves.*

The Second Law of Nature

From this fundamental law of nature, by which men are commanded to endeavour peace, is derived this second law; *that a man be willing, when others are so too, as far-forth, as for peace, and defense of himself shall think it necessary, to lay down this right to all things; and be contented with so much liberty against other men, as he would allow other men against himself.* For as long as every man holds this right, of doing any thing he likes, so long are all men in the condition of war. But if other men will not lay down their right, as well as he; then there is no reason for any one, to divest himself of his: for that were to expose himself to prey, which no man is bound to, rather than to dispose himself to peace. This is that law of the Gospel; *whatsoever you require that others should do to you, that do ye to them.* And that law of all men, "What you do not want done to you, do not do to others."

Giving Up a Right

To *lay down* a man's *right* to any thing, is to *divest* himself of the *liberty,* of hindering another of the benefit of his own right to the same. For he that renounces, or passes away his right, gives not to any other man a right which he had not before; because there is nothing to which every man had not right by nature: but only stands out of his way, that he may enjoy his own original right, without hindrance from him; not without hindrance from another. So that the effect which redounds to one man, by another man's defect of right, is but so much diminution of impediments to the use of his own right original.

Right is laid aside, either by simply renouncing it; or by transferring it to another. By *simply* RENOUNCING; when he cares not to whom the benefit thereof redounds. By TRANSFERRING; when he intends the benefit thereof to some certain person, or persons. And when a man has in either manner abandoned, or granted away his right; then is he said to be obliged, or bound, not to hinder those, to whom such right is granted, or abandoned, from the benefit of it: and that he *ought,* and it is his duty, not to make void that voluntary act of his own: and that such hindrance is injustice, and injury, as being "without right," the right being before renounced, or transferred. So that *injury,* or *injustice,* in the controversies of the world, is somewhat like to that, which in the disputations of scholars is called *absurdity.* For as it is there called an absurdity, to contradict what one maintained in the beginning: so in the world, it is called injustice, and injury, voluntarily to undo that, which from the beginning he had voluntarily done. The way by which a man either simply renounces, or transfers his right, is a declaration, or signification, by some voluntary and sufficient sign, or signs, that he does so renounce, or transfer; or has so renounced, or transferred the same, to him that accepts it. And these signs are either words only, or actions only; or, as it happens most often, both words, and actions. And the same are the bonds, by which men are bound, and obliged: bonds, that have their strength, not from their own nature, for nothing is more easily broken than a man's word, but from fear of some evil consequence upon the rupture.

Some Rights Are Inalienable

Whensoever a man transfers his right, or renounces it; it is either in consideration of some right reciprocally transferred to himself; or for some other good he hopes for thereby. For it is a voluntary act: and of the voluntary acts of every man, the object is some *good to himself.* And therefore there be some rights, which no man can be understood by any words, or other signs, to have abandoned, or transferred. At first a man cannot lay down the right of resisting them, that assault him by force, to take away his life; because he cannot be understood to aim thereby, at any good to himself. The same may be said of wounds, and chains, and imprisonment; both because no benefit proceeds from such patience; as there is to the patience of suffering another to be wounded, or imprisoned: as also because a man cannot tell, when he seeth men proceed against him by violence, whether they intend his death or not. And lastly the motive, and end for which this renouncing, and transferring of right is introduced, is nothing else but the security of a man's person, in his life, and in the means of so preserving life, as not to be weary of it. And therefore if a man by words, or other signs, seem to despoil himself of the end, for which those signs were intended; he is not to be understood as if he meant it, or that it was his will; but that he was ignorant of how such words and actions were to be interpreted.

The Contract

The mutual transferring of right, is that which men call CONTRACT.

There is a difference between transferring of right to the thing; and transferring, or tradition, that is delivery of the thing itself. For the thing may be delivered together with the translation of the right; as in buying and selling with ready money; or exchange of goods, or lands: and it may be delivered some time after.

The Covenant

Again, one of the contractors, may deliver the thing contracted for on his part, and leave the other to perform his part at some determinate time after, and in the mean time be trusted; and then the contract on his part, is called PACT, or COVENANT: or both parts may contract now, to perform hereafter: in which cases, he that is to perform in time to come, being trusted, his performance is called *keeping of promise*, or faith; and the failing of performance, if it be voluntary, *violation of faith*.

When the transferring of right, is not mutual: but one of the parties transferreth, in hope to gain thereby friendship, or service from another, or from his friends; or in hope to gain the reputation of charity, or magnanimity; or to deliver his mind from the pain of compassion; or in hope of reward in heaven, this is not contract, but GIFT, FREE-GIFT, GRACE: which words signify one and the same thing.

Signs of contract, are either *express*, or by *inference*. Express, are words spoken with understanding of what they signify: and such words are either of the time *present*, or *past*; as, *I give, I grant, I have given, I have granted, I will that this be yours*: or of the future; as, *I will give, I will grant*: which words of the future are called promise.

When Covenant of Mutual Trust Become Invalid

If a covenant be made, wherein neither of the parties perform presently, but trust one another; in the condition of mere nature, which is a condition of war of every man against every man, upon any reasonable suspicion, it is void: but if there be a common power set over them both, with right and force sufficient to compel performance, it is not void. For he that performs first, has no assurance the other will perform after; because the bonds of words are too weak to bridle men's ambition, avarice, anger, and other passions, without the fear of some coercive power; which in the condition of mere nature, where all men are equal, and judges of the justness of their own fears, cannot possibly be supposed. And therefore he which performs first, does but betray himself to his enemy; contrary to the right, he can never abandon, of defending his life, and means of living.

But in a civil estate, where there is a power set up to constrain those that would otherwise violate their faith, that fear is no more reasonable: and for that cause, he which by the covenant is to perform first, is obliged so to do.

The cause of fear, which maketh such a covenant invalid, must be always something arising after the covenant made; as some new fact, or other sign of the will not to perform: else it cannot make the covenant void. For that which could not hinder a man from promising, ought not to be admitted as a hindrance of performing. . . .

ON THE OTHER LAWS OF NATURE

The Ninth, Against Pride

The question who is the better man has no place in the condition of mere nature, where, as has been shown before, all men are equal. The inequality that now is has been introduced by the civil laws. I know that Aristotle in the first book of his *Politics*, for a foundation of his doctrine, makes men by nature some more worthy to command, meaning the wiser sort such as he thought himself to be for his philosophy, others to serve, meaning those that had strong bodies but were not philosophers as he; as if master and servant were not introduced by consent of men but by difference of wit, which is not only against reason but also against experience. For there are very few so foolish that had not rather govern themselves than be governed by others; nor when the wise in their own conceit contend by force with them who distrust their own wisdom, do they always, or often, or almost at any time, get the victory. If nature therefore have made men equal, that equality is to be acknowledged; or if nature have made men unequal, yet because men that think themselves equal will not enter into conditions of peace but upon equal terms, such equality must be admitted. And therefore for the ninth law of nature, I put this: *that every man acknowledge another for his equal by nature.* The breach of this precept is pride.

The Tenth, Against Arrogance

On this law depends another: *that at the entrance into conditions of peace, no man require to reserve to himself any right which he is not content should be reserved to every one of the rest.* As it is necessary for all men that seek peace to lay down certain rights of nature—that is to say, not to have liberty to do all they [desire]—so is it necessary for man's life to retain some, as right to govern their own bodies, enjoy air, water, motion, ways to go from place to place, and all things else without which a man cannot live or not live well. If in this case, at the making of peace, men require for themselves that which they would not have to be granted to others, they do contrary to the precedent law that commands the acknowledgement of natural equality and therefore also against the law of nature. The observers of this law are those we call *modest*, and the breakers *arrogant* men. The Greeks call the violation of this law *pleonexia*—that is, a desire of more than their share.

The Eleventh, Equity

Also if *a man be trusted to judge between man and man*, it is a precept of the law of nature *that he deal equally between them.* For without that, the controversies of men cannot be determined but by war. He, therefore, that is partial in judgment does what in him lies to deter men from the use of judges and arbitrators, and consequently, against the fundamental law of nature, is the cause of war.

The observance of this law, from the equal distribution to each man of that which in reason belongs to him, is called EQUITY and, as I have said before, distributive justice; the violation, [*exception*] *of persons.*

The Twelfth, Equal Use of Things Common

And from this follows another law: *that such things as cannot be divided be enjoyed in common, if it can be; and if the quantity of the thing permit, without stint; otherwise proportionably to the number of them that have right.* For otherwise the distribution is unequal and contrary to equity.

OF THE CAUSES, GENERATION, AND DEFINITION OF A COMMONWEALTH

The end of common-wealth, particular security. The final cause, end, or design of men, who naturally love liberty and dominion over others, in the introduction of that restraint upon themselves in which we see them live in commonwealths is the foresight of their own preservation, and of a more contented life thereby—that is to say, of getting themselves out from that miserable condition of war which is necessarily consequent, as has been shown, to the natural passions of men when there is no visible power to keep them in awe and tie them by fear of punishment to the performance of their covenants and observation of those laws of nature set down in the fourteenth and fifteenth chapters.

Which is not to be had from the law of nature. For the laws of nature—as *justice, equity, modesty, mercy,* and, in sum, *doing to others as we would be done to*—of themselves, without the terror of some power to cause them to be observed, are contrary to our natural passions, that carry us to partiality, pride, revenge, and the like. And covenants without the sword are but words, and of no strength to secure a man at all. Therefore, notwithstanding the laws of nature (which everyone has then kept when he has the will to keep them, when he can do it safely), if there be no power erected, or not great enough for our security, every man will—and may lawfully—rely on his own strength and art for caution against all other men . . .

The generation of a commonwealth.

The definition of a commonwealth.

Sovereign and subject, what. The only way to erect such a common power as may be able to defend them from the invasion of foreigners and the injuries of one another, and thereby to secure them in such sort as that by their own industry and by the fruits of the earth they may nourish themselves and live contentedly, is to confer all their power and strength upon one man, or upon one assembly of men that may reduce all their wills, by plurality of voices, unto one will; which is as much as to say, to appoint one man or assembly of men to bear their person, and everyone to own and acknowledge himself to be author of whatsoever he that so bears their person shall act or cause

to be acted in those things which concern the common peace and safety, and therein to submit their wills every one to his will, and their judgments to his judgment. This is more than consent or concord; it is a real unity of them all in one and the same person, made by covenant of every man with every man, in such manner as if every man should say to every man, I authorize and give up my right of governing myself to this man, or to this assembly of men, on this condition that you give up your right to him and authorize all his actions in like manner. This done, the multitude so united in one person is called a COMMONWEALTH, in Latin CIVITAS. This is the generation of that great LEVIATHAN (or rather, to speak more reverently, of that mortal god) to which we owe, under the immortal God, our peace and defense. For by this authority, given him by every particular man in the commonwealth, he has the use of so much power and strength conferred on him that, by terror thereof, he is enabled to form the wills of them all to peace at home and mutual aid against their enemies abroad. And in him consists the essence of the commonwealth, which, to define it, is *one person, of whose acts a great multitude, by mutual covenants one with another, have made themselves every one the author, to the end he may use the strength and means of them all as he shall think expedient for their peace and common defense.* And he that carries this person is called SOVEREIGN and said to have *sovereign power*; and everyone besides, his SUBJECT.

The Discourse on the Origins of Inequality
JEAN-JACQUES ROUSSEAU

Jean-Jacques Rousseau (1712–1778) submitted *The Discourse on the Origins of Inequality* to the Academy of Dijon in Dijon, France, in 1755. While his essay failed to win the academy's prize, it established Rousseau as a leading social philosopher. In this essay Rousseau opposes Hobbes's gloomy assessment of humans in the state of nature, where life is "solitary, poor, nasty, brutish and short." In contrast to Hobbes, Rousseau describes the life of primitive humans as filled with spontaneous and simple pleasures, where healthy and hearty individuals, free and equal, far stronger and self-sufficient than civilized, domesticated beings, wander through forests, picking up food from nature's abundance. Enter property and with it the origins of inequality.

> The first person who, having enclosed a plot of land, took it into his head to say *this is mine* and found people simple enough to believe him, was the true founder of civil society. What crimes, wars, murders, what miseries and horrors would the human race have been spared, had someone pulled up the stakes or filled in the ditch and cried out to his fellow men: "Do not listen to this impostor. You are lost if you forget that the fruits of the earth belong to all and the earth to no one!"

The halcyon existence of the noble savage ends and a new stage of existence commences, one based on vanity, the need for recognition, respect, and social status, which, in turn, leads to acquisitiveness and even greater social inequality. Reason replaces natural sympathy, competition and violence are the result. As Rousseau says in his *Social Contract*, "Man is born free but is everywhere in chains." Yet Rousseau does not think it possible to go back to the state of nature. One must enter into a social contract to flourish in this artificial state of existence.

QUESTION PROPOSED BY THE ACADEMY OF DIJON: WHAT IS THE ORIGIN OF INEQUALITY AMONG MEN, AND IS IT AUTHORIZED BY THE NATURAL LAW?

I conceive of two kinds of inequality in the human species: one which I call natural or physical, because it is established by nature and consists in the difference of age, health, bodily strength, and qualities of mind or soul. The other may be called moral or political inequality, because it depends on a kind of convention and is established, or at least authorized, by the consent of men. This latter type of inequality consists in the different privileges enjoyed by some at the expense of others, such as being richer, more honored, more powerful than they, or even causing themselves to be obeyed by them.

There is no point in asking what the source of natural inequality is, because the answer would be found enunciated in the simple definition of the word. There is still less of a point in asking whether there would not be some essential connection between the two inequalities, for that would amount to asking whether those who command are necessarily better than those who obey, and whether strength of body or mind, wisdom or virtue are always found in the same individuals in proportion to power or wealth. Perhaps this is a good question for slaves to discuss within earshot of their masters, but it is not suitable for reasonable and free men who seek the truth.

Precisely what, then, is the subject of this discourse? To mark, in the progress of things, the moment when, right taking the place of violence, nature was subjected to the law. To explain the sequence of wonders by which the strong could resolve to serve the weak, and the people to buy imaginary repose at the price of real felicity.

PART ONE

When I strip that being, thus constituted, of all the supernatural gifts he could have received and of all the artificial faculties he could have acquired only through long progress; when I consider him, in a word, as he must have left the hands of nature, I see an animal less strong than some, less agile than others, but all in all, the most advantageously organized of all. I see him satisfying his hunger under an oak tree, quenching his thirst at the first stream, finding his bed at the foot of the same tree that supplied his meal; and thus all his needs are satisfied.

When the earth is left to its natural fertility and covered with immense forests that were never mutilated by the axe, it offers storehouses and shelters at every step to animals of every species. Men, dispersed among the animals, observe and imitate their industry, and thereby raise themselves to the level of animal instinct, with the advantage that, whereas each species has only its own instincts, man, who may perhaps have none that belongs to him, appropriates all of them to himself, feeds himself equally well on most of the various foods which the other animals divide among themselves, and consequently finds his sustenance more easily than any of the rest can.

Accustomed from childhood to inclement weather and the rigors of the seasons, acclimated to fatigue, and forced, naked and without arms, to defend their lives and their prey against other ferocious beasts, or to escape them by taking flight, men develop a robust and nearly unalterable temperament. Children enter the world with the excellent constitution of their parents and strengthen it with the same exercises that produced it, thus acquiring all the vigor that the human race is capable of having. Nature treats them precisely the way the law of Sparta treated the children of its citizens: it renders strong and robust those who are well constituted and makes all the rest perish, thereby differing from our present-day societies, where the state, by making children burdensome to their parents, kills them indiscriminately before their birth.

Since the savage man's body is the only instrument he knows, he employs it for a variety of purposes that, for lack of practice, ours are incapable of serving. And our industry deprives us of the force and agility that necessity obliges him to acquire. If he had had an axe, would his wrists break such strong branches? If he had had a sling, would he throw a stone with so much force? If he had had a ladder, would he climb a tree so nimbly? If he had had a horse, would he run so fast? Give a civilized man time to gather all his machines around him, and undoubtedly he will easily overcome a savage man. But if you want to see an even more unequal fight, pit them against each other naked and disarmed, and you will soon realize the advantage of constantly having all of one's forces at one's disposal, of always being ready for any event, and of always carrying one's entire self, as it were, with one.

Hobbes maintains that man is naturally intrepid and seeks only to attack and to fight. On the other hand, an illustrious philosopher thinks, and Cumberland and Pufendorf also affirm, that nothing is as timid as man in the state of nature, and that he is always trembling and ready to take flight at the slightest sound he hears or at the slightest movement he perceives. That may be the case with regard to objects with which he is not acquainted. And I do not doubt that he is frightened by all the new sights that present themselves to him every time he can neither discern the physical good and evil he may expect from them nor compare his forces with the dangers he must run: rare circumstances in the state of nature, where everything takes place in such a uniform manner and where the face of the earth is not subject to those sudden and continual changes caused by the passions and inconstancy of peoples living together. But since a savage man lives dispersed among the animals and, finding himself early on in a position to measure himself against them, he soon makes the comparison; and, aware that he surpasses them in skillfulness more than they surpass him in strength, he learns not to fear them any more. Pit a bear or a wolf against a savage who is robust, agile, and courageous, as they all are, armed with stones and a hefty cudgel, and you will see that the danger will be at least equal on both sides, and that after several such experiences, ferocious beasts, which do not like to attack one another, will be quite reluctant to attack a man, having found him to be as ferocious as themselves. With regard to animals that actually have more strength than man has skillfulness, he is in the same position as other weaker species, which nevertheless subsist. Man has the advantage that, since he is no less adept than they at running and at finding almost certain refuge in trees, he always has the alternative of accepting or leaving the encounter and the choice of taking flight or entering into combat. Moreover, it appears that no animal naturally attacks man, except in the case of self-defense or extreme hunger, or shows evidence of those violent antipathies toward him that seem to indicate that one species is destined by nature to serve as food for another. . . .

With regard to illnesses, I will not repeat the vain and false pronouncements made against medicine by the majority of people in good health. Rather, I will ask whether there is any solid observation on the basis of which one can conclude that the average lifespan is shorter in those countries where the art of medicine is most neglected than in those where it is cultivated most assiduously. And how could that be the case, if we give ourselves more ills than medicine can furnish us remedies? The extreme inequality in our lifestyle: excessive idleness among some, excessive labor among others; the ease with which we arouse and satisfy our appetites and our sensuality; the overly refined foods of the wealthy, which nourish them with irritating juices and overwhelm them with indigestion; the bad food of the poor, who most of the time do not have even that, and who, for want of food, are inclined to stuff their stomachs greedily whenever possible; staying up until all hours, excesses of all kinds, immoderate outbursts of every passion, bouts of fatigue and mental exhaustion; countless sorrows and afflictions which are felt in all levels of society and which perpetually gnaw away at souls: these are the fatal proofs that most of our ills are of our own making, and that we could have avoided nearly all of them by preserving the simple, regular and solitary lifestyle prescribed to us by nature. If nature has destined us to be healthy, I almost dare to affirm that the state of reflection is a state contrary to nature and that the man who meditates is a depraved animal. When one thinks about the stout constitutions of the savages, at least of those whom we have not ruined with our strong liquors; when one becomes aware of the fact that they know almost no illnesses but wounds and old age, one is strongly inclined to believe that someone could easily write the history of human maladies by following the history of civil societies. . . .

With so few sources of ills, man in the state of nature hardly has any need therefore of remedies, much less of physicians. The human race is in no worse condition than all the others in this respect; and it is easy to learn from hunters whether in their chases they find many sick animals. They find quite a few that have received serious wounds that healed quite nicely, that have had bones or even limbs broken and reset with no other surgeon than time, no other regimen than their everyday life, and that are no less perfectly cured for not having been tormented with incisions, poisoned with drugs, or exhausted with fasting. Finally, however correctly administered medicine may be among us, it is still certain that although a sick savage, abandoned to himself, has nothing to hope for except from nature, on the other hand, he has nothing to fear except his illness. This frequently makes his situation preferable to ours.

Therefore we must take care not to confuse savage man with the men we have before our eyes. Nature treats all animals left to their own devices with a predilection that seems to show how jealous she is of that right. The horse, the cat, the bull, even the ass, are usually taller, and all of them have a more robust constitution, more vigor, more strength, and more courage in the forests than in our homes. They lose half of these advantages in becoming domesticated; it might be said that all our efforts at feeding them and treating them well only end in their degeneration. It is the same for man himself. In becoming habituated to the ways of society and a slave, he becomes weak, fearful, and servile; his soft and effeminate lifestyle completes the enervation of both his strength and his courage. Let us add that the difference between the savage man and the domesticated man should be still greater than that between the savage animal and the domesticated animal; for while animal and man have been treated equally by nature, man gives more comforts to himself than to the animals he tames, and all of these comforts are so many specific causes that make him degenerate more noticeably.

So far I have considered only physical man. Let us now try to look at him from a metaphysical and moral point of view. . . . Every animal has ideas, since it has senses; up to a certain point it even combines its ideas, and in this regard man differs from an animal only in degree. Some philosophers have even suggested that there is a greater difference between two given men than between a given man and an animal. Therefore it is not so much understanding which causes the specific distinction of man from all other animals as it is his being a free agent. Nature commands every animal, and beasts obey. Man feels the same impetus, but he knows he is free to go along or to resist; and it is above all in the awareness of this freedom that the spirituality of his soul is made manifest. For physics explains in some way the mechanism of the senses and the formation of ideas; but in the power of willing, or rather of choosing, and in the feeling of this power, we find only purely spiritual acts, about which the laws of mechanics explain nothing.

But if the difficulties surrounding all these questions should leave some room for dispute on this difference between man and animal, there is another very specific quality which distinguishes them and about which there can be no argument: the faculty of self-perfection, a faculty which, with the aid of circumstances, successively develops all the others, and resides among us as much in the species as in the individual. On the other hand, an animal, at the end of a few months, is what it will be all its life; and its species, at the end of a thousand years, is what it was in the first of those thousand years. Why is man alone subject to becoming an imbecile? Is it not that he thereby returns to his primitive state, and that, while the animal which has acquired nothing and which also has nothing to lose, always retains its instinct, man, in losing through old age or other accidents all that his perfectibility has enabled him to acquire, thus falls even lower than the animal itself? It would be sad for us to be forced to agree that this distinctive and almost unlimited faculty is the source of all man's misfortunes; that this is what, by dint of time, draws him out of that original condition in which he would pass tranquil and innocent days; that this is what, through centuries of giving rise to his enlightenment and his errors, his vices and his virtues, eventually makes him a tyrant over himself and nature.

Savage man, left by nature to instinct alone, or rather compensated for the instinct he is perhaps lacking by faculties capable of first replacing them and then of raising him to the level of instinct, will therefore begin with purely animal functions. Perceiving and feeling will be his first state, which he will have in common with all animals. Willing and not willing, desiring, and fearing will be the first and nearly the only operations of his soul until new circumstances bring about new developments in it.

Whatever the moralists may say about it, human understanding owes much to the passions, which, by common consensus, also owe a great deal to it. It is by their activity that our reason is perfected. We seek to know only because we desire to find enjoyment; and it is impossible to conceive why someone who had neither desires nor fears would go to the bother of reasoning. The passions in turn take their origin from our needs, and their progress from our knowledge. For one can desire or fear things only by virtue of the ideas one can have of them, or from the simple impulse of nature; and savage man, deprived of every sort of enlightenment, feels only the passion of this latter sort. His desires do not go beyond his physical needs. The only goods he knows in the universe are nourishment, a woman and rest; the only evils he fears are pain and hunger. I say pain and not death because an animal will never know what it is to die; and knowledge of death and its terrors is one of the first acquisitions that man has made in withdrawing from the animal condition. . . .

Whatever these origins may be, it is clear, from the little care taken by nature to bring men together through mutual needs and to facilitate their use of speech, how little she prepared them for becoming habituated to the ways of society, and how little she contributed to all that men have done to establish the bonds of society. In fact, it is impossible to imagine why, in that primitive state, one man would have a greater need for another man than a monkey or a wolf has for another of its respective species; or, assuming this need, what motive could induce the other man to satisfy it; or even, in this latter instance, how could they be in mutual agreement regarding the conditions. I know that we are repeatedly told that nothing would have been so miserable as man in that state; and if it is true, as I believe I have proved, that it is only after many centuries that men could have had the desire and the opportunity to leave that state, that would be a charge to bring against nature, not against him whom nature has thus constituted. But if we understand the word miserable properly, it is a word which is without meaning or which signifies merely a painful privation and suffering of the body or the soul. Now I would very much like someone to explain to me what kind of misery can there be for a free being whose heart is at peace and whose body is in good health? I ask which of the two, civil or natural life, is more likely to become insufferable to those who live it? We see about us practically no people who do not complain about their existence; many even deprive themselves of it to the extent they are able, and the combination of divine and human laws is hardly enough to stop this disorder. I ask if anyone has ever heard tell of a savage who was living in liberty ever dreaming of complaining about his life and of killing himself. Let the judgment therefore be made with less pride on which side real misery lies. On the other hand, nothing would have been so miserable as savage man, dazzled by enlightenment, tormented by passions, and reasoning about a state different from his own. It was by a very wise providence that the latent faculties he possessed should develop only as the occasion to exercise them presents itself, so that they would be neither superfluous nor troublesome to him beforehand, nor underdeveloped and useless in time of need. In instinct alone, man had everything he needed in order to live in the state of nature; in a cultivated reason, he has only what he needs to live in society. . . .

Above all, let us not conclude with Hobbes that because man has no idea of goodness he is naturally evil; that he is vicious because he does not know virtue; that he always refuses to perform services for his fellow men he does not believe he owes them; or that, by virtue of the right, which he reasonably attributes to himself, to those things he needs, he foolishly imagines himself to be the sole proprietor of the entire universe. Hobbes has very clearly seen the defect of all modern definitions of natural right, but the consequences he draws from his own definition show that he takes it in a sense that is no less false. Were he to have reasoned on the basis of the principles he establishes, this author should have said that since the state of nature is the state in which the concern for our self-preservation is the least prejudicial to that of others, that state was consequently the most appropriate for peace and the best suited for the human race. He says precisely the opposite, because he had wrongly injected into the savage man's concern for self-preservation the need to satisfy a multitude of passions which are the product of society and which have made laws necessary.

Man is weak when he is dependent, and he is emancipated from that dependence before he is robust. Hobbes did not see that the same cause preventing savages from using their reason, as our jurists claim, is what prevents them at the same time from abusing their faculties, as he himself maintains. Hence we could say that savages are not evil precisely because they do not know it is to be good; for it is neither the development of enlightenment nor the restraint imposed by the law, but the calm of the passions and the ignorance of vice which prevents them from doing evil. *So much more profitable to these is the ignorance of vice than the knowledge of virtue is to those.* Moreover, there is another principle that Hobbes failed to notice, and which, having been given to man in order to mitigate, in certain circumstances, the ferocity of his egocentrism or the desire for self-preservation before this egocentrism of his came into being, tempers the ardor he has for his own well-being by an innate repugnance to seeing his fellow men suffer. I do not believe I have any contradiction to fear in granting the only natural virtue that the most excessive detractor of human virtues was forced to recognize. I am referring to pity, a disposition that is fitting for beings that are as weak and as subject to ills as we are; a virtue all the more universal and all the more useful to man in that it precedes in him any kind of reflection, and so natural that even animals sometimes show noticeable signs of it. . . .

Reason is what turns man in upon himself. Reason is what separates him from all that troubles him and afflicts him. Philosophy is what isolates him and what moves him to say in secret, at the sight of a suffering man, "Perish if you will; I am safe and sound." No longer can anything but danger to the entire society trouble the tranquil slumber of the philosopher and yank him from his bed. His fellow man can be killed with impunity underneath his window. He has merely to place his hands over his ears and argue with himself a little in order to prevent nature, which rebels within him, from identifying him with the man being assassinated. Savage man does not have this admirable talent, and for lack of wisdom and reason he is always seen thoughtlessly giving in to the first sentiment of humanity. When there is a riot or a street brawl, the populace gathers together;

the prudent man withdraws from the scene. It is the rabble, the women of the marketplace, who separate the combatants and prevent decent people from killing one another.

It is therefore quite certain that pity is a natural sentiment, which, by moderating in each individual the activity of the love of oneself, contributes to the mutual preservation of the entire species. Pity is what carries us without reflection to the aid of those we see suffering. Pity is what, in the state of nature, takes the place of laws, mores, and virtue, with the advantage that no one is tempted to disobey its sweet voice. Pity is what will prevent every robust savage from robbing a weak child or an infirm old man of his hard-earned subsistence, if he himself expects to be able to find his own someplace else. Instead of the sublime maxim of reasoned justice, *Do unto others as you would have them do unto you*, pity inspires all men with another maxim of natural goodness, much less perfect but perhaps more useful than the preceding one: *Do what is good for you with as little harm as possible to others*. In a word, it is in this natural sentiment, rather than in subtle arguments that one must search for the cause of the repugnance at doing evil that every man would experience, even independently of the maxims of education. Although it might be appropriate for Socrates and minds of his stature to acquire virtue through reason, the human race would long ago have ceased to exist, if its preservation had depended solely on the reasonings of its members. . . .

PART TWO

The first person who, having enclosed a plot of land, took it into his head to say this is mine and found people simple enough to believe him, was the true founder of civil society. What crimes, wars, murders, what miseries and horrors would the human race have been spared, had someone pulled up the stakes or filled in the ditch and cried out to his fellow men: "Do not listen to this impostor. You are lost if you forget that the fruits of the earth belong to all and the earth to no one!" But it is quite likely that by then things had already reached the point

where they could no longer continue as they were. For this idea of property, depending on many prior ideas which could only have arisen successively, was not formed all at once in the human mind. It was necessary to make great progress, to acquire much industry and enlightenment, and to transmit and augment them from one age to another, before arriving at this final stage in the state of nature. Let us therefore take things farther back and try to piece together under a single viewpoint that slow succession of events and advances in knowledge in their most natural order.

Man's first sentiment was that of his own existence; his first concern was that of his preservation. The products of the earth provided him with all the help he needed; instinct led him to make use of them. With hunger and other appetites making him experience by turns various ways of existing, there was one appetite that invited him to perpetuate his species; and this blind inclination, devoid of any sentiment of the heart, produced a purely animal act. Once this need had been satisfied, the two sexes no longer took cognizance of one another, and even the child no longer meant anything to the mother once it could do without her.

Such was the condition of man in his nascent stage; such was the life of an animal limited at first to pure sensations, and scarcely profiting from the gifts nature offered him, far from dreaming of extracting anything from her. But difficulties soon presented themselves to him; it was necessary to learn to overcome them. The height of trees, which kept him from reaching their fruits, the competition of animals that sought to feed themselves on these same fruits, the ferocity of those animals that wanted to take his own life: everything obliged him to apply himself to bodily exercises. It was necessary to become agile, fleet-footed and vigorous in combat. Natural arms, which are tree branches and stones, were soon found ready at hand. He learned to surmount nature's obstacles, combat other animals when necessary, fight for his subsistence even with men, or compensate for what he had to yield to those stronger than himself.

In proportion as the human race spread, difficulties multiplied with the men. Differences in soils, climates and seasons could force them to inculcate these differences in their lifestyles.

Barren years, long and hard winters, hot summers that consume everything required new resourcefulness from them. Along the seashore and the riverbanks they invented the fishing line and hook, and became fishermen and fisheaters. In the forests they made bows and arrows, and became hunters and warriors. In cold countries they covered themselves with the skins of animals they had killed. Lightning, a volcano, or some fortuitous chance happening acquainted them with fire: a new resource against the rigors of winter. They learned to preserve this element, then to reproduce it, and finally to use it to prepare meats that previously they devoured raw.

This repeated appropriation of various beings to himself, and of some beings to others, must naturally have engendered in man's mind the perceptions of certain relations. These relationships which we express by the words "large," "small," "strong," "weak," "fast," "slow," "timorous," "bold," and other similar ideas, compared when needed and almost without thinking about it, finally produced in him a kind of reflection, or rather a mechanical prudence which pointed out to him the precautions that were most necessary for his safety.

The new enlightenment which resulted from this development increased his superiority over the other animals by making him aware of it. He trained himself to set traps for them; he tricked them in a thousand different ways. And although several surpassed him in fighting strength or in swiftness in running, of those that could serve him or hurt him, he became in time the master of the former and the scourge of the latter. Thus the first glance he directed upon himself produced within him the first stirring of pride; thus, as yet hardly knowing how to distinguish the ranks, and contemplating himself in the first rank by virtue of his species, he prepared himself from afar to lay claim to it in virtue of his individuality.

Although his fellowmen were not for him what they are for us, and although he had hardly anything more to do with them than with other animals, they were not forgotten in his observations. The conformities that time could make him perceive among them, his female, and himself, made him judge those he did not perceive. And seeing that they all acted as he would have done under similar circumstances, he concluded that their way of thinking and feeling was in complete conformity with his own. And this important truth, well established in his mind, made him follow, by a presentiment as sure as dialectic and more prompt, the best rules of conduct that it was appropriate to observe toward them for his advantage and safety.

Taught by experience that love of well-being is the sole motive of human actions, he found himself in a position to distinguish the rare occasions when common interest should make him count on the assistance of his fellowmen, and those even rarer occasions when competition ought to make him distrust them. In the first case, he united with them in a herd, or at most in some sort of free association, that obligated no one and that lasted only as long as the passing need that had formed it. In the second case, everyone sought to obtain his own advantage, either by overt force, if he believed he could, or by cleverness and cunning, if he felt himself to be the weaker.

This is how men could imperceptibly acquire some crude idea of mutual commitments and of the advantages to be had in fulfilling them, but only insofar as present and perceptible interests could require it, since foresight meant nothing to them, and far from concerning themselves about a distant future, they did not even give a thought to the next day. Were it a matter of catching a deer, everyone was quite aware that he must faithfully keep to his post in order to achieve this purpose; but if a hare happened to pass within reach of one of them, no doubt he would have pursued it without giving it a second thought, and that, having obtained his prey, he cared very little about causing his companions to miss theirs. . . .

Having previously wandered about the forests and having assumed a more fixed situation, men slowly came together and united into different bands, eventually forming in each country a particular nation, united by mores and characteristic features, not by regulations and laws, but by the same kind of life and foods and by the common influence of the climate. Eventually a permanent proximity cannot fail to engender some intercourse among different families. Young people of different sexes live in neighboring huts; the passing intercourse demanded by nature soon leads to another, through frequent contact with one another, no less sweet and more permanent. People become accustomed to consider different objects and to make comparisons. Imperceptibly they acquire the ideas of merit and beauty which produce feelings of preference. By dint of seeing one another, they can no longer get along without seeing one another again. A sweet and tender feeling insinuates itself into the soul and at the least opposition becomes an impetuous fury. Jealousy awakens with love; discord triumphs, and the sweetest passion receives sacrifices of human blood.

In proportion as ideas and sentiments succeed one another and as the mind and heart are trained, the human race continues to be tamed, relationships spread and bonds are tightened. People grew accustomed to gather in front of their huts or around a large tree; song and dance, true children of love and leisure, became the amusement or rather the occupation of idle men and women who had flocked together. Each one began to look at the others and to want to be looked at himself, and public esteem had a value. The one who sang or danced the best, the handsomest, the strongest, the most adroit or the most eloquent became the most highly regarded. And this was the first step toward inequality and, at the same time, toward vice. From these first preferences were born vanity and contempt on the one hand, and shame and envy on the other. And the fermentation caused by these new leavens eventually produced compounds fatal to happiness and innocence.

As soon as men had begun mutually to value one another, and the idea of esteem was formed in their minds, each one claimed to have a right to it, and it was no longer possible for anyone to be lacking it with impunity. From this came the first duties of civility, even among savages; and from this every voluntary wrong became an outrage, because along with the harm that resulted from the injury, the offended party saw in it contempt for his person, which often was more insufferable than the harm itself. Hence each man punished the contempt shown him in a manner proportionate to the esteem in which he held himself; acts of revenge became terrible, and men became bloodthirsty and cruel. This is precisely the stage reached by most of the savage people known to us; and it is for want of having made adequate distinctions among their ideas or of having noticed how far these peoples already were from the original state of nature that many have hastened to conclude that man is naturally cruel, and that he needs civilization in order to soften him. On the contrary, nothing is so gentle as man in his primitive state, when, placed by nature at an equal distance from the stupidity of brutes and the fatal enlightenment of civil man, and limited equally by instinct and reason to protecting himself from the harm that threatens him, he is restrained by natural pity from needlessly harming anyone himself, even if he has been harmed. For according to the axiom of the wise Locke, *where there is no property, there is no injury.* . . .

From the cultivation of land, there necessarily followed the division of land; and from property once recognized, the first rules of justice. For in order to render everyone what is his, it is necessary that everyone can have something. Moreover, as men began to look toward the future and as they saw that they all had goods to lose, there was not one of them who did not have to fear reprisals against himself for wrongs he might do to another. This origin is all the more natural as it is impossible to conceive of the idea of property arising from anything but manual labor, for it is not clear what man can add, beyond his own labor, in order to appropriate things he has not made. It is labor alone that, in giving the cultivator a right to the product of the soil he has tilled, consequently gives him a right, at least until the harvest, and thus from year to year. With this possession continuing uninterrupted, it is easily transformed into property. . . .

Things in this state could have remained equal, if talents had been equal, and if the use of iron and the consumption of foodstuffs had always been in precise balance. But this proportion, which was not maintained by anything, was soon broken. The strongest did the most work; the most adroit turned theirs to better advantage: the most ingenious found ways to shorten their labor. The farmer had a greater need for iron, or the blacksmith had a greater need for wheat; and in laboring equally, the one earned a great deal while the other barely had enough to live. Thus it is that natural inequality imperceptibly manifests itself together with inequality occasioned by the socialization process. Thus it is that the differences among men, developed by those of circumstances, make themselves more noticeable, more permanent in their effects, and begin to influence the fate of private individuals in the same proportion. . . .

Thus we find here all our faculties developed, memory and imagination in play, egocentrism looking out for its interests, reason rendered active, and the mind having nearly reached the limit of the perfection of which it is capable. We find here all the natural qualities put into action, the rank and fate of each man established not only on the basis of the quantity of goods and the power to serve or harm, but also on the basis of mind, beauty, strength or skill, on the basis of merit or talents. And since these qualities were the only ones that could attract consideration, he was soon forced to have them or affect them. It was necessary, for his advantage, to show himself to be something other than what he in fact was. Being something and appearing to be something became two completely different things; and from this distinction there arose grand ostentation, deceptive cunning, and all the vices that follow in their wake. On the other hand, although man had previously been free and independent, we find him, so to speak, subject, by virtue of a multitude of fresh needs, to all of nature and particularly to his fellowmen, whose slave in a sense he becomes even in becoming their master; rich, he needs their services; poor, he needs their help; and being midway between wealth and poverty does not put him in a position to get along without them. It is therefore necessary for him to seek incessantly to interest them in his fate and to make them find their own profit, in fact or in appearance, in working for his. This makes him two-faced and crooked with some, imperious and harsh with others, and puts him in the position of having to abuse everyone he needs when he cannot make them fear them and does not find it in his interests to be of useful service to them. Finally, consuming ambition, the zeal for raising the relative level of his fortune, less out of real need than in order to put himself above others, inspires in all men a wicked tendency to harm one another, a secret jealousy all the more dangerous because, in order to strike its blow in greater safety, it often wears the mask of benevolence; in short, competition and rivalry on the one hand, opposition of interest[s] on the other, and always the hidden desire to profit at the expense of someone else. All these ills are the first effect of property and the inseparable offshoot of incipient inequality. . . .

I have tried to set forth the origin and progress of inequality, the establishment and abuse of political societies, to the extent that these things can be deduced from the nature of man by the light of reason alone, and independently of the sacred dogmas that give to sovereign authority the sanction of divine right. It follows from this presentation that, since inequality is practically non-existent in the state of nature, it derives its force and growth from the development of our faculties and the progress of the human mind, and eventually becomes stable and legitimate through the establishment of property and laws. Moreover, it follows that moral inequality, authorized by positive right alone, is contrary to natural right whenever it is not combined in the same proportion with physical inequality: a distinction that is sufficient to determine what one should think in this regard about the sort of inequality that reigns among all civilized people, for it is obviously contrary to the law of nature, however it may be defined, for a child to command an old man, for an imbecile to lead a wise man, and for a handful of people to gorge themselves on superfluities while the starving multitude lacks necessities.

Justice and Equality
DAVID HUME

David Hume (1711–1776), a Scottish empiricist, was one of the greatest philosophers of the Enlightenment. In this selection he describes justice as a human convention caused by the intersection of people's tendencies toward "selfishness and limited generosity" with conditions of scarcity in the world. Eliminate any of these conditions and justice would disappear. He goes on to discuss the problem of equality in relation to justice.

I have already observed, that justice takes its rise from human conventions; and that these are intended as a remedy to some inconveniences, which proceed from the concurrence of certain qualities of the human mind with the situation of external objects. The qualities of the mind are selfishness and limited generosity: and the situation of external objects is their easy change, joined to their scarcity in comparison of the wants and desires of men. But however philosophers may have been bewildered in those speculations, poets have been guided more infallibly, by a certain taste or common instinct, which, in most kinds of reasoning, goes further than any of that art and philosophy with which we have been yet acquainted. They easily perceived, if every man had a tender regard for another, or if nature supplied abundantly all our wants and desires, that the jealousy of interest, which justice supposes, could no longer have place; nor would there be any occasion for those distinctions and limits of property and possession, which at present are in use among mankind. Increase to a sufficient degree the benevolence of men, or the bounty of nature, and you render justice useless, by supplying its place with much nobler virtues, and more valuable blessings. The selfishness of men is animated by the few possessions we have, in proportion to our wants; and it is to restrain this selfishness, that men have been obliged to separate themselves from the community, and to distinguish betwixt their own goods and those of others.

Nor need we have recourse to the fictions of poets to learn this; but, beside the reason of the thing, may discover the same truth by common experience and observation. It is easy to remark, that a cordial affection renders all things common among friends; and that married people, in particular, mutually lose their property, and are unacquainted with the mine and thine, which are so necessary, and yet cause such disturbance in human society. The same effect arises from any alteration in the circumstances of mankind; as when there is such a plenty of any thing as satisfies all the desires of men: in which case the distinction of property is entirely lost, and every thing remains in common. This we may observe with regard to air and water, though the most valuable of all external objects; and may easily conclude, that if men were supplied with every thing in the same abundance, or if every one had the same affection and tender regard for every one as for himself, justice and injustice would be equally unknown among mankind.

Here then is a proposition, which, I think, may be regarded as certain, that it is only from the selfishness and confined generosity of men, along with the scanty provision nature has made for his wants, that justice derives its origin. If we look backward we shall find, that this proposition bestows an additional force on some of those observations which we have already made on this.

First, we may conclude from it, that a regard to public interest, or a strong extensive benevolence, is not our first and original motive for

46

the observation of the rules of justice; since it is allowed, that if men were endowed with such a benevolence, these rules would never have been dreamed of.

Secondly, we may conclude from the same principle, that the sense of justice is not founded on reason, or on the discovery of certain connexions and relations of ideas, which are eternal, immutable, and universally obligatory. For since it is confessed, that such an alteration as that above mentioned, in the temper and circumstances of mankind, would entirely alter our duties and obligations, it is necessary upon the common system, that the sense of virtue is derived from reason, to shew the change which this must produce in the relations and ideas. But it is evident, that the only cause why the extensive generosity of man, and the perfect abundance of every thing, would destroy the very idea of justice, is, because they render it useless; and that, on the other hand, his confined benevolence, and his necessitous condition, give rise to that virtue, only by making it requisite to the public interest, and to that of every individual. It was therefore a concern for our own and the public interest which made us establish the laws of justice; and nothing can be more certain, than that it is not any relation of ideas which gives us this concern, but our impressions and sentiments, without which every thing in nature is perfectly indifferent to us, and can never in the least affect us. The sense of justice, therefore, is not founded on our ideas, but on our impressions.

Thirdly, we may further confirm the foregoing proposition, that those impressions, which give rise to this sense of justice, are not natural to the mind of man, but arise from artifice and human conventions. For, since any considerable alteration of temper and circumstances destroys equally justice and injustice; and since such an alteration has an effect only by changing our own and the public interest, it follows that the first establishment of the rules of justice depends on these different interests. But if men pursued the public interest naturally, and with a hearty affection, they would have never dreamed of restraining each other by these rules; and if they pursued their own interest, without any precaution, they would run head-

long into every kind of injustice and violence. These rules, therefore, are artificial, and seek their end in an oblique and indirect manner; nor is the interest which gives rise to them of a kind that could be pursued by the natural and inartificial passions of men.

To make this more evident, consider, that, though the rules of justice are established merely by interest, their connexion with interest is somewhat singular, and is different from what may be observed on other occasions. A single act of justice is frequently contrary to public interest; and were it to stand alone, without being followed by other acts, may, in itself, be very prejudicial to society. When a man of merit, of a beneficent disposition, restores a great fortune to a miser, or a seditious bigot, he has acted justly and laudably; but the public is a real sufferer. Nor is every single act of justice, considered apart, more conducive to private interest than to public; and it is easily conceived how a man may impoverish himself by a signal instance of integrity, and have reason to wish, that, with regard to that single act, the laws of justice were for a moment suspended in the universe.

But, however single acts of justice may be contrary, either to public or private interest, it is certain that the whole plan or scheme is highly conducive, or indeed absolutely requisite, both to the support of society, and the well-being of every individual. It is impossible to separate the good from the ill. Property must be stable, and must be fixed by general rules. Though in one instance the public be a sufferer, this momentary ill is amply compensated by the steady prosecution of the rule, and by the peace and order which it establishes in society. And even every individual person must find himself a gainer on balancing the account; since, without justice, society must immediately dissolve, and every one must fall into that savage and solitary condition, which is infinitely worse than the worst situation that can possibly be supposed in society. When, therefore, men have had experience enough to observe, that, whatever may be the consequence of any single act of justice, performed by a single person, yet the whole system of actions concurred in by the whole society, is infinitely advantageous to the whole, and to every part, it is not long before justice and property take place. Every member of society is sensible of this interest: every one expresses this sense to his fellows, along with the resolution he has taken of squaring his actions by it, on condition that others will do the same. No more is requisite to induce any one of them to perform an act of justice, who has the first opportunity. This becomes an example to others; and thus justice establishes itself by a kind of convention or agreement, that is, by a sense of interest, supposed to be common to all, and where every single act is performed in expectation that others are to perform the like. Without such a convention, no one would ever have dreamed that there was such a virtue as justice, or have been induced to conform his actions to it. Taking any single act, my justice may be pernicious in every respect; and it is only upon the supposition that others are to imitate my example, that I can be induced to embrace that virtue; since nothing but this combination can render justice advantageous, or afford me any motives to conform myself to its rules. . . .

If we examine the particular laws, by which justice is directed, and property determined; we shall still be presented with the same conclusion. The good of mankind is the only object of all these laws and regulations. Not only is it requisite, for the peace and interest of society, that men's possessions should be separated; but the rules, which we follow, in making the separation, are such as can best be contrived to serve farther the interests of society.

We shall suppose, that a creature, possessed of reason, but unacquainted with human nature, deliberates with himself what RULES of justice or property would best promote public interest, and establish peace and security among mankind: His most obvious thought would be, to assign the largest possessions to the most extensive virtue, and give every one the power of doing good, proportioned to his inclination. In a perfect theocracy, where a being, infinitely intelligent, governs by particular volitions, this rule would certainly have place, and might serve to the wisest purposes: But were mankind to execute such a law; so great is the uncertainty of merit, both from its natural obscurity, and from the self-conceit of each individual, that no determinate rule of conduct would ever result

from it; and the total dissolution of society must be the immediate consequence. Fanatics may suppose, that dominion is founded on grace, and that saints alone inherit the earth; but the civil magistrate very justly puts these sublime theorists on the same footing with common robbers, and teaches them by the severest discipline, that a rule, which, in speculation, may seem the most advantageous to society, may yet be found, in practice, totally pernicious and destructive.

That there were religious fanatics of this kind in ENGLAND, during the civil wars, we learn from history; though it is probable, that the obvious tendency of these principles excited such horror in mankind, as soon obliged the dangerous enthusiasts to renounce, or at least conceal their tenets. Perhaps, the levellers, who claimed an equal distribution of property, were a kind of political fanatics, which arose from the religious species, and more openly avowed their pretensions; as carrying a more plausible appearance, of being practicable in themselves, as well as useful to human society.

It must, indeed, be confessed, that nature is so liberal to mankind, that, were all her presents equally divided among the species, and improved by art and industry, every individual would enjoy all the necessaries, and even most of the comforts of life; nor would ever be liable to any ills, but such as might accidentally arise from the sickly frame and constitution of his body. It must also be confessed, that, wherever we depart from this equality, we rob the poor of more satisfaction than we add to the rich, and that the slight gratification of a frivolous vanity, in one individual, frequently costs more than bread to many families, and even provinces. It may appear withal, that the rule of equality, as it would be highly useful, is not altogether impracticable; but has taken place, at least in an imperfect degree, in some republics; particularly that of SPARTA; where it was attended, it is said, with the most beneficial consequences. Not to mention, that the AGRARIAN laws, so frequently claimed in ROME, and carried into execution in many GREEK cities, proceeded, all of them, from a general idea of the utility of this principle.

But historians, and even common sense, may inform us, that, however specious these ideas of perfect equality may seem, they are really, at bottom, impracticable; and were they not so, would be extremely pernicious to human society. Render possessions ever so equal, men's different degrees of art, care, and industry will immediately break that equality. Or if you check these virtues, you reduce society to the most extreme indigence; and instead of preventing want and beggary in a few, render it unavoidable to the whole community. The most rigorous inquisition too is requisite to watch every inequality on its first appearance; and the most severe jurisdiction, to punish and redress it. But besides, that so much authority must soon degenerate into tyranny, and be exerted with great partialities; who can possibly be possessed of it, in such a situation as is here supposed? Perfect equality of possessions, destroying all subordination, weakens extremely the authority of magistracy, and must reduce all power nearly to a level, as well as property.

We may conclude, therefore, that, in order to establish laws for the regulation of property, we must be acquainted with the nature and situation of man; must reject appearances which may be false, though specious; and must search for those rules, which are, on the whole, most useful and beneficial. Vulgar sense and slight experience are sufficient for this purpose; where men give not way to too selfish avidity, or too extensive enthusiasm.

The Manifesto of Equality
FRANCOIS-NOEL BABEUF AND
SYLVAIN MARECHAL

After the death of Robespierre in 1794 and the fall of the French Revolution, a group of revolutionaries conspired to overthrow the reactionary regime. Their leader was Francois-Noel Babeuf (1760–1797), called "Gracchus" (after the Roman reformer, 153–121 B.C.). Their statement "Manifeste des Egaux" (Manifesto of Equals) based on Babeuf's principles was written by the revolutionary journalist Sylvain Marechal (1750–1803). Babeuf was born in Fauborg, France, November 23, 1760, the son of a poor civil servant. Babeuf worked as a journalist and when the revolution took place he opposed the extremes of the Jacobins, who were led by Robespierre, and whom he thought to be power hungry.

Babeuf's first principle was simply: Everyone has a right to survive. His second principle was: There is in everyone an innate disposition to dominate. He would have subscribed to Lord Acton's "Power corrupts and absolute power corrupts absolutely." His dominant question was: How can this innate corrupting power be prevented from developing? His answer was *democracy*. He thought of democracy as revolutionary and communistic. In the beginning he advocated not full equality but a welfare floor in order to ensure survival. But in the spirit of democracy he espoused universal male suffrage, referendum, and recall. He held that anyone who could not fend for himself should be aided by the state—meaning mainly infants, the disabled, and the elderly. To fulfill their needs, the state should enact a progressive income tax, and if the state fails to protect the survival needs of the poor, the poor have a right to use violence to obtain their due.

By 1791 he expanded his program to include land reform and redistribution—something anathema during the revolution itself. In 1793 he was part of the Revolutionary Government's program to requisition food for the starving in Paris. It was a grand success and led Babeuf to believe that the state could make a difference for good in people's lives. It could ensure a welfare system. After Thermador (term meaning "heat" and given to the eleventh month in the French Revolutionary Calendar, corresponding to our mid-summer) 1794 and the fall of the Jacobins, Babeuf converted to complete communism. He believed that there must be complete equality, for people are equal. There must be equality of status in a classless society in order to prevent jealousy and the abuse of power. All goods must be in a common storehouse and redistributed by the government through rations. Men are basically equal because their stomachs are the same size. There must be no difference in pay, for all such differences are due merely to opinion.

But what about those who work harder than others? Should not they be rewarded differentially? No, answers Babeuf. They must be restrained from overproducing, otherwise they would deserve more, and this would upset the egalitarian balance.

There is no chance of bringing this ideal state of affairs about peacefully, so there must be a revolution—but, he assures us, it will only be allowed to last three months. In April 1796 Babeuf, joined by Jacobins, organized an insurrection of the government, the Babeuf Plot. It failed. Babeuf and fellow conspirators were arrested and Babeuf was sent to the guillotine on May 27, 1797, not yet 37. His ideas influenced Marx and Engels, who paid tribute to him in *The Holy Family* and in *The Communist Manifesto*, and at the beginning of the Russian Revolution in October 1919 Leon Trotsky proclaimed Babeuf the first hero and martyr of the Communist Revolution, a true spokesman of the proletariat in the French Revolution. His ideas have represented the most uncompromising egalitarianism ever advocated.

Here is the *Manifesto of Equality*:

People of France!

For fifteen centuries you have lived as slaves and therefore in misery. For six years you have stood breathless, waiting for independence, happiness and equality.

Equality!! the first desire of nature, the first need of man, chief bond of all legitimate society!

People of France! you have not been favored above other nations which vegetate in this unhappy world! . . .

From time immemorial we have been told—hypocritically—that men are equal; and from time immemorial inequality of the most degrading and most monstrous kind has insolently weighed on mankind. Ever since there have been civil societies man's finest birthright has been recognized without contradiction but so far has not once been carried into effect: equality was nothing more than a legal fiction, beautiful but sterile.

Today when our clamor for it is more resolute, we are told "Hold your tongues, wretches! real equality is only an illusion; content yourselves with conditional equality: you are equal before the law. *Canaille!* what more do you need?" Well! what more do we need? Now listen in your turn, legislators, rulers and rich proprietors. . . .

We claim in future to live and die, as we are born, equals: we want true equality or death; that is what we must have. And we will have equality whatever the price. Woe to those who stand between it and us! Woe to whoever would resist a wish so pronounced!

The French Revolution is only the forerunner of another revolution far greater, far more solemn, which will be the last.

The people have trampled on the bodies of kings and priests allied against them: it will be the same for the new tyrants, the new political hypocrites sitting in the places of the old.

What is it that we need in addition to equality of rights?

We need not only that equality be written out in the Declaration of the Rights of Man and of the Citizen, we want it in our very midst, in our hearths and homes. We will pay any price for it, to make a clean sweep so that we can cherish it alone. If need be let all the arts perish so long as true equality remains!

The agrarian law or the distribution of lands was the unconsidered wish of a few unprincipled soldiers, of a few small groups prompted by instinct rather than reason. We aspire to something more sublime and more just, THE COMMON GOOD OR THE

COMMUNITY OF GOODS! No more individual ownership of land, the land belongs to nobody. We lay claim to, we demand, common enjoyment of the fruits of the earth: these fruits exist for all.

We declare that we can no longer suffer the great majority of men to toil and sweat in the service of the few and for the pleasure of the small minority. . . . Begone, henceforth, monstrous distinctions of rich and poor, of great and small, of masters and servants, of rulers and ruled.

Let there be no differences between human beings other than age and sex. Since all have the same needs and the same faculties, let there be one education, one fare for all. They are satisfied with one sun, one air, why should not the same quantity and quality of food suffice for each?

People of France!

No more vast design has ever been conceived and carried out. On rare occasions a few men of genius, a few wise men, have spoken of it in whispers, trembling. Not one had the courage to tell the whole truth.

The time for greatness has come. The evil is at its height; it covers the face of the earth. . . . The moment has come to found the REPUBLIC OF EQUALS, the great hospice open to all men. The days of general restitution have come. Come all ye in distress and be seated at the common table set by nature for all her children.

People of France!

The highest of all glories is yours! Yes, it is you who must be the first to offer the world this moving sight. . . .

On the morrow of this true revolution, men will say to each other in amazement: What! was the common good to be had for so little? We had only to will it. Ah! why did we not will it sooner? Why had we to be told so many times? Without doubt while there is still a single man in the whole world who is richer and more powerful than his fellows or equals, he destroys this equilibrium: crime and misery remain upon the earth.

People of France!

By what sign then will you henceforth recognize the excellence of a constitution? Only one that rests entirely on real equality will be good enough for you and will satisfy all your desires. The aristocratic charters of 1791 and 1795 rivet your chains instead of breaking them. That of 1793 made a real stride towards true equality; never before had it been so closely approached; but it still had not attained the goal, and did not begin to realize the common good, although it was solemnly consecrated to that great principle.

People of France!

Open your eyes and hearts to full felicity: recognize and proclaim with us the REPUBLIC OF EQUALS.

Equality is the highest value, a necessary condition for freedom and well-being. Following the manifesto was the Analysis of the Doctrine of Babeuf, probably written by Babeuf, consisting of twelve theses:

1. Nature has given every man an equal right to the enjoyment of all wealth.
2. The aim of society is to defend this equality, often attacked by the strong and the wicked in the state of nature, and to increase, by the cooperation of all, this enjoyment.
3. Nature has imposed on each man the duty to work; no one can, without committing a crime, abstain from working.
4. Labor and enjoyment ought to be in common.
5. Oppression exists when one man exhausts himself working and wants for everything, while another wallows in abundance without doing anything.
6. No one can, without committing a crime, appropriate to himself alone the wealth of the earth or of industry.
7. In a true society there should be neither rich nor poor.
8. The rich who will not give up their superfluity to help the needy are enemies of the people.
9. No one should be able, by monopolizing the means, to deprive another of the education necessary for his happiness; education ought to be in common.
10. The aim of the Revolution is to destroy inequality and establish the common happiness.
11. The Revolution is not finished, because the rich absorb all wealth and rule exclusively, while the poor work like veritable

slaves, languishing in poverty and counting for nothing in the State.

12. The constitution of 1793 is the true law of the French nation, because the People have solemnly accepted it.

Additional ideas of this utopian communism included (1) belief in the natural goodness of man, hampered only by the evils of environment, by bad economic and political structures, which allowed the vices of greed and tyranny to domi-nate; (2) the immediate cessation of all inheri-tance; (3) the provision that private property would revert to the community on the death of the owner; (4) the idea that there must be com-pletely equal distribution of goods—even where a shortage occurs. The hardship must be distributed equally; and (5) the organization of communal meals. Although the manifesto con-tains universalist language, the communist structure was meant to he confined to France alone.

PART II
ON THE CONCEPT OF
EQUALITY ITSELF

Egalitarianism as a Descriptive Concept
FELIX E. OPPENHEIM

Like "democracy" or "freedom," the term "equality" has a laudatory connotation. Hence the tendency to apply it to those, and only those, institutions or policies which one wishes to commend, and to qualify as inegalitarian those of which one disapproves. The question then arises: Is saying that, say, a sales tax or a graduated income tax is egalitarian like maintaining that one or the other is equitable? If so, persons with different views as to whether a certain policy is equitable are bound to disagree as to whether it is egalitarian, and communication is likely to break down. If, on the other hand, it were possible to set down descriptive criteria of equality, it would become possible to discuss in a meaningful way whether egalitarianism in general is just, or whether egalitarian principles of a particular kind are desirable. It seems, therefore, worthwhile trying to explicate the concept of egalitarianism so that it yields criteria which are not only empirical, but also general. Then we can ascertain whether any given rule—sales tax or graduated income tax, universal military training or student deferment, to each according to his work or need—is egalitarian or inegalitarian, regardless of whether it is equitable or just or desirable on some other grounds.

I. "EQUALITY" IN THE EXPRESSION TO BE DEFINED

First, let us determine the expression we want to define. Here we must distinguish. "Equality" can be predicated either of certain characteristics of persons, or of distributions made by one actor to at least two others, or of rules stipulating how such distributions are to be made. "Equality" in the first two meanings presents no problem from the point of view of our topic, and we shall be mainly concerned with equality as a property of rules of distribution.

A. Equality of Personal Characteristics

When two or more persons are said to be equal with respect to age or citizenship or race or income or aptitude or need, this simply means that they have the same age or nationality or color or income or ability or need—or that they are substantially similar in such respects. When Hobbes says that "nature has made men so equal in the faculties of the body and mind"[1] that anyone can kill, but not outwit, another, he means that all men have substantially the same physical and mental power, and that differences are insignificant. Persons of different age or race or ability are considered unequal in those respects. Human beings can be said to be equal or unequal only with respect to certain characteristics which must be specified. It is elliptic, and hence meaningless to say that "all men are equal." With respect to any given characteristic, some men may be equal, but all are unequal. The only characteristic which they all share is a common "human nature," but that is a tautological statement.

Equality and inequality of characteristics are no doubt descriptive concepts. Indeed, whether A and B have the same age or nationality or income can be empirically ascertained. So can assertions that A has greater ability or aptitude

Reprinted from Felix Oppenheim, "Egalitarianism as a Descriptive Concept," *American Philosophical Quarterly*, 7 (1970) 143–152.

than *B*. These are characterizing value judgments: such statements are descriptive, not normative.

B. Equality of Treatment

Whether two or more persons are being "treated equally" or not is also an empirical question. *A* and *B* are treated equally by *C*, if *C* allots to *A* and *B* the same specified benefit (e.g., one vote) or burden (e.g., one year's military service), or the same amount of some specified benefit or burden (e.g., salary, tax burden). If *A* is let to vote but not *B*, if *A* is drafted but *B* exempted, if *A* receives a higher salary than *B*, then *A* and *B* are treated unequally in those respects.

Whether *A* and *B* are to receive the same treatment will often depend on some general rule of distribution. *With respect to a given rule*, *A* and *B* are treated equally, not if they receive the same treatment, but if the rule is applied impartially to both. This is the concept of "Equality *before* the law, which lays down that we should treat each case in accordance with an antecedently promulgated rule."[2] Equality before a law limiting suffrage to whites requires that any white and no black citizen be allowed to vote. Equality before the law does not demand that the law itself be egalitarian.

C. Egalitarian Rules of Distribution

Our concern is not with egalitarian or inegalitarian treatment relative to a given rule, but with the egalitarian or inegalitarian character of the rules themselves.

Like "just," "egalitarian" can be predicated only of those rules which stipulate how certain benefits or burdens are to be allocated among persons. One may ask whether it is morally right or wrong to legalize or to outlaw abortion or divorce, but not whether such policies are just or unjust, or whether they are egalitarian or inegalitarian. These latter categories can be applied to principles which stipulate how benefits (e.g., voting rights, salaries) or burdens (e.g., the duty to pay taxes, or to serve in the armed forces) are to be allotted.

Rules of distribution have the general form: some specified benefit (e.g., franchise) or burden (e.g., a sales tax) is to be allocated or withheld from any person, depending on whether he has or lacks some specified characteristic (e.g., being a citizen over twenty-one, being white, buying cigarettes). Or: the amount of some specified benefit (e.g., salary) or burden (e.g., income tax) to anyone shall be a function of the amount or degree to which he has a certain characteristic (e.g., his ability, his income). Our question then is: Is there a criterion which permits us to classify any actual or conceivable rule of distribution into egalitarian and inegalitarian ones, independently of any valuational or normative considerations?

II. TRADITIONAL CRITERIA OF EGALITARIANISM

Let us examine some of the criteria which have traditionally been applied, if often only implicitly.

A. Equal Shares to All

According to the most extreme view, a moral or legal system is egalitarian if *all* benefits and burdens are to be distributed in equal amounts to *all*. This is Aristotle's principle of numerical equality—"being treated equally or identically in the number and volume of things you get"[3]— applied to all things anyone is to receive—or has to relinquish. It is the utilitarian principle— "everybody to count for one, nobody to count for more than one"—in the distribution of all benefits and burdens. Equal treatment of all in every respect has been advocated by some 19th century anarchists: equality of occupation (intellectuals to participate in manual work), of consumption (all to eat and dress alike), and especially of education would ultimately wipe out existing inequalities of personal characteristics such as those of talent and intelligence and would eventually mold a uniform human species.

However, practically all rules of distribution are concerned with *certain* benefits or burdens, to be allocated to *certain* persons. Even principles as general as those of the American and French Revolutions proclaim that the same basic legal *rights* are to be given to all, and that means to all citizens in any given political system by their respective governments. If egalitarianism meant equal shares of everything to all, practically all existing rules would be inegalitarian.

B. Equal Shares to Equals

Aristotle himself enlarged the criterion of egalitarianism to include rules which allot "equal shares to equals"; i.e., equal shares of some specified kind to all who are equal with respect to some specified characteristic. Conversely, a rule is inegalitarian "when either equals are awarded unequal shares or unequals equal shares."[4]

Here, the opposite criticism applies. Every existing, and even every conceivable rule of distribution turns out to be egalitarian in this sense, since every one allocates the same benefit or burden to all who have the same specified characteristic, but not to those who are unequal in that respect. Universal suffrage means that every adult citizen shall have one vote, but that minors and aliens shall have none. Suffrage to whites means that the right to vote is given to all white adult citizens, but not to colored persons. Conversely, an inegalitarian rule in this sense is a logical impossibility. A rule cannot stipulate that equals—in the sense of: those who have the characteristic specified by the rule— shall be awarded unequal shares, and unequals equal shares. To practice racial discrimination is to give the same treatment to those of the same color, and to give unequal shares to those who are unequal with respect to this characteristic.

C. Equal Shares to a Relatively Large Group

Since every rule of distribution designates a certain class of persons who are to be treated equally, it could be argued, as it is by Isaiah Berlin, that one rule is more egalitarian than another if it insures "that a larger number of persons (or classes of persons) shall receive similar treatment in specified circumstances."[5] To be more specific: a distribution of *benefits* is the more egalitarian, the larger the class of persons who receive it, as compared with the number of those excluded. Universal suffrage which excludes only minors and aliens is more egalitarian than a system which excludes Negroes in addition. Disenfranchising women is more inegalitarian than disenfranchising Negroes if the latter constitute less than half the population, but less inegalitarian if the majority is colored. Locke, who advocated equal political rights for property owners, was more egalitarian than his predecessors, but less so than later advocates of universal suffrage. On the other hand, a rule which allots *burdens* is the more egalitarian the larger the class of persons on whom it is imposed. Exempting students from the draft is less egalitarian than drafting them also.

This criterion has the great advantage that egalitarianism and inegalitarianism become comparative concepts. From the point of view of empirical science, this is an advance from merely classificatory concepts, possibly leading to quantification. The disadvantage is that all rules of the type, "to each according to his need" would become highly inegalitarian, unless it so happens that a fairly large proportion of the population had the same, and high, degree of need. A sales tax would be very egalitarian; but a graduated income tax, very inegalitarian, since it divides taxpayers not merely into two classes but into a large number of brackets and imposes the greatest tax burden on the usually small number of those with the highest income. Only in the unlikely case that the great majority falls within the highest bracket would a graduated income tax become more egalitarian. Even the principle of equality of opportunity would, in spite of its name, be inegalitarian, since it provides greater advantages to those who lack certain opportunities than to those who already have them.

D. Proportional Equality

Yet, we are inclined to consider more benefits for the needier or a graduated income tax egalitarian. They would be, if egalitarianism were taken in the sense of Aristotle's "proportional equality" or "equality of ratios." A rule of distribution may be said to fulfill this requirement, provided the amount of benefit or burden allotted to anyone is a monotonically increasing function of the personal characteristic specified by the rule; i.e., the more of the characteristic, the greater the share. Any two persons are treated equally in this sense, provided the difference in the amount allotted to each is similarly correlated to the degree to which they differ with respect to the specified characteristic.

However, every conceivable rule would become egalitarian by this criterion, just as it would according to the principle of equal shares to equals. Indeed, all rules of distribution not only allot "equal shares to equals" and "unequal shares to unequals," but also allots them "in proportion to" the latter's inequalities. Both rules, "to each according to his need" and "to each according to his height," assign different shares to different persons in the proportion in which they differ as to need or height. A flat rate and a graduated income tax both fulfill the requirement of proportional equality. Marx's ideal was the principle, "to each according to his need," rather than "to each according to his work." Yet, he did not deny that the latter rule, too, is egalitarian, since "the right of the producers [to receive means of consumption] is *proportional* to the labor they supply; the equality consists in the fact that measurement is made with an *equal standard*, labor." It is, therefore, an egalitarian principle, even though "it tacitly recognizes unequal individual endowment and thus productive capacity as natural privileges."[6] Rules which establish only two categories are also egalitarian by this standard. Both universal suffrage and suffrage for whites only treat all persons in proportion to their inequality, with respect to the specified characteristic. Numerical equality is then but a special case of proportional equality.

E. To Each According to His Desert

Aristotle sometimes contrasts equality, not with proportional equality in general, but with "equality proportionate to desert." Amounts of benefits are to be proportionate to the degree to which beneficiaries have—not whatever characteristic a rule might specify—but one specific characteristic; namely, relative desert. The more deserving a person, the greater his reward, and equal shares to persons of equal desert. Any criterion of distribution which disregards desert is then not truly egalitarian.

This time, it can, of course, not be argued that every rule turns out to be egalitarian. The criticism is rather that egalitarianism is here defined in valuational rather than in descriptive terms. Aristotle himself considers a distribution egalitarian in this sense, if "the relative values of the things given correspond to those of the persons receiving." Now, the relative value of *things* given can usually be objectively ascertained and measured; and so can personal characteristics such as age or income, and even intelligence or aptitude for a certain task. On the other hand, the relative value of a *person* (receiving); i.e., the degree of his desert is clearly a matter of subjective valuation, not of objective assessment. Statements to the effect that *A* is more deserving than (or twice as deserving as) *B*, in the sense that *A* is of greater value or moral worth, are genuine, not characterizing, value judgments.

Implicit here is the Platonic–Aristotelian doctrine that men are essentially of unequal value or desert, in contrast to the later Stoic view of the equal worth or dignity of every human being. On the basis of the criterion under discussion, equality, e.g., of political rights, would be egalitarian to the latter and inegalitarian according to the former view. Again, if whites are considered "superior" to Negroes (in overall desert, not, e.g., in intelligence), then racial discrimination is egalitarian; the same policy would be inegalitarian to those who do not regard a person's worth as depending on his color.

F. Unequal Distributions Corresponding to Relevant Differences

At present the most widely held version of proportional equality is the following: a rule of distribution is egalitarian if, and only if, differences in allotments correspond to *relevant* differences in personal characteristics; in other words, provided the specified characteristic is relevant to the kind of benefits or burdens to be distributed. Thus, age and citizenship are said to be relevant to voting rights; it is, therefore, egalitarian to limit the franchise to adult citizens. Wealth is relevant to taxation; hence, a flat rate or a graduated income tax is egalitarian. Conversely, a rule is inegalitarian if it is either based on irrelevant differences of characteristics or disregards relevant ones. Sex or color or wealth are irrelevant to voting; restricting the franchise to men or whites or poll tax payers is inegalitarian. Wealth *is* relevant to taxation; hence, a sales tax is inegalitarian, since it taxes poor and wealthy buyers at the same rate.

Like personal desert, relevance of a personal characteristic is an evaluative, not a descriptive, term. While the ascription of characteristics such as a certain age or income to a person is a matter of fact, judgments to the effect that such characteristics are relevant or irrelevant to some kind of distribution are valuational, not factual. That age is relevant to voting, but color not, means nothing more than that it is just to require a minimum age for voting, but unjust to base franchise on color. It is inegalitarian—and that means that it is unjust—to treat persons unequally who share a "relevant" characteristic; but unequal awards to persons who differ in some "relevant" respect are egalitarian, i.e., just. Or, in a recent formulation, "a difference in treatment requires *justification* in terms of *relevant* and sufficient differences between the claimants."[7] Advocates and opponents of racial discrimination are likely to disagree as to whether race is a "relevant" difference and whether discrimination is just. On the basis of the definition under discussion, they also would have to disagree as to whether such a policy is egalitarian.

This valuational interpretation of the concept of relevance has recently been challenged. For example, Bernard Williams holds it "quite certainly false" to claim "that the question whether a certain consideration is *relevant* to a moral issue is an evaluative question." He argues as follows:

> The principle that men should be differentially treated in respect to welfare merely on grounds of their color is not a special sort of moral principle, but (if anything) a purely arbitrary assertion of will, like of some Caligulan ruler who decided to execute everyone whose name contained three 'R's.[8]

A racist's advocacy of racial discrimination in welfare matters need not be arbitrary at all, but may well be rational—in the sense of consistent with his overall evaluations and other normative principles. To deny that such principles are *moral* ones is to apply the term "moral" itself in an emotive sense to only those normative views to which one happens to subscribe.

Perhaps Williams means only to assert that the grounds on which such a normative principle would be defended, or criticized, reduces to purely empirical propositions. Indeed, he argues that, "if any reasons are given at all" for racial discrimination

> they will be reasons that seek to correlate the fact of blackness with certain other considerations which are at least candidates for relevance to the question of how a man should be treated: such as insensitivity, brute stupidity, ineducable irresponsibility, etc.

I do not deny that a statement such as "color is relevant to intelligence" is descriptive. It means that intelligence is a function of color, and this statement can be empirically tested, and disconfirmed. But here it is intelligence, not color, which is considered relevant; e.g., to voting rights. Unlike "color is relevant to intelligence," "intelligence is relevant to voting rights" is normative, just as "color is relevant to voting rights" is normative. It means that franchise ought to depend on intelligence or on color, and that a rule to that effect is just. To call a rule based on differences judged relevant *egalitarian* (rather than just) does not alter the normative character of the statement.

More recently, W. T. Blackstone has explicated the concept of relevance as follows:[9]

> To say "*x* is relevant," when we are speaking about the treatment of persons, means "*x is* actually or potentially rated in an instrumentally helpful or harmful way to the attainment of a given end and *consequently ought* to be taken into consideration in the decision to treat someone in a certain way."

I agree with the author that the first part of this definition is descriptive and the second part prescriptive. But I disagree with "consequently." I deny that a statement of the "is" type of relevance entails one of the "ought" type. Let us take his own example:

> If, for example, race or color were cited as grounds for the differential treatment of per-

sons in regard to educational opportunities and it were shown that color or race has nothing to do with educability, then the factual presupposition of those who invoke these criteria would have been shown to be false and those criteria themselves to be irrelevant (in the factual sense of "relevant").

"Color is relevant to educability" is a factual statement, and "educability is relevant to educational opportunity" is normative. But the former statement does not entail the latter. Someone may agree that color "has nothing to do with"; i.e., is not relevant to, educability. Yet, he may hold without inconsistency that greater educational opportunities should be given to the more educable, *or to whites*, or that all should have the same education (i.e., that no group should receive preferential treatment). Blackstone himself concedes:

> It could easily be the case that individuals agree on the factual part of a judgment of relevance (i.e., that certain facts are instrumentally related to certain goals) and yet disagree on the prescriptive part of that judgment (i.e., on what goal is desirable).

This seems to contradict the first-quoted statement ("consequently"). "Relevance" is not a descriptive criterion of egalitarianism as a characteristic of rules of distribution.

G. Unequal Distributions Which Are Just

Egalitarianism is sometimes defined directly in terms of justice (rather than indirectly, via relevance). According to a recent article by a political theorist, "the true opposite of equality is arbitrary, i.e., unjustifiable or inequitable inequality of treatment."[10] It would follow that justifiable or equitable inequality of treatment is "truly" egalitarian. Whether racial discrimination is egalitarian or inegalitarian would again depend on whether it is considered just or unjust.

This is an instance of what I should like to call "the definist fallacy in reverse." The definist fallacy itself consists of defining a value word; e.g., "good" or "desirable," by reference to descriptive terms; e.g., "happiness" or "approval." Now, if "good" means the same as "conducive to happiness," or "desirable" the same as "approved by the majority," it would be self-contradictory to say that something which promotes happiness is bad, or that something is undesirable but approved by the majority. Aristotle's statement that "the unjust is unequal, the just is equal" is another instance of this fallacy. Here the normative concept of justice is defined in terms of egalitarianism which Aristotle himself considers a descriptive term, as we have seen ("giving equal shares to equals"). Again, it is not self-contradictory to say that a graduated income tax is inegalitarian yet just.

Here we have the reverse procedure. Egalitarianism, a concept which we want to function descriptively, is defined by the normative concept of justice. If "rule x is egalitarian" means the same as "rule x is just (or justifiable or equitable)," then it is self-contradictory to consider a graduated income tax just and inegalitarian, or a sales tax inequitable but egalitarian.

Egalitarianism has been identified, even more broadly, with moral rightness. According to J. R. Lucas, a law may

> be said to be unequal, in that the categories are wrongly specified, or the distinctions wrongly drawn, so that the law ... discriminates between classes of people who ought not to be discriminated between.[11]

Accordingly, people who disagree as to the rightness or wrongness of some discrimination are bound to disagree as to whether a law to that effect is egalitarian or inegalitarian.

H. Procedural Equality

Equality is also linked with justice by those who regard egalitarianism as a "procedural" principle: "Treat people equally unless and until there is a justification for treating them unequally."[12] Taken in this sense, "egalitarianism" does not refer to a *characteristic* of rules of distribution at all, but to a rule of distribution itself; namely: "All persons are to be treated alike, unless good reasons can be found for treating them differently."[13] It is true that this "Equality Injunction is not itself a positive rule of ethics, but a rule for adopting rules."[14] It is, nevertheless, a *normative* rule (for adopting substantive rules).

This principle is not only purely normative but also purely procedural, compatible with whatever substantive discriminatory rules of distribution may be held "justified" or based on "good reasons." Such a criterion of egalitarianism does not enable us to classify substantive rules of distribution into egalitarian and inegalitarian ones.[15]

The search for an adequate explication of the concept of equality has been fruitless so far. To repeat briefly: if egalitarianism were defined by "equal shares to all," hardly any rule would be egalitarian; if it meant "equal shares to equals" or "proportional equality," *every* rule would be; and *any* rule could be egalitarian on the basis of definitions referring to desert, or relevant differences, or justice. Procedural equality does not even designate a characteristic of rules of distribution. "Equal shares to a relatively large group" remains the least unsatisfactory definition, but I have indicated that its application leads to results which are often counter-intuitive. Indeed, even advocates of racial discrimination are likely to consider it inegalitarian (yet just) to restrict welfare benefits to whites regardless of need (even if the great majority of the population is white), but egalitarian (though unjust) to make welfare payments to the needy regardless of race (even if the needy are a small minority). I believe that it is possible to find a general descriptive criterion of egalitarianism which captures such distinctions.

III. PROPOSED CRITERION OF EGALITARIANISM

All the definitions we have examined so far consider only how much of some specified benefit or burden is to be allotted to any two persons, A and B. Rules of distribution may also be considered from the point of view of the end result. How much will A and B retain after the rule has been applied to them? How are benefits or burdens to be redistributed between A and B? We must then distinguish between three

stages: (1) the original distribution, (2) some rule of redistribution being applied, and (3) the final distribution resulting from 2. *Example* 1: (1) A has 8 units; B has 2; (2) take 3 from A; give 3 to B; (3) both A and B end up with 5.

A. Simple Criterion

A rule of redistribution might be said to be egalitarian, if it equalizes, or at least reduces the difference between initial holdings. Example. 1 would be an instance of an egalitarian redistribution, since the initial difference between the holdings of A and B, namely, 6 (8 − 2), is reduced to o (5 − 5). So would *Example* 2: Take 3 from A (who has 8) and nothing from B (who has 2)—since the difference between their holdings at the end (5 − 2 = 3) is smaller than it was at the start (8 − 2 = 6). Conversely, a redistribution which leaves previous inequalities of benefits or burdens unaffected or increases the difference would be inegalitarian. *Example* 3: Take 1 from A and 1 from B (the initial difference between their holdings, namely, 6, remains unaffected). *Example* 4: Take 1 from A and 2 from B (the difference increases from 6 to 7).

These examples show that a rule of redistribution can be said to be egalitarian or inegalitarian only relative to some previous distribution. Egalitarianism becomes an ordering concept, an advantage which it shares with the "least unsatisfactory definition" examined under IIC. With respect to a given distribution, a rule of redistribution is the more egalitarian, the smaller the difference between holdings at the end in comparison with those at the start. The redistribution in example 1 is more egalitarian than in example 2, more inegalitarian in example 4 than in example 3.

The examples also illustrate that equal allotments may lead to inegalitarian redistributions, and vice versa. A sales tax (example 3) is inegalitarian, since it weighs heavier on the poorer buyers and does not reduce differences in wealth. Conversely, a graduated income tax (example 2) tends to equalize previous holdings and is as such egalitarian by this criterion. This definition of an egalitarian rule does then remedy precisely the defects of the definition examined under IIC.[16] Like the former, it is couched exclusively in descriptive terms, and is therefore valuationally neutral.

B. More Adequate Criterion

This rather simple criterion does, however, lead to counter-intuitive results in certain instances. *Example* 5: A has 97 units and B has 3; the difference between their holdings is 94. Taking 3 from A and 2 from B reduces their holdings to 94 and 1, respectively, and the difference between their holdings is now smaller than before; namely, 93 (instead of 94). Although more is taken from A who starts with more than from B who starts with less, we hardly would consider such a redistribution egalitarian.

Now, let us look at percentage differences between holdings. If the total of units at the beginning is 100, taking 3 from A (who has 97) and 2 from B (who has 3) reduces this total to 95. A is then left with about 99 per cent of this total (94/95), and B with about 1 per cent (1/95). The percentage difference between the final holdings of A and B (99 − 1) is 98; this is *larger* than 94, the percentage difference between their initial holdings. According to this criterion, the redistribution turns out to be inegalitarian.

This result is more in line with our general conception of egalitarianism. Indeed, if the difference between initial holdings is very large, taking more from those who have more does not necessarily make the redistribution egalitarian. I propose, therefore, to consider a rule of redistribution egalitarian if it reduces and inegalitarian if it increases the *percentage* difference between the holdings of those to whom the rule is being applied. With respect to a given initial distribution, a rule of redistribution is then the more egalitarian, the smaller the difference between the percentage holdings at the end in comparison with the difference at the start. A sales tax is more clearly inegalitarian according to the present criterion than according to the previous.[17] Even a graduated income tax may be inegalitarian according to the present criterion (as in example 5). To be egalitarian, those in the highest brackets must pay proportionally very much, and those in the lower very little (or nothing, as in example 2).

IV. SOME EGALITARIAN AND INEGALITARIAN PRINCIPLES

Let us examine a few of the more important rules of redistribution in the light of the proposed criterion of egalitarianism.

A. Equalization of Wealth

Full equalization of commodities, even when it is held desirable, is generally considered utopian. Even if this goal were realized at one moment, differences would soon reappear, if only because "men are unequal" as to personal endowments; hence, power and influence are bound to remain unequally distributed under every political and economic system. Equalization of wealth usually means merely reducing rather than removing existing inequalities of possessions. According to the proposed definition, this kind of redistribution, although less egalitarian, is egalitarian just the same. In Rousseau's words:

> By equality, we should understand, not that the degree of power and riches be absolutely identical for everybody, but that . . . no citizen be wealthy enough to buy another, and none poor enough to be forced to sell himself. [social contract]

On the other hand, "not even the equal distribution of money will lead to equal happiness."[18] Besides, happiness or satisfaction or utility are not tangible benefits which can be distributed or redistributed to A and B by C, either equally or unequally.

B. Equality of Opportunity

Like utilities, opportunities cannot, strictly speaking, be given or distributed to A and B by C. "A has the opportunity to achieve x" means that there are no obstacles in his way of achieving x, so that he can do x if he wants to. C gives A the opportunity to reach x if he removes such obstacles and thereby enables A to achieve x, so that, whether A reaches x depends only on his native and acquired ability and on his effort. A and B have equal opportunity to win a race if they start from the same line. If A is initially behind B, he must be moved forward to the common starting line to have the same opportunity as *B*.

The principle of equality, or rather equalization, of opportunities is thus concerned with the redistribution of access to the various positions in society, not with the allocation of the positions themselves. The problem is: how to match individuals with unequal endowments with positions yielding unequal remuneration or power and prestige. The solution is to open them up to all on a competitive basis. The assumption is that, if everyone is given an equal start, the position everyone will occupy at the end will depend exclusively on how fast and how far he can run.

Classical liberalism held that equality of opportunity could be implemented by means of an *equal* allocation of the basic legal rights of "life, liberty, and property." If only legal privileges are abolished and equality of legal rights established, no obstacle will stand in the way of everyone's *pursuit* of happiness; i.e., everyone's ability to accede to the position commensurate with his highest ability.

Later it was realized that equality of rights is not sufficient to open up to the socially disadvantaged the opportunities open to the socially privileged. Unequal distributions are required to bring the former up to the common starting level: legal privileges and material benefits for the economically underprivileged, such as "head start" programs. To the extent to which such policies lead to an equalization of opportunities, they are egalitarian.

C. Equal Satisfaction of Basic Needs

The principle of equalization of opportunities is linked to another principle of equalization: the equal satisfaction of basic needs. While personal needs vary in kind and extent, there is a minimum of basic needs which are substantially identical for all in a given society at a given time. However, persons are unequal with respect to their *unsatisfied* basic needs. "Unequal distribution of resources would be required to equalize benefits in cases of unequal need.[19] The greater someone's unsatisfied basic need, the greater the benefits he receives. Those whose basic needs are already more nearly satisfied may not receive anything

and may even have to give up some superfluities to provide for the former's necessities. The end result of such unequal distributions is, again, greater equalization of wealth and of opportunities.

D. To Each According to His Merit

Contemporary proponents of the democratic welfare state tend to combine the two egalitarian principles of equal satisfaction of basic needs and of equality of opportunity with another rule of redistribution: to each according to his merit. Once everyone's minimum needs have been taken care of, and all have been given an equal chance, the race is on, and the position everyone occupies at the end will depend only on his aptitude or "merit," again in theory at least. Unlike a person's "desert," his "merit" in the sense of proficiency at some specified task can in principle be objectively determined. But like "to each according to his desert," "to each according to his merit" is an inegalitarian rule of redistribution.

Schematically, we may then distinguish between the following stages: (1) an initial unequal distribution of commodities; (2) giving more to the needier, resulting in (3) a more egalitarian redistribution: equal satisfaction of basic needs, equality of opportunity; (4) from there on: an inegalitarian final redistribution: to each according to his merit.

This concept of equality is not only general and descriptive, but also valuationally neutral. For example, the author of *The Rise of Meritocracy* advocates "not an aristocracy of birth, not a plutocracy of wealth, but a true meritocracy of talent." By the proposed criterion, all three of these principles are inegalitarian, the one he propounds as well as the two he rejects. On the other hand, advocates of "meritocracy" do in general not want to extend this principle to political participation; they remain in favor of equal suffrage, regardless of "merit."

This leads to the conclusion that modern democratic theory as a whole cannot be qualified as either egalitarian or inegalitarian, but is a mixture of both kinds of principles: equalization up to a certain level (by means of unequal distributions); inegalitarian redistributions beyond. It is, therefore, less inegalitarian than ideologies which base inequality of treatment on hereditary status, color, religion, or wealth.

There is, of course, no contradiction in calling meritocracy both inegalitarian and just. It may also be deemed unjust, yet desirable for other reasons—unjust because a person's merit depends in part on factors over which he has no control, such as innate intelligence and education or training (at least in the absence of full equality of educational opportunities)—desirable nevertheless on utilitarian grounds, because incentives to higher productivity will increase the welfare of all.

It has often been argued that men are equal and, therefore, egalitarianism just, or that inegalitarianism is equitable because men are unequal. For example, John Schaar, in a recent article, takes "the large discrepancy between the observed facts of inequality and the policy or value of equality as a serious intellectual embarrassment."[20] As if it were inconsistent to hold that men should be given equal opportunities even though they are of unequal intelligence—or unequal salaries in spite of their equal basic needs. Normative principles cannot be derived from factual generalizations; equality or inequality of some personal characteristic does not entail the desirability of either egalitarianism or inegalitarianism.

Mistaken arguments of this kind are often the result of confused language. There is the tendency to use factual statements for expressing normative views. We have seen that the allegation that "men are equal," if taken in the factual sense, is either meaningless, or tautological, or false. However, this adage serves more often as a rhetorical device to disguise the normative principle that men should be treated equally—in some respect which is often left unspecified. Then there is the temptation to use the factual statement that such and such a principle is egalitarian for the purpose of commending that particular rule. Conversely, valuational terms are being used to refer to some advocated goal; e.g., persons are to be treated according to their *desert*, or treated equally unless there are *relevant* differences, or unless unequal treatment is *justified*. When such value words are left unspecified, no substantive normative principle is being propounded.

Value words should be used exclusively to express the *advocacy* of some goal or principle; the *advocated* state of affairs should be characterized exclusively by descriptive terms. Following this practice would make for much-needed clarity in our moral discourse.

NOTES

1. Thomas Hobbes, *Leviathan*, ch. XIII.
2. J. R. Lucas, *The Principles of Politics* (Oxford: Clarendon Press, 1966), p. 246.
3. Aristotle, *Politics* 1301b.
4. Aristotle, *Ethics* 1131a.
5. Isaiah Berlin, "Equality as an Ideal" (in this volume).
6. Karl Marx, "Critique of the Gotha Program," in Lewis Feuer, ed., *Karl Marx and Friedrich Engels, Basic Writings in Politics and Philosophy* (Garden City, N.Y.: Anchor Books, 1959), p. 118.
7. Morris Ginsberg, *On Justice in Society* (Baltimore: Penguin Books, 1965), p. 79.
8. Bernard Williams, "The Idea of Equality," in P. Laslett and W. G. Runciman, eds., *Philosophy, Politics, and Society* (Oxford: Basil Blackwell, 1962), p. 113 [reprinted in this volume].
9. W. T. Blackstone, "On the Meaning and Justification of the Equality Principle," *Ethics* 77 (1967), 239–253.
10. W. Von Leydon, "On Justifying Inequality," *Political Studies*, vol. 11 (1963), 56–70.
11. J. R. Lucas, *op. cit.*, p. 256.
12. William Frankena, *Some Beliefs About Justice* (Department of Philosophy, University of Kansas, 1966), p. 8.
13. Monroe Beardsley, "Equality and Obedience to Law," in Sidney Hook, ed., *Law and Philosophy* (New York: New York University Press, 1964), p. 36.
14. Ibid.
15. Furthermore, as we have seen, no rule stipulates that "all persons are to be treated alike." Every rule of distribution treats *some* people equally and others unequally.
16. Definition IIC remains applicable when benefits and burdens are not quantifiable. For example, extending the franchise from white to black citizens, or lowering the voting age, is egalitarian, since there is an increase in the proportion of citizens who receive the benefit relative to those who do not. This also satisfies the present criterion of egalitarianism, since the difference between initial position (having or lacking the franchise) is being reduced.
17. The percentage difference between the initial holdings of A and B in example 3 is 60 (i.e.,

80 − 20). The total of their holdings is reduced from 100 percent to 80 percent. A ends up with 87.5 percent (70/80) and B with 12.5 percent (10/80). The percentage difference between their holdings has *increased* from 60 to 75 (whereas the absolute difference between their holdings remains the same).

18. John Hospers, *Human Conduct* (New York:

Harcourt, Brace & World, 1961), p. 424.

19. Gregory Vlastos, "Justice and Equality," in Richard Brandt, ed., *Social Justice* (Englewood Cliffs, N.J: Prentice-Hall, 1961) [reprinted in this volume].

20. John H. Schaar, "Some Ways of Thinking About Equality," *Journal of Politics*, vol. 29 (1964), 867–895. See p. 868.

Equality and Time
DENNIS McKERLIE

An egalitarian moral view must make certain choices in formulating principles to explain our particular egalitarian judgments. The first choice concerns the form of the egalitarian principle, the particular way in which it differs from a principle simply telling us to maximize what is good across all lives. One kind of egalitarianism aims at equality between different lives. It uses a measure of inequality and requires us to minimize the inequality recorded by the measure. A second kind of egalitarianism gives priority to helping those who are badly off. This view has a tendency toward equality, but not because it believes that equality itself has value. It furthers equality because that will be the result of helping the badly off, and it believes that improving a bad life takes priority over improving better lives. I will use "maximin egalitarianism" as a general name for this kind of view, even though some of the principles it covers are not exclusively concerned with the interests of the very worst off. A third version of egalitarianism believes that everyone should receive at least a specified minimum share of advantages or benefits. It could be called "minimum entitlement egalitarianism."

Each view puts constraints on the distribution of good and bad things across different lives. An egalitarian theory must also specify the things to which the constraints apply. To take the first kind of egalitarianism as an example, which things should be distributed equally across different lives? Some views apply the requirement of equality to possessions and services like wealth, property, and medical care. In Ronald Dworkin's terms these views aim at equality in resources.[1] Other views say that lives should be equal in terms of happiness or the extent to which people's desires are satisfied—equality of welfare in Dworkin's terms. Yet other views start with a list of objective features that give lives value—knowledge, achievements, relationships with others, and so on—and say that we should try to make lives equal in these value-conferring respects.

These two choices have been extensively discussed. A third question is less familiar. As well as specifying the things to be distributed, an egalitarian theory must also specify the units across which the distribution is to take place, or the items with a claim to an equal share of what is distributed. For almost all egalitarians

Reprinted from *Ethics* 99 (April 1989). © 1989 by The University of Chicago, by permission of the author and publisher. Footnotes edited.

people are the units of distribution. The things to be distributed, whatever they are, should be divided equally among the lives of different people. But our lives are lived through time. Because of this fact there are different ways in which the egalitarian requirement could be applied to us.

These different possibilities have been neglected because egalitarians seem to agree on a particular view about how the egalitarian constraint should be applied. I will call it the "complete lives view."[2] It says that different people's shares of resources, or welfare, should be equal when we consider the total amounts of those things that they receive over the complete course of their lives. To apply this view we would begin by estimating the size of a person's share of the relevant good things at each temporal stage of that person's life. Then we would add these figures together to determine that person's share in terms of a complete life. Finally this share would be compared with the shares of other people over their complete lives in order to test for equality.

The complete lives view has two features. It applies distributional constraints only to shares over complete lives, and it considers the total amounts of the relevant good and bad things that different lives contain. I think that both features can be questioned. Most of this paper will be concerned with the first feature, but I will begin with a brief discussion of the second feature.

It is well known that utilitarians must choose between maximizing the total sum of happiness across all lives or maximizing the average happiness of lives. These two goals can differ if the population size is not constant. Egalitarians face a similar choice. Should we equalize the average happiness of different lives, where the average happiness of a life is the total amount of happiness that it contains divided by its length, or should we equalize the total amounts of happiness that lives contain (assuming, for the sake of simplicity, that happiness is the good which should be distributed equally)? These two goals can differ when lives have different lengths. If one life will be longer than another, is it fair if they have the same average happiness per year, or would it be fairer if the shorter life had a higher average so that the total amounts of happiness in the two lives would be the same? If someone must die in ten years of an incurable disease should egalitarianism say that this person is entitled to a higher average happiness during the ten years?

I think that most people would find a strict version of the average view implausible. If one person has a happy life of an ordinary length while someone else dies at thirty, this does seem a natural unfairness that egalitarianism should at least regret, even though the average happiness of the two lives might be the same. But it might also be thought unfair if one person lives a very long life with a miserably low average happiness—for example, an octogenarian peasant in a Third World country—even though the total sum of happiness in that life equals that of a middle-class North American who dies at fifty-five. So it may seem that the best view will be a compromise between the total view and the average view.

Perhaps we can at least conclude that this is not a question for egalitarianism as such to answer. We must decide what we value in lives, choosing between such things as a high average happiness and a large total amount of happiness. This question can be answered by one person thinking about his or her own life. Once an answer is obtained, egalitarians will use it in ensuring that different lives go equally well. But the choice between the average view and the total view will not be made for distinctively egalitarian reasons, reasons concerned with the relationship that should hold between different lives.

The average view and the total view agree in only considering shares of resources or happiness over complete lives, and this is the feature of complete lives egalitarianism that I will criticize. I will begin with examples where the complete lives view draws conclusions that I find implausible. I will then describe some alternative views that would assess the examples differently. Finally, I will briefly discuss the philosophical issues raised by what seems to me the most attractive alternative view.[3]

If egalitarianism takes complete lives as the units across which we should distribute equally, the past will be important for egalitarianism in a way that it is not important for moral views like utilitarianism. The past does not matter for those views because it cannot be changed. We need only consider the consequences of our actions in the present and the future.[4] But if we aim at equality between complete lives the past history of those lives will partly determine which present action would do best at achieving equality.

Derek Parfit has discussed an example that illustrates this feature of complete lives egalitarianism.[5] A doctor has two patients feeling pain. Patient A's suffering is not as severe as the suffering of B, but in the past A has suffered much more than B. The doctor can only help one patient, and the treatment would relieve more suffering if it were given to B.

Complete lives egalitarianism would tell the doctor to help A. It makes this choice because of the past even though there would be less suffering if B were helped instead. Many people would disagree with this conclusion. But the example is not a decisive objection against the complete lives view. If we combine complete lives egalitarianism with a principle of minimizing suffering we are not forced to agree that, all things considered, helping A would be best. We might decide that the good done by relieving more suffering outweighs the loss in terms of equality.[6]

There are simpler examples in which the complete lives view makes the past matter, and I think that many egalitarians would doubt the conclusions it draws. If we judge equality in the complete lives way we will think that past inequality calls for a certain response. If in the past A's life has been worse than B's life, complete lives egalitarianism will tell us not merely to end the inequality but to reverse it—to create a new inequality in A's favor so that their complete lives will be equal. Suppose that one person's childhood was very unhappy, involving the loss of parents, poverty, and suffering. But these tragedies left no scars, and today that person is happy with a bright future. A second person has equally good prospects after a happy childhood. Complete lives egalitarianism will say that it would be a good thing if the first person's future went better than that of the second person, in order to compensate for the difference in their childhoods. I think that many egalitarians would resist that conclusion.

The question raised by the example is whether we should always compensate for past inequality. This policy seems especially inappropriate in the example of the two childhoods. It might be suggested that the example can be handled by slightly modifying the complete lives view. We should aim at equality between complete lives, but we may ignore inequalities in the distant past. But the restriction seems arbitrary. If we only care about inequality between complete lives, why should the fact that the inequality was in the distant past matter? If we think that compensation is not appropriate we should look for a different kind of egalitarian view to explain our judgment.

The complete lives view has another consequence. It does not see any disvalue in inequality between parts of lives as long as the inequality is compensated for at earlier or later times so that there is no inequality between complete lives. This enables us to imagine a new kind of egalitarian society. It contains great inequality, with happier lives attached to certain social positions. But at a fixed time people change places and switch from a superior position to an inferior one or vice versa. One example would be a feudal society in which peasants and nobles exchange roles every ten years. The result is that people's lives as wholes are equally happy. Nevertheless during a given time period the society contains great inequality, and in one sense this always remains true. I will call this system "changing places egalitarianism." If equality between complete lives were all that mattered, an egalitarian could not object to it. But I think that many egalitarians would find it objectionable.

A realistic example is in some respects analogous to changing places egalitarianism. In our society the elderly generally have worse lives than those who are younger.[7] Perhaps that has always been so, but today it is a more serious problem. Retirement policies and medical advances mean that for most people old age begins sooner and lasts longer than it did in the past. Consider the different futures of a thirty-five-year-old and someone who has just retired at the age of sixty-five. The first life might be happy and affluent, the second life might be equivalent to that of a welfare recipient. This inequality is very great, and it might last for as long as twenty-five years.

Some people think the inequality is an injustice and should be mitigated. But according to the complete lives view it is not necessarily unjust. The inequality is not objectionable unless the two lives as wholes differ in quality. If the earlier years of the person who is now old were just as happy as the current life of the middle-aged person, their complete lives might not differ in quality. If the appropriate things happen before it and afterward, the twenty-five-year inequality has no moral importance.

I would not claim that these examples should destroy our confidence in the complete lives view. But I think they are strong enough to motivate an examination of alternative versions of egalitarianism that would reach different conclusions about the examples.

In the example of the two childhoods the complete lives view makes the past important. An obvious alternative is what might be called "future-directed egalitarianism." It ignores the past and tells us to aim at equality in the present and future.

This view makes the present a dividing line for moral significance. But the present is a boundary that moves. Consequently, the view faces a formal problem. It gives us the goal "equality from now on." But this is not a single goal. It changes as the reference of "now" changes. And if we pursue different goals at different times our effort to achieve our goal at one time may interfere with our effort to achieve another goal at another time.

For example, at T1 we have the goal of equality from T1 on. We may decide that the best way to achieve this goal is to make one person, A, bear a burden until a later time T2 while another person, B, enjoys a benefit until T2. After T2 A will receive the benefit and B will bear the burden. But when it is T2 we have a new goal, equality from T2 on. A's burden and B's benefit are now in the past and do not count. So at T2 we might abandon the policy of switching, with the result that A will go on bearing the burden and B will continue to enjoy the benefit. I do not think an egalitarian would accept these consequences of future-directed egalitarianism.

It is true that if at T1 we anticipate our later decision at T2 future-directed egalitarianism would not tell us to begin the policy at T1. The example is not one in which the view, applied at different times with full knowledge of the

facts (including facts about the future), has clearly unacceptable consequences. But future-directed egalitarianism might tell us to begin the policy at T1 if we can also take measures that will make it very difficult to reverse the policy at T2. And then at T2 it will tell us to do all we can to defeat those measures, with the aim of allowing the inequality between A and B to continue. Is it reasonable to adopt a view which gives us this advice about how to achieve equality in the lives of A and B?

Future-directed egalitarianism takes time into account by supposing that there is a fundamental difference in moral importance between the past on the one hand and the present and future on the other. The second way for egalitarianism to give weight to facts about time is to apply the requirement of equality to temporal parts of lives, not just to complete lives.

Consider the lives of A and B during the time periods T1, T2, and T3.

$$
\begin{array}{cccc}
 & T1 & T2 & T3 \\
A & (3 & + \ 4 & + \ 2 = 9) \\
B & (1 & + \ 4 & + \ 4 = 9)
\end{array}
$$

The numbers measure the happiness of A and B during those periods. The complete lives view measures inequality in the following way: it first adds the numbers to measure the happiness of the complete lives of A and B and then compares them to determine the inequality. In this example the inequality is zero.

But there is another way of measuring the inequality. It begins by measuring the inequality across lives within each time period and then adds these figures to measure the total inequality through time.

$$
\begin{array}{ccccccc}
 & T1 & & T2 & & T3 \\
A & \begin{pmatrix}3\\1\\2\end{pmatrix} & + & \begin{pmatrix}4\\4\\0\end{pmatrix} & + & \begin{pmatrix}2\\4\\2\end{pmatrix} & = 4 \\
B & & & & &
\end{array}
$$

The two ways of measuring inequality can lead to different conclusions. For example the first method would prefer A = 2 and B = 4 during T3 to A = 3 and B = 3, but the second method would reach the opposite conclusion.

The second method tells us to minimize the sum total of inequality-at-a-time. I will call it the "simultaneous segments view." It would not compensate for past inequality. It does not see A = 2 and B = 4 during T3 as compensating for the inequality during T1 but rather as adding to the inequality between the lives of A and B. What we do now cannot change the inequality at past times, so this view would agree with future-directed egalitarianism about the example of the two childhoods. It rejects changing places egalitarianism because that system would involve a very high sum total of inequality-at-a-time. The view would recognize a claim to equality between the simultaneously lived final twenty-five years of one person's life and the middle twenty-five years of another person's life. It would see this inequality as something regrettable in itself, and as something whose importance could not be entirely erased by what happens before or after the twenty-five years. The view escapes the formal problem because it gives us the same goal—minimizing the sum total of inequality-at-a-time—at every time.

There are two more egalitarian views that use parts of lives in judging equality. The first begins with a segment of A's life and compares it, not just with the simultaneous segment of B's life, but with every segment of B's life. It repeats this procedure with every other segment of A's life and it adds the results of all the comparisons to determine the total amount of inequality between A's life and B's life. I will call it the "total segments view."

Like the simultaneous segments view, the total segments view would not compensate for past inequality. But its verdict about a present inequality favoring B depends on comparing this segment of B's life with the past segments of A's life, not just with the simultaneous segment of A's life. If A has been better off than B in the past, a present inequality favoring B might do best at minimizing the inequality among all the parts of their lives. Because it values equality in all segments of all lives, the total segments view does recognize a claim to equality between the simultaneously lived final twenty-five years of one life and the middle twenty-five years of another life. However, it does not see any importance in the fact that the unequal parts are simultaneous. So the view's

consequences for the treatment of the elderly should resemble those of the simultaneous segments view, although they will not be as strong.

I will call the second alternative to the simultaneous segments view the "corresponding segments view." It divides all lives into the same series of temporal parts. For the sake of simplicity we can suppose that they are youth, maturity, and old age. It measures equality by comparing the corresponding stages, rather than the simultaneous stages, of different lives. In the following example it would compare A's middle years with B's middle years, while the simultaneous segments view compares A's middle years with B's youth.

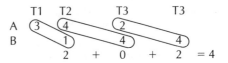

Concerning the elderly, the corresponding segments view requires that their lives should be as happy as ours will be when we reach their age, but it does not object to inequalities between their final years and the middle-age of others.

In the examples in which we seem to care about inequality between parts of lives I think that we care specifically about inequality in the simultaneous parts of different lives. We are disturbed because the elderly are poor and unhappy while others prosper. So I will concentrate on the simultaneous segments view in the next part of the paper, although similar points could be made about the other segments views.

How should the simultaneous segments view divide lives into parts to measure inequality? The view will seem implausible if the time periods within which the inequality is measured are too short. If two people will see a dentist tomorrow, it would tell them to schedule simultaneous appointments so that there will be equality in suffering at that time. Are there serious egalitarian reasons for preferring two 10:30 appointments to an appointment at 10 and an appointment at 11?

We might claim that the inequality in the dental appointments example does have some small importance. This claim would not have implausible consequences since the inequality would not count for much in the context of all the other simultaneous parts of the lives of the people concerned. But the view would still face a difficult example. Suppose that the lives of A and B consist of very short periods of enjoyment alternating with very short periods of intense pain. Perhaps they are the prisoners of a sadistic regime and are alternately tortured and pampered. If their periods of suffering are not synchronized, their lives will involve a very high total sum of inequality-at-a-time. Is it really important that their periods of suffering should be synchronized?

To defend the simultaneous segments view we might claim that, given the nature of the relevant goods and evils, lives cannot change radically within short periods of time in the respects that matter for egalitarianism. For example, if the egalitarian principle requires equality in happiness, perhaps it is not possible for a life to change from happy to unhappy in an afternoon. However, some people may not be convinced by these claims about happiness or welfare, and it would be desirable if the simultaneous segments view were independent of particular views about which good things should be equally distributed.

A different reply claims that an inequality must include a significant portion of the lives in question to be morally important. This reply also faces difficulties. It is difficult to suggest a plausible threshold to pick out the inequalities which last long enough to matter. If the time periods used to measure inequality are too long, there could be intuitively objectionable changing places arrangements inside them. The threshold must be low enough to avoid this problem but high enough to avoid the dental appointments example. And if we are sympathetic to the simultaneous segments view it is difficult to understand why short-term inequalities should not count at all, as opposed to having some slight disvalue. These difficulties are serious, but I do not think the problem of choosing time periods is a decisive objection against the simultaneous segments view.

How persuasive is the simultaneous segments view as an alternative to complete lives egalitarianism? Many people will reject it because it does not give any weight to equality between complete lives. It will not compensate

for past inequality, no matter how long the inequality has lasted and no matter how extreme it has been. If we believe that sometimes we owe those who have been badly off in the past more than just equality with others in the future, we will see this as an objection to the view. And if for some reason there must be inequality in the future, the simultaneous segments view does not distinguish between an inequality favoring those who previously were badly off and an inequality favoring the people who had better lives in the past.

On the other hand, we may be persuaded by the examples which seem to show us caring about inequality between parts of lives. A society in which peasants and nobles change places after twenty-five years does seem worse than a society without gross inequality between large parts of people's lives. Even if the second society contained slightly more inequality between complete lives than changing places egalitarianism, I think that egalitarians should prefer it.

In the case of the elderly, the complete lives view could in principle justify very great inequality between the simultaneous parts of different lives. I would support reducing the current inequality even if this means that those who are now old will have better complete lives than those who are now younger. If it is plausible to think that resources would do more good in utilitarian terms if they were given to younger people (because of the intractable nature of their problems the elderly, like the handicapped, are difficult to help), this conclusion could not be explained by a mixture of complete lives egalitarianism and utilitarianism.

One possibility is that we care about equality between complete lives, but we also accept some principle that gives weight to inequalities between parts of lives. Faced with a choice about whether to compensate for past inequality, we would have to balance the gain in equality between complete lives against the loss in terms of equality between parts of lives. In some examples we might think that one consideration was stronger, in different examples the other consideration.[8]

I have considered some alternatives to complete lives egalitarianism, and I have described their implications in a series of examples. I will now discuss some questions about the ways of thinking about our lives and time that might lie behind the alternative views.

The simultaneous segments view values equality in temporal segments of lives. It might be thought that any such view must depend on revising the ordinary view of personal identity. If we believe that inequality between the later years of A and B does not morally cancel an inequality in their youth, it must be because we believe that in some sense A and B are not the same people in age that they were in youth. Some theories of personal identity divide the life of a person into the lives of a series of different but related 'selves.' The suggestion I will consider is that the plausibility of this kind of egalitarianism depends on the plausibility of some such way of thinking of personal identity.

If the egalitarian views did have this basis certain consequences would follow. First, the views should require equality between the different parts of a single person's life. If an inequality disadvantaging A as a youth cannot be compensated for by an inequality benefiting the elderly A, because the young A and the elderly A are like different persons, then there should also be a claim to equality between the young A and the elderly A.

Second, the theory of personal identity would change our prudential judgments as well as our moral judgments. If the young A and the elderly A are like different people, then A as a youth should not believe that happiness in the distant future would reward him for sacrifices made now.

In fact this view of personal identity would not support the simultaneous segments version of egalitarianism. If different selves should be treated as we now treat different persons, it is natural to suppose that we should aim at minimizing the inequality among all of those distinct selves. The total segments view would give us this goal, once it had been extended to apply to the parts of a single life. But the simultaneous segments view has a different goal. To use the language of selves, it tells us to measure the inequality among each simultaneously existing group of selves and then requires us to minimize the sum total of these inequalities through time.

The difference between the two views is shown by the example of gradual progress. A and B share lives of poverty and sacrifice during T1, modest prosperity during T2, and considerable happiness during T3.

	T1	T2	T3
A	1	3	6
B	1	3	6

The simultaneous segments view (and the complete lives view) would not see any objectionable inequality in this example. But if we aim at minimizing inequality among selves, we will object (for example) to the inequality between A during T1 and B during T2.

I do not think the inequality in the example is objectionable (this is one reason for preferring the simultaneous segments view to the total segments view). And I am not convinced that there is a claim to equality between the different stages of a single life. In the examples where I disagree with complete lives egalitarianism, I do not think that the disagreement results from a special view of personal identity. Objecting to changing places egalitarianism does not require believing that there is some kind of weakening of personal identity in the lives of the people who are in turn peasants and nobles. So I would deny that the plausibility of the simultaneous segments view depends on revising the ordinary view of personal identity.

If it is not supported by a new way of thinking of personal identity, the simultaneous segments view might seem open to serious objections. I will discuss them using the simple example of changing places egalitarianism in which the quality of the lives of A and B is reversed at the midpoint of those lives.

	T1	T2
A	5	2
B	2	5

If A and B are the same people during T1 and T2, why doesn't the inequality in T2 morally cancel the inequality in T1? The connections between A during T1 and A during T2 are stronger than the connections between A during T1 and B during T1, so that it seems more appropriate to group the segments of lives horizontally rather than vertically in order to measure the inequality.

Moreover, the simultaneous segments view might seem to be ruled out by the judgments we make about single lives. We think that what fundamentally matters for a single life is the overall quality of the complete life. The quality of a temporal part of the life matters only to the extent that it contributes to the quality of the complete life. It would be unreasonable for B to choose a better next twenty years at the cost of a worse complete life. But when it compares lives the simultaneous segments view seems to give independent importance to what happens in temporal parts of lives. It objects to inequalities between parts of lives even if these inequalities are made good over complete lives. We also believe that the timing of benefits and harms does not affect the quality of a life. B should not reject a life because its good features would be concentrated in one temporal part while its bad features would be concentrated in a different temporal part. If the timing of benefits and harms is not important in considering a single life, why should it matter in making egalitarian judgments about different lives? Finally, according to prudence a harm at one temporal stage of a life can be outweighed by benefits at other times. Prudence might judge that B's unhappiness in T1 is outweighed by B's happiness in T2. But if B's unhappiness in T1 is compensated for by later events in B's life, why should we give it any weight when we compare B's life with A's life? It might seem that if we agree with the way in which prudential reasoning assesses single lives we must reject simultaneous segments egalitarianism.

However, I think the simultaneous segments view can be explained in a way that answers these objections. Egalitarianism cares about minimizing the inequality between different lives. Because those lives extend through time there can be more than one view about how to do this. The complete lives view and the simultaneous segments view can both be regarded as built around ways of measuring the inequality between lives. Understood in this way the simultaneous segments view is also concerned with achieving equality between complete lives. But it supposes that the inequality between two lives equals the sum of the inequalities between the simultaneous parts of those lives. Thinking about the example of changing places egalitarianism, it denies that the answer to the question, "How much inequality was there in all between A's life and B's life?" is "Absolutely none." According to it, A and B live all of their lives as unequals. And it claims that the sense in which there was inequality was morally important.

That is why the view does not need to deny the fact of personal identity through time or question the importance of this fact. It does not reach its life in T2. It applies the requirement of equality to the temporal parts of the lives of A and B. It objects to the inequality in T1, and it objects because of the difference in A's life and B's life during T1. According to it, following T1 by an inequality in T2 favoring B could at most be a second-best alternative to not allowing the inequality in T1 in the first place.

If it is understood in this way the view is not inconsistent with prudence. It does not give independent importance to parts of lives. Like the complete lives view, its fundamental concern is equality between complete lives, but it takes a different view of how inequality in parts of lives contributes to inequality between complete lives. It treats time as important, but it does not claim that the timing of benefits and harms influences the quality of the individual lives which contain them. Time becomes important in making egalitarian judgments about the relationship between different lives, and it is important because of the way in which the simultaneous segments view measures inequality. The view does not depend on thinking that benefits and harms cannot outweigh one another across time. It can agree that B's happiness in T2 might outweigh B's unhappiness in T1 if we are considering B's life. But it would claim that this does not mean that what happens in T1 cannot have any kind of importance. It might matter when we make egalitarian judgments which compare B's life with A's life.

Explained in this way the simultaneous segments view does not clash with prudential judgments about single lives. But the explanation suggests a different objection. The simultaneous segments view seems to undermine the connection between egalitarianism and the quality of individual lives. It objects to inequalities between the temporal parts of the lives of A and B even though the inequalities are compensated for at earlier or later times. But if the inequalities are compensated for at other times, they do not make the lives of A and B worse than they would have been without the inequalities. (We could say that they make parts of the lives of A and B worse, but this reply would suggest that the view did after all care independently about segments of lives.) It might even be true that both A and B have better complete lives because the inequalities exist. Why should we believe that inequalities that do not make people's lives worse are morally objectionable?

However, it is important to remember that I have been discussing a particular kind of egalitarianism, an egalitarian view that values equality as a relationship holding between different lives. It does not object to the poor quality of B's life during T1, it objects to the difference between A's life and B's life. Because its judgments are not based directly on the contents of the lives of A and B, it is easier to understand why there can be differences between judgments about the quality of individual lives and egalitarian judgments. This kind of egalitarianism might object to inequalities even if they did not make people's lives worse.

If we are forced to treat the simultaneous segments view as a time-relative version of this kind of egalitarianism, some people might take this to be a reason for rejecting the view. But I am not convinced that the view has unacceptable consequences. For example, it is arguable that a health care system and a social security system providing only minimal support for the very old would increase equality over complete lives and use resources in the most efficient way. It is even possible that we would all be better off if we lived our complete lives under these institutions. But this system would create gross inequality between the very old and their younger contemporaries, and I would object to it for that reason despite its advantages.

The simultaneous segments view must also claim that the fact of simultaneity can itself have moral importance.[9] It registers the inequality between A's life during T1 and B's life during T1 as something that should be avoided. But it would not have said the same about an inequality between A's life during T1 and B's

life during T2, because those segments of the two lives are not simultaneous. The example of gradual progress, which the view finds unobjectionable, would turn into an objectionable case of changing places egalitarianism if we imagine that B had instead been born twenty-five years before A, so that the happy and unhappy periods of their lives would not be simultaneous.

Many people would reject this claim about the importance of simultaneity. Could a mere difference in the timing of B's birth have these moral consequences? They might base their objection on the general claim that facts about time do not have intrinsic moral significance. What matters for morality is what happens, not when it happens. If something good happens it would have had the same value if it had occurred instead at some other time. The view that time is morally irrelevant has apparently been held by many moral philosophers. If simultaneous segments egalitarianism contradicts their view this might seem a sufficient reason for rejecting it.

But it is not clear that those writers really do think that no fact about timing can have any kind of moral importance. They discuss particular ways of making time important. Sidgwick says that the consciousness of one moment is not more important than the consciousness of any other moment.[10] Rawls says that in making decisions about our own lives, or other people's lives, we should not be influenced by a pure time preference which gives more weight to the near future than the distant future.[11]

The simultaneous segments view does not make the mistakes that Sidgwick and Rawls warn us against. It objects to inequality in the simultaneous parts of different lives. But it makes the same judgment about this kind of inequality whenever it occurs, and whether it belongs to the past, present, or future. The view can agree that good and bad things have the same value whenever they occur.

The view gives importance to relative temporal position, not to absolute temporal position. For this reason I think it is appropriate to compare it to the view that punishment should follow and not precede an offense. People might disagree over this claim about punishment, depending on their general views about the justification for punishment. But it would be un-reasonable for those who believe it to give it up because they are told that facts about time cannot be morally important.

The situation is analogous with the simultaneous segments view. If we find the view attractive it is because we think that inequality in the simultaneous parts of lives is significant, even if the inequality is compensated for at earlier or later times. This view gives moral importance to the relative timing of benefits and harms in different lives. But if these facts do seem important, we should not be dissuaded by the general claim that time is morally irrelevant.

I have discussed some examples in which I disagree with the conclusions drawn by the complete lives version of egalitarianism. There are two ways in which the complete lives view could be changed: by denying importance to the past or by applying egalitarian constraints directly to parts of lives. I have argued that the second change is preferable.

I have argued that the most plausible time-relative view about equality will require equality in the simultaneous segments of different lives. Our lives are lived serially through time, and the simultaneous segments view responds to this fact by valuing equality in the simultaneous parts of lives rather than by merely requiring that lives should be equal when viewed timelessly as completed wholes. If we find this view persuasive we will probably care both about equality assessed in the complete lives way and equality in the temporal parts of lives. Someone might care about both and still believe that a gain in equality in terms of complete lives is always more important than a gain in equality between the parts of lives. But if we do care about equality in the simultaneous segments way, I think we should believe that a large gain in equality between parts of lives would outweigh a small gain in equality between complete lives.

I have argued that the plausibility of the simultaneous segments view is independent of theories about personal identity. And I have claimed that the view does not conflict with a requirement of timelessness when we are considering good and bad features within one life, or with the thought that what fundamentally matters for a single life is the overall quality of the complete life. I have applied the view to the practical problem of the treatment of the elderly, where I find its consequences intuitively appealing.

NOTES

1. Ronald Dworkin, "What Is Equality? Part I: Equality of Welfare," *Philosophy and Public Affairs* 10 (1981): 185–246; and "What Is Equality? Part 2: Equality of Resources," *Philosophy and Public Affairs* 10 (1981): 283–345.

2. For example, Rawls describes the hypothetical contractors in the original position as considering the life prospects and long-term expectations of representative people from different social classes, so it seems that his difference principle would deal with shares of primary goods over complete lives (John Rawls, *A Theory of Justice*, pp. 78, 178). Dworkin explicitly says that his egalitarian principle requires equal shares of resources over complete lives ("What Is Equality? Part 2: Equality of Resources," pp. 304–305).

3. This paper mainly discusses the kind of egalitarianism that aims at equality and how it might give weight to temporal considerations. But I will also briefly discuss how the other kinds of egalitarianism might handle the issue. My discussion is intended to be neutral between different views about which goods should be equally distributed.

4. Utilitarians could give importance to satisfying past desires directed at the future (past desires are discussed by Derek Parfit in *Reasons and Persons* [Oxford: Clarendon Press, 1984], pp. 149–158). But the fact that such a desire is satisfied is not simply a fact about the past.

5. Derek Parfit, "Comments," *Ethics* 96 (1986): 832–872, esp. pp. 869–870.

6. Parfit also discusses a version of the example in which the medicine would relieve more suffering in the long run if it were given to A, although B's current suffering is more intense than A's suffering will ever be ("Comments," p. 870). Parfit thinks that it would not be absurd to decide to help B. This conclusion could not be explained by a combination of complete lives egalitarianism and the principle of minimizing suffering. If the conclusion is an egalitarian judgment it must be based on what Parfit calls a "times-relative" principle of equality.

7. This claim is disputable if it is applied to all those over sixty-five. But if it is restricted to the 'old old'—those seventy-five or older—it has more force.

8. If we also value equality between complete lives

we can recognize a claim to equality between members of different generations whose lives have no simultaneous parts. In this case there would be no egalitarian constraints applying to the parts of their lives.

9. Some versions of complete lives egalitarianism also make simultaneity important. These views hold that the claim to equality between lives that belong to the same generation is stronger than the claim to equality between lives belonging to generations widely separated in time. If social cooperation were a necessary condition for the applicability of egalitarian principles we could perhaps reach the same conclusion without attributing importance to simultaneity. However, I do not think egalitarian principles are subject to this condition of applicability, and I do think that the claim to equality is stronger among contemporaries.

10. Henry Sidgwick, *The Methods of Ethics* (London: Macmillan, 1907), p. 381.

11. Rawls, pp. 293–294.

Inequality
LARRY S. TEMKIN

I. INTRODUCTION

The notion of equality has long been among the most potent of human ideals, and it continues to play a prominent role in political argument. Views about equality inform much of the debate about such wide-ranging issues as racism, sexism, obligations to the poor or handicapped, relations between the developed and underdeveloped countries, and the justification of competing political, economic and ideological systems.

Most discussions of equality have focused on two questions: Is equality really desirable? And, what kind of inequality do we want to avoid (that is, insofar as we are egalitarians, do we want equality of opportunity, or primary goods, or need satisfaction, or welfare, or what)? These are important questions. But I shall be asking a third question. When is one situation *worse* than another with respect to inequality? It is only by addressing this question, I believe, that one can begin to understand the nature and complexity of the notion of inequality.

Of course, in some cases the answer to my question can easily be given. We know, for instance, that among equally deserving people, the inequality in a situation would be worse if the gaps between the better- and worse-off people were large, than if they were small. Consider, however, a situation where many are better off, and a few are worse off. How would the inequality in such a situation compare to the inequality in a situation where a few are better off and many are worse off? How would both of these compare to a situation where the better-off and worse-off groups were equal in size? It is with questions such as these that I shall be concerned. As we shall see, they are complicated questions, and ones to which several plausible but conflicting answers might be given.

II. PRELIMINARY COMMENTS

I shall mainly discuss inequality of *welfare*, but this does not affect my arguments. Analogous arguments could be made in terms of inequal-

Reprinted from *Philosophy and Public Affairs* 15 (1986) by permission of Princeton University Press and the author. Footnotes edited.

ity of opportunity, or primary goods, or need satisfaction, or whatever.

For each of my examples, where some people are better off than others, I shall assume that the better- and worse-off are equally skilled, hard-working, morally worthy, and so forth. While it would not be necessary, I shall also assume that the better-off are not responsible for the plight of the worse-off, either directly, through exploitation, or indirectly, through unwillingness to share their good fortune. This would be so, for instance, if the inequality were due to irremediable differences in health. Since my concern is with what we might say about these examples with respect to inequality, I make these assumptions in order to insure that our judgments about them are as free as possible from the disturbing influence of our other moral beliefs and ideals.[1]

Although there may be many differences between them, as I shall use the term, an *egalitarian* is any person who attaches *some* value to equality *itself* (that is, any person that cares *at all* about equality, over and above the extent it promotes other ideals). So, equality needn't be the only ideal the egalitarian values, or even the ideal she values most. Still, throughout this article, when I consider what one might say about a situation with respect to inequality, I shall be considering what an egalitarian would say about it *if* equality *were* the only ideal she valued.

There is, I believe, an intimate connection between people's views about equality and certain of their views about justice and fairness. In particular, I believe egalitarians have the deep and (for them) compelling view that it is a bad thing—unjust and unfair—for some to be worse off than others through no fault of their own. Unfortunately, as we shall see, it is one matter to note that egalitarians have such a view, and quite another to unpack what it involves.[2]

In this article, I assume that egalitarians should care about natural, and not merely social, inequality (cf. note 2). However, even if one only cared about social inequality, most of the same questions and considerations would apply. (My own view is that most concern about social inequality must ultimately ride piggyback on concern about natural inequality. It is difficult to see why social inequality would be intrinsically bad, if natural inequality is not.)

I am concerned with inequality from a *moral* perspective. This is why my question is not "When is there *more* inequality in one situation than another?" but rather, "When is one situation *worse* than another with respect to inequality?" There is, I believe, good reason to allow for the possibility that in some cases one situation might be *worse* than another with respect to inequality, though in a certain objective sense it has *less* inequality.[3]

Finally, although I think most of the arguments that have been offered against equality can be refuted, let me emphasize that this article is neither a defense of, nor an attack on, the ideal of equality. I do not address the question of whether one *should* care about inequality, or the question of *how much* one should care about inequality. It seems to me that until one understands the notion of inequality, these questions are premature.

III. INDIVIDUAL COMPLAINTS

My main aim is to consider our judgments about how situations compare with respect to inequality. However, there is another, more particular kind of judgment it will help to consider first. This kind of judgment is about how bad the inequality in a situation is from the standpoint of particular individuals in that situation.

Such judgments can be made using the terminology of "complaints." Thus, for any situation where some people are better off than others, we can say that the best-off have nothing to complain about, while the worst-off have the most to complain about. (Here, and in what follows, I often drop the locution "with respect to inequality." Henceforth all references to complaints are to be understood as complaints with respect to inequality, unless stated otherwise.)

To say that the best-off have nothing to complain about is in no way to impugn their moral sensibilities. They may be just as concerned about the inequality in their world as anyone else. Nor is it to deny that, insofar as one is concerned about inequality, one might have a complaint *about* them being as well off as they are. It is only to recognize that, since they are at least as well off as every other member of their world, *they* have nothing to complain about.

Similarly, to say that the worst-off have a complaint is not to claim that they will in fact complain (they may not). It is only to recognize that it is a bad thing (unjust or unfair) for them to be worse off than the other members of their world through no fault of their own.

For any situation, then, in which some people are worse off than others, two questions arise. Who is it that has a complaint, and, how should we compare the seriousness of different people's complaints? To the first question there seem to be two natural but competing answers, neither of which can easily be dismissed.

According to the first answer, only those people who are *worse off than the average* have a complaint. This answer might be defended as follows. In a world of *n* equally deserving people, the fairest distribution would be for each person to receive one *nth* of the total, since among equally deserving people, a fair share is an *equal* share. Those who receive less than one *nth* of the total would thus have a complaint, since they are receiving *less* than their fair share. Moreover, they are the only people who have a complaint, since those who receive one *nth* or more of the total are *already* receiving their fair share or *more* than their fair share. But, in a world of *n* people, one *nth* of the total welfare is the average level of welfare. Hence, all and only those people below the average have a complaint.

This line of reasoning often expresses itself in our thinking. Thus, whatever someone is complaining about, the lament "Why me?!" will tend to meet with a sympathetic response if she is below average in the relevant respect, but ring hollow otherwise. So, for instance, given that the second best-off person is *already* much better off than the average member of her world, most people would tend to think that such a person has *nothing* to complain about with respect to her level of welfare.

There is another natural answer to the question of who has a complaint: *all but the very best-off* have complaints. A defense of this answer may be made with the aid of diagram I.[4]

In A, we may judge that q has a complaint, because, among equally deserving people, we think it is a bad thing (unjust or unfair) for one person to be at q's level, while another is at p's. In B, for instance, it may seem that q would have just as much to complain about as in A, since she is no better off than she was in A, and since p is no worse off than she was in A. True, in B there is another person who is as bad off relative to p as q is. However, that doesn't lessen the injustice of q's being worse off than p—it only makes it the case that instead of there being *one* instance of injustice there are two!

Consider C. From q's perspective, it seems the inequality in C might appear worse than the inequality in A, since p is just as well off as she was in A, while q is worse off. More particularly, it appears that q's complaint would be larger in C than in A, since it is worse to be at level 20 while another is at level 100, than it is

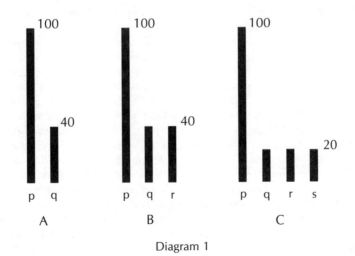

Diagram 1

to be at level 40 while another is at level 100. Again, the presence in C of r and s may not seem to lessen the injustice of q's being worse off than p through no fault of her own; their presence only makes it the case that instead of there being one person with a larger complaint than q had in A, there are three. But note, in C, q fares better relative to the average than she did in A. Hence, the view that q would have a larger complaint indicates that we determine q's complaint by comparing her to p, and not to the average.

Extended, such reasoning yields the conclusion that all but the very best-off have a complaint. And on reflection, it is clear that this, too, often expresses itself in our thinking.[5] Applied to our earlier example, this reasoning suggests that even if we admit that *relatively speaking* the second best-off person has "nothing" to complain about, when we focus on the individual comparison between the best-off person and that person, it will appear to be unfair or unjust for the one to be worse off than the other through no fault of her own. So, even the second best-off person will have a complaint; though her complaint may be small, both in absolute terms, and relative to the complaints of others. Thus, on the question of *who* has a complaint, there appear to be two plausible answers: those below the average, and all but the very best-off.

Let us next consider the question of how we assess the seriousness, or size, of someone's complaint. To this question there seem to be three plausible answers. The first two parallel the division in our thinking about who has a complaint. Thus we might think that the size of someone's complaint will depend upon how she compares to either *the average member of her world,* or *the best-off member of her world.*

These two ways of regarding the size of someone's complaint correspond to two natural ways of viewing an unequal world: as a deviation from the situation which would have obtained if the welfare had been distributed equally, and as a deviation from the situation in which each is as well off as the best-off person. On both views it would be natural to determine the size of someone's complaint by comparing her level to the level at which she would cease to have a complaint. On the first view, this would be the average level of her world—the level she would be at if fate had treated each person equally. On the second view, it would be the level of the best-off person—the level at which she would no longer be worse off than another.

There is a third way of measuring the size of someone's complaint. This way accepts the view that all but the very best-off have a complaint, but contends that the size of someone's complaint depends not on how she fares relative to the best-off person, but on how she fares relative to *all of the other people who are better off than she.*

This view might be defended as follows. It is bad for someone to be worse off than another through no fault of her own. This is why any person who is in such a position will have a complaint. But if it is bad to be worse off than one person through no fault of your own, it should be even worse to be worse off than two such people. And, in general, the more people there are who are better off than someone (and the larger the gap between them), the more that person should have to complain about with respect to inequality. Therefore, to determine the size of someone's complaint, one must compare her level to those of *all* people who are better off than she, and not only to the level of the very best-off person.

Although this third way of regarding the size of someone's complaint may seem less natural than the first two, it does not seem less plausible. Indeed, it is arguable that this position captures certain of the most plausible features of the first two views, while avoiding their most implausible features.

Let us summarize the argument so far. Our notion of inequality allows us to focus on particular individuals, and make judgments about whether or not, and the extent to which, they have a complaint with respect to inequality. There is, however, a division in our thinking concerning who has a complaint, and how we determine the magnitude of a complaint. Specifically, one might plausibly maintain that only people below the average have a complaint, and the size of their complaint depends upon (1) how they fare relative to the average (henceforth, I shall call this the *relative to the average* view of complaints). Alternatively, one may claim that all but the best-off have a complaint, and the size of their complaint depends either upon (2) how they fare relative to the best-off person (henceforth, the *relative to the best-off person* view of complaints), or upon (3) how they fare relative to all those better off than they (henceforth, the *relative to all those better off* view of complaints).

With respect to how we actually measure the size of someone's complaint on the views given above, I shall make the simplifying assumption that we merely subtract her level of welfare from the level of the average person, or the best-off person, or the levels of all those better off than she. I believe that the figures thus arrived at should be differentially weighted to reflect the view that inequality matters more at low levels than at high levels. But for my purposes here, we can ignore this complication. Doing so will not affect the main conclusion I shall reach.

IV. THE SEQUENCE

We are now in a position to consider our most general judgments about how situations compare with respect to inequality. In order to explore the reasoning underlying and influencing such judgments, I shall be looking at a group of artificially simple worlds, which I shall refer to as the *Sequence*. This consists of 999 outcomes, or *worlds*, each of which contains two groups of people, the better-off and the worse-off. In each world the total size of the population is 1,000, but the ratio between the two groups steadily changes. In the first world there are 999 people better off and one person worse off, in the second 998 better off and two worse off, and so on.

By the end world one person is better off and 999 are worse off. The first, middle, and last worlds of the Sequence are represented below.

How do the worlds of the Sequence compare with respect to inequality? Notice, I am *not* asking how they compare "all things considered."[6] These are very different questions. Consider the worlds shown in diagram 3. We may think that "all things considered" A is better off than B, since everybody in A is better off than everybody in B, and since the inequality in A is fairly slight. Nevertheless, *with respect to inequality*, B is better than A. In B there is perfect equality. In A there is not.[7]

I emphasize this point because the Sequence is getting progressively worse in terms of both total and average utility. This is an unavoidable feature of the Sequence, but one which should not mislead us as long as we bear in mind the question we are interested in. Similarly, there is a danger in looking at such neatly divided worlds in that some of the conclusions reached may not be generalizable to the real world. However, if we are careful we should be able to prevent that feature of the Sequence from leading us astray.

Bearing in mind, then, that all comparisons are with respect to inequality unless stated otherwise, there are five judgments about the Sequence I would like to consider. As we shall see, though these judgments conflict, most can be plausibly supported.

V. BETTER AND BETTER

When one first considers the Sequence, one might judge that the worlds are getting *better*

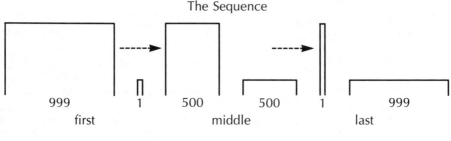

The Sequence

999   1   500   500   1   999

first   middle   last

Diagram 2

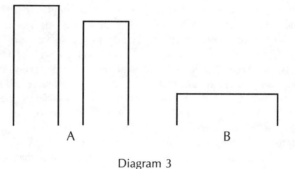

Diagram 3

and better, partly, because as the Sequence progresses, it appears to be less and less the case that anyone is being especially victimized by the situation. In the *first* world, for instance, it is as if the entire burden of the inequality in that world is borne by the one, lone member of the worse-off group. Given that that person is worse off than *every other* member of her world, it may seem both that she has a very large complaint, and that the inequality is especially offensive. By contrast, the inequality in the last world may seem relatively inoffensive. In *that* world, each member of the worse-off group is as well off as *all* but *one* of the other members of her world. Hence, in that world it may seem as if nobody has much to complain about with respect to inequality.

This view is plausible, and it expresses itself in the way we react to the actions of bullies or tyrants. Though, all things considered, we may prefer the mistreatment of a small group to the mistreatment of a large group, certain of our egalitarian views are especially attuned to cases where a particular person or small group is singled out for harmful treatment.[8] Indeed, I think it is the singling out in this way of an individual or small group that is the paradigm of a harmful discrimination which is grossly unjust and unfair (and not merely bad). Having seen that certain elements of our thinking support the "better and better" ordering, let us next try to get clearer about what those elements might involve.

One principle which might seem relevant here is the *maximin* principle of justice. This principle states that a society's political, social, and economic institutions are just if they maximize the average level of the worst-off group.

In one form or another, many philosophers have come to advocate a maximin principle of justice, and one can see why. There is strong appeal to the view that just as it would be right for a mother to devote most of her effort and resources to her neediest child, so it would be right for a society to devote most of *its* effort and resources to its neediest members. This view is captured by the maximin principle which, in essence, maintains that it would be unjust for society to benefit the "haves," if instead it could benefit the "have-nots."

Now, strictly speaking, a Rawlsian version of the maximin principle is not relevant to our discussion. The main reason for this is simply that it has been offered as a principle of *justice*, *not* as a principle of equality. According to Rawls, a society's principles would be better, and not *unjust*, if they were altered to improve the lot of the worst-off group. This is so even if in order to effect a small improvement, the lot of the better-off had to be improved immensely. Clearly, then, the maximin principle of justice is *not* a plausible principle of *equality*, for whether or not such an alteration in a society's institutions would make that society more *just*, it would certainly *not* make it better with respect to inequality.

Still, while Rawls's maximin principle may not itself be relevant to our discussion, the spirit of that principle is relevant. This is because the same basic concern for the worst-off people which supports a maximin principle of justice would also support a maximin principle of equality.

One version of the maximin principle of equality might be stated as follows: How bad a world is with respect to inequality will depend upon how bad the worst-off group in that world fares with respect to inequality, so, if the level of complaint of the worst-off group is larger in one of two worlds, that is the world which is worse. If the level of complaint of the worst-off group is the same in both worlds, then that world will be better whose worst-off group is smallest; if the two worst-off groups are the same size, then the next worst-off groups are similarly compared, and so forth.

Notice the second clause of this principle comes into play *only* if the worst-off groups fare the same in two worlds. This is important, for depending upon which view of complaints one adopts, the magnitude of the worst-off group's complaint may decrease as the size of the worst-off group increases. In such a case the first clause of the maximin principle would tell us that the situation was improving, and the second clause would not apply. Intuitively, then, the maximin principle of equality would first have us maximize the relative position of the worst-off group, and then minimize the number of people in that group, as long as we were not thereby increasing the complaint of the remaining members of the worst-off group. It would then have us do the same thing for the next worst-off group (as long as this did not increase the complaints of the worst-off group), and so on, until all of the groups were as well off and as small as they could be.

We can now see one reason why the "better and better" ordering seems plausible. In accordance with certain plausible positions, the members of the worst-off group have less and less to complain about as the Sequence progresses. This is true on both the "relative to all those better offs" and the "relative to the average" views of complaints (since as the ratio between the better- and worse-off groups decreases, the members of the worst-off group fare better and better with respect both to the number of people who are better off than they [by a certain amount], and to the average level of people in their world). Therefore, insofar as we accept a maximin principle of equality, there will be reason to think that the Sequence is getting better and better.

It is worth noting that the advocate of the maximin principle of equality is concerned not with the sum total of complaints, but with the *distribution* of those complaints. Specifically, he wants the inequality to be distributed in such a way that the "load" which each member of the worst-off group has to "bear" is as small as possible.

There is another line of thought which might support the "better and better" ordering. In the earlier worlds, the inequality may seem particularly offensive, as there seems to be virtually nothing gained by it. If a redistribution of the sources of welfare took place, the better-off group would hardly lose anything, and the worse-off group would gain tremendously. Moreover, the unavoidability of the inequality in those worlds may do nothing to lessen the feeling that it is so pointless and unnecessary. We may still feel that the worse-off have been especially unfortunate; and we still fully recognize that a situation of complete equality would have obtained *if only* each better-off person had received a tiny bit less welfare, and *if only* the "extra table scraps" of welfare had gone to the worse-off people. In the middle worlds, on the other hand, a redistribution of the sources of welfare would be "costly." Many would have to lose a lot to achieve complete equality. In the end worlds, redistribution would involve a tremendous loss in the quality of life for some, with virtually no gain to those thus "benefited." Therefore, the inequality might seem least offensive in the end worlds of the Sequence, as in those worlds the "cost" of the inequality might seem smallest, and the "gain" highest.

This position might be summed up as follows. Whether or not anything could be done about it, it will offend us as egalitarians for some to be badly off, while others are well off. But from one perspective, at least, we will be most offended if just a few are badly off, while the vast majority are well off, since the inequality then seems particularly gratuitous. In accordance with this way of thinking, it will seem that the Sequence is getting better and better.

VI. WORSE AND WORSE

I would next like to suggest that certain elements of our thinking support the judgment that the Sequence is getting, not better and better, but *worse and worse*. One principle which can yield this ordering is what I shall call the *additive* principle of equality. According to this principle, the inequality in a world is measured by summing up each of the complaints that the individuals in that world have; where the larger that sum is, the worse the world is. This kind of principle involves two natural and plausible assumptions: (1) given any two situations, the best situation with respect to some factor f will be the one in which the *most* f obtains if f is something desirable (for example, pleasure, happiness, equality), and the one in which the *least* f obtains if f is something undesirable (for example, pain, misery, inequality); and (2) to determine how much f obtains in a situation one needs only to determine the magnitude of the individual instances of f which obtain and then add them together. Since this kind of principle is—understandably enough—associated with utilitarianism, let me note that where people usually disagree with utilitarianism is *not* with its claim that the best world with respect to utility is the one where the sum total of utilities is greatest, but with its claim that total utility is all that matters.

So, like the maximin principle, an additive principle of equality represents certain plausible positions. It captures the view that it is bad for one person to be in such a position that she has a complaint, and the corresponding view that it should be even worse if, in addition to the first person with her complaint, there is a second person who has a complaint.

As with the maximin principle, the additive principle does not *itself* yield an ordering of the Sequence. However, when combined with the "relative to the best-off person" view of complaints, it supports the judgment that the Sequence is getting worse and worse. After all, on that view, more and more people will have a complaint of a certain constant amount as the Sequence progresses, and according to the additive principle, the more people there are with a given amount to complain about, the worse the situation is with respect to inequality.

There is another view which supports the "worse and worse" ordering. Since the main elements of this view have already been examined, I can be brief. Earlier I noted how the max-

imin principle of equality could be combined with either of two plausible views about complaints to support the "better and better" ordering. However, when combined with the "relative to the best-off person" view, the maximin principle will yield the "worse and worse" ordering. This is because on this view of complaints, the worst-off groups fare the same throughout the Sequence, and according to the most plausible version of the maximin principle of equality, if the worst-off groups fare the same in two worlds, that world will be best whose worst-off group is smallest. Thus, there is a second set of plausible views which combine to support the "worse and worse" ordering.

There is yet another position which would support the "worse and worse" ordering. One might arrive at this position by reasoning as follows. Despite its appeal, the maximin principle is less plausible when applied to more realistic worlds where people are spread out over a continuum of welfare levels. No matter what level is chosen to separate the worst-off group from the rest of society, it seems implausible to contend that we should be genuinely concerned with the complaints of the people at that level, but shouldn't be concerned at all (except in the case of ties) with the complaints of those who are just above that level. More generally, while it may seem reasonable to be more concerned about those with large complaints than those with small complaints, it seems implausible to contend that the complaints of the one group matter, but those of the other do not (except in the case of ties). Thus, an additive principle might seem preferable to a maximin principle, insofar as it is concerned with the complaints of *all* those who have a complaint, and not just with the complaints of some arbitrarily selected worst-off group. Yet a maximin principle might seem preferable to an additive principle, insofar as it is concerned with the *distribution* rather than merely the sum total of complaints. This suggests that a principle which plausibly combined these two elements would have great appeal.

Here is one such principle: We measure the inequality in a world by adding together people's complaints, after first attaching extra weight to them in such a way that the larger someone's complaint is, the more weight is attached to it. Let us call this the *weighted additive* principle of equality. Like the additive principle and the maximin principle, the weighted additive principle appears to be a plausible principle of equality. Combined with the "relative to the best-off person" view of complaints, such a principle supports the "worse and worse" ordering. This is because no matter how the individual complaints are weighted, since the complaints are non-negative, $n + 1$ weighted complaints will always be larger than n weighted complaints.

VII. FIRST WORSE, THEN BETTER

We have seen that certain plausible positions support the "better and better" ordering, and that others support the "worse and worse" ordering. Still others support the judgment that the Sequence, *first gets worse, then gets better*.

It is easy to be drawn to such an ordering by reasoning as follows. In the first world of the Sequence everyone is perfectly equal except, regrettably, for one, isolated individual. As there is just an ever so slight deviation from absolute equality, that world may seem nearly perfect with respect to inequality. In the second world, there are two people who are not at the level of everyone else. The deviation from a state of absolute equality has become more pronounced; hence that world may seem worse than the first. As the Sequence progresses this reasoning continues for a while. The deviations from absolute equality become larger, and as they do so, the Sequence appears to be worsening. After the midpoint, however, the deviations from absolute equality begin to get smaller. By the end world, there is once again just an ever so slight deviation from absolute equality. Everyone is equal except, regrettably, for one, isolated individual. Like the first world, therefore, the last world may appear to be almost perfect with respect to inequality. In sum, since it seems almost tautological that the less a situation deviates from absolute equality the better it is with respect to inequality, it seems natural and plausible to judge that the Sequence first gets worse, then gets better.

There is another line of thought which supports the "worse, then better" ordering. In the first world, only *one* person has a complaint, so as large as this complaint may be, this world's inequality may not seem too bad. Specifically, it may not seem as bad as the inequality in the second, where it may seem that *two* people have *almost* as much to complain about as the one person had in the first world. And these two may not seem *nearly* as bad as the inequality in the middle world. In the middle world, it may seem *both* that a large number have a complaint (half of the population), *and* that the magnitude of their complaints will be quite large (they are, after all, worse off than half of the population through no fault of their own). In the last world, on the other hand, the situation may seem analogous to, though the reverse of, the one obtaining in the first. Although almost everyone has *something* to complain about, it may seem that the size of their complaints will be virtually negligible. Hence, as with the first world, the inequality may not seem too bad.

This reasoning involves two by now familiar elements: the view that the size of someone's complaint depends upon how she fares relative to all those better off than she, and the additive principle of equality. According to the "relative to all those better off" view of complaints, the size of individual complaints will decrease as the Sequence progresses, as there will be fewer and fewer better off than those who have a complaint. According to the additive principle, how bad a world is depends upon both the magnitude *and* the number of complaints. Combined, these views support the judgment that, with respect to inequality, the middle worlds, where a fairly large number have fairly large complaints, will be worse than either the initial worlds, where just a few have very large complaints, or the end worlds, where many have very small complaints. Indeed, on the view assumed here, according to which the size of someone's complaint is measured by summing up the difference between her level of welfare and that of each person better off than she, it is a simple task to verify that the combination of views I have been discussing will support the judgment that the Sequence first gets worse, then gets better.

Similar reasoning would lead one to expect that the additive principle would also support the "worse, then better" ordering when combined with the "relative to the average" view of complaints. As the Sequence progresses, the situation changes from there being a few much worse off than the average, to there being many only a little worse off than the average. So, combining the two views in question, it might seem that the middle worlds, where a fairly large number have fairly large complaints, will be worse than either the initial worlds, where just a few have very large complaints, or the end worlds, where many have very small complaints. And it is easy to verify that the "worse, then better" ordering is yielded by these views, if one makes the assumption that how bad it is for someone to deviate from the average can be measured by taking the difference between her level of welfare and that of the average person.

I believe that the *weighted* additive principle, in any plausible version, would also support the "worse, then better" ordering when combined with either the "relative to all those better off" or the "relative to the average" view of complaints. But while the additive principle would combine with the "relative to all those better off" and the "relative to the average" views of complaints to yield an ordering of the Sequence corresponding to a *symmetrical* curve—like A of diagram 4—the weighted additive principle would combine with those views to yield a *skewed* curve—like B of diagram 4. The extent

to which the curve would be skewed would depend on the exact weighting system employed by the weighted additive principle. If larger complaints receive lots of extra weight it will be greatly skewed; if they only receive a little extra weight it will only be slightly skewed.

VIII. FIRST BETTER, THEN WORSE

By now it may seem that there are *bound* to be several plausible positions supporting the judgment that the Sequence *first gets better, then gets worse*. If there *are* such elements, however, I am not aware of them.

IX. ALL EQUIVALENT

Do any plausible views support the judgment that the worlds of the Sequence are *all equivalent*? One Principle which would support this ordering when combined with the "relative to the best-off person" view of complaints would be a maximin principle of equality which lacked the tie-breaking clause that if the worst-off groups in two worlds fare the same, then that world will be best whose worst-off group is smallest.

I believe that the version of the maximin principle with the tie-breaking clause is more plausible than the version without it. However, it

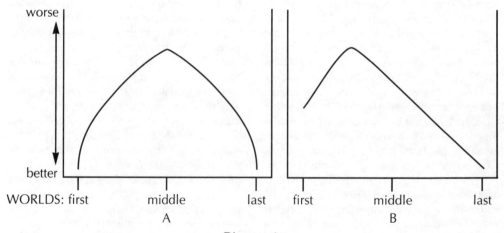

Diagram 4

might be charged that it is the latter version which actually captures our *maximin* views, and that the former version just represents an ad hoc attempt to reconcile our maximin views with certain other views. I think this charge cannot be sustained, and shall briefly suggest why.

The claim that we are especially concerned about the worst-off group is misleading insofar as it suggests a concern on our part about the *group itself* as opposed to the *members* of that group. We do not have a special concern for some real or abstract entity "the worst-off group." What we have, is a special concern for the worst-off members of our world, and it is *this* concern which a maximin principle expresses. But surely, insofar as we are especially concerned with the worst-off members of our world, we would want to raise as many of them as possible above their present level, as long as by doing that we were not increasing the complaints of the others. This suggests that of the two competing versions, it is indeed the one first considered which accurately expresses our maximin views. Thus, one must look elsewhere to support the judgment that the worlds of the Sequence are all equivalent.

There is one sense in which it could be plausibly claimed that the worlds are equivalent. *If* the "relative to the best-off person" view of complaints is adopted, and *if* the worlds of the Sequence represented societies whose principles and institutions were responsible for the size of the gaps between the better- and worse-off groups, but not the *number* of people in those groups, then one might regard each of those societies as equivalent in that with respect to inequality the principles and institutions governing those worlds might seem equally unjust. Such a position would express the view that there is a sense in which two societies can be equally unjust, though in other respects one may be worse than the other. This is analogous to the view that two judges who accepted bribes in all of their cases might be equally corrupt, even if one tried fewer cases.

Thus, given certain assumptions, I think the "all equivalent" ordering would be plausible. However, let me add that the sense in which this is so is one where *social* justice is concerned. Where natural or cosmic justice is concerned, I am not aware of any independently

plausible view which would support this ordering.

X. CONCLUSION

I have examined the question of how we judge one situation to be worse than another with respect to inequality. I have suggested that a number of plausible positions might influence our egalitarian judgments. Specifically, I have suggested that the additive, weighted additive, and maximin principles could each be combined with the relative to the average, the relative to the best-off person, and the relative to all those better off views of complaints, to yield a judgment about how good or bad a situation is with respect to inequality. I have also suggested that in accordance with certain other plausible views, we might judge a situation's inequality in terms of either how gratuitous it appears to be, or how much it deviates from a state of absolute equality. Finally, I have suggested that we may judge how good or bad a society is with respect to inequality in terms of the principles and institutions of that society responsible for the inequality.

I have focused on situations where the levels of the better- and worse-off groups remain the same, but the ratios between those groups vary. It is important to bear in mind that many positions yielding the same judgment about these cases nevertheless represent different (combinations of) views. Hence, in more complicated cases, their judgments will often diverge.

Among the questions that still need to be explored are: What happens to our egalitarian judgments when (a) the better- and worse-off are spread out among a number of groups? (b) the levels between the better- and worse-off groups vary? and (c) the total number of people in the societies vary, and not merely the relative numbers of the better- and worse-off groups? These questions concern important elements of the egalitarian's thinking. However, their answers do not affect my main conclusions, as the arguments presented here are largely independent of the issues in question.

In addition to the theoretical arguments presented, there are other, perhaps less significant, factors which support the conclusions I have reached. Of these, let me briefly note two.

First, there are many cases where people disagree as to which of two situations is worse with respect to inequality. Moreover, even among those who agree that one situation is better than another, there is often disagreement about the degree to which this is so. Such disagreements support my claims, as they can be explained by the complexity of the notion of inequality, and people's focusing on different elements of that notion in their (naive) judgments.

Second, economists have widely advocated a number of statistical measures of inequality, for example, the *range*, the *relative mean deviation*, the *gini coefficient*, the *variance*, the *coefficient of variation*, and the *standard deviation of the logarithm*. Unfortunately, they have mainly focused on these measures' judgments, but have not adequately pursued *why* these measures have the plausibility they do. On examination, these measures can be seen to give (rough) expression to, and derive their plausibility from, some of the positions I have argued for. Specifically, I believe the range gives expression to the relative to the best-off person view of complaints and the maximin principle of equality; the relative mean deviation gives expression to the relative to the average view of complaints and the additive principle of equality; the gini coefficient gives expression to the relative to all those better off view of complaints and the additive principle of equality; and the variance, the coefficient of variation, and the standard deviation of the logarithm each give expression, in their own way, to the relative to the average view of complaints and the weighted additive principle. Thus, between them, the standard statistical measures give expression to each of the three principles of equality, as well as each of the three ways of measuring complaints. Hence, the extent to which these measures have been regarded as plausible, despite its being recognized that they face numerous shortcomings and often conflict, is further independent support for the different elements underlying them.

In suggesting that many different positions underlie and influence egalitarian judgments, I am *not* suggesting that each of these positions is equally appealing, much less that everyone will find them so. But I do think that each represents certain plausible views which cannot easily be dismissed. Because these views often conflict, it may be possible, for each of the positions discussed, to construct examples where the judgment yielded by that position seems implausible. This does *not* show that the various positions are not plausible, nor does it show that they are not involved in people's egalitarian judgments. What it shows is that each position does not *itself* underlie each such judgment.

One conclusion this article suggests which the *non*-egalitarian might readily embrace can be put as follows. Upon examination, the notion of inequality turns out to involve a hodgepodge of different and often conflicting positions. Moreover, and more importantly, many of these positions are fundamentally incompatible, resting as they do on contrary views. It simply cannot be true, for instance, *both* that everybody but the best-off person has a complaint, *and* that only those below the average have a complaint. Nor can it be true that the size of someone's complaint should be measured by comparing her to the average, *and* by comparing her to the best-off person, *and* by comparing her to all those better off than she. The notion of inequality may thus be largely inconsistent and severely limited. While it may permit certain rather trivial judgments such as the judgment that an equal world is better than an unequal one, and that "other things equal" large gaps between people are worse than small ones, in many (and perhaps most) realistic cases, one cannot compare situations with respect to inequality.

Understandably, the egalitarian might try to resist this conclusion. She might contend that each of the positions presented in this article represents a different *aspect* of the notion of inequality, and she might insist that what the conflict between these aspects illustrates is just how complex and multifaceted that notion truly is. What we need, it might be claimed, is to arrive at a measure of our notion of inequality which accurately captures each of the aspects involved in that notion, according them each their due weight. Such a measure would give us a way of accurately comparing many, though perhaps not all, situations with respect to inequality.

It appears, then, that once we see what the notion of inequality involves, we may come to think it is largely inconsistent and severely limited. Alternatively, we may come to think that it is complex, multifaceted, and partially incomplete. Either way, many of our commonsense egalitarian judgments will have to be revised. Few moral ideals have been more widely discussed, yet less well understood, than the notion of inequality.

NOTES

1. One might think that if one assumes people are equally deserving, the concern for equality reduces to a special instance of the more general concern for proportional justice—the concern that each person receives what she deserves, or that there ought to be a proportion between doing well and faring well. But although equally deserving people will be equal if they each get what they deserve, on reflection I think it is apparent that the concern for equality is distinct in both its foundations and implications from the concern for proportional justice. In any event, even if our concern for equality *were* a special instance of our concern for proportional justice, this would not affect the importance of the issues I address or the arguments I present.

2. A word about the notion of injustice. Some people think that the notion of injustice can be applied to a situation only if something could be done to prevent or improve that situation. They regard the concept of natural injustice as bogus. I believe it is a natural injustice that some people are born blind while others are not. However, the difference between these positions is, at least for some writers, largely terminological. Even if one wants to say, with Rawls or Nozick, that an *injustice* has been suffered only where there is a perpetrator of the injustice, we can still recognize that a situation is such that if someone *had* deliberately brought it about she would have been perpetrating an injustice. This tells us something about the situation. It tells us that if the situation were such that we *could* do something to improve it, we *should*, or, more accurately, that there would at least be some reason to do so. (Rawls would, I think, agree with this, though perhaps Nozick would not.)

3. One reason I say this is I think the egalitarian is not committed to the view that deserved inequalities—if there are any—are as bad as undeserved ones. In fact, I think deserved inequalities are not bad *at all*. Rather, what is objectionable is some being worse off than others *through no fault of*

their own. Thus, while objectively there may be *more* inequality in one situation than another, that needn't be *worse* if the greater inequality is deserved, but the lesser inequality is not. (This is another reason why I make the assumption that people are equally skilled, hardworking, morally worthy, and so forth.)

It is, of course, extremely difficult to decide when people are worse off than others through no fault of their own. Some think this is nearly always the case, others, almost never the case. Fortunately, one need not decide this issue in order to recognize that only undeserved inequalities are bad.

Another reason for couching my question in normative rather than purely quantitative terms is presented obliquely in Section V.

4. In the following discussion, it will be easier if I assign numbers to the levels of welfare represented in my diagram. This naturally suggests that the bottoms in the diagram represent the zero-level of welfare—the point at which life ceases to be worth living. While presumably there *is* such a zero-level, there are large disagreements about where that level is. Let me note, therefore, that neither here, nor elsewhere in the article do my results depend upon our being able to determine the zero-level precisely. In this respect my work differs significantly from that of most economists.

5. For example, most people who earn $10,000 a year are better off than the vast majority of people alive today, people who have ever lived, and the other living organisms. But this doesn't stop us from comparing such people to the relatively few who are much better off than they, and thinking they have a complaint with respect to inequality.

6. In this respect, then, as the reader may be aware, I am addressing a different question than the one Derek Parfit addresses when he employs similar diagrams in his work on future generations. Parfit is concerned with overall judgments of better and worse. I am concerned only with inequality.

7. Throughout this article, when I say that x is better than y with respect to inequality, I mean that the inequality in x is not as bad as the inequality in y.

A word about my terminology. Where philosophers talk in terms of *equality*, most economists talk in terms of *inequality*. The issues are the same, but not the words. On this point, I think the economists' terminology is more perspicuous, and for the most part I follow their practice. However, in a concession to more standard philosophical usage, I refer below to several principles of *equality*.

8. Whether we would actually prefer the mistreatment of a large group to that of a small group, all things considered, would depend upon what the

mistreatment consisted of. All things considered, we must be glad that Hitler only ordered the mass murder of the Jews, Gypsies, and homosexuals, and not of all the occupied peoples. However, it might have been better if he had made all of the occupied peoples shave their heads and wear yellow armbands, instead of just dehumanizing the Jews in such a manner.

Unfortunately, this example is not pure. Partly, we may think it would have been better if more people had to shave their heads and wear yellow armbands because we may think that would have lessened the humiliation accompanying those practices. My position is that even if this were *not* so, it still would have been better with respect to certain important elements of the notion of inequality if Hitler had made more people shave their heads and wear yellow armbands.

PART III
GENERAL
CONSIDERATIONS
ON THE IDEAL
OF EQUALITY

THE IDEA OF EQUALITY
BERNARD A. O. WILLIAMS

The idea of equality is used in political discussion both in statements of fact, or what purport to be statements of fact—that men *are* equal—and in statements of political principles or aims—that men *should* be equal, as at present they are not. The two can be, and often are, combined: the aim is then described as that of securing a state of affairs in which men are treated as the equal beings which they in fact already are, but are not already treated as being. In both these uses, the idea of equality notoriously encounters the same difficulty: that on one kind of interpretation the statements in which it figures are much too strong, and on another kind much too weak, and it is hard to find a satisfactory interpretation that lies between the two.

To take first the supposed statement of fact: it has only too often been pointed out that to say that all men are equal in all those characteristics in respect of which it makes sense to say that men are equal or unequal, is a patent falsehood; and even if some more restricted selection is made of these characteristics, the statement does not look much better. Faced with this obvious objection, the defender of the claim that all men are equal is likely to offer a weaker interpretation. It is not, he may say, in their skill, intelligence, strength or virtue that men are equal, but merely in their being men: it is their common humanity that constitutes their equality. On this interpretation, we should not seek for some special characteristics in respect of which men are equal, but merely remind ourselves that they are all men. Now to this it might

be objected that being men is not a respect in which men can strictly speaking be said to be *equal*; but, leaving that aside, there is the more immediate objection that if all that the statement does is to remind us that men are men, it does not do very much, and in particular does less than its proponents in political argument have wanted it to do. What looked like a paradox has turned into a platitude.

I shall suggest in a moment that even in this weak form the statement is not so vacuous as this objection makes it seem; but it must be admitted that when the statement of equality ceases to claim more than is warranted, it rather rapidly reaches the point where it claims less than is interesting. A similar discomfiture tends to overcome the practical maxim of equality. It cannot be the aim of this maxim that all men should be treated alike in all circumstances, or even that they should be treated alike as much as possible. Granted that, however, there is no obvious stopping point before the interpretation which makes the maxim claim only that men should be treated alike in similar circumstances; and since "circumstances" here must clearly include reference to what a man is, as well as to his purely external situation, this comes very much to saying that for every difference in the way men are treated, some general reason or principle of differentiation must be given. This may well be an important principle; some indeed have seen in it, or in something very like it, an essential element of morality itself. But it can hardly be enough to constitute the principle that was advanced in the name of *equality*.

Reprinted from B. A. O. Williams, "The Idea of Equality," in Peter Laslett and W. G. Runciman, eds., *Philosophy, Politics and Society*, Series II, pp. 110–131. Copyright © Basil Blackwell, 1962. Reprinted by permission. Footnotes edited.

It would be in accordance with this principle, for example, to treat black men differently from others just because they were black, or poor men differently just because they were poor, and this cannot accord with anyone's idea of equality.

In what follows I shall try to advance a number of considerations that can help to save the political notion of equality from these extremes of absurdity and of triviality. These considerations are in fact often employed in political argument, but are usually bundled together into an unanalysed notion of equality in a manner confusing to the advocates, and encouraging to the enemies, of that ideal. These considerations will not enable us to define a distinct third interpretation of the statements which use the notion of equality; it is rather that they enable us, starting with the weak interpretations, to build up something that in practice can have something of the solidity aspired to by the strong interpretations. In this discussion, it will not be necessary all the time to treat separately the supposedly factual application of the notion of equality, and its application in the maxim of action. Though it is sometimes important to distinguish them, and there are clear grounds for doing so, similar considerations often apply to both. The two go significantly together: on the one hand, the point of the supposedly factual assertion is to back up social ideals and programmes of political action; on the other hand—a rather less obvious point, perhaps—those political proposals have their force because they are regarded not as gratuitously egalitarian, aiming at equal treatment for reasons, for instance, of simplicity or tidiness, but as affirming an equality which is believed in some sense already to exist, and to be obscured or neglected by actual social arrangements.

1. COMMON HUMANITY

The factual statement of men's equality was seen, when pressed, to retreat in the direction of merely asserting the equality of men as men; and this was thought to be trivial. It is certainly insufficient, but not, after all, trivial. That all men are human is, if a tautology, a useful one,

serving as a reminder that those who belong anatomically to the species *homo sapiens*, and can speak a language, use tools, live in societies, can interbreed despite racial differences, etc., are also alike in certain other respects more likely to be forgotten. These respects are notably the capacity to feel pain, both from immediate physical causes and from various situations represented in perception and in thought; and the capacity to feel affection for others, and the consequences of this, connected with the frustration of this affection, loss of its objects, etc. The assertion that men are alike in the possession of these characteristics is, while indisputable and (it may be) even necessarily true, not trivial. For it is certain that there are political and social arrangements that systematically neglect these characteristics in the case of some groups of men, while being fully aware of them in the case of others; that is to say, they treat certain men as though they did not possess these characteristics, and neglect moral claims that arise from these characteristics and which would be admitted to arise from them.

Here it may be objected that the mere fact that ruling groups in certain societies treat other groups in this way does not mean that they neglect or overlook the characteristics in question. For, it may be suggested, they may well recognize the presence of these characteristics in the worse-treated group, but claim that in the case of that group, the characteristics do not give rise to any moral claim; the group being distinguished from other members of society in virtue of some further characteristic (for instance, by being black), this may be cited as the ground of treating them differently, whether they feel pain, affection, etc., or not.

This objection rests on the assumption, common to much moral philosophy that makes a sharp distinction between fact and value, that the question whether a certain consideration is *relevant* to a moral issue is an evaluative question: to state that a consideration is relevant or irrelevant to a certain moral question is, on this view, itself to commit oneself to a certain kind of moral principle or outlook. Thus, in the case under discussion, to say (as one would naturally say) that the fact that a man is black is, by itself, quite irrelevant to the issue of how he should be treated in respect of welfare, etc., would, on this view, be to commit oneself to a certain sort of moral principle. This view, taken generally, seems to me quite certainly false. The principle that men should be differentially treated in respect of welfare merely on grounds of their colour is not a special sort of moral principle, but (if anything) a purely arbitrary assertion of will, like that of some Caligulan ruler who decided to execute everyone whose name contained three "R"s.

This point is in fact conceded by those who practice such things as colour discrimination. Few can be found who will explain their practice merely by saying, "But they're black: and it is my moral principle to treat black men differently from others." If any reasons are given at all, they will be reasons that seek to correlate the fact of blackness with certain other considerations which are at least candidates for relevance to the question of how a man should be treated: such as insensitivity, brute stupidity, ineducable irresponsibility, etc. Now these reasons are very often rationalizations, and the correlations claimed are either not really believed, or quite irrationally believed, by those who claim them. But this is a different point; the argument concerns what counts as a moral reason, and the rationalizer broadly agrees with others about what counts as such—the trouble with him is that his reasons are dictated by his policies, and not conversely. The Nazis' "anthropologists" who tried to construct theories of Aryanism were paying, in very poor coin, the homage of irrationality to reason.

The question of relevance in moral reasons will arise again, in a different connexion, in this paper. For the moment its importance is that it gives a force to saying that those who neglect the moral claims of certain men that arise from their human capacity to feel pain, etc., are *overlooking* or *disregarding* those capacities; and are not just operating with a special moral principle, conceding the capacities to these men, but denying the moral claim. Very often, indeed, they have just persuaded themselves that the men in question have those capacities in a lesser degree. Here it is certainly to the point to assert the apparent platitude that these men are also human.

I have discussed this point in connexion with very obvious human characteristics of feeling pain and desiring affection. There are, however, other and less easily definable characteristics universal to humanity, which may all the more be neglected in political and social arrangements. For instance, there seems to be a characteristic which might be called "a desire for self-respect;" this phrase is perhaps not too happy, in suggesting a particular culturally limited, bourgeois value, but I mean by it a certain human desire to be identified with what one is doing, to be able to realize purposes of one's own, and not to be the instrument of another's will unless one has willingly accepted such a role. This is a very inadequate and in some ways rather empty specification of a human desire; to a better specification, both philosophical reflection and the evidences of psychology and anthropology would be relevant. Such investigations enable us to understand more deeply, in respect of the desire I have gestured towards and of similar characteristics, what it is to be human; and of what it is to be human, the apparently trivial statement of men's equality as men can serve as a reminder.

2. MORAL CAPACITIES

So far we have considered respects in which men can be counted as all alike, which respects are, in a sense, negative: they concern the capacity to suffer, and certain needs that men have, and these involve men in moral relations as the recipients of certain kinds of treatment. It has certainly been a part, however, of the thought of those who asserted that men were equal, that there were more positive respects in which men were alike: that they were equal in certain things that they could do or achieve, as well as in things that they needed and could suffer. In respect of a whole range of abilities, from weight lifting to the calculus, the assertion is, as was noted at the beginning, not plausible, and has not often been supposed to be. It has been held, however, that there are certain other abilities, both less open to empirical test and more essential in moral connexions, for which it is true that men are equal. These are certain sorts of moral ability or capacity, the capacity for virtue or achievement of the highest kind of moral worth.

The difficulty with this notion is that of identifying any purely moral capacities. Some human capacities are more relevant to the achievement of a virtuous life than others: intelligence, a capacity for sympathetic understanding, and a measure of resoluteness would generally be agreed to be so. But these capacities can all be displayed in non-moral connexions as well, and in such connexions would naturally be thought to differ from man to man like other natural capacities. That this is the fact of the matter has been accepted by many thinkers, notably, for instance, by Aristotle. But against this acceptance, there is a powerful strain of thought that centres on a feeling of ultimate and outrageous absurdity in the idea that the achievement of the highest kind of moral worth should depend on natural capacities, unequally and fortuitously distributed as they are; and this feeling is backed up by the observation that these natural capacities are not themselves the bearers of the moral worth, since those that have them are as gifted for vice as for virtue.

This strain of thought has found many types of religious expression; but in philosophy it is to be found in its purest form in Kant. Kant's view not only carries to the limit the notion that moral worth cannot depend on contingencies, but also emphasizes, in its picture of the Kingdom of Ends, the idea of *respect* which is owed to each man as a rational moral agent—and, since men are equally such agents, is owed equally to all, unlike admiration and similar attitudes, which are commanded unequally by men in proportion to their unequal possession of different kinds of natural excellence. These ideas are intimately connected in Kant, and it is not possible to understand his moral theory unless as much weight is given to what he says about the Kingdom of Ends as is always given to what he says about duty.

The very considerable consistency of Kant's view is bought at what would generally be agreed to be a very high price. The detachment of moral worth from all contingencies is achieved only by making man's characteristic as a moral or rational agent a transcendental characteristic; man's capacity to will freely as a rational agent is not dependent on any empirical capacities he may have—and, in particular, is not dependent on empirical capacities

which men may possess unequally—because, in the Kantian view, the capacity to be a rational agent is not itself an empirical capacity at all. Accordingly, the respect owed equally to each man as a member of the Kingdom of Ends is not owed to him in respect of any empirical characteristics that he may possess, but solely in respect of the transcendental characteristic of being a free and rational will. The ground of the respect owed to each man thus emerges in the Kantian theory as a kind of secular analogue of the Christian conception of the respect owed to all men as equally children of God. Though secular, it is equally metaphysical: in neither case is it anything empirical *about* men that constitutes the ground of equal respect.

This transcendental, Kantian conception cannot provide any solid foundation for the notions of equality among men, or of equality of respect owed to them. Apart from the general difficulties of such transcendental conceptions, there is the obstinate fact that the concept of "moral agent," and the concepts allied to it such as that of responsibility, do and must have an empirical basis. It seems empty to say that all men are equal as moral agents, when the question, for instance, of men's responsibility for their actions is one to which empirical considerations are clearly relevant, and one which moreover receives answers in terms of different degrees of responsibility and different degrees of rational control over action. To hold a man responsible for his actions is presumably the central case of treating him as a moral agent, and if men are not treated as equally responsible, there is not much left to their equality as moral agents.

If, without its transcendental basis, there is not much left to men's equality as moral agents, is there anything left to the notion of the *respect* owed to all men? This notion of "respect" is both complex and unclear, and I think it needs, and would repay, a good deal of investigation. Some content can, however, be attached to it; even if it is some way away from the ideas of moral agency. There certainly is a distinction, for instance, between regarding a man's life, actions or character from an aesthetic or technical point of view, and regarding them from a point of view which is concerned primarily with what it is *for him* to live that life and do those actions in that character. Thus from the technological point of view, a man who has spent his life in trying to make a certain machine which could not possibly work is merely a failed inventor, and in compiling a catalogue of those whose efforts have contributed to the sum of technical achievement, one must "write him off": the fact that he devoted himself to this useless task with constant effort and so on, is merely irrelevant. But from a human point of view, it is clearly not irrelevant: we are concerned with him, not merely as "a failed inventor," but as a man who wanted to be a successful inventor. Again, in professional relations and the world of work, a man operates, and his activities come up for criticism, under a variety of professional or technical titles, such as "miner" or "agricultural labourer" or "junior executive." The technical or professional attitude is that which regards the man solely under that title, the human approach that which regards him as *a man who has* that title (among others), willingly, unwillingly, through lack of alternatives, with pride, etc.

That men should be regarded from the human point of view, and not merely under these sorts of titles, is part of the content that might be attached to Kant's celebrated injunction "treat each man as an end in himself, and never as a means only." But I do not think that this is all that should be seen in this injunction, or all that is concerned in the notion of "respect." What is involved in the examples just given could be explained by saying that each man is owed an effort at identification: that he should not be regarded as the surface to which a certain label can be applied, but one should try to see the world (including the label) from his point of view. This injunction will be based on, though not of course fully explained by, the notion that men are conscious beings who necessarily have intentions and purposes and see what they are doing in a certain light. But there seem to be further injunctions connected with the Kantian maxim, and with the notion of "respect," that go beyond these considerations. There are forms of exploiting men or degrading them which would be thought to be excluded by these notions, but which cannot be excluded merely by considering how the exploited or degraded men see the situation. For it is precisely a mark of extreme exploitation or degradation that those who suffer it do *not* see themselves differently from the way they are seen by the exploiters; either they do not see themselves as anything at all, or they acquiesce passively in the role for which they have been cast. Here we evidently need something more than the precept that one should respect and try to understand another man's consciousness of his own activities; it is also that one may not suppress or destroy that consciousness.

All these I must confess to be vague and inconclusive considerations, but we are dealing with a vague notion: one, however, that we possess, and attach value to. To try to put these matters properly in order would be itself to try to reach conclusions about several fundamental questions of moral philosophy. What we must ask here is what these ideas have to do with equality. We started with the notion of men's equality as moral agents. This notion appeared unsatisfactory, for different reasons, in both an empirical and a transcendental interpretation. We then moved, *via* the idea of "respect," to the different notion of regarding men not merely under professional, social or technical titles, but with consideration of their own views and purposes. This notion has at least this much to do with equality: that the titles which it urges us to look behind are the conspicuous bearers of social, political and technical *inequality*, whether they refer to achievement (as in the example of the inventor), or to social roles (as in the example of work titles). It enjoins us not to let our fundamental attitudes to men be dictated by the criteria of technical success or social position, and not to take them at the value carried by these titles and by the structures in which these titles place them. This does not mean, of course, that the more fundamental view that should be taken of men is in the case of every man the same: on the contrary. But it does mean that each man is owed the effort of understanding, and that in achieving it, each man is to be (as it were) abstracted from certain conspicuous structures of inequality in which we find him.

These injunctions are based on the proposition that men are beings who are necessarily to some extent conscious of themselves and of the world they live in. (I omit here, as throughout the discussion, the clinical cases of people who are mad or mentally defective, who always constitute special exceptions to what is in general true of men.) This proposition does not assert that men are equally conscious of themselves and of their situation. It was precisely one element in the notion of exploitation considered above that such consciousness can be decreased by social action and the environment; we may add that it can similarly be increased. But men are at least potentially conscious, to an indeterminate degree, of their situation and of what I have called their "titles," are capable of reflectively standing back from the roles and positions in which they are cast; and this reflective consciousness may be enhanced or diminished by their social condition.

It is this last point that gives these considerations a particular relevance to the political aims of egalitarianism. The mere idea of regarding men from "the human point of view," while it has a good deal to do with politics, and a certain amount to do with equality, has nothing specially to do with political equality. One could, I think, accept this as an ideal, and yet favour, for instance, some kind of hierarchical society, so long as the hierarchy maintained itself without compulsion, and there was human understanding between the orders. In such a society, each man would indeed have a very conspicuous title which related him to the social structure; but it might be that most people were aware of the human beings behind the titles, and found each other for the most part content, or even proud, to have the titles that they had. I do not know whether anything like this has been true of historical hierarchical societies; but I can see no inconsistency in someone's espousing it as an ideal, as some (influenced in many cases by a sentimental picture of the Middle Ages) have done. Such a person would be one who accepted the notion of "the human view," the view of each man as something more than his title, as a valuable ideal, but rejected the ideals of political equality.

Once, however, one accepts the further notion that the degree of man's consciousness about such things as his role in society is itself in some part the product of social arrangements, and that it can be increased, this ideal of a stable hierarchy must, I think, disappear. For what keeps stable hierarchies together is the idea of necessity, that it is somehow foreordained or inevitable that there should be these orders; and this idea of necessity must be eventually undermined by the growth of people's reflective consciousness about their role, still more when it is combined with the thought that what they and the others have always thought about their roles in the social system was the product of the social system itself.

It might be suggested that a certain man who admitted that people's consciousness of their roles was conditioned in this way might nevertheless believe in the hierarchical ideal: but that in order to preserve the society of his ideal, he would have to make sure that the idea of the conditioning of consciousness did not get around to too many people, and that their consciousness about their roles did not increase too much. But such a view is really a very different thing from its naïve predecessor. Such a man, no longer himself "immersed" in the system, is beginning to think in terms of compulsion, the deliberate *prevention* of the growth of consciousness, which is a poisonous element absent from the original ideal. Moreover, his attitude (or that of rulers similar to himself) towards the other people in the ideal society must now contain an element of condescension or contempt, since he will be aware that their acceptance of what they suppose to be necessity is a delusion. This is alien to the spirit of human understanding on which the original ideal was based. The hierarchical idealist cannot escape the fact that certain things which can be done decently without self-consciousness can, with self-consciousness, be done only hypocritically. This is why even the rather hazy and very general notions that I have tried to bring together in this section contain some of the grounds of the ideal of political equality.

3. EQUALITY IN UNEQUAL CIRCUMSTANCES

The notion of equality is invoked not only in connexions where men are claimed in some sense all to be equal, but in connexions where they are agreed to be unequal, and the question arises of the distribution of, or access to, certain goods to which their inequalities are relevant. It may be objected that the notion of equality is in fact misapplied in these connexions, and that the appropriate ideas are those of fairness or justice, in the sense of what Aristotle called "distributive justice," where (as Aristotle argued) there is no question of regarding or treating everyone as equal, but solely a question of distributing certain goods in proportion to men's recognized inequalities.

I think it is reasonable to say against this objection that there is some foothold for the notion of equality even in these cases. It is useful here to make a rough distinction between two different types of inequality, inequality of *need* and inequality of *merit*, with a corresponding distinction between goods—on the one hand, goods demanded by the need, and on the other, goods that can be earned by the merit. In the case of needs, such as the need for medical treatment in case of illness, it can be presumed for practical purposes that the persons who have the need actually desire the goods in question, and so the question can indeed be regarded as one of distribution in a simple sense, the satisfaction of an existing desire. In the case of merit, such as for instance the possessions of abilities to profit from a university education, there is not the same presumption that everyone who has the merit has the desire for the goods in question, though it may, of course, be the case. Moreover, the good of a university education may be legitimately, even if hopelessly, desired by those who do not possess the merit; while medical treatment or unemployment benefit are either not desired, or not legitimately desired, by those who are not ill or unemployed, that is do not have the appropriate need. Hence the distribution of goods in accordance with merit has a competitive aspect lacking in the case of distribution according to need. For these reasons, it is appropriate to speak, in the case of merit, not only of the distribution of the good, but of the distribution of the opportunity of achieving the good. But this, unlike the good itself, can be said to be distributed equally to everybody, and so one does encounter a notion of *general* equality, much vaunted in our society today, the notion of equality of opportunity.

Before considering this notion further, it is worth noticing certain resemblances and differences between the cases of need and of merit. In both cases, we encounter the matter (mentioned before in this paper) of the relevance of reasons. Leaving aside preventive medicine, the proper ground of distribution of medical care is ill health: this is a necessary truth. Now in very many societies, while ill health may work as a necessary condition of receiving treatment, it does not work as a sufficient condition, since such treatment costs money, and not all who are ill have the money; hence the possession of sufficient money becomes in fact an additional necessary condition of actually receiving treatment. Yet more extravagantly, money may work as a sufficient condition by itself, without any medical need, in which case the reasons that actually operate for the receipt of this good are just totally irrelevant to its nature; however, since only a few hypochondriacs desire treatment when they do not need it, this is, in this case, a marginal phenomenon.

When we have the situation in which, for instance, wealth is a further necessary condition of the receipt of medical treatment, we can once more apply the notions of equality and inequality: not now in connexion with the inequality between the well and the ill, but in connexion with the inequality between the rich ill and the poor ill, since we have straightforwardly the situation of those whose needs are the same not receiving the same treatment, though the needs are the ground of the treatment. This is an irrational state of affairs.

It may be objected that I have neglected an important distinction here. For, it may be said, I have treated the ill health and the possession of money as though they were regarded on the same level, as "reasons for receiving medical treatment," and this is a muddle. The ill health is, at most, a ground of the *right* to receive medical treatment; whereas the money is, in certain circumstances, the causally necessary condition of securing the right, which is a different thing. There is something in the distinction that this objection suggests: there is a distinction between a man's rights, the reasons why he should be treated in a certain way, and his power to secure those rights, the reasons why he can in fact get what he deserves. But this objection does not make it inappropriate to call the situation of inequality an "irrational" situation: it just makes it clearer what is meant by so calling it. What is meant is that it is a situation in which reasons are insufficiently *operative*; it is a situation insufficiently controlled by reasons—and hence by reason itself. The same point arises with another form of equality and equal rights, equality before the law. It may be said that in a certain society, men have equal rights to a fair trial, to seek redress from the law for wrongs committed against them, etc. But if a fair trial or redress from the law can be secured in that society only by moneyed and educated persons, to insist that everyone *has* this right, though only these particular persons can *secure* it, rings hollow to the point of cynicism: we are concerned not with the abstract existence of rights, but with the extent to which those rights govern what actually happens.

Thus when we combine the notions of the *relevance* of reasons, and the *operativeness* of reasons, we have a genuine moral weapon, which can be applied in cases of what is appropriately called unequal treatment, even where one is not concerned with the equality of people as a whole. This represents a strengthening of the very weak principle mentioned at the beginning of this paper, that for every difference in the way men are treated, a reason should be given: when one requires further that the reasons should be relevant, and that they should be socially operative, this really says something.

Similar considerations will apply to cases of merit. There is, however, an important difference between the cases of need and merit, in respect of the relevance of reasons. It is a matter of logic that particular sorts of needs constitute a reason for receiving particular sorts of good. It is, however, in general a much more disputable question whether certain sorts of merit constitute a reason for receiving certain sorts of good. For instance, let it be agreed, for the sake of argument, that the [private] school system provides a superior type of education, which it is a good thing to receive. It is then objected that access to this type of education is unequally distributed, because of its cost: among boys of equal promise or intelligence, only those from wealthy homes will receive it,

and, indeed, boys of little promise or intelligence will receive it, if from wealthy homes; and this, the objection continues, is irrational.

The defender of the [private] school system might give two quite different sorts of answer to this objection; besides, that is, the obvious type of answer which merely disputes the facts alleged by the objector. One is the sort of answer already discussed in the case of need: that we may agree, perhaps, that boys of promise and intelligence have a right to a superior education, but in actual economic circumstances, this right cannot always be secured, etc. The other is more radical: this would dispute the premise of the objection that intelligence and promise are, at least by themselves, the grounds for receiving this superior type of education. While perhaps not asserting that wealth itself constitutes the ground, the defender of the system may claim that other characteristics significantly correlated with wealth are such grounds; or, again, that it is the purpose of this sort of school to maintain a tradition of leadership, and the best sort of people to maintain this will be people whose fathers were at such schools. We need not try to pursue such arguments here. The important point is that, while there can indeed be genuine disagreements about what constitutes the relevant sort of merit in such cases, such disagreements must also be disagreements about the nature of the good to be distributed. As such, the disagreements do not occur in a vacuum, nor are they logically free from restrictions. There is only a limited number of reasons for which education could be regarded as a good, and a limited number of purposes which education could rationally be said to serve; and to the limitations on this question, there correspond limitations on the sorts of merit or personal characteristic which could be rationally cited as grounds of access to this good. Here again we encounter a genuine strengthening of the very weak principle that, for differences in the way that people are treated, reasons should be given.

We may return now to the notion of equality of opportunity; understanding this in the normal political sense of equality of opportunity for *everyone in society* to secure certain goods. This notion is introduced into political discussion when there is question of the access to certain goods which, first, even if they are not desired by everyone in society, are desired by large numbers of people in all sections of society (either for themselves, or, as in the case of education, for their children), or would be desired by people in all sections of society if they knew about the goods in question and thought it possible for them to attain them; second, are goods which people may be said to earn or achieve; and third, are goods which not all the people who desire them can have. This third condition covers at least three different cases, however, which it is worth distinguishing. Some desired goods, like positions of prestige, management, etc., are *by their very nature* limited: whenever there are some people who are in command or prestigious positions, there are necessarily others who are not. Other goods are *contingently* limited, in the sense that there are certain conditions of access to them which in fact not everyone satisfies, but there is no intrinsic limit to the numbers who might gain access to it by satisfying the conditions: university education is usually regarded in this light nowadays, as something which requires certain conditions of admission to it which in fact not everyone satisfies, but which an indefinite proportion of people might satisfy. Third, there are goods which are *fortuitously* limited, in the sense that although everyone or large numbers of people satisfy the conditions of access to them, there is just not enough of them to go round; so some more stringent conditions or system of rationing have to be imposed, to govern access in an imperfect situation. A good can, of course, be both contingently and fortuitously limited at once: when, due to shortage of supply, not even the people who are qualified to have it, limited in numbers though they are, can in every case have it. It is particularly worth distinguishing those kinds of limitation, as there can be significant differences of view about the way in which a certain good is limited. While most would now agree that high education is contingently limited, a Platonic view would regard it as necessarily limited.

Now the notion of equality of opportunity might be said to be the notion that a limited good shall in fact be allocated on grounds which do not *a priori* exclude any section of those that desire it. But this formulation is not really very clear. For suppose grammar school education (a good perhaps contingently, and certainly fortuitously, limited) is allocated on grounds of ability as tested at the age of 11; this would normally be advanced as an example of equality of opportunity, as opposed to a system of allocation on grounds of parents' wealth. But does not the criterion of ability exclude *a priori* a certain section of people, namely those that are not able—just as the other excludes *a priori* those who are not wealthy? Here it will obviously be said that this was not what was meant by *a priori* exclusion: the present argument just equates this with exclusion of anybody, that is, with the mere existence of some condition that has to be satisfied. What then is *a priori* exclusion? It must mean exclusion on grounds *other* than those appropriate or rational for the good in question. But this still will not do as it stands. For it would follow from this that so long as those allocating grammar school education on grounds of wealth thought that such grounds were appropriate or rational (as they might in one of the ways discussed above in connexion with private schools), they could sincerely describe their system as one of equality of opportunity—which is absurd.

Hence it seems that the notion of equality of opportunity is more complex than it first appeared. It requires not merely that there should be no exclusion from access on grounds other than those appropriate or rational for the good in question, but that the grounds considered appropriate for the good should themselves be such that people from all sections of society have an equal chance of satisfying them. What now is a "section of society?" Clearly we cannot include under this term sections of the populace identified just by the characteristics which figure in the grounds for allocating the good— since, once more, any grounds at all must exclude some section of the populace. But what about sections identified by characteristics which are *correlated* with the grounds of exclusion? There are important difficulties here: to illustrate this, it may help first to take an imaginary example.

Suppose that in a certain society great prestige is attached to membership of a warrior class, the duties of which require great physical strength. This class has in the past been recruited from certain wealthy families only; but egalitarian reformers achieve a change in the rules, by which warriors are recruited from all sections of the society, on the results of a suitable competition. The effect of this, however, is that the wealthy families still provide virtually all the warriors, because the rest of the populace is so undernourished by reason of poverty that their physical strength is inferior to that of the wealthy and well nourished. The reformers protest that equality of opportunity has not really been achieved; the wealthy reply that in fact it has, and that the poor now have the opportunity of becoming warriors—it is just bad luck that their characteristics are such that they do not pass the test. "We are not," they might say, "excluding anyone *for* being poor; we exclude people for being weak, and it is unfortunate that those who are poor are also weak."

This answer would seem to most people feeble, and even cynical. This is for reasons similar to those discussed before in connexion with equality before the law; that the supposed equality of opportunity is quite empty—indeed, one may say that it does not really exist—unless it is made more effective than this. For one knows that it could be made more effective; one knows that there is a causal connexion between being poor and being undernourished, and between being undernourished and being physically weak. One supposes further that something could be done—subject to whatever economic conditions obtain in the imagined society—to alter the distribution of wealth. All this being so, the appeal by the wealthy to the "bad luck" of the poor must appear as disingenuous.

It seems then that a system of allocation will fall short of equality of opportunity if the allocation of the good in question in fact works out unequally or disproportionately between different sections of society, if the unsuccessful sections are under a disadvantage which could be removed by further reform or social action. This was very clear in the imaginary example that was given, because the causal connexions involved are simple and well known. In actual fact, however, the situations of this type that arise are more complicated, and it is easier to overlook the causal connexions involved. This is particularly so in the case of educational se-

lection, where such slippery concepts as "intellectual ability" are involved. It is a known fact that the system of selection for grammar schools by the "11+" examination favours children in direct proportion to their social class, the children of professional homes having proportionately greater success than those from working class homes. We have every reason to suppose that these results are the product, in good part, of environmental factors; and we further know that imaginative social reform, both of the primary educational system and of living conditions, would favourably affect those environmental factors. In these circumstances, this system of educational selection falls short of equality of opportunity.

This line of thought points to a connexion between the idea of equality of opportunity, and the idea of equality of persons, which is stronger than might at first be suspected. We have seen that one is not really offering equality of opportunity to Smith and Jones if one contents oneself with applying the same criteria to Smith and Jones at, say, the age of 11; what one is doing there is to apply the same criteria to Smith as affected by favourable conditions and to Jones as affected by unfavourable but curable conditions. Here there is a necessary pressure to equal up the conditions: to give *Smith* and *Jones* equality of opportunity involves regarding their conditions, where curable, as themselves part of what is done to Smith and Jones, and not part of Smith and Jones themselves. Their identity, for these purposes, does not include their curable environment, which is itself unequal and a contributor of inequality. This abstraction of persons in themselves from unequal environments, is a way, if not of regarding them as equal, at least of moving recognizably in that direction; and is itself involved in equality of opportunity.

One might speculate about how far this movement of thought might go. The most conservative user of the notion of equality of opportunity is, if sincere, prepared to abstract the individual from some effects of his environment. We have seen that there is good reason to press this further, and to allow that the individuals whose opportunities are to be equal should be abstracted from more features of social and family background. Where should this stop? Should it even stop at the boundaries of heredity? Suppose it were discovered that when all curable environmental disadvantages had been dealt with, there was a residual genetic difference in brain constitution, for instance, which was correlated with differences in desired types of ability; but that the brain constitution could in fact be changed by an operation. Suppose further that the wealthier classes could afford such an operation for their children, so that they always came out [at the] top of the educational system; would we then think that poorer children did not have equality of opportunity, because they had no opportunity to get rid of their genetic disadvantages?

Here we might think that our notion of personal identity itself was beginning to give way; we might well wonder *who were* the people whose advantages and disadvantages were being discussed in this way. But it would be wrong, I think, to try to solve this problem simply by saying that in the supposed circumstances our notion of personal identity would have collapsed in such a way that we could no longer speak of the individuals involved—in the end, we could still pick out the individuals by spatio-temporal criteria, if no more. Our objections against the system suggested in this fantasy must, I think, be moral rather than metaphysical. They need not concern us here. What is interesting about the fantasy, perhaps, is that if one reached this state of affairs, the individuals would be regarded as in all respects equal in themselves—for in themselves they would be, as it were, pure subjects or bearers of predicates, everything else about them, including their genetic inheritance, being regarded as a fortuitous and changeable characteristic. In these circumstances, where everything about a person is controllable, equality of opportunity and absolute equality seem to coincide; and this itself illustrates something about the notion of equality of opportunity.

I said that we need not discuss here the moral objections to the kind of world suggested in this fantasy. There is, however, one such point that is relevant to the different aspects of equality that have been discussed in this paper as a whole. One objection that we should instinctively feel about the fantasy world is that far too much emphasis was being placed on achiev-ing high ability; that the children were just being regarded as locations of abilities. I think we should still feel this even if everybody (with results hard to imagine) was treated in this way; when not everybody was so treated, the able would also be more successful than others, and those very concerned with producing the ability would probably also be over-concerned with success. The moral objections to the excessive concern with such aims are, interestingly, not unconnected with the ideal of equality itself; they are connected with equality in the sense discussed in the earlier sections of this paper, the equality of human beings despite their differences, and in particular with the complex of notions considered in the second section under the heading of "respect."

This conflict within the ideals of equality arises even without resort to the fantasy world. It exists to-day in the feeling that a thorough-going emphasis on equality of opportunity must destroy a certain sense of common humanity which is itself an ideal of equality. The ideals that are felt to be in conflict with equality of opportunity are not necessarily other ideals of equality—there may be an independent appeal to the values of community life, or to the moral worth of a more integrated and less competitive society. Nevertheless, the idea of equality itself is often invoked in this connexion, and not, I think, inappropriately.

If the idea of equality ranges as widely as I have suggested, this type of conflict is bound to arise with it. It is an idea which, on the one hand, is invoked in connexion with the distribution of certain goods, some at least of which are bound to confer on their possessors some preferred status or prestige. On the other hand, the idea of equality of respect is one which urges us to give less consideration to those structures in which people enjoy status or prestige, and to consider people independently of those goods, on the distribution of which equality of opportunity precisely focuses our, and their, attention. There is perhaps nothing formally incompatible in these two applications of the idea of equality: one might hope for a society in which there existed both a fair, rational and appropriate distribution of these goods, and no contempt, condescension or lack of human communication between persons who were more and less successful recipients of the distribution. Yet in actual fact, there are deep psychological and social obstacles to the realization of this hope; as things are, the competitiveness and considerations of prestige that surround the first application of equality certainly militate against the second. How far this situation is inevitable, and how far in an economically developed and dynamic society, in which certain skills and talents are necessarily at a premium, the obstacles to a wider realization of equality might be overcome, I do not think that we know: these are in good part questions of psychology and sociology, to which we do not have the answers.

When one is faced with the spectacle of the various elements of the idea of equality pulling in these different directions, there is a strong temptation, if one does not abandon the idea altogether, to abandon some of its elements: to claim, for instance, that equality of opportunity is the only ideal that is at all practicable, and equality of respect a vague and perhaps nostalgic illusion; or, alternatively, that equality of respect is genuine equality, and equality of opportunity an inegalitarian betrayal of the ideal—all the more so if it were thoroughly pursued, as now it is not. To succumb to either of these simplifying formulæ would, I think, be a mistake. Certainly, a highly rational and efficient application of the ideas of equal opportunity, unmitigated by the other considerations, could lead to a quite inhuman society (if it worked—which, granted a well-known desire of parents to secure a position for their children at least as good as their own, is unlikely). On the other hand, an ideal of equality of respect that made no contact with such things as the economic needs of society for certain skills, and human desire for some sorts of prestige, would be condemned to a futile Utopianism, and to having no rational effect on the distribution of goods, position and power that would inevitably proceed. If, moreover, as I have suggested, it is not really known how far, by new forms of social structure and of education, these conflicting claims might be reconciled, it is all the more obvious that we should not throw one set of claims out of the window; but should rather seek, in each situation, the best way of eating and having as much cake as possible. It is an uncomfortable situation, but the discomfort is just that of genuine political thought. It is no greater with equality than it is with liberty, or any other noble and substantial political ideal.

Justice does Not Imply Equality
ROBERT NOZICK

The legitimacy of altering social institutions to achieve greater equality of material condition is, though often assumed, rarely *argued* for. Writers note that in a given country the wealthiest N percent of the population holds more than that percentage of the wealth, and the poorest N percent holds less; that to get to the wealth of the top N percent from the poorest, one must look at the bottom P percent (where P is vastly greater than N), and so forth. They then proceed immediately to discuss how this might be altered. On the entitlement conception of jus-

Reprinted from *Anarchy: State and Utopia* (New York: Basic Books, 1974) by permission of HarperCollins Publisher.

tice in holdings, one *cannot* decide whether the state must do something to alter the situation merely by looking at a distributional profile or at facts such as these. It depends upon how the distribution came about. Some processes yielding these results would be legitimate, and the various parties would be entitled to their respective holdings. If these distributional facts *did* arise by a legitimate process, then they themselves are legitimate. This is, of course, *not* to say that they may not be changed, provided this can be done without violating people's entitlements. Any persons who favor a particular end-state pattern may choose to transfer some or all of their own holdings so as (at least temporarily) more nearly to realize their desired pattern.

The entitlement conception of justice in holdings makes no presumption in favor of equality, or any other overall end state or patterning. It cannot merely be *assumed* that equality must be built into any theory of justice. There is a surprising dearth of arguments for equality capable of coming to grips with the considerations that underlie a nonglobal and nonpatterned conception of justice in holdings. (However, there is no lack of unsupported statements of a presumption in favor of equality.) I shall consider the argument which has received the most attention from philosophers in recent years; that offered by Bernard Williams in his influential essay "The Idea of Equality." (No doubt many readers will feel that all hangs on some other argument; I would like to see *that* argument precisely set out, in detail.)

> Leaving aside preventive medicine, the proper ground of distribution of medical care is ill health; this is a necessary truth. Now in very many societies, while ill health may work as a necessary condition of receiving treatment, it does not work as a sufficient condition, since such treatment costs money, and not all who are ill have the money; hence the possession of sufficient money becomes in fact an additional necessary condition of actually receiving treatment.... When we have the situation in which, for instance, wealth is a further necessary condition of the receipt of medical treatment, we can once more apply the notions of equality and inequality: not now in connection with the in-

> equality between the well and the ill, but in connection with the inequality between the rich ill and the poor ill, since we have straightforwardly the situation of those whose needs are the same not receiving the same treatment, though the needs are the ground of the treatment. This is an irrational state of affairs ... it is a situation in which reasons are insufficiently operative; it is a situation insufficiently controlled by reasons—and hence by reason itself.

Williams seems to be arguing that if among the different descriptions applying to an activity, there is one that contains an "internal goal" of the activity, then (it is a necessary truth that) the only proper grounds for the performance of the activity, or its allocation if it is scarce, are connected with the effective achievement of the internal goal. If the activity is done upon others, the only proper criterion for distributing the activity is their need for it, if any. Thus it is that Williams says (it is a necessary truth that) the only proper criterion for the distribution of medical care is medical need. Presumably, then, the only proper criterion for the distribution of barbering services is barbering need. But why must the internal goal of the activity take precedence over, for example, the person's particular purpose in performing the activity? (We ignore the question of whether one activity can fall under two different descriptions involving different internal goals.) If someone becomes a barber because he likes talking to a variety of different people, and so on, is it unjust of him to allocate his services to those he most likes to talk to? Or if he works as a barber in order to earn money to pay tuition at school, may he cut the hair of only those who pay or tip well? Why may not a barber use exactly the same criteria in allocating his services as someone else whose activities have no internal goal involving others? Need a gardener allocate his services to those lawns which need him most?

In what way does the situation of a doctor differ? Why must his activities be allocated via the internal goal of medical care? (If there was no "shortage," could some *then* be allocated using other criteria as well?) It seems clear that *he* needn't do that; just because he has this skill, why should *he* bear the costs of the desired allocation, why is he less entitled to pursue his own goals, within the special circumstances of practicing medicine, than everyone else? So it is *society* that, somehow, is to arrange things so that the doctor, in pursuing his own goals, allocates according to need; for example, the society pays him to do this. But why must the society do this? (Should they do it for barbering as well?) Presumably, because medical care is important, people need it very much. This is true of food as well, though farming does *not* have an internal goal that refers to other people in the way doctoring does. When the layers of Williams' argument are peeled away, what we arrive at is the claim that society (that is, each of us acting together in some organized fashion) should make provision for the important needs of all of its members. This claim, of course, has been stated many times before. Despite appearances, Williams presents no argument for it.[1] Like others, Williams looks only to questions of allocation. He ignores the question of where the things or actions to be allocated and distributed come from. Consequently,

he does not consider whether they come already tied to people who have entitlements over them (surely the case for service activities, which are people's *actions*), people who therefore may decide for themselves to whom they will give the thing and on what grounds.

NOTES

1. We have discussed Williams' position without introducing an essentialist view that some activities necessarily involve certain goals. Instead we have tied the goals to *descriptions* of the activities. For essentialist issues only becloud the discussion, and they still leave open the question of why the only proper ground for allocating the activity is its essentialist goal. The motive for making such an essentialist claim would be to avoid someone's saying: let "schmoctoring" be an activity just like doctoring except that *its* goal is to earn money for the practitioner; has Williams presented any reason why *schmoctoring* services should be allocated according to need?

Against Equality

J. R. LUCAS

Equality is the great political issue of our time. Liberty is forgotten: Fraternity never did engage our passions: the maintenance of Law and Order is at a discount: Natural Rights and Natural Justice are outmoded shibboleths. But Equality— there men have something to die for, kill for, agitate about, be miserable about. The demand for Equality obsesses all our political thought. We

are not sure what it is—indeed, as I shall show later, we are necessarily not sure what it is—but we are sure that whatever it is, we want it: and while we are prepared to look on frustration, injustice or violence with tolerance, as part of the natural order of things, we will work ourselves up into paroxysms of righteous indignation at the bare mention of Inequality.

Reprinted from J. R. Lucas, "Against Equality," *Philosophy,* XL (October 1965), pp. 296–307. Reprinted by permission of the author and The Royal Institute of Philosophy.

For my own part, I think the current obsession with Equality deplorable. There are problems enough in all conscience, to occupy our minds for the rest of this century, without inculcating in each man's breast a feeling of resentment because in some respect or other he compares unfavourably with somebody else. But it is not enough to deplore; and my attack will take the more insidious form of understanding Equality. I shall show why it is that we are tempted to demand Equality, and in what sense the demand is rational; and how we have been confused into thinking that our demand is for something else; and how this demand is incoherent, because what is demanded is both internally inconsistent and incompatible with other more precious ideals.

We are tempted to demand Equality when we set out to give a moral or rational critique of society. Not that it is wrong to try to give a rational account of one's society, although one should not be too doctrinaire about it; the crude realist, who is concerned only with what he can get away with, is not an estimable creature. And although the historical approach is estimable, and adequate for explaining why things are as they are, yet since the future can never be exactly like the past, it gives us only inadequate guidance on how political choices are to be made. To this extent at least, we ought to attempt a moral and rational critique of our society. Of those who have done so, most have laid it down either that men are all equal really, or that they ought to be. This Equality, which is a by-product of rationality, is nothing other than the principle of Universalisability. I shall call it the principle of Formal Equality. It requires that if two people are being treated, or are to be treated, differently, there should be some relevant difference between them. Otherwise, in the absence of some differentiating feature, what is sauce for the goose is sauce for the gander, and it would be wrong to treat the two unequally, that is, not the same.

It is clear that Formal Equality by itself establishes very little. Indeed, if we accept the infinite variety of human personality, that no two people, not even identical twins, are qualitatively identical, then there will always be differences between any two people, which might be held to justify a difference of treatment. Many of these differences we may wish to rule out as not being relevant, but since the principle of Formal Equality does not provide, of itself, any criteria of relevance, it does not, by itself, establish much. It gives a line of argument, but not any definite conclusion.

Egalitarians, however, profess to be less concerned with differences than with samenesses. The ways in which men resemble one another are much more important, they hold, than the ways in which they differ, and a corresponding similarity of treatment is the only one that can be justified. It seems at first sight to be a natural corollary—a contraposition almost—of the principle of Formal Equality. The latter states that people may properly be treated differently only if they are different: the former that since people are, in fact, similar, their treatment should be similar too. A moment's reflection, however, will show that the equivalence is spurious. It is spurious because the respects in which people are, in the one case the same, in the other different, are not themselves the same. Human beings are the same in respect of being featherless bipeds, of being sentient agents, perhaps rational ones, perhaps children of God. They are not the same in respect of height, age, sex, intellectual ability, strength of character. These latter differences may be irrelevant, as the egalitarians assert: but they are not proved not to be differences by the fact that in other respects men are similar.

The argument from sameness is thus seen to be independent of the principle of Formal Equality. It is often expressed by the words "After all, all men are men" or "A man is a man for a' that." It would be difficult to deny what is stated in these words, but difficult also to derive very convincingly from it any principle of Equality. The argument, inasmuch as there is one, seems to run thus:

> All men are men
> <u>All men are equally men</u>
[therefore]   All men are equal.

It is not, on the face of it, a cogent form of argument. That it is in fact fallacious is shown by the parody which can be obtained by replacing the word "men" by the word "numbers."

All numbers are numbers
<u>All numbers are equally numbers</u>
[therefore] All numbers are equal.

An implicit and illegitimate extension is being made of the respects in virtue of which the men (or numbers) are being said to be equal; it has been assumed that because they are equal in some respects—in possessing those character-istics in virtue of which they are said to be men—therefore they are equal in all. And this does not follow.

Nevertheless, we do think that *something* follows from the fact that men are men, and that all men share a common humanity. We do think that men, because they are men, ought not to be killed, tortured, imprisoned, exploited, frustrated, humiliated; that they should never be treated merely as means but always also as ends in themselves. Exactly what is meant is unclear, but at least two things are clear: that all men are entitled to such treatment; and that their entitlement derives from their possession of certain features, such as sentience and rationality, which are characteristic of the human species. And therefore it is proper to view the argument as one which starts from the universal common humanity of men—that all men are men—and ends with an injunction about how men are to be treated—that all men are to be treated alike, *in certain respects*. Although thus set out, the argument would not find favour with tough-minded philosophers, it is a sound argument so far as it goes. Only, it has little to do with Equality. It is, rather, an argument of Universal Humanity, that we should treat human beings, because they are human beings, humanely. To say that all men, because they are men, are equally men, or that to treat any two persons as ends in themselves is to treat them as equally ends in themselves is to import a spurious note of egalitarianism into a perfectly sound and serious argument. We may call it, if we like, the argument from Equality of Respect, but in this phrase it is the word "Respect"—respect for each man's humanity, respect for him as a human being—which is doing the logical work, while the word "Equality" adds nothing to the argument and is altogether otiose.

The principle of Formal Equality or Universalisability, and the principle of Equality of Respect, or Universal Humanity, are two extremes, bounding the range in which seriously egalitarian principles of Equality operate. We have two universes of discourse to correlate: one consists of human beings, the other of possible treatments of human beings. Each human being is characterised by an infinite (or at least indefinitely large) number of characteristics, and we correlate (or "map") the universe of possible treatments with the universe of human beings thus characterised. One principle, the principle of Universalisability, expresses for one type of correlation the fact that it is one-valued; that is, that every distinction which can be drawn between treatments corresponds to some distinction which can be drawn between human beings; but this is always possible since no two people are qualitatively identical: the other principle, that of Universal Humanity, expresses for another type of correlation the fact that it correlates characteristics common to all human beings with characteristics common to all humane treatments. The principle of Universalisability specifies the treatment as fully as any one, egalitarian or non-egalitarian, could want, but in doing this for the treatments, is committed to drawing too many distinctions among the human beings for the egalitarian to stomach. The principle of Universal Humanity manages not to distinguish between men, so as to gladden the heart of the egalitarian: but in saying so little about men as not to differentiate between them, it says too little about treatments to characterise them in more than a very minimal way—too little to ensure that they all will be equal in the way that the egalitarian wants. The egalitarian wants a map of the logical possibilities which is very detailed—in order to have everybody treated alike *in all respects*—and at the same time a crude outline sketch—in order to include all men together in only one constituency: but the logical manoeuvres which will give him the one will preclude him from having the other, and *vice versa*. More than logical considerations will be required to lead us from the minimal specification of human beings, which is the only one in respect of which we are all alike, to the maximal specification of the treatments we are to receive, which is necessary if they are all to be thought to be the same.

The central argument for Equality is a muddle. There are two sound principles of political reasoning, the principle of Universalisability and the principle of Universal Humanity, and each has been described as a sort of Equality, Formal Equality in the one case and Equality of Respect in the other. But they are not the same Equality, nor are they compatible, and they cannot be run in harness to lead to a full-blooded egalitarianism. Each, however, by itself can lead to some conclusions which an egalitarian would endorse. Though these conclusions are less, and necessarily less, than all that an egalitarian would wish, they represent the only Equalities that are obtainable and are reasonable to seek.

The principle of Universalisability is not vacuous in political reasoning because a polity is governed by laws, and laws involve universal terms. Laws are couched in universal terms partly for practical reasons, though not for them alone. There is not time to take into account all the characteristics of each person or all the features of each case: we cannot give separate orders to 50 million people individually, but have to make relatively few and blunt discriminations, lumping people together in categories and applying general rules to them, laying down what *motorists* are required to do, what *householders* are entitled to do, what *customers'* rights are. Exceptions[1] must be rare: for the most part laws must be no respectors of persons.

Practical considerations apart, there are two other reasons for laws being couched in universal terms. The first is that laws ought to be just: not absolutely just—we realise that absolute justice, like any other absolute ideal, is unattainable in this imperfect world—but guided by a certain aspiration towards justice. It is—and here I part company with many modern writers on jurisprudence—essential to our notion of law and our being willing to obey it, that it should be administered by courts which are courts of *justice*, and determined by judges having as their ideal the blind goddess who holds the scales and is no respector of persons but gives her decision in accordance with the merits of the case. But if the decisions of the court are to have any semblance of justice, they must be based on certain general features of the case, held to be relevant; and therefore laws themselves ought to be couched in universal terms, so that the justice dispensed in accordance with them shall conform at least to this necessary condition of being just.

The second reason for couching laws in general terms is to protect the subject from the government, and to enable him to know what the law requires of him so that he may be free to plan his life accordingly. It is an argument from imperfection: imperfection of the governors, imperfection of the governed. We want to make sure that our governors, our rulers, our judges cannot abuse their authority, or subject any one man to covert pressure to conform to their wishes: and we know that many men are not motivated altogether by ideals of absolute morality, and may want to do things which another man might regard as wrong, and that therefore they need to know in advance where they stand, and what things they may, and what things they may not, do. And so we require that laws shall be published beforehand, and apply to people generally, and not pick out any one person rather than another except in so far as he falls under some universal description.

Formal Equality thus becomes, in political reasoning, something much more substantial, namely Equality before the Law; but the Equality it establishes is still not an egalitarian Equality. Justice has her eyes blindfolded: only those considerations which go into the scales are weighed. That is to say, not every factor is relevant. Thus Equality before the Law will secure men equal treatment in some respects at the cost of necessarily not securing men equal treatment in all respects: the guilty are not treated the same as the innocent; the rich are often, and rightly, not fined the same as the poor; the mere fact of conviction may ruin a schoolmaster or a civil servant while constituting only a small penalty to a man of independent means. Equality before the Law is nonetheless valuable for that. It secures to all the protection of the law—no man is to be outside the law, and everyone shall have access to the courts to vindicate his rights against every other man. It secures the uniform administration of the law without fear or favour. It gives the subject protection against arbitrary decisions by those in authority, and it gives him freedom to make rational plans. These are reasons enough to value Equality before the Law and on occasion to enact further measures—the provision of Legal Aid, for example—the better to secure it. But the Equality vouchsafed us by Equality before the Law, although valuable and not vacuous, is still much less than the Equality the egalitarian seeks.

Equality before the Law does not of itself secure that the laws themselves are equal. In one sense, they cannot be. Laws must pick out particular classes of people, actions, situations. The Traffic Acts apply, for instance, mainly to motorists, not to motorists and nonmotorists alike. Nevertheless, we can criticise certain laws, not for discriminating, but for discriminating irrelevantly. It is irrelevant to a man's right to own property or to travel in buses that his skin is of a certain colour, though not, presumably, to his being employed as an actor in the part of Iago. It is irrelevant to whether a man should be allowed to exceed the speed limit that he is rich or that he is not rich, though not that he is a policeman in pursuit of a criminal, and arguably not that he is a doctor going to the scene of an accident. Many of the discriminations the egalitarian objects to, we can object to too, but because they offend against the canons of rationality and justice. Laws ought to be, so far as possible, rational and just, and therefore the distinctions drawn by each law should be relevant ones with regard to the general purpose of the law. But—and here is the rub—there is no sharp criterion of relevance, and sometimes, indeed, the mere fact that some people think something is relevant is enough to make it so. Many of the most serious disputes of our age are really disputes about relevance. The superficial slogans of the egalitarian are no help. If we want to have fruitful discussions about political matters, we must replace controversies about Equality by detailed arguments about *criteria of relevance*.[2] Being arguments, they are naturally two-sided, and one side may be right without the other being unreasonable, and an opponent may be wrong without being necessarily wrongheaded. In the detailed assessment of argument we shall see the important truth which the idiom of egalitarianism conceals, that on most political questions we are presented with a balance of argument rather than a simple black-

and-white issue. Our arguments, therefore, will yield conclusions that are more solidly based, yet more tolerant in tone. Some, but not all, the conclusions the egalitarian yearns for can be maintained on nonegalitarian grounds, better established, but less censoriously affirmed.

In a similar vein the argument from Equality of Respect, Universal Humanity, will produce some of the conclusions the egalitarian looks for, but not the essentially egalitarian ones. Whenever inequality results in some people having *too little*, the humanitarian will protest as well as the egalitarian. Human life cannot be properly lived in very straitened circumstances, and we do not show respect for human beings as such if we do not try to alleviate those conditions. Moreover, wealth and poverty are, in part, relative terms: it is not just that there is a certain minimum requirement of food and fuel—true though this is: there is also a varying, and in our age rising, level of normality in each particular community, and to be too far below this will preclude a man from participation in the normal life of that community. The pre-war poor scholars in Oxford did not usually suffer from undernourishment: but their poverty did prevent them living the normal life of an undergraduate, and could be objected to on those grounds alone. Not only bread, but Nescafé and books are necessaries of university life—of social existence rather than bare physical subsistence.

This argument, the argument of the rising minimum as I shall call it, is by far the most pervasive argument in political thought today. It is a telling argument, but it is open to abuse. It may be a good thing that nobody should be without a television set: but it is only one *desideratum* among many; it does not have, though sometimes pretends to have, the compelling force of the claim that nobody should be without food.

The argument of the rising minimum ought not only to be tentative in its forcefulness, but moderate in its claims, and ought not to set its sights too high. We may say that people ought not to fall too far below the average: we must be careful not to be led into saying that people must not fall at all below the average. The latter would entail a strict Equality: but it cannot be justified on any argument from humanity, however much extended. For there are differences too small to make any substantial difference—for example, if I can afford to invite only thirty-nine people to a party, whereas the average is forty. If negligible differences are to matter, it must be because comparisons are being made, not because their consequences are important. People are feeling put upon *not* because they cannot join in normal activities, but because they *mind* that they have got less than other people. But then the argument has ceased to be an argument from humanity plus, and has become an argument from envy, an argument strong no doubt in many breasts, but a different one, nonetheless, and of a different degree of cogency.

The argument from extended humanity cannot set the minimum acceptable level too close to the average. It therefore cannot require that there should not be any people getting more than the average, and in particular, that there should not be some people getting much more than the average. This is the acid test for distinguishing the true egalitarian from the humanitarian. The true egalitarian will object on principle to any one man having much more than any others, even if, by reducing the one man's possessions, the others would attain only a negligible benefit, or none at all. The humanitarian has no such objection in principle. He may on occasion play Robin Hood, but only if he is convinced that the beneficiaries are in real need and will be substantially benefited by redistribution and that the arguments against intervening are less weighty than the arguments for. Equality of Respect will produce some but not all the conclusions the egalitarian desires, not the peculiarly egalitarian ones.

Having gone thus far in pursuit of Equality, we have gone as far as we can reasonably go. Legality, Justice, Fairness, Equity, Humanity, all will on occasion produce a measure of Equality, but the measure is never exact, and they are none of them essentially egalitarian. The Equality that goes further than this, the Equality that the egalitarian yearns for, is unattainable and, to my mind, undesirable. It may be partly a matter of taste; I like variety more than I like uniformity: but it is also an inescapable conclusion from the nature of society and a consideration of the *desiderata* we

have for a society's being a good one. If men, as we now know them, are to co-exist in civil society there must be sanctions: this follows from the fact that some people are bloody-minded, and will do violence to others unless restrained by force or the threat of force. Civil society is, therefore, dependent on there being a system of coercion, and hence on there being certain people in a position to coerce others, people, that is, with power. Power cannot be equally divided and distributed over the whole population. It is necessarily concentrated in few hands. Egalitarians may take steps to make the possession of power in some sense more equal, but even in so doing they admit its natural inequality. Power is concentrated in some hands rather than others, and since power is one of the goods that men desire, it follows that in any society in which there are, or may be, bloody-minded men, there must be some people who possess more of the good that is constituted by power than do others.

Besides an inequality of power, there is an inequality of prestige, which will arise in any society which is in Durkheim's phrase "a moral community"—whose members, that is, share values and have some ideals in common. It will stem from men's natural inequality of ability resulting in their being able, some to a greater, others to a lesser, extent to be successful in achieving their ideals. There will thus be an inequality of success, and therefore also of prestige, which has nothing to do with power or sanctions. There are many sanctionless sub-societies which form moral communities and are correspondingly stratified. Undergraduates provide one example. There are no sanctions, no undergraduates "in power," but some undergraduates do succeed more than others in realising some undergraduate ideal of excellence. The President of the Union, of University Dramatic Society, of the Junior Common Room, are each top of his own particular tree and have more prestige than the rest of us. Again, in the world of science or in the republic of letters, there is no parity of esteem between all members. In these societies the members are not even located in one place, so there is no possibility of force being used or coercion required. Nevertheless there is a loosely established hierarchy, with all its inevitable inequalities. Shared ideals and inequality of ability is thus enough to bring about this sort of inequality, inequality of prestige. Whereas even if all men were of equal ability, or had no community of ideals, we should still, provided only that they lived in the same place and some of them might be tempted to use force, have an inequality of power.

It follows, then, that we shall never be able to avoid some inequalities; we can never avoid some inequality of power and we cannot avoid an inequality of prestige, unless we are prepared to have our society not be a moral community, but only a minimal civil society—and one of the lessons we can draw from political history since the time of John Locke is that most people will not be content with so bare a form of coexistence. They look to society not merely for security but for the opportunity of realising themselves in social existence, and are always creating the conditions for inequality of prestige.

Since men value power and prestige as much as the possession of wealth—indeed, these three "goods" cannot be completely separated—it is foolish to seek to establish an equality of wealth on egalitarian grounds. It is foolish first because it will not result in what egalitarians really want. It is foolish also because if we do not let men compete for money, they will compete all the more for power; and whereas the possession of wealth by another man does not hurt me, unless I am made vulnerable by envy, the possession of power by another is inherently dangerous; and furthermore if we are to maintain a strict equality of wealth we need a much greater apparatus of state to secure it and therefore a much greater inequality of power. Better have bloated plutocrats than omnipotent bureaucrats.

It might be tempting to deal with power the way the Athenians did—accept that it must be of its nature unequal, but distribute it by lot. If we cannot all have an equal share of power, at least we can all have an equal chance of it. It is noteworthy that this is the method adopted by our egalitarian age of distributing another essentially unequal good in an egalitarian fashion. Great wealth is obviously inegalitarian; but nonetheless coveted for that. The pools create fortunes at negligible cost to their "investors,"

and distribute them at random. The unintelligent and unindustrious have just as much a chance as the energetic and the thrifty. This is their attraction—there is no damned merit about them. And so we do not tax winnings in the way we tax earnings. Our objection to non-random assignments of wealth is the same as the Athenians' objection to elective office: some people are more likely to get rich or get elected than others, and the others know it, and do not like it. Justice is not blind enough: only Ernie is truly no respector of persons.

But there is a snag. Just as we pay a heavy price for preferring Equality to efficiency, and assigning economic rewards on the impartial basis of chance rather than any criteria of effort or enterprise, so the Athenians found the lot producing ineffectual rulers. And power must follow ability. So the *strategoi*, who were elected and could be chosen for their merits, came to exercise power, not the Archons, selected as they were by lot from a large field. The lesson holds good for us. We demand too much of government, we depend too much on its being tolerably competent, for us to be able to sacrifice all considerations of efficiency upon the altar of Equality. We can, and should, take special measures to prevent the abuse of power; but we cannot confine that essentially unequal concept in an egalitarian mould, and if we attempt to do so, we shall find that power has fled from our equalled hands, and has taken on some new, and much less controllable, form.

Even where we can secure Equality, it is often not desirable. The administration of justice is better served by selecting good judges and putting them in a highly unequal position *vis-à-vis* the litigants, than by having a large number of equally eligible *dikastai*, who have no powers to secure the fair conduct of the case. Better laws are likely to be enacted if legislators are unequally privileged in the matter of free speech, and can say in Parliament all sorts of things which would be actionable elsewhere. The choice between economic efficiency and economic Equality is one we are all familiar with, and one that is likely to become more and more pressing in the next decade. If we are to attach any weight to merit—and it is difficult to claim that fairness is preserved where merit is disregarded—we are committed to possible inequalities of some sort, because although it cannot be shown *a priori* that people do have different deserts, it does follow from the nature of the concept that they could. In the same way, Equality of opportunity, whatever the other difficulties of that dubious concept, clearly precludes the certainty of Equality of achievement. If, as is sometimes demanded by politicians, everybody ought to have an equal chance of getting into Oxford, it still means (unless the chance is either unity or zero) that some people will, and others will not, get in. The 18-plus is going the same way as the 11-plus, and from having been the ark of the egalitarian covenant is becoming the symbol of inegalitarian wickedness. This change of front reflects neither dishonesty nor outstanding stupidity on the part of egalitarians, but the internal inconsistency of their ideal, absolute Equality. We can secure Equality in certain respects between members of certain classes for certain purposes and under certain conditions; but never, and necessarily never, Equality in all respects between all men for all purposes and under all conditions. The egalitarian is doomed to a life not only of grumbling and everlasting envy, but of endless and inevitable disappointment.

These, perhaps, are arguments which appeal more to conservatives than radicals. Let me end therefore by pointing out the incompatibility of Equality with the other two traditional ideals of radicalism, Fraternity and Liberty.

Fraternity does in part involve one of our concepts of Equality, Equality of Respect, Universal Humanity. But it demands the negation of other Equalities, Formal Equality and the various egalitarian Equalities. It demands that we treat each person as a person for him-, or her-, self and not simply as the bearer of certain characteristics; the demand is that I should "love you for yourself alone, and not your yellow hair." Whatever the logical difficulties in this, at least it amounts to a protest against the paper world in which people are treated not as people but as beings conforming to specifications. We regard ourselves as individuals, each one different, each one a whole person, knobbly, not fitting exactly into any mould: and we do not like it if, in the name of Equality or anything else, we are wrapped up and put in a carton and labelled, indistinguishably from a lot of others. We want to be ourselves, and to be able to get through to other people, rough uncut diamonds though they may be, not separated from them by layers of tissue paper establishing a flabby uniformity between us all. Inevitably in a large society the demand for Fraternity cannot be pushed very far. Personal relationships are emotionally absorbing and time-consuming; we cannot have them with many people. With most people our relationship must be to some extent official, to some extent formal, based on incomplete knowledge and incomplete attention, and therefore determined by only some of the characteristics of the person concerned, not by them all. We cannot be fully fraternal with the public. But we can resist the attempt to make all our private arrangements subject to the formalities that properly pertain only to public ones, and we can resist public encroachment on private affairs; and in so far as we do, we shall be denying the Equalities that egalitarians strive for.

Liberty imposes like limitations. Only, whereas Fraternity limits Equality at the receiving end—the person dealt with wants to be considered as himself, not as the possessor of certain characteristics—, Liberty limits Equality at the doing end—the person who is doing the dealing wants to be free to make his own choices, and not required always to treat similar cases similarly. Equality lays down how we are to treat people: but Liberty entitles us to act as we choose, not as some rule lays down. If I have any Liberty then there are some decisions I am allowed to make on my own; I am free in some cases to act arbitrarily. And if that is so, I may in such cases arbitrarily choose one person rather than another, without there being any ground to justify discrimination. I may choose Jane, and take her to wife, while passing over Bess, her equally well-favoured sister. This is what it is to be free. Freedom is inherently unfair. If we place any value on Freedom at all, we must to that extent compromise the principle of Equality. And we must place some value on Freedom, for to be free in some respects is a necessary condition of discovering oneself as a moral and rational agent. And only for such can the question of Equality arise.

NOTES

1. E.g. in a monarchy, the monarch: Elizabeth II has no private existence and is quite unlike anybody else. Our laws are not couched altogether in universal terms, and do pay peculiar respect to the person of the Monarch.
2. Or to be exact, both criteria of *relevance* and criteria of *irrelevance*. Sometimes the onus of proof is on the man who claims that a certain factor is relevant, sometimes on him who denies it. Differences of skin-pigmentation may be presumed irrelevant, unless the contrary is shown, on any question of employment: differences of hair-pigmentation may be presumed relevant, unless the contrary is shown, in a beauty contest. Very roughly, in public life there is a presumption of irrelevance, and we will not be happy about any distinction in the Law, in public service, in the conditions of public employment, or in the award of public contracts unless it can be shown to be relevant: whereas in private life there is a presumption of relevance, and we are disposed to accept any distinction a private individual draws, unless it is clearly an irrelevant one.

Egalitarianism and the Equal Consideration of Interests
STANLEY I. BENN

Egalitarians persist in speaking of human equality, as a principle significant for action, in the face of all the evident human inequalities of stature, physique, intellect, virtue, merit, and desert. Claims pressed so tenaciously, in the face of seemingly manifest and overwhelming objections, can hardly be summarily dismissed as naive absurdities. The task for the philosopher is to look for ways of construing such claims, consistent with the evident inequalities, compatible with commonly accepted conceptions of justice, yet still with bite enough to make a difference to behavior worth contending for. I shall argue that in many contexts the claim to human equality is no more than a negative egalitarianism, a denial, a limited criticism of some specific existing arrangements. If one were to interpret such claims as implying a universal positive assertion about human rights and social organization, one would be going beyond what was necessary to make good sense of them. But because such a negative interpretation does not seem to exhaust the possibilities of egalitarianism, I shall formulate a principle that, while satisfying the aforementioned criteria, can still be applied quite generally, and can be properly expressed in the formula "all men are equal." This is the *principle of equal consideration of human interests*. I shall further maintain that this principle is required by current conceptions of social justice. It can be effective in public policy-making, however, only to the extent that agreement can be reached on the proper order of priority of human interests.

Things or persons can be equal in several different ways. In one sense equality presupposes an ordering of objects according to some common natural property or attribute that can be possessed in varying degrees. So, although objects said to be equal occupy interchangeable places in such an ordering, their equality in this respect is necessarily implied neither by their possessing this property in common nor by their common membership of a larger class of which all members possess the property. Although two cabbages happen, for instance, to be of equal weight, their equality is not a necessary feature of their both being cabbages, even though every cabbage has weight. In this sense at least, not all cabbages are equal. Things can be equal in a second sense according to some standard of value or merit. Two students' essays may be equally good, though their properties may differ, one being detailed and painstaking, the other original and imaginative. Here, differences in their properties are weighed against one another in assessing their relative merit; however, in a final ordering of all essays, in which some stand high and others low, these two occupy interchangeable places. Here, again, their equality is not a necessary feature of their both being essays. A third kind of equality is that of need, entitlement, or desert; the remuneration to which a man is entitled for his work or the dose of medicine he needs for his cough may be equal to another's, though it could conceivably have been different without prejudice to their common status as workers or sick men.

These three ways of ascribing equality—descriptive, evaluative, and distributive—are not of course independent of one another. There may be a logical connection: two knives, equally sharp, equally well-tempered, possessing indeed all relevant properties in the same degree, are equally good knives, sharpness, temper, and the like, being the criteria of a good knife. However, the equal merit of the students' essays does not follow necessarily from a list of their properties but depends on a complex appraisal in the light of multiple standards. Different again is the case of two men entitled to equal pay for doing equal amounts of work. In this case, their equality depends on a particular convention; according to a different practice, if one man worked longer than the other, their deserts would be different, even though the results might be the same. In all these instances, however, though the possibility of

comparison depends on the subjects being members of the same class, it is not a necessary condition of their membership that they possess the property by virtue of which they are equals in the precise degree that they do. Mere membership of the same class does not entail, therefore, that the subjects are equals in any of the three senses discussed. Consequently, although two members of a class happen to qualify for equal treatment, this is not a necessary result of their common membership.

To say, then, that two things are in some respect equal is to say that they are, in that and perhaps related respects, interchangeable—that no rational ground exists for treating them in those respects differently from each other. Egalitarians would maintain, however, that the reason for considering them equal need not always be that they satisfy some qualifying condition to the same degree; it may be because, with regard to some manner of treating them, the qualifying condition does not admit of degrees; it may be enough simply to possess the properties necessary to make them members of that class. There may then be something to which all members of a class have an equal claim, in the sense that none has a better claim than another, nor could have, given their common membership. If, for instance, all sane adults have the right to vote, and there are no other qualifying (or disqualifying) conditions, no qualified member of the class of sane adults has any better right than another, nor has any member a right to any more votes than another, by virtue of some further property that they possess in varying degrees. All qualified voters, qua voters, are equal.

Those who demand social equality do not necessarily take universal adult equal suffrage as a paradigm for all social institutions and practices. There may be egalitarians for whom a society without differences is both a possibility and an ideal; most, however, have more limited aims. When egalitarianism is translated into concrete political programs, it usually amounts to a proposal to abandon existing inequalities, rather than to adopt some positive principle of social justice. The egalitarian in politics usually has quite specific objectives and is critical of quite specific kinds of differentiation rather than of every kind of social discrimination. Indeed, differences are rarely called "inequalities" unless, in the first place, they affect the things which men value and for which they compete, like power, wealth, or esteem. One complains of inequality if one has to pay more tax than another man but not if, for some administrative reason, the demands arrive in differently colored envelopes. Egalitarians protest when, in the second place, they see no rational justification for differentiating a particular class for the purpose of allocating certain specific privileges or burdens. The campaign for equal pay for women is a case in point. To treat people according to their skill or productivity would not be to discriminate between the sexes, even though some women might in fact receive less than some men (or, conceivably, all women less than all men), for skill and productivity are generally recognized as relevant and legitimate criteria. Sex differentiation as such is intolerable because, it is argued, no one has yet shown good enough reasons for thinking a person's sex relevant to the income he should earn—and the burden of proof rests on the discriminator. On the other hand, discrimination according to sex for military service has been generally accepted without much question and is usually considered well-grounded; so it is rarely called an inequality.

A race, sex, religious, or class egalitarianism denies the justice, then, of some existing modes of discrimination, possibly in a relatively limited range of social practices; it does not press for the removal of all forms of differentiation. Or it may endorse existing grounds of discrimination but question whether they ought to make as much difference as they do. Of course, the conditions under attack, and the related forms of differentiation not under attack, may be contextually supplied and not explicitly stated; nevertheless, they may be perfectly well understood by all parties to the debate.

Although most movements for equality can be interpreted in terms of protests against specific inequalities, a strong disposition nonetheless exists, among philosophers and others, to argue that whatever men's actual differences and whatever their genuine relevance for certain kinds of differentiation, there yet remain important values in respect of which all men's claims are equal. Whatever these may be—and

catalogs of natural and human rights are attempts to formulate them—they are such that no difference in properties between one man and another could affect them; all men qualify simply by virtue of belonging to the class *man*, which admits of no degrees (just as, in my earlier examples, all voters are equally qualified provided they are sane adults). This certainly looks like a positive and quite general claim to equality rather than a denial of specific irrelevant inequalities.

In a recent article, "Against Equality,"[1] J. R. Lucas contends that egalitarianism rests on a confusion of two principles, each sound in itself but which, if pressed, together lead to incompatible conclusions. One, the principle of formal equality, is the familiar principle underlying all forms of what I have called negative egalitarianism: if two people are to be treated differently there should be some relevant difference between them. Lucas does not regard this as really an egalitarian principle at all, because in itself it prescribes neither equality nor inequality, but, taking it for granted that there might be good reasons for treating men differently in some respects, it lays down the form that a justificatory argument must take. The other principle, that Lucas calls the principle of universal humanity, makes this assertion:

> men, because they are men, ought not to be killed, tortured, imprisoned, exploited, frustrated, humiliated; . . . they should never be treated merely as means but always as ends in themselves. . . . We should treat human beings, because they are human beings, humanely.

But this, he says, has little to do with equality:

> To say that all men, because they are men, are equally men, or that to treat any two persons as ends in themselves is to treat them as equally ends in themselves is to import a spurious note of egalitarianism into a perfectly sound and serious argument. We may call it, if we like, the argument for Equality of Respect, but in this phrase it is the word "Respect"—respect for each man's humanity, respect for him as a human being—which is doing the logical work, while the word "Equality" adds nothing to the argument and is altogether otiose.

I suspect that Lucas has dealt too shortly with positive egalitarianism, in representing it simply as rules about how we ought to behave in relation to objects or persons of a given class. He is perfectly right in saying, for instance, that the duty not to inflict torture has nothing to do with equality, but then, it is not a duty in respect of human beings alone but also of animals. This is not a duty we *owe* to men as men, for it is doubtful whether, properly speaking, we *owe* it to the object at all. Inflicting needless pain is simply wrong; it would not be a case of unequal treatment, but simply of cruelty. It would be a case lacking altogether the characteristic feature that makes inequality objectionable—namely, unfairness or injustice.

But some of Lucas' examples of inhumanity do seem to have more to do with equality than that. In particular, the injunction to respect all men, simply as men or as ends in themselves, unlike the injunction not to torture them, involves recognizing them as subjects of claims, and not merely as objects, albeit objects that ought to be handled in one way rather than another. To treat a man not as an end but simply as a means is to give no consideration to his interests, but to consider him only insofar as he can promote or frustrate the interests of someone else—to treat him, in short, like Aristotle's "natural slave," with no end not derived from that of a master. Now to adopt such an attitude can be said to be not merely wrong (as is cruelty), but wrong in the special way that it disregards a fundamental equality of *claim*—the claim to have one's interests considered alongside those of everyone else likely to be affected by the decision.

Now this *principle of equal consideration of interests* seems to me to involve an assertion of equality that is neither purely formal nor otiose. It *resembles*, it is true, another principle, which is deducible from the principle of formal equality—therefore itself formal—and which is often called the principle of equal consideration. The principle of formal equality states that where there is no relevant difference between two cases, no rational ground exists for not treating them alike; but, conversely, where there is a relevant difference, there is a reasonable ground for treating them differently. This involves, as a corollary, that equal considera-

tion must be given to the relevant features of each, for to have good reasons for favoring one person or course of action rather than another surely implies that there are no conclusively better reasons on the other side; and how could one know that, without having given them equal consideration? This is certainly, then, a purely formal or procedural principle, for it offers no criterion for good reasons nor makes any substantive recommendation for action. The principle of equal consideration of interests, on the other hand, is specific at least to the extent that it directs consideration to the *interests* of those affected, and so lays down, as the other principle does not, a criterion of relevance. After all, if I preferred A to B because A could be of more use to me, I should still be acting consistently with the formal principle of equal consideration, provided I had first considered how useful to me B could be. But this would not be consistent with the equal consideration of interests, for I would have given thought to the interests of neither A nor B, but only to my own.

If the principle is not purely formal, neither is it otiose. For it would be perfectly possible to consider the interests of everyone affected by a decision without giving them *equal* consideration. Elitist moralities are precisely of this kind. Although the elitist would allow that ordinary men have interests deserving some consideration, the interests of the super-man, super-class, or super-race would always be preferred. Some men, it might be said, are simply worth more than others, in the sense that any claim of theirs, whatever it might be and whatever its specific ground, would always take precedence. Such a morality would maintain that there was some criterion, some qualifying condition, of race, sex, intellect, or personality, such that a person once recognized as satisfying it would automatically have prior claim in every field over others.

The egalitarian would deny that there is any such criterion. Whatever priority special circumstances or properties confer on a man in particular fields, no one of them, neither a white skin, male sex, Aryan ancestry, noble birth, nor any other whatsoever, would entitle a man to move to the head of *every* queue. That is not to imply that any man can always claim the same treatment as any other, nor, indeed, that one man's interest could never have priority over another's, as, for instance, when we tax the rich to assist the poor. But every claim must be grounded on criteria specifically appropriate to it, and every demand for privilege must be argued afresh, since arguments valid in one field have no necessary consequential validity in others. This, I think, is the claim fundamental to the idea of social equality or equality of esteem. It is related to the claim to self-respect, which J. C. Davies has put in these words: "I am as good as anybody else; I may not be as clever or hard-working as you are, but I am as good as you are."[2] It bears also on the concept of equality of respect. No one could respect all men equally; nor does it seem likely, leaving aside the differences in respect we have for men on account of their different virtues and merits, that there is still a residual respect we owe to each merely as a man. What is there to respect in what alone is common to all men—membership of this particular biological species? It makes perfectly good sense, however, to say that, whereas we respect different men for different things, there is no property, such as a white skin, which is a necessary condition of a man's being worthy, whatever his other merits, of any respect at all. So every man is entitled to be taken on his own merits; there is no generally disqualifying condition.

That this is not mere empty formalism is clear when we contrast the case of men with that of animals. For not to possess human shape *is* a disqualifying condition. However faithful or intelligent a dog may be, it would be a monstrous sentimentality to attribute to him interests that could be weighed in an equal balance with those of human beings. The duties we have in respect to dogs would generally be discounted when they conflict with our duties to human beings— discounted, not set aside, for we might well decide to waive a minor obligation to a human being rather than cause intense suffering to an animal. But if the duties were at all commensurate, if, for instance, one had to decide between feeding a hungry baby or a hungry dog, anyone who chose the dog would generally be reckoned morally defective, unable to recognize a fundamental inequality of claims.

This is what distinguishes our attitude to animals from our attitude to imbeciles. It would be odd to say that we ought to respect equally the dignity or personality of the imbecile and of the rational man; it is questionable indeed whether one can treat with respect someone for whom one's principal feeling is pity. But there is nothing odd about saying that we should respect their interests equally, that is, that we should give to the interests of each the same serious consideration as claims to conditions necessary for some standard of well-being that we can recognize and endorse.

The imbecile has been something of an embarrassment to moral philosophers.[3] There is a traditional view, going back to the Stoics, that makes rationality the qualifying condition on which human freedom and equality depend. But if equal consideration of interests depended on rationality, imbeciles would belong to an inferior species, whose interests (if they could properly be allowed to have interests) would always have to be discounted when they competed with those of rational men. What reason could then be offered against using them like dogs or guinea pigs for, say, medical research? But, of course, we do distinguish imbeciles from animals in this regard, and although it would be quite proper to discriminate between imbeciles and rational men for very many purposes, most rationalist philosophers would concede that it would be grossly indecent to subordinate the interests of an imbecile to those of normal persons for *all* purposes, simply on the ground of his imbecility.

Nevertheless, the link between rationality and our moral concern for human interests cannot be disregarded. If the human species is more important to us than other species, with interests worthy of special consideration, each man's for his own sake, this is possibly because each of us sees in other men the image of himself. So he recognizes in them what he knows in his own experience, the potentialities for moral freedom, for making responsible choices among ways of life open to him, for striving, no matter how mistakenly and unsuccessfully, to make of himself something worthy of his own respect. It is because this is the characteristically human enterprise, requiring a capacity for self-appraisal and criticism normal to men but not to dogs, that it seems reasonable to treat men as more important than dogs.

Still, we respect the interests of men and give them priority over dogs not *insofar* as they are rational, but because rationality is the human norm. We say it is *unfair* to exploit the deficiencies of the imbecile, who falls short of the norm, just as it would be unfair, and not just ordinarily dishonest, to steal from a blind man. If we do not think in this way about dogs, it is because we do not see the irrationality of a dog as a deficiency or a handicap but as normal for the species. The characteristics, therefore, that distinguish the normal man from the normal dog make it intelligible for us to talk of other men as having interests and capacities, and therefore claims, of precisely the same kind as we make on our own behalf. But although these characteristics may provide the point of the distinction between men and other species, they are not in fact the qualifying conditions for membership, or the distinguishing criteria of the class of morally considerable persons; and this is precisely because a man does not become a member of a different species, with its own standards of normality, by reason of not possessing these characteristics. On the other hand, the deficiency is more than an accidental fact, for it has a bearing on his moral status. For if someone is deficient in this way, he is falling short of what, in some sense, he *ought* to have been, given the species to which by nature he belongs; it is, indeed, to be deprived of the possibility of fully realizing his nature. So where the mental limitations of the dog can be amusing, without lapse of taste, those of an imbecile are tragic and appalling. Moreover, so far from being a reason for disregarding his interests, they may be grounds for special compensatory consideration, to meet a special need.

I said earlier that an egalitarian would deny that any property could confer an automatic general priority of claim on anyone possessing it, but that this need not preclude one man's interests having priority over others' in certain respects. I want to enlarge on this point and in doing so to compare the principle of equal consideration of interests with John Rawls' account of justice as fairness.[4]

Rawls asserts that "inequalities are arbitrary unless it is reasonable to expect that they will work out for everyone's advantage, and provided the positions and offices to which they attach . . . are open to all." He then seeks to show that only a practice that satisfied these conditions could be accepted by free, equal, rational, and prudent participants in it, given that they knew their own interests and that each ran the risk of filling the least favored roles. Rawls' model appears to derive justice from consent. However, what really counts is not what a man would actually accept but what, understanding his interests, he could reasonably accept. Thus objections to a practice based purely on envy of a privileged position would not be admissible, because avoiding the pangs of envy would not be an interest of a rational, prudent man. Rawls' model looks like a way of saying that a practice is just if it sacrifices no one's interest to anyone else's and makes only such distinctions as would promote the interests of everyone, given that the interests are not simply desires but conditions of well-being that rational men could endorse as such. This in turn looks rather like the egalitarian principle of equal consideration of interests. There are, however, difficulties in trying to equate the two accounts.

Rawls' model suggests an adequate schema for justifying discrimination in terms of desert or merit (the traditional problems of justice); it can be fitted, however, to modern conceptions of social justice, only at the cost of so abstracting from reality that the model loses most of its suggestiveness. These conceptions are characteristically compensatory and distributive; they are implicit in the institutions and policies of welfare states, which provide for the needs of the handicapped by taxing the more fortunate. At first glance, at least, Rawls' principles of justice would give wealthy but sterile people who are taxed to help educate the children of poor but fertile people legitimate grounds for complaint, as victims of a discriminatory practice that imposes sacrifices without corresponding advantages.

It could be argued, perhaps, that Rawls meets the case by presupposing in his model that all participants start equal, and that all roles are interchangeable. The restrictions that the community's practices would put on individual interests, or the sacrifices that would be accepted by some for the benefit of others, would then be such as "a person would keep in mind if he were designing a practice in which his enemy were to assign him his place." Rawls may argue that it is always prudent for the fortunate to insure against misfortune; it would be reasonable, in that case, for a man to consent to a tax for someone else's advantage, if there were a risk of his finding himself in that person's place. But which of all the features of a man's situation, character, talents, and incapacities, by which he could be at a disadvantage, are to be taken as intrinsic and irremediable, and which conjecturally subject to reallocation, as part of the "place" to which his enemy might assign him? Need the normal, healthy person really reckon with the risk of being called upon to fill the role of the congenitally handicapped? Similar questions can be asked of some socially conferred disadvantages. While the rich must, perhaps, take account of the risk of poverty, need a white man take seriously the risk of having to fill the role of a colored man in a racially prejudiced society? To meet these arguments, Rawls would need to postulate as one of the conditions of his model, not that the participants are equal but that they are completely ignorant of all their inequalities.

When pressed, then, the model becomes increasingly remote from reality. Rawls' account of justice seems to rely, at first glance, on the conception of principles to which self-interested individuals would agree; it soon becomes evident, however, that these are principles to which such individuals *could reasonably* agree. Moreover, if the primary motivation of self-interest is to be preserved, we must suppose these individuals ignorant of their identities and thus unaware of any circumstances that would distinguish their own interest from anyone else's. What they are really called upon to do, then, is to safeguard a paradigmatic set of interests from a number of typical hazards. We need not now suppose a collection of egotists, so much as creatures with standards of human well-being and with both a concern for and a knowledge of the conditions necessary for achieving or maintaining it. Now the lack of some of these conditions, food and shelter for instance, would frustrate the attainment of such standards more completely than the lack of others, such as holidays or books. One must arrange human interests, then, in an order of priority, distinguishing basic from other less urgent needs. So a

participant in one of Rawls' practices would be well advised to reckon with the possibility of being deprived of basic needs, as well as of being subject to a range of natural and social handicaps that would impair his capacity to supply them. Consequently, he would be rash to concur in any practice that (subject to certain provisos considered below) does not guarantee the satisfaction of basic needs and compensate for handicaps before conceding less urgent advantages to others, even if that means giving the handicapped special treatment at the expense of the normal and healthy.

Developed in this way, Rawls' model would take account of the fact that questions of social justice arise just because people are unequal in ways they can do very little to change and that only by attending to these inequalities can one be said to be giving their interests equal consideration. For their interests are not equal in the sense that every interest actually competing in a given situation is of equal weight, irrespective of how far each claimant's interests have already been attended to; they are equal, instead, in the sense that two men lacking similar conditions necessary to their well-being would, *prima facie*, have equally good claims to them.

This analysis throws some light on the paradoxical problems of compensatory welfare legislation on behalf of Negroes. A recent collection of essays[5] has drawn attention to the ambiguous implications of the notion of equality and, in particular, of the "equal protection" clause of the Fourteenth Amendment, for the desegregation and social integration of Negroes. Even liberal friends of the Negro have been known to argue, it seems, that the law should be color-blind, and that compensatory legislation on the Negro's behalf is discrimination in reverse. If (it is said) color is irrelevant to eligibility for jobs, housing, education, and social esteem, to make special provisions for the Negro as such would be to reinstate an irrelevant criterion, and so to treat equals unequally, or alternatively, to deny the human equality that it is so important to affirm. This argument disregards, however, a vital ambiguity. Negroes and whites are equal in the sense that their interests deserve equal consideration; they are painfully unequal in the sense that society imposes on the Negro special disabilities. So although black and white may equally need housing or education, the obstacles placed by society in the black man's way add extra weight to his claim to public assistance to meet these needs. Where society imposes handicaps, it can hardly be unjust for the state to compensate for them. Nor is it far-fetched to call this a way of providing equal protection for the interests of black and white. Where the interests of a group are subject to discriminatory social handicaps on the irrational ground of color, it is not irrational for the state to apply the same criterion in giving them protection on an appropriately more generous scale. Equal protection ought not to mean an equal allocation of the means of protection—for the protection must be commensurate with the threat or impediment.[6]

Finally, it is necessary to qualify the principle of equal consideration of interests in two respects, the first theoretical, the second practical.

The first corresponds to Rawls' qualification that "an inequality is allowed only if there is reason to believe that the practice with the inequality, or resulting in it, will work for the advantage of every party engaging in it."[7] The principle of equal consideration of interests provides for the satisfaction of interests in order of urgency, every individual's claim being otherwise equal. A departure from this principle could be defended by showing that it would increase the capacity to satisfy interests in general and that it would not weaken the claims of someone who, without the adoption of the variant practice, could reasonably claim satisfaction under the main principle. It may be expedient, but not just, that one man should starve that others might grow fat; but there is no injustice if, in allowing some to grow fat, we can reduce the number that would otherwise starve. In this way we take account of incentive arguments for distribution by desert, as well as of claims to special treatment to meet functional needs.

The second qualification applies to the practical application of the principle. I have argued that it prescribes that interests be satisfied in order of their urgency, men without food and clothes falling further short of some presupposed conception of well-being than men who have these things but lack guitars. But clearly,

this principle works as a practical guide for social policy only so long as there is a very wide measure of agreement on priorities. And there is such agreement in that range of interests we most commonly call "needs," those, in fact, from which most of my examples have been drawn. But it is not easy to see how a society that had solved the problem of providing for everyone's generally agreed needs could go much further in applying equal consideration of needs as a direct distributive principle.

Throughout this paper I have been relying on a conception of interests as conditions necessary to a way of life or to forms of activity that are endorsed as worthwhile, or (what probably amounts to the same thing) as conditions necessary to the process of making of oneself something worthy of respect.[8] Now, hermits and ascetics apart, we shall probably agree on the basic conditions necessary for any good life at all. Once given those preliminary conditions, however, we shall encounter very diverse opinions on the absolute eligibility of certain ways of life, on their relative worth, on the conditions necessary for them, and on the relative urgency of such conditions, as claims to our attention. This would make it very difficult indeed to put a schedule of interests into a socially acceptable order of priority. Furthermore, it is difficult to see how an authoritative and general allocation of resources according to interests could avoid laying down an official ruling on what ways of life were most eligible. Yet, as Charles Fried has argued,[9] the freedom to judge, even mistakenly, what is in one's own interests is itself an important human interest.

This may, however, point the way out of the dilemma. My main criticism of Rawls has been that, unless amended along the lines I have indicated, his postulate of equality is either unrealistic or restrictive, removing some of the most insistent problems of social justice from the scope of his principles, by presupposing a condition that is in the interests of justice to bring about. But in the conditions of affluence I am now considering, where basic interests are already being satisfied, and there is no further common ground on priorities, the postulate of equality would come much closer to reality. If there are equal opportunities to pursue one's interests, and freedom to determine what they are is recognized as itself an important interest, even at the risk of error, Rawls' principles of justice come into their own. Rawls lays it down that a practice is just if everyone is treated alike, unless a discrimination in favor of some is of advantage to everyone. We can now translate this into the language of equal interests: If all basic interests are already being satisfied and if there is no universally acknowledged order of priority as between further interests competing for satisfaction, then, given that the individual has a fundamental interest in determining what are his own interests, a practice would be just that gave all interests actually competing in a situation equal satisfaction, save insofar as an inequality made possible a greater degree of satisfaction without weakening claims that would be satisfied without it. On this interpretation, Rawls' original account of the criteria of a just practice turns out to be a special application, in conditions where all handicaps have already been remedied, of the principle of the equal consideration of interests.

NOTES

1. *Philosophy*, XL (1965), pp. 296–307.
2. J. C. Davies, *Human Nature in Politics*, New York, 1963, p. 45.
3. For example, Bernard Williams, "I omit here, as throughout the discussion, the clinical cases of people who are mad or mentally defective, who always constitute special exceptions to what is in general true of men." "The Idea of Equality," in P. Laslett and W. G. Runciman, eds., *Philosophy, Politics, and Society*, Oxford, 1962, p. 118.
4. John Rawls, "Justice as Fairness," reprinted in C. J. Friedrich and J. W. Chapman, eds., *Justice: Nomos VI*, New York, 1963, pp. 98–125.
5. R. L. Carter, D. Kenyon, Peter Marcuse, Loren Miller, *Equality*, New York, 1965.
6. G. Vlastos makes a similar point in connection with the right to security, "Justice and Equality," *Social Justice*, R. B. Brandt, ed., Englewood Cliffs, N.J.: Prentice-Hall, 1962. Reprinted in this volume.
7. "Justice as Fairness," op. cit., p. 135.
8. It is not necessary for my present purposes to discuss what could be good reasons for approving some ways of life, or forms of activity, or kinds of personality, and rejecting others. I ask the reader's assent only to the following propositions: that we do in fact make judgments of this kind, and that the notion of what is in a man's interest must ultimately be related to such a judgment, at any rate at the stage at which it is said that he is mistaking where his real interest lies. There may be sufficient consensus in a society for "interests" to function descriptively; but this is only because, at that level, the normative element is not in dispute and not therefore obtrusive.
9. Charles Fried, "Justice and Liberty," in *Justice Nomos VI*, op. cit.

JUSTICE AND EQUALITY
GREGORY VLASTOS

I

The close connection between justice and equality is manifest in both history and language. The great historic struggles for social justice have centered about some demand for equal rights: the struggle against slavery, political absolutism, economic exploitation, the disfranchisement of the lower and middle classes and the disfranchisement of women, colonialism, racial oppression. On the linguistic side let me mention a curiosity that will lead us into the thick of our problem. When Aristotle in Book V of the *Nicomachean Ethics* comes to grips with distributive justice, almost the first remark he has to make is that "justice is equality, as all men believe it to be, quite apart from any argument." And well they might if they are Greeks, for their ordinary word for equality, to *ison* or *isotes*, comes closer to being the right word for "justice" than does the word *dikaiosyne*, which we usually translate as "justice." Thus, when a man speaks Greek he will be likely to say "equality" and *mean* "justice." But it so happens that Aristotle, like Plato and others before him, believed firmly that a just distribution is in general an unequal one. And to say this, if "equal" is your word for "just," you would have to say that an "equal" distribution is an *unequal* one. A way had been found to hold this acrobatic linguistic posture by saying that in this connection *isotes* meant "geometrical equality," i.e., proportionality; hence the "equal" (just, fair) distribution to persons of unequal merit would have to be unequal. This tour de force must have provoked many an honest man at the time as much as it has enraged Professor Popper in ours. We may view it more dispassionately as classical testimony to the strength of the tie between equality and justice: even those who meant to break the conceptual link could not, or would not, break the verbal one. The meritarian view of justice paid reluctant homage to the equalitarian one by using the vocabulary of equality to assert the justice of inequality.

But when the equalitarian has drawn from this what comfort he may, he still has to face the fact that the expropriation of his word "equality" could be carried through so reputably and so successfully that its remote inheritance has made it possible for us to speak now in a perfectly matter of fact way of "equitable inequalities" or "inequitable equalities." This kind of success cannot be wholly due to the tactical skill of those who carried out the original maneuver; though one may envy the virtuosity with which Plato disposes of the whole notion of democratic equality in

a single sentence (or rather less, a participial clause) when he speaks of democracy as "distributing an odd sort of equality to equals and unequals." The democrats themselves would have been intellectually defenseless against that quip. Their faith in democracy had no deep roots in any concept of human equality; the *isonomia* (equality of law) on which they prided themselves was the club-privilege of those who had had the good judgment to pick their ancestors from free Athenian stock of the required purity of blood. But even if we could imagine a precocious humanitarian in or before Plato's time, founding the rights of the citizen on the rights of man, it is not clear that even he would be proof against Plato's criticism. For what Plato would like to know is whether his equalitarian opponent really means to universalize equality: would he, would anyone, wish to say that there are no just inequalities? That there are no rights in respect of which men are unequal?

One would think that this would be among the first questions that would occur to equalitarians, and would have had long since a clear and firm answer. Strange as it may seem, this has not happened. The question has been largely evaded. Let me give an example: Article I of the Declaration of Rights of Man and Citizen (enacted by the Constituent Assembly of the First French Republic in 1791) reads: "Men are born and remain free and equal in rights. Social distinctions can be based only upon public utility." Bentham takes the first sentence to mean that men are equal in *all* rights. One would like to think that this was a wilful misunderstanding. For it would be only too obvious to the drafters of the Declaration that those "social distinctions" of which they go on to speak would entail many inequalities of right. Thus the holder of a unique political office (say, the president of a republic) would not be equal in all rights to all other men or even to one other man: no other man would have equal right to this office, or to as high an office; and many would not have equal right to any political office, even if they had, as they would according to the republican constitution, equal right of eligibility to all offices. But if this is in the writers' minds, why don't they come out and say that men are born and remain equal in some rights, but are either not born or do not remain equal in a great many others? They act as though they were afraid to say the latter on this excessively public occasion, lest their public construe the admission of some unequal rights as out of harmony with the ringing commitment to human rights which is the keynote of the Declaration. What is this? Squeamishness? Confusion? Something of both? Or has it perhaps a sound foundation and, if so, in what? Plato's question is not answered. It is allowed to go by default.

There is here, as so often in the tradition of natural rights, a lack of definiteness which is exasperating to those who look for plain and consecutive thinking in moral philosophy. Coming back to this tradition fresh from the systems of Plato or Hobbes or Hume, with their clean, functional lines, one feels that whether or not the case for inequality has ever been proved, it has at least been made clear from both the aristocratic and the utilitarian side; while the case for equality, housed in the rambling and somewhat rundown mansion of natural rights, has fared so poorly that when one puts a question like the one I just raised, one can't be sure of what the answer is, or even that there is supposed to be one. And much the same is true of several other questions that remain after one has completely cut out one earlier source of confusion: the mythological prehistory of a supposed state of nature. Taking "natural rights" to mean simply *human* rights— that is to say, rights which are human not in the trivial sense that those who have them are men, but in the challenging sense that in order to have them they need only be men—one would still like to know:

(1) What is the range of these rights? The French Declaration states: "these rights are liberty, property, security, and resistance to oppression." The imprudent beginning—"these rights are" instead of Jefferson's more cautious, "among these rights are"—makes it look as though the four natural rights named here are meant to be all the rights there are. If so, what happened to the pursuit of happiness? Is that the same as liberty? As for property, this was not a natural right before Locke, and not always after him, e.g., not for Jefferson. And what of welfare rights? They are not mentioned in the French document, nor are they implied by "security."

(2) Can the doctrine of natural rights find a place for each of the following well-known maxims of distributive justice:

1. To each according to his *need*.
2. To each according to his *worth*.
3. To each according to his *merit*.
4. To each according to his *work*.

And we might add a fifth which does not seem to have worked its way to the same level of adage-like respectability, but has as good a claim as some of the others:

5. To each according to the *agreements* he has made.

By making judicious selections from this list one can "justicize" extreme inequalities of distribution. It is thus that Plato concludes that the man who can no longer work has lost his right to live, and Bentham that no just limits can be set to the terms on which labor can be bought, used, and used up. Hobbes, most frugal of moral philosophers, operates with just the last of these maxims; making the keeping of covenants the defining element of justice, he decimates civil liberties *more geometrico*. These premises were not, of course, the only ones from which such morally dismal results were reached by these clearheaded and upright men; but they were the controlling ones. If merit or work or agreement, or any combination of the three, are made the final principles of distributive justice, it will not be hard to find plausible collateral premises from which to get such results. What then should a natural rights philosopher do with these maxims? Must he regard them as fifth-columnists? Or can he keep them as members of his working team, useful, if subordinate, principles of his equalitarian justice? Can this be done without making concessions to inequality which will divide his allegiance to equality?

(3) Finally, are natural rights "absolute," i.e., are their claims unexceptionable? If I have a natural right to a given benefit does it follow that I ought to be granted that benefit in all possible circumstances no matter how my other rights or those of others might be affected? Is this the meaning of the well-known statements

that natural rights are "inalienable" and "imprescriptible"?

I believe that all these questions admit of reasonable answers which, when worked out fully, would amount to a revised theory of natural rights or, what is the same thing, a theory of human rights: I shall use the two expressions interchangeably. Progress has been made in this direction in recent years in a number of important essays. I shall borrow freely results reached by various contributors to this work, though without taking time to make explicit acknowledgments or register specific disagreements.

Let me begin with the answer to the third of the questions I raised. Are human rights absolute? All of these writers would say, "No." I am convinced that in this they are right, and am even prepared to add that neither is there anything explicitly contrary to this in that branch of the classical theory which is of greatest interest to us today: in Locke, for example. Locke has indeed been understood to mean that natural rights are absolute. But nowhere does Locke *say* this. Contrariwise he believes many things which imply the opposite. For example, he would certainly approve of imprisonment as a punishment for crime; and we hear him recommending that beggars be detained in houses of correction or impressed in the navy. Such constraints he would have to reckon justified exceptions to that freedom of movement which all persons claim in virtue of their natural right to liberty. So too he would have to think of the death penalty for convicted criminals, or of a military order which would bring death to many of those obeying it, as justified exceptions to some men's natural right to life. Even the right to property—indeed, that special form of it which is upheld more zealously than any other right in the *Second Treatise*, one's right not to be deprived of property without consent—could not be unconditional; Locke would have to concede that it should be over-ruled, e.g., in a famine when stores of hoarded food are requisitioned by public authority. We would, therefore, improve the consistency of Locke's theory if we understood him to mean that natural rights are subject to justified exceptions. In any case, I shall adhere to his view here and, borrowing from current usage, shall speak of human rights as "prima facie" rights to mean that

the claims of any of them may be over-ruled in special circumstances. Can one say this without giving away the radical difference which the traditional doctrine fixed between natural rights and all others? To this the answer would be that, though in this respect all rights are alike, the vital difference remains untouched: one need only be a man to have *prima facie* rights to life, liberty, welfare, and the like; but to be a man is not all one needs to have a *prima facie* right to the house he happens to own or the job he happens to hold. As for the "inalienability" and "imprescriptibility" of natural rights, we may understand them with this proviso to mean exactly what they say: that no man can alienate (i.e., sign away, transfer by contract) a *prima facie* natural right, his own or anyone else's; and that no people can lose *prima facie* natural rights by prescription, e.g., in virtue of the time-hallowed possession of despotic power over them by a royal dynasty.

II

Let me begin with the first on my list of maxims of distributive justice: "To each according to his need." Since needs are often unequal, this looks like a precept of unequal distribution. But this is wrong. It is in fact *the most perfect form of equal distribution*. To explain this let me take one of the best established rights in the natural law tradition: the right to the security of life and person. Believing that this is an equal right, what do we feel this means in cases of special need?

Suppose, for instance, New Yorker X gets a note from Murder, Inc., that looks like business. To allocate several policemen and plainclothesmen to guard him over the next few weeks at a cost a hundred times greater than the per capita cost of security services to other citizens during the same period, is surely *not* to make an exception to the equal distribution required by the equal right of all citizens to the security of their life and person; it is not done on the assumption that X has a greater right to security or a right to greater security. If the visitor from Mars drew this conclusion from the behavior of the police, he would be told that he was just mistaken. The greater allocation of community resources in X's favor, we would have to explain, is made precisely *because* X's security rights are equal to those of other people in New York. This means that X is entitled to the same level of police-made security as is maintained for other New Yorkers. Hence in these special circumstances, where his security level would drop to zero without extra support, he should be given this to bring his security level nearer the normal. I say "nearer," not "up to" the normal, because I am talking of New York as of 1961. If I were thinking of New York with an ideal municipal government, ideally supplied with police resources, I *would* say "up to the normal," because that is what equality of right would ideally mean. But as things are, perhaps the best that can be done for X without disrupting the general level of security maintained for all the other New Yorkers is to decrease his chances of being bumped off in a given week to, say, one to ten thousand, while those of ordinary citizens, with ordinary protection are, say, one to ten million—no small difference. Now if New York were more affluent, it would be able to buy more equality of security for its citizens (as well as more security): by getting more, and perhaps also better paid, policemen, it would be able to close the gap between security maintained for people in ordinary circumstances and that supplied in cases of special need, like that of X in his present jam. Here we stumble on something of considerable interest: that approximation to the goal of completely equal security benefits for all citizens is a function of two variables: first, and quite obviously, of the pattern of distribution of the resources; second, and less obviously, of their size. If the distributable resources are so meager that they are all used up to maintain a general level barely sufficient for ordinary needs, their reallocation to meet exceptional need will look too much like robbing Peter to pay Paul. In such conditions there is likely to be little, if any, provision for extremity of need and, what is more, the failure to meet the extremity will not be felt as a social injustice but as a calamity of fate. And since humanity has lived most of its life under conditions of general indigence, we can understand why it has been so slow to connect provision for special need with the notion of justice, and has so often made it a mat-

ter of charity; and why "to each according to his need" did not become popularized as a precept of justice until the first giant increase in the productive resources, and then only by men like Blanc and Marx, who projected an image of a super-affluent, machine-run society on the grid of an austerely equalitarian conception of justice.

So we can see why distribution according to personal need, far from conflicting with the equality of distribution required by a human right, is so linked with its very meaning that under ideal conditions equality of right would coincide with distribution according to personal need. Our visitor misunderstood the sudden mobilization of New York policemen in favor of Mr. X, because he failed to understand that it is benefits to persons, not allocation of resources as such, that are meant to be made equal; for then he would have seen at once that unequal distribution of resources would be required to equalize benefits in cases of unequal need. But if he saw this he might then ask, "But why do you want this sort of equality?" My answer would have to be: Because the human worth of all persons is equal, however unequal may be their merit. To the explanation of this proposition I shall devote the balance of this Section.

By "merit" I shall refer throughout this essay to all the kinds of valuable qualities or performances in respect of which persons may be graded. The concept will not be restricted to moral actions or dispositions. Thus wit, grace of manner, and technical skill count as meritorious qualities fully as much as sincerity, generosity, or courage. Any valuable human characteristic, or cluster of characteristics, will qualify, provided only it is "acquired," i.e., represents what its possessor has himself made of his natural endowments and environmental opportunities. Given the immense variety of individual differences, it will be commonly the case that of any two persons either may excel the other in respect of different kinds or sub-kinds of merit. Thus if A and B are both clever and brave men, A may be much the cleverer as a business man, B as a literary critic, and A may excel in physical, B in moral, courage. It should be clear from just this that to speak of "a person's merit" will be strictly senseless except insofar as this is an elliptical way of referring to that person's merits, i.e., to those specifiable qualities or activities in which he rates well. So if there is a value attaching to the person himself as an integral and unique individual, *this* value will not fall under merit or be reducible to it. For it is of the essence of merit, as here defined, to be a grading concept; and there is no way of grading individuals as such. We can only grade them with respect to their qualities, hence only by abstracting from their individuality. If *A* is valued for some meritorious quality, *m*, his individuality does not enter into the valuation. As an individual he is then dispensable; his place could be taken without loss of value by any other individual with as good an *m*-rating. Nor would matters change by multiplying and diversifying the meritorious qualities with which *A* is endowed. No matter how enviable a package of well-rounded excellence *A* may represent, it would still follow that, if he is valued only for his merit, he is not being valued as an individual. To be sure individuals *may* be valued only for their merits. This happens all too commonly. *A* might be valued in just this way by *P*, the president of his company, for whom *A*, highly successful vice-president in charge of sales, amusing dinner-guest, and fine asset to the golf club, is simply high-grade equipment in various complexes of social machinery which *P* controls or patronizes. On the other hand, it is possible that, much as *P* prizes this conjunct of qualities (*M*), he values *A* also as an individual. *A* may be his son, and he may be genuinely fond of him. If so, his affection will be for *A*, not for his *M*-qualities. The latter *P* approves, admires, takes pride in, and the like. But his affection and good will are for *A*, and *not only because*, or *insofar as*, *A* has the *M*-qualities. For *P* may be equally fond of another son who rates well below *A* in *P*'s scoring system. Moreover, *P*'s affection for *A*, as distinct from his approval or admiration of him, need not fluctuate with the ups and downs in *A*'s achievements. Perhaps *A* had some bad years after graduating from college, and it looked then as though his brilliant gifts would be wasted. It does not follow that *P*'s love for *A* then lapsed or even ebbed. Constancy of affection in the face of variations of merit is one of the surest tests of whether or not a parent does love a child. If he feels fond of it only

when it performs well, and turns coldly indifferent or hostile when its achievements slump, then his feeling for the child can scarcely be called *love*. There are many relations in which one's liking or esteem for a person are strictly conditional on his measuring up to certain standards. But convincing evidence that the relation is of this type is no evidence that the relation is one of parental love or any other kind of love. It does nothing to show that one has this feeling, or any feeling, for an *individual*, rather than for a place-holder of qualities one likes to see instantiated by somebody or other close about one.

Now if this concept of value attaching to a person's individual existence, over and above his merit—"individual worth," let me call it— were applicable *only* in relations of personal love, it would be irrelevant for the analysis of justice. To serve our purpose its range of application must be coextensive with that of justice. It must hold in all human relations, including (or rather, especially in) the most impersonal of all, those to total strangers, fellow-citizens or fellow-men. I must show that the concept of individual worth does meet this condition.

Consider its role in our political community, taking the prescriptions of our laws for the treatment of persons as the index to our valuations. For merit (among other reasons) persons may be appointed or elected to public office or given employment by state agencies. For demerit they may lose licences, jobs, offices; they may be fined, jailed, or even put to death. But in a large variety of law-regulated actions directed to individuals, either by private persons or by organs of the state, the question of merit and demerit does not arise. The "equal protection of the laws" is due to persons not to meritorious ones, or to them in some degree above others. So too for the right to vote. One does not have it for being intelligent and public-spirited, or lose it for being lazy, ignorant, or viciously selfish. One is entitled to exercise it as long as, having registered, one manages to keep out of jail. This kind of arrangement would look like whimsy or worse, like sheer immoralism, if the only values recognized in our political community were those of merit. For obviously there is nothing compulsory about our political system; we could certainly devise, if we so wished, workable alternatives which would condition fundamental rights on certain kinds of merit. For example, we might have three categories of citizenship. The top one might be for those who meet high educational qualifications and give definite evidence of responsible civic interest, e.g., by active participation in political functions, tenure of public office, record of leadership in civic organizations and support to them, and the like. People in this *A*-category might have multiple votes in all elections and exclusive eligibility for the more important political offices; they might also be entitled to a higher level of protection by the police and to a variety of other privileges and immunities. At the other end there would be a *C*-category, disfranchised and legally underprivileged, for those who do not meet some lower educational test or have had a record of law-infraction or have been on the relief rolls for over three months. In between would be the *B*'s with ordinary suffrage and intermediate legal status.

This "*M*-system" would be more complicated and cumbersome than ours. But something like it could certainly be made to work if we were enamoured of its peculiar scheme of values. Putting aside the question of efficiency, it gives us a picture of a community whose political valuations, conceived entirely in terms of merit, would never be grounded on individual worth, so that this notion would there be politically useless. For us, on the other hand, it is indispensable. We have to appeal to it when we try to make sense of the fact that our legal system accords to all citizens an identical status, carrying with it rights such as the *M*-system reserves to the *B*'s or the *A*'s, and some of which (like suffrage or freedom of speech) have been denied even to the nobility in some caste-systems of the past. This last comparison is worth pressing: it brings out the illuminating fact that in one fundamental respect our society is much more like a caste society (with a *unique* caste) than like the *M*-system. The latter has no place for a rank of dignity which descends on an individual by the purely existential circumstance (the "accident") of birth and remains his unalterably for life. To reproduce this feature of our system we would have to look not only to caste-societies, but to extremely rigid ones, since most of them make some provision for elevation in rank for rare merit or degradation for extreme demerit. In our legal system no such thing can happen: even a criminal may not be sentenced to second-class citizenship. And the fact that first-class citizenship, having been made common, is no longer a mark of distinction does not trivialize the privileges it entails. It is the simple truth, not declamation, to speak of it, as I have done, as a "rank of dignity" in some ways comparable to that enjoyed by hereditary nobilities of the past. To see this one need only think of the position of groups in our society who have been cheated out of this status by the subversion of their constitutional rights. The difference in social position between Negroes and whites described in Dollard's classic is not smaller than that between, say, bourgeoisie and aristocracy in the *ancien régime* of France. It might well be greater.

Consider finally the role of the same value in the moral community. Here differences of merit are so conspicuous and pervasive that we might even be tempted to *define* the moral response to a person in terms of moral approval or disapproval of his acts or disposition, i.e., in terms of the response to his moral merit. But there are many kinds of moral response for which a person's merit is as irrelevant as is that of New Yorker *X* when he appeals to the police for help. If I see someone in danger of drowning I will not need to satisfy myself about his moral character before going to his aid. I owe assistance to any man in such circumstances, not merely to good men. Nor is it only in rare and exceptional cases, as this example might suggest, that my obligations to others are independent of their moral merit. To be sincere, reliable, fair, kind, tolerant, unintrusive, modest in my relations with my fellows is not due them because they have made brilliant or even passing moral grades, but simply because they happen to be fellow-members of the moral community. It is not necessary to add, "members in good standing." The moral community is not a club from which members may be dropped for delinquency. Our morality does not provide for moral outcasts or halfcastes. It does provide for punishment. But this takes place *within* the moral community and under its rules. It is for this reason that, for example, one has no right to be cruel to a cruel person. His offense against the moral law has not put him outside the law. He is still protected by its prohibition of cruelty—as much so as are kind persons. The pain inflicted on him as punishment for his offense does not close out the reserve of good will on the part of all others which is his birthright as a human being; it is a limited withdrawal from it. Capital punishment, if we believe in it, is no exception. The fact that a man has been condemned to death does not license his jailors to beat him or virtuous citizens to lynch him.

Here, then, as in the single-status political community, we acknowledge personal rights which are not proportioned to merit and could not be justified by merit. Their only justification could be the value which persons have simply because they are persons: their "intrinsic value as individual human beings," as Frankena calls it; the "infinite value" or the "sacredness" of their individuality, as others have called it. I shall speak of it as "individual human worth"; or "human worth," for short. What these expressions stand for is also expressed by saying that men are "ends in themselves." This latter concept is Kant's. Some of the kinks in his formulation of it can be straightened out by explaining it as follows: Everything other than a person can only have value *for* a person. This applies not only to physical objects, natural or manmade, which have only instrumental value, but also to those products of the human spirit which have also intrinsic, no less than extrinsic, value: an epic poem, a scientific theory, a legal system, a moral disposition. Even such things as these will have value only because they can be (a) experienced or felt to be valuable by human beings and (b) chosen by them from competing alternatives. Thus of everything without exception it will be true to say: if *x* is valuable and is not a person, then *x* will have value for some individual other than itself. Hence even a musical composition or a courageous deed, valued for their own sake, as "ends" not as means to anything else, will still fall into an entirely different category from that of the *valuers*, who do not need to be valued as "ends" by someone else in order to have value. In just this sense persons, and only persons, are "ends in themselves."

The two factors in terms of which I have described the value of the valuer—the capacities answering to (a) and (b) above—may not be exhaustive. But their conjunction offers a translation of "individual human worth" whose usefulness for working purposes will speak for itself. To (a) I might refer as "happiness," if I could use this term as Plato and Aristotle used *eudaimonia*, i.e., without the exclusively hedonistic connotations which have since been clamped on it. It will be less misleading to use "well-being" or "welfare" for what I intend here; that is, the enjoyment of value in all the forms in which it can be experienced by human beings. To (b) I shall refer as "freedom," bringing under this term not only conscious choices and deliberate decisions but also those subtler modulations and more spontaneous expressions of individual preference which could scarcely be called "choices" or "decisions" without some forcing of language. So understood, a person's well-being and freedom are aspects of his individual existence as unique and unrepeatable as is that existence itself: If *A* and *B* are listening to the same symphony with similar tastes and dispositions, we may speak of their enjoying the "same" good, or having the "same" enjoyment, and say that each has made the "same" choice for this way of spending his time and money. But here "same" will mean no more than "very similar"; the two enjoyments and choices, occurring in the consciousness of *A* and *B* respectively, are absolutely unique. So in translating "*A*'s human worth" into "the worth of *A*'s well-being and freedom" we are certainly meeting the condition that the former expression is to stand for whatever it is about *A* which, unlike his merit, has *individual* worth.

We are also meeting another condition: that the equality of human worth be justification, or ground, of equal human rights. I can best bring this out by reverting to the visitor from Mars who had asked a little earlier why we want equalization of security benefits. Let us conjure up circumstances in which his question would spring, not from idle curiosity, but from a strong conviction that this, or any other, right entailing such undiscriminating equality of benefits, would be entirely *un*reasonable. Suppose then that he hails from a strict meritarian community, which maintains the *M* system in its political life and analogous patterns in other associations. And to make things simpler, let us also suppose that he is shown nothing in New York or elsewhere that is out of line with our formal professions of equality, so that he imagines us purer, more strenuous, equalitarians than we happen to be. The pattern of valuation he ascribes to us then seems to him fantastically topsy-turvy. He can hardly bring himself to believe that rational human beings should want equal personal rights, legal and moral, for their "riff-raff" and their elites. Yet neither can he explain away our conduct as pure automatism, a mere fugue of social habit. "These people, or some of them," he will be saying to himself, "must have some reasons for this incredible code. What could these be?" If we volunteered an answer couched in terms of human worth, he might find it hard to understand us. Such an answer, unglossed, would convey to him no more than that we recognize something which is highly and equally valuable in all persons, but has nothing to do with their merit, and constitutes the ground of their equal rights. But this might start him hunting—snark-hunting—for some special quality named by "human worth" as honesty is named by "honesty" and kindness by "kindness," wondering all the while how it could have happened that he and all his tribe have had no inkling of it, if all of them have always had it.

But now suppose that we avail ourselves of the aforesaid translation. We could then tell him: "To understand our code you should take into account how very different from yours is our own estimate of the relative worth of the welfare and freedom of different individuals. We agree with you that not all persons are capable of experiencing the same values. But there is a wide variety of cases in which persons are capable of this. Thus, to take a perfectly clear case, no matter how *A* and *B* might differ in taste and style of life, they would both crave relief from acute physical pain. In that case we would put the same value on giving this to either of them, regardless of the fact that *A* might be a talented, brilliantly successful person, *B* 'a mere nobody.' On this we would disagree sharply. You would weigh the welfare of members of the elite more highly than that of 'riff-raff,' as you call them. We would not. If

A were a statesman, and giving him relief from pain enabled him to conclude an agreement that would benefit millions, while *B*, an unskilled laborer, was himself the sole beneficiary of the like relief, we would, of course, agree that the *instrumental* value of the two experiences would be vastly different—but not their *intrinsic* value. In all cases where human beings are capable of enjoying the same goods, we feel that the intrinsic value of their enjoyment is the same. In just this sense we hold that (1) *one man's well-being is as valuable as any other's.* And there is a parallel difference in our feeling for freedom. You value it only when exercised by good persons for good ends. We put no such strings on its value. We feel that choosing for oneself what one will do, believe, approve, say, see, read, worship, has its own intrinsic value, the same for all persons, and quite independently of the value of the things they happen to choose. Naturally, we hope that all of them will make the best possible use of their freedom of choice. But we value their exercise of that freedom, regardless of the outcome; and we value it equally for all. For us (2) *one man's freedom is as valuable as any other's.*"

This sort of explanation, I submit, would put him in a position to resolve his dilemma. For just suppose that, taking this homily at face-value, he came to think of us as believing (1) and (2). No matter how unreasonable he might think of us he would feel it entirely reasonable that, since we do believe in equal *value* of human well-being and freedom, we should also believe in the *prima facie* equality of men's *right* to well-being and to freedom. He would see the former as a good reason for the latter; or, more formally, he could think of (1) and (2) respectively as the crucial premises in justification arguments whose respective conclusions would be: (3) One man's (*prima facie*) right to well-being is equal to that of any other, and (4) One man's (*prima facie*) right to freedom is equal to that of any other. Then, given (4), he could see how this would serve as the basis for a great variety of rights to specific kinds of freedom: freedom of movement, of association, of suffrage, of speech, of thought, of worship, of choice of employment, and the like. For each of these can be regarded as simply a specification of the general right to freedom, and would thus be covered by the justification of the latter. Moreover, given (3), he could see in it the basis for various welfare-rights, such as the right to education, medical care, work under decent conditions, relief in periods of unemployment, leisure, housing, etc. Thus to give him (1) and (2) as justification for (3) and (4) would be to give him a basis for every one of the rights which are mentioned in the most complete of currently authoritative declarations of human rights, that passed by the Assembly of the United Nations in 1948. Hence to tell him that we believe in the equal worth of individual freedom and happiness would be to answer, in terms he can understand, his question, "What is your reason for your equalitarian code?"

Nowhere in this defense of the translation of "equal human worth" into "equal worth of human well-being and freedom" have I claimed that the former can be *reduced* to the latter. I offered individual well-being and freedom simply as two things which do satisfy the conditions defined by individual human worth. Are there others? For the purposes of this essay this may be left an open question. For if there are, they would provide, at most, additional grounds for human rights. The ones I have specified are grounds enough. They are all I need for the analysis of equalitarian justice as, I trust, will appear directly.

III

I offer the following definition: An action is *just* if, and only if, it is prescribed exclusively by regard for the rights of all whom it affects substantially. This definition could be discussed at length. I shall make, and with the utmost brevity, just two general points by way of elucidation:

(a) The standard cases are clearly covered, e.g., that of the judge adjudicating a dispute. To perform justly this strictly judicial function he must (i) seek to determine with scrupulous care what, in these circumstances, are the rights of the litigants and of others, if any, who are substantially affected, and then (ii) render a verdict determined by regard for those rights and by nothing else. He may be unjust by failing at (i) through ignorance, carelessness, impatience,

laziness, addiction to stereotypes of race or class, and the like; at (ii) by any sort of partiality, even if this is due to nothing so low as venality or prejudice, but perhaps even to humane and generous sentiments. Thus, if in the case before him an honest and upright man has trespassed on the rights of a well-known bully (perhaps only to protect one of the latter's victims), the judge will have no choice but to find for the bully: he must be "blind" to anything but the relevant rights when making up his verdict. This is the commonsense view of the matter, and it accords perfectly with what follows from the definition.

(b) The definition does not flout common usage by making "just" *interchangeable* with "right," and "unjust" with "wrong." Whenever the question of regard, or disregard, for substantially affected rights does not arise, the question of justice, or injustice, does not arise. We see a man wasting his property and talents in dissolute living. It would not occur to us to think of his conduct as unjust, unless we see it as having a substantial effect on somebody's rights, say, those of dependents: it is unfair or unjust *to* them. Again, whenever one is in no position to govern one's action by regard for rights, the question of justice, or injustice, does not arise. Two strangers are in immediate danger of drowning off the dock on which I stand. I am the only one present, and the best I can do is to save one while the other drowns. Each has a right to my help, but I cannot give it to both. Hence regard for rights does not prescribe what I am to do, and neither "just" nor "unjust" will apply: I am not unjust to the one who drowns, nor just to the one I save.

A major feature of my definition of "just" is that it makes the answer to "Is *x* just?" (where *x* is any action, decision, etc.) strictly dependent on the answer to another question: "What are the rights of those who are substantially affected by *x*?" The definition cannot, and does not pretend that it can, give the slightest help in answering the latter question, with but one exception: it does tell us that the substantially affected rights, whatever they may be, should all be impartially respected. Thus it does disclose one right, though a purely *formal* one: the right to have one's *other* rights respected as impartially as those of any other interested party.

But what are these other rights? Are they equal or unequal? On this the definition is silent. It is thus completely neutral in the controversy between meritarians and equalitarians, and should prove equally acceptable to either party. Its neutralism should not be held against it. The words "just" and "unjust" are not the private property of the equalitarians; they may be used as conscientiously by those who reject, as by those who share, their special view of justice. We are not compelled to provide for this in our definitions; but there are obvious advantages in doing so. For we thereby offer our opponents common ground on which they too may stand while making their case. We allow Aristotle, for instance, to claim, without misusing language, that slavery and the disfranchisement of manual workers are just institutions. It allows us to rebut his claim, not by impugning its linguistic propriety, but by explaining that we affirm what his claim implicitly denies: that all human beings have the right to personal and political freedom.

It should now be plain to the reader why I have been so heavily preoccupied with the question of human rights throughout the first half of this essay, and content to write most of Section II without even mentioning the word "justice." I have done so precisely because my purpose in this essay is not to discuss justice in general, but equalitarian justice. As should now be obvious, had I tried to reason from the concept of justice to that of equalitarian justice I would have been reasoning in a circle. I did allude at the start to important historical and linguistic ties of justice with equality. But these, while perfectly relevant, are obviously not conclusive. They would be dismissed by a determined and clear-headed opponent, like Plato, as mere evidences of a widespread *mis*conception of justice. I am not suggesting that we should yield him this point or that, conversely, there is any good reason to think that he would come around to our view if we presented him with the argument of Section II (or a stronger one to the same effect). My contention is rather that we would be misrepresenting our view of justice if we were to give him the idea that it is susceptible of proof by that kind of historical and linguistic evidence. To explain our position to him so that, quite apart from his coming to

agree with it, he would at least have the chance to *understand* it, one thing would matter above all: to show that we believe in human rights, and why.

That is why the weight of the argument in the preceding Section II fell so heavily on the notion of human worth, understood to mean nothing less than the equal worth of the happiness and freedom of all persons. Given this, we have equal welfare-rights and freedom-rights; and this puts us in a position to cover the full range of human rights which the natural rights tradition left so perplexingly indeterminate. I did not stop to argue for this contention when I made it in Section II, and will not do so now, for I have more important business ahead of me. I have not forgotten the task I set myself at the close of Section I, and wish to proceed to it as soon as possible. But before proceeding to this in Section IV, there is a major item of still unfinished business that must be attended to. It concerns a feature of equalitarian justice that must be made fully explicit, if only because it will play an important role in the argument that is to follow in Section IV.

Consider the following very simple rule of just distribution: *If* A *and* B *have sole and equal right to* x, *they have a joint right to the whole of* x. This rule (R_1) would be normally taken as axiomatic. Thus if A and B had sole and equal right to an estate, no executor bent on making a just settlement of their claims would think of giving away a part of the estate to some other person, C. But why not? Can it be shown that the consequent of R_1 does follow from its antecedent? It can. *Only* A *and* B *have any right to* x entails *anyone other than* A *or* B *has no right to* x and hence C *has no right to* x. Hence if some part of *x* were distributed to *C*, it would be going to someone who has no right to it. Such a distribution would not conform to our definition of "just": it would not be the one prescribed by impartial regard for the relevant rights. Now what if the executor withheld some part of *x* from *A* or *B*, without giving it to a third party? But how could that happen? Did he perhaps abandon it in a deserted place? He has no right to do that with any property unless it happens to be *his own*. So if he did such a foolish thing with a part of the estate, he has acted as though *he* is the third party to whom this has been distributed, and most unjustly, since he has no right to it. But what if he actually destroyed a part, perhaps throwing it overboard in a strong-box stuffed with valuables to sink to the bottom of the ocean? This too he would have no right to do, unless this part of the property were already *his*. So this action would be as unjust as before and for the same reason. And there is no other possibility, unless a part of the estate were lost, or destroyed through some natural calamity, in which case the question of its being *withheld* by the executor from A and B would not arise. If he does withhold it, he would have to give it to some third party or else act as though he had already given it to himself, hence in either case to someone who has no right to x, hence unjustly. To act justly he must give the whole of it to those who have sole right to it.

Now let us think of an allied case. A man leaves a will containing many marks of his affection for his two sons and sole heirs and of his wish to benefit them. The terms of his will provide, *inter alia*, that a large industrial property is to be used, at the direction of trustees, to produce income for the sole and equal benefit of D and E, the income to be divided annually between them. Here the annual distribution of the income will fall directly under R_1. But another decision, in which D and E have as big a stake, will not: how the property is to be used to yield the desired income. Let L and M be the only known feasible dispositions of the property for this purpose between which the trustees must decide at a given time: each, let us say, would involve a five-year commitment, but L would assure the estate twice the income, security, etc. being the same. L is obviously a windfall for the estate, and the trustees are not likely to waste a second thought on M as a possibly just decision in the circumstances. Why not? Why is it that in fairness to D and E they *should* choose L? Not in virtue of R_1, since that does not apply here: L is not a whole of which M is a part. What the trustees must be invoking (or would be, if they were thinking out the basis of their decision) is an analogue to R_1, covering cases such as this, where the right is not to an already existing object but to a future benefit which may be secured at any one of several possible levels: *if* D *and* E *have sole and*

equal right to benefit from x, *they have a joint right to the benefit at the highest level at which it may be secured*. If we were asked to justify this rule (R_2), how would we go about it? If the trustees' reason for preferring M to L were to benefit a third party, C, the reasoning would be the same as before: since only D and E have the right to benefit from x, C has no such right; hence M cannot be the disposition prescribed by regard for the relevant rights. But what if the trustees were to prefer M, without aiming to benefit a third party? This possibility would be analogous to the case above in which R_1 was violated by the wilful loss or destruction of part of x. For a preference for M would be fully as injurious to D and E, and as unjust to them, as if the trustees had voted for L with the diabolical rider that half the annual income during the next five years was to be withheld from D and E and destroyed. The loss to D and E would be exactly the same, and the injustice would be the same: the trustees might have the right to forgo a benefit to *themselves* equivalent to the difference between L and M, but only if *they* had the right to this benefit in the first place. In choosing M over L they would be acting as though they did have this right, hence in clear violation of D's and E's *sole* right.

Now the validity of R_2 is obviously unaffected by the number of those who have sole and equal right to a benefit. It would hold for any number; hence for the whole of humanity, or any lesser part of it. Consider then the total benefit derivable by humanity from men's use of what we may call "the means of well-being," i.e., of their own bodies and minds and of the resources of the natural universe. Since men have an equal right to well-being (apart from special property-rights, and the like, with which we are not now concerned), they have an equal right to the means of well-being. And the right of humanity to these means is exclusive. We are, therefore, entitled to assert that *men have sole and equal right to benefit from the means of well-being*. From this we may conclude, in conformity with R_2 that *men are jointly entitled to this benefit at the highest level at which it may be secured*.

This conclusion affects importantly the concept of equalitarian justice. It implies that the fundamental and distinctive idea in its notion of just distribution is (i) not equal distribution of benefits, but (ii) their equal distribution at the highest obtainable level. (i) has already been argued for in Frankena's essay when he considered, and rejected, Hourani's attractive formula, "Justice is equality, evident or disguised," as an over-simplification. But on Frankena's view neither can (ii) constitute the needed corrective. It is an obligation of beneficence, not of justice, he argues, "to promote the greatest possible good." He writes: "even if we allow . . . that society has an obligation to be beneficent, then we must insist that such beneficence, at least if it exceeds a certain minimum, is no part of social justice as such." Now there is no difference of opinion between us as to the importance of distinguishing sharply the concept of beneficence (or of benevolence) from that of equalitarian justice. But I submit that this can be done perfectly by adhering to the concept of equalitarian justice I have given here, and is in no way imperilled by my thesis here at (ii). To go back to the definition of "just" at the start: this leaves plenty of scope for acts which might be beneficent but *un*just, as, e.g., when *A* defrauds *B* to help *C*; or beneficent and *non*-just (neither just nor unjust: "just" does not apply), as when *A* helps one needy person, disregarding the claim of millions of others for the simple reason that he is in no position to help more than one out of all these millions. Conversely, neither would it follow from my theory of equalitarian justice that every just act, decision, practice, etc., will be beneficent. A large number will be non-beneficent (neither beneficent nor maleficent; "beneficent" will not apply): the repayment of debts, the rendering of ordinary judicial verdicts, or the enforcement of punishments. So *equalitarian justice* and *beneficence* will have different extensions, and their meanings will be as different as is that of *justice* on the present definition from that of *beneficence* on the usual view. Hence the concepts are entirely distinct, both intensionally and extensionally. But distinct concepts may, of course, overlap. And this is precisely what I maintain in the present case: (ii) above certainly falls under beneficence; but that, of itself, is no reason whatever why it *may* not *also* fall under equalitarian justice. That it does is what the foregoing argument for the validity of R_2 and its ap-

plicability to human rights, was designed to show.

One way of stating the thesis of that argument would be that equalitarian justice has a direct stake not only in equalizing the distribution of those goods whose enjoyment constitutes well-being, but also in promoting their creation. That it would have an indirect stake in the latter even if it were concerned *only* with equalizing their distribution could be argued independently by an obvious generalization of the point I made at the start of Section II, where I argued that a more affluent society could "buy more equality." The reasoning for and from R_2 provides a stronger and more general argument that *given any two levels of the production of good known to be possible in given circumstances, then*, other things being equal, *the higher should be preferred on grounds of justice.* "Goods" here, as throughout this essay, is a general expression for a class of which economic goods would be a sub-class. We may thus use an economic test-case of the underlined proposition: Suppose that the supreme policy-maker of the *N*'s (whose economy resembles closely that of the U.S.A.) had to choose between two policies, P(*L*) and P(*M*), knowing that (a) the effect of P(*M*) would be to maintain throughout the next five years the current rate of annual increase of the gross national product (which is, say, 2.5 per cent), while that of P(*L*) would *double* that rate; (b) the pattern of distribution of the national income would remain the same; (c) the greater wealth produced under P(*L*) would not be offset by aggravation of the risk of war, cultural deterioration, corruption of morals, or of any other significant evil. (c) is, of course, a strong restriction; but, like (b), it is built into the hypothesis to insure that the *only* appreciable difference between the two policies would be in the lesser, or fuller, utilization and expansion of the economic resources of the nation. This, and the artificiality of the whole model, by no means trivializes the contention that in such circumstances equalitarian justice would leave the policy-maker no choice but P(*L*). To say that beneficence (or benevolence) would leave him no other choice *would* be trivial: no one would care to dispute this. But the same thing said for equalitarian justice can be, and is being, disputed. This asserts that the N's have *rights* in this matter which the policy-maker would violate if he were to choose P(M)—as much so as the trustees in the example would violate the rights of D and E if they chose M. That the rights of the N's, unlike those of D and E, are moral, not legal, is immaterial: *only* the moral justice of the decision is here in view. The moral rights in question are those of the N's to well-being, hence to the means of well-being: to anything which would enrich their life, save it from pain, disease, drudgery, emptiness, ugliness. Given (a) in the hypothesis, an enormously larger quantity of such means would be made available to the N's under P(L) in the course of the five-year period; and given (b) their distribution would be no more unequal than that of the smaller volume of goods produced under P(M). Hence the N's have jointly a right to P(L). They have this for just the reasons which justify the inference from the antecedent of R_2 to its consequent. The crux of the inference is that since the N's, and only they, have a right to the benefits obtainable under either alternative, they have a right to that alternative which produces the greater benefit. Only (and at most) if the policy-maker had *himself* the right to the aggregate benefit represented by the difference between P(L) and P(M) would he have the right to frustrate the realization of that benefit. But he does not have that right. So if he were to choose P(M) he would violate the right of those who do. That is why that decision would be unjust.

Two more points:

(A) That not equality as such, but equality at the highest possible level, is the requirement of equalitarian justice may be argued as strongly in the case of the right to freedom. Thus if a legislature had before it two bills, B(L) and B(M), such that B(L) would provide for greater personal freedom than would B(M), then, other things remaining equal, they would be voting unjustly if they voted for the second: they would be violating the human right to freedom of those affected by the legislation. *A* vote for B(M) would be tantamount to a vote for the needless *restriction* of freedom. And since *freedom* is a personal (or individual) right, to equalize its restriction would be to aggravate, not to alleviate, its injustice. Would any of us feel that no injustice was suffered by Soviet citizens by the suppression of *Doctor Zhivago* if we were reliably informed that no one, not even Khrushchev, was exempted, and that the censors themselves had been foreign mercenaries?

(B) The conjunction of equalitarian justice and benevolence could have been argued at a still deeper level if we had gone down to the ultimate *reasons* for the equal right to well-being and freedom, i.e., to (1) and (2) at the close of Section II above. What could be a stronger expression of benevolence towards one's fellow-men, than to say that the well-being and freedom of every one of them is worth as much as one's own and that of those few persons one happens to love? At this level equalitarian justice is as deeply committed to two notions which it does not display in its title, benevolence and freedom, as to the notion of equality, which it does. It now remains to show how, given this threefold commitment, it can *also* recognize claims of *un*equal distribution.

PART IV
EQUAL OPPORTUNITY

Equality of Opportunity, and Beyond
JOHN H. SCHAAR

I

Equality is a protean word. It is one of those political symbols—liberty and fraternity are others—into which men have poured the deepest urgings of their hearts. Every strongly held theory or conception of equality is at once a psychology, an ethic, a theory of social relations, and a vision of the good society.

Of the many conceptions of equality that have emerged over time, the one that today enjoys the most popularity is equality of opportunity. The formula has few enemies—politicians, businessmen, social theorists, and freedom marchers all approve it—and it is rarely subjected to intellectual challenge. It is as though all parties have agreed that certain other conceptions of equality, and notably the radical democratic conception, are just too troublesome to deal with because they have too many complex implications, too broad a scope perhaps, and a long history resonant of violence and revolutionary fervor. Equal opportunity, on the other hand, seems a more modest proposal. It promises that the doors to success and prosperity will be opened to us all yet does not imply that we are all equally valuable or that all men are really created equal. In short, this popular and relatively new concept escapes many of the problems and pitfalls of democratic equality and emphasizes the need for an equal opportunity among men to develop and be paid for their talents, which are of course far from being equal.

The doctrine itself is attractively simple. It asserts that each man should have equal rights and opportunities to develop his own talents and virtues and that there should be equal rewards for equal performances. The formula does not assume the empirical equality of men. It recognizes that inequalities among men on virtually every trait or characteristic are obvious and ineradicable, and it does not oppose differential evaluations of those differences. Nor is the formula much concerned with complex chains of normative reasoning: It is practical and policy-oriented. In addition, equal opportunity is not, in principle, confined to any particular sector of life. It is held to be as applicable to politics as to law, as suitable for education as for economics. The principle is widely accepted as just and generous, and the claim is often made that application of the principle unlocks the energies necessary for social and economic progress.

Whereas this conception of equality answers or evades some questions, it raises others. Who is to decide the value of a man's talents? Are men to be measured by the commercial demand for their various abilities? And if so, what happens to the man whose special gifts are not recognized as valuable by the buying public? And most important, is the resulting inequality, based partly on natural inequalities and partly on the whims of consumers, going to bury the ideal of democratic equality, based on a philosophy of equal human worth transcending both nature and economics?

These are serious questions, and it is my intention in this essay to probe their deeper meanings, as well as to clarify some major assumptions, disclose the inner spirit, and explore some of the moral and political implications of the principle of equal opportunity.

From NOMO SIX: *Equality*, eds. J. Chapman, R. Pennock, New York: Atherton Press, 1967.

II

The first thing to notice is that the usual formulation of the doctrine—equality of opportunity for all to develop their capacities—is rather misleading, for the fact always is that not all talents can be developed equally in any given society. Out of the great variety of human resources available to it, a given society will admire and reward some abilities more than others. Every society has a set of values, and these are arranged in a more or less tidy hierarchy. These systems of evaluation vary from society to society: Soldierly qualities and virtues were highly admired and rewarded in Sparta, while poets languished. Hence, to be accurate, the equality of opportunity formula must be revised to read: equality of opportunity for all to develop those talents which are highly valued by a given people at a given time.

When put in this way, it becomes clear that commitment to the formula implies prior acceptance of an already established social-moral order. Thus, the doctrine is, indirectly, very conservative. It enlists support for the established pattern of values. It also encourages change and growth, to be sure, but mainly along the lines of tendency already apparent and approved in a given society. The doctrine is "progressive" only in the special sense that it encourages and hastens progress within a going pattern of institutions, activities, and values. It does not advance alternatives to the existing pattern. Perhaps we have here an example of those policies that Dwight D. Eisenhower and the theorists of the Republican Party characterized as the method of "dynamic conservatism."

If this argument is correct, then the present-day "radicals" who demand the fullest extension of the equal-opportunity principle to all groups within the society, and especially to Negroes and the lower classes, are really more conservative than the "conservatives" who oppose them. No policy formula is better designed to fortify the dominant institutions, values, and ends of the American social order than the formula of equality of opportunity, for it offers *everyone* a fair and equal chance to find a place within that order. In principle, it excludes no man from the system if his abilities can be put to use within the system. We have here another example of the repeated tendency of American radicals to buttress the existing framework of order even while they think they are undermining it, another example of the inability of those who see themselves as radical critics of the established system to fashion a rhetoric and to formulate ends and values that offer a genuine alternative to the system. Time after time, never more loyally than at the present, America's radicals have been her best conservatives.

Before one subscribes to the equality-of-opportunity formula, then, he should be certain that the dominant values, institutions, and goals of his society are the ones he really wants. The tone and content of much of our recent serious literature and social thought—thought that escapes the confines of the conservative-radical framework—warn that we are well on the way toward building a culture our best men will not honor. The facile formula of equal opportunity quickens that trend. It opens more and more opportunities for more and more people to contribute more and more energies toward the realization of a mass, bureaucratic, technological, privatized, materialistic, bored, and thrill-seeking, consumption-oriented society—a society of well-fed, congenial and sybaritic monkeys surrounded by gadgets and pleasure-toys.

Secondly, it is clear that the equal-opportunity policy will increase the inequalities among men. In previous ages, when opportunities were restricted to those of the right birth and station, it is highly probable, given the fact that nature seems to delight in distributing many traits in the pattern of a normal distribution, and given the phenomenon of regression toward the mean, that many of those who enjoyed abundant opportunities to develop their talents actually lacked the native ability to benefit from their advantages. It is reasonable to suppose that many members of ascribed elites, while appearing far superior to the ruck, really were not that superior in actual attainment. Under the regime of equal opportunity, however, only those who genuinely are superior in the desired attributes will enjoy rich opportunities to develop their qualities. This would produce, within a few generations, a social system where the members of the elites really were immensely superior in ability and attainment to the masses. We should then have a condition where the natural and social aristocracies would be identical—a meritocracy, as Michael Young has called it.[1]

Furthermore, the more closely a society approaches meritocracy, the wider grows the gap in ability and achievement between the highest and the lowest social orders. This will happen because in so many fields there are such huge quantities of things to be learned before one can become certified as competent that only the keenest talents, refined and enlarged by years of devoted study and work, can make the grade.[2] We call our age scientific, and describe it further as characterized by a knowledge explosion. What these labels mean from the perspective of equalitarianism is that a handful of men possess a tremendous fund of scientific knowledge, while the rest of us are about as innocent of science as we have always been. So the gap widens: The disparity between the scientific knowledge of an Einstein and the scientific knowledge of the ordinary man of our day is greater than the disparity between a Newton and the ordinary man of his day.

Another force helps widen the gap. Ours is an age of huge, complex, and powerful organizations. Those who occupy positions of command in these structures wield enormous power over their underlings, who, in the main, have become so accustomed to their servitude that they hardly feel it for what it is. The least efficient of the liberal-social welfare states of our day, for example, enjoys a degree of easy control over the ordinary lives of its subjects far beyond the wildest ambitions of the traditional "absolute" rulers. As the commanding positions in these giant organizations come to be occupied increasingly by men who have been generously endowed by nature and, under the equal-opportunity principle, highly favored by society, the power gap between the well- and the poorly-endowed widens. The doctrine of equality of opportunity, which in its origins was a rather nervous attempt to forestall moral criticisms of a competitive and inequalitarian society while retaining the fiction of moral equality, now ironically magnifies the natural differences among men by policies based on an ostensibly equalitarian rationale. The doctrine

of equal opportunity, social policies and institutions based on it, and advances in knowledge all conspire with nature to produce more and more inequality.

This opens a larger theme. We untiringly tell ourselves that the principle of equality of opportunity is a generous one. It makes no distinctions of worth among men on any of the factitious grounds, such as race, religion, or nationality, that are usually offered for such distinctions. Nor does it set artificial limits on the individual. On the contrary, it so arranges social conditions that each individual can go as high as his natural abilities will permit. Surely, nothing could be fairer or more generous.

The generosity dissolves under analysis. The doctrine of equal opportunity, followed seriously, removes the question of how men should be treated from the realm of human responsibility and returns it to "nature." What is so generous about telling a man he can go as far as his talents will take him when his talents are meager? Imagine a footrace of one mile in which ten men compete, with the rules being the same for all. Three of the competitors are forty years old, five are overweight, one has weak ankles, and the tenth is Roger Bannister. What sense does it make to say that all ten have an equal opportunity to win the race? The outcome is predetermined by nature, and nine of the competitors will call it a mockery when they are told that all have the same opportunity to win.

The cruelty of the jest, incidentally, is intensified with each increase in our ability to measure traits and talents at an early age. Someday our measuring instruments may be so keen that we will be able to predict, with high accuracy, how well a child of six or eight will do in the social race. Efficiency would dictate that we use these tools to separate the superior from the inferior, assigning the proper kinds and quantities of growth resources, such as education, to each group. The very best training and equipment that society can afford would, of course, go to those in the superior group—in order to assure equality of opportunity for the development of their talents. It would seem more generous for men themselves to take responsibility for the matter, perhaps by devising a system of handicaps to correct for the accidents of birth, or even by abandoning the competitive ethic altogether.

Three lines of defense might be raised against these criticisms of the equality-of-opportunity principle.

It might be replied, first, that I have misstated the principle of equal opportunity. Correctly stated, the principle only guarantees equal opportunity for all to *enter* the race, not to *win* it. That is certainly correct: Whereas the equal-opportunity principle lets each individual "go as high as his natural abilities will permit," it does not guarantee that all will reach to the same height. Thus, the metaphor of the footrace twists the case in that it shows fools, presumably deluded by the equal-opportunity doctrine, trying to stretch hopelessly beyond their natural reach. But there is no reason to think that fat men who foolishly compete against Roger Bannister are deluded by a doctrine. They are deluded because they are fools.

These reservations are entirely proper. The metaphor of the footrace does misrepresent the case. But it was chosen because it also expresses some features of the case which are often overlooked. The equal-opportunity principle probably does excite a great many men to dreams of glory far beyond their real capabilities. Many observers of American life have pointed to the frequency of grand, bold, noble "first acts" in the drama of American life, and the scarcity of any "second acts" at all. The equal-opportunity principle, with its emphasis on success, probably does stir many men to excesses of hope for winning and despair at losing. It certainly leaves the losers with no external justification for their failures, and no amount of trying can erase the large element of cruelty from any social doctrine which does that. Cases like that of the footrace, and our growing ability to measure men's abilities, makes it clear that the equal-opportunity principle really is not very helpful to many men. Under its regime, a man with, say, an Intelligence Quotient of ninety, is given equal opportunity to go as far as his native ability will take him. That is to say, it lets him go as far as he could have gone without the aid of the doctrine—to the bottom rung of the social ladder—while it simultaneously stimulates him to want to go farther.

Secondly, it might be argued that the equality-of-opportunity principle need not be interpreted and applied, as it has been in this treatment, within a setting and under the assumptions of social competitiveness. The principle could be construed as one that encourages the individual to compete against himself, to compare what he is with what he might become. The contest takes place between one's actual and potential selves, rather than between oneself and others.

This is an interesting, and hopeful, revision of the principle. It would shift the locus of judgment from society to the individual, and it would change the criteria of judgment from social utility to personal nobility. This shift is possible, but it would require a revolution in our present ways of thinking about equality, for those ways are in fact socially oriented and utilitarian. Hence, this defense against the criticisms is really no defense at all. It is irrelevant in the strict sense that instead of meeting the specific charges it shifts the question to a different battleground. It is an alternative to the existing, operative theory, not a defense of it. In fact, the operative doctrine, with its stress on overcoming others as the path of self-validation, is one of the toughest obstacles in the way of an ethic of personal validation through self-transcendence. The operative doctrine specifies success as the test of personal worth, and by success is meant victory in the struggle against others for the prizes of wealth and status. The person who enters wholeheartedly into this contest comes to look upon himself as an object or commodity whose value is set, not by his own internal standards of worth but by the valuations others placed on the position he occupies. Thus, when the dogma of equal opportunity is effectively internalized by the individual members of a society, the result is as humanly disastrous for the winners as for the losers. The winners easily come to think of themselves as beings superior to common humanity, while the losers are almost forced to think of themselves as something less than human.

The third defense is a defense, though not a strong one. It consists in explaining that the metaphor of the footrace oversimplifies the reality that is relevant to an appraisal of the equal-opportunity principle. What actually occurs in a society is not just one kind of contest but many kinds, so that those who are not good at one thing need only look around for a different contest where they have a better chance of winning. Furthermore, there is not just one prize in a given contest but several. Indeed, in our complex and affluent society, affairs might even be so arranged that everyone would win something: There need be no losers.

This reply has some strength, but not enough to touch the basic points. Although there are many avenues of opportunity in our society, their number is not unlimited. The theory of equal opportunity must always be implemented within a set of conventions which favors some potentialities and discourages others. Persons who strive to develop potentialities that are not admired in a given society soon find their efforts tagged silly, or wrongheaded, or dangerous, or dysfunctional. This is inherent in any society, and it forms an insurmountable barrier to the full development of the principle of equal opportunity. Every society encourages some talents and contests, and discourages others. Under the equal opportunity doctrine, the only men who can fulfill themselves and develop their abilities to the fullest are those who are able and eager to do what society demands they do.

There is, furthermore, a hierarchy of value even among those talents, virtues, and contests that are encouraged: The winners in some contests are rewarded more handsomely than the winners in other contests. Even in a complex society, where many contests take place, and even in an affluent society, where it might seem that there had to be no losers, we know full well that some awards are only consolation prizes, not the real thing, and a bit demeaning to their winners. When the fat boy who finishes last in the footrace gets the prize for "best try," he has lost more than he has won.

The formula of equality of opportunity, then, is by no means the warm and generous thing it seems to be on first view. Let us now examine the doctrine from another perspective.

III

The equal-opportunity principle is widely praised as an authentic expression of the de-mocratic ideal and temper. I shall argue, to the contrary, that it is a cruel debasement of a genuinely democratic understanding of equality. To argue that is also to imply, of course, that a genuinely democratic conception of equality is not widely held in the United States.

The origins and development of the principle are enough to throw some doubt on its democratic credentials. Plato gave the principle its first great statement, and he was no democrat. Nor was Napoleon, who was the first to understand that the doctrine could be made the animating principle of the power state. In the United States, the Jacksonian demand for equal rights was assimilated by the Whigs and quickly converted into the slogan of equal opportunity. It soon won a secure place in popular political rhetoric. Whig politicians used the slogan to blunt popular demands for equality—interpreted as "levelling equality"—while defending the advantages of the wealthy.

This argument from origins is, of course, merely cautionary, not conclusive, but other, more systematic considerations, lead toward the same conclusion.

The doctrine of equality of opportunity is the product of a competitive and fragmented society, a divided society, a society in which individualism, in Tocqueville's sense of the word,[3] is the reigning ethical principle. It is a precise symbolic expression of the liberal-bourgeois model of society, for it extends the marketplace mentality to all the spheres of life. It views the whole of human relations as a contest in which each man competes with his fellows for scarce goods, a contest in which there is never enough for everybody and where one man's gain is usually another's loss. Resting upon the attractive conviction that all should be allowed to improve their conditions as far as their abilities permit, the equal-opportunity principle insists that each individual do this by and for himself. Thus, it is the perfect embodiment of the Liberal conception of reform. It breaks up solidaristic opposition to existing conditions of inequality by holding out to the ablest and most ambitious members of the disadvantaged groups the enticing prospect of rising from their lowly state into a more prosperous condition. The rules of the game remain the same: The fundamental character of the social-economic system is unaltered. All that happens is that individuals are given the chance to struggle up the social ladder, change their position on it, and step on the fingers of those beneath them.

A great many individuals do, in fact, avail themselves of the chance to change sides as offered by the principle of equality of opportunity.[4] More than that, the desire to change sides is probably typical of the lower and middle classes, and is widely accepted as a legitimate ethical outlook. In other words, much of the demand for equality, and virtually all of the demand for the kind of equality expressed in the equal-opportunity principle, is really a demand for an equal right and opportunity to become unequal. Very much of what goes by the name of democratic sentiment—as that sentiment is molded within the framework of an individualistic, competitive society and expressed in the vocabulary of such a society—is really envy of those who enjoy superior positions combined with a desire to join them.[5]

This whole way of thinking leads effortlessly to the conclusion that the existence of hierarchy, even of oligarchy, is not the antithesis of democracy but its natural and necessary fulfillment. The idea of equality of opportunity assumes the presence of a mass of men of average talents and attainments. The talents and attainments of the superior few can be measured by comparison with this average, mass background. The best emerge from the democracy, the average, and set themselves over it, resting their position securely on the argument from merit and ability. Those on top are automatically justified because they owe their positions to their natural superiority of merit, not to any artificial claim derived from birth, or wealth, or any other such basis. Hence, the argument concludes, the workings of the equal-opportunity principle help the democracy discover its own most capable masters in the fairest and most efficient way. Everybody gains: the average many because they are led by the superior few; the superior few because they can legitimately enjoy rewards commensurate with their abilities and contributions.

So pervasive and habitual is this way of thinking today that it is virtually impossible to criticize it with any hope of persuading others of its weaknesses. One is not dealing with a set of specific propositions logically arrayed, but with an atmospheric condition, a climate of opinion that unconsciously governs articulate thought in a variety of fields. Something like this cluster of opinions and sentiments provides the framework for popular discussion of the origins and legitimacy of economic inequality. We are easily inclined to think that a man gets what he deserves, that rewards are primarily products of one's talents and industry, secondarily the consequences of luck, and only in small part the function of properties of the social-cultural structure. Somewhere around three-fourths of all personal wealth in the United States belongs to the richest fifth of our families. There is no evidence, in the form of major political movements or public policies, that this distribution shocks the American democratic conscience— a fact suggesting that the American conscience on this matter simply is not democratic but is, rather, formed by the rhetoric of equal opportunity. Similarly, the giant public and private bureaucracies of our day could not justify for a minute their powers over the lives of men if the men so used did not themselves believe in the justness of hierarchy based on merit—merit always defined as tested competence in a special subject matter, tested mastery of a special skill or craft. Most modern writers on the theory of democracy accept this argument for elitism and point out happily that no serious moral or political problems arise so long as avenues for the movement of members into and out of the hierarchies are freely provided. The principle of equal opportunity, of course, does just that.

The basic argument is not new. What is new is the failure to appreciate the profoundly antidemocratic spirit of the argument. This failure is the specific novelty of the "democratic" thought and sentiment of our day, and it makes today's democrats as amenable to domination as any men have ever been. It is only necessary to persuade the masses (usually an easy task) that the hierarchs possess superior merit and that anyone (one naturally thinks of himself at this point) with the requisite ability can join them.

All that can be said against this orientation is that a genuinely democratic ethic and vision rejects oligarchy *as such*. The democrat rejects in principle the thesis that oligarchy of merit (special competence) is in some way different in kind from oligarchy of any other sort, and that this difference makes it nobler, more reasonable, more agreeable to democracy, than oligarchies built on other grounds. The democrat who understands his commitment holds oligarchy itself to be obnoxious, not merely oligarchy of this or that kind.

The argument for hierarchy based on merit and accomplished by the method of equal opportunity is so widespread in our culture that there seems no way to find a reasonable alternative to it. We automatically think that the choice is either-or: *either* hierarchy and orderly progress *or* anarchy and disorderly stalemate. But that is not so. It is hardly even relevant. The fact that it is thought to be so is a reflection of the crippling assumptions from which modern thought on these matters proceeds. It is thought that there must be hierarchies and masses, elites and non-elites, and that there can be no more democratic way of selecting elites than by the method of equal opportunity. The complexity of affairs demands elites; and democracy and justice require selection of those elites by merit and equal opportunity.

Of course there must be hierarchy, but that does not imply a hierarchical and bureaucratic mode of thinking and acting. It need imply no more than specialization of function. Similarly, the fact that complexity demands specialization of function does not imply the unique merit and authority of those who perform the special functions. On the contrary: A full appreciation of complexity implies the need for the widest possible diffusion of knowledge, sharing of views, and mutual acceptance of responsibility by all members of the affected community.

Of course there must be organization, and organization implies hierarchy. Selection of the hierarchs by the criterion of merit and the mechanism of equal opportunity seems to reassure the worried democrat that his values are not being violated. But hierarchy may or may not be consonant with the democratic spirit. Most of today's democratic thinkers soothe themselves on this question of democracy and organization with the assertion that everything that can be done is being done when organizations permit factions, provide channels of consultation, and protect individual rights by establishing quasi-judicial bodies for hearing and arbitrating disputes. Certainly these guarantees are valuable, but they have little to do with making organizations democratic. They are constitutionalist devices, not democratic ones.

Before there can be a democratic organization, there must first be a democratic mentality—a way of thinking about the relations among men which stresses equality of being and which strives incessantly toward the widest possible sharing of responsibility and participation in the common life. A democratic orientation does not grow from and cannot coexist with the present bureaucratic and "meritorian" ethic. It is an alternative to the present ethic, not an expansion or outgrowth of it. When the democratic mentality prevails, it will not be too hard to find the mechanisms for implementing it.

IV

I hope my argument will not be interpreted as some sort of mindless demand for the abolition of distinctions or as a defense of the ethic of mutual aid against the ethic of competition. The argument was mainly negative in intention, attempting to show that the idea of equality of opportunity is a poor tool for understanding even those sectors of life to which the notion of equality is applicable. It is a poor tool in that, whereas it seems to defend equality, it really only defends the equal right to become unequal by competing against one's fellows. Hence, far from bringing men together, the equal-opportunity doctrine sets them against each other. The doctrine rests on a narrow theory of motivation and a meager conception of man and society. It reduces man to a bundle of abilities, an instrument valued according to its capacity for performing socially valued functions with more or less efficiency. Also, the doctrine leads inevitably to hierarchy and oligarchy, and tries to soften that hard outcome by a new form of the ancient argument that the best should rule. In all these ways, the idea of equality of opportunity constitutes a thorough misunderstanding of a democratic conception of equality.

It is not the primary task of this essay to set forth a genuinely democratic conception of equality: that is a work for another time. Still, enough should be done in the second part of this essay to arrest the most obvious and most likely objections to the first part.

The equal-opportunity principle is certainly not without value. Stripped of its antagonistic and inequalitarian overtones, the formula can be used to express the fundamental proposition that no member of the community should be denied the basic conditions necessary for the fullest possible participation in the common life, insofar as those conditions can be provided for by public action and through the use of public resources. This formulation will take one some distance toward a democratic conception of equality, but it must be interpreted carefully, for it can easily turn into just another defense of the equal right to become unequal.

Still, the formulation does provide some useful guidelines. It obviously implies equality in and before the law. It also implies a far greater measure of economic equality than is the case today. The issue here is not material comfort. Nor does it have anything to do with the notion that justice is served when economic goods are allocated according to the actual work (in the customary definition) each man does. That is impossible. We may urge that each should contribute according to his ability; we must surely insist that each be provided for according to his need.

What the criterion of a substantial degree of economic equalization requires is the establishment of the material conditions necessary for a generous measure of freedom of choice for all members of the community and the establishment of the conditions necessary for relations of mutual respect and honesty among the various economic and social groups within a society. This is not some kind of levelling demand for equality of condition. It is no more than a recognition of the obvious fact that the great material inequality that prevails in America today produces too much brutishness, impotence, and rage among the lower classes, and too much nervous vulgarity among the middle classes. There is no assertion here that economic equalization is the sufficient condition for the democratic New Jerusalem. Rather, the assertion is negative. As Arnold put it, "equality will never of itself alone give us a perfect civilisation. But, with such inequality as ours, a perfect civilisation is impossible."[6]

The equality-of-opportunity principle, as formulated above, also implies the equal right of each member to share in the political life of the community to the fullest extent of his interest and ability. But this is the point at which the principle, no matter how carefully formulated, easily leads one away from a democratic view. The equal-opportunity principle as employed today in, for example, discussions of representation and voting rights, really does nothing more than fortify the prevailing conception of political action as just another of the various steps individuals and groups take to secure and advance their own interests and advantages. In this view, politics is but another aspect of the struggle for competitive advantage, and men need political power in order to protect and advance their private powers. This conception of politics is drawn from the economic sphere, and never rises above the ethical and psychological possibilities of that sphere.

When it is understood that the principle of equal opportunity is in our time an expression of the competitive, capitalistic spirit, and not of the democratic spirit, then the boundaries of its applicability begin to emerge. To the extent that competition is inescapable, or socially useful, all competitors should have the same advantages, and this the equal-opportunity principle guarantees. In any competitive situation, some will do better than others, and it seems just that those who do well should be rewarded more generously than those who do poorly. This too the principle guarantees.

The basic question, however, is not whether competition should be praised or condemned, but where and under what conditions competition is a desirable principle of action and judgment and where and under what conditions it is not. Some kinds of competition actually draw men more closely together whereas others produce antagonism and isolation. The problem is to distinguish between these kinds, encouraging the former and discouraging the latter. Peace is but a euphemism for slavery unless men's competitive energies are given adequate outlet. Most people probably have some need for both inward and outward striving. Perhaps the struggles against other people and the struggles within the self can be brought to some kind of balance in each individual and in society as a whole. Ideally, we might strive toward a truly pluralistic society in which nearly everybody could find a specialty he could do fairly well and where he would enjoy friendly competition with others. Judged by this imaginative possibility, our present social order is a mean thing. It is a kind of institutionalized war game, or sporting contest, in which the prizes are far too limited in kind, the referees and timekeepers far too numerous, and the number of reluctant and ill-adjusted players far too high. We need a social order that permits a much greater variety of games. Such a social order could, I think, be based on an effort to find a place for the greatest possible range of natural abilities among men. The variety of available natural abilities is enormous and worth much more exploration than any of the currently dominant conceptions of social order are willing to undertake. In the United States today, the fundamental justification of the equal-opportunity principle is that it is an efficient means for achieving an indefinite expansion of wealth and power. Many men are unsuited by nature for that competition, so that nature herself comes to seem unjust. But many of the injustices we regard nature as having perpetrated on individuals are actually no more than artifacts of the narrow view we take of nature's possibilities and a consequent distortion of the methods and ideals by which we attempt to transcend nature. For example, in defining intelligence as what I.Q. tests measure, we constrict the meanings of intelligence, for there are many modes of intelligence that the tests do not capture—nature is more protean than man's conception of her. Furthermore, having defined intelligence in a certain way, we then proceed to reward the people who have just that kind of intelligence and encourage them to use it in the pursuit of knowledge, which they are likely to do by building computers, which in turn give only certain kinds of knowledge. Thus our constricted definition of nature is confirmed by the methods we use to study nature. In this special sense, there might still be something to say for the eighteenth-century idea that society should imitate nature.

We must learn to ask questions like these about the method of competition and the principle of equal opportunity. The task is to define their proper spheres of action, not to treat them as blocks to be totally accepted or rejected. At the outer limit, it seems clear that whereas every society is to some extent competitive and competition in some spheres is socially and individually valuable, no society ought to exalt the competitive spirit as such, and the equal-opportunity principle that implements it. Both conceptions tend naturally toward selfishness unless carefully controlled.

V

In addition to equality of opportunity, there is another kind of equality that is blind to all questions of success or failure. This is the equality that obtains in the relations among the members of any genuine community. It is the feeling held by each member that all other members, regardless of their many differences of function and rank, belong to the community "as fully as he does himself."[7] Equal opportunity, far from strengthening this kind of equality, weakens it.

When this point is reached, when the discussion turns to the meanings of equality involved in a democratic conception of membership and a democratic conception of ruling and being ruled, the equal-opportunity principle—no matter how carefully formulated—begins to mislead. A fuller conception of equality is needed, one stripped of the antagonistic and privatistic overtones of the equal-opportunity principle. That fuller conception, in turn, requires a broader view of politics than is afforded by the "who gets what, when, how" perspective.

Political life occupies a middle ground between the sheer givens of nature and society on the one side, and the transcendental "kingdom of ends" on the other. Through political action men publicly strive to order and transform the givens of nature and society by the light of values drawn from a realm above or outside the order of the givens. Men, acting together, define the ideal aims of the common life and try to bend realities toward them. Through acting with others to define and achieve what can be called good for all, each realizes part of his own meaning and destiny. Insofar as man is a being that wants not merely to live but to live well, he is a political being. And insofar as any man does not participate in forming the common definition of the good life, to that degree he falls short of the fullest possibilities of the human vocation. No man can assign to another dominion over how he shall live his life without becoming something less than a man. This way of thinking about political action leads to an idea of equality whose tone and implications are very different from those of the equal-opportunity formulation.

Other features of political action lead in the same direction, and, specifically, require a rejection of all claims to rulership based on the ancient analogies between the art of ruling and other arts. When one contracts with a carpenter to build a house, he may assume that the carpenter's skills are sufficient to the work that is to be done. But when citizens elevate some among them to places of political authority the case is different. Politics has so few givens and so many contingencies and complexities, contains so many dangerous possibilities and so few perfect solutions, and is such a baffling mixture of empirical, prudential, and ethical considerations that no man or group of men has knowledge and skill sufficient for all situations. As John Winthrop said, no man can "profess nor undertake to have sufficient skill for that office."[8]

Winthrop's comment, grounded as it is on a solid understanding of the political vocation, is a just rebuke to all claims for political authority based on technical competence. Relations between politician and citizen are very different from those between craftsman and employer. Politicians cannot be said to serve or to execute the will of citizens in the way that craftsmen can be said to serve their employers. Nor can politicians claim authority over their work and over other persons engaged in that work on the grounds of technical competence. The relations between politicians and citizens, in sum, are relations among equals in a number of important senses. Above all, their relations are built on premises that, when properly understood, encourage genuine conversation among the participants, not merely the transmission of information and commands up and down a line. This way of thinking about the matter presumes equality among citizens in the sense most basic to a democratic understanding

of the relations among the members of a political community—in the sense of equality of being—and hence presumes the widest possible participation in and sharing of responsibility for the policies that govern the whole community.

Just as political authorities may not lay claim to superior rights on the ground of special merit, neither may ordinary citizens absolve themselves from partial responsibility for public policies on the ground that their task is done when they have selected those who will take active charge of the affairs of the polity. The democratic idea offers no such easy absolution from shared responsibility and guilt.

This sharing of responsibility and guilt may be one of the reasons why a genuinely democratic conception of equality is not easy to accept even by those who call themselves democrats. It is comforting to men to think that someone else is competently in charge of the large and dangerous affairs of politics: Somebody else rules; I just live here. Hierarchy and oligarchy provide subjects with that comfort and with easy escapes from shared responsibility and guilt. This freedom from political responsibility is very valuable to men who would much rather devote themselves to their private interests anyway, than share the burden of caring for the public good. The doctrine of equality of opportunity, tied as it is to the principle of hierarchy, easily leads to moral arrogance on the part of the winners and to the taking of moral holidays by the losers.

A proper view of equality still leaves wide scope for the existence of necessary and just superiorities and differences, but it brings a different mentality to their appraisal. Certainly, some things *are* better than others, and more to be preferred. Some vocations and talents are more valuable than others, and more to be rewarded. The implication here is only that the more highly skilled, trained, or talented man has no ground either for thinking himself a better *man* than his less-favored fellows, or for regarding his superiorities as providing any but the most temporary and limited justification for authority over others. The paradigmatic case is that of the relation between teacher and student. The teacher's superior knowledge gives him a just claim to authority over his students. But central to the ethic of teaching is the conviction that the teacher must impart to students not only his substantive knowledge but also the critical skills and habits necessary for judging and contributing to that knowledge. The teacher justifies his authority and fulfills his duty by making himself unnecessary to the student.

Perhaps this at least suggests the outlines of a democratic conception of equality and draws the boundaries of its applicability. The heart of such a view of equality is its affirmation of equality of being and belonging. That affirmation helps identify those sectors of life in which we should all be treated in a common or average way, so that the minimal conditions of a common life are made available to all: legal equality, equal rights of participation in political life, equal right to those average material provisions necessary for living together decently at all. It also stresses the greatest possible participation in and sharing of the common life and culture while striving to assure that no man shall determine or define the being of any other man.

This is what equality is all about, and it is a great deal.[9] But it is far from everything. Beyond the realm of the average and the comparable lies another realm of relations among men where notions of equality have no relevance. Hence, a fair understanding of equality requires a sense of the boundaries of that realm in which equalitarian categories do not apply.

Those boundaries begin where we try to define man himself. Every attempted formulation of equality stumbles on the mystery and the indefinability of the creature for and about whom the formulation is made. In the end, it makes no sense to say that all men are equal, or that any two men are, because it is impossible to say what a man is. It is easy to abstract a part from the whole, and define that part in terms that make it commensurable with the same parts abstracted from other whole men. Thus, one can define an American citizen in terms that impart perfect sense to the proposition that all American citizens are equal. But when it comes to talking about whole men and about man, the concept of equality is mute. Then there is only the mystery of being, the recognition of self and others. Lawrence has expressed the idea perfectly, and he should be permitted the last word:

One man is neither equal nor unequal to another man. When I stand in the presence of another man, and I am my own pure self, am I aware of the presence of an equal, or of an inferior, or of a superior? I am not. When I stand with another man, who is himself, and when I am truly myself, then I am only aware of a Presence, and of the strange reality of Otherness. There is me, and there is *another being*. . . . There is no comparing or estimating. . . . Comparison enters only when one of us departs from his own integral being, and enters the material mechanical world. Then equality and inequality starts at once.[10]

NOTES

1. Michael Young, *The Rise of the Meritocracy*, London: Thames and Hudson, 1958.
2. Success is a function of both inborn talent and the urge to do well, and it is often impossible to tell which is the more important in a particular case. It is certain that the urge to do well can be stimulated by social institutions. How else can we account for Athens or Florence, or the United States?
3. *Democracy in America.* New York: Vintage, 1945, vol. 2, pp. 104–105.
4. Some civil rights leaders are suspicious of open enrollment plans to combat *de facto* segregation for precisely this reason.
5. "The greatest obstacle which equality has to overcome is not the aristocratic pride of the rich, but rather the undisciplined egoism of the poor." Proudhon, as quoted in James Joll, *The Anarchists*, Boston: Little, Brown, 1964, p. 67.
6. Matthew Arnold, essay on "Equality" (1878) in *Matthew Arnold: Prose and Poetry*, ed. A. L. Bouton, N.Y.: Scribner's, 1927, p. 362.
7. John Plamenatz, *Man and Society*, New York: McGraw-Hill, 1963, vol. 2, p. 120.
8. John Winthrop, "Speech to the General Court," July 3, 1645, in Perry Miller, ed., *The American Puritans: Their Prose and Poetry*, Garden City, N.Y.: Doubleday Anchor, 1956, pp. 91–92.
9. As Paine said with permissible exaggeration, "inequality of rights has been the cause of all the disturbances, insurrections, and civil wars, that ever happened . . ." Thomas Paine, *Works*, ed. J. P. Mendum, Boston: 1878, vol. 1, pp. 454–455.
10. D. H. Lawrence, "Democracy," as quoted in Raymond Williams, *Culture and Society, 1780–1950*, New York: Columbia University Press, 1958, p. 211.

Liberty Versus Equal Opportunity
JAMES S. FISHKIN

1. INTRODUCTION

Liberalism has often been viewed as a continuing dialogue about the relative priorities between liberty and equality. When the version of equality under discussion requires equalization of outcomes, it is easy to see how the two ideals might conflict. But when the version of equality requires only equalization of opportunities, the conflict has been treated as greatly muted since the principle of equality seems so meager in its implications. However, when one looks carefully at various versions of equal opportunity and various versions of liberty, the conflict between them is, in fact, both dramatic and inescapable. Each version of the conflict poses hard choices which defy any *systematic* pattern granting priority to one of these basic values over the other. In this essay, I will flesh out and argue for this picture of fundamental conflict, and then turn to some more general issues about the kinds of answers we should expect to the basic questions of liberal theory.

I will explore the conflicts between liberty and equal opportunity by focusing on three positions, each of which can be considered in terms of its corresponding account of liberty and equal opportunity. Charts 1 and 2 below illustrate the relation among these concepts. I will term the three positions Laissez Faire, Meritocracy, and Strong Equality. While these labels are in some respects arbitrary, the positions they represent will turn out, I believe, to be familiar ones even though they travel under various banners.

2. LAISSEZ FAIRE

A good recent example of the laissez-faire position is the one Nozick takes in *Anarchy, State, and Utopia.* One of the more provocative examples in the book compares decisions to marry with decisions by prospective employers and employees:

> Suppose there are twenty-six women and twenty-six men each wanting to be married. For each sex, all of that sex agree on the same ranking of the twenty-six members of the opposite sex in terms of desirability as marriage partners: call them A to Z and A′ to Z′ respectively in decreasing preferential order. A and A′ voluntarily choose to get married. . . . When B and B′ marry, their choices are not made nonvoluntary merely by the fact that there is something else they each would rather do. . . . This contraction of the range of options continues down the line until we come to Z and Z′, who each face a choice between marrying the other or remaining unmarried.

Nozick explicitly develops his account of liberty in market exchanges on analogy with these mating decisions:

> Similar considerations apply to market exchanges between workers and owners of capital. Z is faced with working or starving; the choices and actions of all other persons do not add up to providing Z with some other options. . . . Does Z choose to work voluntarily? . . . Z does choose voluntarily if the

Reprinted from James Fishkin, "Liberty vs Equal Opportunity", *Social Philosophy & Policy* 5:1 (1978) 32–48, © Blackwell Publishers, Ltd.

Chart 1: Notions of Negative Liberty

Bench mark for Harm includes:	Laissez Faire	Meritocracy	Strong Equality
Lockean Rights	+	+	+
Right to Equal Consideration in Job Market	–	+	+
Right to Conditions for an Equal Life Chance	–	–	+

Chart 2: Notions of Equal Opportunity

Negative Liberty:	Laissez Faire	Meritocracy	Strong Equality
Unfettered in Private Sphere	+	+	–
Unfettered in Public Sphere	+	–	–

other individuals A through Y each acted voluntarily and within their rights.

In both the market and the mating cases, "A person's choice among differing degrees of unpalatable alternatives is not rendered nonvoluntary by the fact that others voluntarily chose and acted within their rights in a way that did not provide him with a more palatable alternative." Others acting within their rights cannot, on this view, do me harm. If we think of harm in the core negative-liberty sense of people individually or collectively being able to do as they please so long as they do not harm or violate the rights of others (with rights violations being construed as harms for these purposes), then one can easily subsume both the right to marry and the right to get a job within the same conception of liberty and the same conception of justice. Nozick's slogan "From each as they choose, to each as they are chosen" works perfectly for the selection of mates under modern conditions. Nozick's extension of it to the market means only that the welfare state and other redistributional devices seem objectionable because they would prohibit capitalist acts between consenting adults.

Because A and A' are fully within their rights to marry, we do not think of their action as harming B and B' even though it does, obviously, limit their options. So far, the analogy between mating and employment retains some plausibility. However, there is also a crucial disanalogy, at least from the perspective of any advocate of equal opportunity.

In modern, secular, Western moral culture, we commonly think that members of the same ethnic group, race, or religion can, *if they choose*, select mates only from the same ethnic group, race, or religion. In fact, we commonly think they can marry more or less whomever they like. Those who would like to marry others who are similar in those respects are fully within their rights to do so; those who have other views are free to follow them as well.

In the job market, by contrast, if employers hire only members of the same ethnic group, race, or religion, we commonly view that not as an exercise of liberty but, rather, as an act of blatant discrimination. The laissez-faire view includes Lockean rights but not the right to equal consideration in the job market within the bench mark for relevant harms (see Chart 1). Another way of making this point is to say that negative liberty is completely unfettered in both the private and public spheres on the laissez-faire view (completely unfettered in that so long as no one is harmed in the relevant sense, people may do as they please in both areas). Nozick's analogy between the distribution of mates and that of jobs (or, more generally, of goods) is exemplified by the two pluses in the laissez-faire column in Chart 2. The two spheres are treated in the same way. But treating them in the same way trivializes equal opportunity in the job market because it eliminates any basis for complaints against discrimination and sheer arbitrariness. For this reason, the bench mark on harm compatible with meritocratic notions of equal opportunity can be thought of as the same as the laissez-faire notion—except for the incorporation of an additional right defining relevant harms, the right to equal consideration of one's qualifications in the job market.

Now it might be argued in defense of the laissez-faire view that rational employers will not discriminate; they will not hire less "qualified" people merely on the basis of irrelevant factors such as race, ethnicity, or religion. They will not do so because it will cost them something in terms of efficiency, productivity, or the like. There are two replies worth noting briefly. First, the rational behavior of economic actors is a theoretical idealization which some firms and some people approximate under some conditions, but fall far short of in others. There is no reason to assume that departures from rationality of this sort will not occur. Furthermore, within the laissez-faire theory, these actors are within their rights to be irrational, just as any prospective couple about to make an unwise decision to marry would also be within its rights to be irrational. (If, say, they were on any objective assessment really incompatible, they would still be within their rights to get married if they wished to do so.)

Second, statistical discrimination will, in fact, be rational for economic actors under some conditions. If members of a given group generally perform badly, then firms may decide to forgo the decision costs of individual evaluation and substitute group membership as a fairly reliable proxy for whatever individual factors they would have tested. If they do, they will be right most of the time, but at the cost of some serious injustices (in the meritocratic sense) to some individuals. Discrimination can be economically rational. The self-interest of economic actors is not sufficient protection if nondiscrimination is an important goal.

3. MERITOCRACY

The second position in Charts 1 and 2, meritocracy, is designed to rule out discrimination. Roughly, this position entails that there should be widespread procedural fairness in the evaluation of qualifications for positions. Qualifications must be job-relevant for the positions to be filled, and they must represent actual efforts of the individual, not merely group membership (shared, arbitrary native characteristics).

On the meritocratic position, an additional right has been added to the standard Lockean rights for determining the bench mark for harm. If I am discriminated against, then I am harmed in the sense that my right to equal consideration of my qualifications has been violated. This addition represents a sharp departure from the kind of negative liberty we presume in the private sphere. If Jane prefers John to Joseph as a mate, Joseph does not have grounds for complaint that his qualifications were not given equal consideration. Jane's preference is decisive, regardless of her reasons. But if Company X prefers John to Joseph as an employee, Joseph would have grounds for complaint if he could show that, because of his race or religion, a less qualified person (John) was hired instead. Under meritocracy, negative liberty is not unfettered in the public sphere as it is in the private, while under laissez faire, the two spheres are treated in the same way (see Chart 2).

4. STRONG EQUALITY

From the standpoint of advocates of strong equality, meritocracy does not go far enough. I believe its limitations are nicely captured by an example which I adopt from Bernard Williams. Imagine a warrior society, one which, from generation to generation, has been dominated by a warrior class. At some point, advocates of equal opportunity are granted a reform. From now on, new membership in the warrior class will be determined by a competition which tests warrior skills. A procedurally fair competition is instituted, but the children of the present warriors triumph overwhelmingly. To make it simple, let us assume that children from the other classes are virtually on the verge of starvation, and children from the warrior class have been exceedingly well-nourished. Hence, in the warrior's competition we might imagine three-hundred pound Sumo wrestlers vanquishing ninety pound weaklings. While this competition is procedurally fair in that, we will assume, it really does select the best warriors, it does not embody an adequate ideal of equal opportunity. The Sumo wrestlers have been permitted to develop their talents under such favorable conditions, while the weaklings have developed theirs under such unfavorable conditions, that measuring the results of such overwhelmingly predictable (and manipulable) causal processes does not represent an equal opportunity for the less advantaged to compete. The causal conditions under which they prepare for the competition deny them an effective opportunity. This criticism holds despite the fact that, on meritocratic grounds, the competition may operate perfectly so as to select the best warriors—as those warriors have developed under such unequal conditions.

A principle which captures the injustice embodied in the warrior society is the criterion of equal life chances. According to this principle, I should not be able to enter a hospital ward of newborn infants and predict what strata they will eventually reach merely on the basis of their arbitrary native characteristics such as race, sex, ethnic origin, or family background. To the extent that I can reliably make such predictions about a society, it is subject to a serious kind of inequality of opportunity. Obviously, inequality of life chances would be compatible with strictly meritocratic assignment. The warrior society scenario, where family background perfectly predicts success in the competition, illustrates how one sort of equal opportunity is entirely separable from the other. By contrast, the position I label "Strong Equality" in Charts 1 and 2 is committed to both forms—meritocratic assignment and, in addition, equality of life chances.[1]

The difficulty with strong equality is that it is only realizable at an even more severe cost in liberty than that required for meritocracy. A clue as to the issues at stake can be found in the restriction of negative liberty by strong equality, not only in the public sphere but also in the private sphere (the two minuses in the last column in Chart 2). The liberty at stake in the private sphere turns out to be the autonomy of the family—the liberty of families, acting consensually, to benefit their children.

5. THE TRILEMMA

When family autonomy is combined with the two demanding components of equal opportunity considered thus far—meritocratic assignment and equal life chances—a pattern of conflicting and difficult choices emerges, a kind of dilemma with three corners which I term a "trilemma." It is a trilemma because realization of any two of these principles can realistically be expected to preclude the third. This pattern of conflict applies even under the most optimistic scenarios of ideal theory. If equal opportunity is to provide a coherent ideal which we should aspire to implement, then certain hard choices need to be faced. The options in this trilemma are pictured in Chart 3.

Chart 3: Options in the Trilemma

	Meritocracy	Reverse Discrimination	Strong Equality
Merit	+	−	+
Equal Life Chances	−	+	+
Family Autonomy	+	+	−

The trilemma of equal opportunity can be sketched quickly. Let us assume favorable and realistic conditions—only moderate scarcity, and good faith efforts at strict compliance with the principles we propose (both in the present and in the relevant recent past). However, to be realistic, let us also assume background conditions of inequality, both social and economic. The issue of equal opportunity—the rationing of chances for favored positions—would be beside the point if there were no favored positions, i.e., if there were strict equality of result throughout the society. Every modern developed country, whether capitalist or socialist, has substantially unequal payoffs to positions. The issue of equal opportunity within liberal theory is *how* people get assigned to those positions—by which I mean both their *prospects* for assignment and the *method* of assignment (whether, for example, meritocratic procedures are employed guaranteeing equal consideration of relevant claims).

The trilemma consists in a forced choice among three principles.

Merit: There should be widespread procedural fairness in the evaluation of qualifications[2] for positions.
Equality of Life Chances: The prospects of children for eventual positions in the society should not vary in any systematic and significant manner with their arbitrary native characteristics.[3]
The Autonomy of the Family: Consensual relations within a given family governing the development of its children should not be coercively interfered with except to ensure for the children the essential prerequisites for adult participation in the society.[4]

Given background conditions of inequality, implementing any two of these principles can reasonably be expected to preclude the third. For example, implementing the first and third undermines the second. The autonomy of the family protects the process whereby advantaged families differentially contribute to the development of their children. Given background conditions of inequality, children from the higher strata will have been systematically subjected to developmental opportunities which can reliably be expected to give them an advantage in the process of meritocratic competition. Under these conditions, the principle of merit—applied to talents as they have developed under such unequal conditions—becomes a mechanism for generating unequal life chances. Hence, the difficulty with the meritocratic option in Chart 3 is the denial of equal life chances.

Suppose one were to keep the autonomy of the family in place but attempt to equalize life chances. Fulfilling the second and third principles would require sacrifice of the first. Given background conditions of inequality, the differential developmental influences just mentioned will produce disproportionate talents and other qualifications among children in the higher strata. If they must be assigned to positions so as to equalize life chances, then they must be assigned regardless of these differential claims. Some process of "reverse discrimination" in favor of those from disadvantaged backgrounds would have to be applied systematically throughout the society if life chances were to be equalized (while also maintaining family autonomy). Hence, the difficulty with the second option in Chart 3, which I have labeled reverse discrimination, is the cost in merit.

Suppose one were to attempt to equalize life chances while maintaining the system of meritocratic assignment. Given background conditions of inequality, it is the autonomy of families that protects the process by which advantaged families differentially influence the development of talents and other qualifications in their children. Only if this process were interfered with in a systematic manner could both the principles of merit and of equal life chances be achieved. Perhaps a massive system of collectivized child rearing could be devised. Or perhaps a compulsory schooling system could be devised so as to even out home-inspired developmental advantages and prevent families from making any *differential* investments in human capital in their children, either through formal or informal processes. In any case, achieving both merit and equal life chances would require a systematic sacrifice in family autonomy. Hence, the difficulty with the third scenario, the strong equality position in Chart 3, is the sacrifice in family autonomy.

Implementation of any two of these principles precludes the third. While inevitable conflicts might be tolerated by systematic theorists in the nonideal world, these conflicts arise within ideal theory. This argument is directed at the aspiration to develop a rigorous solution even if it is limited to the ideal theory case. Given only moderate scarcity and strict compliance with the principles chosen, and given that there is no aftermath of injustice from the immediate past, we are applying these principles in our thought experiment to the best conditions that could realistically be imagined for a modern, large-scale society.

Of course, liberalism has long been regarded as an amalgam of liberty and equality. And liberals and libertarians have long been fearful of the sacrifices in liberty that would be required to achieve equality of result. Equality of opportunity, by contrast, has been regarded as a weakly reformist, tame principle which avoids such disturbing conflicts. However, even under the best conditions, it raises stark conflicts with the one area of liberty which touches most of our lives most directly. Once we take account of the family, equal opportunity is an extraordinarily radical principle, and achieving it would require sacrifices in liberty which most of us would regard as grossly illiberal.

The force of the trilemma argument depends on there being independent support for each of the principles. Merit makes a claim to procedural fairness. However, as Brian Barry has argued, procedural fairness is a thin value without what he calls "background fairness," and background fairness would be achieved by equality of life chances. Family autonomy can be rationalized within a broader private sphere of liberty; it protects the liberty of families, acting consensually, to benefit their children through developmental influences. The principle leaves plenty of room for the state to intervene when some sacrifice in the essential interests of the child is in question or when consensual relations within the family have broken down (raising issues of child placement or children's rights). Without the core area of liberty defined by this narrow principle, the family would be unrecognizably different.

Hence, these principles are not demanding by themselves; they are demanding in combination. Each of the trilemma scenarios which fully implements two of the principles leads to drastic sacrifice of the third. To blithely assume that we can realize all three is to produce an incoherent scenario for equal opportunity, even under ideal conditions.

One reasonable, but unsystematic response to this pattern of conflict would be to trade off small increments of each principle without full realization of any. But this is to live without a systematic solution. The aspiration fueling the reconstruction of liberal theory has been that some single solution in clear focus can be defined for ideal conditions, and then policy can be organized so as to approach this vision asymptotically. But if trade-offs are inevitable, even for ideal theory, then we have ideals without an ideal, conflicting principles without a unifying vision.

6. POLICY IMPLICATIONS

My position is, first, that equal opportunity is a prime case for this result; second, that despite the lack of a systematic solution for ideal theory, there are significant policy prescriptions which can be derived without solving the priority relations among these principles; and third, that the lack of a systematic solution exemplifies the special difficulties facing liberalism in our contemporary culture.

Having sketched the first point, let us turn to the second: the issue of policy implications. There are two kinds of policy implications we can evaluate without having to solve the problem of priority relations among these three principles for ideal theory—without, in other words, employing the model of an asymptotic aspiration to a single unified and coherent ideal which we should, as best we can, approach through partial realization. The first kind of policy implication involves cases in which we can achieve a major *improvement* in the realization of one of these values without a major loss in any of the others (or in any other new values which the proposal impinges upon). The second kind of policy implication involves cases in which a proposal would impose a major *loss* in one of these values without any comparable gain in any of the other values (or in any new values which the proposal impinges upon).

The first kind of policy implication is exemplified by all those things we could do to improve equality of life chances, family autonomy, or meritocratic assignment. In the U.S. for example, we are far from the possibility frontier in achieving any of these values and, in some cases, we have moved further away rather than closer in recent years. We blithely tolerate the perpetuation of an urban underclass; a whole generation of urban youth is growing up with blighted life chances and with few opportunities to make it into the mainstream economy, and with few policy initiatives now focused on their problem. Family autonomy is protected for middle-class families, but poor families have far greater difficulty in forming and maintaining themselves intact. By neglecting job prospects among the poor, the Reagan administration has also affected the incentives for family formation, as well as the ability of poor families to provide essential prerequisites for child development and socialization. We are also far from achieving meritocratic assignment. Discrimination persists against blacks, Hispanics, women, and other minorities, including homosexuals. There is no justification for tolerating job discrimination on the basis of arbitrary factors which are irrelevant to the roles in question. In other words, despite Reagan's talk of protecting "the family" and of creating an "opportunity society," his policies have promoted middle-class families and middle-class opportunities at the expense of the disadvantaged.

The second kind of policy implication is exemplified by the major quick fix for the first set of problems—preferential treatment based *merely* on arbitrary native characteristics. When it is applied in competitive meritocratic contexts, this policy yields a major sacrifice in one of our values, meritocratic assignment, without a significant gain in either of the others. The difficulty is that preferential treatment, when it is based merely on arbitrary native characteristics, is mistargeted as a policy which could have any effect on equality of life chances. It is mistargeted because, in competitive meritocratic contexts (e.g., admissions to graduate and professional schools) there are strong institutional pressures to accept the most qualified applicants with the specified arbitrary native characteristics. Just as family background provides disproportionate opportunities to develop qualifications among advantaged white children, it does so among relatively advantaged minority children. This policy only serves to widen the gap between the urban underclass and the black middle class—despite the fact that it is typically justified as special consideration for those who are from disadvantaged backgrounds.

My objection does not apply to policies which apply preferential treatment to those who are actually from disadvantaged backgrounds. In that case, meritocratic assignment is sacrificed for a gain in equal life chances. Rather, my objection applies to programs which are applied *merely* on the basis of arbitrary native characteristics, so as to reward the most qualified members of the group (who will, as a statistical matter, tend to come from its more advantaged portions). Hence, the irony of the De

Funis and Bakke cases. De Funis, a Sephardic Jew from a relatively poor background, was not admitted to the University of Washington Law School while most of the minority students admitted on the basis of preferential treatment were, apparently, from more advantaged backgrounds (or, at least, were the children of black professionals). On the other hand, the program at the University of California at Davis which the Court struck down in the Bakke case was unusual for having procedures in place to direct special consideration to those who actually came from economically disadvantaged backgrounds. Theoretically, the program which the Court struck down in *Bakke* was defensible within our framework, while the program on which it avoided making a decision in *De Funis* (providing preferential treatment for race as such) would not be.

We should mention one persistent counterargument to this conclusion about preferential treatment. Preferential treatment based merely on race (or on other arbitrary native characteristics) is sometimes supported not as a remedy for developmental disadvantages in the present, but as a form of *compensation* for injustices in the past. However, the mistargeting objection has force here as well, but with additional complications.

First, the list of groups which were historically victims of discrimination is much broader than the groups now demanding compensation. Consistent pursuit of this argument would produce a host of other ethnic claims—Irish, Polish, and Italian, Catholic as well as Jewish, in addition to the more familiar arguments made on behalf of Hispanics, Native Americans, and Orientals. This proliferation is not fanciful. The AntiDefamation League discovered one American law school which had no less than sixteen racial and ethnic categories for admissions classifications.[5]

Second, the very notion of compensation raises conceptual challenges—unacknowledged by its proponents—when it is applied to this kind of problem. An individual X is supposed to be compensated by returning him to the level of well-being he would have reached had some identifiable injustice in the past (against his forebears) not occurred. In tracing back through the generations, however, it soon becomes clear that X would usually not now exist were it not for the historical injustice. If we try to imagine the world which would have existed had the historical injustices not occurred, we cannot return X to the level he would have reached, because he would not have reached any level at all. For example, let us take the well-documented case of Kunta Kinte. If Kunta Kinte, Alex Haley's ancestor in *Roots*, had not been brutally kidnapped and sold as a slave, there is no likelihood that the author of *Roots* would have come to exist in the twentieth century. The mating and reproduction of each generation, in turn, depends on a host of contingencies. If the chain were to have been broken at any point, by a parent, grandparent, or great-grandparent, we would get a different result in this generation. If it were not for the initial injustice, Kunta Kinte's descendants might well have been native Africans, perhaps residents today of Juffure (Kunta Kinte's village in West Africa).

Hence, we cannot employ the straightforward notion of compensation (returning people to the level they would have reached had the injustice not occurred) when the injustice spans several generations. Perhaps some compelling version of the argument might be created which confronts this difficulty. Rather than deny this possibility I wish merely to claim that such an argument, if it were developed, should, at the least, accept my objection to mistargeting.

Compensation is not compatible with the mistargeting which results from preferential treatment applied *merely* to racial categories in competitive meritocratic contexts. Compensation cannot plausibly mean benefiting some blacks (who may be already well-off) for earlier injustices to *other* blacks—particularly when those who do *not*, by and large, benefit from the compensatory argument (the urban underclass) are experiencing extremely disadvantaged conditions. To take a provocative analogy, would it not have been outrageous if the German government, after World War II, had paid "compensation" to well-off American Jews, ignoring the orphans and other direct victims of the Holocaust? It would not have been compensation to benefit Jews indiscriminately or, even worse, to benefit disproportionately those who were untouched by the injustices at issue. For this reason, I conclude that the compensation argument does not alter the general conclusion about preferential treatment reached earlier. When it is directed at those who are themselves from disadvantaged backgrounds, it is admissible within our framework, for then the gain in equal life chances may balance the loss in strictly meritocratic assignment. But when, in competitive meritocratic contexts, it is applied merely on the basis of arbitrary native characteristics, then we have grounds for objecting to it.

7. THE LIMITS OF THEORY

Turning to our third general issue, I believe these arguments show that equal opportunity is a useful test case for contemporary liberalism. First, it provides an area of social choice where major substantive commitments of liberalism inevitably clash, even for ideal theory. Hence, it should affect our conception of the appropriate connections between ideal theory and the real world of policy prescriptions. It should discredit the model according to which we make asymptotic approaches to a single, unified, and coherent ideal. Rather, we have conflicting principles, any one of which, if given further emphasis, would take policy in a different direction. Even for the best of circumstances, we have to balance conflicting principles. We are left with ideals without an ideal.

Second, the intuitionism which results is not trivial in its implications. The two clearest routes to substantive implications—embracing substantial gains without a loss and rejecting substantial losses without a gain—yield significant results on the contemporary scene. They do not add up to a systematic theory, but they should assist us in rethinking important policies.

Third, these results reveal the vulnerable position in which liberalism finds itself within our contemporary moral culture. In my recent book on the psychology of moral reasoning, I classify moral reasoners according to the seven ethical positions listed across the top of Chart 4. The six ethical claims listed at the left can be combined, consistently, only into the seven possibilities listed across the top. There are, of course, many other possible ways of dividing

Chart 4: Seven Ethical Positions

	I Absolutism	II Rigorism	III Minimal Objectivism	IV Subjective Universalism	V Relativism	VI Personalism	VII Amoralism
The Absolutist Claim	+	−	−	−	−	−	−
The Inviolability Claim	+	+	−	−	−	−	−
The Objective Validity Claim	+	+	+	−	−	−	−
The Universalizability Claim	+	+	+	+	−	−	−
The Interpersonal Judgment Claim	+	+	+	+	+	−	−
The Judgment of Self Claim	+	+	+	+	+	+	−

Chart 5: Six Ethical Claims

Claim 1: One's judgments are *absolute*, i.e., their inviolable character is rationally unquestionable.

Claim 2: One's judgments are *inviolable*, i.e., it would be objectively wrong ever to violate (permit exceptions to) them.

Claim 3: One's judgments are *objectively valid*, i.e., their consistent application to everyone is supported by considerations that anyone should accept were he to view the problem from what is contended to be the appropriate moral perspective.

Claim 4: One's judgments apply *universalizably*, i.e., they apply consistently to everyone, so that relevantly similar cases are treated similarly.

Claim 5: One's judgments apply *interpersonally*, i.e., to others as well as to oneself.

Claim 6: One's judgments apply to oneself.

up the terrain. But this particular map purports to be exhaustive in the sense that it captures the consistent possibilities on the issues which it classifies.

The focus of my study is an investigation into the rationales motivating adoption of any of the subjectivist positions (IV through VII). It turns out that the rationales for subjectivism all depend on failed absolutist expectations. It is the difficulty or unavailability of positions I or II—Absolutism or Rigorism—which appears to support the conclusion that the only possible alternative is subjectivism in the form of positions IV through VII. The arguments of ordinary reasoners rely on absolutist expectations which specify that principles must be rationally unquestionable and must hold without exception, thereby ruling out the intuitionist balancing of conflicting principles, in order to avoid subjectivism.

However, the main burden of our substantive argument here has been that positions I or II are not plausible interpretations of liberal theory—at least for the crucial issue of equal opportunity. Even for ideal theory, we cannot establish inviolable priority relations. Unless we abandon one of our initial, central commitments, we find ourselves faced with interminable conflicts even under the best conditions which could realistically be imagined for a modern industrial society. If we are correct in this substantive conclusion, this result is profoundly disappointing for liberal theoretical aspirations.

However, this result also poses a crucial challenge to the viability of liberalism as a form of moral culture. If my empirical study is correct,

we live in a moral culture imbued with absolutist expectations. When those expectations for rationally unquestionable, inviolable, and complete principles are combined with the inevitable conflicts and indeterminacies of liberalism—even under the best conditions—liberal ideology becomes vulnerable to a legitimacy crisis. The ingredients are the clash between expectations and inevitable limits. The expectations define the assumption that, in our scheme, moral positions must either live up to the requirements of positions I or II or be relegated to the moral arbitrariness of IV, V, VI or VII. The thrust of our substantive analysis has been that the best liberalism can reasonably aspire to achieve is position III. In this middle ground position, liberalism lays claim to valid principles but embraces their conflicting and controversial character. At this position, principles are not arbitrary, but neither are they inviolable or beyond reasonable question—as at positions I or II. The inevitability of moral conflict about equal opportunity makes it a good substantive case for the general problem confronting liberalism.

Either we must learn to expect less, or liberalism undermines itself as a coherent moral ideology; it undermines itself by robbing itself of moral legitimacy, of claims to moral validity. It seems to lead to the unavoidable conclusion that all value judgments are arbitrary, a matter of mere personal taste—including all value judgments which can be made on behalf of the liberal state itself. Balancing conflicting principles is widely seen in our culture as a kind of nonanswer, just as intuitionism is seen as a non-theory. The difficulty facing liberalism arises if we are right about the limits of liberal theory and if we accept the absolutist expectations. I reject the latter step. My solution is to jettison the absolutist expectations and to embrace, by contrast, a limited liberalism, one which confines itself to position III in my scheme. As a matter of public ideology this requires a revision of expectations, a revision of moral culture. As for equal opportunity, we do not need a *systematic* theory and the demand for one is a part of the problem.

NOTES

1. Rawls's principle of fair equality of opportunity approximates strong equality, but without confronting the implications for family autonomy. See John Rawls, *A Theory of Justice* (Harvard University Press, 1971), especially pp. 73–74.
2. By "qualifications" I mean criteria that are job-related in that they can fairly be interpreted as indicators of competence or motivation for an individual's performance in a given position. Education, job history, fairly administered test results, or other tokens of ability or effort might all be included. Inferences that because one is a member of a group which generally does poorly, one is unlikely to do well would not be included within my account of qualifications. Such inferences would constitute statistical discrimination.
3. By a "native characteristic," I mean any factor

knowable at birth that could be employed to differentiate adult persons of at least normal health and endowment. As I note in *Justice*, these characteristics are not necessarily unalterable: "Even though native characteristics can be ascribed to an individual at birth, they are not necessarily unalterable, as cases of sex change illustrate dramatically" (p. 28, n. 20). What do I mean by "arbitrary"? A native characteristic will be considered arbitrary unless it predicts the development of qualifications to a high degree among children who have been subjected to equal developmental conditions. Race, sex, ethnic origin and family background are considered arbitrary here. I employ the characteristic liberal assumption that under equal developmental conditions, knowledge of these factors would not permit us to reliably predict qualifications of individuals for desirable positions in the society. I am giving liberalism the benefit of the doubt here, since my point is to establish the conundrums of the trilemma under optimistic conditions for a liberal thought experiment.
4. By "essential prerequisites," I mean the physical and psychological health of the child and his or her knowledge of those social conventions necessary for participation in adult society. Literacy, the routines of citizenship, and other familiar elements of secondary education would count among the essential prerequisites (absence of which could justify coercive interference by the state).
5. See Anti-Defamation League of B'Nai B'rith, "A Study of Post-Bakke Admissions Policies in Medical, Dental and Law Schools," *Rights*, vol. 10, no. 1 (Summer 1979), pp. 11–12.

The Concept of Equal Opportunity
PETER WESTEN

The concept of equal opportunity represents something of a paradox for Americans. We profess to believe in equal opportunity, yet we allow unequal opportunity to abound. Some observers may conclude, with R. H. Tawney, that we are simply hypocritical—that, while we pay "homage" to equal opportunity, we also "resist most strenuously attempts to apply it."[1] I be-

Reprinted from *Ethics* 95 (July 1985): 837–850. © 1985 by The University of Chicago by permission.

lieve that the paradox of equal opportunity is more complex and the solution more interesting. I believe, not that we say one thing and hypocritically do another, but that the rhetoric of "equality" and "opportunity" confounds what we really mean by equal opportunity. The rhetoric suggests that equal opportunity is a single and ideal state of affairs—difficult to attain, perhaps, but definitely to be desired.[2] The truth is quite the opposite. Equal opportunity is neither a single state of affairs nor ideal—neither difficult to attain nor inherently desirable.

To see why this is so, we must pierce the rhetoric of "equal opportunity" and examine its constituent elements. Equal opportunity is a "verbal formula"[3] consisting of four simple and recurring elements. The formula is treacherous[4] because three of the elements are covert and the fourth term is derivative. Once the four elements are identified, equal opportunity loses much of its mystery and most of its rhetorical appeal.

THE MEANING OF OPPORTUNITY: THREE COVERT ELEMENTS

The difficulties of equal opportunity do not begin with the word "equal." "Equal" presents challenges, as we shall see; but the puzzle of equal opportunity inheres less in the meaning of "equal" than in the meaning of "opportunity."[5]

Every statement of opportunity consists of three covert elements. The first covert element is the agent, or class of agents, to whom the opportunities belong. Opportunities do not float freely about, unattached to persons. Opportunities, by definition, are of people—whether the people be black people alone, or blacks and whites together, or women, or rich people, or poor people, or rich and poor together, or people from one region alone, or older people, or children, or whatever.[5] The particular agent or class of agents will differ from one opportunity to another, but every opportunity entails an agent or a class of agents. As T. D. Campbell has said, "We may therefore always intelligibly ask about an opportunity—as we may always ask about any liberty or freedom—to whom it belongs."[6]

The second covert element in all statements of opportunity is the goal or set of goals toward which the opportunities are directed. An opportunity is a relationship of some agent to some desired thing. "All opportunities are opportunities to do or enjoy some benefit or activity."[7] The goal of an opportunity may be a job, or an education, or medical care, or a political office, or land to settle, or housing, or a financial investment, or a military promotion, or a life of "culture," or the development of one's natural abilities, or whatever. The particular goal or set of goals will differ from one opportunity to another, but every opportunity is a relationship of a specific agent or class of agents (whether explicit or implicit) to a specific goal or set of goals (whether explicit or implicit).

The last and most elusive of the covert elements is the relationship that connects the agent of an opportunity, say, X, to the goal of the opportunity, say Y. An opportunity of X to attain Y is not a guarantee that X will succeed in attaining Y if he so chooses. An opportunity is not a guarantee because agents are rarely (if ever) guaranteed that they will attain their desired goals. Every child born in America has an "opportunity" to become president of the United States, but he has no guarantee of becoming president because he has no assurance that he will overcome the many possible obstacles that stand in the way. Every president-elect in America has an even better opportunity to become president, but he has no guarantee either because he has no assurance that he will overcome the obstacles—illness, natural catastrophe, the discovery of vote fraud, constitutional crisis, death, and so forth—that may stand in the way of his taking the oath of office on January 20. It seems, therefore, that, when we talk about opportunities, we are not necessarily talking about the absence of all possible obstacles between a given agent and a given goal.

Conversely, while an opportunity is something less than a guarantee, it is something more than a mere possibility—more, that is, than merely the possible absence of all obstacles between a given agent and a given goal. An opportunity is more than mere possibility because nearly everything is possible. We might say every foreign-born citizen of the United States has a "possibility" of becoming president because it is possible to remove the constitutional requirement that candidates for president be native-born. Yet we would not say foreign-born citizens have an opportunity to become president because an opportunity requires something more than the possible absence of all obstacles between a given agent and a given goal.

It thus appears that an opportunity falls somewhere between a guarantee and a mere possibility—that is, somewhere between the absence of all possible obstacles between X and Y, on the one hand, and the possible absence of all obstacles between X and Y, on the other hand. But that is not so because one can remove a specified obstacle in the way of X's attaining Y without also granting X an opportunity to do Y. Assume, for example, that having formerly required candidates for governor to be native-born males, a state removes the sex requirement, thus leaving the governorship open to all native-born men and women. We might then say that, by removing one insurmountable obstacle in the way of foreign-born women, the state has given all foreign-born women an increased possibility of becoming governor. But we would not say that the state has also given all foreign-born women an opportunity of becoming governor because, by retaining the requirement that candidates be native-born, the state has explicitly left an insurmountable obstacle directly in their way—an obstacle which, unless removed, permanently precludes foreign-born women from attaining their goal. It thus appears that an opportunity requires at a minimum that an agent have a chance to attain his goal, that is, that no insurmountable obstacles explicitly stand in the way of his attaining his goal.

This may suggest that an opportunity, being no less than a chance, is also no more than a chance, that is, no more than the absence of insurmountable obstacles in the way of X's attaining Y. But that is not so either, for opportunities are not confined to the absence of insurmountable obstacles. Suppose, for example, that, having formerly required airline stewardesses to be unmarried women, an airline company removes the marital obstacle, thus opening stewardess jobs to all women. The marital obstacle differs from insurmountable obstacles like race, color, and sex because marriage in America is a legal status that a person himself may change. Yet we would surely use the language of opportunity to describe the airline company's action. We would surely say that, by removing the marital obstacle, the airline company had given married women an opportunity to become airline stewardesses.

What, then, is the relationship between the agent of an opportunity and the goal of an opportunity? The answer should now be clear. An opportunity is not solely the absence of a specified obstacle or solely the absence of insurmountable obstacles. It is a combination of both. "Opportunity" is the word we use to refer to the absence of a specified obstacle or set of obstacles, the absence of which leaves no insurmountable obstacles explicitly in the way of X's attaining Y. We say someone has an opportunity when we have in mind a particular obstacle or set of obstacles that is not there, an obstacle the absence of which gives X a chance he did not previously possess to attain Y if he so chooses. The particular obstacle or set of obstacles the opportunity removes may be insurmountable (e.g., race, color, sex, ancestry, or place of birth), or surmountable (e.g., religious belief, wealth, social class, marital status, minimum age, high school diploma, or residency), or a combination of surmountable and insurmountable obstacles; it may be the obstacle of being excluded from a competitive race altogether, or the obstacle of being admitted to the competition but having to run further than other runners, or the obstacle of running the same distance but having to overcome the "social" disadvantage of poorer training and motivation than other runners,[8] or the obstacle of having the same social advantages but having to overcome the "natural" disadvantage of lesser natural ability than other runners;[9] or the obstacle may be the totality of all the features that distinguish one person from another,[10] or whatever. The particular obstacle will differ from one opportunity to another, but every opportunity is a chance of a specified agent or class of agents, X, to choose to attain a specified goal or set of goals, Y, without the hindrance of a specified obstacle or set of obstacles, Z.

As an illustration, consider the Illinois Human Rights Act of 1979.[11] The act provides statutory opportunities for people in Illinois by making it unlawful for labor organizations to limit the employment of persons in Illinois by discriminating against them on the basis of "race, color, religion, sex, national origin, ancestry, age, marital status, [or] physical or mental handicap." Like all opportunities, the Illinois statutory opportunity consists of a specified agent, X, a specified goal, Y, and a specified obstacle, Z, the absence of which gives X a chance he did not previously possess to attain Y if he so chooses. The agents, X, are the class of persons in Illinois; the goal, Y is employment; and the obstacle, Z, is discrimination by labor organizations on the basis of race, color, religion, sex, national origin, ancestry, marital status, or physical or mental handicap. Moreover, like all opportunities, the statutory opportunity consists of a certain relationship between agents, goals, and obstacles. The relationship is less than a guarantee and more than a possibility: less than a guarantee because the act provides for less than the removal of all possible obstacles to employment; more than a possibility because the act provides for more than the possible removal of all obstacles. The relationship does more than simply remove an obstacle because it does so in such a way as to leave no insurmountable obstacles explicitly in the way of X's attaining Y; yet the relationship also does more than simply remove insurmountable obstacles because it removes some obstacles (e.g., marital status and religion) that are not insurmountable. In a word (and, indeed, in the words of the act), the relationship constitutes an "opportunit[y]." It gives people in Illinois a chance they did not previously possess to attain employment by removing specified obstacles that would otherwise stand in their way.

To be sure, legislatures do not always specify as explicitly as Illinois did the precise terms of the opportunities they mean to prescribe. Indeed, the obfuscations of opportunity result from expressing opportunities without specifying their three constituent terms. Consider, for example, the statement, Every child in America should have an opportunity to graduate from high school. Like all statements of opportunity, the latter states a relationship between agent X, a goal, Y, and an obstacle, Z. X and Y, being both explicit, are obvious. X is the class of all

children in America, and Y is the goal of graduating from high school. Z, being implicit, is ambiguous. Z may be something educationally uncontroversial, like the obstacles of indigency or race, or something educationally controversial, like the obstacle of passing a competency examination. By leaving the content of Z unspecified, the statement masks a wide range of possible prescriptions—from the most acceptable prescription of opportunity to the most controversial.

The foregoing analysis supports several conclusions. First, an opportunity is not a particular state of affairs. It is a formal relationship—a relationship of an agent, X, to a goal, Y, with respect to an obstacle, Z. It is a chance on the part of X, if he so chooses, to attain Y without the hindrance of Z. The concept of opportunity can be particularized into specific conceptions of opportunity by replacing the variables X, Y, and Z with specific agents, specific goals, and specific obstacles. One conception of opportunity will differ from another. Some conceptions of opportunity may be more just, or unjust, than others. But every conception of opportunity, qua opportunity, is as much an opportunity as every other.

Second, while opportunities may be divided into subclasses, the subclasses themselves remain relationships of agents, goals, and obstacles. Thus, "descriptive" opportunities are relationships that actually obtain, that is, agents who actually possess chances to attain specified goals without the hindrance of specified obstacles if they so choose. (Descriptively, Americans have an opportunity to engage in national political debate without the hindrance of widespread illiteracy or polyglot because, descriptively, Americans are highly literate in a single common language.) "Prescriptive" opportunities are relationships that ought to obtain, that is, agents who ought to have a chance to attain specified goals without the hindrance of specified obstacles if they so choose. The two subclasses are conceptually distinct. One cannot infer that given agents ought to have an opportunity from the description that they actually have an opportunity or that given agents actually have an opportunity from the prescription that they ought to have an opportunity. Yet as subclasses of opportunity, descriptive and prescriptive opportunities are both chances of agents, X, to attain goals, Y, without the hindrance of obstacles, Z.

Third, one cannot grant prescriptive opportunities to some people without denying prescriptive opportunities to other people. In stating that X ought to have a chance to attain Y without the obstacle of Z, one necessarily states that W ought not to have a chance to prevent X from attaining Y by means of Z. This does not mean that one should refrain from creating prescriptive opportunities. It means, rather, that the significant question is, not whether opportunities should be prescribed, but which opportunities should be prescribed and which opportunities proscribed.

THE MEANING OF EQUALITY: A DERIVATIVE ELEMENT

The rhetoric of opportunity accounts for much of the confusion surrounding equal opportunity, but not all. Some confusion derives from the other half of the phrase—from the rhetoric of equality. The confusions of equality, however, are the converse of those of opportunity. Opportunity tends to confuse because it tends to leave essential elements unsaid. Equality confuses because it repeats what opportunity already fully says. The rhetoric of opportunity suffers from being incomplete. The rhetoric of equality suffers from being derivative.

The derivative nature of the word "equal" in "equal opportunity" inheres in the dictionary meaning of "equal." "Equal" means the same thing in the phrase "equal opportunity" as it does everywhere else. To say two persons or things are equal does not mean that they are identical by every possible descriptive or prescriptive measure because no two persons or things can be identical by every possible measure. Nor does it mean that they are identical by any one possible descriptive or prescriptive measure because all persons and things are identical by some measures. It means, rather, that they are identical by the relevant descriptive or prescriptive measure—the relevant measure being the particular measure one stipulates as applicable. To say two persons are equal

means that (1) they have each been measured by a stipulated standard of measure, (2) their respective measures have been compared with one another, and (3) the comparison shows their measures to be identical to one another. The same applies to "equal" in "equal opportunity." To say two persons possess (or ought to possess) opportunities means that they possess (or ought to possess) chances to attain given goals without the hindrance of given obstacles. To say further that their opportunities are equal means that (1) their respective opportunities have each been measured by a stipulated standard for measuring opportunities, (2) the opportunities so measured have been compared with one another, and (3) the comparison shows the opportunities to be identical by that standard of measure. Now, what is the standard of "measur[e]," or "predicate," by which equality of opportunity is ascertained? The standard can be any stipulated opportunity—any "specification"[12] of the three variable terms of which opportunities consist. The specification may be descriptive, that is, it may identify agents who actually possess a chance to attain a specified goal without the hindrance of a specified obstacle. Or the specification may be prescriptive, that is, it may identify the class of agents who ought to possess a chance to attain a specified goal without the hindrance of a specified obstacle. In either event, equality of opportunity is simply the identity that obtains among two or more persons by virtue of their all falling within a class of agents who all possess (or ought to possess) a chance to attain a specified goal or goals without the hindrance of a specified obstacle or obstacles.

It follows, therefore, that two persons can have an equal opportunity to attain a specified goal even though each faces different obstacles of his own, provided that they are both free from the same specified obstacles. Assume, for example, that two runners with different training and talent are both given a chance to win a race by both being allowed to start at the same time and place and run the same distance; assume, too, that the measure of opportunity is the chance to win the race without the obstacles of starting at different times and running different distances; the two runners in that event can truly be said to have an equal opportunity to win the race even though they face different obstacles regarding talent and the training that make it unlikely that both will actually win because they are identical in both being free from the same specified obstacles to attain the same specified goal. Similarly, two persons can lack an equal opportunity to attain a specified goal even though they are identical in both being free from the same obstacles, provided that the obstacles from which they are free are not specified as relevant obstacles. Thus, if the measure of opportunity for the two runners is the chance to win the race without the obstacles of lack of training, the two runners do not have an equal opportunity to win the race even though they both start from the same time and place because they are not identical in both being free from the specified obstacles regarding training. People who have equal opportunity by one measure of opportunity will have unequal opportunities by other measures. No two people can have an equal opportunity to attain a specified goal by every measure of opportunity unless they are both guaranteed the result of attaining the goal if they so wish.

It also follows from this that the word "equal" in "equal opportunity" occurs derivatively. It tells us nothing we do not already know about who possesses (or ought to possess) a chance to attain what goal without the hindrance of which obstacle. It refers us, derivatively, to the consequences of measuring agents by stipulated descriptive or prescriptive standards of opportunity. In the absence of stipulated standards of opportunity, one has no way of identifying agents who are equal in respect of possessing such opportunities. Yet in the presence of stipulated standards of opportunity, one has no need to identify equality among agents because the standards themselves tell us everything we need to know: the standards themselves tell us who has (or ought to have) such opportunities and who lacks (or ought to lack) them. If two or more people fall within the class of agents who possess (or ought to possess) a chance to attain a relevant goal without the hindrance of a relevant obstacle, it follows that they are (or ought to be) equals in respect of possessing that opportunity. If two people do not fall within the class of agents who possess (or ought to possess) a chance to attain a relevant goal without

the hindrance of a relevant obstacle, it follows that they are not (or ought not to be) equal in respect of possessing that opportunity. In either event, to say that two people possess (or do not possess) equal opportunities is simply a derivative way of saying that they both fall (or do not both fall) within the class of agents who possess specified opportunities in common.

The Public Telecommunications Act of 1978 nicely illustrates the derivative nature of "equal" in "equal opportunity." The operative provision of the act can be divided into two parts: part 1 prescribes "equal opportunity in employment" and part 2 prescribes that "no person" seeking employment with the Public Broadcasting Service (PBS) or National Public Radio (NPR) shall be subjected to "discrimination" on grounds of "race, color, religion, national origin, or sex." The prescription of equal opportunity in part 1 is meaningless without part 2 because without part 2 one has no prescriptive standard of opportunity for determining equality among agents—no stipulation of specified goals and specified obstacles by which one can identify the class of agents who are identical in respect of the opportunity they possess. Yet with part 2, one has no need for part 1 because part 2 contains everything one needs to know. Part 2 specifies the three essential terms of the opportunity by which equality of opportunity obtains. Part 2 specifies that a specified class of agents (i.e., "all persons" desiring employment) shall have a chance to attain a specified goal (i.e., "employment" at PBS or NPR) without being hindered by a specified obstacle (i.e., discrimination "on grounds of race, color, religion, national origin, or sex"). Given the prescription in part 2, it follows that all members of the agent class are equal in respect of the opportunity the act proscribes. (It also follows that, as far as the Public Telecommunications Act is concerned, they are not prescriptively equal in respect of opportunities the act does not proscribe, for example, the opportunity to work for PBS without discrimination on grounds of sexual preference.) The equality of opportunity that thus obtains among members of the agent class does not add anything to the opportunity that exists without it. The act would continue to mean everything it now means if "equal" were simply deleted from the text and the statute stated without it: "No person shall be subjected to discrimination in employment by [PBS or NPR] on grounds of race, color, religion, national origin, or sex."

To be sure, like statements of opportunity, statutes that prescribe equal opportunity sometimes omit one or more of the essential terms of which the constituent opportunity consists. Some equal opportunity statutes fail to specify essential terms altogether, while other statutes use "equal opportunity" as a surrogate for implied terms. Yet even where "equal opportunity" is used as a surrogate for implied terms, "equal" still occurs derivatively because it still refers, derivatively, to the identity that obtains among agents by virtue of their falling within a common class of agents for whom the statute implicitly prescribes a particular opportunity.

Now it might be asked, What difference does it make that "equal" works derivatively? Why does it matter whether one specifies the three essential terms of an opportunity directly or uses "equal" to imply them derivatively? It makes a difference because statements of equal opportunity are less perspicuous—and, hence, more "ambiguous"—than are direct specifications of the opportunities for which they stand.

The ambiguities of equal opportunity take two forms: (1) cases in which "equal opportunity" obscures the precise obstacles the prescribed opportunity eliminates and (2) cases in which "equal opportunity" also obscures the precise class of agents who possess the prescribed opportunity. The first confusion occurs with statutes of the form, A shall have an equal opportunity with B to attain goal Y. Such statutes tend to be ambiguous because, while they specify the agents of the prescribed opportunity (i.e., the combined class of A and B) and the goal of the opportunity (i.e., Y), they do not specify the precise obstacle the prescribed opportunity removes. By using "equal opportunity" as a surrogate for the unstated obstacle, they imply that the obstacle consists of one of three things—(1) the obstacle of being classified as A (as opposed to B), (2) the obstacle of being classified as B (as opposed to A), or (3) the obstacle of being classified either as A (as opposed to B) or as B (as opposed to A). Yet by not specifying which of the three obstacles

they have in mind, the statutes obscure their own content.

To illustrate, assume a statute takes the following form:

> American women shall have an equal opportunity with American men to serve as astronauts in the space-shuttle program.

The statute specifies two terms of the prescribed opportunity but uses "equal opportunity" as an ambiguous surrogate for the third term. It specifies the agents who possess the prescribed opportunity and the goal of the prescribed opportunity; and it uses "equal opportunity" in conjunction with "men" and "women" to imply that the obstacle being removed consists of sex discrimination of one form or another. Unfortunately, because there are at least three different kinds of sex discrimination, there are also at least three kinds of prescribed opportunity:

O_1: American men and women shall have whatever chances are otherwise prescribed for men to serve as astronauts in the space-shuttle program without the hindrance of any special preference for men.

O_2: American men and women shall have whatever chances are otherwise prescribed for women to serve as astronauts in the space-shuttle program without the hindrance of any special preference for women.

O_3: American men and women shall have a chance to serve as astronauts in the space-shuttle program without the hindrance of any special preference for persons of a particular sex.

The foregoing prescriptions of opportunity each differ significantly from one another. O_1 protects women, but not men, from discrimination; O_2 protects men, but not women, from discrimination; O_3 protects men and women both from discrimination. Yet each prescription creates equal opportunity between men and women because each of them defines men and women as members of an agent class possessing a common opportunity. Each prescription squares with what the statute says. To know which prescription squares with what the statute means, one would have to pierce the "vague" language of equal opportunity for the unspecified prescription that underlies it.

The second major confusion occurs with statutes of the form, A and B shall have an equal opportunity to attain Y. Such statutes tend to be ambiguous because they fail to specify either the agents who possess the prescribed opportunity or the obstacle the opportunity removes. The statutes mask three distinct prescriptive standards of opportunity by which A and B may be rendered equal: (1) A and B may be equal to one another in their chances to attain Y without being disfavored vis-à-vis one another; (2) A and B may be equal to an unnamed but implied third-party agent, C, in their chances to attain Y without being disfavored vis-à-vis C; or (3) A and B may be equal to C in their chances to attain Y without being disfavored vis-à-vis one another. Instead of specifying the particular prescriptive opportunity A and B share in common, the statutes obscure the pertinent opportunity by referring instead to the equality that obtains between A and B by virtue of their possessing the unspecified opportunity in common.

The Export Expansion Finance Act of 1971 is a good example. The Act requires the Export-Import Bank (Eximbank) to accord "equal opportunity to . . . independent export firms [and] small commercial banks in the formulation and implementation of its programs." Like all prescriptive statements of equal opportunity, the act necessarily presupposes a prescriptive standard of opportunity by which the equality obtains. Unfortunately, instead of specifying the three essential terms of the prescribed opportunity, the act specifies only one of them, leaving two of them to be inferred. The act specifies the goal of the prescribed opportunity (i.e., the formulation and implementation of Eximbank programs): and it uses "equal opportunity" in conjunction with "independent export firms" and "small commercial banks" in such a way as to raise implications about both the agents who possess the prescribed opportunity and the obstacles the prescribed opportunity removes; but its implications are sufficiently ambiguous to encompass at least three distinct prescriptions of opportunity:

O_1: Independent export agents and small commercial banks shall have a chance, if they so choose, to participate in the formulation and implementation of Eximbank programs without being disfavored vis-à-vis one another.

O_2: Independent export agents, small commercial banks, and large commercial banks shall have a chance, if they so choose, to participate in the formulation and implementation of Eximbank programs on whatever terms are otherwise open to large commercial banks without being disfavored vis-à-vis large commercial banks.

O_3: Independent export agents, small commercial banks, and large commercial banks shall have a chance, if they so choose, to participate in the formulation and implementation of Eximbank policy programs without being disfavored vis-à-vis one another.

Each of the three prescribed opportunities creates a class of agents who are identical—and, hence, equal—in their chances to attain the specified goals. Each of the prescribed opportunities includes independent export agents and small commercial banks within its respective class of agents. Each of the three prescriptions thus accords equal opportunity to independent export agents and small commercial banks. Yet the three prescriptions differ significantly. Legislative history in fact suggests that the act was enacted to codify O_2 rather than O_1 or O_3.[13] Without independent information of that sort, however, one has no way of knowing from the language of equal opportunity which of the three opportunities the act actually prescribes.

CONCLUSION

Popular wisdom on equal opportunity turns it upside down. People commonly think of equal opportunity as a desideratum—a single state of affairs that is highly desirable in theory, though perhaps unattainable in practice. The truth is rather the contrary. Equal opportunity is not a single state of affairs, not unattainable, and not necessarily desirable.

"'Equality of Opportunity' is no more the name of a single ideal than is 'Liberty.' "[14] Rather it is a way of talking about countless states of affairs—about the countless opportunities, descriptive and prescriptive, that groups of people everywhere possess in common. An opportunity is a chance of an agent, X, to choose to attain a goal, Y, without the hindrance of an obstacle, Z. Equal opportunity is the identity of opportunity that obtains among any two persons who fall within a common class of agents. One cannot conceive of particular opportunities without first substituting specified agents, specified goals, and specified obstacles in the place of the variable terms X, Y, and Z. Once one specifies the variables, one can talk about the resulting opportunity in one of two ways: one can talk about the opportunity directly, by speaking directly to the agents' chances to attain their specified goal without being hindered by the pertinent obstacle, or one can talk about the opportunity indirectly, by speaking of the identity—the equality—that obtains among its agents by virtue of their possessing a common chance to attain the goal without being hindered by the pertinent obstacle. The reference to equality does not add to the content of the opportunity. It is simply a way of talking about the opportunity by reference to the identity that obtains among the agents who possess it in common.

It thus follows, then, that although particular opportunities may indeed be unattainable,[15] equal opportunity itself is unavoidable. Equal opportunity exists everywhere two or more people have a chance to attain a specified goal without being hindered by a specified obstacle. Descriptively, equal opportunity exists wherever two or more people fall within a class of agents who are all free from the same obstacle to attain the same goal. Prescriptively, equal opportunity exists wherever two or more people fall within a class of agents who we believe ought to be all free from the same obstacle to attain the same goal. Equal opportunity exists prescriptively wherever we wish to prescribe it.

It also follows from the meanings of "opportunity" and "equal" that equal opportunity itself (in contrast to particular equal opportunities) is neither desirable nor undesirable. Equality of opportunity is the identity of opportunity that obtains between two persons by virtue of their both being free from a specified obstacle to attain a specified goal. The desirability of their equality of opportunity thus depends entirely on the desirability of their both being free from the pertinent obstacle to pursue the pertinent goal. Just as opportunities can be good or bad, equal opportunities can be good or bad. The equal descriptive opportunity Americans possess to commit homicide without the hindrance of a national handgun shortage seems to many people to be bad; the equal descriptive opportunity they possess to live a long life without the hindrance of smallpox seems to be good. The equal prescriptive opportunity American property holders possessed under *Dred Scott* to take chattel property into the free territories today seems bad; the equal prescriptive opportunity they still possess to receive just compensation for takings of their property today seems good. The equalities and inequalities that obtain among people under given descriptions and prescriptions of opportunity are as good (and as bad) as the descriptions and prescriptions from which they derive.

The American paradox of equal opportunity—namely, that we profess to believe in equal opportunity and, yet, allow unequal opportunity to prevail in many spheres of life—rests on false premises. We do not really believe in equal opportunity as such. We believe in particular equal opportunities, just as we believe in particular unequal opportunities. We believe in prescribing particular opportunities, and, hence, we believe in the respective equalities and inequalities that obtain among those who do and do not possess such opportunities in common. We do not contradict our professed values by prescribing unequal opportunity. We vindicate them. Logically, we cannot prescribe equal opportunity for some persons without prescribing unequal opportunity for other persons. Logically, we cannot prescribe equal opportunity in respect of some goals and obstacles without withholding equal opportunity in respect of other goals and obstacles. Ultimately, we prescribe equal opportunities for the same reasons we prescribe unequal opportunities—because equal and unequal opportunities obtain as a logical consequence of the opportunities we wish to prescribe.

NOTES

1. R. H. Tawney, *Equality*, 4th ed. (London: G. Allen & Unwin, 1964), p. 103.
2. See, e.g., William Galston, *Justice and the Human Good* (Chicago: University of Chicago Press, 1980), p. 17, referring to equality of opportunity as "one ... principl[e]"; Michael Levin, "Equality of Opportunity," *Philosophical Quarterly* 31 (1983): 110–25, p. 110: "Everyone agrees that opportunities should be equal"; John Schaar, "Equality of Opportunity," in *Nomos IX: Equality*, ed. James Pennock and John Chapman (New York: Atherton Press, 1967): 228–49, p. 228: "The one [conception of equality] that today enjoys the most popularity is equality of opportunity. The formula has few enemies—politicians, businessmen, social theorists, and freedom marchers all approve of it."
3. Charles Frankel, "Equality of Opportunity," *Ethics* 81 (1971): 191–211, p. 192.
4. John Lucas, *The Principles of Politics* (Oxford: Clarendon Press, 1966), p. 249.
5. See Levin: "Before attempting to say what equality of opportunity, or opportunity rights, are, one must say something about what an opportunity is" (p. 110).
6. T. D. Campbell, "Equality of Opportunity," *Proceedings of the Aristotelian Society* 75 (1975): 51–68, pp. 51–52.
7. Onora O'Neill, "How Do We Know When Opportunities Are Equal?" in *Feminism and Philosophy*, ed. Mary Vetterling-Braggin, Frederick Elliston, and Jane English (Totowa, NJ.: Rowman & Littlefield, 1977), pp. 177–89, p. 178.
8. See, e.g., Alan Goldman, "The Principle of Equal Opportunity," *Southern Journal of Philosophy* 15 (1977): 473–85, p. 475, advocating a standard of opportunity by which people are given handicaps to correct for "socially relative initial disadvantages."
9. Compare Frankel (p. 204), advocating a standard of opportunity in which people are judged on the basis of their "abilities," with Goldman (p. 474), discussing a "sense" of opportunity by which persons are allowed to compete without the obstacles of their "natural" disadvantages.
10. See Edwina Dorn, *Rules and Racial Equality* (New Haven, Conn.: Yale University Press, 1979), p. 112, advocating a standard of opportunity by which people have a chance to attain their goals without any hindrance other than a pure lottery.
11. Illinois Human Rights Act, Ill. Ann. Stat., ch. 68, Sec. 1–101 (1979) (Smith-Hurd, 1982 Supp.).
12. Alistair MacCleod, "Equality of Opportunity: Some Ambiguities in the Ideal," in *Equality and Freedom*, ed. Gray Dorsey (New York: Oceana Publications, 1975), vol. 3, p. 1083: one cannot talk about "equality of opportunity" without making a "careful specification of the type of opportunity to be equalized."
13. See H. Rpt. No. 92–303, accompanying H.R. 8181, 92d Congress, 1st session, in *1971 U.S. Congressional and Administrative News* (St. Paul, Minn.: West Publishing Co., 1972), vol. 2, pp. 1414, 1427; Hearings on H.R. 8181, House Subcommittee on International Trade, 92d Congress, 1st session, pp. 513, 514, 517, 522–23, 524.
14. Macleod, p. 1077.
15. See, e.g., James Fishkin, *Justice, Equal Opportunity, and the Family* (New Haven, Conn.: Yale University Press, 1983), pp. 51, 106–107, 132, 145, arguing that "family autonomy" is irreconcilable with a certain specification of equal opportunity.

Life is Not a Race
ROBERT NOZICK

Equality of opportunity has seemed to many writers to be the minimal egalitarian goal, questionable (if at all) only for being too weak. (Many writers also have seen how the existence of the family prevents fully achieving this goal.) There are two ways to attempt to provide such equality: by directly worsening the situations of those more favored with opportunity, or by im-

Reprinted from *Anarchy: State and Utopia:* [Basic Books, 1974] by permission of HarperCollins Publishers.

proving the situation of those less well-favored. The latter requires the use of resources, and so it too involves worsening the situation of some: those from whom holdings are taken in order to improve the situation of others. But holdings to which these people are entitled may not be seized, even to provide equality of opportunity for others. In the absence of magic wands, the remaining means toward equality of opportunity is convincing persons each to choose to devote some of their holdings to achieving it.

The model of a race for a prize is often used in discussions of equality of opportunity. A race where some started closer to the finish line than others would be unfair, as would a race where some were forced to carry heavy weights, or run with pebbles in their sneakers. But life is not a race in which we all compete for a prize which someone has established; there is no unified race, with some person judging swiftness. Instead, there are different persons separately giving other persons different things. Those who do the giving (each of us, at times) usually do not care about desert or about the handicaps labored under; they care simply about what they actually get. No centralized process judges people's use of the opportunities they had; that is not what the processes of social cooperation and exchange are *for*.

There is a reason why some inequality of opportunity might seem *unfair*, rather than merely unfortunate in that some do not have every opportunity (which would be true even if no one else had greater advantage). Often the person entitled to transfer a holding has no special desire to transfer it to a particular person; this contrasts with a bequest to a child or a gift to a particular person. He chooses to transfer to someone who satisfies a certain condition (for example, who can provide him with a certain good or service in exchange, who can do a certain job, who can pay a certain salary), and he would be equally willing to transfer to anyone else who satisfied that condition. Isn't it unfair for one party to receive the transfer, rather than another who had less opportunity to satisfy the condition the transferrer used? Since the giver doesn't care to whom he transfers, provided the recipient satisfies a certain general condition, equality of opportunity to be a recipient in such circumstances would violate no entitlement of

the giver. Nor would it violate any entitlement of the person with the greater opportunity; while entitled to what he has, he has no entitlement that it be more than another has. Wouldn't it be *better* if the person with less opportunity had an equal opportunity? If one so could equip him without violating anyone else's entitlements (the magic wand?) shouldn't one do so? Wouldn't it be fairer? If it *would* be fairer, can such fairness also justify overriding some people's entitlements in order to acquire the resources to boost those having poorer opportunities into a more equal competitive position?

The process is competitive in the following way. If the person with greater opportunity didn't exist, the transferrer might deal with some person having lesser opportunity who then would be, under those circumstances, the best person available to deal with. This differs from a situation in which unconnected but similar beings living on different planets confront different difficulties and have different opportunities to realize various of their goals. There, the situation of one does *not* affect that of another; though it would be better if the worse planet were better endowed than it is (it also would be better if the better planet were better endowed than *it* is), it wouldn't be *fairer*. It also differs from a situation in which a person does not, though he could, choose to *improve* the situation of another. In the particular circumstances under discussion, a person having lesser opportunities would be better off if some particular person having better opportunities didn't exist. The person having better opportunities can be viewed not merely as someone better off, or as someone not choosing to aid, but as someone *blocking* or *impeding* the person having lesser opportunities from becoming better off. Impeding another by being a more alluring alternative partner in exchange is not to be compared to directly *worsening* the situation of another, as by stealing from him. But still, cannot the person with lesser opportunity justifiably complain at being so impeded by another who does not *deserve* his better opportunity to satisfy certain conditions? (Let us ignore any similar complaints another might make about *him*.)

While feeling the power of the questions of the previous two paragraphs (it is *I* who ask them), I do not believe they overturn a thoroughgoing entitlement conception. If the woman who later became my wife rejected another suitor (whom she otherwise would have married) for me, partially because (I leave aside my lovable nature) of my keen intelligence and good looks, neither of which did I earn, would the rejected less intelligent and less handsome suitor have a legitimate complaint about unfairness? Would my thus impeding the other suitor's winning the hand of fair lady justify taking some resources from others to pay for cosmetic surgery for him and special intellectual training, or to pay to develop in him some sterling trait that I lack in order to equalize our chances of being chosen? (I here take for granted the impermissibility of worsening the situation of the person having better opportunities so as to equalize opportunity; in this sort of case by disfiguring him or injecting drugs or playing noises which prevent him from fully using his intelligence.) *No such consequences follow.* (Against whom would the rejected suitor have a legitimate complaint? Against what?) Nor are things different if the differential opportunities arise from the accumulated effects of people's acting or transferring their entitlement as they choose. The case is even easier for consumption goods which cannot plausibly be claimed to have any such triadic impeding effect. *Is* it unfair that a child be raised in a home with a swimming pool, using it daily even though he is no more *deserving* than another child whose home is without one? Should such a situation be prohibited? Why then should there be objection to the transfer of the swimming pool to an adult by bequest?

The major objection to speaking of everyone's having a right *to* various things such as equality of opportunity, life, and so on, and enforcing this right, is that these "rights" require a substructure of things and materials and actions; and *other* people may have rights and entitlements over these. No one has a right to something whose realization requires certain uses of things and activities that other people have rights and entitlements over. Other people's rights and entitlements to *particular things* (*that* pencil, *their* body, and so on) and how they choose to exercise these rights and entitlements fix the external environment of any given individual and the means that will be available to him. If his goal requires the use of means which others have rights over, he must enlist their voluntary cooperation. Even to *exercise* his right to determine how something he owns is to be used may require other means he must acquire a right to, for example, food to keep him alive; he must put together, with the cooperation of others, a feasible package.

There are particular rights over particular things held by particular persons, and particular rights to reach agreements with others, *if* you and they together can acquire the means to reach an agreement. (No one has to supply you with a telephone so that you may reach an agreement with another.) No rights exist in conflict with this substructure of particular rights. Since no neatly contoured right to achieve a goal will avoid incompatibility with this substructure, no such rights exist. The particular rights over things fill the space of rights, leaving no room for general rights to be in a certain material condition. The reverse theory would place only such universally held general "rights to" achieve goals or to be in a certain material condition into its substructure so as to determine all else; to my knowledge no serious attempt has been made to state this "reverse" theory.

A Liberal Defense of Equality of Opportunity
WILLIAM GALSTON

I

Every society embodies a conception of justice. The modern liberal society is no exception. Two principles are of particular importance. First, goods and services that fall within the sphere of basic needs are to be distributed on the basis of need, and the needs of all individuals are to be regarded as equally important. Second, many opportunities outside the sphere of need are to be allocated to individuals through a competition in which all have a fair chance to participate.

The latter principle entered American political thought under the rubric of "equality of opportunity." Much of American social history can be interpreted as a struggle between those who wished to widen the scope of its application and those who sought to restrict it. Typically, its proponents have promoted *formal* equality of opportunity by attacking religious, racial, sexual, and other barriers to open competition among individuals. And they have promoted *substantive* equality of opportunity by broadening access to the institutions that develop socially valued talents.

Recently, equality of opportunity has come under renewed attack. Conservatives charge that it fosters excessive public intervention in essentially private or voluntary relations. Radicals point with scorn to the competitive selfishness it fosters and to the unequal outcomes it permits. In the face of such assaults, liberals seem bewildered and defensive.

In this paper I want to sketch the grounds on which I believe equality of opportunity can be defended, and on that basis reply to the strictures of its critics. In the course of doing so I shall revise the generally accepted understanding of this principle in several respects. As I interpret it, equality of opportunity is less juridical and more teleological than is commonly supposed. It rests on an understanding of human equality more substantive than "equality of concern and respect." It is broader than the traditional concept of meritocracy. And it is embedded in a larger vision of a good society.

My argument proceeds in four steps. First, I shall examine in summary fashion some propositions that provide the philosophical foundation for equality of opportunity. Next I shall explore the strengths and limits of four kinds of arguments commonly offered in defense of this principle. Third, I shall discuss some difficulties that attend the translation of the abstract principle into concrete social practices. Finally, I shall briefly respond to three recent critics of equality of opportunity.

II

Let me begin my foundational argument with two propositions about individuals. Proposition 1: *All judgments concerning justice and injustice are ultimately relative to individuals* who are benefited or harmed, honored or dishonored in the distribution of contested goods. When we say that a group has been treated unjustly, we mean that the individuals comprising that group have been so treated. It would make no sense to say that every member of a group has been treated justly but that nevertheless the group has been treated unjustly. Membership in the group does not constitute an additional basis of entitlement beyond individual circumstances.

The insistence on the individual as the benchmark of justice is essential to the principle of equality of opportunity and to liberal theory as a whole. Not surprisingly, this premise has been sharply questioned. Communitarian critics of liberalism contend that the physical boundaries of individuals do not correspond to the social unities from which we ought to take our bearings. We become human only in society, they argue. Our language, our customs, our ambitions—everything that defines us is formed in social interchange. To be human is to participate in activities that are essentially social and relational. We are inextricably fused with others through that participation. It is impossible to say "I" without meaning "we."

This argument is, I believe, a non sequitur. While the formative power of society is surely decisive, it is nevertheless *individuals* that are being shaped. I may share everything with others. But it is *I* that shares them—an independent consciousness, a separate locus of pleasure and pain, a demarcated being with interests to be advanced or suppressed. My interpretation of my own good may be socially determined, but it is still *my* good, and it may well not be fully congruent with the good of others. Thus, as we counter the hyperindividualism of those who deny the existence of any social bonds with or moral obligations to others, it is important not to fall into the hyperorganicism that denies the ineradicable separateness of our individual existences.[1]

I turn now to my second proposition: *All principles of justice—including liberal principles—rest on some view of the good life for individuals*. It is now widely believed that principles of justice need not rest on this foundation, and that liberalism is precisely the theory that rests on the studied refusal to specify the human good. This is the premise underlying John Rawls's so-called priority of the right over the good, as well as the neutrality thesis of Ronald Dworkin and Bruce Ackerman.[2] But it is mistaken. Let me cite just one reason why.

Every principle of justice is intended to guide human conduct. Confronted with such a principle, the skeptic is entitled to ask, "Why should I be just?" It certainly won't do to reply, "Be just because the moral point of view requires it." A well-formed answer, I suggest, must link justice to intelligible motives for action. That is, it must invoke some conception of the good as the end of action—happiness, perfection, moral freedom, or the like. Even the strong claim that justice is a requirement of reason derives its hortatory force from the assumed goodness of the rational life.[3]

Some views of the human good argue for a summum bonum—one best way of life on the basis of which all others can be judged and rank-ordered. It may well be possible to defend such a view. For my present purposes, however, a more latitudinarian approach will suffice, along the following lines.

Every human being is born with a wide range of potential talents. Some ought not to be encouraged—a capacity for ingenious and guiltless cruelty, for example. Among the capacities of an individual that are in some sense worth developing, a small subset are comprehensive enough to serve as organizing principles for an entire life. The fullest possible development of one or more of these capacities is an important element of the good life for that individual.

Experience teaches us that individuals vary widely. Each of us is naturally gifted along some dimensions and inept along others. Some are naturally good at many things, others at few. Experience also suggests that talents vary qualitatively. Some are common and rudimentary, others are rare and highly prized.

Here I want to propose a notion of human equality that is essential to equality of opportunity as I understand it. I want to suggest that in spite of profound differences among individuals, the full development of each individual—however great or limited his or her natural capacities—is equal in moral weight to that of every other. For any individuals A and B, a policy that leads to the full development of A and partial development of B is, *ceteris paribus*, equal in value to a policy that fully develops B while restricting A's development to the same degree. Thus a policy that neglects the educable retarded so that they do not learn how to care for themselves and must be institutionalized is, considered in itself, as bad as one that reduces extraordinary gifts to mere normality.

On one level, this proposal runs counter to our moral intuitions. It seems hard to deny that the full realization of high capacities is preferable to the full development of lower, more limited capacities. But this consideration is not decisive.

We would of course prefer a world in which everyone's innate capacities were more extensive than they are at present, and we would choose to be (say) mathematically talented rather than congenitally retarded. Accordingly, we would prefer *for ourselves* the full development of more extensive capacities to the full development of lesser ones. But it does not follow that whenever the developmental interests of different individuals come into conflict, the development of higher or more extensive capacities is to be given priority. A policy that focuses exclusively on the intrinsic worth of our capacities treats the characteristics of separate individuals as an artificial, disembodied unity, ignoring the fact that they have no existence apart from the individuals in whom they inhere.

It may be argued, nonetheless, that there is something more horrible about the incomplete development of great capacities than about the waste of lesser gifts. Perhaps so. But one might say with equal justice that it is more horrible for someone who can be taught to speak to be condemned to a life of inarticulate quasi-animality than it is for someone who could have been a great mathematician to lead an ordinary life. Our intuitions about the relative desirability of the best cases are more or less counterbalanced by the relative unacceptability of the worst.

I can now offer a partial definition of a good society. In such a society, the range of social possibilities will equal the range of human possibilities. Each worthy capacity, that is, will find a place within it. No one will be compelled to flee elsewhere in search of opportunities for development, the way ambitious young people had to flee farms and small towns in nineteenth-century societies. Further, each worthy capacity will be treated fairly in the allocation of resources available for individual development within that society.

These criteria, I suggest, are more fully satisfied in a liberal society than in any other. Historically, liberal societies have come closer than any others to achieving the universality that excludes no talent or virtue. The development of great gifts encounters few material or political impediments. The development of ordinary gifts is spurred by education and training open to all. Warriors, statesmen, poets, philosophers, men and women of devoted piety—all are welcomed and accommodated. The fundamental argument for a diverse society is not—as some believe—that our reason is incompetent to judge among possible ways of life. It is rather that the human good is not one thing but many things.

Although the principle of equality of opportunity is embedded in this kind of society, it is nonetheless commonly thought to presuppose a sharp distinction between the natural endowments of individuals and their social environment. The life chances of individuals, it is argued, should not be determined by such factors as race, economic class, and family background. To the extent that these factors do tend to affect the development and exercise of individual talents, it is the task of social policy to alleviate their force. If malnutrition stunts mental and physical development, then poor children must be fed by the community. If social deprivation leaves some children irreparably behind before they start first grade, then compensatory preschool programs are essential.

The proposition that natural but not social differences should affect individual life chances raises a number of difficult problems. To begin with, natural differences are usually viewed as genetic endowments not subject to external intervention. But increasingly, natural endowments are malleable, and the time may not be far off when they can be more predictably altered than can social circumstances. This eventuality will transform not only the distinction between the natural and the social but also its normative consequences. To that extent that, for example, modern techniques can overcome genetic defects or even determine genetic endowments, disputes will arise among families over access to these scarce and expensive techniques. Before the opportunity to develop one's capacities will come the opportunity to have certain capacities to develop. At this point—as

Bernard Williams rightly suggests—equality of opportunity will merge into broader issues of absolute equality and the morality of genetic intervention.[4]

Assuming that we are still some time away from the obliteration of the naturally given, we can still ask why differences of social background are thought to be impermissible determinants of social outcomes and, conversely, why natural differences are thought to be appropriate determinants.

Why shouldn't the chief's eldest child be the next chief? This question is seldom asked because it seems absurd to us. We take it for granted that a competitive system ought to winnow out the candidate "best qualified" and that family membership is utterly irrelevant to this selection. But of course it need not be. If the tribe is held together by shared loyalty based in part on family sentiments, the chief's child may be uniquely qualified. Descent may be an important ingredient of social legitimacy and therefore an important claim to rule, especially when other sources of legitimacy have been weakened. Contemporary Lebanon, where sons gain power from fathers and assume their murdered brothers' burdens, typifies this sort of society.

Underlying the usual distinction between social and natural differences is the moral intuition that social outcomes should be determined by factors over which individuals have control. But the wealth and social standing of one's family are facts over which individuals cannot exercise control, and therefore they shouldn't matter.

The difficulty with this argument is that individuals don't control their natural endowments any more than they do their ancestry. The requirement that the basis on which we make claims must somehow be generated through our own efforts amounts to a nullification of the very procedure of claiming *anything*.

The costs of this conclusion are very high. Every conception of justice presupposes the distinction between valid and invalid claims, which in turn rests on some facts about individuals. There can be no theory of justice without some notion of individual desert, and no notion of individual desert that doesn't eventually come to rest on some "undeserved" characteristics of individuals.

Some may wish to conclude that the cause of justice is lost. I disagree, because I reject the premise of the preceding argument. The world's fastest sprinter doesn't "deserve" his natural endowment of speed, but surely he deserves to win the race established to measure and honor this excellence. There is nothing in principle wrong with a conception of individual desert that rests on the possession of natural gifts.

I would conclude, rather, that the normative distinction between social facts and natural endowments is not so sharp as most interpretations of equality of opportunity presuppose. This distinction provided the historical impetus for the development of the principle: the triumph of meritocratic over patriarchal and hereditary norms is an oft-told tale. But philosophically, the social/natural distinction must be reinterpreted as the distinction between relevant and irrelevant reasons for treating individuals in certain manners.

To further this reinterpretation, I want to examine four ways in which equality of opportunity can be defended.

III

First—and most obviously—equality of opportunity can be justified as a principle of *efficiency*. Whatever the goals of a community may be, they are most likely to be achieved when the individuals most capable of performing the tasks that promote those goals are allowed to do so. Such efficiency, it may be argued, requires a system that allows individuals to declare their candidacy for positions they prefer and then selects the ablest. From this standpoint, equality of opportunity is a dictate of instrumental rationality, a measure of collective devotion to social goals.

But a complication crops up immediately. Competition among individuals to fill social roles may not produce aggregate efficiency, even if the most talented is chosen to fill each individual role.

To see why, consider a two-person society with two tasks. Suppose that person *A* can perform both tasks better than person *B* and is by an absolute measure better at the first task than at the second. If A is only slightly better than B at the first but much better at the second, it is more productive for the society as a whole to allocate the first task to B, even though A will then not be doing what he does best.

In actual societies, the differential rewards attached to tasks can produce comparable distortions. If (say) lawyers are paid much more than teachers, the talent pool from which lawyers are selected is likely to be better stocked. Teachers will then tend to be mediocre, even if the best are selected from among the candidates who present themselves. This circumstance may well impose aggregate costs on society, at least in the long run.

These difficulties arise for two reasons. First, applying equality of opportunity to a society characterized by division of labor produces a set of individual competitions whose aggregate results will fall short of the best that society could achieve through more centralized coordination among these contests. Second, equality of opportunity embodies an element of individual liberty. Individuals can choose neither the rules of various competitions nor their outcomes. But they can choose which game to play. The fact that society as a whole will benefit if I perform a certain task does not mean that I can be coerced to perform it. Within limits, I can choose which talents to develop and exercise, and I can refuse to enter specific competitions, even if I would surely emerge victorious. "From each according to his ability" is not the principle of a liberal society, for the simple reason that the individual is regarded as the owner of his or her capacities. Equality of opportunity is a meritocratic principle, but it is applied to competitions among self-selected individuals.

I do not wish to suggest that this liberty is anything like absolute. Duties to other individuals, particularly family members who have made sacrifices on my behalf, may require me to develop and exercise certain abilities. Similarly, duties to my country may require me to become a first-rate general or physicist, if I am capable of doing so. But after all such duties are taken into account, there will still be a range of choice into which a liberal society should not intrude. This will always be a bar-

rier to the single-minded pursuit of efficiency, and to the use of coercive meritocracy to achieve it.

The second justification of equality of opportunity focuses on the notion of *desert*. For each social position, it is argued, a certain range of personal qualities may be considered relevant. Individuals who possess these qualities to an outstanding degree deserve those positions. A fair competition guided by equality of opportunity will allow exemplary individuals to be identified and rewarded.

Many critics have objected to this line of reasoning. It is a mistake, they argue, to regard social positions as prizes. In athletic competition, first prize goes to the one who has performed best. It would be inappropriate to take future performance into account or to regard present performance in the context of future possibilities. The award of the prize looks only backward to what has already happened. The prize winner has established desert through completed performance. In the case of social positions, on the other hand, the past is of interest primarily as an index of future performance. The alleged criterion of desert is thus reducible to considerations of efficiency.

This critique contains elements of truth, but I believe that the sharp contrast it suggests is overdrawn. After all, societies do not just declare the existence of certain tasks to be performed. They also make known, at least in general terms, the kinds of abilities that will count as qualifications to perform these tasks. Relying on this shared public understanding, young people strive to acquire and display these abilities. If they succeed in doing so, they have earned the right to occupy the corresponding positions. They deserve them. It would therefore be wrong to breach these legitimate expectations, just as it would be wrong to tell the victorious runner, "Sorry. We know you crossed the finish line first, but we've decided to give the prize to the runner who stopped to help a fallen teammate."

To be sure, circumstances may prevent society from honoring legitimate desert claims. Individuals may spend years preparing themselves for certain occupations, only to find that economic or demographic changes have rendered their skills outmoded. Socially established expectations cannot be risk-free—a fact that security-seeking young people are not always quick to grasp. But this fact does not distinguish social competition from athletic competition. The Americans who worked so hard for the 1980 Olympic Games, only to be denied the right to compete, were deeply disappointed, but they could not maintain that they had been treated unjustly.

In short, no clear line can be drawn between tasks and prizes. Many tasks *are* prizes—opportunities to perform activities that are intrinsically or socially valuable. These prizes are of a special character—forward-looking rather than complete in themselves—and this gives rise to legitimate disagreement about the criteria that should govern their distribution. There is no science that permits completely reliable inferences from past to future performance in any occupation. But once criteria, however flawed, have been laid down, they create a context within which claims of desert can be established and must be honored if possible. Performance criteria may be altered, but only after existing claims have been discharged, and only in a manner that gives all individuals the fairest possible chance to redirect their efforts.

A third kind of justification of equality of opportunity focuses on *personal development*. When a society devotes resources to education and training, when it encourages individuals to believe that their life chances will be significantly related to their accomplishments, and when it provides an attractive array of choices, there is good reason to believe that individuals will be moved to develop some portion of their innate capacities. Thus, it may be argued, equality of opportunity is the principle of task allocation most conducive to a crucial element of the human good.

I accept this argument. But it has significant limitations. It ignores, for example, ways in which individuals may benefit from performing certain tasks even if they are less competent to do so than others. If an apprentice is not permitted to perform the activities of his craft, he cannot increase his competence. In this process, the master craftsman must be willing to accept errors and inefficiencies. This is true even if the learner can never achieve the full competence of the best practitioner. Even individuals of mediocre talents can increase their knowledge,

skill, and self-confidence when they are allowed to discharge demanding responsibilities. Thus developmental considerations may suggest rotating some tasks fairly widely rather than restricting them to the most able.

In addition, most individuals can achieve excellence in specific demanding tasks only when they concentrate on mastering that task to the exclusion of all others. Equality of opportunity is thus linked to the division of labor, to specialization, and to the principle of "one person, one job." An argument of considerable antiquity questions the human consequences of this principle. Perhaps it is better for individuals to be minimally competent and developed in many areas rather than allowing most of their capacities to lie fallow. Perhaps a system of task assignment that deemphasized competence in favor of variety would be preferable.

These considerations raise a broader issue. Human activities have both external and internal dimensions. On the one hand, they effect changes in the natural world and in the lives of others. On the other hand, they alter—develop, stunt, pervert—the character and talent of those who perform them. Neither dimension can be given pride of place; neither can be ignored.

Without a measure of physical security and material well-being, no society can afford to devote resources to individual development or to exempt individuals from material production for any portion of their lives. In societies living at the margin, child labor is a necessity and scholarly leisure is an unaffordable luxury. But structuring a social and economic system to promote productive efficiency is justified only by physical needs and by the material preconditions of development itself. Thus a fundamental perversion occurs when the subordination of development to production continues beyond that point. A wealthy community that determines the worth of all activities by the extent to which they add to its wealth has forgotten what wealth is for. A system of training, education, and culture wholly subservient to the system of production denies the fuller humanity of its participants.

For these reasons, I suggest, a prosperous society must carefully consider not only how it allocates its tasks but also how it defines and organizes the tasks it allocates. The very concern for individual development that makes equality of opportunity so attractive leads beyond that principle to basic questions of social structure.

Finally, equality of opportunity may be defended on the grounds that it is conducive to *personal satisfaction*. Within the limits of competence, individuals are permitted to choose their lives' central activity, and they are likely to spend much of their time in occupations they are competent to perform. No system can guarantee satisfaction, of course. But one that reduces to a minimum the compulsory elements of labor and allows individuals to feel competent in the course of their labor will come closer than any alternative.

While this argument is probably correct, it is important to keep its limits in mind. To begin with, the satisfaction derived from an activity is not always proportional to our ability to perform it. We may want to do what we cannot do very well, and we may obtain more pleasure from doing what we regard as a higher task in a mediocre manner than from doing a lower task very well. In addition, in a system fully governed by equality of opportunity, there would be no external causes of failure and no alternative to self-reproach for the inability to achieve personal ambitions.

An equal opportunity system stimulates many to strive for what they cannot attain. By broadening horizons, it may well increase frustration. Of course, this is not necessarily a bad thing. Such a system does induce many who can excel to develop themselves more fully. It is not clear that a system that increases both achievement and frustration is inferior to one that increases the subjective satisfaction of the less talented only by decreasing the motivation of the more talented to realize their abilities. And many people not capable of the highest accomplishments will nevertheless develop and achieve more in a context that infuses them with a desire to excel. A permanent gap between what we are and what we want to be need not be debilitating. On the contrary, it can be a barrier to complacency, a source of modesty, an incentive for self-discipline, and a ground of genuine respect for excellence.

IV

I remarked at the outset that the principle of equality of opportunity gains both content and justification from the society in which it is embedded. There are, I believe, four major dimensions along which this abstract principle is rendered socially concrete: first, the range of possibilities available within a society; second, the manner in which these activities are delimited and organized; third, the criteria governing the assignment of individuals to particular activities; and finally, the manner in which activities are connected to external goods such as money, power, and status.

I need not add much to the previous discussion of possibilities. A good society is maximally inclusive, allowing the greatest possible scope for the development and exercise of worthy talents.

Opportunities for development are affected not just by the kinds of activities that take place within a society but also by their manner of organization. Consider the provision of health care. At present in the United States, doctors, nurses, orderlies, and administrators perform specific ranges of activities, linked to one another by rigid lines of authority. It is possible—and probably desirable—to redraw these boundaries of specialization. Nurses, for example, could well be given more responsibility for tasks now performed by doctors, particularly in areas where judgment, experience, and sensitivity to the needs of specific individuals are more significant than are high levels of technical training. Similarly, it is possible to reorganize the process of production. At some plants, small groups of workers collectively produce entire automobiles, performing the required operations sequentially in the group's own area rather than along an assembly line. Proposals to expand managerial decision making to include production workers have been tried out in a number of European countries.

Behind all such suggestions lies the belief that the existing organization of social tasks rests more on habit and special privilege than on an impartial analysis of social or individual benefit. Occupational hierarchies in which all creativity and authority are confined to a few tasks while all the rest enforce routine drudgery are typically justified on the grounds of efficiency. Maintaining a certain quality and quantity of goods and services is said to demand this kind of hierarchy. In general, there is little evidence to support this proposition and much to question it. Besides, as we have seen, there are other things to consider—in particular, the effect of tasks on the development and satisfaction of the individuals who perform them. Equal opportunity requires an appropriate balance between the preconditions of productive efficiency and the internal consequences of tasks— a balance that may well depend on a far-reaching reorganization of social tasks.

Let me assume that a society has actually reached agreement on such a balance. The assignment of individuals to the tasks embodied in that agreement will remain controversial, because criteria of assignment aré open to reasonable dispute. Some considerations are clearly irrelevant. Barring aberrant background circumstances, such factors as the color of one's hair or eyes should have no bearing on one's chances of becoming a doctor, because they have no bearing on one's capacity to practice the medical art. But beyond such obvious cases, there is disagreement about the nature of the good doctor. In the prevailing view the good doctor is one who is capable of mastering a wide variety of techniques and employing them appropriately. But dissenters suggest that moral criteria should be given equal weight: the good doctor cares more about her patients' welfare than about her own material advancement, gives great weight to need in distributing her services, never loses sight of the humanity of her patients. Still others believe that the willingness to practice where medical needs are greatest is crucial. They urge that great weight be given to the likelihood—or the promise— that a prospective doctor will provide health care to rural areas, small towns, urban ghettos, or other localities lacking adequate care. From this standpoint, otherwise dubious criteria such as geographical origin or even race might become very important.

This dispute cannot be resolved in the abstract. The relative weight accorded the technical, moral, and personal dimensions will vary with the needs and circumstances of particular societies. It will also vary among specialties within professions. In the selection of brain surgeons, technical mastery is probably paramount. For pediatricians, human understanding is far more important. Whatever the criteria, they must be made as explicit as possible, so that individuals can make informed commitments to courses of training and preparation. Those who control the selection are not free to vary publicly declared criteria once they have engendered legitimate expectations.

I turn now to the connection between activities and external goods. Here my point is simple. A fair competition may demonstrate my qualification for a particular occupation. But the talents that so qualify me do not entitle me to whatever external rewards happen to be attached to that occupation. I may nevertheless be entitled to them, but an independent line of argument is needed to establish that fact. So, for example, in accordance with public criteria, my technical competence may entitle me to a position as a brain surgeon. It does not follow that I am entitled to half a million dollars a year. Even if we grant what is patently counterfactual in the case of doctors—that compensation is determined by the market—the principle of task assignment in accordance with talents does not commit us to respect market outcomes. Indeed, the kind of competition inherent in a system of equal opportunity bears no clear relation to the competition characteristic of the market.

This distinction has an important consequence. Many thinkers oppose meritocratic systems on the ground that there is no reason why differences of talent should generate or legitimate vast differences in material rewards. They are quite right. But this is not an objection to meritocracy as such. It is an objection to the way society assigns *rewards* to tasks, not to the way it assigns *individuals* to tasks.

Indeed, one could argue that current salary inequalities should be reversed. Most highly paid jobs in our society are regarded as intrinsically desirable by the people who perform them. In moments of candor, most business executives, doctors, lawyers, generals, and college professors admit that they would want to continue in their professions even at considerably lower income levels. The incomes generally associated with such occupations cannot then be justified as socially necessary incentives.

There are, however, some rewards that are intrinsically related to tasks themselves. The most obvious is the gratification obtained from performing them. Another is status. Although I cannot prove it, it seems likely that there is a hierarchy of respect and prestige independent of income, correlated with what is regarded as the intrinsic worth of activities. Tasks involving extraordinary traits of mind and character or the ability to direct the activities of others are widely prized.

Finally, certain activities may entail legitimate claims to some measure of power and authority. As Aristotle pointed out, there are inherent hierarchical relations among specialized functions. The architect guides the work of the bricklayer and the plasterer. Moreover, if members of a community have agreed on a goal, knowledge that conduces to the achievement of that goal provides a rational basis for authority. If everyone wishes to cross the ocean and arrive at a common destination, then the skilled navigator has a rational claim to the right to give orders. But the navigator's proper authority is limited in both extent and time. It does not regulate the community's nonnavigational activities, and it vanishes when all reach their destination.

V

At the outset of this paper I said that I would employ my analysis of equality of opportunity to reply to its critics, radical and conservative. I wish, in conclusion, to touch on three arguments that are frequently brought against equality of opportunity.

The first objection is the *libertarian*, raised in its purest form by Robert Nozick. According to Nozick, equality of opportunity understates the individualistic character of human existence. Life is not a race with a starting line, a finish line, a clearly designated judge, and a complex of attributes to be measured. Rather, there are only individuals, agreeing to give to and receive from each other.[5]

I believe that this contention overlooks important social facts. Within every community, certain kinds of abilities are generally prized. Being excluded from an equal chance to develop them means that one is unlikely to have much of value to exchange with others: consider the problem of hard-core unemployment when the demand for unskilled labor is declining. To be sure, there is more than one social contest, but the number is limited. In a society in which rising educational credentials are demanded even for routine tasks, exclusion from the competition for education and training—or inclusion on terms that amount to a handicap— will make it very difficult to enter the system of exchange. Equality of opportunity acknowledges these prerequisites to full participation in social competition, and it therefore legitimates at least some of the social interventions needed to permit full participation.

The second objection is the *communitarian*. According to this view, advanced by John Schaar among others, even the most perfect competition is insufficient, because competition is a defective mode of existence. It sets human beings apart from each other and pits them against one another, in an essentially destructive struggle.[6]

Certainly an equal opportunity system contains some competitive elements. But not all forms of competition are bad. Some competition brings human beings closer together, into communities of shared endeavor and mutual respect. Consider the embrace of two exhausted boxers at the end of a match, or even the spontaneous bond between Anwar Sadat and Golda Meir at their first face-to-face encounter. Moreover, competition can be mutually beneficial. Scientific competition may produce simultaneous discoveries, neither of which would have occurred without the presence of the competitor; gymnastic competition may inspire two perfect performances. And finally, the traditional antithesis between competition and community is too simple. Community rests on some agreement. A competitive system can be a form of community if most participants are willing to accept the principle of competition.

The third objection to equality of opportunity is the *democratic*. According to this objection— articulated by Michael Walzer, among others— equality of opportunity is at best a limited principle because it cannot apply to the sphere of politics. Technical expertise may confer a limited authority. But because there is no rationally binding conception of the good, there is no technique for selecting the ends of political life. Political power does not look *up* to Platonic ideas, but rather *around* to prevailing opinions: "The proper exercise of power is nothing more than the direction of the city in accordance with the civic consciousness or public spirit of the citizens."[7]

I do not believe that any contemporary political thinker has adequately defended the crucial premise of this argument: that no rational theory of political ends is available. But let me set this question to one side and focus briefly on what it means to direct a community in accordance with its own self-understanding.

At one juncture Walzer notes that a majority of citizens "might well misunderstand the logic of their own institutions or fail to apply consistently the principles they professed to hold." There may, then, be a kind of expertise in the understanding of civic consciousness that cuts against simply majoritarian institutions and democratic procedures. In *Brown* v. *Board of Education*, for example, the U.S. Supreme Court rendered a decision that would certainly have been rejected by majority vote at the time, but that was ultimately accepted as the authoritative interpretation of American principles.

More broadly: I would argue there are distinctive political excellences and virtues; they are necessary for the success of all political orders, including democracies; and they do constitute one claim—though not the only claim—to political authority, because they contribute to needed cooperation and to the achievement of shared purposes. Without them, a political community will lose its bearings and its self-confidence. It would be very fortunate if these virtues were widely distributed. But experience suggests that the percentage of individuals who possess them to any significant degree within a given community will be small.

This does not necessarily mean that democracy is based on a mistake. As Jefferson saw, the problem of democracy is to achieve some convergence of participation, consent, and excellence. He believed that this problem is soluble—in part through social and political institutions that single out the natural *aristoi*, develop their special gifts, and reliably promote them to high office. From this standpoint, the purpose of elections is not just to register opinion but also to identify excellence. Indeed, the test of an electoral system is its propensity to confer the mantle of leadership on those most worthy to lead. Properly understood, the distribution of power in democracies is not wholly distinct from, but rather partly governed by, the merit-based principle of equal opportunity.

NOTES

1. For the best example of what I call "hyperindividualism," see Robert Nozick, *Anarchy, State, and Utopia* (New York: Basic Books, 1974), pp. 30–33.
2. John Rawls, *A Theory of Justice* (Harvard University Press, 1971); Ronald Dworkin, "Liberalism" in Stuart Hampshire, ed., *Public and Private Morality* (Cambridge University Press, 1978); Bruce Ackerman, *Social Justice in the Liberal State* (Yale University Press, 1980).
3. For a fuller discussion, see William Galston, *Justice and the Human Good* (University of Chicago Press, 1980), pp. 55–56; 279–280; and "Defending Liberalism," *American Political Science Review* 76 (1982): 621–629.
4. Bernard Williams, "The Idea of Equality" (see reading 9 in this volume).
5. Robert Nozick, *op. cit.*, pp. 235–238 (see previous reading).
6. John Schaar, "Equality of Opportunity and Beyond," in J. Roland Pennock and John W. Chapman, eds., *Nomos 9: Equality* (New York: Atherton, 1967) (see reading 14 in this volume).
7. Michael Walzer, *Spheres of Justice: A Defense of Pluralism and Equality* (New York: Basic Books, 1983), p. 287.

PART V
THE CONTEMPORARY
DEBATE ON THE
NATURE AND VALUE
OF EQUALITY

Justice and Equality
JOHN RAWLS

HUMAN BEINGS POSSESS INTRINSIC WORTH

Each person possesses an inviolability founded on justice that even the welfare of society as a whole cannot override. For this reason justice denies that the loss of freedom for some is made right by a greater good shared by others. It does not allow that the sacrifices imposed on a few are outweighed by the larger sum of advantages enjoyed by the many. Therefore, in a just society the liberties of equal citizenship are taken as settled; the rights secured by justice are not subject to political bargaining or the calculus of social interests. . . .

It seems reasonable to suppose that the parties in the original position are equal. That is, all have the same rights in the procedure for choosing principles; each can make proposals, submit reasons for their acceptance, and so on. Obviously the purpose of these conditions is to represent equality between human beings as moral persons, as creatures having a conception of their good and capable of a sense of justice. The basis of equality is taken to be similarity in these two respects. Systems of ends are not ranked in value; and each man is presumed to have the requisite ability to understand and act upon whatever principles are adopted. Together with the veil of ignorance, these conditions define the principles of justice as those which rational persons concerned to advance their interests would consent to as equals when none are known to be advantaged or disadvantaged by social and natural contingencies. . . .

THE MAIN IDEA OF THE THEORY OF JUSTICE

My aim is to present a conception of justice which generalizes and carries to a higher level of abstraction the familiar theory of the social contract as found, say, in Locke, Rousseau, and Kant. In order to do this we are not to think of the original contract as one to enter a particular society or to set up a particular form of government. Rather, the guiding idea is that the principles of justice for the basic structure of society are the object of the original agreement. They are the principles that free and rational persons concerned to further their own interests would accept in an initial position of equality as defining the fundamental terms of their association. These principles are to regulate all further agreements; they specify the kinds of social cooperation that can be entered into and the forms of government that can be established. This way of regarding the principles of justice I shall call *justice as fairness*.

Thus we are to imagine that those who engage in social cooperation choose together, in one joint act, the principles which are to assign basic rights and duties and to determine the division of social benefits. Men are to decide in advance how they are to regulate their claims against one another and what is to be the foundation charter of their society. Just as each person must decide by rational reflection what constitutes his good, that is, the system of ends which it is rational for him to pursue, so a group of persons must decide once and for all what is to count among them as just and unjust. The choice which rational men would make in this hypothetical situation of equal liberty, assuming for the present that this choice problem has a solution, determines the principle of justice.

In *justice as fairness* the original position of equality corresponds to the state of nature in the traditional theory of the social contract. This original position is not, of course, thought of as an actual historical state of affairs, much less as a primitive condition of culture. It is understood as a purely hypothetical situation characterized so as to lead to a certain conception of justice. Among the essential features of this situation is that no one knows his place in society, his class position or social status, nor does any one know his fortune in the distribution of natural assets and abilities, his intelligence, strength, and the like. I shall even assume that the parties do not know their conceptions of the good or their special psychological propensities. The principles of justice are chosen behind the *veil of ignorance*. This ensures that no one is advantaged or disadvantaged in the choice of principles by the outcome of natural chance or the contingency of social circumstances. Since all are similarly situated and no one is able to design principles to favor his particular condition, the principles of justice are the result of a fair agreement or bargain. For given the circumstances of the original position, the symmetry of everyone's relations to each other, this initial situation is fair between individuals as moral persons, that is, as rational beings with their own ends and capable, I shall assume, of a sense of justice. The *original position* is, one might say, the appropriate initial status quo, and thus the fundamental agreements reached in it are fair. This explains the propriety of the name "justice as fairness": it conveys the idea that the principles of justice are agreed to in an initial situation that is fair. The name does not mean that the concepts of justice and fairness are the same, any more than the phrase "poetry as metaphor" means that the concepts of poetry and metaphor are the same. . . .

Nor, again, does anyone know his conception of the good, the particulars of his rational plan of life, or even the special features of his psychology such as his aversion to risk or lia-

bility to optimism or pessimism. More than this, I assume that the parties do not know the particular circumstances of their own society. That is, they do not know its economic or political situation, or the level of civilization and culture it has been able to achieve. The persons in the original position have no information as to which generation they belong.

Justice as fairness begins, as I have said, with one of the most general of all choices which persons might make together, namely, with the choice of the first principles of a conception of justice which is to regulate all subsequent criticism and reform of institutions. Then, having chosen a conception of justice, we can suppose that they are to choose a constitution and a legislature to enact laws, and so on, all in accordance with the principles of justice initially agreed upon. Our social situation is just if it is such that by this sequence of hypothetical agreements we would have contracted into the general system of rules which defines it. Moreover, assuming that the original position does determine a set of principles (that is, that a particular conception of justice would be chosen), it will then be true that whenever social institutions satisfy these principles those engaged in them can say to one another that they are cooperating on terms to which they would agree if they were free and equal persons whose relations with respect to one another were fair. They could all view their arrangements in an initial situation that embodies widely accepted and reasonable constraints on the choice of principles. The general recognition of this fact would provide the basis for a public acceptance of the corresponding principles of justice. No society can, of course, be a scheme of cooperation which men enter voluntarily in a literal sense; each person finds himself placed at birth in some particular position in some particular society, and the nature of this position materially affects his life prospects. Yet a society satisfying the principles of justice as fairness comes as close as a society can to being a voluntary scheme, for it meets the principles which free and equal persons would assent to under circumstances that are fair. In this sense its members are autonomous and the obligations they recognize self-imposed. . . .

THE PRINCIPLES OF JUSTICE

1. Everyone will have an equal right to the most extensive basic liberties compatible with similar liberty for others.
2. Social and economic inequalities must satisfy two conditions:
   (a) They are to the greatest benefit of the least advantaged (the difference principle).
   (b) They are attached to positions open to all under conditions of fair equality of opportunity.

The basic liberties of citizens are, roughly speaking, political liberty (the right to vote and to be eligible for public office) together with freedom of speech and assembly; freedom of the person along with the right to hold property; and freedom from arbitrary arrest and seizure as defined by the concept of the rule of law. These liberties are all required to be equal by the first principle, since citizens of a just society are to have the same basic rights.

The second principle applies to the distribution of income and wealth and to the design of organizations that make use of differences in authority and responsibility, or chains of command. While the distribution of wealth and income need not be equal, it must be to everyone's advantage, and at the same time, positions of authority and offices of command must be accessible to all. . . .

A society should try to avoid the region where the marginal contributions of those better off are negative, since, other things equal, this seems a greater fault than falling short of the best scheme when these contributions are positive. The even larger difference between rich and poor makes the latter even worse off, and this violates the principle of mutual advantage as well as democratic equality. . . .

A person in the original position would concede the justice of these inequalities. Indeed, it would be shortsighted of him not to do so. He would hesitate to agree to these regularities only if he would be dejected by the bare knowledge or perception that others were better situated; and I have assumed that the parties decide as if they are not moved by envy. In order to make the principle regulating inequalities determinate, one looks at the system from the standpoint of the least advantaged representative man. Inequalities are permissible when they maximize, or at least contribute to, the long-term expectations of the least fortunate group in society.

There is no more reason to permit the distribution of income and wealth to be settled by the distribution of natural assets than by historical and social fortune. Furthermore, the principle of fair opportunity can be only imperfectly carried out, at least as long as the institution of the family exists. The extent to which natural capacities develop and reach fruition is affected by all kinds of social conditions and class attitudes. Even the willingness to make an effort, to try, and so to be deserving in the ordinary sense is itself dependent upon happy family and social circumstances. It is impossible in practice to secure equal chances of achievement and culture for those similarly endowed, and therefore we may want to adopt a principle which recognizes this fact and also mitigates the arbitrary effects of the natural lottery itself. . . .

THE TENDENCY TO EQUALITY

I wish to conclude this discussion of the two principles by explaining the sense in which they express an egalitarian conception of justice. Also I should like to forestall the objection to the principle of fair opportunity that it leads to a callous meritocratic society. In order to prepare the way for doing this, I note several aspects of the conception of justice that I have set out.

First we may observe that the difference principle gives some weight to the considerations singled out by the principle of redress. This is the principle that undeserved inequalities call for redress; and since inequalities of birth and natural endowment are undeserved, these inequalities are to be somehow compensated for. Thus the principle holds that in order to treat all persons equally, to provide genuine equality of opportunity, society must give more attention to those with fewer native assets and to those born into the less favorable social positions. The idea is to redress the bias of contingencies in the direction of equality. In pursuit of this principle greater resources might be spent on the education of the less rather than the more intelligent, at least over a certain time of life, say the earlier years of school.

Now the principle of redress has not to my knowledge been proposed as the sole criterion of justice, as the single aim of the social order. It is plausible as most such principles are only as a prima facie principle, one that is to be weighed in the balance with others. For example, we are to weigh it against the principle to improve the average standard of life, or to advance the common good. But whatever other principles we hold, the claims of redress are to be taken into account. It is thought to represent one of the elements in our conception of justice. Now the difference principle is not of course the principle of redress. It does not require society to try to even out handicaps as if all were expected to compete on a fair basis in the same race. But the difference principle would allocate resources in education, say, so as to improve the long-term expectation of the least favored. If this end is attained by giving more attention to the better endowed, it is permissible; otherwise not. And in making this decision, the value of education should not be assessed solely in terms of economic efficiency and social welfare. Equally if not more important is the role of education in enabling a person to enjoy the culture of his society and to take part in its affairs, and in this way to provide for each individual a secure sense of his own worth.

Thus although the difference principle is not the same as that of redress, it does achieve some of the intent of the latter principle. It transforms the aims of the basic structure so that the total scheme of institutions no longer emphasizes social efficiency and technocratic values. We see then that the difference principle represents, in effect, an agreement to regard the distribution of natural talents as a common asset and to share in the benefits of this distribution whatever it turns out to be. Those who have been favored by nature, whoever they are, may gain from their good fortune only on terms that improve the situation of those who have lost out. The naturally advantaged are not to gain merely because they are more gifted, but only to cover the costs of training and education and for using their endowments in ways that help the less fortunate as well. No one deserves his greater natural capacity nor merits a more favorable starting place in society. But it does not follow that one should eliminate these distinctions. There is another way to deal with them. The basic structure can be arranged so that these contingencies work for the good of the least fortunate. Thus we are led to the difference principle if we wish to set up the social system so that no one gains or loses from his arbitrary place in the distribution of natural assets or his initial position in society without giving or receiving compensating advantages in return.

In view of these remarks we may reject the contention that the ordering of institutions is always defective because the distribution of natural talents and the contingencies of social circumstance are unjust, and this injustice must inevitably carry over to human arrangements. Occasionally this reflection is offered as an excuse for ignoring injustice, as if the refusal to acquiesce in injustice is on a par with being unable to accept death. The natural distribution is neither just nor unjust; nor is it unjust that persons are born into society at some particular position. These are simply natural facts. What is just and unjust is the way that institutions deal with these facts. Aristocratic and caste societies are unjust because they make these contingencies the ascriptive basis for belonging to more or less enclosed and privileged social classes. The basic structure of these societies incorporates the arbitrariness found in nature. But there is no necessity for men to resign themselves to these contingencies. The social system is not an unchangeable order beyond human control but a pattern of human action. In justice as fairness men agree to share one another's fate. In designing institutions they undertake to avail themselves of the accidents of nature and social circumstance only when doing so is for the common benefit. The two principles are a fair way of meeting the arbitrariness of fortune; and while no doubt imperfect in other ways, the institutions which satisfy these principles are just.

A further point is that the difference principle expresses a conception of reciprocity. It is a principle of mutual benefit. We have seen that, at least when chain connection holds, each representative man can accept the basic structure as designed to advance his interests. The social order can be justified to everyone, and in particular to those who are least favored; and in this sense it is egalitarian. But it seems necessary to consider in an intuitive way how the condition of mutual benefit is satisfied. Consider any two representative men A and B, and let B be the one who is less favored. Actually, since we are most interested in the comparison with the least favored man, let us assume that B is this individual. Now B can accept A's being better off since A's advantages have been gained in ways that improve B's prospects. If A were not allowed his better position, B would be even worse off than he is. The difficulty is to show that A has no grounds for complaint. Perhaps he is required to have less than he might since his having more would result in some loss to B. Now what can be said to the more favored man? To begin with, it is clear that the well-being of each depends on a scheme of social cooperation without which no one could have a satisfactory life. Secondly, we can ask for the willing cooperation of everyone only if the terms of the scheme are reasonable. The difference principle, then, seems to be a fair basis on which those better endowed, or more fortunate in their social circumstances, could expect others to collaborate with them when some workable arrangement is a necessary condition of the good of all.

There is a natural inclination to object that those better situated deserve their greater advantages whether or not they are to the benefit of others. At this point it is necessary to be clear about the notion of desert. It is perfectly true that given a just system of cooperation as a scheme of public rules and the expectations set up by it, those who, with the prospect of improving their condition, have done what the system announces that it will reward are entitled to their advantages. In this sense the more fortunate have a claim to their better situation; their claims are legitimate expectations established by social institutions, and the community is obligated to meet them. But this sense of desert presupposes the existence of the cooperative scheme; it is irrelevant to the question whether in the first place the scheme is to be designed in accordance with the difference principle or some other criterion.

Perhaps some will think that the person with greater natural endowments deserves those assets and the superior character that made their development possible. Because he is more worthy in this sense, he deserves the greater advantages that he could achieve with them. This view, however, is surely incorrect. It seems to be one of the fixed points of our considered judgments that no one deserves his place in the distribution of native endowments, any more than one deserves one's initial starting place in society. The assertion that a man deserves the superior character that enables him to make the effort to cultivate his abilities is equally problematic; for his character depends in large part upon fortunate family and social circumstances for which he can claim no credit. The notion of desert seems not to apply to these cases. Thus the more advantaged representative man cannot say that he deserves and therefore has a right to a scheme of cooperation in which he is permitted to acquire benefits in ways that do not contribute to the welfare of others. There is no basis for his making this claim. From the standpoint of common sense, then, the difference principle appears to be acceptable both to the more advantaged and to the less advantaged individual. Of course, none of this is strictly speaking an argument for the principle, since in a contract theory arguments are made from the point of view of the original position. But these intuitive considerations help to clarify the nature of the principle and the sense in which it is egalitarian.

I noted earlier that a society should try to avoid the region where the marginal contributions of those better off to the well-being of the less favored are negative. It should operate only on the upward rising part of the contribution curve (including of course the maximum). One reason for this, we can now see, is that on this segment of the curve the criterion of mutual benefit is always fulfilled. Moreover, there is a natural sense in which the harmony of social interests is achieved; representative men do not gain at one another's expense since only reciprocal advantages are allowed. To be sure, the shape and slope of the contribution curve is determined in part at least by the natural lottery in native assets, and as such it is neither just nor unjust. But suppose we think of the forty-five degree line as representing the ideal of a perfect harmony of interests; it is the contribution curve (a straight line in this case) along which everyone gains equally. Then it seems that the consistent realization of the two principles of justice tends to raise the curve closer to the ideal of a perfect harmony of interests. Once a society goes beyond the maximum it operates along the downward sloping part of the curve and a harmony of interests no longer exists. As the more favored gain the less advantaged lose, and vice versa. The situation is analogous to being on an efficiency frontier. This is far from desirable when the justice of the basic structure is involved. Thus it is to realize the ideal of the harmony of interests on terms that nature has given us, and to meet the criterion of mutual benefit, that we should stay in the region of positive contributions.

A further merit of the difference principle is that it provides an interpretation of the principle of fraternity. In comparison with liberty and equality, the idea of fraternity has had a lesser place in democratic theory. It is thought to be less specifically a political concept, not in itself defining any of the democratic rights but conveying instead certain attitudes of mind and forms of conduct without which we would lose sight of the values expressed by these rights. Or closely related to this, fraternity is held to represent a certain equality of social esteem manifest in various public conventions and in the absence of manners of deference and servility. No doubt fraternity does imply these things, as well as a sense of civic friendship and social solidarity, but so understood it expresses no definite requirement. We have yet to find a principle of justice that matches the underlying idea. The difference principle, however, does seem to correspond to a natural meaning of fraternity: namely, to the idea of not wanting to have greater advantages unless this is to the benefit of others who are less well off. The family, in its ideal conception and often in practice, is one place where the principle of maximizing the sum of advantages is rejected. Members of a family commonly do not wish to gain unless they can do so in ways that further the interests of the rest. Now wanting to act on the differ-

ence principle has precisely this consequence. Those better circumstanced are willing to have their greater advantages only under a scheme in which this works out for the benefit of the less fortunate.

The ideal of fraternity is sometimes thought to involve ties of sentiment and feeling which it is unrealistic to expect between members of the wider society. And this is surely a further reason for its relative neglect in democratic theory. Many have felt that it has no proper place in political affairs. But if it is interpreted as incorporating the requirements of the difference principle, it is not an impracticable conception. It does seem that the institutions and policies which we most confidently think to be just satisfy its demands, at least in the sense that the inequalities permitted by them contribute to the well-being of the less favored. On this interpretation, then, the principle of fraternity is a perfectly feasible standard. Once we accept it we can associate the traditional ideas of liberty, equality, and fraternity with the democratic interpretation of the two principles of justice as follows: liberty corresponds to the first principle, equality to the idea of equality in the first principle together with equality of fair opportunity, and fraternity to the difference principle. In this way we have found a place for the conception of fraternity in the democratic interpretation of the two principles, and we see that it imposes a definite requirement on the basic structure of society. The other aspects of fraternity should not be forgotten, but the difference principle expresses its fundamental meaning from the standpoint of social justice.

Now it seems evident in the light of these observations that the democratic interpretation of the two principles will not lead to a meritocratic society. This form of social order follows the principle of careers open to talents and uses equality of opportunity as a way of releasing men's energies in the pursuit of economic prosperity and political dominion. There exists a marked disparity between the upper and lower classes in both means of life and the rights and privileges of organizational authority. The culture of the poorer strata is impoverished while that of the governing and technocratic elite is securely based on the service of the national ends of power and wealth. Equality of opportunity means an equal chance to leave the less fortunate behind in the personal quest for influence and social position. Thus a meritocratic society is a danger for the other interpretations of the principles of justice but not for the democratic conception. For, as we have just seen, the difference principle transforms the aims of society in fundamental respects. This consequence is even more obvious once we note that we must when necessary take into account the essential primary good of self-respect and the fact that a well-ordered society is a social union of social unions. It follows that the confident sense of their own worth should be sought for the least favored and this limits the forms of hierarchy and the degrees of inequality that justice permits. Thus, for example, resources for education are not to be allotted solely or necessarily mainly according to their return as estimated in productive trained abilities, but also according to their worth in enriching the personal and social life of citizens, including here the less favored. As a society progresses the latter consideration becomes increasingly more important.

THE BASIS OF EQUALITY

We have yet to consider what sorts of beings are owed the guarantees of justice. . . . The natural answer seems to be that it is precisely the moral persons who are entitled to equal justice. Moral persons are distinguished by two features: first they are capable of having (and are assumed to have) a conception of their good (as expressed by a rational plan of life); and second they are capable of having (and assumed to acquire) a sense of justice, a normally effective desire to apply and to act upon the principles of justice, at least to a certain minimum degree. We use the characterization of the persons in the original position to single out the kind of beings to whom the principles chosen apply. After all, the parties are thought of as adopting these criteria to regulate their common institutions and their conduct toward one another; and the description of their nature enters into the reasoning by which these principles are selected. Thus equal justice is owed to those who

have the capacity to take part in and to act in accordance with the public understanding of the initial situation. One should observe that moral personality is here defined as a potentiality that is ordinarily realized in due course. It is this potentiality which brings the claims of justice into play. . . .

We see, then, that the capacity for moral personality is a sufficient condition for being entitled to equal justice. Nothing beyond the essential minimum is required. . . .

It should be stressed that the sufficient condition for equal justice, the capacity for moral personality, is not at all stringent. When someone lacks the requisite potentiality either from birth or accident, this is regarded as a defect or deprivation. There is no race or recognized group of human beings that lacks this attribute. Only scattered individuals are without this capacity, or its realization to the minimum degree, and the failure to realize it is the consequence of unjust and impoverished social circumstances, or fortuitous contingencies. Furthermore, while individuals presumably have varying capacities for a sense of justice, this fact is not a reason for depriving those with a lesser capacity of the full protection of justice. Once a certain minimum is met, a person is entitled to equal liberty on a par with everyone else. . . . It is sometimes thought that basic rights and liberties should vary with capacity, but justice as fairness denies this: provided the minimum for moral personality is satisfied, a person is owed all the guarantees of justice.

This account of the basis of equality calls for a few comments. First of all, it may be objected that equality cannot rest on natural attributes. There is no natural feature with respect to which all human beings are equal, that is, which everyone has (or which sufficiently many have) to the same degree. It might appear that if we wish to hold a doctrine of equality, we must interpret it in another way, namely as a purely procedural principle. Thus to say that human beings are equal is to say that none has a claim to preferential treatment in the absence of compelling reasons. The burden of proof favors equality: it defines a procedural presumption that persons are to be treated alike. Departures from equal treatment are in each case to be defended and judged impartially by the same system of principles that hold for all; the essential equality is thought to be equality of consideration.

There are several difficulties with this procedural interpretation. For one thing, it is nothing more than the precept of treating similar cases similarly applied at the highest level, together with an assignment of the burden of proof. Equality of consideration puts no restrictions upon what grounds may be offered to justify inequalities. There is no guarantee of substantive equal treatment, since slave and caste systems (to mention extreme cases) may satisfy this conception. The real assurance of equality lies in the content of the principles of justice and not in these procedural presumptions. The placing of the burden of proof is not sufficient. But further, even if the procedural interpretation imposed some genuine restriction on institutions, there is still the question why we are to follow the procedure in some instances and not others. Surely it applies to creatures who belong to some class, but which one? We still need a natural basis for equality so that this class can be identified.

Moreover, it is not the case that founding equality on natural capacities is incompatible with an egalitarian view. All we have to do is select a range property (as I shall say) and to give equal justice to those meeting its conditions. For example, the property of being in the interior of the unit circle is a range property of points in the plane. All points inside this circle have this property although their coordinates vary within a certain range. And they equally have this property, since no point interior to a circle is more or less interior to it than any other interior point. Now whether there is a suitable range property for singling out the respect in which human beings are to be counted equal is settled by the conception of justice. But the description of the parties in the original position identifies such a property, and the principles of justice assure us that any variations in ability within the range are to be regarded as any other natural asset. There is no obstacle to thinking that a natural capacity constitutes the basis of equality.

Mutual respect is a natural duty due to a moral agent as a being with a sense of justice and a conception of the good. . . . Mutual respect is shown in several ways: in our willingness to see the situation of others from their point of view, from the perspective of their conception of their good; and in our being prepared to give reasons for our actions whenever the interests of others are materially affected.

[T]he public recognition of the two principles gives greater support to men's self-respect and this in turn increases the effectiveness of social cooperation. Both effects are reasons for choosing these principles. It is clearly rational for men to secure their self-respect. A sense of their own worth is necessary if they are to pursue their conception of the good with zest and to delight in its fulfillment. Self-respect is not so much a part of any rational plan of life as the sense that one's plan is worth carrying out. Now our self-respect normally depends upon the respect of others. Unless we feel that our endeavors are honored by them, it is difficult if not impossible for us to maintain the conviction that our ends are worth advancing. Hence for this reason the parties would accept the natural duty of mutual respect which asks them to treat one another civilly and to be willing to explain the grounds of their actions, especially when the claims of others are overruled. Moreover, one may assume that those who respect themselves are more likely to respect each other and conversely. Self-contempt leads to contempt of others and threatens their good as much as envy does. Self-respect is reciprocally self-supporting.

[People need] to be assured by the esteem of their associates. Their self-respect and their confidence in the value of their own system of ends cannot withstand the indifference much less the contempt of others. Everyone benefits then from living in a society where the duty of mutual respect is honored. The cost to self-interest is minor in comparison with the support for the sense of one's own worth.

Justice: A Funeral Oration
WALLACE MATSON

The auncient Ciuilians do say justice is a wille perpetuall and constaunt, which gyueth to euery man his right.

—Sir Thomas Elyot, 1531

TAX JUSTICE: IT'S IN YOUR INTEREST!
. . . The military budget seems to have replaced human needs as a priority. . . . UC employees have a right to a job and a living wage. . . . To insure this right, AFSCME is asking UC employees to support the *Split Roll Tax Initiative*, which will redistribute the benefits of Proposition 13 among residents and renters, while taking a fair share from commerce. Along with other tax equality measures . . . this will put the state budget back on its feet. . . .
PUBLIC EMPLOYEES NEED TAX JUSTICE IN CALIFORNIA!

—From a manifesto handed out in Berkeley, 1982

1. THRENODY

Is it any longer possible to talk seriously about justice and rights? Are these words corrupted and debased beyond redemption? There is no need to multiply examples of how anything that any pressure group has the chutzpah to lay claim to forthwith becomes a right, *nemine contradicente*. Nor is this Newspeak restricted to the vulgar. The President of the Pacific Division of the American Philosophical Association has granted permission to misuse words like *rights* and *justice* if you do so in the service of desirable political ends.[1] Our most universally acclaimed theoretician of justice has shown at length that justice is a will perpetual and constant to forcibly take goods from those who have earned them and give them to those who have not;[2] and the leading light of Anglo-American jurisprudence has constructed a 'straightforward' argument proving that a citizen's right to equal protection of the laws is fully satisfied if only the bureaucrat denying him or her a public benefit on racial grounds shows 'respect and concern' while processing the forms.[3]

Linguistic entropy makes it as futile to try to rehabilitate mutilated words as to put toothpaste back in the tube. The semantic battle has been lost; and with it a lot more than perspicuous speech. From Plato onward ideologues have sought to capture the vocabulary of justice, the paradigm of OK words, and tie it to schemes aiming at doing away with rights and justice. Now they have brought it off. A single generation has witnessed the movement of enlightened thought away from the position that any discrimination in treatment based merely on race is a grievous wrong, all the way to a consensus that forgetting about race and treating people as individuals is proof positive of racism, and people who advocate it should be ostracized and deprived of the protection of the First Amendment. It took the Supreme Court hardly a decade to discover that the Civil Rights Act of 1964, which in the plainest and clearest language ever seen in a statute condemned racial quotas, really encouraged or even mandated them. Scarcely less abrupt has been the transformation of admiration and fostering of

Reprinted from *Social Philosophy and Policy* I (1983) by permission of the author.

excellence into the vice of elitism. The deepest philosophico-legal thinker of the western United States has preached against the immorality of requiring any applicant for any job to possess qualifications for it.[4] At the other end of the country lives another heavyweight moralist who can imagine no worse injustice than paying smart people more than dumb people.[5]

Why then am I writing about justice? What can arguments accomplish anyway? The windmills of the *Zeitgeist* ("spirit of the times"— ED.) keep right on turning. I write also about the interpretation of Parmenides (5th century B.C.). The one activity is likely to produce about as much change in the world as the other.

2. A TALE OF THE SOUTH SEAS

The island of Alpha is not on any chart and is claimed by no nation. It is a delightful place with abundant vegetation which when properly cultivated yields delicious groceries. The lagoon abounds in succulent fish. There are plenty of materials for shelter, clothing, whatever you need or desire and know how to make.

A, the sole inhabitant, who arrived on Alpha quite by accident, works a not excessively fatiguing forty-hour week producing all he wants save companionship, and being satisfied, makes no attempt to attract rescuers.

In this situation, Aristotle has told us, no questions of just and unjust can arise. One cannot be unjust to oneself "except metaphorically" and there is no one else for A to be unjust to, or vice versa.

Beta is an island near Alpha but quite unlike it: barren, plagued by vermin. It too has but one inhabitant, B, who also arrived by accident. B lives at the brink of starvation, laboriously scratching the soil to grow the single, foul-tasting, barely edible plant found on the island.

A and B do not communicate nor even know of each other's existence.

The condition of B is pitiable, but there is no more cause for talk of injustice on Beta than on Alpha. Can it be said, however, that the state of affairs consisting of A on Alpha and B on Beta is an unjust state of affairs? A and B are certainly unequal, which condition benefits nei-

ther of them, and it has been said that injustice is simply inequalities that are not to the advantage of all. Nevertheless, it would be bizarre to contend that the situation contains injustice. B's condition is unfortunate but not unjust (nor just either). The mere coexistence of A without interaction cannot add a new moral dimension.

So let us add some interaction and see what happens.

There are no materials on Beta for making a boat or raft, and the strait between the islands is shark-infested. So B cannot go to Alpha. And A has no incentive to go to Beta. But now a volcano emerges from the sea, and when it has cooled there is a land bridge making Alpha and Beta one island.

Let us consider the time interval when B can enter the Alpha district but has not actually done so. We have then a single territory containing two inhabitants, one of whom is in possession of fewer goods than the other. Is this a condition of injustice?

The difference is only that now it is feasible to equalize the conditions of A and B whereas previously it was not. If there is injustice it consists in the unequal possessions of A and B and can be remedied by taking from A and giving to B. But then it cannot be the case that the injustice arose when the islands became connected; it must rather have existed previously but only at that moment become remediable. (Murder is murder whether or not it can be punished.) But this would be contrary to our conclusion that no injustice arose from the mere comparison of the two conditions.

None of this will surprise us. We knew that justice is a social concept; so as long as A and B were incommunicado the notion had no application. If we now arrange for them to meet and converse, no injustice can be deemed to have arisen here either. How could it? B is now conscious of being worse off than A, and will no doubt feel envy, will want to share in A's bounty. B may even complain of "unjust fate," but that can only be poetry. The change has been only in knowledge; and the previous absence of injustice did not depend on ignorance.

Various things may happen when B sets foot on Alpha territory. Let us consider some of the possibilities.

Case I. Suppose the Alpha territory is a land of such abundance that it cannot be exploited by A alone; there are resources that A does not need and cannot make use of. It is no injustice if B now appropriates some or all of these goods. Nothing has been taken to which A has established any claim, nor has A been harmed.

But what if A regards B as a threat or nuisance? Would injustice be committed if A chased B out of the area or took even more drastic measures? It is hard to see what the charge could be based on, if A and B have held no converse. On a right to be let alone if one is behaving peaceably? But what if A is a lady and B is a tiger?—a possibility not ruled out by any of our suppositions. Is it not permissible to drive tigers away from one's vicinity, even if in fact the tiger has only peaceable intentions? If so, how is the situation changed if instead of a tiger one is confronted with another human being of unknown intent?

Case II. Zucchini does not grow wild in Alpha; all that there is has been cultivated by A, but there is more of it than A can possibly make use of. Would injustice arise if B should appropriate some of the surplus without A's consent? Hardly, for the surplus does not constitute a good for A, even though he produced it. Whatever happens to it is a matter of indifference as far as A is concerned; and if A is not made any worse off there can be no injustice.

Case III. Is the moral situation altered if the produce with which B absconds is something necessary for A's dinner? Well, again, if B is a tiger, we should not want to say that it is guilty of injustice, however inconvenient its conduct may be for A. And how should it differ if B is human? Both the tiger and the man are hungry, perceive an opportunity to eat, and take it. If they do fight it out, "like animals," no question of justice arises. But if A and B are human (as we shall henceforth assume) they may have an alternative not generally available to the brute creature: they can communicate, talk things over, and reach some settlement of the question "Who gets what?" that is more advantageous for one or the other or both than direct and, perhaps, uncertain combat.

3. INTERMISSION

There are in Alpha two classes of things: those which exist, or exist in altered form, or in the place where they are, because of the labor of A; and those that do not, but would be just as they are even if A had never been there. The first class of things consists of cultivated plants, constructed shelter, utensils, fish hooks, woodpiles, and the like. Call them the Artifacts. It is characteristic of human beings to labor to produce artifacts. The essence of life—any kind of life—consists in doing, acting; production of things is one important kind of doing. This means, in the human case, experiencing a need or at least a desire for something; picturing to oneself the advantage of possessing that thing; making a plan to bring it into existence or into one's possession; and expending effort to that end according to a developed pattern of skill. We speak of this in terms of the Will and its satisfaction. When all goes well we end up having what we want, and sometimes we are better off thereby. Not to be able to carry out one's own projects in this way but to serve only the interests of others, is so far not to live a human life. Extreme deprivation of this kind is slavery.

Most projects are recognized to be more or less chancy. The compassing of material ends may be frustrated by droughts, earthquakes, diseases, wild beasts, etc. Any animal can be viewed as a device for sorting out its dinner and other necessities from an environment in which the constituents occur more or less at random. And the whole process may be got through successfully and then at the last moment the desired product is snatched away, as with the Old Man in Hemingway's story. None of these frustrations is literally immoral. Tigers are not murderers and coyotes are not thieves.

To a certain extent the same attitude may be taken to other human beings, if they are strangers, not in one's group: forces of nature to be coped with as best one can. It is different, however, within the tribe. That is a group within which it is taken for granted that at least some cooperation will be extended.

People may help one another because they are forced to by threats or punishment, but that negates essential humanity. Voluntary assistance must be based on some community of goals.

4. THE TALE CONTINUED

Case IV. Let us now suppose that A and B confer. Let us suppose further that A has not produced any more artifacts than he can himself use and consume, but he has been so skillful and industrious that his production comprises considerably more than he requires for mere survival. Let us refer to the difference between A's total store and what he needs for bare survival as A's quasi-surplus.

This is what A has to bargain with. It seems that he cannot concede more than it to B, for if he does he cannot survive, so he might as well fight. A's aim in negotiating will be to give up as little of the quasi-surplus as possible to B, and to get in exchange for it as much as he can from B.

What can B bargain with? He has no surplus at all; indeed, to make the situation even starker we may assume that the earthquake destroyed Beta so that B is entirely destitute. This would, however, merely increase A's problem, for if no bargain can be struck, B will fight, which we assume A wants to avoid. Let us suppose that B can survive only if ceded 150% of A's quasi-surplus. Does it follow that there must be war to the death? No, fortunately, because if B pitches in and helps, the production of artifacts in Alpha may increase to the point where both A and B can survive. In other words, B can contribute his labor even if he lacks material resources. It turns out, then, that A can cede more than his quasi-surplus as long as the excess is made up by the added effort.

The upshot is that both A and B may be individually better off for making an agreement to share goods and labor than either one would have been if they fought winner-take-all.

Perhaps truce would be a better word than agreement for the arrangement that A and B set up. For the question of course arises, What is to prevent either party from violating the provisions of the pact when he sees fit? And the answer can only be: Nothing. We can expect no

more than that each party will abide by the pact as long as it is in his interest to do so. But it was in the interest of both parties to conclude the treaty in the first place; it remains in the interest of each party to see to it that the other one remains in the same situation; and it will not be impossible in general for him to do so. Covenants without the sword are but words, true; but each of our covenantors has and retains his sword.

Even in this simplified situation the particulars of the compact might take indefinitely many different forms, depending on the amount of A's armaments and other resources in relation to B's, their bargaining skills, and their preferences. They might agree to pool their resources (nonwithstanding A's initial advantage) and share alike; or erect a fence across the island not henceforth to be crossed by either without the other's permission; or agree that B should go to work for A five days in seven at a fixed wage. Or B might consent to become A's slave. What any such compact is, though, is an acquiescence of wills in the restriction of their own future objects. For A to cede a shovel to B is for A to renounce the satisfaction of any future desire he might have to dig with that particular shovel. B in his turn denies himself liberty to kill, disable, or maim A.

The transaction is fraught with momentous consequences. *First*, there are now obligations—bonds—between A and B; to this extent at least they form a community. They have set up rules, and they ought to abide by them. This ought, to be sure, is a prudential ought: the sanction, the consequence of nonconformity, is that the truce will be called off, and the parties will again be in danger of physical attack by each other, which they both want to avoid. To avoid resumption of war over minor infractions of the truce conditions, they may agree on methods of restitution. There will be problems about determining when a rule has been violated, as there are in tennis without an umpire, but they need not be insurmountable.

Second, A and B have invented property, at least if there are any clauses in the treaty specifying that any artifacts or other objects, or parcels of land, are to be off limits to one party without the consent of the other. Ownership is acknowledged, exclusive control of use or access.

But was there not already property before the truce? What about the artifacts A had labored to produce? Were not they, at least, already his?

John Locke's argument is that a man owns his own body; therefore he owns the labor of his body; therefore whatever he "mixes" that labor with becomes *pro tanto* an extension of his body; therefore he owns it too. The argument gets off to a bad start: "I own my own body" may look like a truism but it hardly is. It is a question of fact whether one has acknowledged, exclusive control of the use of one's body, and there are people for whom the answer is No. No doubt that is not as it should be; but we are talking of how things are. And while it is true that before B appeared on the scene A had exclusive control of the use of his own body, the exclusive control was not acknowledged. It takes two to make property.

When A and B draw up their treaty there is no limitation in principle to what they may agree to be the property of one and of the other, or to be held in common or left subject to subsequent claim. There is nothing about the axe that A has laboriously constructed from scratch that makes it his property, or property at all: no more than a tree that he plans to cut down, perhaps, some time next year and saw into boards. Nevertheless, there is something more than sentiment making the relation between a man and that with which he has "mixed his labor" particularly intimate and fit to be legitimized, as it were, by acknowledgment of ownership. Labor need not be unpleasant always, but it is generally engaged in not for its own sake but because some comprehensive plan requires it; the agent envisages some end, the production of something, the enjoyment of which is viewed a good in itself; he plans how to get it; and realizing that work is indispensable, he works. To deprive a man of some good thing that he got by luck, without effort, is indeed to frustrate him; but to take away the product of his labor is to do double damage. He has undergone the hardship of toil, and in vain. He would not have put up with the drudgery if he had known of the outcome in advance. So it is impossible to suppose that anyone would voluntarily forgo the enjoyment—which means the ownership—of what he has mixed his labor with, unless in exchange for some other good perceived as of at least equivalent value. This means that in the terms of the truce between A and B, possession of their respective artifacts will be guaranteed to them unless they receive compensation. And since A and B begin their negotiations with each in physical possession of his artifacts, it is, to be sure, as if they had property to begin with. Moreover, this concern that each has for what he produces shapes the form that their agreement will take. It is to the continuing interest of each that each should keep on producing things. Therefore the truce will contain provisions for maintaining production, which must recognize and respect the producer's ownership of his product or allow compensation if it is to be taken from him; otherwise there could remain no motive to keep it going, unless sheer fear, which is incompatible with the primary aim of the agreement.

And so, *third* and finally, we see in this agreement the genesis of rights and justice. The truce once agreed to will remain in force only as long as both parties find its continuance to their advantage. Now, some truces are made for stipulated, definite periods of time, but not this one, since the motive for making it is to avoid combat altogether. Hence it has no expiration date and cannot be abrogated by mutual consent. Breaking it is a unilateral act of war and will provoke the indignation of the other party, who was willing to continue it and was living up to it. This is enough to generate the use of moral language, supposing it has not up to now been current. One has a *right* to have the terms adhered to; failure to observe the terms on which one has agreed is *injustice*. Even if derelictions in this regard are initially only violations of a prudential ought, they are very serious, as tending to bring about the dissolution of community. Moreover the prudence they offend against is primarily not that of the agent himself but of his fellow citizen; in consequence of which objections are bound to take on a moral tone.

Thomas Hobbes held that to enter into society is to give up at least some rights, whereas I am claiming that there are no rights outside community. This is perhaps a verbal point, but hardly of no consequence. Hobbes's Right of Nature, an absolute "right to all things," is anomalous in that it has no correlative duty. In the state of nature I have the right to appropriate your shovel or hit you over the head, but that does not mean that you have any duty to submit or to refrain from doing the same to me. The sense of "right" in this context, then, seems to be only "not subject to moral censure" or as a hockey player not in the penalty box has a right to pass the puck. But this is at least a misleading way of speaking; the thought is more straightforwardly conveyed simply by saying that before any agreements have been made, questions of right and wrong in the moral sense cannot arise.

The objection might be raised that this truce cannot be the origin of justice and rights, for it might be asked of the truce itself, Is it a just agreement? Does it not, or could it not, infringe on the rights of a party?

But it is a logical point about justice that injustice cannot be suffered voluntarily, as Aristotle saw. And the truce is not only concluded but maintained voluntarily.

This reply may be thought unsatisfactory on the ground that the parties are not equal in their bargaining positions. Hence one (A) may get the better of the bargain, i.e. be in a better position after concluding it than the other party (B). Indeed, as I admitted, one form the agreement might take would be for B to make himself A's slave. But this or any other inequitable arrangement would be manifestly unjust. And it is not only absurd but morally repugnant to suggest that a slave would be behaving unjustly, violating his master's rights, if he subsequently rebelled (broke the truce). Furthermore, no such desperate engagement could be voluntarily undertaken.

I answer: First, the view that any inequality is *ipso facto* unjust is mere dogma. It is certainly not self-evidently true, for *prima facie* it is not unjust to pay travel money and honoraria to learned persons who participate in enlightening conferences on justice. The objection based on slavery is more serious. I do not assert with complete confidence that a person might voluntarily agree to become a slave. In practice there are, of course, degrees of slavery; but I suppose the concept is of one whose will is entirely subordinate to another's, one who never makes plans of his own and carries them out. Galley slavery must approximate this

condition. If that is so, then the question whether one can voluntarily become a slave seems to be the same as whether the will can voluntarily negate itself permanently. If as I maintain the essence of life is the exertion of will, then the slave is as good as dead.

But not quite. Where there is life there is hope. Probably the only circumstances in which one would choose slavery would be where the only alternative was death. And a choice's being between unpleasant alternatives does not make it no choice. If the terms of our truce involve my becoming your slave, then we form a community within which you have a right to all my services and I have no right to pursue any interest of mine independent of yours; and *within that community* I act unjustly if I do anything for myself. But let us not forget that according to the view being presented I may choose at any time to abrogate the truce and bring the community to an end. In practice, then, a community consisting of one master and one slave is likely to be unstable, the slave always on the lookout for the opportune moment to get out of that status. In other words, it is a sort of degenerate ease of community, hardly distinguishable from a lull in a state of war.

5. MORALS OF THE STORY

A novelist would tell the tale differently, but to much the same effect. Actual people in this sort of situation, if not murderously inclined or forced by extreme scarcity to eliminate competition, will come to some agreement, perhaps tacit, of the form "I'll let you alone if you let me alone; and I'll help you out from time to time if you reciprocate." Appropriation by one of things the other had made, or even just found, would be regarded as stealing and if serious would lead to conflict.

That is to say, they would establish a community and a system of justice based on agreement. This can be called justice "from the bottom up": it is not imposed on them by any superior force, for there isn't any. It comes from their mutual apprehension of necessary conditions for human beings, each with his own interests and plans, to dwell in close proximity without fighting. It can fittingly be called natural, being a direct consequence of what human life is about, the expression of human capabilities in achieving planned goals in those universal and unavoidable circumstances of existence of a semigregarious species.

However, there is, as we have seen, no constraint on the particular form of the truce. It must represent what the parties to it, not in some hypothetical and abstract condition but in concrete circumstances of their existence, can agree on as preferable to direct physical confrontation. In particular it does not presuppose equality of power in the bargaining situation, or of talents or industry, or of luck, or of the distribution of goods that result, or of anything except that all parties have equal rights to insist on the equal observance of those clauses of the treaty in which their particular interests are safeguarded. Nevertheless, natural justice if it does not (necessarily) start from an initial position of equality and does not guarantee eventual achievement of it, yet facilitates betterment of the individual's position through effort. That is what its main purpose is: to make it possible for plans to be carried out without arbitrary interference and frustration by fellow members of the community. Even in our story, destitute B will probably be able to come to terms with prosperous A that will make it possible for him through hard work to approach A's level of luxurious consumption. Remember: the harsher the terms A attempts to impose on B, the greater danger he runs of B's abrogating the truce.

The story is not a myth of the origin of government; it is Lockean, not Hobbist. There is no Sovereign set up to whom all owe deference and who has a monopoly of power wherewith to coerce the intractable; there are only the individuals with whatever resources they happen to command. As Locke noted, such an arrangement will be attended with certain inconveniences showing, for example, a need for impartial umpires and arbitrators. How it might come about (after a few more castaways had landed) that a central authority would be set up, and what its functions would or should be, is another topic. But the institutions and conceptions of right and justice would antedate the formation of such an authority, the operations of which would be liable to criticism from the

standpoint of justice. So much seems incontrovertible; the Hobbesian contention to the contrary is paradoxical and carries no conviction.

Lest this analysis be regarded as excessively hard-boiled, note that the conception of justice as observance of rules agreed on from the motive of self-interest by no means precludes the existence and importance in the community of interactions in which the requirements of justice are voluntarily held in abeyance: love and charity. Indeed it is what makes them possible: one cannot simultaneously make love and war.

Finally we observe that nothing precludes the extension of the truce to later arrivals. The conditions may have to be modified for their benefit; the arrival of a third castaway would so perturb the relations of A and B that there might have to be a new constitutional convention, as it were. But not for every new immigrant; as population grows we may expect the weight of existing agreement to impose itself on latecomers in a take-it-or-leave-it fashion.

And what is the bearing of this story and its morals on actual human affairs? This: We have been examining the kinds of relations other than out-and-out no-holds-barred conflict that can subsist between human beings; we have concluded that peace might be based on agreement; that the agreement cannot be expected to outlast its advantageousness to all parties; that the terms of agreement define what justice is, and what the rights of the parties are, within the community of those in agreement—in particular and most importantly it creates the rights of property. The normative character of the rights so specified is derived from the fact—so we have contended—that persons wishing each to attain his own goals in the context of association with other persons, would agree to them.

However, we have been assuming that human plans to achieve particular separate goals sometimes lead to conflict; and that conflict if serious will be settled by force unless the rivals can arrive at some compromise. But is it the case that human animals are necessarily motivated by individual "selfish" interests? Is it not possible—maybe sometimes actual—that they could as it were submerge their own interests into one big interest, the general welfare, the pursuit of which would involve only peaceful cooperation?

6. SOUTH SEAS TALE II

B, oppressed by the harsh terms of the truce with A but impotent to revolt, has thought of a way out. Every week he spends the one afternoon he has to himself in collecting branches and vines from the little forest plot that A has not claimed. At last one day, having secretly made a raft, he scratches in the sand an insulting note to A and paddles off into the open sea.

After many hardships he struggles onto the shore of another island. From between the palms a majestic bearded figure appears.

Alas, B thinks to himself, here we go again. More truce terms!

But no. "Welcome to Gamma, O stranger" the figure intones in a kindly voice. "I am G. You must be hungry and thirsty. Won't you join us for dinner?"

At the groaning board B is introduced to the other islanders: F, an old man confined to a wheelchair; H, a mature and handsome woman; J, a lad of seventeen or so; and two children, K and L.

Over the coffee and liqueurs B deems the time opportune for discussing their future arrangements. "I'm grateful for your tacit temporary truce," he begins, "and hope you can make it permanent."

"Truce? What ever do you mean?"

"Why, the usual—I won't try to kill you as long as you don't—"

Consternation and alarm among the Gammanians. H grasps K and L protectively in her arms. Desperately trying to scurry out of the way, F overturns his wheelchair. J grabs a silver candlestick and advances menacingly on B but is restrained by G, who at last restores a modicum of calm.

B then explains how things are done on Alpha. The Gammanians weep at the sad tale. H comforts him that he has arrived finally in a civilized community.

"But how can you get along without a truce?" B is still puzzled. "Don't you have your individual interests and goals, and don't you have to have some means of reconciling the conflicts to which they inevitably give rise?"

"Well," the youthful J begins to reply, "Sometimes I—"

But G cuts him off. "Not at all. We have only one goal, which is the good life for us all. Each of us helps to achieve it in any way that he or she can, and each gets all the help he or she needs from all the rest. From each according to his ability; to each according to his need."

"Just like one big happy family," B muses, dimly recalling childhood scenes.

"Of course," says G. "That's what we are—a family!"

"But what happens if you have different ideas about what your needs are?"

A suggestion of a frown appears on J's face, and he seems to exchange a significant glance with H; but G replies: "Oh, sometimes there is some perplexity about that, but when there is, we handle it democratically."

"You mean, you have a discussion and then vote on the different proposals?"

"Not exactly," says G. "I listen to what everybody has to say, and then I explain what the wise thing to do is. As everybody here is rational, they all concur, and that's that.—From now on, we all want you to feel that you are one of the family.—You must be tired. H will make your bed in the dormitory. Tomorrow after breakfast J will show you the woodpile and get you started—I take it you know something about woodchopping?—"

And so they lived happily ever after.

7. ANOTHER BATCH OF MORALS

Within the family—I mean the "traditional" family as found (say) in the novels of Jane Austen and Samuel Butler—there is little concern for justice in the sense of giving each member his or her rights. Ordinarily there is one "breadwinner," the father, who is the sole or at least principal source of income, most of which is disbursed for the common benefit of all. Where it is used to buy things for individuals, the principle of distribution is need not merit: the snaggle-toothed daughter must have her orthodontia before the musical prodigy acquires a Steinway. And if the old folks and infants are helpless and only a drain on resources, their needs must nevertheless be provided. Competitiveness plays no part, or at

least it is deplored when it does. This is called Love.

Most philosophers now writing experienced family life more or less along these lines when they were young, or at least were able to view it close up. And it may seem a more satisfactory way to order relations between people than "justice" with its stern judgments and devil-take-the-hindmost attitude. The transition from the warm nurturing environment of the family to the cold and impersonal rat-race in which the independent individual is caught up may be as traumatic as birth itself. That is doubtless one reason why the family is preferred by so many to the treaty as the proper model for human relationships.

Another is that it is inherently equalitarian. Within the ideal family all members are equal in a number of respects. There is no distinction of rich and poor; if one member has more expended on him, it is not so that he can enjoy a higher "standard of living." One does not have higher status than another or receive more deference. (Again, this is the ideal; but it is why we feel that something is wrong in the household where Cinderella lives.) Parents are careful to treat all their children fairly, which means dividing up benefits equally unless one has greater need than another; the notion of "earning" hardly enters except in comparatively trivial ways mostly concerned with putative training for the rat-race to come; and even here the experts tend to deprecate it. Granted that intrafamilial conflicts, notably sibling rivalry, have always occurred, they are—or used to be—considered superficial and due to immaturity. Universal brotherhood has been taken as synonymous with the elimination of human conflicts.

"Why can't the whole human race, or at least the whole nation, be like that?" the philosopher asks, and so do the plain man and woman. The plain man is likely to answer, "Because family relations are based on affection, which won't stretch that far." So do some philosophers, e.g. Hobbes in commenting on the perpetual state of war "in many places of *America*, except the government of small Families, the concord whereof dependeth on naturall lust".[6] But many others, of whom the first and greatest was Plato, have maintained that the project is not impossible; all that is needed is a salutary revision of education and institutional arrangement, whereupon paternal, maternal, filial, fraternal and sororal affection will become the cement binding together a completely unified and therefore, happy social order in which everyone cares for everyone else.

These philosophers base their optimism on the belief that so-called human nature is all nurture, there is no limit to how outlooks and motivations can be altered by training. This is held as a dogma by many social thinkers, like creationism among fundamentalists. But also like creationism, it is an empirical question whether it is true. A lot of evidence is in, all of it adverse: the utter failure of every attempt which, on a large scale or small, to produce the requisite changes (with the doubtful and minor exception of Israeli kibbutzim). The explanation of this dismal history is provided by the science of sociobiology. But is it altogether regrettable that human beings cannot be improved to fill the bill? If we scrutinize the family model more closely we may find that it has less pleasant aspects.

If there is no conflict within the ideal family, it is because there is only one will, or only one that counts: father's. Husband and wife being "one flesh," the woman's will is held to coincide with her man's. ("Man's happiness is: I will. Woman's happiness is: He wills"—Nietzsche.) The children are under tutelage, their wills are being formed, and are not to be regarded as competent in their own right. When in adolescence they begin to develop wills of their own and assert them, that is the well known revolt against parental authority and first step in exit from the familial hearth.

The totalitarian implications, when the family is held up as a model for emulation by the larger community, are obvious. If they are not seen immediately it is because within the family the will of the father is (sometimes) regarded as merely the expression of the dominant family member, but as the voice of Reason. "Father knows best." His macrocosmic analogue, then, is not looked upon as a tyrant but as the Philosopher King. And his subjects, that is, all the children in Philosopher Father's extended family, agree entirely with him insofar as they are ra...

d that is all that matters, of course. Who ants to be irrational? Nevertheless, there is no etting around the fact that the expanded family, unlike the microcosm, must maintain its children" in tutelage not for fifteen or twenty years but for all their lives. They cannot be allowed to grow up; all their important decisions must be made for them from above.

This has not bothered philosophers from Plato to Pol Pot who saw themselves as the loving fathers. It is, however, a stumbling block to Professor John Rawls (to his credit), and accounts for some incoherencies in his philosophy, as I shall explain presently.

Now, what will the conception of justice be according to the family model?

The short answer to this question is that there will be no such conception, although the word will be retained for propaganda effect. As we saw, there is little use for a notion of justice within the real family; and this will carry over. However, let us go the long way around to this conclusion.

The first thing to notice is that the adjective in the phrase "distributive justice" now receives emphasis. On the agreement model of justice the question of *distributing* anything hardly arises. The main idea of justice from the bottom up is that people are to keep what they produce unless they voluntarily exchange it for what others have made. It is no part of the agreement model that there will be a Master Distributor at all, distinct from the producers. That is one reason for calling it justice from the bottom up.

It is otherwise with the family model. In the (real) family there is a divorce between production and acquisition on the one hand and distribution on the other. With unimportant exceptions property is held in common; where all can make use of it they do; where they cannot it is distributed (by Father, or at least according to his will) without special consideration for who in particular made, earned, or acquired it. The *fundamentum distributionis* being need, things will be thought of as rightly distributed when they go to the neediest; or if they are such that one member's need for them is no greater than another's, when the distribution is fair, that is, equal.

Second, fathers are *ex officio* utilitarians. The loving father's aim is that all his dependents should be happy, and equally so. He is a "good provider" and what he provides is satisfactions. That does not mean of course that he caters to every whim; he does not "spoil" his dependents. He may on occasion be judgmental and punishing, but it is for their own good; when he birches the unruly offspring it really does hurt him more than the wailing lad. If family members are in trouble, he is automatically on their side and will do all he can to get them out of it regardless of whether it is "their own fault."

Magnified to the scale of society this concern becomes what in contemporary jargon is called "compassion." Anyone who is hard up for whatever reason is to have his or her needs met at the expense of all who are not hard up. And so in this regard the paternalistic society will equate justice with compassion (a term which itself has undergone a curious transformation— one hardly tends to picture sleek politicians and bureaucrats as "suffering with" the objects of their solicitude). It is held that need entails the right to its fulfillment.

Natural justice on the other hand has no conceptual connection to utility, only a factual one. The idea of justice is that people should get what they deserve, what they have earned, and to find out what fits this specification it is not relevant to calculate the consequences of the award. But since the prospect of enjoying the fruits of one's labors is by and large the most potent incentive to labor, and labor by and large is what produces goods that satisfy desires, the observance of natural justice promotes utility demonstrably better for all concerned than "compassionate" redistribution.

Third, the characteristic concern of the father for his dependents is positive in the sense that it is not enough for him to keep them from harm, he must actively promote their welfare. Writ large, this means that the Philosopher King has not discharged his duty to his subjects when he has prevented or redressed wrongdoing among them; he must improve them, make them positively better off than they were, even if he knows that in so doing some inconveniences are regrettably bound to occur. Thus Dr. Goebbels mused:

There can be no peace in Europe until the last Jews are eliminated from the continent.

That, of course, raises a large number of exceedingly delicate questions. What is to be done with the half-Jews? What with those related to Jews? In-laws of Jews? Persons married to Jews? Evidently we still have quite a lot to do and undoubtedly a multitude of personal tragedies will ensue within the framework of the solution of this problem. But that is unavoidable. . . . We are doing a good work in proceeding radically and consistently. The task we are assuming today will be an advantage and a boon to our descendants.[7]

In contrast, the partisan of natural justice does not suppose that the reign of justice and the millennium are necessarily one and the same thing. Justice is no doubt desirable for its own sake, but its main value is instrumental: it is one important condition for the productive release of human energy. And in a way the negative is primary: all that the champion of justice is called upon to do is to eliminate *in*justice; once that has been done he can rest and allow those whom he has liberated from its shadow to go about the task of making a better world.

In sum: Every society must have some recognized rules for deciding questions of ownership. In a social structure based on agreement the rules will be those of natural justice, justice from the bottom up, providing for initial ownership and subsequent voluntary exchange of the products of one's own labor. In a paternalistic society, on the other hand, such considerations will not be decisive or paid much attention. The term "justice" will nevertheless be retained on account of its favorable associations to refer to the principles observed by the persons who have the power, authority, and wisdom to redistribute the goods taken from the producers and put into a common pot. These principles will emphasize the satisfaction of needs, the most urgent getting the highest priority. Where needs are equal, distribution will be equal as far as possible. Moreover the distribution is to be handled in such a way that a harmonious social pattern is produced, a "better world." This last principle applies especially to the distribution of intangibles such as status. A person will be said to have a "right" to X if and only if the distribution pattern assigns X to that person.

This is artificial justice or justice from the top down.

8. ILLUSTRATION: AFFIRMATIVE ACTION

Philosophy is sometimes said to have no practical consequences. If so, the theory of justice is not philosophy, for whether one holds one view or another of justice makes an enormous difference in practice: As an example, let us consider the ways in which justice from the bottom up and from the top down deal with the problem of racial discrimination in employment.

First, justice from the bottom up:

In a society recognizing this norm, citizens may make whatever agreements they choose, for any reason or none, as long as they do not infringe on the rights of other citizens. So if I am a Ruritanian widgetmaker, a manufacturer of widgets who detests Ruritanians may legitimately refuse to hire me. And if there are many more of his sort, we Ruritanian widgetmakers will be at a disadvantage, we will be discriminated against just because we are Ruritanians, and that is bad. But happily the problem will solve itself. We will offer our services to non-Ruritanophobe entrepreneurs for wages lower than the bigots must pay; and if we really are just as good workers, our unbiased employers will be put at a competitive advantage over the prejudiced ones. In the not very long run, then, the gap between Ruritanian and non-Ruritanian wage levels will disappear. And in the somewhat longer run the very idea of this sort of discrimination will begin to look silly, and we will be welcomed as fellow club members and sons-in-law by the former meanies. At any rate this is the pattern that has hitherto manifested itself time and again in the United States. It is well to note in this connection that slavery in the Southern states was, and South African apartheid is, imposed by government edict, i.e. they are interferences with freedom of contract.

Justice from the top down takes a different approach. Everybody is equal to everybody else (dogma), therefore, Ruritanians are just as good at making widgets as anyone else (non sequitur); therefore, if Ruritanian representation in the widget industry is not equal to the statistical expectation, it must be the work of prejudice (non sequitur), which if sincerely denied must be an unconscious aversion (absurdity). This is sin, which must be put down by force, viz. the imposition of a pro-Ruritanian quota (called something else) on widgetmakers. This will, of course, have two effects: it will disrupt the widget industry, already reeling from Japanese competition; and it will exacerbate resentment against Ruritanians.

9. SOME PARADOXES

The derivation of some main tenets of contemporary liberal (another word-corpse) opinion from the family model will no doubt strike some people as absurd, on the ground that liberals hold the old-fashioned family to be a pernicious institution which must be abolished or at least drastically overhauled. But hostility of derivative to original is hardly unheard of. Christianity with its anti-Semitism is after all in origin a Jewish sect. Nazism was a kind of socialism. And no one can deny that Plato's Republic is paternalistic; yet Plato was the first to propose the abolition of the family in order to eliminate emotional competition with his extended political family. Totalitarian liberalism finds no embarrassment in this.

It is otherwise, however, with John Rawls. The celebrated Difference Principle, that "social and economic inequalities are to be arranged so that they are . . . to the greatest benefit of the least advantaged," and its elaboration are all easily deducible from the family model. But we must not forget that there is another Rawlsian Principle of Justice, that of equal liberties—"each person is to have an equal right to the most extensive basic liberty compatible with a similar liberty for others"—which comes first and is required to be satisfied before one even starts thinking about fulfilling the Difference Principle. The sincerity of Rawls's

advocacy of liberty, at least political liberty, and his rejection of a constitution where the Philosopher King runs everything, cannot be called in question. And that is why Rawls bases his philosophy on consent of self-interested parties; as we have seen, that is what generates a free society. But Rawls hedges his commitment. The personages behind the veil of ignorance are deprived of all flesh and blood, what is left being only the abstract Voice of Reason, which might as well be a single Rational Person wishing equal happiness for all—which as we have also seen is central to the paternalistic model.

Rawls's theory thus turns out, unsurprisingly, to be a confection of incompatible elements. The principle of equal liberties is bottom-up, but the difference principle is top-down. It would be humanly impossible to instantiate both principles simultaneously: the redistribution required by the second can only be brought about by force, thereby contravening the equal liberties. Rawls like many thinkers of today has failed to see what was so clear to Locke and his contemporaries, that without property rights there can be no rights at all. For government, not being producer of anything, has to be supported out of citizens' property. So if government has complete control of property there can be no limit on its power. In particular, as the economist Milton Friedman has emphasized, the dissenter from official policy has no base of operations or even of livelihood.

Perhaps the blindness of Rawls and so many others to this point, so obvious both in theory and in practice, results from their having convinced themselves that if ever *they* were in power, of course *they* would never abuse their position by clobbering the opposition, but would behave as exemplary liberals.

10. IN AETERNAM?

We have compared two conceptions that claim the name justice.

One is that of rendering every man his due. A man's due is what he has acquired by his own efforts and not taken from some other man without consent. A community in which this conception is realized will be one in which the members agree not to interfere in the legitimate endeavors of each other to achieve their individual goals, and to help each other to the extent that the conditions for doing so are mutually satisfactory. These agreements obtain at the level of the individual citizens, for which reason I call this conception justice from the bottom up. ("Up": there may develop a hierarchical arrangement with those at the top having special duties of enforcing the agreements; but if so, the decision concerning which agreements to enforce will not originate with them.) Such a community will be one giving the freest possible rein to all its members to develop their particular capacities and use them to carry out their plans for their own betterment. If this activity is The Good for Man (and I hold with the Philosopher that it is), then it is appropriate to call the associated conception of justice natural.

The other conception holds justice to be the satisfaction of needs so as to bring everyone as far as possible onto the same plateau of pleasurable experience. The view of human life underlying it is that life consists of two separable phases, production and consumption; the consumption phase is where The Good lies; there is ultimately no reason why any individual should have any more or less of this Good than any other individual; and the problem of how to secure the requisite production is merely technical. Society based on this conception must be structured as a hierarchy of authority, in order to solve the problem of production and to administer justice, i.e. to adjust the satisfaction quanta. Thus I have called this justice from the top down (though of course I don't think it is really justice at all).

Justice from the top down as I have described it does not sound attractive. I have tried to account for the fact that, nevertheless, it commands the enthusiastic support of so many clever men and women and is everywhere on the march by showing its emotional basis in the structure of the family, an institution that has been felt to be, at its best, a warm, conflict-free, loving refuge from fear and anxiety. Many people do not really *want* to grow up, and when they do they yearn for a return to blissful dependence in the family or even in the stage of development previous to that. I do not think it

can be controverted that this is part of the explanation for the popularity of top-down justice; but nor can it be the whole, for such a complex phenomenon must be due to many factors. Among them are genuine compassion for the unfortunate and altruistic desire to help them; fantasies of omnipotence, to which powerless academic intellectuals are exceptionally liable; and envy. What the proportions are, is anybody's guess.

As there is no hope of lessening the influence of these emotions in human affairs, the triumph of the top-down cannot be stemmed unless there are yet more powerful emotions to pit against them. What might they be? I can think of three possibilities: the desire that everyone has that he himself should be given his due, and the concomitant outrage, with which more and more people are becoming acquainted, when the top-down authority denies it; revulsion witnessing the actual, practical effects of top-down justice, e.g. in Cambodia; and finally the life force itself, Spinoza's *conatus*, the endeavor of each thing to persevere in its being, and not (except in parasites) by sucking forever but by getting proper solid nourishment. I *hope* these are strong enough to prevail and show this funeral oration to have been premature: Justice is not dead, only mugged by intellectual hoods.

NOTES

1. Joel Feinberg, *Rights, Justice, and the Bounds of Liberty* (Princeton: Princeton University Press, 1980), 141, 153. I am indebted to Max Hocutt for this reference.
2. John Rawls, *A Theory of Justice* (Cambridge, MA: Harvard University Press, 1971), 277–280 *et passim*.
3. Ronald Dworkin, *Taking Rights Seriously* (Cambridge: Harvard University Press, 1977), 227–229.
4. Richard Wasserstrom, "A Defense of Programs of Preferential Treatment," in Vincent Barry, ed., *Applying Ethics* (Belmont, CA: Wadsworth, 1982), 332 f.
5. Thomas Nagel, *Mortal Questions* (New Rochelle, N.Y.: Cambridge University Press, 1979), 99 f.
6. *Leviathan*, Chapter 13.
7. *The Goebbels Diaries*, ed. and trans. Louis P. Lochner (Westport, CT: Greenwood, 1971), 135 (March 7, 1942).

Radical Welfare Egalitarianism
KAI NIELSON

I

The argument in this chapter will attempt to show that justice should be linked closely to equality and that, so construed, it is not, as conservatives and even some liberals think, the mortal enemy of liberty. I shall also argue that equality, in an important reading, should be regarded as a goal—indeed as a fundamental human good. Moreover, it is something which is both instrumentally and intrinsically good. There is also a reading—a compatible but distinct reading from the reading mentioned above—in which equality is a right. I shall elucidate and also argue for that reading but I shall principally be concerned with arguing for equality as a fundamental goal, a goal essential for justice, which a perfectly just society would realize. In our class societies, and indeed in our dark times, such justice is not in the immediate offing. It is not the sort of thing we are going to achieve in the next decade or so. But such a conception of justice should remain a heuristic ideal in our emancipatory struggles. . . .

IV

As everybody knows, equality and egalitarianism are unclear notions. Just for a starter: is equality a right or is it a goal or is it in some complicated way both? Moreover, goal or right, what is equality and what are its criteria? What are we demanding when we demand equality? Many people—perhaps now most people—who are anti-egalitarians believe that people have a right to be treated equally in certain respects. Libertarians, though they detest egalitarianism, firmly believe that there are rights (for them negative rights) that *everyone* is supposed to have and so in that way these rights are egalitarian. Most contemporary moralists and social theorists, including even anti-egalitarian thinkers on the right (Flew, Nozick, Friedman, Lucas, Hayek), share with egalitarians "an assumption of moral equality between persons," though they differ in their interpretations of it. They agree that the moral claims of all persons are, at a sufficiently abstract level, the same, but disagree over what these are. . . . They try, in some sense, to give equal weight to each person's point of view. People must all be treated as moral persons of equal worth; in that way they must be treated as equals. But, anti-egalitarians are quick to remind us, that does not mean that we must or even should treat them equally and this is surely right, *if* it means (as anti-egalitarians usually assume) to treat them identically. A child and a very old and ill person should not be treated the same. But no egalitarian thinks that they should.

What then is the distinctively egalitarian commitment to moral equality? What reading should the egalitarian give it and what substantive claims does it involve? There are some things that once defined egalitarians but that now are accepted by conservatives as well. They are certainly conditions that would

Reprinted from Kai Nielsen, *Equality and Liberty: A Defense of Radical Egalitarianism* (Totowa, N.J.: Rowman & Allenheld, 1985) by permission. Footnotes edited.

have to be met in an egalitarian society. I refer to equal legal and political rights for all members of a society. It is now well known, though perhaps not sufficiently taken to heart, that there can be, and indeed are, in our societies great substantive inequalities in legal protection and political power even though there is formal legal and political equality—for example any adult citizen can vote or stand for office, all people can have their day in court, and no caste or class or gender distinctions can be made by the courts. Substantive legal and political equality is in reality importantly dependent on economic factors; questions of legal, political or social equality cannot be detached from questions of economic equality. Yet these formal equalities, as insufficient as they are, are not to be despised, for they are the opening wedge in the struggle tc achieve equality and they must be a part of any adequate specification of the criteria for equality. For there to be equality, these political and legal conditions must obtain. But we must never lose sight of the fact that though they are necessary they are not nearly sufficient conditions for equality.

There is a historical dimension to egalitarianism. Once the commitment to political and legal equality was something that distinguished the egalitarian from the non-egalitarian. Now, in theory at least, even anti-egalitarians accept legal and political equality as readily as do egalitarians and many, provided they could give their own reading to it, would accept the vague notion of social equality as well. They are not like Aristotle or Nietzsche. That their actual concrete political commitments cut against even these equalities is something else again.

However, for contemporary egalitarians some form of economic equality is central as part of a package with legal, political and social equalities, though again what this will come to has been variously interpreted. Part of our task will be to specify what this will come to, as well as to specify clearly what we are talking about in speaking of social equality. We need to ask whether people have a right to equal portions of certain social goods and if so what social goods?

V

In putting it in this way, we should come back to our question of whether equality is a right or a goal or both. Let us assume, for a moment, that egalitarians have successfully specified the equalities they think it is desirable to attain. Then we need to ask, are these desirable things—also things people have a *right* to—or are they simply things that egalitarians, perhaps quite correctly, take it to be desirable that all people, as far as possible, have? Some egalitarians will not defend equality—or at least all the egalitarian conditions it is desirable to attain—as something people have a right to but simply judge it as desirable (morally preferable) that human beings be treated as being equal in certain respects, beyond what is strictly required to treat them as moral equals. These respects might be that people share equally, as far as is reasonably possible, the benefits and burdens of their society or have equal opportunities for self-development or all equally have the institutional bases for having their basic needs satisfied. (It is also debatable whether justice can be so nonglobal. Its scope, arguably, should be the whole world and not just a particular society.)

It is important to see that to take equality as a matter of a set of rights that people have and to take equality as a goal could be importantly different. If we stick to negative rights (rights not to be interfered with), a system of equal rights will predictably lead to very unequal distributions of wealth, power and well-being. If we admit, as genuine rights, positive rights as well, then, depending on what positive rights we admit, there may not be much of a practical difference between the two conceptions.

VI

I want now to consider equality as a goal, though this is not to say that some equalities are not rights, though how this can be needs, of course, to be elucidated. As a goal, as an ideal state of affairs to be obtained, an egalitarian is committed to trying to provide the social basis for an equality of *condition* for all human be-

ings. The ideal, putting it minimally as a first step, is to provide the social basis for an equality of life prospects such that there cannot be anything like the vast disparities in whole life prospects that exist now.

Suppose we ask, "Why should this be thought to be desirable?" We are, I believe, so close to bedrock here that it is diffficult to know what to say. That such a condition is desirable gives expression, to speak autobiographically for a moment, to a root pre-analytical (pre-theoretical) conception of a central element in a good society and to my pre-analytic (pre-theoretical) conception of what fairness between persons comes to. Vis-à-vis fairness/unfairness, I have in mind the sense of unfairness which goes with the acceptance, where something non-catastrophic could be done about it, of the existence of very different life prospects of equally talented, equally energetic children from very different social backgrounds: say the children of a successful businessman and a dishwasher. Their whole life prospects are very unequal indeed and, given the manifest quality of that difference, that this should be so seems to me very unfair. It conflicts sharply with my sense of justice.

My egalitarian ideal is a generalization of that. I can understand someone saying that the existence of such disparities is unfortuante, that life itself in that respect is not fair, but to try to do something about it would be still worse for it would entail an onslaught on the family, the undermining of liberty, the violation of individual rights and the like. That being so, we must just live with these disparities in life prospects. Here we have something we can reason about in a common universe of discourse. But what I do not see, what indeed seems both incredible and morally monstrous, is someone who would honestly think that if none of these consequences obtained, with regard to the family, liberty, rights, and so on, they would *still* not see that there is any unfairness in a society, particularly an abundant society, so structured. There is nothing wrong, they seem at least to think, with such people having such radically unequal life prospects even when something could be done about it without violating anyone's rights or causing a social catastrophe. If someone sees no unfairness here, nothing that,

other things being equal, should be corrected in the direction of equality, then I do not know where to turn. It is almost like a situation in which someone says that he sees nothing wrong with racial bigotry, religious intolerance or torturing people to get them to confess to petty crimes. It seems that there are very basic considered judgments (moral intuitions, if you will) being appealed to here and that there is little likelihood of getting back of them to something more fundamental or evident. It seems to me to be an intrinsic good that fair relations obtain between people and that it is intrinsically desirable that at least between equally deserving people there obtain, if that is reasonably possible, an equality of life conditions. Equality seems to me to be an intrinsic good, though surely not the sole intrinsic good.

VII

However, and perhaps more importantly, equality is also a very important instrumental good. Where there are extensive differences in life prospects between people, at least within a single society, where their condition is markedly unequal, where there are extensive income differentials, the better off people in this respect tend to gain a predominance of power and control in society. It is as evident as anything can be that there is a close correlation between wealth and power. If we are reasonably clearheaded, and if we prize liberty and autonomy, and if we prize democracy, we will also be egalitarians. With those inequalities of power and control, liberty and democracy must suffer. Equality, liberty, autonomy, democracy and justice, I shall argue, come as a packaged deal. To have any of them in any secure or extensive manner we must have all of them.

VIII

I also want to argue that a certain kind of equality is a right. That everyone, where this is reasonably possible, is to have his or her needs equally met is an egalitarian *goal*; that people be treated as equals, that in the design of our

institutions people have an equal right to respect, that none be treated as a means only, are natural *rights*. That kind of equality is something we have by right. (By a "natural right" I mean nothing more arcane than rights which need not be legal rights or rights which must be conventionally acknowledged.) It is not that I am saying that a right is a goal. What I am saying is that *a certain condition of equality* is a goal that we should strive toward and that, quite independently of its attainment, there are certain rights that we all have, the covering formula for which is the claim that we all are to be treated as moral equals. This is something that could obtain now, though it is certainly not observed, and it is something that we could and should claim as a right, while the egalitarian goal I speak of is something for the future when the productive forces are more developed and when the productive relations and parallel political and legal formations have been transformed.

The link between such rights-talk and such goals-talk is this: if we believe that we human beings have an equal right to respect and that our institutions should be designed so as to achieve and sustain this, we are also very likely, when we think about what this comes to, to say that all human beings also have an equal right to concern on the part of society. By this we mean that our social institutions should be impartially concerned with all human beings under their jurisdiction. We cannot allow any playing of favorites here. If we get this far, it is a very short step, or so at least we are going to be naturally inclined to believe, to the belief that we must not construct our lives together in such a way that the needs of any human being are simply ignored. Beyond that we will also be inclined to believe that there must be an equal concern on the part of society for the satisfaction of the needs of all human beings. (I am, of course, talking about situations of plenty where this is possible.) No one in such a circumstance can be treated as being simply expendable. Rather, all needs and all interests must, as far as that is possible, be equally considered. What starts as a goal—what in some historical circumstances is little more than a heuristic ideal—turns into a right when the goal can realistically be achieved. And a just social

order, if such is ever to come into existence, must have these egalitarian commitments.

It is not likely that a condition of moral equality between human beings can be stably sustained where there is not something approaching a rough equality of condition. Where people do not stand in that condition, one person is very likely to have, in various ways, some subtle and some not so subtle, greater power than another. Because of this, it will be the case that in some ways at least some will gain control over others or at least will be in a position to exercise control or partial control, and that in turn limits the autonomy of some and works to undermine their self-respect. If we want a world of moral equals, we also need a world in which people stand to each other in a rough equality of condition. To have a world in which a condition of equal respect and concern obtain, we need, where a person's whole lifetime is the measure, a rough equality of resources. If equality as a right is to be secure; that is, if that is a right that people actually can securely exercise, we must attain the goal of equality of condition. That, of course, is something we are not within a country mile of attaining. To think about justice seriously is to think about what must be done to be on our way to attaining it.

IX

Conservatives reject the identification of the doing of social justice with the bringing about of an equality of condition. They, of course, reject egalitarianism. They are firmly set against what they regard as a horror of horrors, namely any attempt to bring about equality of result (outcome), though contemporary conservatives do accept moral equality where this is read as the doctrine that all people are to be respected equally in the sense that "we are all entitled to choose our own ends and to do our own things."[1]

To identify justice, or at least social justice, with the achieving of a certain equality of result, say a certain equality of condition, is profoundly mistaken, they believe, for it takes equality of result, a forward looking notion, and identifies it with justice, a backward looking no-

tion very much concerned with determining what actually happened in the past. To do justice, we must remember, is to render to each his due; and, as we are not all the same, like identical chocolate drops coming out of a candy machine, what is due to us will vary as we are variable and as our circumstances vary. These conservatives reject the equalizing conception of egalitarian justice. Justice, they argue, is not concerned with the future oriented ideal of making us more equal in some favored respect or respects. Its concern with distribution is only to try to make it the case that everyone gets her due which is, tautologically, what she deserves or is otherwise entitled to.

Antony Flew, one of the most extreme of the conservatives, even goes so far as to deny that a liberal egalitarian such as Rawls is concerned with justice at all. To talk about justice, Flew would have it, is to talk about our true deserts and our legitimate entitlements. To treat, identify or link justice and equality is to fail to understand what justice is. What "traditional justice is all about is the securing of everyone's presumably often different deserts and entitlements." It is, Flew claims, the demand that everyone should have their own, their due: *suum cuique tribuere*. That in turn is necessarily a matter of our all securing or being allotted our several and—that definition would suggest—often different deserts and entitlements. This is, it is claimed, what justice is and this plainly is not anything about equality of result.

Flew's claim, in the first instance at least, is a claim about the use of a term presumably common to many languages. Minimally it is a claim about English and an examination of an assortment of dictionaries will make it evident enough that the term is, in many contexts, used, and pervasively used, as Flew says it is. But there are, as well, usages, displayed in some of those dictionaries, that readily allow of a reading that is compatible with a liberal egalitarian or even a radical egalitarian understanding of justice.

In the various dictionaries I consulted, justice is linked with fairness. And to be fair was construed by some of these dictionaries as "the treating of both or all sides alike, without reference to one's feelings or interests"; to be fair, in short, is to be just to all parties, to be equi-

table. In an important way, fair treatment, some dictionaries tell us, is to put everyone on an equal footing. And this fair dealing is justice.

Now this fair dealing can be understood as giving each his due or giving each what he is entitled to, and in this way it squares with Flew's conceptualization of justice; but there is no mandate in the language requiring us to read it in this way. It can, without any linguistic impropriety, be construed as Rawls and Richards construe it. And there are, as they bring out, theoretical reasons for so treating it.

Specifically, liberal egalitarians such as Rawls, Richards and Hampshire are wary of appealing to the concept of desert. Our social and natural inheritance—that, is what kind of people we are and what our abilities and opportunities are—are in important ways beyond our control and are subject to all sorts of contingencies for which we are not, and indeed cannot be, responsible. It is very problematical, from the point of view of justice, whether we should, where it can reasonably be helped, allow those things to advantage or disadvantage us to the extent they do. Conservatives, such as Robert Nozick and Antony Flew, think that justice requires that we allow the chips to fall where they may, while any kind of egalitarian favors some correction for the imbalances that will result.

Reflection on this might very well incline us not to give any central place, or at least so central a place, as Flew and others like him do, to desert or even to entitlement in our conceptualization of justice. And if we do find these considerations compelling, as Rawls and Hampshire do, there are resources in our language which enable us, without linguistic legerdemain, to construe fairness and with that, justice, without such reference to desert or entitlement. Doing justice can be to make a certain distribution of benefits and burdens in the society, including, as one possibility, providing an equal distribution of benefits and burdens, allowing deviations for the handicapped and the like. That is an intelligible, though perhaps mistaken, conceptualization of justice. Whether it is mistaken or not and whether a more exacting and nuanced statement of it captures adequately the claims of egalitarian justice is a complicated substantive issue. It cannot reasonably be ruled out right from the start on lin-

guistic or conceptual grounds as Flew seeks to do.

This substantive claim of egalitarian justice will be examined in this book as well as the alternative claims of desert and entitlement, but we cannot, rightly, put a full stop to the whole discussion, as conservatives such as Flew seek to do, by claiming that egalitarians are just not talking about justice. . . .

Let me say first crudely and oversimply what I want to do. I want to explicate and defend an egalitarian conception of justice both in production and in distribution that is even more egalitarian than John Rawls's conception of justice. In the course of arguing for this I shall argue that such a conception of justice requires, if it is to be anything other than an ideal which turns no machinery, a socialist organization of society. I am well aware that there are a host of very diverse objections that will immediately spring to mind. I shall try to make tolerably clear what I am claiming and why I want to claim it and I shall try to go some way toward at least considering, and, I hope, in some degree meeting, some of the most salient of these objections.

I shall first give four formulations of such a radical egalitarian conception of justice, formulations which, if there is anything like a concept of social justice, capture something of it, though it is more likely that such a way of putting things is not very helpful and what we have here are four conceptualizations of social justice which together articulate what the Left takes social justice to be. I shall follow that with a statement of what I take to be the two most fundamental principles of radical egalitarian justice.

1

Four Conceptions of Radical Egalitarian Justice

(1)   Justice in society as a whole ought to be understood as requiring that each person be treated with equal respect irrespective of desert and that each person be entitled to self-respect irrespective of desert.[2]

(2)   Justice in society as a whole ought to be understood as requiring that each person be so treated such that we approach, as close as we can, to a condition where everyone will be equal in satisfaction and in such distress as is necessary for achieving our commonly accepted ends.[3]

(3)   Justice in society as a whole ought to be understood as a complete equality of the overall level of benefits and burdens of each member of that society.[4]

(4)   Justice in society as a whole ought to be understood as a structuring of the institutions of society so that each person can, to the fullest extent compatible with all other people doing likewise, satisfy her/his genuine needs.

These conceptualizations are, of course, vague and in various ways indeterminate. What counts as 'genuine needs', 'fullest extent', 'complete equality of overall level of benefits', 'as close as we can', 'equal respect' and the like? Much depends on how these notions function and in what kind of a theory they are placed. However, I will not pursue these matters here. I take it; however, that these conceptualizations will help us locate social justice on the conceptual and moral map.

The stress and intent of these egalitarian understandings of the concept of social justice is on the equal treatment of all people in various crucial respects. The emphasis is in attaining social justice, some central equality of condition for everyone. Some egalitarians stress some prized condition such as self-respect or a good life; others, more mundanely, but at least as crucially, stress an overall equal sharing of the various good things and bad things of the society. And such talk of needs postulates a common condition of life that is to be the common property of everyone.

When egalitarians speak of equality they should be understood as asserting that everyone is to be treated equally in certain respects, namely, that there are certain conditions of life that should be theirs. What they should be understood as saying is that all human beings are to be treated equally in respects $F_1, F_2, F_3, \ldots,$ F_n, where the predicate variable will range over the conditions of life which are thought to be things that all people should have. This is to say that each person has an equal right to them, but it is not to say, or to give to understand, that each person is to have identical or uniform amounts of them. Talking about identical or uniform amounts has no clear sense for respect, self-respect, satisfaction of needs, or attaining the best life of which a person is capable. The equality of condition to be coherently sought is that they all have $F_1, 2_1, F_3, \ldots, F_n$. Not that they must all have them equally, since for some F's this does not even make sense. Everyone has a right to respect and to an equal respect in that none can be treated as second-class people, but this does not mean that in treating them with respect you treat them in an identical way. In treating with equal respect a baby, a young person, or an enfeebled old man out of his mind on his death-bed, we do not treat them equally, that is, identically or uniformly, but with some kind of not very clearly defined proportional equality. (It is difficult to say what we mean here but we know how to work with the notion.) Similarly, in treating an Andaman Islander and a Bostonian with respect, we do not treat them identically, for what counts as treating someone with respect will not always be the same.

I want now to turn to a statement and elucidation of my egalitarian principles of justice. They are principles of just distribution, and it is important to recognize at the outset that they do not follow from any of my specifications of the concept of social justice. Someone might accept one of those specifications and reject my principles, and someone might accept my principles and reject any or all of those specifications or indeed believe that there is no coherent concept of social justice at all and believe that there are only different conceptualizations of justice that different theorists with different aims propound. But there is, I believe, an elective affinity between my principles and the egalitarian understanding of what the concept specified above involves. I think that if one does take justice in this egalitarian way one will find it reasonable to accept my principles.

I state my principles in a way parallel to Rawls's for ease of comparison. I will briefly compare them with his principles and show why I think an egalitarian or someone committed to Dworkin's underlying belief about the moral equality of persons, as both Rawls and I are, should opt for something closer to my principles than to Rawls's.

Principles of Egalitarian Justice

(1) Each person is to have an equal right to the most extensive total system of equal basic liberties and opportunities (including equal opportunities for meaningful work, for self-determination and political participation) compatible with a similar treatment of all. (This principle gives expression to a commitment to attain and/or sustain equal moral autonomy and equal self-respect.)

(2) After provisions are made for common social (community) values, for capital overhead to preserve the society's productive capacity and allowances are made for differing unmanipulated needs and preferences, the income and wealth (the common stock of means) is to be so divided that each person will have a right to an equal share. The necessary burdens requisite to enhance well-being are also to be equally shared, subject, of course, to limitations by differing abilities and differing situations (natural environment, not class position).

Principles of Justice as Fairness

(1) Each person is to have an equal right to the most extensive total system of equal basic liberties compatible with a similar system of liberty for all.

(2) Social and economic inequalities are to be arranged so that they are both: (a) to the greatest benefit of the least advantaged, consistent with the just savings principle, and (b) attached to offices and positions open to all under conditions of fair equality of opportunity.[5]

I shall start with a comparison of Rawls's principles and my own, setting out a brief criticism of Rawls's principles as I go along. (I shall be brief here as I have given that criticism at greater length elsewhere.) We both, as a glance at our respective first principles of justice makes clear, have an equal liberty principle, though I do not claim the strict priority for mine over my second principle that Rawls does for his. Over the statement of the equal liberty principle, there is no serious difference between us; and I am plainly indebted to Rawls here. The advantage of my principle is that it makes more explicit what is involved in such a commitment to equal liberty than does Rawls's principle. They both give expression to the importance of moral autonomy and to the equality of self-respect, and they both acknowledge the underlying importance of a commitment to a social order where there is an equal concern and respect for all persons. This must show itself in seeing humankind as a community in which we view ourselves as "a republic of equals." This, at the very least, requires an acceptance of each other's moral autonomy and indeed equal moral autonomy. There can be no popes or dictators, no bosses and bossed; any authority that obtains must be rooted in at least some form of hypothetical consent. ("What one would choose if one were . . ."). The crucial thing about my first principle is its insistence that in a through-and-through just society we must all, if we are not children, mentally defective or senile, be in a position to control the design of our own lives and we must in our collective decisions have the right to an equal say. (The devices for doing this, of course, are numerous and the difficulties in its implementation are staggering. It is here that demanding, concrete socio-political-economic thinking is essential.)

The sharp differences between Rawls and myself come over our second principles of justice. My claim is that, given our mutual commitment to equal self-respect and equal moral autonomy, in conditions of moderate scarcity (conditions similar to those in most of North America, Japan, and much of Europe) equal self-respect and equal moral autonomy require something like my second principle for their attainability. There are circumstances where Rawls's second principle is satisfiable where equal liberty and equal self-respect are not obtainable. In short, I shall argue, his first and second principles clash. Rawls would respond, of course, that, given the lexical priority of the first principle over the second, this just couldn't ob-

tain. But he, on his interpretation of the second principle, allows inequalities which undermine any effective application of the equal liberty principle.

Rawls would argue against a radical egalitarianism such as my own by claiming that "an equal division of all primary goods is irrational in view of the possibility of bettering everyone's circumstances by accepting certain inequalities." The difference principle tells us that if the worst off will be better off—better off in monetary terms—they should accept the inequality. Justice and rationality conspire to require it. The rub, however, is in Rawls's understanding of 'better off' or 'improving the position' of the worst off. He cashes these notions in purely monetary terms. This prompts the response that either this is too narrow a notion of being 'better off' or of 'improving your position', or we are not justified in believing that rational agents, who have a tolerably adequate conception of fairness, will always give first priority to being 'better off' or 'improving their position'. They might very well, in conditions of moderate scarcity, recognize other things to be of greater value. Concerning these alternatives, it is well to remark, as Wittgenstein might, "Say what you will, it still doesn't alter the substance of the matter." Either 'being better off' is being construed too narrowly by Rawls or it does not always have first priority in deliberations about what is desirable. Indeed Rawls's own notion of the good of self-respect provides us with a jarring conception of what can, in circumstances such as ours, be a conflicting assessment of what is most desirable. Self-respect is for Rawls the most important primary good and it is something which is to be shared equally. In situations of moderate scarcity (relative abundance), we cannot, in Rawls's system, trade off a lesser self-respect for more of the other primary goods. But the disparities in power, authority, and autonomy that obtain, even in welfare state capitalism, and are not only allowed but justified by the difference principle, undermine, for the worst off, and indeed for many others as well, their self-respect. Certainly it does not make for a climate of equal self-respect.

Rawls recognizes this as an "unwelcome complication" and tries to show that self-respect need not be undermined or even diminished by the disparities in power and authority allowable in his system by the difference principle. But he concedes that if they did so undermine self-respect the difference principle should be altered. He argues that a well-ordered society, in which his difference principle is in operation, would not be a society in which these inequalities in power, authority and the ability to direct your own life, would, for the worst off, and the strata which are near relatives to them, be particularly visible, hence their self-respect would not be diminished. There would be, as Rawls puts it, a "plurality of associations in a well-ordered society, with their own secure internal life. . . ." The more disadvantaged strata will have their various peer groups in which they will find positions that they regard as relevant to their aspirations. These various associations, Rawls remarks, will "tend to divide into . . . many noncomparing groups," where "the discrepancies between these divisions" will not attract "the kind of attention which unsettles the lives of those less well-placed." This itself is a tendentious sociological description of life in contemporary class societies. It is in particular very innocent about the nature of work in those societies. Such a view of things could hardly withstand reflection on the facts about work in the twentieth century brought out, for example, in Harry Braverman's *Labor and Monopoly Capital*.

However, even if that were not so and even if Rawls's account here is in some way "telling it like it is," it still reflects an incredible elitism and paternalism. People are to be kept in ignorance and are to moderate their own aspirations and to accept their station and its duties with their respective roles—roles which often will not bear comparing, if self-respect is to be retained. However, they can, if they are so deceived, retain self-respect and society will not be destabilized by their agitation. They will not make comparisons and will unreflectively accept their social roles. Here we not only have elitism and paternalism, we have the ghost of aristocratic justice. Rawls's 'realism' here has driven him into what in effect, though I am sure not in intention, is a crass apology for the bourgeois order.

However, Rawls does not retreat here for he sees it as the only acceptable way in which self-respect can be preserved. The equality of self-respect must be preserved or achieved in this way, for we cannot rationally go for a levelling of wealth and status—an alternative way of achieving equal self-respect—because it would be irrational to undermine the incentive value of those limited inequalities of wealth which will produce more goods for all including the worst off. But that appeal, even if the motivational hypothesis behind it is true, begs the question. Some would say—and there are conflicting elements in Rawls's theory which would support them—"Better a greater equality in self-respect than more goods." Even if— indeed particularly if—that claim is made by the worst off in conditions of moderate scarcity (relative abundance), that claim, as far as anything Rawls has shown, is not irrational, or even less rational, than his worst off chaps sticking with the difference principle. (Even with the links stressed by Rawls between self-respect and liberty and given the priority of liberty, this is also what he should say. Indeed, given Rawls's and Dworkin's own deeply embedded belief that there should be equal respect and concern across persons, it would seem here that the response, "Better a greater equality in self-respect than more goods" would be, morally speaking, more appropriate, though, for reasons that Bertolt Brecht has made unforgettable, we must never forget that we are, in making such a claim, talking about conditions of relative abundance.)

Rawls might counter that he was not talking about our societies but, operating from within his ideal theory, about an 'ideal type' called a well-ordered society, where, by definition, there would not be such disparities in authority and power and effective control over one's life. But he also claims that his account is meant (a) to be applicable in the real world and (b) even there to some forms of capitalism. But my point was that his difference principle sanctions inequalities that are harmful to the sense of self-respect of people in the worse off strata of any capitalist society, actual or realistically possible. They simply, if they are being rational, must accept as justified, disparities in power, wealth, and authority which are harmful to them. Indeed these disparities attack their self-respect through undermining their moral autonomy; in such social conditions, men do not have effective control over their own lives. Thus his difference principle, in a way my second more egalitarian principle is not, is in conflict with his first principle and, given Rawls's doctrine of the priority of liberty, should be abandoned.

Rawls tries to square his two principles and provide moral and conceptual space for both liberty and socio-economic inequalities by distinguishing between liberty and the *worth* of liberty. Norman Daniels, in an impressive series of both internal and external criticisms, has, I believe, demolished that defense. So I shall be brief and stick with the simplest and most direct points. Even allowing the coherence and nonarbitrariness of the distinction, it will not help to say that the socio-economic disparities affect the *worth* of liberty but not liberty itself, for a liberty that cannot be exercised is of no value; and, indeed, it is in reality no liberty at all. What is the sense of having something, even assuming it makes sense to say here that you have it, which you cannot exercise? A 'liberty' that we cannot effectively exercise, particularly because of some powerful *external* constraints, is hardly a liberty. Certainly it is of little value. If I have a right to vote but am never allowed to vote, I certainly do not have much of a right. Moreover, a rational contractor, or indeed any thoroughly rational person not bamboozled by ideology, would judge it rational to choose an equal *worth* of liberty, if he judged it rational to choose equal basic liberties. To will the end is to will the necessary means to the end. It is hardly reasonable to opt for equal liberty and then opt for a difference principle which accepts an unequal worth of liberty which, in turn, makes the equal liberty principle inoperable, that is, which makes it impossible for people actually to achieve equal liberty.

I want now to return to Rawls's arguments that equal self-respect in class societies can be achieved when inequalities remain invisible or at least invisible to those who are on the deprived side of the inequality. This hardly accords with Rawls's insistence that the principles of justice are "principles that rational persons with true general beliefs would acknowledge in the original position." As Keat and Miller aptly remark, "a theory is not ac-

ceptable if the stability of a society based upon it depends upon the members of that society not knowing its principles and the way in which it is organized." There is, they continue, something morally distressing—they actually say abhorrent—about a theory of justice relying on "the worse-off members of society continuing not to compare their position with that of the better off. This narrowing of reference groups, and the concomitant lowering of expectations, is something which should be a main object of criticism for any theory of justice which claims, as Rawls's does, to be 'democratic' and 'egalitarian'."

My above arguments—as well as the arguments of Keats and Miller and Daniels—should push Rawls, if they are near their mark, in a more egalitarian direction. Specifically, they should require either an abandonment or an extensive modification of his second principle. If the preservation of self-respect is regarded as a conception at the heart of any theory of social justice and is taken, as Rawls would take it, to be directly relevant to questions about the just distribution of primary goods, then it seems that we would be forced to adopt more egalitarian principles of just distribution than Rawls adopts.

2

However, to go in a more egalitarian direction, is not, of course, necessarily to accept my principles. There are no doubt other alternatives. I shall now directly examine my egalitarian principles, starting with an elucidation of my own second principle and then proceeding to a consideration of some of the criticisms that would naturally be made of it.

What is now at issue is my second principle.

After provisions are made for common social (community) values, for capital overhead to preserve the society's productive capacity and allowances are made for differing unmanipulated needs and preferences, the income and wealth (the common stock of means) is to be so divided that each person will have a right to an equal share. The necessary burdens requisite to enhance well being are also to be equally shared, subject, of course, to limitations by differing abilities and different situations (natural environment, not class position).

A central intent of this principle is to try to reduce inequalities in primary or basic social goods and goods that are the source of or ground for distinctions that give one person power or control over another. All status distinctions should be viewed with suspicion. Everyone should be treated equally as moral persons and, in spite of what will often be rather different moral conduct, everyone should be viewed as having equal moral worth.

The second principle is meant as a tool for attaining a state of affairs where there are no considerable differences in life prospects between different groups of people because some have a far greater income, power, authority, or privilege than others. My second principle tries to distribute the benefits and burdens so that they are, as far as is compatible with people having different abilities, equally shared. It does not say that all wealth should be divided equally, like equally dividing up a pie. Unlike such pie dividing, part of the social product must be used for things that are of collective value, for example, hospitals, schools, roads, clean air, recreation facilities, and the like. And part of it must be used to protect future generations. Another part must be used to preserve the society's productive capacity so that there will be a continuous and adequate supply of goods to be divided. However, all of us—especially those of us who live in an economically authoritarianly controlled capitalist society primarily geared to production for profit and capital accumulation and only secondarily to meeting needs—must be aware of becoming captivated or entrapped by productivism. We need democratically controlled decisions about what is to be produced, who is to produce it and how much is to be produced. The underlying rationale must be to meet (as fully as possible, as equally as possible, and while allowing for different needs) the needs of all the people. Care must be taken, particularly in the period of transition out of a capitalist society, that the needs referred to are needs people would acknowledge if they were fully aware of the various hidden persuaders operating on them. And the satisfaction of a given person's needs must, as far as possible, be compatible with other people being able to similarly so satisfy their needs.

A similar attitude should be taken toward preferences. People at different ages, in different climates, with different needs and preferences will, in certain respects, need different treatment. However, they all must start with a baseline in which their basic needs are met— needs that they will have in common. (Again what exactly they are and how this is to be ascertained is something which needs careful examination.)

Rawls's notion of primary goods captures something of what they are. What more is required will be a matter of dispute and will vary culturally and historically. However, there is enough of a core here to give us a basis for consensus; and, given an egalitarian understanding of the concept of social justice, there will be a tendency to expand what counts as basic needs. Beyond that, the differing preferences and needs should, as far as possible, be equally satisfied, though what is involved in the rider "as far as possible" is not altogether evident. But it is only fair to give them all a voice. No compossible need should be denied satisfaction where the person with the need wants it satisfied and is well-informed and would continue to want it satisfied even after rational deliberation. Furthermore, giving all people a voice has other worthwhile features. It is evident enough that people are different. These differences are sometimes the source of conflict. Attaching the importance to them that some people do, can, in certain circumstances, be ethnocentric and chauvinistic. But it is also true that these differences are often the source of human enrichment. Both fairness and human flourishing are served by the stress on giving equal play to the satisfaction of all desires that are compossible.

So my second principle of justice is not the same as a principle which directs that a pie be equally divided, though it is like it in its underlying intent, namely, that fairness starts with a presumption of equality and only modifies a strict equal division of whatever is to be divided in order to remain faithful to the underlying intent of equal treatment. For example, both children aren't given skates; one is given skates, which is what she wants, and the other is given snowshoes, which is what she wants. Thus both, by being in a way treated differently, are treated with equal concern for the satisfaction of their preferences. Treating people like this catches a central part of our most elemental sense of what fair treatment comes to.

It should also be noted that my second principle says that each person, subject to the above qualifications, has a right to an equal share. But this does not mean that all or even most people will exercise that right or will feel that they should do so. This is generally true of rights. I have a right to run for office and to make a submission to a federal regulatory agency concerning the running of the CBC. But I have yet even to dream of exercising either of those rights, though I would be very aggrieved if they were taken away, and, in not exercising them, I have done nothing untoward. People, if they are rational, will exercise their rights to shares in primary goods, since having them is necessary to achieving anything else they want, but they will not necessarily demand equal shares and they will surely be very unlikely to demand equal shares of all the goods of the world. People's wants and needs are simply too different for that. I have, or rather should have, an equal right to have fish pudding or a share in the world's stock of bubble gum. *Ceteris paribus*, I have an equal right to as much of either as anyone else, but, not wanting or liking either, I will not demand my equal share.

When needs are at issue something even stronger should be said. If I need a blood transfusion, I have, *ceteris paribus*, an equal right to blood as anyone else. But I must actually need it before I have a right to an equal share or, indeed, to any blood plasma at all. Moreover, people who need blood have an equal right to the amount they require, compatible with others who are also in need having the same treatment; but, before they can have blood at all, they must need it. My wanting it does not give me a right to any of the common stock, let alone an equal share. And, even for the people actually getting the blood, a fair share would probably not be an equal share. Their needs here would probably be too different.

How does justice as equality work where it is impossible to give equal shares? Consider the equal right to have a blood transfusion. Suppose at a given time two people in a remote community both need an immediate transfusion to survive, and suppose it is impossible to give them both a transfusion at that time. There is no way of getting blood of the requisite type and there is no way of dividing up the available plasma and giving them each half or something like that. In order to live, each person needs the whole supply. There can be no equal division here. Still are not some distributions just and others unjust? If there are no relevant differences between the people needing the plasma, the only just thing to do is to follow some procedure like flipping a coin. But there almost always are relevant differences and then we are in a somewhat different ball game.

It might be thought that, even more generally in such a situation, the radical egalitarian should say "In such a situation a coin should be tossed," but suppose the two people involved were quite similar in all relevant respects except that A had been a frequent donor of blood and B had never given blood. There is certainly a temptation to bring in desert and say that A is entitled to it and B is not. A had done his fair share in a cooperative situation and B had not, so it is only fair that A gets it. (We think of justice not only as equality but also as reciprocity.) Since 'ought' implies 'can', and since we cannot divide the blood equally, it does not violate my second principle or the conception of justice as equality to so distribute the plasma.

I would not say that to do so is unjust, but also, given my reservations about the whole category of desert, I would hesitate to say that justice requires it. But the central thing to see here is that such a distribution according to desert does not violate my second principle or run counter to justice as equality.

Suppose the individuals involved were A^1 and B^1. They are alike in all relevant respects except that A^1 is a young woman who has three children and who would soon be back in good health after the transfusion, and that B^1 is a woman ninety years of age, severely mentally enfeebled, without dependents and who would most probably die within the year anyway. It seems to me that the right thing to do under the circumstances is to give the plasma to A^1. Again it does not violate my second principle for an equal division is rationally impossible. But it is not correct to say A^1 deserves it more than B^1 or even, in a straightforward way, needs it more. However, we can relevantly say, because of the children and people who would be affected by the children, that more needs would be satisfied if A^1 gets it than B^1. This is bringing in utilitarian reasoning here, but, whatever we would generally say about utilitarianism as a complete moral theory, it seems to me perfectly appropriate to use such reasoning here. We could also say—and notice the role universalizability and role reversal play here—that, after all, B^1 had lived her life to the full, was now quite incapable of having the experiences and satisfactions that we normally can be expected to prize and indeed will soon not have any experiences at all, while A^1, by contrast, has much of the fullness of her life before her. Fairness here, since we have to make such a horrible choice, would seem to require that we give the plasma to A^1 or, if 'fairness' is not the correct notion here, a certain conception of rightness seems to dictate that, everything considered, that is the right thing to do.

Let me briefly consider a final pair A^2 and B^2. Again they are alike in every respect except that A^2 is the community's only doctor while B^2 is an unemployable hopeless drunk. Both are firm bachelors and they are both middle-aged. B^2 is not likely to change his ways or A^2 to abandon what is a competently and conscientiously done practice. Here it seems to me we again quite rightly appeal to social utility—to the overall good of the community—and give the plasma to A^2. Even if, since after all he is the only doctor, A^2 makes the decision himself in his favour, it is still a decision that can be impartially sustained. Again my second principle has not been violated since an equal division is impossible.

I think that all three of those cases—most particularly the last two with their utilitarian rationale—might be resisted because of the feeling that they, after all, violate not my second principle, but, more generally, justice as equality in not giving equal treatment to persons. B, B^1 and B^2 are simply treated as expendable in a utilitarian calculation. They are treated merely as means.

This response seems to me to be mistaken. B, B^1 and B^2 are not being ignored. If the roles were reversed and they had the features of the A they are paired with, then they would get the plasma. They are not being treated differently as *individuals*. We start from a baseline of equality. If there were none of these differences between them, and if there were no other relevant differences, there would be no grounds to choose between them. We could not, from a moral point of view, simply favor A because he was A. Just as human beings, as moral persons or persons who can become capable of moral agency, we do not distinguish between them. We must treat them equally. In the limiting case, where they are only spatiotemporally distinct, this commitment to equality of treatment is seen most clearly. Morality turns into favoritism and privilege when this commitment is broken or ignored. *Within* morality there is no bypassing it; that is fixed by the very language-game of morality (by what the concept is, if you don't like that idiom). . . .

CONCLUSION

Instead of putting out "All people are of equal worth regardless of merit" as some kind of mysterious truth-claim which appears in fact to be at best groundless and at worst false, would it not have been clearer and less evasive of the human-rights advocate simply to remark that he starts with a commitment on which he will not bend, namely a commitment to the treatment of all people as beings who are to have quite unforfeitably an equality of concern and respect? It is that sort of world that he or she most deeply desires and it is there that he stands pat. There are other equally intelligible and no doubt equally rational, moral points of view that do not contain such commitments. But it is with such a commitment that he takes his stand. Given that stand, he can justify certain claims or principles in ethics, but, with that principle, justification for him comes to an end.

It appears at least that the human rights advocate or the defender of a right-based ethic who, claiming more than this, claims his account is in some way grounded in reason or in fact or both and is demonstrably more reasonable than the elitist's view, whether in a Nietzschean form or that of a milder elitism, has made a claim that is not justified by reason. This is not to suggest what is also not the case—that the elitists have any stronger justification for their position. At this level, it appears at least to be the case that commitment rather than reason is king.

It is not that our sentiments are opposed to or unaffected by our reason, but that in such situations reason (together with a knowledge of the facts) is not sufficient to provide an answer which would tell us what is the right view of the matter and give us the principles in accordance with which, at least in such circumstances, we should guide our lives. What I think the above arguments point toward is that we have no good reason to expect that a human-rights position or a right-based ethic is necessarily more reasonable than an aristocratic one which would not accept human rights (i.e., the belief that there are some basic rights that all humans have simply in virtue of being human). I think the reason why this human rights account fails and indeed why all such arguments will fail is that they fail to realize that while many different moral codes, moralities, and moral points of view can be *consistent* with reason (with, if you will, the canons of practical rationality) *none are required by reasons*. It is a great Kantian illusion, and an illusion shared by some who are not Kantians, to think that there is a morality, if only we can unearth or (perhaps) invent it, which is *required by reason*. The fact is that rationality underdetermines morality. There are many moral points of view that can be equally compatible with or in accordance with the principles of rational action and rational belief. There is no Santa Claus of pure reason, including pure practical reason, which will tell us what we must do or even what we should do or what, through and through, would be the most desirable thing for us to do. . . .

What I think can be shown is that in the situation described, for persons with certain moral sentiments, a conception of justice of the type formulated above would be the rational choice. The sentiment I have in mind is the one that leads Rawls to what Ronald Dworkin regards as his deepest moral assumption underlying his commitment to justice as fairness, namely, "the assumption of a natural right of all men and women to an equality of concern and respect, a right they possess not in virtue of birth or characteristic or merit or excellence but simply as human beings with the capacity to make plans and give justice." I do not know how anyone could show this belief to be true—to say nothing of showing it to be self-evident—or in anyway prove it or show that if one is through and through rational, one must accept it. As I was at pains to show . . . a Nietzschean, a Benthamite, or even a classist amoralist who rejects it cannot thereby be shown to be irrational or even in any way necessarily to be diminished in his reason. It is a moral belief that I am committed to and I believe Dworkin is right in claiming that Rawls is too. What I am claiming is that in the circumstances I described if one is so committed and one has the facts straight, reasons carefully, and takes these reasons to heart, one will be led not to utilitarianism or to justice as fairness or even to a form of pluralism, but to some such form of radical egalitarianism.

NOTES

1. Antony Flew, "Who Are the Equals?" *Philosophia* 9, no. 2 (July 1980): 131–153; and Antony Flew, *The Politics of Procrustes* (Buffalo, N.Y.: Prometheus Books, 1981).
2. David Miller, "Democracy and Social Justice," *British Journal of Political Science* 8 (1977): 1–19.
3. Ted Honderich, *Three Essays on Political Violence* (Oxford, England: Basil Blackwell Ltd., 1976), pp. 37–44.
4. Christopher Ake, "Justice as Equality," *Philosophy and Public Affairs* 5, no. 1 (Fall, 1975): 69–89.
5. John Rawls, *A Theory of Justice* (Cambridge: Harvard University Press, 1971), pp.535–537.

Justice and Equality
R. M. HARE

THE SENSES OF 'JUST'

There are several reasons why a philosopher of my persuasion should wish to write about justice. The first is the general one that ethical theory ought to be applied to practical issues, both for the sake of improving the theory and for any light it may shed on the practical issues, of which many of the most important involve questions of justice. This is shown by the frequency with which appeals are made to justice and fairness and related ideals when people are arguing about political or economic questions (about wages for example, or about schools policy or about relations between races or sexes). If we do not know what 'just' and 'fair' mean (and it looks as if we do not) and therefore do not know what would settle questions involving these concepts, then we are unlikely to be able to sort out these very difficult moral problems. I have also a particular interest in the topic: I hold a view about moral reasoning which has at least strong affinities with utilitarianism;[1] and there is commonly thought to be some kind of antagonism between justice and utility or, as it is sometimes called, expediency. I have therefore a special need to sort these questions out.

We must start by distinguishing between different kinds of justice, or between different senses or uses of the word 'just' (the distinction between these different ways of putting the matter need not now concern us). In distinguishing between different kinds of justice we shall have to make crucial use of a distinction between different levels of moral thinking which I have explained at length in other places.[2] It is perhaps simplest to distinguish three levels of thought, one ethical or meta-ethical and two moral or normative-ethical. At the meta-ethical level we try to establish the meanings of the moral words, and thus the formal properties of the moral concepts, including their logical properties. Without knowing these a theory of normative moral reasoning cannot begin. Then there are two levels of (normative) moral thinking which have often been in various ways distinguished. I have myself in the past called them 'level 2' and 'level 1'; but for ease of remembering I now think it best to give them names, and propose to call level 2 the *critical* level and level 1 the *intuitive* level. At the intuitive level we make use of *prima facie* moral principles of a fairly simple general sort, and do not question them but merely apply them to cases which we encounter. This level of thinking cannot be (as intuitionists commonly suppose) self-sustaining; there is a need for a critical level of thinking by which we select the *prima facie* principles for use at the intuitive level, settle conflicts between them, and give to the whole system of them a justification which intuition by itself can never provide. It will be one of the objects of this paper to distinguish those kinds of justice whose place is at the intuitive level and which are embodied in *prima facie* principles from those kinds which have a role in critical and indeed in meta-ethical thinking.

The principal result of meta-ethical enquiry in this field is to isolate a sense or kind of justice which has come to be known as 'formal justice'. Formal justice is a property of all moral principles (which is why Professor Rawls heads his chapter on this subject not 'Formal constraints of the concept of *just*' but 'Formal constraints of the concept of *right*',[3] and why his disciple David Richards is able to make a good attempt to found the whole of morality, and not merely a theory of justice, on a similar hypothetical-contract basis).[4] Formal justice is simply another name for the formal requirement of universality in moral principles on which, as I have explained in detail elsewhere,[5] golden-rule arguments are based. From the formal, logical properties of the moral words, and in particular from the logical prohibition of individual references in moral principles, it is possible to derive formal canons of moral argument, such as the rule that we are not allowed to discriminate morally between individuals unless there is some qualitative difference between them which is the ground for the discrimination; and the rule that the equal interests of different individuals have equal moral weight. Formal justice consists simply in the observance of these canons in our moral arguments; it is widely thought that this observance by itself is not enough to secure justice in some more substantial sense. As we shall see, one is not offending against the first rule if one says that extra privileges should be given to people just because they have white skins; and one is not offending against either rule if one says that one should take a cent from everybody and give it to the man with the biggest nose, provided that he benefits as much in total as they lose. The question is, How do we get from formal to substantial justice?

This question arises because there are various kinds of material or substantial justice whose content cannot be established directly by appeal to the uses of moral words or the formal properties of moral concepts (we shall see later how much can be done indirectly by appeal to these formal properties in *conjunction* with other premises or postulates or presuppositions). There are a number of different kinds of substantial justice, and we can hardly do better than begin with Aristotle's classification of them,[6] since it is largely responsible for the different senses which the word 'just' still has in common use. This is a case where it is impossible to appeal to common use, at

any rate of the word 'just' (the word 'fair' is better) in order to settle philosophical disputes, because the common use is itself the product of past philosophical theories. The expressions 'distributive' and 'retributive' justice go back to Aristotle,[7] and the word 'just' itself occupies the place (or places) that it does in our language largely because of its place in earlier philosophical discussions.

Aristotle first separated off a generic sense of the Greek word commonly translated 'just', a sense which had been used a lot by Plato: the sense in which justice is the whole of virtue in so far as it concerns our relations with other people.[8] The last qualification reminds us that this is not the most generic sense possible. Theognis had already used it to include the whole of virtue, full stop.[9] These very generic senses of the word, as applied to men and acts, have survived into modern English to confuse philosophers. One of the sources of confusion is that, in the less generic sense of 'just' to be discussed in most of this paper, the judgment that an act would be unjust is sometimes fairly easily overridden by other moral considerations ('unjust', we may say, 'but right as an act of mercy'; or 'unjust, but right because necessary in order to avert an appalling calamity'). It is much more difficult for judgments that an act is required by justice in the generic sense, in which 'unjust' is almost equivalent to 'not right', to be overridden in this way.

Adherents of the '*fiat justitia ruat caelum*'[10] school seldom make clear whether, when they say 'Let justice be done though the heavens fall', they are using a more or less generic sense of 'justice'; and they thus take advantage of its non-overridability in the more generic sense in order to claim unchallengeable sanctity for judgments made using one of the less generic senses. It must be right to do the just thing (whatever that may be) in the sense (if there still is one in English) in which 'just' *means* 'right'. In this sense, if it were right to cause the heavens to fall, and therefore just in the most generic sense, it would of course be right. But we might have to take into account, in deciding whether it would be right, the fact that the heavens would fall (that causing the heavens to fall would be one of the things we were doing if we did the action in question). On the other hand, if it were merely the just act in one of the less generic senses, we might hold that, though just, it was not right, because it would not be right to cause the heavens to fall merely in order to secure justice in this more limited sense; perhaps some concession to mercy, or even to common sense, would be in order.

This is an application of the 'split-level' structure of moral thinking sketched above. One of the theses I wish to maintain is that principles of justice in these less generic senses are all *prima facie* principles and therefore overridable. I shall later be giving a utilitarian account of justice which finds a place, at the intuitive level, for these *prima facie* principles of justice. At this level they have great importance and utility, but it is in accordance with utilitarianism, as indeed with common sense, to claim that they can on unusual occasions be overriden. Having said this, however, it is most important to stress that this *does not* involve conceding the overridability of either the generic kind of justice, which has its place at the critical level, or of formal justice, which operates at the metaethical level. These are preserved intact, and therefore defenders of the sanctity of justice ought to be content, since these are the core of justice as of morality. We may call to mind here Aristotle's[11] remarks about the 'better justice' or 'equity' which is required in order to rectify the crudities, giving rise to unacceptable results in particular cases, of a justice whose principles are, as they have to be, couched in general (i.e. simple) terms. The lawgiver who, according to Aristotle, 'would have' given a special prescription if he had been present at this particular case, and to whose prescription we must try to conform if we can, corresponds to the critical moral thinker, who operates under the constraints of formal justice and whose principles are not limited to simple general rules but can be specific enough to cover the peculiarities of unusual cases.

RETRIBUTIVE AND DISTRIBUTIVE JUSTICE

After speaking briefly of generic justice, Aristotle goes on[12] to distinguish two main kinds of justice in the narrower or more particular sense in which it means 'fairness'. He calls these retributive and distributive justice. They have their place, respectively, in the fixing of penalties and rewards for bad and good actions, and in the distribution of goods and the opposite between the possible recipients. One of the most important questions is whether these two sorts of justice are reducible to a single sort. Rawls, for example, thinks that they are, and so do I. By using the expression 'justice as fairness', he implies that all justice can be reduced to kinds of distributive justice, which itself is founded on procedural justice (i.e. on the adoption of fair procedures) in distribution.[13]

We may (without attempting complete accuracy in exposition) explain how Rawls might effect this reduction as follows. The parties in his 'original position' are prevented by his 'veil of ignorance' from knowing what their own positions are in the world in which they are to live; so they are unable when adopting principles of justice to tailor them to suit their own individual interests. Impartiality (a very important constituent, at least, of justice) is thus secured. Therefore the principles which govern *both* the distribution of wealth and power and other good things and the assignment of rewards and penalties (and indeed all other matters which have to be regulated by principles of justice) will be impartial as between individuals, and in this sense just. In this way Rawls in effect reduces the justice of acts of retribution to justice in distributing between the affected parties the good and bad effects of a system of retributions, and reduces this distributive justice in turn to the adoption of a just procedure for selecting the system of retributions to be used.

This can be illustrated by considering the case of a criminal facing a Judge (a case which has been thought to give trouble to me too, though I dealt with it adequately, on the lines which I am about to repeat here, in my book *Freedom and Reason*).[14] A Rawlsian judge, when sentencing the criminal, could defend himself against the charge of injustice or unfairness by saying that he was faithfully observing the principles of justice which would be adopted in the original position, whose conditions are procedurally fair. What these principles would be requires, no doubt, a great deal of discussion, in the course of which I might find myself in disagreement with Rawls. But my own view on how the judge should justify his action is, in its formal properties, very like his. On my view likewise, the judge can say that, when he asks himself what universal principles he is prepared to adopt for situations exactly like the one he is in, and considers examples of such logically possible situations in which *he* occupies, successively, the positions of judge, and of criminal, and of all those who are affected by the administration and enforcement of the law under which he is sentencing the criminal, including, of course, potential victims of possible future crimes—he can say that when he asks himself this, he has no hesitation in accepting the principle which bids him impose such and such a sentence in accordance with the law.

I am assuming that the judge is justifying himself at the critical level. If he were content with justifying himself at the intuitive level, his task would be easier, because, we hope, he, like most of us, has intuitions about the proper administration of justice in the courts, embodying *prima facie* principles of a sort whose inculcation in judges and in the rest of us has a high social utility. I say this while recognizing that *some* judges have intuitions about these matters which have a high social *dis*utility. The question of what intuitions judges ought to have about retributive justice is a matter for *critical* moral thinking.

On both Rawls' view and mine retributive justice has thus been reduced to distributive; on Rawls' view the principles of justice adopted are those which *distribute* fairly between those affected the good and the evil consequences of having or not having certain enforced criminal laws; on my own view likewise it is the impartiality secured by the requirement to universalize one's prescriptions which makes the judge say what he says, and here too it is an impartiality in distributing good and evil consequences between the affected parties. For the judge to let off the rapist would not be *fair* to all those who would be raped if the law were not enforced. I conclude that retributive justice can be reduced to distributive, and that therefore we shall have done what is required of us if we can give an adequate account of the latter.

What is common to Rawls' method and my own is the recognition that to get solutions to particular questions about what is just or unjust, we have to have a way of selecting principles of justice to answer such questions, and that to ask them in default of such principles is senseless. And we both recognize that the method for selecting the principles has to be founded on what he calls 'the formal constraints of the concept of right'. This measure of agreement can extend to the method of selecting principles of distributive justice as well as retributive. Neither Rawls nor I need be put off our stride by an objector who says that we have not addressed ourselves to the question of what acts are just, but have divagated on to the quite different question of how to select principles of justice. The point is that the first question cannot be answered without answering the second. Most of the apparently intractable conflicts about justice and rights that plague the world have been generated by taking certain answers to the first question as obvious and requiring no argument. We shall resolve these conflicts only by asking what arguments are available for the principles by which questions about the justice of individual acts are to be answered. In short, we need to ascend from intuitive to critical thinking; as I have argued in my review of his book, Rawls is to be reproached with not *completing* the ascent.[15]

Nozick, however, seems hardly to have begun it.[16] Neither Rawls nor I have anything to fear from him, so long as we stick to the formal part of our systems which we in effect share. When it comes to the application of this formal method to produce substantial principles of justice, I might find myself in disagreement with Rawls, because he relies much too much on his own intuitions which are open to question. Nozick's intuitions differ from Rawls', and sometimes differ from, sometimes agree with mine. This sort of question is simply not to be settled by appeal to intuitions, and it is time that the whole controversy ascended to a more serious, critical level. At this level, the answer which both Rawls and I should give to Nozick is that whatever sort of principles of justice we are after, whether structural principles, as Rawls thinks, or historical principles, as Nozick maintains, they have to be supported by critical thinking, of which Nozick seems hardly to see the necessity. This point is quite independent of the structural-historical disagreement.

For example, if Nozick thinks that it is just for people to retain whatever property they have acquired by voluntary exchange which benefited all parties, starting from a position of equality but perhaps ending up with a position of gross inequality, and if Rawls, by contrast, thinks that such inequality should be rectified in order to make the position of the least advantaged in society as good as possible, how are we to decide between them? Not by intuition, because there seems to be a deadlock between their intuitions. Rawls has a procedure, which *need* not appeal to intuition, for justifying distributions; this would give him the game, if he were to base the procedure on firm logical grounds, and if he followed it correctly. Actually he does not so base it, and mixes up so many intuitions in the argument that the conclusions he reaches are not such as the procedure really justifies. But Nozick has no procedure at all: only a variety of considerations of different sorts, all in the end based on intuition. Sometimes he seems to be telling us what arrangements in society would be arrived at if bargaining took place in accordance with games-theory between mutually disinterested parties; sometimes what arrangements would maximize the welfare of members of society; and sometimes what arrangements would strike them as fair. He does not often warn us when he is switching from one of these grounds to another; and he does little to convince us by argument that the arrangements so selected would be in accordance with justice. He hopes that we will think what he thinks: but Rawls at least thinks otherwise.

FORMAL JUSTICE AND SUBSTANTIAL EQUALITY

How then do we get from formal to substantial justice? We have had an example of how this is done in the sphere of retributive justice; but how is this method to be extended to cover distributive justice as a whole, and its relation, if any, to equality in distribution? The difficulty of using formal justice in order to establish principles of substantial justice can indeed be illustrated very well by asking whether, and in

what sense, justice demands equality in distribution. The complaint is often made that a certain distribution is unfair or unjust because unequal; so it looks, at least, as if the substantial principle that goods ought to be distributed equally in default of reasons to the contrary forms part of some people's conception of justice. Yet, it is argued, this substantial principle cannot be established simply on the basis of the formal notions we have mentioned. The following kind of schematic example is often adduced: consider two possible distributions of a given finite stock of goods, in one of which the goods are distributed equally, and in the other of which a few of the recipients have nearly all the goods, and the rest have what little remains. It is claimed with some plausibility that the second distribution is unfair, and the first fair. But it might also be claimed that impartiality and formal justice alone will not establish that we ought to distribute the goods equally.

There are two reasons which might be given for this second claim, the first of them a bad one, the other more cogent. The bad reason rests on an underestimate of the powers of golden-rule arguments. It is objected, for example, that people with white skins, if they claimed privileges in distribution purely on the ground of skin-colour, would not be offending against the formal principle of impartiality or universalizability, because no individual reference need enter into the principle to which they are appealing. Thus the principle that blacks ought to be subservient to whites is impartial as between *individuals*; any individual whatever who has the bad luck to find himself with a black skin or the good luck to find himself with a white skin is impartially placed by the principle in the appropriate social rank. This move receives a brief answer in my *Freedom and Reason*,[17] and a much fuller one in a forthcoming paper.[18] If the whites are faced with the decision, not merely of whether to frame this principle, but of whether to prescribe its adoption universally in all cases, including hypothetical ones in which their own skins turn black, they will at once reject it.

The other, more cogent-sounding argument is often used as an argument against utilitarians by those who think that justice has a lot to do with equality. It could also, at first sight, be used as an argument against the adequacy of formal justice or impartiality as a basis for distributive justice. That the argument could be leveled against both these methods is no accident; as I have tried to show elsewhere,[19] utilitarianism of a certain sort is the embodiment of—the method of moral reasoning which fulfils in practice—the requirement of universalizability or formal justice. Having shown that neither of these methods can produce a direct justification for equal distribution, I shall then show that both can produce indirect justifications, which depend, not on a priori reasoning alone, but on likely assumptions about what the world and the people in it are like.

The argument is this. Formal impartiality only requires us to treat everybody's interest as of equal weight. Imagine, then, a situation in which utilities are equally distributed. (There is a complication here which we can for the moment avoid by choosing a suitable example. Shortly I shall be mentioning the so-called principle of diminishing marginal utility, and shall indeed be making important use of it. But for now let us take a case in which it does not operate, so that we can, for ease of illustration, treat money as a linear measure of utility.) Suppose that we can vary the equal distribution that we started with by taking a dollar each away from everybody in the town, and that the loss of purchasing power is so small that they hardly notice it, and therefore the utility enjoyed by each is not much diminished. However, when we give the resulting large sum to one man, he is able to buy himself a holiday in Acapulco, which gives him so much pleasure that his access of utility is equal to the sum of the small losses suffered by all the others. Many would say that this redistribution was unfair. But we were, in the required sense, being impartial between the equal interests of all the parties; we were treating an equal access or loss of utility to any party as of equal value or disvalue. For, on our suppositions, the taking away of a dollar from one of the unfortunate parties deprived him of just as much utility as the addition of that dollar gave to the fortunate one. But if we are completely impartial, we have to regard *who has* that dollar or that access of utility as irrelevant. So there will be nothing to choose, from an impartial point of view, between our original equal distribution and our later highly unequal one, in which everybody else is deprived of a cent in order to give one person a holiday in Acapulco. And that is why people say that formal impartiality alone is not enough to secure social justice, nor even to secure impartiality itself in some more substantial sense.

What is needed, in the opinion of these people, is some principle which says that it is unjust to give a person more when he already has more than the others—some sort of egalitarian principle. Egalitarian principles are only one possible kind of principles of distributive justice; and it is so far an open question whether they are to be preferred to alternative inegalitarian principles. It is fairly clear as a matter of history that different principles of justice have been accepted in different societies. As Aristotle says, 'everybody agrees that the just distribution is one in accordance with desert of some kind; but they do not call desert the same thing, but the democrats say it is being a free citizen, the oligarchs being rich, others good lineage, and the aristocrats virtue'.[20] It is not difficult to think of some societies in which it would be thought unjust for one man to have privileges not possessed by all men, and of others in which it would be thought unjust for a slave to have privileges which a free man would take for granted, or for a commoner to have the sort of house which a nobleman could aspire to. Even Aristotle's democrats did not think that slaves, but only citizens, had equal rights; and Plato complains of democracy that it 'bestows equality of a sort on equals and unequals alike'.[21] We have to ask, therefore, whether there are any reasons for preferring one of these attitudes to another.

At this point some philosophers will be ready to step in with their intuitions, and tell us that some distributions or ways of achieving distributions are *obviously* more just than others, or that *everyone will agree on reflection* that they are. These philosophers appeal to our intuitions or prejudices in support of the most widely divergent methods or patterns of distribution. But this is a way of arguing which should be abjured by anybody who wishes to have rational grounds for his moral judgments. Intuitions prove nothing; general consensus proves nothing; both have been used to support conclusions which *our* intuitions and our consensus may well find outrageous. We want arguments, and in this field seldom get them.

However, it is too early to despair of finding some. The utilitarian, and the formalist like me, still have some moves to make. I am supposing that we have already made the major move suggested above, and have ruled out discrimination on grounds of skin colour and the like, in so far as such discrimination could not be accepted by all for cases where they were the ones discriminated against. I am supposing that our society has absorbed this move, and contains no racists, sexists or in general discriminators, but does still contain economic men who do not think it wrong, in pursuit of Nozickian economic liberty, to get what they can, even if the resulting distribution is grotesquely unequal. Has the egalitarian any moves to make against them, and are they moves which can be supported by appeal to formal justice, in conjunction with the empirical facts?

TWO ARGUMENTS FOR EQUAL DISTRIBUTION

He has two. The first is based on that good old prop of egalitarian policies, the diminishing marginal utility, within the ranges that matter, of money and of nearly all goods. Almost always, if money or goods are taken away from someone who has a lot of them already, and given to someone who has little, total utility is increased, other things being equal. As we shall see, they hardly ever are equal; but the principle is all right. Its ground is that the poor man will get more utility out of what he is given than the rich man from whom it is taken would have got. A millionaire minds less about the gain or loss of a dollar than I do, and I than a pauper.

It must be noted that this is not an *a priori* principle. It is an empirical fact (if it is) that people are so disposed. The most important thing I have to say in this paper is that when we are, as we now are, trying to establish *prima facie* principles of distributive justice, it is enough if they can be justified in the world as it actually is, among people as they actually are.

It is a wholly illegitimate argument against formalists or utilitarians that states of society or of the people in it could be *conceived of* in which gross inequalities could be justified by formal or utilitarian arguments. We are seeking principles for practical use in the world as it is. The same applies when we ask what qualifications are required to the principles.

Diminishing marginal utility is the firmest support for policies of progressive taxation of the rich and other egalitarian measures. However, as I said above, other things are seldom equal, and there are severe empirical, practical restraints on the equality that can sensibly be imposed by governments. To mention just a few of these hackneyed other things: the removal of incentives to effort may diminish the total stock of goods to be divided up; abrupt confiscation or even very steep progressive taxation may antagonize the victims so much that a whole class turns from a useful element in society to a hostile and dangerous one; or, even if that does not happen, it may merely become demoralized and either lose all enterprise and readiness to take business risks, or else just emigrate if it can. Perhaps one main cause of what is called the English sickness is the alienation of the middle class. It is an empirical question, just when egalitarian measures get to the stage of having these effects; and serious political argument on this subject should concentrate on such empirical questions, instead of indulging in the rhetoric of equal (or for that matter of unequal) rights. Rights are the offspring of *prima facie*, intuitive principles, and I have nothing against them; but the question is, What *prima facie* principles ought we to adopt? What intuitions ought we to have? On these questions the rhetoric of rights sheds no light whatever, any more than do appeals to intuition (i.e. to prejudice, i.e. to the *prima facie* principles, good or bad, which our upbringings happen to have implanted in us). The worth of intuitions is to be known by their fruits; as in the case of the principles to be followed by judges in administering the law, the best principles are those with the highest acceptance-utility, i.e. those whose general acceptance maximizes the furtherance of the interests, in sum, of all the affected parties, treating all those interests as of equal weight, i.e. impartially, i.e. with formal justice.

We have seen that, given the empirical assumption of diminishing marginal utility, such a method provides a justification for moderately egalitarian policies. The justification is strengthened by a second move that the egalitarian can make. This is to point out that inequality itself has a tendency to produce envy, which is a disagreeable state of mind and leads people to do disagreeable things. It makes no difference to the argument whether the envy is a good or a bad quality, nor whether it is justified or unjustified—any more than it makes a difference whether the alienation of the middle class which I mentioned above is to be condemned or excused. These states of mind are facts, and moral judgments have to be made in the light of the facts as they are. We have to take account of the actual state of the world and of the people in it. We can very easily think of societies which are highly unequal, but in which the more fortunate members have contrived to find some real or metaphorical opium or some Platonic noble lie[22] to keep the people quiet, so that the people feel no envy of privileges which we should consider outrageous. Imagine, for example, a society consisting of happy slave-owners and of happy slaves, all of whom know their places and do not have ideas above their station. Since there is *ex hypothesi* no envy, this source of disutility does not exist, and the whole argument from envy collapses.

It is salutary to remember this. It may make us stop looking for purely formal, *a priori* reasons for demanding equality, and look instead at the actual conditions which obtain in particular societies. To make the investigation more concrete, albeit oversimplified, let us ask what would have to be the case before we ought to be ready to push this happy slave-owning society into a revolution—peaceful or violent—which would turn the slaves into free and moderately equal wage-earners. I shall be able only to sketch my answer to this question, without doing nearly enough to justify it.

ARGUMENTS FOR AND AGAINST EGALITARIAN REVOLUTIONS

First of all, as with all moral questions, we should have to ask what would be the actual consequences of what we were doing—which is the same as to ask what we should be *doing*, so that accusations of 'consequentialism'[23] need not be taken very seriously. Suppose, to simplify matters outrageously, that we can actually predict the consequences of the revolution and what will happen during its course. We can then consider two societies (one actual and one possible) and a possible process of transition from one to the other. And we have to ask whether the transition from one to the other will, all in all, promote the interests of all those affected more than to stay as they are, or rather, to develop as they would develop if the revolution did not occur. The question can be divided into questions about the process of transition and questions about the relative merits of the actual society (including its probable subsequent 'natural' development) and the possible society which would be produced by the revolution.

We have supposed that the slaves in the existing society feel no envy, and that therefore the disutility of envy cannot be used as an argument for change. If there *were* envy, as in actual cases is probable, this argument *could* be employed; but let us see what can be done without it. We have the fact that there is gross inequality in the actual society and much greater equality in the possible one. The principle of diminishing marginal utility will therefore support the change, provided that its effects are not outweighed by a reduction in total utility resulting from the change and the way it comes about. But we have to be sure that this condition is fulfilled. Suppose, for example, that the actual society is a happy bucolic one and is likely to remain so, but that the transition to the possible society initiates the growth of an industrial economy in which everybody has to engage in a rat-race and is far less happy. We might in that case pronounce the actual society better. In general it is not self-evident that the access of what is called wealth makes people happier, although they nearly always think that it will.

Let us suppose, however, that we are satisfied that the people in the possible society will be better off all round than in the actual. There is also the point that there will be more generations to enjoy the new regime than suffer in the transition from the old. At least, this is what revolutionaries often say; and we have set them at liberty to say it by assuming, contrary to what is likely to be the case, that the future state of society is predictable. In actual fact, revolutions usually produce states of society very different from, and in most cases worse than, what their authors expected—which does not always stop them being better than what went before, once things have settled down. However, let us waive these difficulties and suppose that the future state of society can be predicted, and that it is markedly better than the existing state, because a greater equality of distribution has, owing to diminishing marginal utility, resulted in greater total utility.

Let us also suppose that the more enterprising economic structure which results leads to increased production without causing a rat-race. There will then be more wealth to go round and the revolution will have additional justification. Other benefits of the same general kind may also be adduced; and what is perhaps the greatest benefit of all, namely liberty itself. That people like having this is an empirical fact; it may not be a fact universally, but it is at least *likely* that by freeing slaves we shall *pro tanto* promote their interests. Philosophers who ask for *a priori* arguments for liberty or equality often talk as if empirical facts like this were totally irrelevant to the question. Genuine egalitarians and liberals ought to abjure the aid of these philosophers, because they have taken away the main ground for such views, namely the fact that people are as they are.

The arguments so far adduced support the call for a revolution. They will have to be balanced against the disutilities which will probably be caused by the process of transition. If heads roll, that is contrary to the interests of their owners; and no doubt the economy will be disrupted at least temporarily, and the new rulers, whoever they are, may infringe liberty just as much as the old, and possibly in an even more arbitrary manner. Few revolutions are pleasant while they are going on. But if the revolution can be more or less smooth or even peaceful, it may well be that (given the arguments already adduced about the desirability of the future society thereby achieved) revolution can have a utilitarian justification, and therefore

a justification on grounds of formal impartiality between people's interests. But it is likely to be better for all if the same changes can be achieved less abruptly by an evolutionary process, and those who try to persuade us that this is not so are often merely giving way to impatience and showing a curious indifference to the interests of those for whom they purport to be concerned.

The argument in favour of change from a slave-owning society to a wage-earning one has been extremely superficial, and has served only to illustrate the lines on which a utilitarian or a formalist might argue. If we considered instead the transition from a capitalist society to a socialist one, the same forms of argument would have to be employed, but might not yield the same result. Even if the introduction of a fully socialist economy would promote greater equality, or more equal liberties (and I can see no reason for supposing this, but rather the reverse; for socialism tends to produce very great inequalities of *power*), it needs to be argued what the consequences would be, and then an assessment has to be made of the relative benefits and harms accruing from leaving matters alone and from having various sorts of bloody or bloodless change. Here again the rhetoric of rights will provide nothing but inflamatory material for agitators on both sides. It is designed to lead to, not to resolve, conflicts.

REMARKS ABOUT METHODS

But we must now leave this argument and attend to a methodological point which has become pressing. We have not, in the last few pages, been arguing about what state of society would be just, but about what state of society would best promote the interests of its members. All the arguments have been utilitarian. Where then does justice come in? It is likely to come into the propaganda of revolutionaries, as I have already hinted. But so far as I can see it has no direct bearing on the question of what would be the better society. It has, however, an important indirect bearing which I shall now try to explain. Our *prima facie* moral principles and intuitions are, as I have already said, the products of our upbringings; and it is a very important question *what* principles and intuitions it is best to bring up people to have. I have been arguing on the assumption that this question is to be decided by looking at the consequences for society, and the effects on the interests of people in society, of inculcating different principles. We are looking for the set of principles with the highest acceptance-utility.

Will these include principles of justice? The answer is obviously 'Yes', if we think that society and the people in it are better off with *some* principles of justice than without any. A 'land without justice' (to use the title of Milovan Djilas' book)[24] is almost bound to be an unhappy one. But what are the principles to be? Are we, for example, to inculcate the principle that it is just for people to perform the duties of their station and not envy those of higher social rank? Or the principle that all inequalities of any sort are unjust and ought to be removed? For my part, I would think that neither of these principles has a very high acceptance-utility. It may be that the principle with the highest acceptance-utility is one which makes just reward vary (but not immoderately) with desert, and assesses desert according to service to the interests of one's fellow-men. It would have to be supplemented by a principle securing equality of opportunity. But it is a partly empirical question what principles would have the highest acceptance-utility, and in any case beyond the scope of this paper. If some such principle is adopted and inculcated, people will *call* breaches of it unjust. Will they *be* unjust? Only in the sense that they will be contrary to a *prima facie* principle of distributive justice which we ought to adopt (not because it is itself a just principle, but because it is the best principle). The only sense that can be given to the question of whether it is a just principle (apart from the purely circular or tautological question of whether the principle obeys itself), is by asking whether the procedure by which we have selected the principle satisfies the logical requirements of critical moral thinking, i.e. is *formally* just. We might add that the adoption of such a formally just procedure and of the principles it selects is just in the *generic* sense mentioned at the beginning of this paper: it is the right thing to do; we morally ought to do it. The reason is that critical thinking, because it follows the re-

quirements of formal justice based on the logical properties of the moral concepts, especially 'ought' and 'right', can therefore not fail, if pursued correctly in the light of the empirical facts, to lead to principles of justice which are in accord with morality. But because the requirements are all formal, they do not by themselves determine the content of the principles of justice. We have to do the thinking.

What principles of justice are best to try to inculcate will depend on the circumstances of particular societies, and especially on psychological facts about their members. One of these facts is their readiness to accept the principles themselves. There might be a principle of justice which it would be highly desirable to inculcate, but which we have no chance of successfully inculcating. The best principles for a society to *have* are, as I said, those with the highest acceptance-utility. But the best principles to *try to inculcate* will not necessarily be these, if these are impossible to inculcate. Imagine that in our happy slave-society both slaves and slave-owners are obstinately conservative and know their places, and that the attempt to get the slaves to have revolutionary or egalitarian thoughts will result only in a very few of them becoming discontented, and probably going to the gallows as a result, and the vast majority merely becoming unsettled and therefore more unhappy. Then we ought not to try to inculcate such an egalitarian principle. On the other hand, if, as is much more likely, the principle stood a good chance of catching on, and the revolution was likely to be as advantageous as we have supposed, then we ought. The difference lies in the dispositions of the inhabitants. I am not saying that the probability of being accepted is the same thing as acceptance-utility; only that the rationality of trying to inculcate a principle (like the rationality of trying to do anything else) varies with the likelihood of success. In this sense the advisability of trying to inculcate principles of justice (though not their merit) is relative to the states of mind of those who, it is hoped, will hold them.

It is important to be clear about the extent to which what I am advocating is a kind of relativism. It is certainly not relativistic in any strong sense. Relativism is the doctrine that the truth of some moral statement depends on whether people accept it. A typical example would be the thesis that if in a certain society people think that they ought to get their male children circumcised, then they ought to get them circumcised, full stop. Needless to say, I am not supporting any such doctrine, which is usually the result of confusion, and against which there are well-known arguments. It is, however, nearly always the case that among the facts relevant to a moral decision are facts about people's thoughts or dispositions. For example, if I am wondering whether I ought to take my wife for a holiday in Acapulco, it is relevant to ask whether she would like it. What I have been saying is to be assimilated to this last example. If we take as given certain dispositions in the members of society (namely dispositions not to accept a certain principle of justice however hard we work at propagating it) then we have to decide whether, in the light of these facts, we ought to propagate it. What principles of justice we ought to propagate will vary with the probable effects of propagating them. The answer to this 'ought'-question is not relative to what we, who are asking it, think about the matter; it is to be arrived at by moral thought on the basis of the facts of the situation. But among these facts are facts about the dispositions of people in the society in question.

The moral I wish to draw from the whole argument is that ethical reasoning *can* provide us with a way of conducting political arguments about justice and rights rationally and with hope of agreement; that such rational arguments have to rest on an understanding of the concepts being used, *and* of the facts of our actual situation. The key question is 'What principles of justice, what attitudes towards the distribution of goods, what ascriptions of rights, are such that their acceptance is in the general interest?' I advocate the asking of this question as a substitute for one which is much more commonly asked, namely 'What rights do I have?' For people who ask this latter question will, being human, nearly always answer that they have just those rights, whatever they are, which will promote a distribution of goods which is in the interest of their own social group. The rhetoric of rights, which is engendered by this question, is a recipe for class war, and civil war. In pursuit of these rights, people will, because they have

convinced themselves that justice demands it, inflict almost any harms on the rest of society and on themselves. To live at peace, we need principles such as critical thinking can provide, based on formal justice and on the facts of the actual world in which we have to live. It is possible for all to practise this critical thinking in cooperation, if only they would learn how; for all share the same moral concepts with the same logic, if they could but understand them and follow it.

NOTES

1. See my 'Ethical Theory and Utilitarianism' (*ETU*) in *Contemporary British Philosophy 4*, ed. H. D. Lewis (London, 1976).
2. See, e.g., my 'Principles', *Ar. Soc.* 72 (1972/3), 'Rules of War and Moral Reasoning', *Ph. and Pub. Aff.* 1 (1972) and *ETU*.
3. Rawls, J., *A Theory of Justice* (Cambridge, Mass., 1971), p. 130.
4. Richards, D. A. J., *A Theory of Reasons for Action* (Oxford, 1971).
5. See my *Freedom and Reason*, pt. II (Oxford, 1963) and *ETU*.
6. *Nicomachean Ethics*, bk. V.
7. ib. 1130 b 31, 1131 b 25.
8. ib. ll30 a 8.
9. Theognis 147; also attr. to Phocylides by Aristotle, ib. 1129 b 27.
10. The earliest version of this tag is attr. by the *Oxford Dictionary of Quotations* to the Emperor Ferdinand I (1503–64).
11. ib. ll37 b 8.
12. ib. 1130 a 14 ff.
13. *A Theory of Justice*, p. 136.
14. Pp. 115–7, 124.
15. *Ph. Q.* 23 (1973), repr. in *Reading Rawls*, ed. N. Daniels (Oxford, 1975).
16. Nozick, R. D., *Anarchy, State and Utopia* (New York, 1974).
17. Pp. 106f.
18. 'Relevance', in a volume in honour of R. Brandt, W. Frankena and C. Stevenson, eds. A. Goldman and J. Kim (Reidel, forthcoming).
19. See note 2 above.
20. ib. 1131 a 25.
21. *Republic* 558 c.
22. ib. 414 b.
23. See, e.g., Anscombe, G. E. M., 'Modern Moral Philosophy', *Philosophy* 33 (1958) and Williams, B. A. O., in Smart, J. J. C. and Williams, B. A. O., *Utilitarianism: For and Against* (Cambridge, Eng., 1973), p. 82.
24. Djilas, M., *Land without Justice* (London, 1958).

Equality and Equal Opportunity For Welfare
RICHARD J. ARNESON

Insofar as we care for equality as a distributive ideal, what is it exactly that we prize? Many persons are troubled by the gap between the living standards of rich people and poor people in modern societies or by the gap between the average standard of living in rich societies and that prevalent in poor societies. To some extent at any rate it is the gap itself that is troublesome, not just the low absolute level of the standard of living of the poor. But it is not easy to decide what measure of the "standard of living" it is appropriate to employ to give content to the ideal of distributive equality. Recent discussions by John Rawls[1] and Ronald Dworkin[2] have debated the merits of versions of equality of welfare and equality of resources taken as interpretations of the egalitarian ideal. In this paper I shall argue that the idea of equal opportunity for welfare is the best interpretation of the ideal of distributive equality.

Consider a distributive agency that has at its disposal a stock of goods that individuals want to own and use. We need not assume that each good is useful for every person, just that each good is useful for someone. Each good is homogeneous in quality and can be divided as finely as you choose. The problem to be considered is: How to divide the goods in order to meet an appropriate standard of equality. This discussion assumes that some goods are legitimately available for distribution in this fashion, hence that the entitlements and deserts of individuals do not predetermine the proper ownership of all resources. No argument is provided for this assumption, so in this sense my article is addressed to egalitarians, not their opponents.

1. EQUALITY OF RESOURCES

The norm of equality of resources stipulates that to achieve equality the agency ought to give everybody a share of goods that is exactly identical to everyone else's and that exhausts all available resources to be distributed. A straightforward objection to equality of resources so understood is that if Smith and Jones have similar tastes and abilities except that Smith has a severe physical handicap remediable with the help of expensive crutches, then if the two are accorded equal resources, Smith must spend the bulk of his resources on crutches whereas Jones can use his resource share to fulfill his aims to a far greater extent. It seems forced to claim that any notion of equality of condition that is worth caring about prevails between Smith and Jones in this case.

At least two responses to this objection are worth noting. One, pursued by Dworkin,[3] is that in the example the cut between the individual and the resources at his disposal was made at the wrong place. Smith's defective legs and Jones's healthy legs should be considered among their resources, so that only if Smith is assigned a gadget that renders his legs fully serviceable in addition to a resource share that is otherwise identical with Jones's can we say that equality of resources prevails. The example then suggests that an equality of resources ethic should count personal talents among the resources to be distributed. This line of response swiftly encounters difficulties. It is impossible for a distributive agency to supply educational and technological aid that will offset inborn dif-

Philosophical Studies 56:77–93, 1989. © 1989 *Kluwer Academic Publishers. Printed in the Netherlands.*

ferences of talent so that all persons are blessed with the same talents. Nor is it obvious how much compensation is owed to those who are disadvantaged by low talent. The worth to individuals of their talents varies depending on the nature of their life plans. An heroic resolution of this difficulty is to assign every individual an equal share of ownership of everybody's talents in the distribution of resources.[4] Under this procedure each of the N persons in society begins adult life owning a tradeable 1/N share of everybody's talents. We can regard this share as amounting to ownership of a block of time during which the owner can dictate how the partially owned person is to deploy his talent. Dworkin himself has noticed a flaw in this proposal, which he has aptly named "the slavery of the talented."[5] The flaw is that under this equal distribution of talent scheme the person with high talent is put at a disadvantage relative to her low-talent fellows. If we assume that each person strongly wants liberty in the sense of ownership over his own time (that is, ownership over his own body for his entire lifetime), the high-talent person finds that his taste for liberty is very expensive, as his time is socially valuable and very much in demand, whereas the low-talent person finds that his taste for liberty is cheap, as his time is less valuable and less in demand. Under this version of equality of resources, if two persons are identical in all respects except that one is more talented than the other, the more talented will find she is far less able to achieve her life plan than her less talented counterpart. Again, once its implications are exhibited, equality of resources appears an unattractive interpretation of the ideal of equality.

A second response asserts that given an equal distribution of resources, persons should be held responsible for forming and perhaps reforming their own preferences, in the light of their resource share and their personal characteristics and likely circumstances.[6] The level of overall preference satisfaction that each person attains is then a matter of individual responsibility, not a social problem. That I have nil singing talent is a given, but that I have developed an aspiration to become a professional opera singer and have formed my life around this ambition is a further development that was to some extent within my control and for which I must bear responsibility.

The difficulty with this response is that even if it is accepted it falls short of defending equality of resources. Surely social and biological factors influence preference formation, so if we can properly be held responsible only for what lies within our control, then we can at most be held to be partially responsible for our preferences. For instance, it would be wildly implausible to claim that a person without the use of his legs should be held responsible for developing a full set of aims and values toward the satisfaction of which leglessness is no hindrance. Acceptance of the claim that we are sometimes to an extent responsible for our preferences leaves the initial objection against equality of resources fully intact. For if we are sometimes responsible we are sometimes not responsible.

The claim that "we are responsible for our preferences" is ambiguous. It could mean that our preferences have developed to their present state due to factors that lay entirely within our control. Alternatively, it could mean that our present preferences, even if they have arisen through processes largely beyond our power to control, are now within our control in the sense that we could now undertake actions, at greater or lesser cost, that would change our preferences in ways that we can foresee. If responsibility for preferences on the first construal held true, this would indeed defeat the presumption that our resource share should be augmented because it satisfies our preferences to a lesser extent than the resource shares of others permit them to satisfy their preferences. However, on the first construal, the claim that we are responsible for our preferences is certainly always false. But on the second, weaker construal, the claim that we are responsible for our preferences is compatible with the claim that an appropriate norm of equal distribution should compensate people for their hard-to-satisfy preferences at least up to the point at which by taking appropriate adaptive measures now, people could reach the same preference satisfaction level as others.

The defense of equality of resources by appeal to the claim that persons are responsible for their preferences admits of yet another interpretation. Without claiming that people have caused their preferences to become what they are or that people could cause their preferences to change, we might hold that people can take responsibility for their fundamental preferences in the sense of identifying with them and regarding these preferences as their own, not as alien intrusions on the self. T. M. Scanlon has suggested the example of religious preferences in this spirit.[7] That a person was raised in one religious tradition rather than another may predictably affect his lifetime expectation of preference satisfaction. Yet we would regard it as absurd to insist upon compensation in the name of distributive equality for having been raised fundamentalist Protestant rather than atheist or Catholic (a matter that of course does not lie within the individual's power to control). Provided that a fair (equal) distribution of the resources of religious liberty is maintained, the amount of utility that individuals can expect from their religious upbringings is "specifically not an object of public policy."[8]

The example of compensation for religious preferences is complex, and I will return to it in section II below. Here it suffices to note that even if in some cases we do deem it inappropriate to insist on such compensation in the name of equality, it does not follow that equality of resources is an adequate rendering of the egalitarian ideal. Differences among people including sometimes differences in their upbringing may render resource equality nugatory. For example, a person raised in a closed fundamentalist community such as the Amish who then loses his faith and moves to the city may feel at a loss as to how to satisfy ordinary secular preferences, so that equal treatment of this rube and city sophisticates may require extra compensation for the rube beyond resource equality. Had the person's fundamental values not altered, such compensation would not be in order. I am not proposing compensation as a feasible government policy, merely pointing out that the fact that people might in some cases regard it as crass to ask for indemnification of their satisfaction-reducing upbringing does not show that in principle it makes sense for people to assume responsibility (act as though they were responsible) for what does not lie within their control. Any policy that attempted to ame-

liorate these discrepancies would predictably inflict wounds on innocent parents and guardians far out of proportion to any gain that could be realized for the norm of distributive equality. So even if we all agree that in such cases a policy of compensation is inappropriate, all things considered, it does not follow that so far as distributive equality is concerned (one among the several values we cherish), compensation should not be forthcoming.

Finally, it is far from clear why assuming responsibility for one's preferences and values in the sense of affirming them and identifying them as essential to one's self precludes demanding or accepting compensation for these preferences in the name of distributive equality. Suppose the government has accepted an obligation to subsidize the members of two native tribes who are badly off, low in welfare. The two tribes happen to be identical except that one is strongly committed to traditional religious ceremonies involving a psychedelic made from the peyote cactus while the other tribe is similarly committed to its traditional rituals involving an alcoholic drink made from a different cactus. If the market price of the psychedelic should suddenly rise dramatically while the price of the cactus drink stays cheap, members of the first tribe might well claim that equity requires an increase in their subsidy to compensate for the greatly increased price of the wherewithal for their ceremonies. Advancing such a claim, so far as I can see, is fully compatible with continuing to affirm and identify with one's preferences and in this sense to take personal responsibility for them.

In practise, many laws and other public policies differentiate roughly between preferences that we think are deeply entrenched in people, alterable if at all only at great personal cost, and very widespread in the population, versus preferences that for most of us are alterable at moderate cost should we choose to try to change them and thinly and erratically spread throughout the population. Laws and public policies commonly take account of the former and ignore the latter. For example, the law caters to people's deeply felt aversion to public nudity but does not cater to people's aversion to the sight of tastelessly dressed strollers in public spaces. Of course, current American laws and policies are not designed to achieve any strongly egalitarian ideal, whether resource-based or not. But in appealing to common sense as embodied in current practises in order to determine what sort of equality we care about insofar as we do care about equality, one would go badly astray in claiming support in these practises for the contention that equality of resources captures the ideal of equality. We need to search further.

II. EQUALITY OF WELFARE

According to equality of welfare, goods are distributed equally among a group of persons to the degree that the distribution brings it about that each person enjoys the same welfare. (The norm thus presupposes the possibility of cardinal interpersonal welfare comparisons.) The considerations mentioned seven paragraphs back already dispose of the idea that the distributive equality worth caring about is equality of welfare. To bring this point home more must be said to clarify what "welfare" means in this context.

I take welfare to be preference satisfaction. The more an individual's preferences are satisfied, as weighted by their importance to that very individual, the higher her welfare. The preferences that figure in the calculation of a person's welfare are limited to self-interested preferences—what the individual prefers insofar as she seeks her own advantage. One may prefer something for its own sake or as a means to further ends; this discussion is confined to preferences of the former sort.

The preferences that most plausibly serve as the measure of the individual's welfare are hypothetical preferences. Consider this familiar account: The extent to which a person's life goes well is the degree to which his ideally considered preferences are satisfied.[9] My ideally considered preferences are those I would have if I were to engage in thoroughgoing deliberation about my preferences with full pertinent information, in a calm mood, while thinking clearly and making no reasoning errors. (We can also call these ideally considered preferences "rational preferences.")

To avoid a difficulty, we should think of the full information that is pertinent to ideally considered preferences as split into two stages corresponding to "first-best" and "second-best" rational preferences. At the first stage one is imagined to be considering full information relevant to choice on the assumption that the results of this ideal deliberation process can costlessly correct one's actual preferences. At the second stage one is imagined to be considering also information regarding (a) one's actual resistance to advice regarding the rationality of one's preferences, (b) the costs of an educational program that would break down this resistance, and (c) the likelihood that anything approaching this educational program will actually be implemented in one's lifetime. What it is reasonable to prefer is then refigured in the light of these costs. For example, suppose that low-life preferences for cheap thrills have a large place in my actual conception of the good, but no place in my first-best rational preferences. But suppose it is certain that these low-life preferences are firmly fixed in my character. Then my second-best preferences are those I would have if I were to deliberate in ideal fashion about my preferences in the light of full knowledge about my actual preferences and their resistance to change. If you are giving me a birthday present, and your sole goal is to advance my welfare as much as possible, you are probably advised to give me, say, a bottle of jug wine rather than a volume of Shelley's poetry even though it is the poetry experience that would satisfy my first-best rational preference.[10]

On this understanding of welfare, equality of welfare is a poor ideal. Individuals can arrive at different welfare levels due to choices they make for which they alone should be held responsible. A simple example would be to imagine two persons of identical tastes and abilities who are assigned equal resources by an agency charged to maintain distributive equality. The two then voluntarily engage in highstakes gambling, from which one emerges rich (with high expectation of welfare) and the other poor (with low welfare expectation). For another example, consider two persons similarly situated, so they could attain identical welfare levels with the same effort, but one chooses to pursue personal welfare zealously while the other pursues an aspirational preference (e.g., saving the whales), and so attains lesser fulfillment of self-interested preferences. In a third example, one person may voluntarily cultivate an expensive preference (not cognitively superior to the preference it supplants), while another person does not. In all three examples it would be inappropriate to insist upon equality of welfare when welfare inequality arises through the voluntary choice of the person who gets lesser welfare. Notice that in all three examples as described, there need be no grounds for finding fault with any aims or actions of any of the individuals mentioned. No imperative of practical reason commands us to devote our lives to the maximal pursuit of (self-interested) preference satisfaction. Divergence from equality of welfare arising in these ways need not signal any fault imputable to individuals or to "society" understood as responsible for maintaining distributive equality.

This line of thought suggests taking equal opportunity for welfare to be the appropriate norm of distributive equality.

In the light of the foregoing discussion, consider again the example of compensation for one's religious upbringing regarded as affecting one's lifetime preference satisfaction expectation. This example is urged as a reductio ad absurdum of the norm of equality of welfare, which may seem to yield the counterintuitive implication that such differences do constitute legitimate grounds for redistributing people's resource shares, in the name of distributive equality. As I mentioned, the example is tricky; we should not allow it to stampede us toward resource-based construals of distributive equality. Two comments on the example indicate something of its trickiness.

First, if a person changes her values in the light of deliberation that bring her closer to the ideal of deliberative rationality, we should credit the person's conviction that satisfying the new values counts for more than satisfying the old ones, now discarded. The old values should be counted at a discount due to their presumed greater distance from deliberative rationality. So if I was a Buddhist, then become a Hindu, and correctly regard the new religious preference as cognitively superior to the old, it is not

the case that a straight equality of welfare standard must register my welfare as declining even if my new religious values are less easily achievable than the ones they supplant.

Secondly, the example might motivate acceptance of equal opportunity for welfare over straight equality of welfare rather than rejection of subjectivist conceptions of equality altogether. If equal opportunity for welfare obtains between Smith and Jones, and Jones subsequently undergoes religious conversion that lowers his welfare prospects, it may be that we will take Jones's conversion either to be a voluntarily chosen act or a prudentially negligent act for which he should be held responsible. (Consider the norm: Other things equal, it is bad if some people are worse off than others through no voluntary choice or fault of their own.) This train of thought also motivates an examination of equal opportunity for welfare.

III. EQUAL OPPORTUNITY FOR WELFARE

An opportunity is a chance of getting a good if one seeks it. For equal opportunity for welfare to obtain among a number of persons, each must face an array of options that is equivalent to every other person's in terms of the prospects for preference satisfaction it offers. The preferences involved in this calculation are ideally considered secondbest preferences (where these differ from first-best preferences). Think of two persons entering their majority and facing various life choices, each action one might choose being associated with its possible outcomes. In the simplest case, imagine that we know the probability of each outcome conditional on the agent's choice of an action that might lead to it. Given that one or another choice is made and one or another outcome realized, the agent would then face another array of choices, then another, and so on. We construct a decision tree that gives an individual's possible complete life-histories. We then add up the preference satisfaction expectation for each possible life history. In doing this we take into account the preferences that people have regarding being confronted with the particular range of options given at each decision point. Equal opportunity for welfare obtains among persons when all of them face equivalent decision trees—the expected value of each person's best (= most prudent[11]) choice of options, second-best, ... nth-best is the same. The opportunities persons encounter are ranked by the prospects for welfare they afford.

The criterion for equal opportunity for welfare stated above is incomplete. People might face an equivalent array of options, as above, yet differ in their awareness of these options, their ability to choose reasonably among them, and the strength of character that enables a person to persist in carrying out a chosen option. Further conditions are needed. We can summarize these conditions by stipulating that a number of persons face *effectively* equivalent options just in case one of the following is true: (1) the options are equivalent and the persons are on a par in their ability to "negotiate" these options, or (2) the options are nonequivalent in such a way as to counterbalance exactly any inequalities in people's negotiating abilities, or (3) the options are equivalent and any inequalities in people's negotiating abilities are due to causes for which it is proper to hold the individuals themselves personally responsible. Equal opportunity for welfare obtains when all persons face effectively equivalent arrays of options.

Whether or not two persons enjoy equal opportunity for welfare at a time depends only on whether they face effectively equivalent arrays of options at that time. Suppose that Smith and Jones share equal opportunity for welfare on Monday, but on Tuesday Smith voluntarily chooses or negligently behaves so that from then on Jones has greater welfare opportunities. We may say that in an extended sense people share equal opportunity for welfare just in case there is some time at which their opportunities are equal and if any inequalities in their opportunities at later times are due to their voluntary choice or differentially negligent behavior for which they are rightly deemed personally responsible.

When persons enjoy equal opportunity for welfare in the extended sense, any actual inequality of welfare in the positions they reach is due to factors that lie within each individual's control. Thus, any such inequality will be nonproblematic from the standpoint of distributive equality. The norm of equal opportunity for welfare is distinct from equality of welfare only if some version of soft determinism or indeterminism is correct. If hard determinism is true, the two interpretations of equality come to the same.

In actual political life under modern conditions, distributive agencies will be staggeringly ignorant of the facts that would have to be known in order to pinpoint what level of opportunity for welfare different persons have had. To some extent it is technically unfeasible or even physically impossible to collect the needed information, and to some extent we do not trust governments with the authority to collect the needed information, due to worries that such authority, will be subject to abuse. Nonetheless, I suppose that the idea is clear in principle, and that in practise it is often feasible to make reliable rough-and-ready judgments to the effect that some people face very grim prospects for welfare compared to what others enjoy.

In comparing the merits of a Rawlsian conception of distributive equality as equal shares of primary goods and a Dworkinian conception of equality of resources with the norm of equality of opportunity for welfare, we run into the problem that in the real world, with imperfect information available to citizens and policymakers, and imperfect willingness on the part of citizens and officials to carry out conscientiously whatever norm is chosen, the practical implications of these conflicting principles may be hard to discern, and may not diverge much in practise. Familiar information-gathering and information-using problems will make us unwilling to authorize government agencies to determine people's distributive shares on the basis of their preference satisfaction prospects, which will often be unknowable for all practical purposes. We may insist that governments have regard to primary good share equality or resource equality as rough proxies for the welfarist equality that we are unable to calculate. To test our allegiance to the rival doctrines of equality we may need to consider real or hypothetical examples of situations in which we do have good information regarding welfare prospects and opportunities for welfare, and consider whether this information affects our judgments as to what counts as egalitarian policy. We also need to consider cases in which we gain new evidence that a particular resource-based standard is a much more inaccurate proxy for welfare equality than we might have thought, and much less accurate than another standard now available. Indifference to these considerations would mark allegiance to a resourcist interpretation of distributive equality in principle, not merely as a handy rough-and-ready approximation.

IV. STRAIGHT EQUALITY VERSUS EQUAL OPPORTUNITY; WELFARE VERSUS RESOURCES

The discussion to this point has explored two independent distinctions: (1) straight equality versus equal opportunity and (2) welfare versus resources as the appropriate basis for measuring distributive shares. Hence there are four positions to consider. On the issue of whether an egalitarian should regard welfare or resources as the appropriate standard of distributive equality, it is important to compare like with like, rather than, for instance, just to compare equal opportunity for resources with straight equality of welfare. (In my opinion Ronald Dworkin's otherwise magisterial treatment of the issue in his two-part discussion of "What Is Equality?" is marred by a failure to bring these four distinct positions clearly into focus.[12])

The argument for equal opportunity rather than straight equality is simply that it is morally fitting to hold individuals responsible for the foreseeable consequences of their voluntary choices, and in particular for that portion of these consequences that involves their own achievement of welfare or gain or loss of resources. If accepted, this argument leaves it entirely open whether we as egalitarians ought to support equal opportunity for welfare or equal opportunity for resources.

For equal opportunity for resources to obtain among a number of persons, the range of lotteries with resources as prizes available to each

of them must be effectively the same. The range of lotteries available to two persons is effectively the same whenever it is the case that, for any lottery the first can gain access to, there is an identical lottery that the second person can gain access to by comparable effort. (So if Smith can gain access to a lucrative lottery by walking across the street, and Jones cannot gain a similar lottery except by a long hard trek across a desert, to this extent their opportunities for resources are unequal.) We may say that equal opportunity for resources in an extended sense obtains among a number of persons just in case there is a time at which their opportunities are equal and any later inequalities in the resource opportunities they face are due to voluntary choices or differentially negligent behavior on their part for which they are rightly deemed personally responsible.

I would not claim that the interpretation of equal opportunity for resources presented here is the only plausible construal of the concept. However, on any plausible construal, the norm of equal opportunity for resources is vulnerable to the "slavery of the talented" problem that proved troublesome for equality of resources. Supposing that personal talents should be included among the resources to be distributed (for reasons given in section I), we find that moving from a regime of equality of resources to a regime that enforces equal opportunity for resources does not change the fact that a resource-based approach causes the person of high talent to be predictably and (it would seem) unfairly worse off in welfare prospects than her counterpart with lesser talent.[13] If opportunities for resources are equally distributed among more and less talented persons, then each person regardless of her native talent endowment will have comparable access to identical lotteries for resources that include time slices of the labor power of all persons. Each person's expected ownership of talent, should he seek it, will be the same. Other things equal, if all persons strongly desire personal liberty or initial ownership of one's own lifetime labor power, this good will turn out to be a luxury commodity for the talented, and a cheap bargain for the untalented.

A possible objection to the foregoing reasoning is that it relies on a vaguely specified idea of how to measure resource shares that is shown to be dubious by the very fact that it leads back to the slavery of the talented problem. Perhaps by taking personal liberty as a separate resource this result can be avoided. But waiving any other difficulties with this objection, we note that the assumption that any measure of resource equality must be unacceptable if applying it leads to unacceptable results for the distribution of welfare amounts to smuggling in a welfarist standard by the back door.

Notice that the welfare distribution implications of equal opportunity for resources will count as intuitively unacceptable only on the assumption that people cannot be deemed to have chosen voluntarily the preferences that are frustrated or satisfied by the talent pooling that a resourcist interpretation of equal opportunity enforces. Of course it is strictly nonvoluntary that one is born with a particular body and cannot be separated from it, so if others hold ownership rights in one's labor power one's individual liberty is thereby curtailed. But in principle one's self-interested preferences could be concerned no more with what happens to one's own body than with what happens to the bodies of others. To the extent that you have strong self-interested hankerings that your neighbors try their hand at, say, farming, and less intense desires regarding the occupations you yourself pursue, to that extent the fact that under talent pooling your own labor power is a luxury commodity will not adversely affect your welfare. As an empirical matter, I submit that it is just false to hold that in modern society whether any given individual does or does not care about retaining her own personal liberty is due to that person's voluntarily choosing one or the other preference. The expensive preference of the talented person for personal liberty cannot be assimilated to the class of expensive preferences that people might voluntarily cultivate.[14] On plausible empirical assumptions, equal opportunity for welfare will often find tastes compensable, including the talented person's taste for the personal liberty to command her own labor power. Being born with high talent cannot then be a curse under equal opportunity for welfare (it cannot be a blessing either).

V. SEN'S CAPABILITIES APPROACH

The equal opportunity for welfare construal of equality that I am espousing is similar to a "capabilities" approach recently defended by Amartya Sen.[15] I shall now briefly sketch and endorse Sen's criticisms of Rawls's primary social goods standard and indicate a residual welfarist disagreement with Sen.

Rawls's primary social goods proposal recommends that society should be concerned with the distribution of certain basic social resources, so his position is a variant of a resource-based understanding of how to measure people's standard of living. Sen holds that the distribution of resources should be evaluated in terms of its contribution to individual capabilities to function in various ways deemed to be objectively important or valuable. That is, what counts is not the food one gets, but the contribution it can make to one's nutritional needs, not the educational expenditures lavished, but the contribution they make to one's knowledge and cognitive skills. Sen objects to taking primary social goods measurements to be fundamental on the ground that persons vary enormously from one another in the rates at which they transform primary social goods into capabilities to function in key ways. Surely we care about resource shares because we care what people are enabled to be and do with their resource shares, and insofar as we care about equality it is the latter that should be our concern.

So far, I agree. Moreover, Sen identifies a person's well-being with the doings and beings or "functionings" that he achieves, and distinguishes these functionings from the person's capabilities to function or "well-being freedom."[16] Equality of capability is then a notion within the family of equality of opportunity views, a family that also includes the idea of equal opportunity for welfare that I have been attempting to defend. So I agree with Sen to a large extent.

But given that there are indefinitely many kinds of things that persons can do or become, how are we supposed to sum an individual's various capability scores into an overall index? If we cannot construct such an index, then it would seem that equality of capability cannot qualify as a candidate conception of distributive equality. The indexing problem that is known to plague Rawls's primary goods proposal also afflicts Sen's capabilities approach.[17]

Sen is aware of the indexing problem and untroubled by it. The grand theme of his lectures on "Well-being, Agency and Freedom" is informational value pluralism: We should incorporate in our principles all moral information that is relevant to the choice of actions and policies even if that information complicates the articulation of principles and precludes attainment of a set of principles that completely orders the available alternative actions in any possible set of circumstances. "Incompleteness is *not* an embarrassment," Sen declares.[18] I agree that principles of decision should not ignore morally pertinent matters but I doubt that the full set of my functioning capabilities does matter for the assessment of my position. Whether or not my capabilities include the capability to trek to the South Pole, eat a meal at the most expensive restaurant in Omsk, scratch my neighbor's dog at the precise moment of its daily maximal itch, matters not one bit to me, because I neither have nor have the slightest reason to anticipate I ever will have any desire to do any of these and myriad other things. Presumably only a small subset of my functioning capabilities matter for moral assessment, but which ones?

We may doubt whether there are any objectively decidable grounds by which the value of a person's capabilities can be judged apart from the person's (ideally considered) preferences regarding those capabilities. On what ground do we hold that it is valuable for a person to have a capability that she herself values at naught with full deliberative rationality? If a person's having a capability is deemed valuable on grounds independent of the person's own preferences in the matter, the excess valuation would seem to presuppose the adequacy of an as yet unspecified perfectionist doctrine the like of which has certainly not yet been defended and in my opinion is indefensible.[19] In the absence of such a defense of perfectionism, equal opportunity for welfare looks to be an attractive interpretation of distributive equality.

NOTES

1. John Rawls, 'Social Unity and Primary Goods,' in Amartya Sen and Bernard Williams, eds., *Utilitarianism and Beyond* (Cambridge: Cambridge University Press, 1982), pp.159–185.
2. Ronald Dworkin, 'What Is Equality? Part 1: Equality of Welfare,' *Philosophy and Public Affairs* 10 (1981): 185–246; and 'What Is Equality? Part 2: Equality of Resources,' *Philosophy and Public Affairs* 10 (1981): 283–345. See also Thomas Scanlon, 'Preference and Urgency,' *Journal of Philosophy* 72 (1975): 655–669.
3. Dworkin, 'Equality of Resources.'
4. Hal Varian discusses this mechanism of equal distribution, followed by trade to equilibrium, in 'Equity, Envy, and Efficiency,' *Journal of Economic Theory* 9 (1974): 63–91. See also John Roemer, 'Equality of Talent,' *Economics and Philosophy* I (1985): 151–186; and 'Equality of Resources Implies Equality of Welfare,' *Quartery Journal of Economics* 101(1986): 751–784.
5. Dworkin, 'Equality of Resources,' p.312. It should be noted that the defender of resource-based construals of distributive equality has a reply to the slavery of the talented problem that I do not consider in this paper. According to this reply, what the slavery of the talented problem reveals is not the imperative of distributing so as to equalize welfare but rather the moral inappropriateness of considering all resources as fully alienable. It may be that equality of resources should require that persons be compensated for their below-par talents, but such compensation should not take the form of assigning individuals full private ownership rights in other people's talents, which should be treated as at most partially alienable. See Margaret Jane Radin, 'Market-Inalienability,' *Harvard Law Review* 100 (1987): 1849–1937.
6. Rawls, 'Social Unity and Primary Goods,' pp.167–170.
7. Thomas Scanlon 'Equality of Resources and Equality Of Welfare: A Forced Marriage?', *Ethics* 97 (1986): 111–118; see esp. pp.115–117.
8. Scanlon, 'Equality of Resources and Equality of Welfare,' p.116.
9. See, e.g., John Rawls, *A Theory of Justice* (Cambridge, MA: Harvard University Press, 1971), pp. 416–424; Richard Brandt, *A Theory of the Good and the Right* (Oxford: Oxford University Press, 1979), pp. 110–129; David Gauthier, *Morals by Agreement* (Oxford: Oxford University Press, 1986), pp. 29–38; and Derek Parfit, *Reasons and Persons* (Oxford: Oxford University Press, 1984), pp.493–499.

10. In this paragraph I attempt to solve a difficulty noted by James Griffin in 'Modern Utilitarianism,' *Revue Internationale de Philosophie* 36 (1982): 331–375; esp. pp. 334–335. See also Amartya Sen and Bernard Williams, 'Introduction' to *Utilitarianism and Beyond* p. 10.

11. Here the most prudent choice cannot be identified with the choice that maximizes lifelong expected preference satisfaction, due to complications arising from the phenomenon of preference change. The prudent choice as I conceive it is tied to one's actual preferences in ways I will not try to describe here.

12. See the articles cited in note 2. Dworkin's account of equality of resources is complex, but without entering into its detail I can observe that Dworkin is discussing a version of what I call "equal opportunity for resources." By itself, the name chosen matters not a bit. But confusion enters because Dworkin neglects altogether the rival doctrine of equal opportunity for welfare. For a criticism of Dworkin's objections against a welfarist conception of equality that do not depend on this confusion, see my 'Liberalism, Distributive Subjectivism, and Equal Opportunity for Welfare.'

13. Roemer notes that the person with high talent is cursed with an involuntary expensive preference for personal liberty. See Roemer, 'Equality of Talent.'

14. As Rawls writes," . . . those with less expensive tastes have presumably adjusted their likes and dislikes over the course of their lives to the income and wealth they could reasonably expect; and it is regarded as unfair that they now should have less in order to spare others from the consequences of their lack of foresight or self-discipline." See Social Unity and Primary Goods,' p. 169.

15. Amartya Sen, 'Well-being, Agency and Freedom: The Dewey Lectures 1984,' *Journal of Philosophy* 82 (1985): 169–221; esp. pp. 185–203. See also Sen, 'Equality of What?', in his *Choice, Welfare and Measurement* (Oxford: Basil Blackwell, 1982), pp. 353–369.

16. Sen, 'Well-being, Agency and Freedom,' p. 201.

17. See Allan Gibbard, 'Disparate Goods and Rawls' Difference Principle: A Social Choice Theoretic Treatment,' *Theory and Decision* 11 (1979): 267–288; see esp. pp. 268–269.

18. Sen, 'Well-being, Agency and Freedom ,' p. 200.

19. However, it should be noted that filling out a preference-satisfaction approach to distributive equality would seem to require a normative account of healthy preference formation that is not itself preference-based. A perfectionist component may thus be needed in a broadly welfarist egalitarianism. For this reason it would be mis-

guided to foreclose too swiftly the question of the possible value of a capability that is valued at naught by the person who has it. The development and exercise of various capacities might be an important aspect of healthy preference formation, and have value in this way even though this value does not register at all in the person's preference satisfaction prospects.

POSTSCRIPT (1995)

My 1989 essay contains an unclear presentation of the norm of equal opportunity for welfare and hence might convey the impression to the reader that the idea is inherently confused. It is not. For the sake of clarity it might be of use to restate the idea in several stages.

Roughly, we can say that equal opportunity for welfare obtains among a group of persons at a time just in case the highest level of expected welfare that each person could gain if she were to behave with perfect prudence is the same for all persons. But it would be implausible for the norm of equal opportunity for welfare to require that people have equal opportunity throughout their lives, because people who are initially equally favorably situated can make choices that result in some having diminished opportunities for welfare compared to the opportunities enjoyed by the rest. The intuitive idea that lies behind the equal opportunity norm is that each individual makes choices that affect her life prospects, and it is morally legitimate that each should bear the consequences of her choices, at least when society has provided a fair menu of options from which to choose. So the equal opportunity norm may provisionally be formulated so: equal opportunity for welfare obtains among a group of persons just in case at the onset of adulthood each person can choose among a set of life strategies, and if the person chooses prudently from this set, her expected welfare over the course of her life is the same as everyone else's.[1]

One further refinement is needed to capture the equal opportunity norm. Two people may have equal opportunity as defined above even though their abilities to make use of these opportunities efficiently to advance their welfare are quite different. For example, suppose that in order to choose prudently one must carry out a mathematical calculation. One person can do it easily, a second cannot do it, a third can do it only with great difficulty, or with acute discomfort. In order to carry out the prudent choice, one must resist a certain temptation, and again we may imagine that people differ markedly in their native "choice-following" talents. I will say that *true equal opportunity for welfare* obtains among a number of persons when society compensates and adjusts for individuals' different abilities to negotiate options, so that if from the onset of adulthood each person behaved as prudently as could reasonably be expected in the light of her choice-making and choice-following abilities, she would have the same expected welfare over the course of her life as anyone else.

Society might compensate for differential choice-making and choice-following ability by providing extra resources to those with lesser abilities. Such compensation can take many forms besides provision of money. Guardrails and warning signs in front of obvious cliff edges at national parks provide no benefit to alert and prudently cautious park visitors but may prevent some injuries to the dull-witted, inattentive, and negligent. Compulsory government programs that require savings for old age tend to equalize opportunities for welfare among myopic and farsightedly prudent citizens. In some cases paternalistic restrictions of liberty such as bans on dangerous recreational drugs serve a similar function. Since there are various dimensions of personal decision-making talent, and given the difficulty of separating a person's native endowment of prudential talent from the part of a person's present disposition to prudence that is due to her own hard-earned efforts at character transformation for which she should be given credit, it may be unclear what constitutes the level of prudent conduct that it is reasonable to expect of someone. In the simplest case, imagine that individuals differ only in their native willpower, so that individuals who make equal good faith efforts to be prudent may via unequal willpower end up behaving with different degrees of prudence. In this case compensation and adjustment produces equal opportunity for welfare when it is the case that if each person made good faith efforts to be prudent, all would have equal expected welfare.

In 1989 I wrote that when people enjoy equal opportunity for welfare as characterized just above, "any actual inequality of welfare in the positions they reach is due to factors that lie within each individual's control." But this is obviously false. Equality of opportunity for welfare obtains between Smith and Jones if their expected welfare given reasonably prudent conduct is the same. Facing these equal prospects, Smith and Jones may make exactly the demanded reasonably prudent choices, yet one enjoys better luck, and Smith ends up leading a miserable existence, while Jones lives well. Equal prospects prior to choice are compatible with unequal welfare as individuals lead their lives that comes about through sheer brute luck. (A lightning bolt strikes Smith and misses Jones, who is standing next to her.) Hence equal opportunity for welfare can obtain among a group of persons even though it also turns out to be the case that some of these persons are worse off than others through no fault or voluntary choice of their own.

This discussion suggests an alternate ideal of equal opportunity, call it *equal opportunity for welfare in the strict sense*. Strict equal opportunity obtains among a number of people just in case at the onset of adulthood they face option sets such that if each behaves as prudently as could reasonably be expected, all will attain the same level of welfare over the course of their lives. When strict equal opportunity obtains, no one is worse off than others through no fault or voluntary choice of her own.

Which version of the equal opportunity for welfare norm is ethically more appealing? This is a tricky matter. One might object to strict equal opportunity on the ground that it is violated if two individuals have identical initial prospects and identical tastes and abilities, then engage voluntarily in high-stakes gambling, a game of sheer chance, from which one emerges with high welfare prospects and the other with low welfare prospects. Even though strict equal opportunity is violated here, one might argue that in the morally relevant sense, these two individuals did have equal opportunities for welfare, because the eventual differences in their welfare prospects came about only through a process that both mutually agreed to undergo under conditions of full information against a background of equal initial prospects.

On the other hand, equal opportunity as I characterized it in 1989 (what I am calling here *true equal opportunity for welfare*) can be fully satisfied in circumstances in which some people become worse off than others through processes that entirely bypass their own choice. This difficulty is described three paragraphs back. A vivid illustration of the possibility is provided by an example suggested by Brian Barry: Imagine that in a class-stratified capitalist society marked by great inequalities in life prospects social science researchers discover that for many years nurses in hospitals have been conspiring to switch babies randomly just after birth so that at birth each person faces equal lifetime prospects of welfare, which resolve into very unequal prospects as soon as the nurses' lottery is concluded and you are placed either with a poor family or a rich family. After discovering this odd fact, would we then say that we had thought the society was terribly unjust, but now we see that since everyone had initially equal prospects, the society was just in its distributive practices after all? The inegalitarian society adjusted by the nurses' conspiracy seems to me far from just in its distributive practices, but more nearly just than an otherwise similar society minus the nurses' conspiracy. The implication of this story does not carry over in a completely smooth way to a society regulated by the norm of what I am calling "true" equal opportunity for welfare, because of the wrinkle about requiring equal prospects at the onset of adulthood. But it would be easy to invent a similar story about true equal opportunity for welfare that shows it vulnerable to Barry's criticism. As mentioned above, the point is that in a society in which the norm of true equal opportunity for welfare is perfectly satisfied, it may yet be the case that some people end up worse off than others through no fault or voluntary choices of their own. The ethical imperative of undoing the effects of unchosen luck on the quality of human lives is only incompletely satisfied in a society that fully satisfies true equal opportunity for welfare.

Up to this point I have been engaged in an intramural dispute among rival versions of equal opportunity for welfare. This family of equal opportunity for welfare norms has been subjected to attack, and the question arises to what extent the criticisms discredit the norm.

One criticism charges that the ideal of equal opportunity for welfare is utopian. We could not actually design and operate a society that would fulfill it. This criticism inflicts no significant damage. The ideal that everyone in the world should enjoy good health and longevity is also utopian, but this does not gainsay the desirability of the state of affairs posited as ideal. If a goal is worthwhile but unattainable, but we can approach it to greater or lesser extent, then a utopian ideal may dictate the eminently practical imperative that we ought to act so that we come as close to achieving the goal as is feasible.

A more significant worry is that given that some unfortunate persons could not be fully compensated for bad luck in their genetic endowments by any means, a serious attempt to attain equal life prospects for all would involve channeling all available resources to a few extremely unfortunate individuals, leaving these resource basin individuals still very badly off and the rest of the human race scarcely better off. The world being as it is, the average level of human welfare prospects would plummet if we tried to make welfare prospects as close to equal for all as possible. This point indicates that the norm of equal opportunity for welfare is one value among other values and that in practice many of these values conflict, so that more of one value means less of the others, and it is arguable that no single value should be given unqualified priority. At least, no version of the value of distributive equality is a likely candidate for the role of the single fundamental value to which all other values are to be subordinated. Any norm of equality, including equal opportunity for welfare, competes with other values and should sometimes lose the competition. My aim in my 1989 essay was not to gauge how important distributive equality is as it competes with other values, but to provide a plausible interpretation of the norm of distributive equality.

Some objections against equal opportunity for welfare are really objections against subjectivist conceptions of welfare. Consider Tiny

Tim, the cripple in Charles Dickens's story *A Christmas Carol*. Being extremely cheerful and prone to appreciate small blessings, Tiny Tim can attain a high level of welfare construed as satisfaction despite his grave handicap and poverty. Yet we may judge he is one of society's unfortunates, entitled to compensation to offset his imposed poverty and physical disability. If equal opportunity for welfare cannot ratify this judgment, so much the worse for this ideal (so runs the objection).

In this example there is an implicit appeal to objectivist convictions about human welfare or well-being. We believe that there are some goods that are important constituents of a good human life, and that if one lacks too many of these constitutive elements one does not enjoy a good life, whatever one's level of preference satisfaction. With respect to this worry, my 1989 essay could have been more clear by stating that the conception of welfare I employed in formulating the equal opportunity norm is an objectivist conception—one according to which the measure of the welfare level that a person reaches is not fixed by that very individual's actual beliefs, desires, and values. After all, the individual could be dead wrong about these matters. At any rate, the issue of whether an objectivist or a subjectivist conception of welfare is more adequate does not impugn the ideal of equal opportunity for welfare as such. This is merely an issue about how best to interpret the ideal.

A more direct challenge to equal opportunity for welfare challenges the normative plausibility of any conception of distributive equality.

Perhaps distributive justice is not concerned with equality at all, beyond the formal equality that requires that whatever the rules in place, they should be applied equally and impartially to all persons within their jurisdiction. Insofar as we are committed to distributive justice, perhaps instead of trying to make everyone's condition the same in any sense we should be trying to make the condition of the worst-off person in society as favorable as it can be made. Or perhaps justice requires arranging social practices so that each person is kept above some minimally acceptable threshold of well-being and beyond this floor, human well-being in the aggregate is maximized. Or, to mention an alternative that strikes me as plausible, perhaps justice requires that practices be set so as to maximize some function of aggregate human well-being that gives extra weight to improving the welfare of those who are badly off and that also gives extra weight to securing improvements for more deserving individuals. To suggest a quite different line, perhaps justice is simply refraining from violating anyone's individual rights understood in a neo-Lockean fashion. None of the ideas of social justice just mentioned include any distributive equality requirement—that all persons' conditions be kept equally desirable. The issues raised here are delicate, complex, tangled, and fundamental. I would note only that the issue of the moral weight of the value of distributive equality is independent of the issue of how best to interpret the ideal of distributive equality. My 1989 essay explores the latter issue.[2]

References

Arneson, Richard. "Liberalism, Distributive Subjectivism, and Equal Opportunity for Welfare," *Philosophy and Public Affairs*, 19, no. 2 (Spring, 1990): 158–194.

——. "Primary Goods Reconsidered," *Nous*, 24, no. 3 (June, 1990): 429–454.

——. "A Defense of Equal Opportunity for Welfare," *Philosophical Studies*, 62, no. 2 (May, 1991): 187–195.

——. "Property Rights in Persons," *Social Philosophy and Policy*, 9, no. 1 (1992): 201–230.

——. "What Do Socialists Want?," *Politics and Society*, 22, no. 4 (December 1994): 549–567.

NOTES

1. A complication here is that prudent conduct for an individual is conduct that maximizes expected welfare given how other people are actually expected to behave, not given the artificial stipulation that all others behave with ideal prudence. I will not try to reformulate the equal opportunity for welfare norm to register this minor complication.
2. I thank Louis Pojman for valuable correspondence on the issues discussed in this "Postscript."

A Critique of Welfare Egalitarianism
ERIC RAKOWSKI

EGALITARIAN WELFARISM

Utilitarianism's chief flaw is its obsession with aggregate quantities of welfare to the neglect of welfare's distribution. Egalitarian welfarism—the view that society should equalize the welfare of its members or contribute equally to their well-being—attempts to remedy this deficiency by regarding individuals as the subject of equal-ity, rather than treating equally the units of preference-intensity spread haphazardly over members of the relevant community. Its appeal is straightforward: personal welfare, one might argue, is what ultimately matters to people; if people matter equally, then they ought to be made (maximally) equal with respect to what they consider fundamentally important. Nevertheless, egalitarian welfarism languishes under three serious infirmities. Because these

Reprinted from Eric Rakowski, *Equal Justice*, Clarendon Press (1991), pp. 19–22; 39–52.

weaknesses are familiar, a short summary will suffice.

The first is utilitarianism's nemesis: the problem of external preferences. Because egalitarian welfarism repudiates utilitarianism's voting analogy and its appeal to constrained hypothetical choice as justificatory devices, it can flatly refuse, without blatant inconsistency, to count external preferences when measuring people's welfare. But the same pressure exists to include them in the measurement. Why should only certain dimensions of a person's welfare be taken into account, if people are entitled to equal consideration? More pointedly, what if the most important thing, for a person's own happiness, is how well *other* people fare? It seems perverse to give someone fewer resources or less assistance just because, though his well-being matters equally, he is less selfish than his fellows. But the inclusion of external preferences, as we have seen, opens the door to manifest injustice.

Egalitarian welfarism's second shortcoming is that it cannot possibly stand alone as a theory of distributive justice; rather, it presupposes a second, more basic theory of fair shares. Egalitarian welfarism cannot conceivably require that equality be attained by reducing everyone's welfare to the level of the most agonized and despondent individual. If one asserts, however, that the theory commands levelling up, not cutting the happy down to size, one needs *another* theory of justice to specify those rights that cannot be infringed in the course of establishing as nearly equal a distribution as possible.

One might reply that egalitarian welfarism should be interpreted to require not that everybody's welfare be equalized, or made more nearly equal subject to certain constraints, but rather that resources should be distributed so as to enhance everyone's welfare to the same degree. That response, however, fails to solve the problem. For in order to advance everyone's welfare to the same extent, one must begin from some approved starting-point, and that baseline perforce presupposes some theory of justice more fundamental than egalitarian welfarism which alone enables it to acquire prescriptive force.

This dependence cannot be avoided by characterizing welfare in terms of preferences or ambitions rather than some psychic state, and not only because a person's relative success is difficult to measure. (What is halfway to becoming Secretary of State?) When considering their ambitions and preferences for purposes of either of the theory's two variants, people must be imagined as choosing and modifying their goals against the backdrop of whatever means and opportunities they reasonably expect to be available to them. Egalitarian welfarism would be a risible proposal if everyone could state a preference for the life of a maharajah. But then egalitarian welfarism must tacitly rely on another theory of justice that defines people's allotments in terms of the value of resources (including opportunities), not welfare. Given this dependence, egalitarian welfarism cannot be the main story, let alone the whole story.

Egalitarian welfarism's third weakness is equally profound. Like utilitarianism, it attaches no significance to the distinction between preferences or needs people have chosen, cultivated, or preserved, and those they have not; similarly, it ignores the distinction between the contributions people make to the community's store of resources, and the extent to which their production owes nothing to their own efforts. The first point is best illustrated by people who foster expensive tastes, that is, tastes the possession of which renders it more expensive for someone to attain a given level of welfare than it would cost were his tastes different. Egalitarian welfarism would require that the allotment of someone who cultivated expensive tastes—for flashy cars, posh restaurants, designer clothes—be increased, in order to reestablish parity of welfare, even though everyone else's stock of resources would have to fall to repair the deficit he created. By contrast, those whose predilections are more cheaply satisfied would receive smaller shares. Yet surely this would be to reward the prodigal unjustly.

A more egregious example is that of a severely handicapped person who remains happy in spite of his infirmity. Somebody who is born or becomes disabled, and who had no opportunity to protect himself physically or financially (by buying insurance), is plainly entitled to special benefits whether or not he greets life with a smile. Egalitarian welfarism, however, says

just the reverse. It commands Tiny Tim to pawn his crutches to add a few coppers to Scrooge's purse, rather than requiring Scrooge to pay for Tim's physiotherapy. This result is intolerable. Why should the cravings or whims somebody has instilled or tolerated and that did or do lie within his control qualify him for larger shares? How can greed generate a right to gold, or envy to possession? Egalitarian welfarism seems to reverse the relation between desires and desert: justice requires that people order their lives, including their desires and emotions, in the knowledge of what they are due on independent grounds. The finicky and the phlegmatic have no valid claim to special favors.

Egalitarian welfarism's unjust treatment of production mirrors its mishandling of consumption. People's choices to labor longer or harder are irrelevant to their material rewards, the theory declares; desires are all that matter, regardless of whether people contribute anything to satisfying them. The woman who slaves away at her job does not necessarily deserve to keep even a part of what she produces, just as someone who imprudently tries and fails may always be entitled to another shot at his fellow workers' expense. What egalitarian welfarism ultimately fails to recognize is that individuals are responsible agents whose tastes, whose efforts, and whose happiness are predominantly their own concern, and who deserve better or worse as the result of their choices. People desire, and decide, and strive, but if egalitarian welfarism is correct, they need never own up to the material consequences of their actions, except to the dilute degree that members of a large insurance pool are affected by the care they take individually. It is hard to imagine a graver affront to our sense of justice and desert. Although we all bear the stamp of our surroundings, our mentors, and our misfortunes, we are, exceptional circumstances apart, autonomous beings who cannot disclaim responsibility for the choices we make or the blemishes we carry. But welfare-based theories cannot acknowledge this fact without ceding priority to a non-welfare-based account of fair shares. Hence, the only serious question is which non-welfare-based theory supports and matches our convictions most faithfully.

OPPORTUNITY-BASED CONCEPTIONS OF EQUALITY WITH WELFARIST ROOTS

One of the fundamental flaws in welfare-based theories is their failure to recognize that responsible individuals are the proper subject of equality for purposes of distribution. They do so either by locating the focus of equality elsewhere than in individual persons, as utilitarianism does in tying prescriptions to the outcome of a joust between preferences, or by denying the relevance (perhaps because they deny the possibility) of people's free choices to the size of their just shares. Yet, despite this decisive failing, welfare-based theories manifest a crucial insight. Material goods, occupational possibilities, and other rights and opportunities that might be apportioned are valuable primarily because they can be used to enhance the well being of those who possess them. No theory of distributive justice that purports to extend equal consideration to all can ignore the impact of a system of allocation on the welfare of those governed by it. On the contrary, the link between, on the one side, resources, rights, and opportunities, and, on the other, their capacity for satisfying people's preferences must be at the forefront of distributive decisions. The question is how to combine this conviction with the equally important thesis that people, as responsible agents (certain exceptional cases apart), should be held accountable for their decisions insofar as they affect the resources and other welfare-enhancing rights and permissions available to others. The two opportunity-based theories discussed in this section provide related answers.

Equality of Opportunity for Welfare

Richard Arneson rejects egalitarian welfarism for one of the reasons advanced above: "Individuals can arrive at different welfare levels due to choices they make for which they alone should be held responsible."[1] Suppose, he says, that two people whose tastes, abilities, and possessions are identical gamble with a sizable portion of their wealth, with one emerging rich and the other impoverished. In consequence,

unless the lucky person's winnings are taken from him and given to the loser, the second person's self-interested preferences will receive much shorter shrift because he now lacks equal means to satisfy them. The fact that the two will subsequently experience different levels of welfare, however, is in Arneson's view no reason to right the resource imbalance they freely created. Similarly, if two persons could satisfy their self-interested preferences with equal effort but one concentrates on saving whales while the other vigorously pursues a hedonistic course, society has no duty to disregard their choices and equalize their personal satisfaction after the fact. Or if one of two identically situated people trades one of his preferences for another that is more expensive to fulfill but that yields no additional pleasure while the second person retains his more humble hankerings, then the diminished happiness of the first person (if resources are not rearranged) provides no reason to take from the second to add to his holdings. Because egalitarian welfarism commands just the opposite, it cannot be correct.[2]

In place of equal welfare, Arneson offers a desideratum he calls "equal opportunity for welfare."[3] Simplifying slightly, two people's opportunity for welfare is the same, in Arneson's view, when the chances they are given over the course of their lives for satisfying their ideally considered, self-interested preferences are such that, if both of those people availed themselves of the maximally satisfying opportunity presented to them at each stage in their lives, their welfare, conceived of as the fulfillment of self-interested preferences, would be identical. In practice, of course, people's welfare might not be the same. As Arneson notes, some people will fritter away their chances, or give precedence to the achievement of goals other than their personal satisfaction, or cultivate tastes that yield less enjoyment per resource unit than the tastes they displace. But so long as the same level of personal satisfaction is made available to everybody, people are treated as equal, autonomous members of a just community. Whether they seize the chances granted them is solely their own business.

Arneson's theory undeniably improves on egalitarian welfarism insofar as it makes a person's entitlements depend on his own free choices. To the extent that under Arneson's theory other people's resources and opportunities are no longer hostage to an individual's profligacy or ill-considered decisions, the resulting pattern of distribution is plainly more just. Arneson's theory, however, is open to several of the same criticisms that egalitarian welfarism is unable to meet. In addition, it raises special problems of its own.

The first difficulty is posed, yet again, by external preferences. Arneson excludes them from consideration in measuring a person's welfare and thus that person's opportunity for welfare. For a theory that accords welfare, or at any rate its possibility, pride of place, this exclusion cannot but seem odd. After all, external preferences are no less potential sources of welfare than are self-interested preferences. Some people assign them considerably more importance than they do all but their most basic self-interested preferences, and adjudge their lives successes or failures to a far greater degree according to the satisfaction or frustration of their most important external preferences than according to how well their self-interested preferences have fared. To one who declares that welfare matters preeminently (whether or not people realize it through their own effort or choices), giving external preferences no weight at all in calculating distributive shares seems an act either of apostasy or of acceptance of the unconvincing claim that personal preferences alone ought to matter to people. But sidestepping this dilemma and giving external preferences equal consideration, as the arguments above have shown, opens the gate to injustice. It would certainly be preferable to avoid the fork, as theories of equality of resources can, by making somebody's claim to distributable resources independent of whether he would use them to bolster his own welfare or to attempt to achieve some non-self-interested aim.

Abstracting from external preferences in setting distributive shares on a welfare-derived basis has another unwelcome consequence that Arneson appears to have overlooked. The self-interested preferences of people whose non-self-interested ambitions are most central to their lives are often weaker than the self-interested preferences of persons whose primary concerns revolve around their own well-being. In cases where this relation obtains, people whose lives are dominated by non-self-interested desires will need, and on Arneson's theory must be given, a more valuable stock of resources or opportunities to put them on the same potential welfare plane. In consequence, more of the community's resources and opportunities would have to be made available to those people who attached the least importance to the goal—personal preference satisfaction—on the basis of which shares were assigned. And since these people would be free to devote their resources to non-self-interested purposes, as Arneson's example of the whale-saver reveals, Arneson's theory would, to the extent preferences develop in the foregoing way, compel community members in effect to subsidize the political, environmental, religious, or other-directed personal projects of people who care most intensely about their non-self-interested preferences, however much those community members might deny the wisdom or propriety of their undertakings and resent contributing to them. In making people choose whether to satisfy non-self-interested preferences in lieu of self-directed desires, Arneson's theory would often (if the above psychological assumption regarding relative preference strength is correct) make that choice much easier for those whose self-directed desires have been pushed aside by outward-directed ambitions, by giving them more resources to divide between their two classes of aims. That consequence hardly seems just.

As Arneson's theory appears likely to bestow excessive rewards on people whose self-interested preferences are faint because they chose to develop, or became convinced that they ought to adopt, preferences not belonging to that class, it conversely appears to deny their fair share of resources to at least some people who are easily pleased. Equal opportunity for welfare seems just as bound as egalitarian welfarism to require Tiny Tim to surrender his crutches to pad Scrooge's wallet in order to equalize their opportunity for welfare. It is, for that reason, equally unacceptable as a theory of distributive justice.

This criticism presupposes, of course, that somebody who remains content, even cheerful,

in spite of disease, infirmity, or other ill fortune may in fact enjoy the same opportunity for welfare, defined as the sum of possibilities over the course of a lifetime for the satisfaction of self-interested preferences, as a physically and materially fortunate curmudgeon. Given the difficulties of comparing two people's opportunity for welfare on Arneson's theory, however, that supposition seems by no means secure. Equal opportunity for welfare shares with preference-satisfaction versions of egalitarian welfarism the difficulty of ascertaining when two persons would enjoy equal welfare once the impact of the satisfaction or denial of external preferences has been distinguished and deleted. That in itself is a formidable problem both of theory and of application, particularly given the often pervasive influence on a person's sense of well-being of how well projects and events turn out that are unconnected to his self-interested designs. But the problem of interpersonal comparisons is still more imposing.

Consider two ambiguities in Arneson's account. First, Arneson does not describe in detail how the huge number of welfare-opportunity cross-sections over the course of a lifetime are to be summed for purposes of comparison. Should one look only to the range of choices confronting somebody at the age of majority (or whenever people are first held accountable for their choices) and ask what his welfare would be if he unfailingly chose the maximally satisfying act at each moment over the rest of his life? Or should one repeat this estimation procedure every moment of the year, looking at the possibilities in fact open to a person each minute of his life given the choices he made earlier, and then add all these calculations together to arrive at an aggregate measure of opportunity for welfare? If the first option is the one Arneson favors, then the measurement problem not only seems impossible, even if crude approximations are used: the result of its implementation could be vastly different levels of welfare (or opportunities for welfare) later in life if some people kept to the straight and narrow whereas other people strayed from the optimal path early on and, although they later regretted their decision, could not retrace their steps. The second option, however, arguably does not hold people fully responsible for their

free choices, because it requires continual re-calculation of opportunities for welfare without regard to whether someone's predicament was his own fault. The second option, moreover, would not appreciably ease the task of mea-surement, although it seems no more unwork-able (which is not to say that it is workable) than egalitarian welfarism in this regard.

The second ambiguity concerns Arneson's requirement that, in adding up the preference satisfaction expectations for each possible life history, "we take into account the preferences that people have regarding being confronted with the particular range of options given at each decision point." Here, too, a familiar dif-ficulty that one class of preference-satisfaction theories must confront, including preference-satisfaction versions of egalitarian welfarism, makes implementation seem an intractable prob-lem. How would this requirement be imple-mented, for example, in the case of Parfit's Russian nobleman? The young Russian knows he will inherit vast estates in several years. He now wants to give the land to his peasants, but he also realizes that by the time he comes into his inheritance, his moral idealism will probably have faded and he will desire to keep his land. Arneson would presumably include in his cal-culus of welfare opportunities the young Russian's preference that he not be allowed to choose later (by making available to him, say, the legal option of giving away now what he will come to own ten years hence). But would Arneson also include the preference of the no-bleman's later self that he not have been given that choice earlier, because his opportunity for welfare would be greater at that later time were that backward-looking preference fulfilled? How are forward- and backward-looking preferences to be combined in judging overall opportunity for welfare? And how is (to take the most ex-treme case of preference alteration by third par-ties) the brainwashing problem to be handled? A person's backward-looking preferences can in some instances be changed radically so that, in duration and intensity, they outweigh his con-trary forward-looking preferences. If those back-ward-looking preferences are to be accounted for in determining a person's opportunity for wel-fare, then forcible brainwashing or other invol-untary conditioning might be condoned, unless

Arneson adds to his theory a supplementary ac-count of personal rights or an account of per-sonal identity that would preclude weighing the opposed forward- and backward-looking pref-erences as those of the same person. Whatever course Arneson would favor, these complica-tions, particularly if some method is employed to discount preferences according to the degree to which personal identity is attenuated or al-tered, would vastly increase the complexity of the necessary calculations. And when these com-plications are superimposed on the preceding measurement difficulties, the calculations essen-tial to establishing a person's just allotment be-come mind-boggling. Try to fit together the ex-pected possibilities open to millions of people on a variety of assumptions about what every other person will want or do, and the difficulties of even a crude sort of measurement seem insu-perable.[4]

The example of Tiny Tim points to yet a fur-ther inadequacy in Arneson's current formula-tion of his theory. Like egalitarian welfarism, equal opportunity for welfare cannot stand alone as a comprehensive theory of justice. In some cases, equal opportunity for welfare is simply impossible, just as equality of welfare is. Some people, through no fault of their own, live short, painful lives that are beyond human power to lengthen or improve. But surely it would be wrong to limit everyone else's op-portunity for welfare just to make all equal, if in limiting the opportunities open to others one could not improve the prospects of those whose opportunities were naturally most restricted. Indeed, it seems wrong to require that resources be transferred to those with limited opportuni-ties where the costs to others are very high and the marginal gains to recipients are negligible. If Arneson would for these reasons impose lim-its on redistribution, however, he needs to im-port ancillary moral principles. Equal opportu-nity for welfare is not a self-sufficient theory of distributive justice.

One final difficulty . . . concerns the types of choices for which Arneson would make people answerable insofar as those choices bear on their opportunities for welfare. As Arneson notes, there are several senses in which people might be said to be responsible for their pref-erences. Two are relevant. Responsibility "could mean that our present preferences, even if they have arisen through processes largely beyond our power to control, are now within our control in the sense that we could now undertake actions, at greater or lesser cost, that would change our preferences in ways that we can foresee." Or people could be said to take responsibility for their preferences "in the sense of identifying with them and regarding these preferences as their own, not as alien intrusions on the self," even though they did not choose those preferences and are powerless to change them. Surprisingly, Arneson does not endorse either formulation (or consider other attractive possibilities), although his theory presupposes *some* account of responsibility for preferences. He does, however, suggest that even the second formulation, which one would expect to license less redistribution than the first because it enlarges the set of preferences that justice ought to ignore, would still require (practical political and administrative considerations apart) the redistribution of resources on account of people's religious beliefs. In my view, this suggestion is incorrect, and it is not borne out by Arneson's examples.

Arneson offers two illustrations. Consider someone "raised in a closed fundamentalist community such as the Amish who then loses his faith and moves to the city." Such a person "may feel at a loss as to how to satisfy ordinary secular preferences, so that equal treatment of this rube and city sophisticates may require extra compensation for the rube beyond resource equality." Arneson does not in fact favor extra compensation because if institutionalized it would "predictably inflict wounds on innocent parents and guardians far out of proportion to any gain that could be realized for the norm of distributive equality." But justice alone, he seems to think, would require it. As a second example, suppose "the government has accepted an obligation to subsidize the members of two native tribes who are badly off, low in welfare." The two tribes are identical, except that the religious ceremonies of the tribes require different types of cactus. If the price of one of the two cacti "rises dramatically" while the other cactus "stays cheap," then members of the first tribe, Arneson says, "might well claim" that equity requires that they receive a higher subsidy on account of the greater cost of the cactus they need; such a claim "is fully compatible with continuing to affirm and identify with one's preferences and in this sense to take personal responsibility for them."

The Amish rube Arneson describes is hard to bring into focus. Given his youth and limited experience, one might think that he would be easily pleased by comparison with his jaded neighbors, and thus qualify for a *smaller* basket of resources on Arneson's theory. Arneson must suppose instead that the Amish convert simply does not know how to enjoy himself— perhaps a perennial feeling of guilt remains as a vestige of his former faith—and that more resources than other people receive, perhaps partly in the form of psychiatric counseling, are necessary to give him the same prospect of happiness as everyone else. If this is the proper description of the rube's predicament, then Arneson has a point. Justice generally requires, I shall argue, that people be compensated for ill fortune against which they were unable to insure adequately and the risk of which they did not choose to run. If the young Amish man was handicapped psychologically by his upbringing, that is, placed at a distinct disadvantage in fulfilling his now mature preferences and realizing his considered aims relative to other people his age, then compensation (probably exclusively in the form of therapeutic services) would be due him, even if other values would prevent our providing free counseling in fact.

In this case, however, compensation would not be attributable to the rube's religious convictions or to other commitments with which he identifies. Its justification would lie in his seeking to escape from feelings and attitudes he did not instill in himself and of which he disapproves. This is as much a handicap as physical and mental infirmities somebody did not bring on himself, and it places equal demands on others to restore an equal distribution of resources, broadly construed to include the opportunity to live untroubled by exceptionally strong, debilitating feelings of guilt induced by the actions of others from whom, for whatever reason, specific damages cannot be sought. It would be wrong to conclude from this example that people's religiously inspired expenditures invariably entitle them to reimbursement by all the rest. Contrast Arneson's case, for example, with that of the Rube's father, who (we can imagine) was aware of other religions and ways of life but who remained true to his Amish heritage until late middle age, when his doubts won out. If he left the Amish community and requested an infusion of cash because he had always lived simply and had not managed to save enough money or acquire the education necessary for him to match his new neighbors' living standards, his claim would, as a matter of justice, probably be rebuffed. Unlike someone just entering his majority who bears diminished responsibility for his desires and ill-considered beliefs, he must answer for his earlier actions and omissions (unless some rule of leniency applies) because he must answer for the beliefs that prompted them. He espoused those beliefs fully recognizing the life to which they would consign him. In making that commitment, he acquired no right to assistance from those who thought him misguided; in repudiating it himself, his claim grew no stronger.

The same is true of Arneson's two tribes. To the extent that his example seems to sustain the conclusion that religiously required actions influence the resources someone justly possesses because they impact on his opportunities for welfare, it does so largely, I think, because Arneson stipulates that both tribes are "badly off, low in welfare," and that the government has already undertaken to subsidize them equally (as a matter of justice or of public charity?). Under the circumstances, it might seem only fair to give members of the tribe whose religious rituals have become much more expensive (presumably through no fault of their own, such as their negligently killing all the nearby cacti) a little more money, since the government has apparently decided to maintain two ways of life at the same level; and the choice might seem especially easy because they have so little money anyway.

It would certainly be too quick, however, to infer from the arguable propriety of an enhanced subsidy in these singular circumstances that all religious beliefs that carry material costs provide adequate grounds for redistribution. The problem is not just that the expenditures actually *required* of most believers by most established religions are either required *because*
they entail sacrifice, which would make compensation self-defeating, or because those burdens are so minimal as not to warrant, as a practical matter, the creation of a formal program of compensation. Soaring cathedrals, elaborately inlaid mosques, gold-capped shrines are not considered necessary for salvation or spiritual health; the majority of large outlays seem rather to be acts of personal charity, praise, or thanksgiving, much more akin to saving the whales, for which Arneson would provide no public subsidy, than coping with a lame leg. Even if an expenditure is large and religiously mandated, and even if Arneson is correct in classifying religious convictions among the self-interested preferences with which (he avers) justice is alone concerned, such an expenditure does not trigger a duty on the part of others to subsidize his faith. Articles of religious faith, like other matters of conviction (e.g. a claimed duty to save the environment, protect future generations, help others beyond what justice demands, foster artistic creativity, preserve a cultural heritage) that seem more accurately described as perceived action-guiding truths than as chosen tastes or preferences, are matters for which a person must assume responsibility once he attains the age at which he can be presumed to have considered his commitments and decided to abide by them. They are not among the chance events that require a reordering of resources so that all are truly treated as equals. They instead represent aims and values people are free to pursue with the resources and opportunities to which they are entitled, as a matter of justice, on other grounds. Contrary to what Arneson appears to suggest, it would be tyrannical to force someone who has rejected for himself goals and beliefs another person has accepted intelligently and freely to advance the second person's ends through his tax payments. Insofar as Arneson's theory considers religious beliefs or other considered commitments as appropriate grounds for redistribution, it betrays an important flaw.

NOTES

1. Richard Arneson, "Equality and Equal Opportunity for Welfare," *Philosophical Studies*, 1989, p.83 (reprinted in this volume).

2. *See* Arneson (1989), pp. 83–84.

3. Arneson's endorsement of this aim is due as well to what he perceives as shortcomings of the goal of equality of resources. His chief complaint is that if equality of resources treats people's physical and mental powers as resources, it cannot easily avoid making talented people slaves of those who are less favorably endowed. Arneson's reason for rejecting equality of resources is, however, inadequate if the theory treats certain resources as inalienable or tempers the pursuit of certain allocative goals with a theory of rights that precludes the adoption of certain redistributive mechanisms. In fact, Arneson himself recognizes the availability of this rejoinder (*see* Arneson (1989), 92 n. 5), although he declines to say why he thinks it fails to save equality of resources (if that is his belief). I rely on such a theory of rights in Chapter 6 in arguing that enslavement of the talented would not occur. Arneson's further contention that equality of resources wrongly fails to take account of certain welfare-decreasing attributes for which a person is not responsible is discussed in text below.

4. It might be possible to escape at least some of these problems if one takes the view that, so long as people could have insured on equal terms against later adversity, their opportunity for welfare was equivalent. Arneson gives no indication that he would endorse this possible resolution of some of these conceptual and measuremental problems. . . .

Equality and Partiality
THOMAS NAGEL

INTRODUCTION

This essay deals with what I believe to be the central problem of political theory. Rather than proposing a solution to it, I shall try to explain what it is, and why a solution is so difficult to achieve. This result need not be thought of pessimistically, since the recognition of a serious obstacle is always a necessary condition of progress, and I believe there is hope that in the future, political and social institutions may develop which continue our unsteady progress toward moral equality, without ignoring the stubborn realities of human nature.

My belief is not just that all social and political arrangements so far devised are unsatisfactory. That might be due to the failure of all actual systems to realize an ideal that we should all recognize as correct. But there is a deeper problem—not merely practical, but theoretical:

We do not yet possess an acceptable political ideal, for reasons which belong to moral and political philosophy. The unsolved problem is the familiar one of reconciling the standpoint of the collectivity with the standpoint of the individual; but I want to approach it not primarily as a question about the relation between the individual and society, but in essence and origin as a question about each individual's relation to himself. This reflects a conviction that ethics, and the ethical basis of political theory, have to be understood as arising from a division in each individual between two standpoints, the personal and the impersonal. The latter represents the claims of the collectivity and gives them their force for each individual. If it did not exist, there would be no morality, only the clash, compromise, and occasional convergence of individual perspectives. It is because a human being does not occupy only his own

Reprinted from Thomas Nagel, *Equality and Partiality* Oxford University Press (1991), pp. 63–74; 130–138. Footnotes deleted.

point of view that each of us is susceptible to the claims of others through private and public morality.

Any social arrangement governing the relations among individuals, or between the individual and the collective, depends on a corresponding balance of forces within the self—its image in microcosm. That image is the relation, for each individual, between the personal and impersonal standpoints, on which the social arrangement depends and which it requires of us. If an arrangement is to claim the support of those living under it—if it is to claim legitimacy, in other words—then it must rely on or call into existence some form of reasonable integration of the elements of their naturally divided selves. The division is rough, and spans a great deal of subordinate complexity, but I believe it is indispensable in thinking about the subject.

The hardest problems of political theory are conflicts within the individual, and no external solution will be adequate which does not deal with them at their source. The impersonal standpoint in each of us produces, I shall claim, a powerful demand for universal impartiality and equality, while the personal standpoint gives rise to individualistic motives and requirements which present obstacles to the pursuit and realization of such ideals. The recognition that this is true of everyone then presents the impersonal standpoint with further questions about what is required to treat such persons with equal regard, and this in turn presents the individual with further conflict.

The same problems arise with respect to the morality of personal conduct, but I shall argue that their treatment must be extended to political theory, where the relations of mutual support or conflict between political institutions and individual motivation are all-important. It emerges that a harmonious combination of an acceptable political ideal and acceptable standards of personal morality is very hard to come by. Another way of putting the problem, therefore, is this: When we try to discover reasonable moral standards for the conduct of individuals and then try to integrate them with fair standards for the assessment of social and political institutions, there seems no satisfactory way of fitting the two together. They respond to opposing pressures which cause them to break apart.

To a considerable extent, political institutions and their theoretical justifications try to externalize the demands of the impersonal standpoint. But they have to be staffed and supported and brought to life by individuals for whom the impersonal standpoint coexists with the personal, and this has to be reflected in their design. My claim is that the problem of designing institutions that do justice to the equal importance of all persons, without making unacceptable demands on individuals, has not been solved—and that this is so partly because for our world the problem of the right relation between the personal and impersonal standpoints within each individual has not been solved.

Most people feel this on reflection. We live in a world of spiritually sickening economic and social inequality, a world whose progress toward the acknowledgment of common standards of toleration, individual liberty and human development has been depressingly slow and unsteady. There are sometimes dramatic improvements, and recent events in Eastern Europe must give pause to all those, like myself, who in response to the dominant events of this century have cultivated a defensive pessimism about the prospects of humanity. But we really do not know how to live together. The professed willingness of civilized persons to slaughter each other by the millions in a nuclear war now appears to be subsiding, as the conflicts of political conviction which fueled it lose their sharpness. But even in the developed world, and certainly in the world taken as a whole, the problems which generated the great political and moral rift between democratic capitalism and authoritarian communism have not been solved by the utter competitive failure of the latter. . . .

TWO STANDPOINTS

Most of our experience of the world, and most of our desires, belong to our individual points of view: We see things *from here*, so to speak. But we are also able to think about the world in abstraction from our particular position in it—in abstraction from who we are. It is possible to abstract much more radically than that from the contingencies of the self. For example, in pursuit of the kind of objectivity needed in the physical sciences, we abstract even from our humanity. But nothing further than abstraction from our identity (that is, *who* we are) enters into ethical theory. Each of us begins with a set of concerns, desires, and interests of his own, and each of us can recognize that the same is true of others. We can then remove ourselves in thought from our particular position in the world and think simply of all those people, without singling out as *I* the one we happen to be.

By performing this deed of abstraction we occupy what I shall call the impersonal standpoint. From that position, the content and character of the different individual standpoints one can survey remain unchanged: One has set aside only the fact that a particular standpoint is one's own, if any of them is. It isn't that one doesn't know; one just omits this fact from the description of the situation.

A great deal emerges from our capacity to view the world in this way, including the great enterprise of trying to discover the objective nature of reality. But since objectivity also has its significance with respect to values and the justification of conduct, the impersonal standpoint plays an essential role in the evaluation of political institutions. Ethics and political theory begin when from the impersonal standpoint we focus on the raw data provided by the individual desires, interests, projects, attachments, allegiances and plans of life that define the personal points of view of the multitude of distinct individuals, ourselves included. What happens at that point is that we recognize some of these things to have impersonal value. Things do not simply cease to matter when viewed impersonally, and we are forced to recognize that they matter not only *to* particular individuals or groups.

I have argued before, and I continue to believe, that it is impossible to avoid this consequence if one juxtaposes personal and impersonal standpoints toward one's own life. You cannot sustain an impersonal indifference to the things in your life which matter to you person-

ally: some of the most important have to be regarded as mattering, period, so that others besides yourself have reason to take them into account. But since the impersonal standpoint does not single you out from anyone else, the same must be true of the values arising in other lives. If you matter impersonally so does everyone.

We can usefully think of the values that go into the construction of a political theory as being revealed in a series of four stages, each of which depends on a moral response to an issue posed by what was revealed at the previous stage. At the first stage, the basic insight that appears from the impersonal standpoint is that everyone's life matters, and no one is more important than anyone else. This does not mean that some people may not be more important in virtue of their greater value for others. But at the baseline of value in the lives of individuals, from which all higher-order inequalities of value must derive, everyone counts the same. For a given quantity of whatever it is that's good or bad—suffering or happiness or fulfillment or frustration—its intrinsic impersonal value doesn't depend on whose it is.

There are so many people one can barely imagine it, and their aims and interests interfere with one another; but what happens to each of them is enormously important—as important as what happens to you. The importance of their lives to them, if we really take it in, ought to be reflected in the importance their lives are perceived to have from the impersonal standpoint, even if not all elements of those lives will be accorded an impersonal value corresponding to its personal value to the individual whose life it is—a qualification I leave aside for the moment.

Given this enormous multitude of things that matter impersonally, values positive and negative pointing in every conceivable direction, the problem for the impersonal standpoint is to determine how the elements should be combined and conflicts among them resolved, so that we can evaluate alternatives that affect different individuals differently in ways that matter to them.

The response to this problem is the second stage in the generation of ethics from its raw material in personal value. I won't try to defend even a partial solution yet, but my belief is that the right form of impersonal regard for everyone is an impartiality among individuals that is egalitarian not merely in the sense that it counts them all the same as inputs to some combinatorial function, but in the sense that the function itself gives preferential weight to improvements in the lives of those who are worse off as against adding to the advantages of those better off—though all improvements will count positively to some degree. This is obviously related to the egalitarian element in Rawls's theory of social justice, but I believe something of the kind is true in ethics more generally. I believe also that the degree of preference to the worst off depends not just on their position relative to the better off, but also on how badly off they are, absolutely. Alleviation of urgent needs and serious deprivation has particularly strong importance in the acceptable resolution of conflicts of interest.

We are talking now about how things appear from an entirely impersonal standpoint, one it would be natural to take up if we were looking from outside at a situation to which we were personally unconnected. The point is that we can also adopt this stance by abstraction toward situations in which we are involved, either personally or by connection with someone else. If we ask ourselves, considering all the lives affected, what would be best, or how to determine which of several alternatives would be better, we are pulled toward the conclusion that what happens to anyone matters the same as if it had happened to anyone else, that the elimination of the worst sufferings and deprivations matters most, that improvements at higher levels matter gradually less, and that at roughly equivalent levels of well-being, larger quantities of improvement or the reverse and larger numbers of individuals matter more.

This is at least consistent with some familiar moral feelings. When we survey the actual world from the impersonal standpoint, its sufferings press in upon us: The alleviation of misery, ignorance, and powerlessness, and the elevation of most of our fellow human beings to a minimally decent standard of existence, seem overwhelmingly important, and the first requirement of any social or political arrangement would seem to be its likelihood of contributing to this goal. That is the clear impersonal judgment as to what matters most—the judgment one would make if one were observing the world from outside. And if one were actually a powerful and benevolent outsider, dispensing benefits to the inhabitants of the world, one would probably try to produce the best result by the impartial and egalitarian measure I have sketched.

However, the story does not stop here, because neither ethics nor political theory have as their aim to provide advice to a powerful and benevolent outsider capable of affecting the welfare of human beings. They aim rather to advise human beings themselves what to do, either as individuals or as the creators, supporters, and inhabitants of social and political institutions. The results depend on the capacity of persons to occupy the impersonal standpoint by abstraction even when they are part of the situation being considered. But that is not the only standpoint they occupy.

The raw material from which ethics begins—the personal aims, interests, and desires of individuals that the impersonal standpoint comprehends—remains fully present as a part of each individual's point of view. Often the personal standpoint also involves strong personal allegiance to particular communities of interest or conviction or emotional identification, larger than those defined by family or friendship, but still far less than universal. This large collection of diverse but essentially perspectival motives, ranging from self-interest to national solidarity, forms the other side of the broad mental conflict with which political theory must deal.

It is clear that in most people, the coexistence of the personal standpoint with the values deriving from the initial judgment of the impersonal standpoint produces a division of the self. From his own point of view within the world each person, with his particular concerns and attachments, is extremely important to himself, and is situated at the center of a set of concentric circles of rapidly diminishing identification with others. But from the impersonal standpoint which he can also occupy, so is everyone else: *Everyone's* life matters as much as his does, and his matters no more than anyone else's. These two attitudes are not easy to combine, particularly (but not only) for someone who is rather well off in a world in which most others are much worse off, with the result that from the impersonal standpoint, their needs are much more urgent than his. But if an ethical or political theory is to tell people how they should live, it must work with this juxtaposition of standpoints, and it must try to give an answer which is *generally* valid, and which everyone can acknowledge to be so.

Of course a limiting possibility is that the values I have described as emerging from the impersonal standpoint should be dominant, at the most basic level of justification, whenever they conflict with more personal values. There is a venerable tradition in ethics, fully developed by utilitarians, according to which we should attempt to become, so far as possible, instruments for the realization of those impartial values that appear from the impersonal standpoint—living, in effect, as if we were under the direction of an impartial benevolent spectator of the world in which we appear as one among billions. But this radical claim would have to be defended, it cannot simply be assumed; and I shall defend the alternative view that the personal standpoint must be taken into account directly in the justification of any ethical or political system which humans can be expected to live by. This is an ethical and not merely a practical claim.

But it will not be a solution to the ethical problem if the two standpoints are simply left to fight it out or reach some kind of individual accommodation within each person. Instead, this situation of conflict must itself be regarded as presenting a further problem for ethical and political theory—a new set of data for which a theory must be constructed. The response to that problem is the third stage in the generation of ethics, and it is the point at which ethics must assume a Kantian form. That is, it must go beyond the question "What can we all agree would be best, impersonally considered?" to address the further question "What, if anything, can we all agree that we should do, given that our motives are not merely impersonal?" That is how we reach the demand for ideal unanimity mentioned earlier, and the attendant doubts as to whether it can be met.

If it were not for fear of the charge of multiplying standpoints beyond necessity, I would be tempted to call the point of view from which this question is asked the Kantian standpoint,

because it attempts to see things simultaneously from each individual's point of view and to arrive at a form of motivation which they can all share, instead of simply replacing the individual perspectives by an impersonal one reached by stepping outside them all—as happens in the attitude of pure impartial benevolence. But perhaps I can refer to it instead as the Kantian development of the impersonal standpoint.

What the impersonal standpoint generates at the first and second stages is a massive impartial addition to each individual's values without any indication of how this is to be combined with the personal values that were already there. The individual is of course counted as one among the many whose life is seen to have value from the impersonal standpoint, but that does not make his special personal interest in his own life go away. This is, I think, an acutely uncomfortable position. There is no obvious way of doing justice to the demands of both these perspectives at the same time—for example, by construing them as subordinate aspects of a single, higher-order evaluative system. Yet fulfillment of the one will almost inevitably clash with fulfillment of the other. That may be true even of the worst off who are most favored by an egalitarian impartiality, since their individual interests may not correspond to what would serve the interests of their fellows. So each of us, after the results of the first stage of impersonal evaluation have been assimilated, is likely to find himself severely torn.

The question is, how can we put ourselves back together? The political problem, as Plato believed, must be solved within the individual soul if it is to be solved at all. This does not mean that the solution will not deal with interpersonal relations and public institutions. But it means that such "external" solutions will be valid only if they give expression to an adequate response to the division of the self, conceived as a problem for each individual.

Something more than the original attitude of impartiality will be required to deal with this issue, even when we think of it from the impersonal standpoint. Impartiality alone could only add the anxieties of inner conflict to the set of human ills, and include their reduction among its aims for everyone. But this would leave the problem essentially unchanged for particular individuals whose more personal aims conflicted with the collective good thus redefined. What is needed instead is some general method of resolving the inner conflict that can be applied universally and that is acceptable to everyone in light of the universality of that conflict. But here the values universally recognized will have a different form, specifying what in light of the full complement of factors it is reasonable for each person to do and want, rather than what results are better or worse. The idea of what is reasonable, which will play a significant part in this discussion, is the object of a Kantian judgment: It is what I can affirm that anyone ought to do in my place, and what therefore everyone ought to agree that it is right for me to do as things are.

Whether this is a well-defined idea is a notoriously difficult question, familiar to anyone who has tried to interpret the categorical imperative. The solution to this problem, if there is one, would constitute the third stage in the progression from the personal to the ethical.

The problem of integration has to be approached both through the morality of individual conduct and through the design of those institutions, conventions, and rules in which it is embedded. We must ask not only what type and degree of contribution to impersonal aims can reasonably be asked of divided creatures like ourselves, but also how we or our circumstances might reasonably hope to be transformed so that a life which better meets both sets of demands would become possible for us. This shows the connection between the ethics of individual conduct and political theory, and brings us finally to the fourth stage in the generation of ethics.

Political institutions can be regarded as in part the response to an ethical demand: the demand for creation of a context in which it will be possible for each of us to live a decent and integrated life, both because the effects of our actions are altered by the context and because we ourselves are transformed by our place in it. Political institutions serve some of the same purposes as moral conventions, though our participation in them, unlike obedience to moral requirements, is not voluntary but coercively imposed. This together with their much greater complexity and role differentiation gives them exceptional powers of transformation, for better or for worse.

The contents of the personal standpoint can be altered not only by changes in the structure of incentives but by changes in the sense of who we are, what our ends are, and where our personal fulfillment is to be found. But it is perfectly clear, as a psychological matter, that the special concern with how one's own life goes cannot be abolished or even, except in unusual cases, minimized. However powerful the impartial, egalitarian values of the impersonal standpoint may be, they have to be realized by institutions and systems of conduct that face up to the irreducibility of the individual point of view which is always present alongside the impersonal standpoint, however highly developed the latter may be. The individual point of view is not only a perspective on the facts and a causal point of contact—essential of course for acting within the world—but a perspective of value. It can distort the perception of impersonal values, but even if it does not, it provides its own, independent version of what matters to each of us.

The ideal, then, is a set of institutions within which persons can live a collective life that meets the impartial requirements of the impersonal standpoint while at the same time having to conduct themselves only in ways that it is reasonable to require of individuals with strong personal motives. But to state this ideal is to see how hard it will be to realize. Its two conditions pull in contrary directions.

The conflict between personal and impersonal standpoints is particularly conspicuous for those who are relatively fortunate, but it forces itself also on the unfortunate, not only through possible opposition between their concern for themselves and the equal claims of others like them, but through the issue of how much they may legitimately ask of others who are better off. At some point the natural demand for egalitarian impartiality has to come to terms with a recognition that legitimate claims of personal life exist even for those who are not in need.

But let me add immediately that we are nowhere near that point. In the grossly unequal world in which we live, the primary significance of the impersonal standpoint for those at the bottom of the social heap is that it compounds their personal wretchedness with a perception that they do not really count in the eyes of the world. To suffer from the unavoidable blows of fate is bad enough; to suffer because others do not accord one's life its true value is worse. We would have to move a considerable distance toward improvement in the condition of most human lives before the claims of the better off presented a serious challenge to the pursuit of further equality at their expense.

There may be those who think that I have exaggerated the problem by exaggerating the strength of the values perceived in the first instance from the impersonal standpoint. Does everyone really matter that much from a detached perspective? There is a genuine philosophical problem here. A skeptic might hold that *nothing* matters from the impersonal standpoint—that all that matters is what matters to this or that individual. I believe as already indicated that this is untenable, but won't try to argue further against it here. More to the point, I believe that if people's lives matter impersonally at all, they matter hugely. They matter so much, in fact, that the recognition of it is hard to bear, and most of us engage in some degree of suppression of the impersonal standpoint in order to avoid facing our pathetic failure to meet its claims.

If the suppression is sufficiently effective, it may give currency to the idea that political theory ought really to concern itself only with the accommodation of individual interests, among parties each of whom cares only about himself and a few other people. But I believe that any political theory that merits respect has to offer us an escape from the self-protective blocking out of the importance of others, which we may find psychologically unavoidable in a badly arranged world but which involves the denial of an essential aspect of ourselves. Suppression of the full force of the impersonal standpoint is denial of our full humanity, and of the basis for a full recognition of the value of our own lives. That is a loss which all of us should want to escape, even if it has to some extent the effect of concealing from us its own cost.

Everyone has reasons deriving from the impersonal standpoint to want the world to be arranged in a way that accords better with the demands of impartiality—whatever may be the relation of such a development to his personal interests. Any political theory that aspires to moral decency must try to devise and justify a form of institutional life which answers to the real strength of impersonal values while recognizing that that is not all we have to reckon with. Any moral theory which is not related to such a political theory must be regarded as incomplete.

7. EGALITARIANISM

Modern political theories agree that a society must treat its members equally in some respects, but they disagree over the respects, and the priorities among them. For someone accustomed to the forms of equality before the law and equality of citizenship that hold first place in a liberal democracy, the natural question is how far it is desirable or possible to extend the rule of equality into the areas of social and economic relations.

This topic has been extensively discussed, and most of what I have to say is not new. I shall present a case for wishing to extend the reach of equality in a legitimate political system beyond what is customary in modern welfare states, and then reflect on the great difficulties, practical and moral, of doing so. I am drawn to a strongly egalitarian social ideal, to whose realization the duality of standpoints seems to present great obstacles. So I do not see how to embody it in a morally and psychologically viable system.

Rawls devotes considerable discussion to the motivational viability of an egalitarian position in the final chapters of *A Theory of Justice*, but I find myself unable to share his psychological expectations. Essentially, my doubts lead me to suspect that Kantian unanimity may not be available over this issue. We can get closer through political institutions, but a gap remains which can be closed only by a human transformation that seems, at the moment, utopian, or by institutional invention beyond anything that is at present imaginable.

It is the motive of impartiality which gives us a reason for wanting more equality than we have. If impartiality is not admitted as an important motive in determining the acceptability of a social system—if every such system is just a bargain struck among self-interested parties—then there will be no call for equality except to the extent needed to ensure stability. But I believe that impartiality emerges from an essential aspect of the human point of view, and that it naturally seeks expression through the institutions under which we live.

There are other ways to conceive of ethics and political theory. If one defines their subject matter solely in terms of the search for possible points of agreement among distinct persons on how they should conduct themselves, important results may be found in the convergence of interests and the striking of bargains for mutual advantage. But it does not disparage the importance of these factors to insist that they are not all we have to rely on, and that a direct concern for others is potentially the most transformative influence on the acceptability of social ideals.

We are so accustomed to great social and economic inequalities that it is easy to become dulled to them. But if everyone matters just as much as everyone else, it is appalling that the most effective social systems we have been able to devise permit so many people to be born into conditions of harsh deprivation which crush their prospects for leading a decent life, while many others are well provided for from birth, come to control substantial resources, and are free to enjoy advantages vastly beyond the conditions of mere decency. The mutual perception of these material inequalities is part of a broader inequality of social status, personal freedom, and self-respect. Those with high income, extensive education, inherited wealth, family connections, and genteel employment are served and in many cultures treated deferentially by those who have none of these things. One cannot ignore the difficulties of escaping from this situation, but that is no reason not to dislike it.

The impartial attitude is, I believe, strongly egalitarian both in itself and in its implications. As I have said, it comes from our capacity to take up a point of view which abstracts from who we are, but which appreciates fully and takes to heart the value of every person's life and welfare. We put ourselves in each person's shoes and take as our preliminary guide to the value we assign to what happens to him the value which it has from his point of view. This gives to each person's well-being very great importance, and from the impersonal standpoint everyone's primary importance, leaving aside his effect on the welfare of others, is the same.

The result is an enormous set of values deriving from individual lives, without as yet any method of combining them or weighing them against one another when they conflict, as they inevitably will in the real world. The question whether impartiality is egalitarian in itself is the question whether the correct method of combination will include a built-in bias in favor of equality, over and above the equality of importance that everyone's life has in the initial set of values to be combined.

Even if impartiality were not in this sense egalitarian in itself, it would be egalitarian in its distributive consequences because of the familiar fact of diminishing marginal utility. Within any person's life, an additional thousand dollars added to fifty thousand will be spent on something less important than an additional thousand added to five hundred—since we satisfy more important needs before less important ones. And people are similar enough in their basic needs and desires so that something roughly comparable holds between one person and another: Transferable resources will usually benefit a person with less more than they will benefit a person with significantly more. So if everyone's benefit counts the same from the impersonal standpoint, and if there is a presumption in favor of greater benefit, there will be a reason to prefer a more equal to a less equal distribution of a given quantity of resources. Although actual alternatives do not in general offer a constant quantity of resources, the rate at which marginal utility diminishes is so rapid that it will still have egalitarian consequences even in many cases in which the better off stand to lose more resources than the worse off stand to gain.

But I believe that impartiality is also egalitarian in itself, and that is a more controversial claim. What it means is that impartiality generates a greater interest in benefiting the worse off than in benefiting the better off—a kind of priority to the former over the latter. Of course impartiality means a concern for everyone's good, so added benefit is desirable, whoever gets it. But when it comes to a choice of whom to benefit, there is still the question of how to combine distinct and conflicting claims, and the pure idea of concern for everyone's good does not answer it.

The answer will depend on many things. We may be able to benefit more persons or fewer, and we may be able to benefit them to a greater or lesser extent. Both of these efficiency factors are certainly relevant, and impartiality will favor the first alternative over the second in each case, other things being equal. But in addition, I believe that the proper form of equal concern for all will sometimes favor benefit to the worse off even when numbers or quantity go the other way. Such a ranking of concern is internal to the attitude, correctly understood, giving the worst off a priority in their claim on our concern.

The reason is that concern for everyone has to be particularized: It must contain a separate and equal concern for each person's good. When we occupy the impersonal standpoint, our impartial concern for each person exists side by side with our concern for every other person. These concerns should not be conglomerated. Even though we cannot contain all these separate lives together in our imagination, their separateness must be preserved somehow in the system of impersonal values which impartiality generates.

The point is famously made by Rawls in his charge that utilitarianism does not take seriously the distinction between persons. Rawls's construal of the moral attitude that underlies the sense of justice, as modeled in the Original Position, includes this strongly individualized impartial concern as an essential element. Because we are asked to choose principles without knowing who we are, we must put ourselves fully into the position of each representative person in the society. While the results of this simultaneous multiple identification may be obscure, it is clearly one of the sources of the egalitarian character of his theory.

This is connected with its Kantian inspiration, even though Kant himself did not draw egalitarian conclusions from the condition of treating each individual as an end in himself. If we try to view things simultaneously from everyone's point of view, as Kant insisted, we are led, I think, in an egalitarian direction. I believe this egalitarian feature is present even in pure, detached benevolence, but it also takes us part of the way toward the conditions of universal acceptability demanded by Kantian universalization: Up to a point, more equality makes it harder for anyone to object.

The fundamental point about individualized impartial concern is that it generates a large set of separate values corresponding to separate lives, and we must then make a further judgment about how to decide the inevitable conflicts among them. We cannot simply assume that they are to be combined like vectors of force, which add together or cancel one another out. That is the utilitarian solution, but it seems in fact the wrong way to treat them. Instead they have to be compared with one another at least partly in accordance with some standard of relative priority.

The separateness of the concerns does not rule out all ranking of alternatives involving different persons, nor does it mean that benefiting more people is not in itself preferable to benefiting fewer. But it does introduce a significant element of nonaggregative, pairwise comparison between the persons affected by any choice or policy, whereby the situation of each and the potential gains of each are compared separately with those of every other. I believe that when this is done, on careful reflection, a ranking of urgency naturally emerges. The claims on our impartial concern of an individual who is badly off present themselves as having some priority over the claims of *each* individual who is better off: as being ahead in the queue, so to speak. And this means there is reason to try to satisfy them first, even at some loss in efficiency, and therefore even beyond the already significant preference that derives from the diminishing marginal utility of resources. (In any case, some of those who are badly off may be suffering from other evils than poverty, and may be *inefficient* targets of resource allocation.)

To some extent the combined claims of larger numbers, or of greater quantity of benefit—particularly if it is greater not just absolutely but relative to what is already there—can pull in the contrary direction. I do not suggest that impartiality imposes an absolute priority for benefit to the worse off. But it includes some priority of this kind as a significant element, and it should incline us to favor the alternative that is least unacceptable to the persons to whom it is most unacceptable.

This is a direct consequence of what I take to be the proper form of imaginative identification with the points of view of others, when we recognize their importance from the impersonal standpoint. Instead of combining all their experiences into an undifferentiated whole, or choosing as if we had an equal chance of being any of them, we must try to think about it as if we were each of them separately—as if each of their lives were our only life. Even though this is a tall order and does not describe a logical possibility, I believe it means something imaginatively and morally: It belongs to the same moral outlook that requires unanimity as a condition of legitimacy.

Pure impartiality is intrinsically egalitarian, then, in the sense of favoring the worse off over the better off. It is not egalitarian in the sense of begrudging advantages to the better off which cost the worse off nothing, since impartial concern is universal. But for more than one reason the impersonal standpoint generates an attitude of impartiality which attracts us strongly to a social ideal in which large inequalities in the distribution of resources are avoided if possible, and in which development of this possibility is an important aim. And economic inequality is only part of the story. It may support stifling social stratification and class or communal oppression, inequality of political rights, and so forth. These are evils to which the equal concern of impartiality responds, favoring those at the bottom of the heap and those institutions which improve their status. All this comes from putting oneself in everyone's shoes, and even if we leave unspecified the strength of the egalitarian factor, measured by these standards the world is clearly a pretty terrible place.

One might of course agree that the world is a pretty terrible place without subscribing to an egalitarianism as general as I have proposed. One might say that all the moral intuitions of which we can be confident would be fully accounted for by a principle of priority to those who are not only worse off than others, but ab-

solutely deprived, because their basic needs for food, shelter, health, and minimal self-respect are not met. This is certainly a possible view, and it could be thought that a more general egalitarianism gains unwarranted support from its overlap with such a requirement of priority to the satisfaction of absolute needs. However, I want to defend the stronger priority of worse over better off, for two reasons.

First, it seems to me intuitively right. Remember that the subject of an egalitarian principle is not the distribution of particular rewards to individuals at some time, but the prospective quality of their lives as a whole, from birth to death (a point stressed by Rawls). Contemplating the differences in life prospects at birth which are built into any system of social stratification, I do not think that our sense of priority for improvements in the position of those lower down on the scale is exhausted by the case of the absolutely needy. Of course they have first priority. But the distinction between the unskilled and the skilled working class, or between the lower middle class and the upper middle class, or between the middle class and the upper class, presents the same intuitive ranking of relative importance.

The only point at which I think it gives out is in the upper reaches of the economic distribution: My moral instincts reveal no egalitarian priority for the well-to-do over the rich and super-rich. But I suspect that is because the marginal utility of wealth diminishes so steeply in those regions (am I being hopelessly unimaginative?) that these categories do not correspond to significant objective differences in well-being, of a kind that is morally important or a serious object of impartial concern. Apart from the separate question of political power, the difference in life prospects between the children of a multimillionaire and the children of a middle-rank manager or professional are morally insignificant. On the other hand differences between the lives of skilled laborers and middle-class managers are substantial, even if neither of them is in serious need.

My second reason for favoring a general egalitarianism is that it is supported by the best theoretical interpretation of impartiality, in terms of individualized concern. The resulting method of pairwise comparison with priority going to the lower member of the pair simply does not cease to apply above the level of basic needs. I conclude that only the rejection of impartiality or another interpretation of it would warrant the rejection of a broad egalitarianism in favor of the more limited principle of abolishing absolute deprivation.

To embody egalitarian values in a political ideal would be an involved task. An essential part of that task would be to introduce an appropriate condition of non-responsibility into the specification of those goods and evils whose equal possession is desirable. What seems bad is not that people should be unequal in advantages or disadvantages generally, but that they should be unequal in the advantages or disadvantages for which they are not responsible. Only then must priority be given to the interests of the worse off. Two people born into a situation which gave them equal life chances can end up leading lives of very different quality as a result of their own free choices, and that should not be objectionable to an egalitarian. But to make sense of such a condition generates notorious problems.

First, there is wide disagreement over when an individual is responsible for what happens to him, ranging from disputes over freedom of the will in general to disputes over the conditions of knowledge and opportunity needed to confer responsibility for an outcome, to disputes over when the use of a natural ability or fortunate circumstance for which one is not responsible nevertheless makes one responsible for the results. These are large issues of moral philosophy into which I shall not enter here. They may themselves bring up considerations of equality in their treatment. Let me simply say that it seems to me clear that, whatever remotely plausible positive condition of responsibility one takes as correct, many of the important things in life—especially the advantages and disadvantages with which people are born or which form the basic framework within which they must lead their lives—cannot be regarded as goods or evils for which they are responsible, and so fall under the egalitarian principle.

Second, there is a problem of consistency. If A gains a benefit for which he is responsible, becoming better off than B, who is not responsible for the change, the resulting inequality is still acceptable, since the principle does not object to *inequalities* for which the parties are not responsible, but only to the parties' being unequal in goods or evils for *the possession of which* they are not responsible—where merely having less than someone else is not in itself counted as an evil. So if A and B are each responsible for how much of a particular good he has, the non-responsibility condition fails and inequality is unobjectionable. It is perfectly all right if A has more of the good, even though B is not responsible for the inequality, since he is not responsible for how much A has.

But suppose A gains a benefit for which he *is* responsible, but that in addition to benefiting A, A's gain positively harms B in a way for which B is *not* responsible (by taking away all his customers or simply making him poor). If the evil for which B is not responsible is always allowed to dominate the good for which A is responsible, rendering the inequality unacceptable, very little will be left. Yet there are cases in which such dominance seems undeniable: Sometimes, for example, inequalities in the conditions of children are clearly not rendered acceptable by the fact that they result from advantages and disadvantages for which their parents are responsible.

This is by way of preliminary acknowledgment that any egalitarian social theory will have to be complex, even though its impersonal sources will certainly demand significant equality as a component of the social ideal. I shall return to these complexities later, since they present major obstacles to the pursuit of equality. But at this point I want to move on to the other side of the story.

In addition to the impersonal standpoint, each of us in reality occupies his own shoes, and we must ask therefore of any concrete social ideal designed to serve the value of equality what it will be like for each of the individuals involved to live under it. The impersonal standpoint and the impartial attitudes that emerge from it form only part of their makeup. Therefore no social system can be run on the motive of impartiality alone. Nor can it be run on the assumption that individuals are motivated by a mixture of personal and impersonal attitudes in which impartiality invariably has the dominant role. A human society is not a community of saints.

Whatever else they do, people will lead their own lives, and an egalitarian ideal can be approached only by creating a system which is more impartial and more egalitarian than they are, taken as whole persons. Such a system will engage their impartiality but it must operate in a way that is consistent with the other things that are true of them.

This topic can be divided into two parts. First, there is the question of the basis for allegiance of complex individuals to an impartial system as a whole. Second, there is the question of how, as individuals, they will be motivated in playing the roles which it assigns to them. This second question in turn has two aspects, the political and the personal.

I shall leave the exact strength of the egal-itarian preference vague. The absolute priority to the worst off of Rawls's Difference Principle is one version, and it can be generalized into the Lexical Difference Principle, suggested by Rawls and modified by Scanlon. I am inclined toward a somewhat weaker preference for the worse off, which can be outweighed by sufficiently large benefit to sufficiently large numbers of those better off. On the other hand I am concerned with the problem of altering those features of individual motivation and human interaction which make it necessary to accept large inequalities in order to benefit the worse off. The kind of egalitarianism I am talking about would require a system much more equal than now exists in most democratic countries.

Equality as a Moral Ideal
HARRY FRANKFURT

First Man: "How are your children?"
Second Man: "Compared to what?"

I

Economic egalitarianism is, as I shall construe it, the doctrine that it is desirable for everyone to have the same amounts of income and of wealth (for short, "money"). Hardly anyone would deny that there are situations in which it makes sense to tolerate deviations from this standard. It goes without saying, after all, that preventing or correcting such deviations may involve costs which—whether measured in economic terms or in terms of non-economic con-siderations—are by any reasonable measure unacceptable. Nonetheless, many people believe that economic equality has considerable moral value in itself. For this reason they often urge that efforts to approach the egalitarian ideal should be accorded—with all due consideration for the possible effects of such efforts in obstructing or in conducing to the achievement of other goods—a significant priority.

In my opinion, this is a mistake. Economic equality is not as such of particular moral importance. With respect to the distribution of economic assets, what is important from the point of view of morality *is* not that everyone should have *the same* but that each should have *enough*. If everyone had enough it would be of no moral consequence whether some had more than others. I shall refer to this alternative to egalitarianism—namely, that what is morally important with respect to money is for everyone to have enough—as "the doctrine of sufficiency."

The fact that economic equality is not in its own right a morally compelling social ideal is in no way, of course, a reason for regarding it as undesirable. My claim that equality in itself lacks moral importance does not entail that equality is to be avoided. Indeed, there may well be good reasons for governments or for individuals to deal with problems of economic distribution in accordance with an egalitarian standard, and to be concerned more with attempting to increase the extent to which people are economically equal than with efforts to regulate directly the extent to which the amounts of money people have are enough. Even if equality is not as such morally important, a commitment to an egalitarian social policy may be indispensable to promoting the enjoyment of significant goods besides equality, or to avoiding their impairment. Moreover, it might turn out that the most feasible approach to the achievement of sufficiency would be by the pursuit of equality.

But despite the fact that an egalitarian distribution would not necessarily be objectionable, the error of believing that there are powerful moral reasons for caring about equality is far from innocuous. In fact, this belief tends to do significant harm. It is often argued as an objection to egalitarianism that there is a dangerous conflict between equality and liberty: if people are left to themselves inequalities of income and wealth inevitably arise, and therefore an egalitarian distribution of money can be achieved and maintained only at the cost of repression. Whatever may be the merit of this argument concerning the relationship between equality and liberty, economic egalitarianism engenders another conflict which is of even more fundamental moral significance.

To the extent that people are preoccupied with equality for its own sake, their readiness to be satisfied with any particular level of income or wealth is guided not by their own interests and needs but just by the magnitude of the economic benefits that are at the disposal of others. In this way egalitarianism distracts people from measuring the requirements to which their individual natures and their personal circumstances give rise. It encourages them instead to insist upon a level of economic support that is determined by a calculation in which the particular features of their own lives are irrelevant. How sizeable the economic assets of others are has nothing much to do, after all, with what kind of person someone is. A concern for economic equality, construed as desirable in itself, tends to divert a person's attention away from endeavoring to discover—within his experience of himself and of his life—what he himself really cares about and what will actually satisfy him, although this is the most basic and the most decisive task upon which an intelligent selection of economic goals depends. Exaggerating the moral importance of economic equality is harmful, in other words, because it is alienating.

To be sure, the circumstances of others may reveal interesting possibilities and provide data for useful judgments concerning what is normal or typical. Someone who is attempting to reach a confident and realistic appreciation of what to seek for himself may well find this helpful. It is not only in suggestive and preliminary ways like these, moreover, that the situations of other people may be pertinent to someone's efforts to decide what economic demands it is reasonable or important for him to make. The amount of money he needs may depend in a more direct way on the amounts others have. Money may bring power or prestige or other competitive advantages. A determination of how much money would be enough cannot intelligently be made by someone who is concerned with such things except on the basis of an estimate of the resources available to those with whose competition it may be necessary for him to contend. What is important from this point of view, however, is not the comparison of levels of affluence as such. The measurement of inequality is important only as it pertains contingently to other interests.

The mistaken belief that economic equality is important in itself leads people to detach the problem of formulating their economic ambitions from the problem of understanding what is most fundamentally significant to them. It influences them to take too seriously, as though it were a matter of great moral concern, a question that is inherently rather insignificant and not directly to the point: viz., how their economic status compares with the economic status of others. In this way the doctrine of equality contributes to the moral disorientation and shallowness of our time.

The prevalence of egalitarian thought is harmful in another respect as well. It not only tends to divert attention from considerations of greater moral importance than equality. It also diverts attention from the difficult but quite fundamental philosophical problems of understanding just what these considerations are and of elaborating, in appropriately comprehensive and perspicuous detail, a conceptual apparatus which would facilitate their exploration. Calculating the size of an equal share is plainly much easier than determining how much a person needs in order to have enough. In addition, the very concept of having an equal share is itself considerably more patent and accessible than the concept of having enough. It is far from self-evident, needless to say, precisely what the doctrine of sufficiency means and what applying it entails. But this is hardly a good reason for neglecting the doctrine or for adopting an incorrect doctrine in preference to it. Among my primary purposes in this essay is to suggest the importance of systematic inquiry into the analytical and theoretical issues raised by the concept of having enough, whose importance egalitarianism has masked.

II

There are a number of ways of attempting to establish the thesis that economic equality is important. Sometimes it is urged that the prevalence of fraternal relationships among the members of a society is a desirable goal and that equality is indispensable to it. Or it may be maintained that inequalities in the distribution of economic benefits are to be avoided because they lead invariably to undesirable discrepancies of other kinds—for example, in social status, in political influence, or in the abilities of people to make effective use of their various opportunities and entitlements. In both of these arguments, economic equality is endorsed because of its supposed importance in creating or preserving certain non-economic conditions. Such considerations may well provide convincing reasons for recommending equality as a desirable social good, or even for preferring egalitarianism as a policy over the alternatives to it. But both arguments construe equality as valuable derivatively, in virtue of its contingent connections to other things. In neither argument is there an attribution to equality of any unequivocally inherent moral value.

A rather different kind of argument for economic equality, which comes closer to construing the value of equality as independent of contingencies, is based upon the principle of diminishing marginal utility. According to this argument, equality is desirable because an egalitarian distribution of economic assets maximizes their aggregate utility. The argument presupposes: (a) for each individual the utility of money invariably diminishes at the margin; and (b) with respect to money, or with respect to the things money can buy, the utility functions of all individuals are the same. In other words, the utility provided by or derivable from an nth dollar is the same for everyone, and it is less than the utility for anyone of dollar $(n - 1)$. Unless (b) were true, a rich man might obtain greater utility than a poor man from an extra dollar. In that case an egalitarian distribution of economic goods would not maximize aggregate utility even if (a) were true. But given both (a) and (b), it follows that a marginal dollar always brings less utility to a rich person than to one who is less rich. And this entails that total utility must increase when inequality is reduced by giving a dollar to someone poorer than the person from whom it is taken.

In fact, however, both (a) and (b) are false. Suppose it is conceded, for the sake of the argument, that the maximization of aggregate utility is in its own right a morally important social goal. Even so, it cannot legitimately be inferred that an egalitarian distribution of money must therefore have similar moral importance. For in virtue of the falsity of (a) and (b), the argument linking economic equality to the maximization of aggregate utility is unsound.

So far as concerns (b), it is evident that the utility functions for money of different individuals are not even approximately alike. Some people suffer from physical, mental, or emotional weaknesses or incapacities that limit the satisfactions they are able to obtain. Moreover, even apart from the effects of specific disabilities, some people simply enjoy things more than other people do. Everyone knows that there are, at any given level of expenditure, large differences in the quantities of utility that different spenders derive.

So far as concerns (a), there are good reasons against expecting any consistent diminution in the marginal utility of money. The fact that the marginal utilities of certain goods do indeed tend to diminish is not a principle of reason. It is a psychological generalization, which is accounted for by such considerations as that people often tend after a time to become satiated with what they have been consuming and that the senses characteristically lose their freshness after repetitive stimulation. It is common knowledge that experiences of many kinds become increasingly routine and unrewarding as they are repeated.

It is questionable, however, whether this provides any reason at all for expecting a diminution in the marginal utility of *money*—that is, of anything that functions as a generic instrument of exchange. Even if the utility of everything money can buy were inevitably to diminish at the margin, the utility of money itself might nonetheless exhibit a different pattern. It is quite possible that money would be exempt from the phenomenon of unrelenting marginal decline because of its limitlessly protean versatility. As Blum and Kalven explain:

> In . . . analysing the question whether money has a declining utility it is . . . important to put to one side all analogies to the observation that particular commodities have a declining utility to their users. There is no need here to enter into the debate whether it is useful or necessary, in economic theory, to assume that commodities have a declining utility. Money is infinitely versatile. And even if all the things money can buy are subject to a law of diminishing utility, it does not follow that money itself is.

From the supposition that a person tends to lose more and more interest in what he is consum-

ing as his consumption of it increases, it plainly cannot be inferred that he must also tend to lose interest in consumption itself or in the money that makes consumption possible. For there may always remain for him, no matter how tired he has become of what he has been doing, untried goods to be bought and fresh new pleasures to be enjoyed.

There are in any event many things of which people do not from the very outset immediately begin to tire. From certain goods, they actually derive more utility after sustained consumption than they derive at first. This is the situation whenever appreciating or enjoying or otherwise benefitting from something depends upon repeated trials, which serve as a kind of "warming up" process: for instance, when relatively little significant gratification is obtained from the item or experience in question until the individual has acquired a special taste for it, or has become addicted to it, or has begun in some other way to relate or respond to it profitably. The capacity for obtaining gratification is then smaller at earlier points in the sequence of consumption than at later points. In such cases marginal utility does not decline; it increases. Perhaps it is true of everything, without exception, that a person will ultimately lose interest in it. But even if in every utility curve there is a point at which the curve begins a steady and irreversible decline, it cannot be assumed that every segment of the curve has a downward slope.

III

When marginal utility diminishes, it does not do so on account of any deficiency in the marginal unit. It diminishes in virtue of the position of that unit as the latest in a sequence. The same is true when marginal utility increases: the marginal unit provides greater utility than its predecessors in virtue of the effect which the acquisition or consumption of those predecessors has brought about. Now when the sequence consists of units of money, what corresponds to the process of warming up—at least, in one pertinent and important feature—is *saving*. Accumulating money entails, as warming up does, generating a capacity to derive at some subsequent point in a sequence gratifications that cannot be derived earlier.

The fact that it may at times be especially worthwhile for a person to save money rather than to spend each dollar as it comes along is due in part to the incidence of what may be thought of as *utility thresholds*. Consider an item with the following characteristics: it is non-fungible, it is the source of a fresh and otherwise unobtainable type of satisfaction, and it is too expensive to be acquired except by saving up for it. The utility of the dollar that finally completes a program of saving up for such an item may be greater than the utility of any dollar saved earlier in the program. That will be the case when the utility provided by the item is greater than the sum of the utilities that could be derived if the money saved were either spent as it came in or divided into parts and used to purchase other things. In a situation of this kind, the final dollar saved permits the crossing of a utility threshold.

It is sometimes argued that, for anyone who is rational in the sense that he seeks to maximize the utility generated by his expenditures, the marginal utility of money must necessarily diminish. Abba Lerner presents this argument as follows:

> The principle of diminishing marginal utility of income can be derived from the assumption that consumers spend their income in the way that maximizes the satisfaction they can derive from the good obtained. With a given income, all the things bought give a greater satisfaction for the money spent on them than any of the other things that could have been bought in their place but were not bought for this very reason. From this it follows that if income were greater the additional things that would be bought with the increment of income would be things that are rejected when income is smaller because they give less satisfaction; and if income were greater still, even less satisfactory things would be bought. The greater the income the less satisfactory are the additional things that can be bought with equal increases of income. That is all that is meant by the principle of the diminishing marginal utility of income.

Lerner invokes here a comparison between the utility of G(n)—the goods which the rational consumer actually buys with his income of n dollars—and "the other things that could have been bought in their place but were not." Given that he prefers to buy G(n) rather than the other things, which by hypothesis cost no more, the rational consumer must regard G(n) as offering greater satisfaction than the others can provide. From this Lerner infers that with an additional n dollars the consumer would be able to purchase only things with less utility than G(n); and he concludes that, in general, "the greater the income the less satisfactory are the additional things that can be bought with equal increases of income." This conclusion, he maintains, is tantamount to the principle of the diminishing marginal utility of income.

It seems apparent that Lerner's attempt to derive the principle in this way fails. One reason is that the amount of satisfaction a person can derive from a certain good may vary considerably according to whether or not he also possesses certain other goods. The satisfaction obtainable from a certain expenditure may therefore be greater if some other expenditure has already been made. Suppose that the cost of a serving of popcorn is the same as the cost of enough butter to make it delectable; and suppose that some rational consumer who adores buttered popcorn gets very little satisfaction from unbuttered popcorn, but that he nonetheless prefers it to butter alone. He will buy the popcorn in preference to the butter, accordingly, if he must buy one and cannot buy both. Suppose now that this person's income increases so that he can buy the butter too. Then he can have something he enjoys enormously: his incremental income makes it possible for him not merely to buy butter in addition to popcorn, but to enjoy buttered popcorn. The satisfaction he will derive by combining the popcorn and the butter may well be considerably greater than the sum of the satisfactions he can derive from the two goods taken separately. Here, again, is a threshold effect.

In a case of this sort, what the rational consumer buys with his incremental income is a good—G(i)—which, when his income was smaller, he had rejected in favor of G(n) because having it alone would have been less satisfying than having only G(n). Despite this, however, it is not true that the utility of the income he uses to buy G(*i*) is less than the utility of the income he used to buy G(*n*). When there is an opportunity to create a combination which is (like buttered popcorn) synergistic in the sense that adding one good to another increases the utility of each, the marginal utility of income may not decline even though the sequence of marginal items—taking each of these items by itself—does exhibit a pattern of declining utilities.

Lerner's argument is flawed in virtue of another consideration as well. Since he speaks of "the *additional* things that can be bought with equal increases of income," he evidently presumes that a rational consumer uses his first *n* dollars to purchase a certain good and that he uses any incremental income beyond that to buy something else. This leads Lerner to suppose that what the consumer buys when his income is increased by *i* dollars (where *i* is equal to or less than *n*) must be something which he could have bought and which he chose not to buy when his income was only *n* dollars. But this supposition is unwarranted. With an income of (*n* + *i*) dollars the consumer need not use his money to purchase both G(*n*) and G(*i*). He might use it to buy something which costs more than either of these goods—something which was too expensive to be available to him at all before his income increased. The point is that if a rational consumer with an income of *n* dollars defers purchasing a certain good until his income increases, this does not necessarily mean that he "rejected" purchasing it when his income was smaller. The good in question may have been out of his reach at that time because it cost more than *n* dollars. His reason for postponing the purchase may have had nothing to do with comparative expectations of satisfaction or with preferences or priorities at all.

There are two possibilities to consider. Suppose on the one hand that, instead of purchasing G(*n*) when his income is *n* dollars, the rational consumer saves that money until he can add an additional *i* dollars to it and then purchases G(*n* + *i*). In this case it is quite evident that his deferral of the purchase of G(*n* + *i*) does not mean that he values it less than G(*n*). On the other hand, suppose that the rational consumer declines to save up for G(*n* + *i*) and

that he spends all the money he has on G(*n*). In this case too it would be a mistake to construe his behavior as indicating a preference for G(*n*) over G(*n* + *i*). For the explanation of his refusal to save for G(*n* + *i*) may be merely that he regards doing so as pointless because he believes that he cannot reasonably expect to save enough to make a timely purchase of it.

The utility of G(*n* + *i*) may not only be greater than the utility either of G(*n*) or of G(*i*). It may also be greater than the sum of their utilities. That is, in acquiring G(*n* + *i*) the consumer may cross a utility threshold. The utility of the increment *i* to his income is then actually greater than the utility of the *n* dollars to which it is added, even though *i* equals or is less than *n*. In such a case, the income of the rational consumer does not exhibit diminishing marginal utility.

IV

The preceding discussion has established that an egalitarian distribution may fail to maximize aggregate utility. It can also easily be shown that, in virtue of the incidence of utility thresholds, there are conditions under which an egalitarian distribution actually minimizes aggregate utility. Thus suppose that there is enough of a certain resource (e.g., food or medicine) to enable some but not all members of a population to survive. Let us say that the size of the population is ten, that a person needs at least five units of the resource in question to live, and that forty units are available. If any members of this population are to survive, some must have more than others. An equal distribution, which gives each person four units, leads to the worst possible outcome: viz., everyone dies. Surely in this case it would be morally grotesque to insist upon equality! Nor would it be reasonable to maintain that, under the conditions specified, it is justifiable for some to be better off only when this is in the interests of the worst off. If the available resources are used to save eight people, the justification for doing this is manifestly not that it somehow benefits the two members of the population who are left to die.

An egalitarian distribution will almost certainly produce a net loss of aggregate utility whenever it entails that fewer individuals than otherwise will have, with respect to some necessity, enough to sustain life—in other words, whenever it requires a larger number of individuals to be below the threshold of survival. Of course, a loss of utility may also occur even when the circumstances involve a threshold that does not separate life and death. Allocating resources equally will reduce aggregate utility whenever it requires a number of individuals to be kept below *any* utility threshold without ensuring a compensating move above some threshold by a suitable number of others.

Under conditions of scarcity, then, an egalitarian distribution may be morally unacceptable. Another response to scarcity is to distribute the available resources in such a way that as many people as possible have enough, or, in other words, to maximize the incidence of sufficiency. This alternative is especially compelling when the amount of a scarce resource that constitutes enough coincides with the amount that is indispensable for avoiding some catastrophic harm—as in the example just considered, where falling below the threshold of enough food or enough medicine means death. But now suppose that there are available, in this example, not just forty units of the vital resource but forty-one. Then maximizing the incidence of sufficiency by providing enough for each of eight people leaves one unit unallocated. What should be done with this extra unit?

It has been shown above that it is a mistake to maintain that *where some people have less than enough, no one should have more than anyone else.* When resources are scarce, so that it is impossible for everyone to have enough, an egalitarian distribution may lead to disaster. Now there is another claim that might be made here, which may appear to be quite plausible, but which is also mistaken: *where some people have less than enough, no one should have more than enough.* If this claim were correct, then— in the example at hand—the extra unit should go to one of the two people who have nothing. But one additional unit of the resource in question will not improve the condition of a person who has none. By hypothesis, that person will die even with the additional unit. What he needs

is not one unit, but five. It cannot be taken for granted that a person who has a certain amount of a vital resource is necessarily better off than a person who has a lesser amount, for the larger amount may still be too small to serve any useful purpose. Having the larger amount may even make a person worse off. Thus it is conceivable that while a dose of five units of some medication is therapeutic, a dose of one unit is not better than none but actually toxic. And while a person with one unit of food may live a bit longer than someone with no food whatever, perhaps it is worse to prolong the process of starvation for a short time than to terminate quickly the agony of starving to death.

The claim that no one should have more than enough while anyone has less than enough derives its plausibility, in part, from a presumption that is itself plausible but that is nonetheless false: to wit, giving resources to people who have less of them than enough necessarily means giving resources to people who need them and, therefore, making those people better off. It is indeed reasonable to assign a higher priority to improving the condition of those who are in need than to improving the condition of those who are not in need. But giving additional resources to people who have less than enough of those resources, and who are accordingly in need, may not actually improve the condition of these people at all. Those below a utility threshold are not necessarily benefitted by additional resources that move them closer to the threshold. What is crucial for them is to attain the threshold. Merely moving closer to it may either fail to help them or be disadvantageous.

By no means do I wish to suggest, of course, that it is never or only rarely beneficial for those below a utility threshold to move closer to it. Certainly it may be beneficial, either because it increases the likelihood that the threshold will ultimately be attained or because, quite apart from the significance of the threshold, additional resources provide important increments of utility. After all, a collector may enjoy expanding his collection even if he knows that he has no chance of ever completing it. My point is only that additional resources do not necessarily benefit those who have less than enough. The additions may be too little to make any difference. It may be morally quite acceptable, accordingly, for some to have more than enough of a certain resource even while others have less than enough of it.

V

Quite often, advocacy of egalitarianism is based less upon an argument than upon a purported moral intuition: economic inequality, considered as such, just seems wrong. It strikes many people as unmistakably apparent that, taken simply in itself, the enjoyment by some of greater economic benefits than are enjoyed by others is morally offensive. I suspect, however, that in many cases those who profess to have this intuition concerning manifestations of inequality are actually responding not to the inequality but to another feature of the situations they are confronting. What I believe they find intuitively to be morally objectionable, in the types of situations characteristically cited as instances of economic inequality, is not the fact that some of the individuals in those situations have *less* money than others but the fact that those with less have *too little*.

When we consider people who are substantially worse off than ourselves, we do very commonly find that we are morally disturbed by their circumstances. What directly touches us in cases of this kind, however, is not a quantitative discrepancy but a qualitative condition— not the fact that the economic resources of those who are worse off are *smaller in magnitude* than ours, but the different fact that these people are so *poor*. Mere differences in the amounts of money people have are not in themselves distressing. We tend to be quite unmoved, after all, by inequalities between the well-to-do and the rich; our awareness that the former are substantially worse off than the latter does not disturb us morally at all. And if we believe of some person that his life is richly fulfilling, that he himself is genuinely content with his economic situation, and that he suffers no resentments or sorrows which more money could assuage, we are not ordinarily much interested—from a moral point of view—in the question of how the amount of money he has compares with the amounts possessed by others. Economic dis-

crepancies in cases of these sorts do not impress us in the least as matters of significant moral concern. The fact that some people have much less than others is morally undisturbing when it is clear that they have plenty.

It seems clear that egalitarianism and the doctrine of sufficiency are logically independent: considerations that support the one cannot be presumed to provide support also for the other. Yet proponents of egalitarianism frequently suppose that they have offered grounds for their position when in fact what they have offered is pertinent as support only for the doctrine of sufficiency. Thus they often, in attempting to gain acceptance for egalitarianism, call attention to disparities between the conditions of life characteristic of the rich and those characteristic of the poor. Now it is undeniable that contemplating such disparities does often elicit a conviction that it would be morally desirable to redistribute the available resources so as to improve the circumstances of the poor. And, of course, that would bring about a greater degree of economic equality. But the indisputability of the moral appeal of improving the condition of the poor by allocating to them resources taken from those who are well off does not even tend to show that egalitarianism is, as a moral ideal, similarly indisputable. To show of poverty that it is compellingly undesirable does nothing whatsoever to show the same of inequality. For what makes someone poor in the morally relevant sense—in which poverty is understood as a condition from which we naturally recoil—is not that his economic assets are simply of lesser magnitude than those of others.

A typical example of this confusion is provided by Ronald Dworkin. Dworkin characterizes the ideal of economic equality as requiring that "no citizen has less than an equal share of the community's resources just in order that others may have more of what he lacks."[1] But in support of his claim that the United States now falls short of this ideal, he refers to circumstances that are not primarily evidence of inequality but of poverty:

> It is, I think, apparent that the United States falls far short now [of the ideal of equality]. A substantial minority of Americans are chronically unemployed or earn wages be-

low any realistic "poverty line" or are handicapped in various ways or burdened with special needs; and most of these people would do the work necessary to earn a decent living if they had the opportunity and capacity. (208)

What mainly concerns Dworkin—what he actually considers to be morally important—is manifestly not that our society permits a situation in which a substantial minority of Americans have *smaller shares* than others of the resources which he apparently presumes should be available for all. His concern is, rather, that the members of this minority *do not earn decent livings*.

The force of Dworkin's complaint does not derive from the allegation that our society fails to provide some individuals with as much as others, but from a quite different allegation: viz., our society fails to provide each individual with "the opportunity to develop and lead a life he can regard as valuable both to himself and to [the community]" (211). Dworkin is dismayed most fundamentally, not by evidence that the United States permits economic inequality, but by evidence that it fails to ensure that everyone has enough to lead "a life of choice and value" (212)—in other words, that it fails to fulfill for all the ideal of sufficiency. What bothers him most immediately is not that certain quantitative relationships are widespread but that certain qualitative conditions prevail. He cares principally about the value of people's lives, but he mistakenly represents himself as caring principally about the relative magnitudes of their economic assets.

My suggestion that situations involving inequality are morally disturbing only to the extent that they violate the ideal of sufficiency is confirmed, it seems to me, by familiar discrepancies between the principles egalitarians profess and the way in which they commonly conduct their own lives. My point here is not that some egalitarians hypocritically accept high incomes and special opportunities for which, according to the moral theories they profess, there is no justification. It is that many egalitarians (including many academic proponents of the doctrine) are not truly concerned whether they

are as well off economically as other people are. They believe that they themselves have roughly enough money for what is important to them, and they are therefore not terribly preoccupied with the fact that some people are considerably richer than they. Indeed, many egalitarians would consider it rather shabby or even reprehensible to care, with respect to their own lives, about economic comparisons of that sort. And, notwithstanding the implications of the doctrines to which they urge adherence, they would be appalled if their children grew up with such preoccupations.

VI

The fundamental error of egalitarianism lies in supposing that it is morally important whether one person has less than another regardless of how much either of them has. This error is due in part to the false assumption that someone who is economically worse off has more important unsatisfied needs than someone who is better off. In fact the morally significant needs of both individuals may be fully satisfied or equally unsatisfied. Whether one person has more money than another is a wholly extrinsic matter. It has to do with a relationship between the respective economic assets of the two people, which is not only independent of the amounts of their assets and of the amounts of satisfaction they can derive from them, but which is also independent of the attitudes of these people toward those levels of assets and of satisfaction. The economic comparison implies nothing concerning whether either of the people compared has any morally important unsatisfied needs at all, nor concerning whether either is content with what he has.

This defect in egalitarianism appears plainly in Thomas Nagel's development of the doctrine. According to Nagel:

> The essential feature of an egalitarian priority system is that it counts improvements to the welfare of the worse off as more urgent than improvements to the welfare of the better off.... What makes a system egalitarian is the priority it gives to the claims of those ... at the bottom.... Each individual with a

more urgent claim has priority . . . over each individual with a less urgent claim.[2]

And in discussing Rawls's Difference Principle, which he endorses, Nagel says the Difference Principle "establishes an order of priority among needs and gives preference to the most urgent." But the preference actually assigned by the Difference Principle is not in favor of those whose needs are most urgent; it is in favor of those who are identified as worst off. It is a mere assumption, which Nagel makes without providing any grounds for it whatever, that the worst off individuals have urgent needs. In most societies the people who are economically at the bottom are indeed extremely poor; and they do, as a matter of fact, have urgent needs. But this relationship between low economic status and urgent need is wholly contingent. It can be established only on the basis of empirical data. There is no necessary conceptual connection between a person's relative economic position and whether he has needs of any degree of urgency.

It is possible for those who are worse off not to have more urgent needs or claims than those who are better off, because it is possible for them to have no urgent needs or claims at all. The notion of "urgency" has to do with what is *important*. Trivial needs or interests, which have no significant bearing upon the quality of a person's life or upon his readiness to be content with it, cannot properly be construed as being urgent to any degree whatever or as supporting the sort of morally demanding claims to which genuine urgency gives rise. From the fact that a person is at the bottom of some economic order, moreover, it cannot even be inferred that he has *any* unsatisfied needs or claims. After all, it is possible for conditions at the bottom to be quite good; the fact that they are the worst does not in itself entail that they are bad, or that they are in any way incompatible with richly fulfilling and enjoyable lives.

Nagel maintains that what underlies the appeal of equality is an "ideal of acceptability to each individual." On his account, this ideal entails that a reasonable person should consider deviations from equality to be acceptable only if they are in his interest in the sense that he would be worse off without them. But a reasonable person might well regard an unequal

distribution as entirely acceptable even though he did not presume that any other distribution would benefit him less. For he might believe that the unequal distribution provided him with quite enough; and he might reasonably be unequivocally content with that, with no concern for the possibility that some other arrangement would provide him with more. It is gratuitous to assume that every reasonable person must be seeking to maximize the benefits he can obtain, in a sense requiring that he be endlessly interested in or open to improving his life. A certain deviation from equality might not be *in* someone's interest, because it might be that he would in fact be better off without it. But as long as it does not *conflict* with his interest, by obstructing his opportunity to lead the sort of life that it is important for him to lead, the deviation from equality may be quite acceptable. To be wholly satisfied with a certain state of affairs, a reasonable person need not suppose that there is no other available state of affairs in which he would be better off.

Nagel illustrates his thesis concerning the moral appeal of equality by considering a family with two children, one of whom is "normal and quite happy" while the other "suffers from a painful handicap." If this family were to move to the city the handicapped child would benefit from medical and educational opportunities that are unavailable in the suburbs, but the healthy child would have less fun. If the family were to move to the suburbs, on the other hand, the handicapped child would be deprived but the healthy child would enjoy himself more. Nagel stipulates that the gain to the healthy child in moving to the suburbs would be greater than the gain to the handicapped child in moving to the city: in the city the healthy child would find life positively disagreeable, while the handicapped child would not become happy "but only less miserable."

Given these considerations, the egalitarian decision is to move to the city; for "it is more urgent to benefit the [handicapped] child even though the benefit we can give him is less than the benefit we can give the [healthy] child." Nagel explains that this judgment concerning the greater urgency of benefitting the handicapped child "depends on the worse off position of the [handicapped] child. An improvement in his situation is more important than an equal or somewhat greater improvement in the situation of the [normal] child." But it seems to me that Nagel's analysis of this matter is flawed by an error similar to the one that I attributed above to Dworkin. The fact that it is preferable to help the handicapped child is not due, as Nagel asserts, to the fact that this child is worse off than the other. It is due to the fact that this child, and not the other, suffers from a painful handicap. The handicapped child's claim is important because his condition is *bad*—significantly undesirable—and not merely because he is *less well off* than his sibling.

This does not imply, of course, that Nagel's evaluation of what the family should do is wrong. Rejecting egalitarianism certainly does not mean maintaining that it is always mandatory simply to maximize benefits, and that therefore the family should move to the suburbs because the normal child would gain more from that than the handicapped child would gain from a move to the city. However, the most cogent basis for Nagel's judgment in favor of the handicapped child has nothing to do with the alleged urgency of providing people with as much as others. It pertains rather to the urgency of the needs of people who do not have enough.

VII

What does it mean, in the present context, for a person to have enough? One thing it might mean is that any more would be too much: a larger amount would make the person's life unpleasant, or it would be harmful or in some other way unwelcome. This is often what people have in mind when they say such things as "I've had enough!" or "Enough of that!" The idea conveyed by statements like these is that *a limit has been reached* beyond which it is not desirable to proceed. On the other hand, the assertion that a person has enough may entail only that a *certain requirement or standard has been met* with no implication that a larger quantity would be bad. This is often what a person intends when he says something like "That should be enough." Statements such as this one characterize the indicated amount as sufficient while leaving open the possibility that a larger amount might also be acceptable.

In the doctrine of sufficiency the use of the notion of "enough" pertains to *meeting a standard* rather than to *reaching a limit*. To say that a person has enough money means that he is content, or that it is reasonable for him to be content, with having no more money than he has. And to say this is, in turn, to say something like the following: the person does not (or cannot reasonably) regard whatever (if anything) is unsatisfying or distressing about his life as due to his having too little money. In other words, if a person is (or ought reasonably to be) content with the amount of money he has, then insofar as he is or has reason to be unhappy with the way his life is going, he does not (or cannot reasonably) suppose that more money would—either as a sufficient or as a necessary condition—enable him to become (or to have reason to be) significantly less unhappy with it.

It is essential to understand that having enough money differs from merely having enough to get along, or enough to make life marginally tolerable. People are not generally content with living on the brink. The point of the doctrine of sufficiency is not that the only morally important distributional consideration with respect to money is whether people have enough to avoid economic misery. A person who might naturally and appropriately be said to have just barely enough does not, by the standard invoked in the doctrine of sufficiency, have enough at all.

There are two distinct kinds of circumstances in which the amount of money a person has is enough—that is, in which more money will not enable him to become significantly less unhappy. On the one hand, it may be that the person is suffering no substantial distress or dissatisfaction with his life. On the other hand, it may be that although the person is unhappy about how his life is going, the difficulties that account for his unhappiness would not be alleviated by more money. Circumstances of this second kind obtain when what is wrong with the person's life has to do with non-economic goods such as love, a sense that life is meaningful, satisfaction with one's own character, and so on. These are goods that money cannot buy; moreover, they are goods for which none of the things money can buy are even approximately adequate substitutes. Sometimes, to be sure, non-economic goods are obtainable or enjoyable only (or more easily) by someone who has a certain amount of money. But the person who is distressed with his life while content with his economic situation may already have that much money.

It is possible that someone who is content with the amount of money he has might also be content with an even larger amount of money. Since having enough money does not mean being at a limit beyond which more money would necessarily be undesirable, it would be a mistake to assume that for a person who already has enough the marginal utility of money must be either negative or zero. Although this person is by hypothesis not distressed about his life in virtue of any lack of things which more money would enable him to obtain, nonetheless it remains possible that he would enjoy having some of those things. They would not make him less unhappy, nor would they in any way alter his attitude toward his life or the degree of his contentment with it, but they might bring him pleasure. If that is so, then his life would in this respect be better with more money than without it. The marginal utility for him of money would accordingly remain positive.

To say that a person is content with the amount of money he has does not entail, then, that there would be no point whatever in his having more. Thus someone with enough money might be quite *willing* to accept incremental economic benefits. He might in fact be *pleased* to receive them. Indeed, from the supposition that a person is content with the amount of money he has it cannot even be inferred that he would not *prefer* to have more. And it is even possible that he would actually be prepared to *sacrifice* certain things that he values (for instance, a certain amount of leisure) for the sake of more money.

But how can all this be compatible with saying that the person is content with what he has? What *does* contentment with a given amount of money preclude, if it does not preclude being willing or being pleased or preferring to have more money or even being ready to make sacrifices for more? It precludes his having an *active interest* in getting more. A contented person regards having more money as *inessential* to his being satisfied with his life. The fact that he is content is quite consistent with his recognizing that his economic circumstances could

be improved and that his life might as a consequence become better than it is. But this possibility is not important to him. He is simply not much interested in being better off, so far as money goes, than he is. His attention and interest are not vividly engaged by the benefits which would be available to him if he had more money. He is just not very responsive to their appeal. They do not arouse in him any particularly eager or restless concern, although he acknowledges that he would enjoy additional benefits if they were provided to him.

In any event, let us suppose that the level of satisfaction that his present economic circumstances enable him to attain is high enough to meet his expectations of life. This is not fundamentally a matter of how much utility or satisfaction his various activities and experiences provide. Rather, it is most decisively a matter of his attitude toward being provided with that much. The satisfying experiences a person has are one thing. Whether he is satisfied that his life includes just those satisfactions is another. Although it is possible that other feasible circumstances would provide him with greater amounts of satisfaction, it may be that he is wholly satisfied with the amounts of satisfaction that he now enjoys. Even if he knows that he could obtain a greater quantity of satisfaction overall, he does not experience the uneasiness or the ambition that would incline him to seek it. Some people feel that their lives are good enough, and it is not important to them whether their lives are as good as possible.

The fact that a person lacks an active interest in getting something does not mean, of course, that he prefers not to have it. This is why the contented person may without any incoherence accept or welcome improvements in his situation and why he may even be prepared to incur minor costs in order to improve it. The fact that he is contented means only that the possibility of improving his situation is not *important* to him. It only implies, in other words, that he does not resent his circumstances, that he is not anxious or determined to improve them, and that he does not go out of his way or take any significant initiatives to make them better.

It may seem that there can be no reasonable basis for accepting less satisfaction when one could have more, that therefore rationality itself entails maximizing, and hence that a person who refuses to maximize the quantity of satisfaction in his life is not being rational. Such a person cannot, of course, offer it as his reason for declining to pursue greater satisfaction that the costs of this pursuit are too high; for if that were his reason then, clearly, he would be attempting to maximize satisfaction after all. But what other good reason could he possibly have for passing up an opportunity for more satisfaction? In fact, he may have a very good reason for this: namely, *that he is satisfied with the amount of satisfaction he already has.* Being satisfied with the way things are is unmistakably an excellent reason for having no great interest in changing them. A person who is indeed satisfied with his life as it is can hardly be criticized, accordingly, on the grounds that he has no good reason for declining to make it better.

He might still be open to criticism on the grounds that he *should not* be satisfied—that it is somehow unreasonable, or unseemly, or in some other mode wrong for him to be satisfied with less satisfaction than he could have. On what basis, however, could *this* criticism be justified? Is there some decisive reason for insisting that a person ought to be so hard to satisfy? Suppose that a man deeply and happily loves a woman who is altogether worthy. We do not ordinarily criticize the man in such a case just because we think he might have done even better. Moreover, our sense that it would be inappropriate to criticize him for that reason need not be due simply to a belief that holding out for a more desirable or worthier woman might end up costing him more than it would be worth. Rather, it may reflect our recognition that the desire to be happy or content or satisfied with life is a desire for a satisfactory amount of satisfaction, and is not inherently tantamount to a desire that the quantity of satisfaction be maximized.

Being satisfied with a certain state of affairs is not equivalent to preferring it to all others. If a person is faced with a choice between less and more of something desirable, then no doubt it would be irrational for him to prefer less to more. But a person may be satisfied without having made any such comparisons at all. Nor is it necessarily irrational or unreasonable for a person to omit or to decline to make comparisons between his own state of affairs and possible alternatives. This is not only because making comparisons may be too costly. It is also because if someone is satisfied with the way things are, he may have no motive to consider how else they might be.

Contentment may be a function of excessive dullness or diffidence. The fact that a person is free both of resentment and of ambition may be due to his having a slavish character or to his vitality being muffled by a kind of negligent lassitude. It is possible for someone to be content merely, as it were, by default. But a person who is content with resources providing less utility than he could have may be neither irresponsible nor indolent nor deficient in imagination. On the contrary, his decision to be content with those resources—in other words, to adopt an attitude of willing acceptance toward the fact that he has just that much—may be based upon a conscientiously intelligent and penetrating evaluation of the circumstances of his life.

It is not essential for such an evaluation to include an *extrinsic* comparison of the person's circumstances with alternatives to which he might plausibly aspire, as it would have to do if contentment were reasonable only when based upon a judgment that the enjoyment of possible benefits has been maximized. If someone is less interested in whether his circumstances enable him to live as well as possible than in whether they enable him to live satisfyingly, he may appropriately devote his evaluation entirely to an *intrinsic* appraisal of his life. Then he may recognize that his circumstances lead him to be neither resentful nor regretful nor drawn to change and that, on the basis of his understanding of himself and of what is important to him, he accedes approvingly to his actual readiness to be content with the way things are. The situation in that case is not so much that he rejects the possibility of improving his circumstances because he thinks there is nothing genuinely to be gained by attempting to improve them. It is rather that this possibility, however feasible it may be, fails as a matter of fact to excite his active attention or to command from him any lively interest.

NOTES

1. Ronald Dworkin, *A Matter of Principle* (Harvard University Press, 1985), p. 206
2. Thomas Nagel, *Mortal Questions* (Cambridge University Press, 1979), p. 118.

A Defense of Resource Equality
ERIC RAKOWSKI

EQUAL SHARES IN
A FREE MARKET

Bearing in mind the failings but also the considerable strengths of the egalitarian proposals discussed above, what principles of distribution are just? It seems easiest to answer this question in stages, beginning with a simple case and adding complications serially. Suppose for now that every member of a group of people is equally healthy, talented, intelligent, and adult, that a finite stock of resources exists for them to divide, and that the stock of resources is not so vast relative to their number that all could realize their every wish if one or several distributions were chosen. How should they divide the resources available to them?

In everyday life, this would seem an odd question, because for all practical purposes everything worth having already has an owner whose property cannot rightfully be taken from him by a gang desirous of additional possessions. But in searching for fundamental principles of distribution, one must abstract from the regime of ownership already in place. Philosophers therefore routinely invoke some vision of a state of nature where everything is up for grabs, or call upon the more familiar images of a band of travelers shipwrecked on a desert island to which none has a prior claim, or of a group of hikers chancing on a bush of berries in the wild and having to decide how the harvest should be apportioned (on the assumption that everybody likes berries). Beginning with these artificially simple cases is

useful, for they capture an important truth. Although we come into the world at different times, and somebody was always there before us, we enter in the same way, without any more right to the bounty of nature than anyone else who sees daylight for the first time. It therefore seems sensible to ask how the world should be carved up among people who are equally able but equally undeserving, before considering what difference it makes if one relaxes the assumptions of equal intelligence, talents, and health, and if one abandons a static world for one in which procreation, risk-taking, and production occur.

As these hypothetical cases frame the initial distributive question, it all but answers itself. Once welfare-based theories have been excluded from consideration, and once one acknowledges that nobody possesses any congenital or acquired advantage that would translate into superior bargaining power if such advantages were permitted by a theory of justice grounded in impartiality to influence the distribution of resources, the natural answer is that everyone should receive an equally valuable share. Nobody would settle for less, because nobody else would have a right to demand more. The presumption must therefore be that people are entitled to equally valuable shares, unless some difference between them justifies a departure from equality.

In stating that everyone would insist on receiving a share at least as large as others receive, I assume, as I said in Chapter 1, that what Rawls terms the "circumstances of justice" ob-

Reprinted from Eric Rakowski, *Equal Justice*. Clarendon Press (1991), pp. 65–77.

tain. More specifically, I assume here and throughout that people generally desire more resources and opportunities than an equal share affords them, or at least that they would ordinarily oppose any individual or collective attempt to take part of that share from them without compensation. Thus, while it is undoubtedly true at *some* level, as Harry Frankfurt says, that what matters "from the point of view of morality is not that everyone should have *the same* but that each should have *enough*,"[1] it seems sensible to assume, in delineating generally applicable principles of distributive justice, that that level has not been reached, because in any contemporary society it is unlikely to be. Contrary to Frankfurt's suggestion, it appears to me that the inequalities existing between the middle class and the wealthy in the world's richer countries *do* raise significant issues of distributive justice, even if the moral imperative of assuring that the indigent have enough to survive is obviously more pressing than correcting any injustice in the holdings of the relatively well-to-do. An egalitarian need *not* suppose, as Frankfurt asserts, "that it is morally important whether one person has less than another regardless of how much either of them has." Past a certain point, everyone might be so comfortable that nobody cared about remaining inequalities, and questions of justice would become aridly academic, if they were even asked. But so long as somebody protests existing inequalities—either because he wants more resources to satisfy his own desires or because he wants more so that he can aid others who desire greater wealth—questions of justice come to the fore, and an egalitarian must confront them.

The evident appropriateness of an equal division under the circumstances described raises numerous problems of application. Some I do not tackle at all; others I leave for later chapters.

The first set of problems stems from the question: what should count as resources subject to equal division? One can imagine that a group of people dividing up resources might want to place at least some of them under collective ownership. Avenues of travel, such as roads and waterways, and scarce but essential natural resources, such as a single source of drinking water or fuel, might serve as examples. I shall not advance a theory either of public goods or of collective decisionmaking here; instead, I assume that at least some, and probably the greater part, of the resources available for division would be held privately, and confine my argument to those resources that are placed in individuals' hands.

The other principal problem growing out of the question what should count as resources is ascertaining whether certain rights that could be held privately should be subject to redistribution in accordance with principles of justice. Under the restrictive assumptions set forth above, the group in question need not decide, for example, whether their talents and body parts (such as kidneys and corneas) are resources to be allocated on an equal basis, since all are assumed to be equally well endowed and equally healthy. But in adapting this model to real-world problems, these questions must be addressed. . . .

The second set of problems is clustered around the question: how are the resources subject to division to be valued? The value of ownership rights depends in part upon the uses to which they may be put. If, for example, the owner of riverfront property has the right to release toxic wastes into the water, or to divert as much of the flow as he wants to irrigate his crops, without compensating those living downstream for the resultant diminution or pollution of their supply of water, then land located upstream is apt to be worth more, other things equal, than land through which water is less likely to flow freely or clearly. Similarly, if strict controls or steep taxes are placed on the emission of sulfur oxides, then the value of coal deposits can be expected to decline relative to cleaner sources of energy. Zoning likewise affects property prices by limiting the activities that may be performed within a given area. And if property-based levies to fund permissible public works vary from region to region, so too will the cost of real estate. Thus, the question what form property and tort law should take, along with the question which tax and regulatory policies not required by principles of justice a government will pursue, must be answered prior to or at least simultaneous with the question how objects of private ownership ought initially to be assigned.

The question of the nature of collective endeavors and of regulatory standards lies beyond the bounds of this book, both because its answer would depend upon the particular preferences and circumstances of a given group of people, and because the broader questions of the ideal form of government and of the moral limits to state power are too sweeping to take up here. . . . Assume for now . . . that real or personal property may be used as its owner likes, provided he does not subject others to substantial risks of injury or invade their rights to bodily integrity and the quiet enjoyment of their possessions. Anyone who violates this rule is liable for the harm he causes, and those who cause or threaten injury may ordinarily be enjoined from pursuing a harmful or potentially dangerous course of conduct. Rights to noninterference or possession may not be expropriated by those who do not own them, upon payment of their value as determined by the state, except in rare cases where the transaction costs associated with a voluntary sale would be exceedingly large and the collective benefits of arranging a forced sale outweigh potential injustices and the loss of autonomy suffered by the involuntary seller.

Another preliminary question is how resources slated for private ownership should be characterized prior to inclusion in people's equal bundles. Should land, for example, be split into tiny plots, forcing neighboring owners to work together or, if exchange is allowed, to buy adjacent blocks? Or should land be required to have multiple owners, necessitating joint decisions on its use? Or should only plots whose size makes their independent cultivation economically sensible be made available for individual distribution?

If people are to be treated as autonomous beings whose happiness and ambitions are, from the community's standpoint, their own concern, then joint ownership of land and divisible resources should not be required, because individual control is essential to ensure the liberty of each. If ownership of a given object had to be shared, then some of its owners might never be able to attract sufficient support among the others to have their way, whereas other people might acquire disproportionate control because their desires were echoed more loudly. This

would be tyranny of the majority in microcosm. People are only treated as equals whose projects deserve equal regard if they are given equally valuable shares and the power to determine how those shares are used, not just a statistically equal chance of having their wishes fulfilled by being in a local majority on a particular issue. Those who enjoy or think they will profit from cooperative ventures should be free to engage in them, subject to whatever morally permissible constraints, such as antitrust laws, the community enacts. But those who prefer to strike out on their own should not be forced to throw in their lot with others if common ownership and communal decisions occupy a small place in their conception of the good life.

Of course, if people are permitted to combine their possessions for whatever purposes they choose, those whose preferences are unpopular and who are therefore unable to find associates may be consigned to a less favorable economic position than they would hold were combinations prohibited. They are, nevertheless, in a better position than if joint ownership were required and, more important, it would be an unjustifiable abridgement of individual freedom to prevent people from acting in concert so long as they do not use their economic clout to reap monopolistic profits. Just as no one may justifiably complain if the prices of those goods he desires are high in a free market in virtue of others' sharing his desires, so too he lacks a legitimate grievance if others do not have the same beliefs or preferences and his influence over how the world goes is lessened in consequence. Individual liberty encompasses the right to compete and cooperate in this way, including the right to solicit assistance or to dissuade others from banding together, so long as any morally permissible limitations (which I leave unexplored) on collective action or market dominance are not exceeded.

Similar reasons dictate that the way in which resources and rights over them are defined prior to the initial bidding should be as sensitive as possible to individuals' desires. Subject to whatever zoning regulations political morality and the configuration of people's preferences allow, those who desire a small plot of land should be able to spend only what is necessary to outbid others for that property; they should

not have to buy more than they want, just because many other people want larger plots. Likewise, those who would like to buy a slice of lake frontage should be free to forgo the purchase of rights to use lake water as a source of irrigation or as a dumping ground, even though most prospective purchasers of such property would prefer the full panoply of rights. And people who would like to become co-owners of a piece of property, or of certain valuable resources or enterprises, should be allowed to combine their purchasing power, subject, as mentioned before, to any morally permissible limits the group imposes, such as antitrust laws. Only if individuals' plans are honored by maximizing their range of choice—both at the time resources are divided and over time, since the (in principle) unlimited separability of property rights gives people more scope to reassess their projects, allegiances, and preferences and to abandon some for others—are they truly treated as persons of equal worth.[2]

Assuming that everybody is entitled to an equally valuable share of resources, and that rights to them are to be characterized as finely as people desire to maximize their freedom of belief and action, how should they be divided up?

Bundles of resources are equally valuable if each of their owners would not prefer to hold someone else's bundle; in that case, nobody could protest that he was given less than anybody else. There are several ways this state might be achieved. People might be given baskets of goods that were exactly the same (fractional interests in indivisible resources would have to be assigned) and left to trade among themselves. Or they might be given baskets that, though not identical, were nevertheless deemed at least as good as any other basket by their several recipients, and permitted to make whatever exchanges they thought desirable. In either case, the distribution that existed once all mutually beneficial exchanges had been completed would perforce be equal and at least as good from everyone's point of view as any other equal division, assuming that everyone knew the composition of all the bundles and the price at which each person would buy or sell all the items found in the various bundles.

The same end could also be reached by holding an auction. Each person might be handed the same large number of currency units and every item not set aside for collective ownership might be put up for bidding. Each participant could demand finer divisions or property rights than the auctioneer made initially (for the sake of convenience), so long as he was prepared to pay more for the right or newly defined resource than all other bidders. In any actual auction, of course, some limit might be necessary on personal redefinition of the objects up for bidding, in order to save time and forestall confusion; but in theory the possibility of redefinition need not be constrained. Participants could also confer and coordinate their bidding, provided that their agreements did not offend any morally required or permissibly adopted constraints—for instance, rules designed to prevent monopolization of important resources. When, after however many runs of the auction were necessary, each person had spent all his cash and no one would gain from yet another auction because no one preferred someone else's bundle of resources to his own and nobody could imagine a set of bundles that could emerge from the auction that would leave him better placed than he presently was, an equal and optimal division of the available resources would have been achieved.

One central feature of these procedures is an economic market. Because the market ensures that traders will be made as well off as they could be consistent with some initial distribution of resources, given perfect information about bid and offer prices and the absence of monopsonistic and monopolistic distortions, the market is efficiency's handmaiden. Equally significant, it poses no threat to the equality of holdings. Although trades among people whose initial shares are equal might enhance their happiness to different degrees, and although they might allow some people to increase their holdings faster than if trades were prohibited and thus to bring about greater disparities in wealth or income than would otherwise arise, no one can possibly be made worse off absolutely by market exchanges, so long as the market remains competitive. Because the market facilitates improvements in people's welfare that do not come at other people's expense—except, of

course, to the extent that it allows some participants to sour competitors' voluntary gambles—it can only be regarded as beneficial, not an accomplice of evil. Trade, like other voluntary cooperative enterprises, is not an affront to justice or a violation of others' rights.

Nor is the fact that some will likely be happier with their initial allotments than others ordinarily any reason for departing from an equal distribution. If someone's tastes are relatively popular, he may benefit over time from economies of scale in the production of what he wants. Equally possibly, he may have to make do with less of what he desires than if fewer people shared his preferences. Similarly, the things someone craves might be rare or difficult to obtain, whereas others find the objects of their longing in lush profusion. None of these facts is generally relevant to the choice of a distributive result or principle. That the world, including the preferences of others, is not always as one would like is simply a fact of life. It may be an instance of divine injustice, but it is usually not the product of human iniquity. After all, people commonly have the power to alter their desires and allegiances, at least to a fairly considerable degree. Those who mope about wishing for a mandarin's mansion, or who choose to cultivate a taste for caviar, cannot blame others who are easier to please or who prize things that they think of meager value. Except in the case of involuntarily induced desires of which a person disapproves, they therefore cannot justly snatch some of their fellow citizens' cash to bring them closer to their dreams.

Of course, in the hypothetical case of an island auction, this last point seems less telling, inasmuch as those who were washed ashore unawares lacked an opportunity to shape their preferences in full cognizance of the likes and dislikes of their colleagues and of the material resources that are available to satisfy or assuage them. Some were simply more fortunate in their desires than others at the time disaster struck, even if the effects of this initial bit of bad luck would taper off to insignificance over time. But while unequal fortune of this kind might furnish a reason for some inequality in the islanders' initial shares if its influence on people's relative happiness were pronounced, it

would not supply a ground for unequal allotments in an ongoing society whose members could take others' preferences and the means to meet them into account when forming their tastes and personalities. It is only right that the resources people command should reflect their cost to the community in the form of production expenses and the unallayed desires of others. Justice does not favor those who pine most ardently for luxury.

Thus, equal consideration in dividing collectively owned resources among equally healthy and able persons means putting an equally valuable bundle of goods at everyone's disposal and allowing them to consume, invest, or gamble away their holdings as they choose, consonant with respect for the rights of others. No one's preferences, whether alone or in combination with the preferences of others, may justly constrain another person's choice of goods or the exercise of his property rights, except insofar as people are willing to pay for their privileges out of their initially equal shares. Unlike welfare-based theories, moreover, equality of fortune holds that there is no necessary connection between people's desires and the size of their just allotments (except, as I mentioned briefly and shall later argue, in the case of certain pathological desires that are best viewed as unchosen afflictions). Each person is entitled to an equally valuable stock of resources, measured by people's collective preferences in the form of market prices, whatever his tastes and ambitions happen to be. Although desires are partially constitutive of a person, they are generally also within his control and thus ultimately his own responsibility. People are free to mold their desires as they choose, given their knowledge of others' preferences, the scarcity of various goods, and the size of people's holdings determined on grounds independent of their preferences. No one deserves more market power simply because his desires are legion, his passions ardent, or his tastes more or less expensive than the norm. Whether other differences among persons—their luck in voluntary undertakings, their health, their effort, their talents, or the generosity of their relatives or friends—can justify differences in market power is the subject of the rest of Part I.

VOLUNTARY CHOICES AND
EMERGENT INEQUALITIES

In Chapter 2, I began from the assumption that theories of distributive justice must be justifiable impartially, that they must treat all conscious bearers of interests as moral subjects with legitimate, if not in all cases equal, claims on unowned resources. I then argued that egalitarian theories of justice that define equal treatment by reference to people's welfare—whether they take the form of an egalitarianism of preferences, as in the case of utilitarianism, or the equalization of happiness or assistance towards the satisfaction of desire—are flawed in conception and counterintuitive in application. People are treated as equals, I contended, when they are given equally valuable opportunities and unowned resources, even if those shares do not leave them equally happy or do not maximize the sum of people's happiness.

My argument ended, however, with a snapshot: the equal division of resources among equally able people at a single instant in time. In actuality, however, people's shares would not stay equal for long. One way in which initially equal holdings may cease to be equal is through luck. Fortune smiles on some people's projects but frowns on others' gambles. A few wildcat drillers find oil, most strike only sand. Lucky farmers enjoy bountiful harvests while their less fortunate competitors struggle with inclement weather and ravenous insects. Some people fall ill, go blind, break bones, or die early, whereas others lead long, trouble-free lives. Does justice require the transfer of resources after initial assignments have been made to repair emergent inequalities of these kinds?

In answering this question, I shall place considerable weight on Ronald Dworkin's distinction between "option luck" and "brute luck." Option luck he defines as "a matter of how deliberate and calculated gambles turn out—whether someone gains or loses through accepting an isolated risk he or she should have anticipated and might have declined." Brute luck, by contrast, is "a matter of how risks fall out that are not in that sense deliberate gambles."[3] The distinction is therefore between, on the one hand, risks that people must ineluctably

bear or that, though they could in principle have avoided running, they had no reason beforehand to associate with an activity in which they engaged, and, on the other hand, all other risks that people knowingly run or of which they should be aware. It may in practice be difficult to say how the favorable or unfavorable outcome of a given activity should be classified, although there are paradigmatic examples of both types of luck to help one pigeonhole. Discussion of some easy and hard cases follows. The general implications of the theory of equality of fortune should be sketched in advance, however, because a single principle specifies the proper response to almost all potential sources of inequality.

Abstract for now from differences in people's intelligence and reasoning ability. My principal claim is that all inequalities in holdings arising from variations in people's option luck are morally unobjectionable, provided that no one who wanted to run the risks associated with such luck lacked an opportunity to do so. But all inequalities resulting from variable brute luck ought to be eliminated, except to the extent that a victim of bad brute luck waived or waives his right to compensation, or someone who enjoyed good brute luck is or was allowed to retain the benefits he received by those who have or would have had a claim to some part of them; and provided, further, that those who suffered bad brute luck would profit significantly at the margin from transfers designed to restore equality by comparison with the marginal cost to those providing compensation, and that any compensation paid is not excessively burdensome.

The basic rationale for adopting this principle is simple. People come into the world equally undeserving. Because no one has a greater claim to the earth or what lies on or beneath it than anyone else, all are entitled to equal shares. In actuality, of course, people enter the world at different times, and parents often desire to bestow some sizable but unequal portion of what we can assume are their just but unequal earnings on their offspring, even though children have no right to more than a certain share of their parents' wealth. For now, however, suppose that all are born contemporaries and all are born adults. It is only just that

each receive an equally valuable lot of resources, measured by the group's collective
preferences, for people must assume responsibility for their likes and aversions and only thus
can no one complain that he received less than
his neighbor. And since exchange benefits those
who find it advantageous without destroying
equality of holdings in the foregoing sense, a
market in goods may justifiably flourish as well,
provided that all may trade on an equal footing
and all have the same opportunity to engage in
the panoply of economic activity. Inequalities
stemming from people's choice of different
jobs are similarly just, for except perhaps in extremely rare instances, if people's endowments
are similar they must take credit or blame for
their decisions and the unequal material rewards that trail them. Only if some avail themselves of opportunities that others lack, whether
because markets fail to function perfectly or because information is not equally available to all,
do those who are disadvantaged have a claim
to relief.

Luck warrants parallel treatment. If an opportunity to risk one's time, energy, or resources is open to everyone, then those who
seize it need not share their gains with those
who are less adventurous. But neither may they
demand assistance if fortune treats them
roughly. As when bidding for goods at an original auction or choosing an occupation, people
cannot escape responsibility for the preferences
they exhibit and cannot complain if others'
preferences lead them to choose goods, or types
of work, or more or less risky activities that
leave them more or less comfortably situated.
Just as somebody cannot object to others' living more leisurely if he could have such an existence with its special joys and material costs
should he so choose, so he cannot object if
someone profits from a gamble he might have
taken but did not. Nor can he complain if others adopt a cautious course and show him no
sympathy when he tries his luck and loses. In
such cases, justice demands that jackpots and
empty purses fall where they may, for only in
this way will it remain true that nobody prefers
anyone else's bundle of resources and labor *and
voluntary gambles* to his own.

But while differential option luck cannot vindicate redistributive taxation, unequal brute

luck typically generates a right to recompense
unless the unlucky waived their claims in advance. For the essence of the theory of equality of fortune is the imperative that people's
shares be kept equal, insofar as that is humanly
possible and not excessively costly, except to
the extent that their voluntary actions give rise
to inequalities; only by eliminating unsolicited
good and bad fortune from the forces shaping
people's holdings can true equality of station
be attained, and the distribution of resources be
made acceptable to a community of persons
who regard one another as moral equals. No one
should have fewer resources than his peers with
which to make his way in the world or to enjoy himself therein except by choice.

Of course, past decisions may affect the
amount of compensation someone deserves in
virtue of his bad brute luck. To the extent that
people increase their chances of contracting a
certain disease through their voluntary actions,
as smokers court cancer, they reduce the compensation to which they are entitled. And they
may choose to waive their right to compensation—to decline what is tantamount to universal
insurance coverage—if they fancy taking
chances and if others agree to release them from
their obligation to assist those whose brute luck
is bad. Independent moral principles, such as a
rule exempting people from making substantial
sacrifices to benefit others in some barely noticeable way, also militate against the unqualified pursuit of equality, while limitations on
human ingenuity might render equality unattainable. The core idea is clear, however. Undeserved, unwagered, unchosen inequalities warrant redress. Whenever the inequitable effects of
brute luck can be cancelled, they ought to be, assuming that people have not chosen to gamble
on their good fortune and paternalistic legislation has not rendered their choice ineffective.

I shall elaborate and reinforce this justification for the differential treatment of brute and
option luck when I consider examples of both.
First, however, one sweeping objection to this
entire enterprise should be dismissed. No ten-
able distinction between brute and option luck
can be drawn, one might argue, because both
kinds of chance event are equally inevitable. Far
from referring to anything real or morally significant, luck is an epistemic concept, a word

we attach to events that we are as yet unable to predict but that, in our fully determined universe, we might have anticipated had we possessed greater knowledge. It signifies nothing more than our ignorance. But if our present ignorance of "brute" future events supplies a moral reason to mend resultant inequalities, should not our equal ignorance before the fact of future occurrences constituting option luck [impose on us a] duty to annul whatever inequalities it causes? Both types of events are equally certain, the ensuing disparities equally real. Consistency demands that equality be maintained throughout or not at all.

The problem with this objection is that one of its assumptions fatally undermines its conclusion. It assumes that, although all events are inevitable, we can avoid certain outcomes if we so choose and that we deserve moral censure if we choose wrongly, for it assumes that it is up to us to decide whether to ensure that people's possessions remain equal, despite the fact that determinism is true. But while these assumptions are perfectly reasonable if one holds a compatibilist account of free will, and while common sense supports them, they can hardly be squared with the claim that we ought not to hold people responsible for their decisions to expose themselves to risks that they need not have faced or to forgo insurance against risks that they cannot help but run. If the choice of principles of distributive justice is subject to moral appraisal, then so are choices such as

these. And if it is possible to avoid certain outcomes or actions but not others while in the grip of an inexorable causal process, there exists some basis for distinguishing risks that people assume voluntarily from risks they must bear willy-nilly. The foregoing objection therefore fails. If moral discourse has any sense at all, the distinction between brute and option luck is firm.

The question, then, is how familiar events giving rise to inequalities should be classified. . . .

NOTES

1. Harry Frankfurt, "Equality as a Moral Ideal," *Ethics* 98 (1987), p. 134. [reprinted in this volume].
2. Ronald Dworkin calls this commitment to the maximum accommodation of individuals' desires "the principle of abstraction." He endorses it "not because costs of particular resources will be either higher or lower in more abstract auctions, nor because welfare will be overall greater or more equal, but rather because the general aim of . . . equality, which is to make distribution as sensitive as possible to the choices different people make in designing their own plans and projects, is better achieved by the flexibility abstraction provides." Dworkin, "What is Equality? Part 3: The Place of Liberty," *Iowa Law Review* 73.
3. Ronald Dworkin, "What is Equality? Part 2: Equality of Resources," *Philosophy and Public Affairs* (1981), vol. 10, no. 4, p. 293.

On Equal Human Worth: A Critique of Contemporary Egalitarianism
LOUIS POJMAN

All human beings are born free and equal in dignity and rights. They are endowed with reason and conscience and should act towards one another in a spirit of brotherhood. (United Nations' Universal Declaration of Human Rights, 1948)

Theories of equal human rights have experienced an exponential growth during the past thirty or forty years. From declarations of human rights, such as the United Nations' Universal Declaration of Human Rights, to arguments about the rights of fetuses versus the rights of women, to claims and counterclaims about the rights of minorities to preferential hiring, the rights of animals to life and well-being, and the rights of trees to be preserved, the proliferation of rights affects every phase of our sociopolitical discourse. Hardly a month goes by without a new book appearing on the subject.[1]

As J. L. Mackie used to say, "Rights are pleasant. They allow us to make claims of others. Duties are onerous. They obligate us to others." Rights threaten to replace responsibility as the central focal point of moral theory. But this need not be the case. A rights theory balanced by a strong sense of the social good and individual responsibility may well be the best kind of moral-political theory we can have.

Virtually the only candidate for a rights theory today is egalitarianism, at least with regard to rational human beings. While there are differences between contemporary egalitarian arguments, they all accept what Ronald Dworkin calls "the egalitarian plateau," the "deepest moral assumption" of our time, that each person is of equal intrinsic value, of "dignity" and thus ought to be treated with equal respect and be given equal rights.[2] The phrase, *dignity of the human person*, signifies in the words of Jacques Maritain, that "the human person has the right to be respected, is the subject of rights, possesses rights. These are things which are owed to [a person] because of the very fact that he is a [person]."[3] Will Kymlicka states that "Every plausible political theory has the same ultimate value, which is equality. They are 'egalitarian theories.' "[4]

Ronald Green says that egalitarianism is the presupposition for morality itself, the precondition of moral discourse and the necessary first assumption of any moral system, whatever its resultant values.[5] Political theories as diverse as Robert Nozick's Libertarianism, John Rawls's Liberalism, Peter Singer's Utilitarianism, and Kai Nielsen's Marxism all share the notion that each person matters and matters equally.

What distinguishes most contemporary egalitarianism from earlier natural law models is its self-conscious secularism. There is no appeal to a God or a transcendental realm. Although Kant's doctrine of Ends ("Human beings qua rational have an inherent dignity and so ought to treat each other as ends and never merely as means") is the touchstone of most egalitarians, they generally distance themselves from the metaphysical grounding of Kant's doctrine. In the words of Dworkin, contemporary egalitarianism is "metaphysically unambitious."[6] Yet it may well be that without some deeper metaphysical underpinnings equal rights theories fail to persuade thoughtful persons.

If a deconstructed Kant is the father of contemporary egalitarians, their enemies are Aristotle and Thomas Hobbes. Aristotle thought that humans were essentially unequal, depending on their ability to reason. Hobbes rejected the notion of humans having any intrinsic worth at all. "The value or worth of a man is, as of all other things, his price—that is to say, so much as would be given for the use of his power—and therefore is not absolute but a thing dependent on the need and judgment of another."[7]

In this paper I want to examine the principal arguments for equal human rights given by contemporary egalitarians. Specifically, I want to explore the basis for attributing *equal worth* to all human beings or all minimally rational persons, since it is the doctrine of equal worth that undergirds most egalitarian theories of both rights and justice. In Part I, I argue that in their present form none of the arguments given for the doctrine of equal human worth are sound. In Part II, I suggest that the doctrine of equal human worth has its home in a deeper metaphysical system than secular egalitarians are able to embrace: non-natural systems, not necessarily religious, but typically so. My conclusion is that on the secularist's naturalistic assumptions, there is reason to give up egalitarianism altogether.

PART I: CONTEMPORARY SECULAR ARGUMENTS FOR EQUAL HUMAN WORTH

Ten arguments (or strategies) for equal human rights based on equal human worth appear in current philosophical literature. They are: (1) The Presumption Argument; (2) The Properly Basic Belief Strategy; (3) The Existential Strategy; (4) The Libertarian Argument; (5) The Family Argument; (6) The Pragmatic Argument; (7) The Utilitarian Argument; (8) The Coherentist Argument; (9) The Rational Agency Argument; and (10) The Argument from Moral Personality. Let me briefly describe

them and point out their deficiencies. I regret the cursory treatment of important theories, but my purpose is primarily to show how little attention has been paid to justifying the egalitarian plateau. Having until recently simply taken egalitarianism for granted, I now am puzzled by this idea or ideal and wonder whether it is simply a leftover from a religious world view now rejected by all of the philosophers discussed in this essay. At any rate, my discussion is meant to be exploratory and provocative, not the final word on the subject.

1. The Presumption of Equality Argument

R. S. Peters, Stanley Benn, Monroe Beardsley, E. F. Carritt, and James Rachels interpret equal worth in terms of equal consideration or impartiality and argue that there is a presumption in favor of treating people equally. "All persons are to be treated alike, unless there are good reasons for treating them differently."[8] But there are problems. First of all, this type of egalitarianism is unduly formal. It lacks a material criterion or metric to guide deliberation. One might as well say that "all sentient beings should be treated alike, unless there are good reasons for treating them differently." The formula only shifts the focus onto the idea of *good reasons*. We need to know by virtue of what material criterion people are to be treated equally or differently. What are the material criteria? Need, effort, contribution, intelligence, sentience, self-consciousness, or moral merit? And if there is more than one, how do we weight them in various circumstances? As far as I know, the problem of material criteria has not been solved.

Plato's hierarchical theory and Aristotle's aristocracy could accommodate this formal notion of equality (treating equals equally and unequals unequally), and even Hitler could have used it to justify his atrocities. Inegalitarians simply claim that there is a good reason for unequal treatment of human beings. They are of unequal worth.

The presumption of equality argument reduces to the notion of impartiality (what R. M. Hare calls "universalizability") and is not really an egalitarian argument at all. It makes no restrictions upon what reasons may be given to warrant inequalities. It merely prescribes that we not act arbitrary, but consistently. We should make our discriminations according to a proper standard, but doing so does not commit us to egalitarianism. For all rational action is governed by the idea of consistency.

Furthermore, there seems something arbitrary about the Presumption Argument. Why should we start off with a bias toward equality and not inequality? Why don't we have a principle presuming unequal treatment: "All persons are to be treated unequally unless there is some reason for treating them equally"? Neither a presumption of equality nor one of inequality is necessary, though there may be pragmatic or utilitarian considerations that incline us to opt for a presumption of equality rather than inequality. We will consider those strategies later.

2. The Properly Basic Belief Strategy

Sometimes, no argument at all is given for the claim of equal human worth and the equal human rights that flow from it. Ronald Dworkin begins *Taking Rights Seriously* with a rejection of metaphysical assumptions.

> Individual rights are political trumps held by individuals. Individuals have rights when, for *some reason*, a collective goal is not a sufficient justification for denying them what they wish, as individuals, to have or to do, or not a sufficient justification for imposing some loss or injury upon them. That characterization of a right is, of course, formal in the sense that it does not indicate what rights people have or guarantee, indeed, that they have any. But it does not suppose that rights have some special metaphysical character, and the theory defended in these essays therefore departs from older theories of rights that do rely on that supposition. (P. xi, italics mine)

Nowhere in his book does Dworkin parse out the notion of "some reason" to override "collective goals." It is a given. The notion of equal human rights based on equal human worth simply becomes the assumption that replaces earlier religious or Kantian metaphysical assump-

tions. Every plausible political theory is egalitarian in that it holds that all members of the community have a right to equal concern and respect. "The Deepest Moral Assumption: the assumption of a natural right of all men and women to an equality of concern and respect, a right they possess not in virtue of birth or characteristic or merit or excellence but simply as human beings with the capacity to make plans and give justice."[9] In other words, we do not need to argue for this thesis. In a series of lengthy articles on welfare and resource egalitarianism Dworkin simply assumes the ideal of equality: that "people matter and matter equally."

Dworkins's view seems similar to what Alvin Plantinga calls "a properly basic belief," a foundational belief which does not need any further justification. But whatever merits this strategy has for religious beliefs, it seems unsatisfactory when employed to justify moral and political equality. At the very least, we should want to know why the capacity to "make plans and give justice" grants all and only humans equal concern and respect.

3. The Existential Strategy

Closely related to Dworkins's view is Kai Nielsen's "Radical Egalitarianism," which holds that the ideal of equal human life prospects is something to which we arbitrarily, that is, existentially, choose to commit ourselves. It enjoins treating equal life prospects as both a goal to be aimed at and a right to be claimed, but one cannot rationally justify these commitments.

> Instead of putting out, "All people are of equal worth regardless of merit" as some kind of mysterious truth-claim which appears in fact to be at best groundless and at worst false, would it not have been clearer and less evasive of the human-rights advocate simply to remark that he starts with a commitment on which he will not bend, namely a commitment to the treatment of all people as beings who are to have quite unforfeitably an equality of concern and respect? It is that sort of world that he or she most deeply desires and it is there that he stands pat. There are

other equally intelligible and no doubt equally rational, moral points of view that do not contain such commitments. But it is with such a commitment that he takes his stand.[10]

Nielsen claims that it is "a great Kantian illusion" to think that one can or should justify our moral views through reason. These views are ultimate commitments, more basic than any of our other beliefs, so they are the grounds of belief which themselves cannot be justified, but must be chosen. That is where he distinguishes himself from Dworkin, who sees equality as a properly basic intuition.[11] Nielsen sees it as an existential and arbitrary choice. Nielsen continues:

> I do not know how anyone could show this belief to be true—to say nothing of showing it to be self-evident—or in any way prove it or show that if one is through and through rational, one must accept it.... A Nietzschean, a Benthamite, or even a classist amoralist who rejects it cannot thereby be shown to be irrational or even in any way necessarily to be diminished in his reason. It is a moral belief that I am committed to . . . [and which leads] to some . . . form of radical egalitarianism.[12]

In other words, equal human worth is a posit of secular faith, but a faith that seems to suffer from counter-examples: the apparent inequalities of abilities of every sort. Furthermore, many moral and political philosophers, myself included, believe that we can provide rational support for our moral and political beliefs. Nothing Nielsen says shows why we must resort to arbitrary existential leaps, but if this is all that can be said for egalitarianism, then the inegalitarian is quite safe. Since he or she does not choose to make the leap of faith into the religion of egalitarianism, we have a standoff. But such a standoff is hardly compelling grounds for demanding universal human rights based on equal human worth.

These first three types of egalitarianism can hardly be called arguments at all. Presumption arguments simply presume, properly basic beliefs stipulate, and existential choices do not claim rational justification. These theories already suppose egalitarian foundations. We turn to more substantive efforts.

4. The Libertarian Argument

At the other end of the political spectrum from Nielsen's Socialism with a rich panoply of positive welfare rights is the Libertarian idea that there is only one natural right: the negative equal right not to be interfered with. Robert Nozick, like Dworkin, simply assumes such a natural right. "Individuals have rights, and there are things no persons or groups may do to them (without violating their rights)." But unlike Dworkin, Nozick believes that only the minimal state, which protects the individual "against force, theft, fraud, [the breaking] of contracts, and so on, is justified.[13] An equal and absolute right to self-ownership gives people an absolute right to their justly acquired property. Tibor Machan formulates the Libertarian position in this way: "In short, a just human community is one that first and foremost protects the individual's right to life and liberty—the sovereignty of human individuals to act without aggressive intrusion from other human beings."[14]

On the face of it, after the rhetoric of absolute rights to property is deflated (Nozick wrongly supposes that the notion of self-ownership entails this absolute right), Libertarian arguments come down to little more than the back side of an ultra-minimalist morality, one which sets up as its single principle: Do no unnecessary harm. But this by itself does not even distinguish humans from animals. We should not cause harm to anyone without a moral justification.

Machan separates himself from Libertarians like Nozick, who does not offer arguments for natural rights, and John Hospers, who is a metaphysical determinist, and grounds his political Libertarianism in metaphysical Libertarianism. For Machan it is our ability to act freely (contra-causally) that separates humans from other animals and gives us value.

This seems a promising move, a departure from the mainstream rejection of metaphysics, but it has problems. The first is that the Libertarian (contra-causal) notion of free seems mysterious and hard to argue for. It seems to presuppose a notion of the self that is metaphysically richer than the physicalist version held by most compatibilists; though if we grant a transcendent notion of agency, the Libertarian notion will be more promising. However, it will probably not be secular in the usual meaning of that term (as disclaiming a notion of the spiritual or transcendent).

Second, even if the property of Libertarian free will is granted, still if it has nothing to *choose*, it is of little practical value. By increasing a person's opportunities (through non-Libertarian institutions such as public education and welfare economics) we enable free will to be exercised.

Third, it seems that people are unequally free. Some people deliberate with great ease and accuracy, while others become muddled in emotion. Some choose according to the best reasons available, while others suffer from weakness of will. Some plan their lives according to long-term goals and are able to execute those plans with consummate skill, while others are driven by circumstances, short-term goals, and impulse. So Libertarianism is not obviously egalitarian. Even if we all possess some free will, we do not possess it equally.

There seems no reason on Libertarian premises to value all humans equally. Here David Gauthier's Libertarian theory of "morals by agreement" is more consistent with a secular world view. People do not have inherent moral value. Indeed, there are no objective values. Values are simply subjective preferences of different individuals, and the "moral artifice" is merely a convention that is mutually advantageous. We refrain from coercing or harming not because people have inherent equal dignity but because it is not mutually advantageous to do so.[15]

5. The Family Metaphor

Gregory Vlastos, in his celebrated article "Justice and Equality," appeals to the metaphor of a "loving family" to defend his egalitarianism. Vlastos has us imagine that we are visited by a Martian unfamiliar with our customs who asks us why we hold to the ideal of equal human rights. Vlastos replies, "Because the human worth of all persons is equal, however unequal may be their merit."[16]

The moral community is not a club from which members may be dropped for delin-

quency. Our morality does not provide for moral outcasts or half-castes. It does provide for punishment. But this takes place within the moral community and under its rules. It is for this reason that, for example, one has no right to be cruel to a cruel person. His offence against the moral law has not put him outside the law. . . . The pain inflicted on him as punishment for his offence does not close out the reserve of goodwill on the part of all others which is his birthright as a human being; it is a limited withdrawal from it. . . . [The] only justification [of human rights is] the value which persons have simply because they are persons: their 'intrinsic value as individual human beings,' as Frankena calls it; the 'infinite value' or the 'sacredness' of their individuality, as others have called it. (p. 48)

Vlastos distinguishes gradable or meritorious traits from nongradable but valuable traits and says that talents, skills, character, and personality belong to the gradable sort, but that our humanity is a nongradable value. Regarding human worth all humans get equal grades. In this regard, human worth is like love. "Constancy of affection in the face of variations of merit is one of the surest tests of whether a parent does love a child." But the family metaphor, which is the closest Vlastos comes to providing an argument for his position, needs further support. It is not obvious that all humans are related to each other as members of a family. If we are all brothers and sisters, who is the parent? By virtue of what property in human beings do we obtain value? Vlastos does not tell us. To the contrary, if we evolved from other animals, there is no more reason to think that we are siblings to all humans than to think that we are siblings to apes and gorillas.

Note that Vlastos offers as evidence for equal worth the fact that "no one has a right to be cruel to a cruel person." But surely these are not evidences for equality, for we should not be cruel—without justification—to anyone, animal or human. Aristotle, certainly no egalitarian, regarded cruelty as a vice.

Nor does the gradable-nongradable distinction make a difference here. There are nongradable properties: all members of the set of books or cats may possess the nongradable property of being equally books or cats, but we can still grade members with respect to specific interests or standards and say from the point of view of aesthetic value some books and cats are better than others. Likewise, we may agree that all homo sapiens equally are homo sapiens but insist that within that type there are important differences which include differences in value. Some humans are highly moral, some moderately moral, and others immoral. Why not make the relevant metric morality rather than species-membership? The point is that Vlastos has not grounded his claim of *equal* worth, or any *worth* for that matter, and until he does, his idea of the family connection remains a mere metaphor.

Finally, one must wonder at the sacerdotal language used of human beings: "sacred," of "infinite value," "inviolability," and so forth. The religious tone is not accidental, but the lack of reference to religion is a serious omission.

Suppose one of Vlastos's Martians, asks the egalitarian why he uses such language of mere animals. He invites Vlastos to consider Smith, a man of low morals and lower intelligence, who abuses his wife and children, who hates exercising or work, for whom novels are dull and art a waste of time, and whose joy it is to spend his days as a couch potato, drinking beer, while watching mud wrestling, violent sports, and soap operas on TV. He is an avid voyeur, devoted to child pornography. He is devoid of intellectual curiosity, eschews science, politics, and religion, and eats and drinks in a manner more befitting a pig than a person. Smith lacks wit, grace, humor, technical skill, ambition, courage, self-control, and wisdom. He is antisocial, morose, lazy, a freeloader who feels no guilt about living on welfare, when he is perfectly able to work, has no social conscience, and barely avoids getting caught for his petty thievery. He has no talents, makes no social contribution, lacks a moral sense, and from the perspective of the good of society, would be better off dead. But Smith is proud of one thing: that he is "sacred," of "infinite worth," of equal intrinsic value as Abraham Lincoln, Mother Teresa, Albert Schweitzer, the Dalai Lama, Jesus Christ, Gandhi, and Einstein. He is inviolable—and proud of it—in spite of any deficiency of merit. From the egalitarian perspective, in spite of appearances to the contrary, Smith is of equal intrinsic worth as the best citizen in his community. We could excuse the Martian if he exhibited amazement at this incredible doctrine.

6. The Pragmatic (or Useful Attitude) Argument

Joel Feinberg, who rejects Vlastos's essentialist position as unpromising, concedes that the notion of human worth is "not demonstrably justifiable." His support for the principle of equal human worth seems based on a combination of existential commitment and pragmatic concerns.

> "Human worth" itself is best understood to name no property in the way that "strength" names strength and "redness" names redness. In attributing human worth to everyone we may be ascribing no property or set of qualities, but rather expressing an attitude—the attitude of respect—towards the humanity in each man's person. That attitude follows naturally from regarding everyone from the "human point of view," but it is not grounded on anything more ultimate than itself, and it is not demonstrably justifiable.

> It can be argued further against the skeptics that a world with equal human rights is a *more just* world, a way of organizing society for which we would all opt if we were designing our institutions afresh in ignorance of the roles we might one day have to play in them. It is also a *less dangerous* world generally, and one with a *more elevated and civilized* tone. If none of this convinces the skeptic, we should turn our backs on him to examine more important problems.[17]

Feinberg may be correct in seeking to disentangle the concept of human worth from a property-view, but his position seems to have problems of its own. He needs to tell us *why* we should take the attitude of regarding everyone as equally worthy. What is this peculiar "human point of view," which supposedly grounds the notion of equal human worth? His pragmatic justification (i.e., that it will result in a less dangerous world and a more elevated and civilized world) simply needs to be argued out, for it is not obvious that acting as if everyone were of equal worth would result in a less dangerous world than one in which we treated people according to some other criteria.

Feinberg's claim that a world with equal human rights based on equal worth "is a more just world" is simply question-begging, since it is exactly the notion of equal worth that is contested in the idea of justice. Formally, we are to treat equals equally and unequals unequally. Feinberg seems to be saying that justice consists in treating everyone as though they were equal whether or not they are.

But ignoring this and supposing that there were good utilitarian reasons to treat people as though they were of equal worth, we would still want to know whether we really were of equal worth. If the evidence is not forthcoming, then the thesis of equal worth would have all the earmarks of Plato's Noble Lie, ironically, asserting the very contrary of the original. Whereas for Plato the Noble Lie specified that we are to teach people that they are really unequal in order to produce social stability in an aristocratic society, in Feinberg's version of the Noble Lie we are to teach people that they are all equal in order to bring social stability to a democratic society.

Feinberg's final comment, "If none of this convinces the skeptic, we should turn our backs on him to examine more important problems," signals a flight from the battle, an admission that the emperor has no clothes, for what could be more important than setting the foundations of sociopolitical philosophy?

7. The Utilitarian Argument for Human Equality

According to Jeremy Bentham, the founder of classical utilitarianism, "Each [is] to count as one and no one to count as more than one." This principle individuates persons (and sentient beings) as loci of utility, and the Utility Principle enjoins us to take everyone's utility function into consideration in the process of producing the highest net utility possible. But if this is all that is said, the alleged egalitarianism is spurious, for it is the net utility that is aimed at, not equal distribution of welfare or resources (except perchance that such a distri-

bution would actually coincide with maximal utility). My ten hedons count as much as yours, but what matters is the hedons, not you or I. While the initial measuring unit is the individual, the relevant goal is aggregative, ignoring any distribution pattern. If I can produce one hundred more hedons by inegalitarian distribution schemes than by egalitarian ones, I should use the inegalitarian ones.

Utilitarian egalitarians, such as R. M. Hare, respond that the doctrine of diminishing marginal utility leads to egalitarian distribution schemes because with respect to many goods, including money, their utility diminishes at the margin.[18] For example, redistributing ten dollars from a millionaire to a hungry person will increase net utility, for the hungry person will be able to sustain his life by what is a mere trifle to the millionaire. The idea is that because people are relevantly similar, egalitarian redistribution of wealth will tend to maximize utility.

The interesting feature of utilitarianism is that it does not need a deep theory of human nature to promote its philosophy—all it needs is the thesis that humans are place holders for hedons and dolors (units of suffering). So this may be a way to get around the problem of grounding the worth of the self in something metaphysical. But this is an illusion. First of all, utility functions apply as much to animals as to humans. If cats or rats get more pleasure from humans for ten dollars worth of food or an artificial stimulation machine, we should redistribute wealth in favor of animals. Of course, utilitarians like Peter Singer would accept such otherwise counterintuitive implications of their theory.

But, more important, the doctrine of diminishing marginal utility has severe restrictions. The utility of money or other good does not invariably diminish at the margin and utility functions for all people are not the same. After a certain threshold point of subsistence needs, people's utility functions diverge radically. A monk needs far less than a corporate executive to meet his needs.

Furthermore, each unit of money (or whatever the good in question is) does not have the same function for each person. Some people, optimists and cheerful folk, are better converters of resources to utility than pessimists and morose people. Some are stoics, who are able to handle adversity nobly and overcome it through resolute courage and wisdom. On the other hand, some people, who are grumpy, greedy or masochistic, may misuse resources to enhance their suffering.

Finally, there is a synergistic effect which causes the unit that crosses the threshold to make the difference between great utility and little or none at all. Frankfurt illustrates this point.

> Suppose that the cost of a serving of popcorn is the same as the cost of enough butter to make it delectable; and suppose that some rational consumer who adores buttered popcorn gets very little satisfaction from unbuttered popcorn, but that he nevertheless prefers it to butter alone. He will buy one and cannot buy both. Suppose now that this person's income increases so that he can buy the butter too. Then he can have something he enjoys enormously: his incremental income makes it possible for him not merely to buy butter in addition to popcorn, but to enjoy buttered popcorn. The satisfaction he will derive by combining the popcorn and the butter may well be considerably greater than the sum of the satisfactions he can derive from the two goods taken separately. Here again, is a threshold effect.[19]

The Principle of Diminishing Marginal Utility is more a principle of utility than one of equality. Consider the following illustration from Frankfurt. Suppose ten people are starving and each one needs five units to survive. We have only forty units of food. If we share it equally all will die, but if we distribute it unequally so that eight people get five units and two are left to die, we at least save eight people. Furthermore, suppose we have forty-one units, the additional unit would not, on utilitarian grounds, go to one of the two who are dying, but to one of the surviving.

But there is an even deeper problem lurking in the background, and that is the problem of a justification of utility as the sole moral principle to guide our behavior. A problem arises when we apply the utilitarian calculus to competing interests. Suppose Aristotle needs slaves to do his manual labor so that he can carry on his philosophical contemplation. It is not in the slaves' interest to be slaves to Aristotle, but if we can maximize utility by subjugating the interests of the slaves to the interests of the whole group (treating the slaves kindly, of course), what becomes of the utilitarian ideal of equal consideration of interests? Does he say to the slaves, "We considered your interests along with Aristotle's and the rest of society and concluded that on balance it's in all our interest that you stay slaves?" Perhaps the same logic can be used to justify some of the harmful animal experiments that the utilitarian Peter Singer condemns in his book *Animal Liberation*. If this is so, it turns out that equal consideration of interests is simply a gloss for total utilitarian calculations in which individual rights are sacrificed for the good of the whole. We can still do the animal experiments if we anesthetize them first, so that they do not feel pain. But we may kill them and anyone else where net utility is expected.

Or suppose that I could create more utility by letting my children starve or go without books and sending my income to the starving people in Ethiopia or Bangladesh or West Virginia. I do not see any reason to follow utilitarian prescriptions here. If we do not find utilitarianism a compelling theory, we certainly will not be tempted to take the doctrine of diminishing marginal utility as an overriding principle—even if it did guarantee egalitarian results.

8. The Coherentist Argument

In a recent article, "On Not Needing to Justify Equality," Kai Nielsen derives a defense of egalitarianism from John Rawls's and Norman Daniels's method of wide reflective equilibrium—a method that aims at providing a fit between our moral theory and particular moral judgments, which results in an overall coherent account of morality. Nielsen claims that the method can be used to show that the principle of equal human worth and equal treatment is justified as part of an overall coherent account of morality.[20]

If an egalitarianism rights theory is to succeed, my guess is that it will be a coherentist theory of the kind that Nielsen adumbrates. But, as things stand, there are two criticisms of Nielsen's argument. First, at best we have only a promissory note for a coherent secular system where equal worth plays a legitimate role. That is, no one has set forth a naturalistic account of morality where human worth, let alone equal human worth, does not have an unduly ad hoc appearance. Second, Coherentist justifications in general are subject to the criticism of not tying into reality. A Nazi world view, a religious fundamentalist theology, and Nielsen's Marxist egalitarianism, not to mention fairy tales, are all coherent and internally consistent; but no more than one of these mutually incompatible world views can be correct. Coherence is a necessary but not sufficient condition for justification. We want to know by which criteria we can distinguish between coherent theories. In scientific theory building empirical observation and other theoretical constraints do this sort of work. But it would seem that the empirical and theoretical data we have count against the notion of equal worth, so that the kind of justification needed for secular egalitarianism is wanting.

9. The Rational Agency Argument

The ninth attempt at getting a deeper argument for equal rights based on equal worth is found in the work of Alan Gewirth. In his book, *Reason and Morality*, his essay, "Epistemology of Human Rights," and elsewhere, Gewirth argues that we can infer equal human rights to freedom and well-being from the notion of rational agency.[21] A broad outline of the argument is as follows: Each rational agent must recognize that a measure of freedom and well-being is necessary for his or her exercise of rational agency. That is, each rational agent must will, if he is to will at all, that he possess that measure of freedom and well-being. Therefore anyone who holds that freedom and well-being are necessary for his exercise of rational agency is logically committed to holding that he has a prudential right to these goods. By the principle of universalizability we obtain the conclusion that all rational agents have a prima facie right to freedom and well-being.

But Gewirth's argument is invalid. From the premise that I need freedom and well-being in order to exercise my will nothing follows by itself concerning a right to freedom and well-being. From the fact that I assert a prudential right to some x does not give anyone else a sufficient reason to grant me that x.

But even if we can make sense of Gewirth's argument, this does not give us a notion of equal human worth, but merely minimal equal prima facie rights to freedom and well-being, which could be overridden for other reasons. Inegalitarians like Aristotle could accept this kind of equal right and argue that the prima facie right to minimal freedom of action should be overridden either when the actions are irrational or when a hierarchically structured society has need of slaves, in which case those who were best suited to this role would have their prima facie right to free action suitably constrained. In like manner Utilitarians could accept Gewirthian equal prima facie rights and override them whenever greater utility was at stake. Gewirthian equal rights reduce to little more than recognizing that noninterference and well-being are values which we have a prima facie moral duty to promote whether in animals or angels, humans or Galacticans. They do not give us a set of thick natural rights.

Tom Nagel has set forth a version of Gewirth's Rational Agency Argument in his books *A View from Nowhere* and *Equality and Partiality,* which may be more promising than Gewirth's own version in that it centers not on free action but on essential value viewed from an impersonal standpoint ("a view from nowhere").

> You cannot sustain an impersonal indifference to the things in your life which matter to you personally. . . . But since the impersonal standpoint does not single you out from anyone else, the same must be true of the value arising in other lives. If you matter impersonally, so does everyone. We can usefully think of the values that go into the construction of a political theory as being revealed in a series of four stages, each of which depends on a moral response to an issue posed by what was revealed at the previous stage. At the first stage, the basic insight that appears from the impersonal standpoint is that everyone's life matters, and no one is more important in virtue of their

greater value for others. But at the baseline of value in the lives of individuals, from which all higher-order inequalities of value must derive, everyone counts the same. For a given quality of whatever it is that's good or bad—suffering or happiness or fulfillment or frustration—its intrinsic impersonal value doesn't depend on whose it is.[22]

The argument goes like this.

1. I cannot help but value myself as a subject of positive and negative experiences (e.g., suffering, happiness, fulfillment, or frustration).
2. All other humans are relevantly similar to me, subjects of positive and negative experiences.
3. Therefore, I must, on pain of contradiction, ascribe equal value to all other human beings.

Although this looks more promising than Gewirth's argument, it too is defective. First of all, it is not necessary to value oneself primarily as a possessor of the capacity for positive and negative experiences. Why cannot I value myself because of a complex of specific properties: excellence of skill, ability to engage in complex deliberation, rationality, discipline and self-control, industriousness, high integrity, athletic ability, creative and artistic talent, or quickness of wit without which I would not deem living worth the effort? I value myself more for actually *having* these properties than I do my *capacity* to suffer. These are what positively make up my happiness and give me a sense of worth—from the *impersonal* (i.e., impartial) point of view. If I were to lose any one of these properties, I, given my present identity, would value myself less than I do now. Should I lose enough of them, my present self would view this future self as lacking positive value altogether, and my future self might well agree. Should I become immoral, insane, or desperately disease ridden, I would be valueless and I hope I would die as swiftly as possible. So it follows that I am under no obligation to value everyone, since not everyone is moral, rational, or healthy. There is no contradiction in failing to value the debauched Smith (section 5 above) or Rawls's blade of grass counter,

the rapist or child molester, the retarded or the senile, since they lack the necessary qualities in question. Furthermore, I may value people *in degrees*, according to the extent that they exhibit the set of positive qualities.

So, letting these positive values be called "traits T," we need to revise the first premise to read:

1A. I cannot help but value myself as the possessor of a set of traits T.

But then 2 becomes false—all other human beings are *not* relevantly similar to me in this regard. And so, Nagel's conclusion does not follow, I do not contradict myself in failing to value people who lack the relevant qualities.

There is a second problem with Nagel's argument. It rests too heavily on the agent's judgment about himself. "If you matter impersonally, so does everyone." There are two ways to invalidate this conditional. The conditional will not go through if you do not value yourself. If I am sick of life and believe that I do not matter, then, on Nagel's premises, I have no reason to value anyone else. Second, I may deny the consequent and thereby reject the antecedent. I may come to believe that no one else does matter and then be forced to acknowledge that I do not matter either. We are all equal—equally worthless. If reflection has any force, Nagel's first premise (i.e., I cannot help but value myself as a subject of positive and negative experiences) seems false. People cease to value themselves when they lose the things which give life meaning.

Third, note the consequentialist tone of the last two sentences of Nagel's statement: ". . . at the baseline of value in the lives of individuals, from which all higher order inequalities of value must derive, everyone counts the same. For a given quantity of whatever it is that's good or bad—suffering or happiness or fulfillment or frustration—its intrinsic impersonal value doesn't depend on whose it is." We hear the echo of Bentham's "each one to count for one and no one for more than one" in this passage. But Nagel, like Bentham before him, cannot both be a maximizer *and* an egalitarian. If it is *happiness* that really is the good to be maximized or *suffering* to be minimized, then individuals are mere place holders for these qualities, so that if we can maximize happiness (or minimize suffering) by subordinating some individuals to others, we should do so. If A can derive ten hedons by eliminating B and C who together can only obtain eight hedons, it would be a good thing for A to kill B and C. If it turns out that a pig satisfied really is happier than Socrates dissatisfied, then we ought to value the pig's life more than Socrates', and if a lot of people are miserable and are making others miserable, we would improve the total happiness of the world by killing them.

I for one confess that I do not care whether cats thrive more than mice or whether all cats are equally prosperous. No one I know cares about this either. But from Nagel's impersonal "View from Nowhere," should not we care as much about them, since cats and mice are subjects to positive and negative experiences—pleasures and suffering? How, on Nagel's premises are humans—themselves animals—intrinsically better than cats and mice? I can appreciate it if a religious person responds that humans are endowed with the image of God, but Nagel, not being religious, cannot use this response. Why should I care that all humans are equally happy anymore than I care whether all cats or mice are equally happy and as equally happy as humans? If the question is absurd, I would like to know why. Do not misunderstand me, I do not want to harm anyone without moral justification, but I do not see any moral reason to treat all humans, let alone all animals, with equal respect.

10. The Argument from Moral Personality

No exposition of egalitarianism has had a greater influence on our generation than John Rawls's A Theory of Justice, which Robert Nisbet has called "the long awaited successor to Rousseau's *Social Contract* . . . the Rock on which the Church of Equality can properly be founded in our time."[23] Rawls sets forth a hypothetical contract theory in which the bargainers go behind a veil of ignorance in order to devise a set of fundamental agreements that are fair.

First of all no one knows his place in society, his class position or social status; nor does he know his fortune in the distribution of natural assets and abilities, his intelligence and the like. Nor, again, does anyone know his conception of the good, the particulars of his rational plan of life, or even the special features of his psychology such as his aversion to risk or liability to optimism or pessimism. More than this, I assume that the parties do not know the particular circumstances of their own society. That is, they do not know its economic or political situation, or the level of civilization and culture it has been able to achieve. The persons in the original position have no information as to which generation they belong. (p. 137)

By denying individuals knowledge of their natural assets and social position Rawls prevents them from exploiting their advantages, thus transforming a decision under risk (where probabilities of outcomes are known) to a decision under uncertainty (where probabilities are not known). To the question, why should the individual acknowledge the principles chosen as morally binding? Rawls would answer, "We should abide by these principles because we all chose them under fair conditions." That is, the rules and rights chosen by fair procedures are themselves fair, since these procedures take full account of our moral nature as equally capable of "doing justice." The two principles that would be chosen, Rawls argues, are (1) everyone will have an equal right to equal basic liberties and (2) social and economic inequalities must satisfy two conditions: (a) they are to attach to positions open to all under conditions of fair equality of opportunity; and (b) they must serve the greatest advantage of the least advantaged members of society (the difference principle).

Michael Sandel has criticized Rawls's project as lacking a notion of intrinsic worth. "Rawls' principles do not mention moral desert because, strictly speaking, no one can be said to deserve anything. . . . On Rawls' view *people have no intrinsic worth*, no worth that is intrinsic in the sense that it is theirs prior to or independent of . . . what just institutions attribute to them."[24]

Although Rawls sometimes lays himself open to this kind of charge, I think that Sandel is wrong here. What grounds Rawls's social contract is a Kantian humanism.

> Each person possesses an inviolability founded on justice that even the welfare of society as a whole cannot override. For this reason justice denies that the loss of freedom for some is made right by a greater good shared by others. It does not allow that the sacrifices imposed on a few are outweighed by the larger sum of advantages enjoyed by the many. Therefore, in a just society the liberties of equal citizenship are taken as settled; the rights secured by justice are not subject to political bargaining or the calculus of social interests. (p. 3f)

At the center of Rawls's project is a respect for the individual as "inviolable," sacred, whose essential rights are inalienable. In section 77 of *A Theory of Justice*, this inviolability is grounded in our having "the capacity for moral personality," that is, the ability to enter into moral deliberation. "It is precisely the moral persons who are entitled to equal justice. Moral persons are distinguished by two features: first they are capable of having . . . a conception of the good; and second they are capable of having . . . a sense of justice. . . . One should observe that moral personality is here defined as a potentiality that is ordinarily realized in due course. It is this potentiality which brings the claims of justice into play."[25]

Members in the original position are not mere utilitarian containers of the good but Kantian "ends in themselves," who are worthy of "equal concern and respect." Rawls already presupposes equal and positive worth at the very beginning of his project. The question is, is this assumption reasonable? Is Rawls's egalitarian starting point justified? I think not. Given the framework in which Rawls writes there is no reason to suppose that we have intrinsic and equal value. Let me explain.

A standard criticism of *A Theory of Justice* is that it fails to take into account the conservative who, as a gambler, would rather take his chances on a meritocratic or hierarchical society and so reject part or all of Rawls's second principle. I think that this objection is even stronger than has been made out, for it is not simply as a *gambler* that the conservative will self-interestedly choose meritocracy, but rather because he or she deems it the essence of justice.

This point becomes highlighted when we examine Rawls's *threshold* principle. "Once a certain minimum is met, a person is entitled to equal liberty on a par with everyone else" (p. 506). This move seems ad hoc. There is no obvious reason why we should opt for tacit equal status (let alone inviolability) rather than an Aristotelian hierarchical structure based on differential ability to reason or deliberate. Even as some life plans are objectively better than others, so some people might well be considered more worthy than others and treated accordingly.

Why would it be wrong to weight the votes behind the veil of ignorance according to criteria of assessment? For example, the deeply reflective with low time preferences would be given more votes than the less reflective with high time preferences. Those with high grades might get four or five votes whereas the minimally reflective might get only one vote. Why have only one threshold between those who pass and those who fail the rationality test, as Rawls proposes? Why not have five or six thresholds?

With different layers of weighted votes one would still expect a benevolent society, but the difference principle might well be replaced by Harsanyi's average utility principle or Frankfurt's sufficiency principles permitting hierarchical arrangements.[26] Rawls's first principle (maximum liberty) and the first half of the second principle (equal opportunity) would very likely result in a hierarchical, elitist society.

Normally we think that each person has a right—based on freedom and moral worth (the very principles Rawls embraces)—to develop his or her capacities and talents and extend one's goals higher and higher. Suppose that I love to travel for both enjoyment and educational purposes. I use the knowledge I receive for education purposes, including writing books, for which I receive generous royalties. Even though I give more than average to charity, I still end up with vastly more wealth than the average person, and thus am enabled to buy more books, do more travelling, and enjoy the good things of life several times that of the average person. Presumably, I am violating the Equality Principle of only having as much resources (or welfare) as the average person. But this seems counterintuitive. In economics the Pareto Principle of Optimality prescribes that an agent should maximize his own welfare so long as no one is thereby made (unjustly) worse off. Either the Pareto Principle is illegitimate and we are not allowed to advance our interests while others have less or the Equality Principle is mistaken and we may advance our interests even when it brings us to a position where we are far better off than others.

But we may go even further than the Pareto Principle. Even if my fulfilling my goals leaves others worse off, that still may not be wrong. Drawing on an illustration from Nozick, suppose that my marrying the most beautiful woman in my community leaves twenty rival suitors in abject despair, on the brink of suicide. Even though each of them is worse off, I am justified in using my superior talents to win my beloved and thus end up in a far better position than my despairing rivals. The situation is unequal, but not unjust.

What would Rawls say to these criticisms? Why does he hold on to a principle of equal intrinsic worth? The closest Rawls comes to addressing this question gets us back to his self-respect argument, discussed in section 8. Self-respect, according to Rawls, is a fundamental human need which his theory satisfies and which hierarchical arrangements fail to satisfy. But we have already seen that this is severely problematic.

It is noteworthy that these matters are not addressed in Rawls's second book, *Political Liberalism*.

Counter-Evidence to Egalitarianism: The Empirical Consideration

Contrary to egalitarians there is good reason to believe that humans are not of equal worth. Given the empirical observation, it is hard to believe that humans are equal in any way at all.

We all seem to have vastly different levels of abilities. Some, like Aristotle, Newton, Shakespeare, and Einstein, are very intelligent; others are imbeciles and idiots. Some are wise like Socrates and Abraham Lincoln; others are very foolish. Some have great powers of foresight and are able to defer gratification, while others can hardly assess their present circumstances, gamble away their future, succumb to immediate gratification, and generally go through life as through a fog. From the perspective of the moral point of view, it looks like Einstein, Gandhi, and Mother Teresa have more value than Jack-the-Ripper or Adolf Hitler. If a research scientist with the cure for cancer is on the same raft with an ordinary person, there is no doubt about who should be saved on the basis of functional value.

Take any capacity or ability you like: reason, a good will, the capacity to suffer, the ability to deliberate and choose freely, the ability to make moral decisions and carry them out, self-control, sense of humor, health, athletic and artistic ability, and it seems that humans (not to mention animals) differ in the degree to which they have those capacities and abilities.

Furthermore, given the purely secular version of the theory of evolution, there does not seem to be any reason to believe that the family metaphor, supposed by philosophers like Vlastos and the United Nations' Declaration on Human Rights (see the beginning of this paper), has much evidence in its favor. If we are simply a product of blind evolutionary chance and necessity, it is hard to see where the family connection comes in. Who is the parent? In fact, given a naturalistic account of the origins of homo sapiens, it is hard to see that humans have intrinsic value at all. If we are simply physicalist constructions, where does intrinsic value emerge?

Of course, most, if not all, of the egalitarians discussed above recognize this empirical consideration. The point is that the empirical problem seems to place its own burden of proof on any theory that would claim that equal rights are based on equal human worth. As far as I can see, none have countered the presumption of inequality.

PART II: THE METAPHYSICAL ORIGINS OF THE IDEA OF EQUAL WORTH: OUR JUDEO-CHRISTIAN TRADITION

The doctrine that all people are of equal worth, and thus endowed with inalienable rights, is rooted in our religious heritage. The language of human dignity and worth implies a great family in which a benevolent and sovereign Father binds together all his children in love and justice. The originators of rights language presupposed a theistic world view, and secular advocates of equal rights are, to cite Tolstoy, like children who see beautiful flowers, grab them, break them at their stems, and try to transplant them without their roots. The egalitarian assertions of the *United Nations' Universal Declaration of Human Rights* are similar to those of our *Declaration of Independence,* with one important difference—God is left out of the former; but that makes all the difference. That posit (or some metaphysical idea which will support equal and positive worth) is not just an ugly appendage or a pious afterthought but a root necessary for the bloom of rights.

While the thesis of equal human worth may not have been clearly recognized, let alone embraced, by ancient Israel or in all Jewish and Christian quarters, the Jewish prophetic tradition and much of the Christian tradition, supports this thesis. In such texts as the first three chapters of Genesis, which speak of God creating man and woman in His image, as "good"; in Malachi 2:10, where the prophet writes, "Have we not all one Father? Has not one God created us? Why then are we faithless to one another?" and in Psalms 8:3–6, where the psalmist asks, "When I look at thy heavens, the work of thy fingers, the moon and the stars which thou has established: What is man that thou are mindful of him, or the son of man that thou does care for him?" and answers his own question, "Thou hast made him a little less than God, and dost crown him with glory and honor. Thou has given him dominion over the works of thy hands; thou has put all things under his feet." The prophets Amos, Micah, and Isaiah speak of God's concern being universal and of a coming universal kingdom wherein all people enjoy peace and prosperity.[27]

In the New Testament and in the early Christian church there are strains that point to the thesis that all humans are loved equally by God and are equally accountable to him for their actions. The moral law is revealed to each person, so that each will be judged according to his or her moral merit (Romans 2). Still, even the sinner is of incalculable worth; like a corroded and distorted coin of the royal mint, he or she still bears the King's image.

Of course, in itself theism is no guarantee of equal worth, for God could have created people unequal. The argument implicit in the Judeo-Christian tradition seems to be that God is the ultimate value and that humans derive their value by being created in his image and likeness. To paraphrase the psalmist, we are a little lower than God, mini-gods the Hebrew seems to suggest. With regard to possessing intrinsic value we all get equal grades.

There are two arguments for equal human worth which I find implicit in the Judeo-Christian tradition: the Essentialist Argument and the Argument from Grace. The Essentialist Argument goes like this: God created all humans with an equal amount of some property P, which constitutes high value. The property may be a natural or a non-natural one. If it is a natural property, then conceivably we could discover it and act upon it without needing God to reveal it. If it a non-natural property, the only reason to suppose that we possess it is that our theory says we do. The fact that we cannot identify it constitutes some evidence against the theory itself, but if there are good reasons to accept the theory as a whole, one might be content to live humbly with this mystery. Since no empirical quality is had by all humans in the same quantity, the naturalistic picture seems foreclosed and the non-natural one wins by default.

The second argument which I find in the Judeo-Christian tradition is the Argument from Grace. Strictly speaking it is not an egalitarian argument, if egalitarianism means that each person has equal intrinsic worth. Here the actual value may be different in different people but grace compensates the differences. It raises the worst-off until they are equal with the best-off.

The Argument from Grace often makes use of the family metaphor, such as we find in Vlastos's article (above)—only in this case the family has a parent. God is the Heavenly Father, and we are all family, brothers and sisters to one another. As our Father, God loves us each equally and unconditionally, and wants his children to love each other. Each person does matter and does matter equally, but not because of some innate property, but simply by virtue of God's gracious love.

The meaning of the Sermon on the Mount, with its prescriptions to love even one's enemies, of the Parable of the Good Samaritan, which enjoins recognizing people of despised groups as capable of moral grandeur, and of the Parable of the Prodigal Son, which teaches us to forgive and restore lost causes, is that God's grace triumphs over human difference, both moral and nonmoral, and raises each of us to an equal pinnacle of sanctity and dignity.

The Argument from Grace is a version of the divine command theory of ethics, though it does not entail reducing all morality to divine commands. Some moral duties may be based on human nature, while the duty to equal concern for the welfare of all persons may be a product of God's command. That is, morality may be a combination of divine commands and rational discoveries.

These two arguments can stand separately or together in making a case for the thesis of equal human rights based on equal human worth. That is, it is the God-relationship that provides the metaphysical basis for this thesis, whether the equality comes in at creation or whether it is due to grace.

I do not mean to imply that the Judeo-Christian tradition is the only logical basis for a doctrine of equal worth. I am simply pointing to the historic origins of our perspective. One could opt for a Stoic pantheism, which maintains that all humans have within them a part of God, the *logos spermatikos* (the divinely rational seed). We are all part of God, chips off the old divine block, as it were. Other religions, such as Islam and Hinduism, also have a notion of the divine origins and high worth of humanity. Perhaps a version of a Platonic system could do the trick as well.

The possibilities are frighteningly innumerable. My point is that you need some metaphysical explanation to ground the doctrine of equal worth, if it is to serve as a basis for equal human rights. It is not enough simply to assert, as philosophers like Dworkin do, that their egalitarian doctrines are "metaphysically unambitious." But, of course, there are severe epistemological difficulties with the kinds of metaphysical systems I have been discussing. My point has not been to defend religion. For purposes of this paper I am neutral on the question of whether any religion is true. Rather my purpose is to show that we cannot burn our bridges and still drive Mack trucks over them. But, if we cannot return to religion, then it would seem perhaps we should abandon egalitarianism and devise political philosophies that reflect naturalistic assumptions, theories which are forthright in viewing humans as differentially talented animals who must get on together.

CONCLUSION

Secular egalitarian arguments for equal rights seem, at best, to be based on a posit of faith that all humans are of equal worth or that it is useful to regard them as such. They have not offered plausible reasons for their thesis, and, given the empirical consideration, inegalitarianism seems plausible. If my analysis of the subject is confirmed by fuller arguments, then there are only two choices for egalitarians and the rest of us: either secular inegalitarian moral/political systems or religious (or comparable metaphysical) systems.

I have suggested that secular egalitarians have inherited a notion of inviolability or intrinsic human worth from a religious tradition which they no longer espouse. The question is whether the kind of democratic ideals that egalitarians espouse can do without a religious tradition. If it cannot, then egalitarians may be living off the borrowed interest of a religious metaphysic, which (in their eyes) has gone bankrupt. The question is: Where is the capital?[28]

NOTES

1. Among the most prominent recent works on equal human rights are: John Baker, *Arguing for Equality* (Verso, 1987); Maurice Cranston, *What are Human Rights?* (Taplinger, 1973); J. Finnis, *Natural Law and Natural Rights* (Clarendon Press, 1980); Alan Gewirth, *Human Rights* (University of Chicago, 1982); Ronald Dworkin, *Taking Rights Seriously* (Harvard University, 1977); Will Kymlicka, *Contemporary Political Philosophy: An Introduction* (Oxford University, 1990); Rex Martin, *Rawls and Rights* (University of Kansas, 1985); Tibor Machan, *Individual Rights* (Open Court, 1989); James Nickel, *Making Sense of Human Rights* (University of California, 1987); Ellen Frankl Paul, Fred Miller, and Jeffrey Paul, eds., *Human Rights* (Basil Blackwell, 1984); Robert Nozick, *Anarchy, State and Utopia* (Basic Books, 1974); John Rawls, *A Theory of Justice* (Harvard, 1971); Jeremy Waldron, ed., *Theories of Rights* (Oxford University, 1984); Carl Wellman, *A Theory of Rights* (Rowman and Allenheld, 1985) and Morton E. Winston, ed., *The Philosophy of Human Rights* (Wadsworth, 1989).

2. Ronald Dworkin, "The Original Position," *University of Chicago Law Review* 40, no. 3 (Spring 1973): 532.

3. Jacques Maritain, *The Rights of Man* (London, 1944), p. 37. For a good introduction to the significance of human rights see the introduction and readings in *The Philosophies of Human Rights*, ed. Morton Winston (Wadsworth, 1989). Mortimer Adler's statement is representative of contemporary egalitarians: "All human beings are equal as human. Being equal as humans, they are equal in the rights that arise from needs inherent in their common human nature. A constitution is not just if it does not treat equals equally. Nor is it just if it does not recognize the equal right of all to freedom—to be ruled as human beings should be ruled, as citizens, not as slaves or subjects." *Aristotle for Everybody* (Bantam, 1978), p. 114.

4. Will Kymlicka, *Contemporary Political Philosophy* (Oxford University Press, 1989), p. 4. Inegalitarianism is often dismissed as a crackpot idea that no self-respecting person would seriously consider. In another work, as though to apply the coup de grace to inegalitarianism, Kymlicka notes, "Some theories, like Nazism, deny that each person matters equally. But such theories do not merit serious consideration." (*Liberalism, Community and Culture* (Oxford University Press, 1989), p. 40. In *The End of Equality* (Basic Books, 1992), Mickey Kaus writes, "I confess I had forgotten that social inegalitarians still existed in this country. Since writing the book I have encountered a few lively specimens. Still, I have confidence that they remain a small minority" (p. viii).

5. Ronald Green, *Morality and Religion* (Oxford University Press, 1988), p. 140. I have challenged Green's idea of moral equality in my article "Equality: The Concept and Its Conceptions," in *Behavior and Philosophy* (forthcoming).

6. Ronald Dworkin, "The Original Position," *University of Chicago Law Review* 40, no. 3 (Spring 1973): 532.

7. Thomas Hobbes, *Leviathan* (Bobbs-Merrill, 1958), ch. 10, p. 79f.

8. R. S. Peters and S. I. Benn, *Social Principles and the Democratic State* (George Allen and Unwin, 1959) ch 5; R. S. Peters, "Equality and Education," S. I. Benn and R. S. Peters, "Justice and Equality," and Monroe Beardsley, "Equality and Obedience to Law," all in *The Concept of Equality*, W. T. Blackstone, ed. (Burgess Publishing Company, 1960). Benn and Peters recognize the negative character of their definition and appeal to the principle of relevance to fill in the positive content (*Social Principles and the Democratic State*, p. 111f). E. F. Carritt in *Ethical and Political Thinking* (Oxford, 1947), p. 156f writes, "Equality of consideration is the only thing to the whole of which men have a right, [and] it is just to treat men as equal until some reason, other than preference, such as need, capacity, or desert, has been shown to the contrary."

9. Ronald Dworkin, *Taking Rights Seriously* (Harvard, 1977), p. 184. In his response to Narveson's request for a supporting argument, Dworkin concedes that he has no argument to convince the skeptic regarding the "egalitarian plateau," but argues that rejecting it has such unwelcome consequences (such as class and caste systems), that we are justified in accepting it. He writes:

> But it is . . . hard to conceive how any of us could think that it matters more, from any kind of objective standpoint, how his life goes than anyone else's, if I am right in supposing that each of us thinks that the course of his own life has *intrinsic* importance. You might want to say, for example, that it is more important how your life goes because you are a more virtuous person. But your convictions about the importance of how your life goes are too deep—too fundamental—to permit this. Your belief provides you with a reason to consider whether to be virtuous, and where virtue lies, which means that you think it important how your life goes for some reason that in this way precedes your virtue. If so, then you cannot say that it is more important how you live

for any reason drawn from your merit or the merit of your life, and no other kind of reason can plausibly distinguish you from anyone else who has a life to lead." ("Comment on Narveson: In Defense of Equality" in *Social Philosophy & Policy* vol. 1: 1983, p. 35).

Dworkin is clearly correct in stating that we *deeply* value our lives and do so prior to imputing moral criteria, but he is wrong if he thinks this must be the basis of political and social arrangements. It is a large step from (1) "I matter most to myself" and "everyone else matters most to him or herself" to (2) everyone should matter *equally* to the State, for when we enter into society, we bring in contractual and/or utilitarian considerations which have normative features of their own. And these normative features may well specify that some interests count more than others, that virtue be rewarded differentially, and that some individual contributions or abilities be valued over others.

10. Kai Nielsen, *Equality and Liberty* (Rowman and Allenheld, 1985), p. 23.

11. Nielsen elsewhere speaks of his view that vast discrepancies in life prospects should be corrected as a "very basic considered judgment (moral intuition)," making his view identical with Dworkin's, p. 8. Nielsen may differ from Dworkin only in emphasizing the role of choice in adopting his intuition. The question remains: what is the basis of the intuition that equality is intrinsically a good thing? Is it a natural intuition constitutive of the human condition, so that those who lack it are fundamentally deficient? Is it the product of a religious system which holds that all humans are made in the image of God with infinite value? Is it an aesthetic principle—similar to a sense of symmetry or unity? If for a secularist it is bad that humans are unequal in ability, why is it not bad that humans and apes or dogs or mice are of unequal ability?

12. Kai Nielsen, op. cit., p. 95.

13. Nozick in *Anarchy, State and Utopia* (Blackwell, 1874), p. ix. In this regard Jeffrie Murphy points out that Nozick's Lockean theory of original acquisition of property (chapter 7) fails because it omits the theological assumptions that supported Locke's own theory. Nozick seeks to prevent hoarding of property by first-comers, so he evokes "The Lockean Proviso" that there be "enough and as good left in common for others." His Lockean justification for this is that no one is worsened by this situation. But what Nozick fails to explain is why anyone should care whether anyone else's position is worsened. As Murphy says, "If nature is unowned and I am bound, why may I not simply say, 'Lucky me I got it all first and unlucky you who came too late'—and let it go at that? What right do you

have with respect to unowned and morally virgin nature?" (Jeffrie Murphy, "Afterword: Constitutionalism, Moral Skepticism, and Religious Belief," in *Constitutionalism*, ed. Alan Rosenbaum (Greenwood Press, 1988), p. 247).

14. Tibor Machan, *Individuals and Their Rights* (Open Court, 1989) xxiv. For Machan's views on freedom of the will, see p. 14f.

15. David Gauthier, *Morals By Agreement* (Oxford University Press, 1986), pp. 55ff; 222. Gauthier seems to hold the Hobbesian idea that people are more or less equal in their ability to harm others, in their vulnerability to being harmed, and in their bargaining power, but I doubt this very much. The strong and clever can do more damage to others and have more to bring to the bargaining table.

16. Gregory Vlastos, "Justice and Equality," in *Social Justice*, ed. Richard Brandt (Prentice-Hall, 1962). (reprinted in this volume).

17. Joel Feinberg, *Social Philosophy* (Prentice-Hall, 1973), p. 93f.

18. R. M. Hare, "Justice and Equality," in *Justice and Economic Distribution*, eds. John Arthur and William H. Shaw (Prentice-Hall, 1978). Thomas Nagel, "Equality" in *Mortal Questions* (Cambridge University Press, 1979), also holds such a position, though he is not a utilitarian.

19. For a cogent criticism of the uses of the doctrine of diminishing marginal utility for egalitarian purposes, see Harry Frankfurt, "Equality as a Moral Ideal," *Ethics* 98 (1987). My work is indebted to Frankfurt.

20. Kai Nielsen, "On Not Needing to Justify Equality," *International Studies in Philosophy*, vol. 20/3 (1988), pp. 55–71.

21. Alan Gewirth, *Reason and Morality* (University of Chicago, 1978), "Epistemology of Human Rights" in *Human Rights,* eds. Ellen Paul, Fred Miller, and Jeffrey Paul (Blackwell, 1984); and *Human Rights: Essays on Justification and Applications* (University of Chicago, 1982).

22. Tom Nagel, *A View from Nowhere* (Oxford University Press, 1986) and *Equality and Impartiality* (Oxford University Press, 1991), p. 11.

23. Robert Nisbet, "The Pursuit of Equality" *The Public Interest*, vol 35 (1974), pp. 103–120.

24. Michael Sandel, *Liberalism and the Limits of Justice* (Cambridge University Press, 1982), p. 88.

25. Rawls, op. cit., p. 505.

26. John Harsanyi, *Essays in Ethics, Social Behavior and Scientific Explanation* (Reidel, 1976), and Harry Frankfurt, "Equality as a Moral Ideal," *Ethics*, vol. 98.1 (October 1987). Reprinted as reading 25 in this volume.

27. See for example Isaiah 2; 19:21–25; 60:1–5; Micah 4 and Revelation 21 and 22. See Lenn

Evan Goodman's "Equality and Human Rights: The Lockean and Judaic Views," in *Judaism* (1984) for an interpretation similar to my own.

28. Parts of this paper were taken from "A Critique of Contemporary Egalitarianism," in *Faith and Philosophy* 8:4 (October 1991); and "Are Human Rights Based on Equal Human Worth?," in *Philosophy and Phenomenological*

Research 52:3 (September 1992). I am indebted to Richard Arneson, Robert Audi, Donald Blackeley, Tziporah Kasachkoff, Michael Levin, Paul Pojman, Steven Ross, William Rowe, Peter Simpson, and Robert Westmoreland for comments on previous versions of this paper.

Complex Equality
MICHAEL WALZER

PLURALISM

Distributive justice is a large idea. It draws the entire world of goods within the reach of philosophical reflection. Nothing can be omitted; no feature of our common life can escape scrutiny. Human society is a distributive community. That's not all it is, but it is importantly that: we come together to share, divide, and exchange. We also come together to make the things that are shared, divided, and exchanged; but that very making—work itself—is distributed among us in a division of labor. My place in the economy, my standing in the political order, my reputation among my fellows, my material holdings: all these come to me from other men and women. It can be said that I have what I have rightly or wrongly, justly or unjustly; but given the range of distributions and the number of participants, such judgments are never easy.

The idea of distributive justice has as much to do with being and doing as with having, as much to do with production as with consumption, as much to do with identity and status as with land, capital, or personal possessions. Different political arrangements enforce, and

different ideologies justify, different distributions of membership, power, honor, ritual eminence, divine grace, kinship and love, knowledge, wealth, physical security, work and leisure, rewards and punishments, and a host of goods more narrowly and materially conceived—food, shelter, clothing, transportation, medical care, commodities of every sort, and all the odd things (paintings, rare books, postage stamps) that human beings collect. And this multiplicity of goods is matched by a multiplicity of distributive procedures, agents, and criteria. There are such things as simple distributive systems—slave galleys, monasteries, insane asylums, kindergartens (though each of these, looked at closely, might show unexpected complexities); but no full-fledged human society has ever avoided the multiplicity. We must study it all, the goods and the distributions, in many different times and places.

There is, however, no single point of access to this world of distributive arrangements and ideologies. There has never been a universal medium of exchange. Since the decline of the barter economy, money has been the most common medium. But the old maxim according to which there are some things that money can't buy is not only normatively but also factually true. What should and should not be up for sale is something men and women always have to decide and have decided in many different ways. Throughout history, the market has been one of the most important mechanisms for the distribution of social goods; but it has never been, it nowhere is today, a complete distributive system.

Similarly, there has never been either a single decision point from which all distributions are controlled or a single set of agents making decisions. No state power has ever been so pervasive as to regulate all the patterns of sharing, dividing, and exchanging out of which a society takes shape. Things slip away from the state's grasp; new patterns are worked out—familial networks, black markets, bureaucratic alliances, clandestine political and religious organizations. State officials can tax, conscript, allocate, regulate, appoint, reward, punish, but they cannot capture the full range of goods or substitute themselves for every other agent of distribution. Nor can anyone else do that: there are market coups and cornerings, but there has never been a fully successful distributive conspiracy.

And finally, there has never been a single criterion, or a single set of interconnected criteria, for all distributions. Desert, qualification, birth and blood, friendship, need, free exchange, political loyalty, democratic decision: each has had its place, along with many others, uneasily coexisting, invoked by competing groups, confused with one another.

In the matter of distributive justice, history displays a great variety of arrangements and ideologies. But the first impulse of the philosopher is to resist the displays of history, the world of appearances, and to search for some underlying unity: a short list of basic goods, quickly abstracted to a single good; a single distributive criterion or an interconnected set; and the philosopher himself standing, symbolically at least, at a single decision point. I shall argue that to search for unity is to misunderstand the subject matter of distributive justice. Nevertheless, in some sense the philosophical impulse is unavoidable. Even if we choose pluralism, as I shall do, that choice still requires a coherent defense. There must be principles that justify the choice and set limits to it, for pluralism does not require us to endorse every proposed distributive criteria or to accept every would-be agent. Conceivably, there is a single principle and a single legitimate kind of pluralism. But this would still be a pluralism that encompassed a wide range of distributions. By contrast, the deepest assumption of most of the philosophers who have written about justice, from Plato onward, is that there is one, and only one, distributive system that philosophy can rightly encompass.

Today this system is commonly described as the one that ideally rational men and women would choose if they were forced to choose impartially, knowing nothing of their own situation, barred from making particularist claims, confronting an abstract set of goods. If these constraints on knowing and claiming are suitably shaped, and if the goods are suitably defined, it is probably true that a singular conclusion can be produced. Rational men and women, constrained this way or that, will choose one, and only one, distributive system. But the force of that singular conclusion is not easy to measure. It is surely doubtful that those same men and women, if they were transformed into ordinary people, with a firm sense of their own identity, with their own goods in their hands, caught up in everyday troubles, would reiterate their hypothetical choice or even recognize it as their own. The problem is not, most importantly, with the particularism of interest, which philosophers have always assumed they could safely—that is, uncontroversially—set aside. Ordinary people can do that too, for the sake, say, of the public interest. The greater problem is with the particularism of history, culture, and membership. Even if they are committed to impartiality, the question most likely to arise in the minds of the members of a political community is not, What would rational individuals choose under universalizing conditions of such-and-such a sort? But rather, What would individuals like us choose, who are situated as we are, who share a culture and are determined to go on sharing it? And this is a question that is readily transformed into, What choices have we already made in the course of our common life? What understandings do we (really) share?

Justice is a human construction, and it is doubtful that it can be made in only one way. At any rate, I shall begin by doubting, and more than doubting, this standard philosophical assumption. The questions posed by the theory of distributive justice admit of a range of answers, and there is room within the range for cultural diversity and political choice. It's not only a matter of implementing some singular principle or set of principles in different historical settings. No one would deny that there is a range of morally permissible implementations. I want to argue for more than this: that the principles of justice are themselves pluralistic in form; that different social goods ought to be distributed for different reasons, in accordance with different procedures, by different agents; and that all these differences derive from different understandings of the social goods themselves—the inevitable product of historical and cultural particularism. . . .

Autonomy is a matter of social meaning and shared values, but it is more likely to make for occasional reformation and rebellion than for everyday enforcement. For all the complexity of their distributive arrangements, most societies are organized on what we might think of as a social version of the gold standard: one good or one set of goods is dominant and determinative of value in all the spheres of distribution. And that good or set of goods is commonly monopolized, its value upheld by the strength and cohesion of its owners. I call a good dominant if the individuals who have it, because they have it, can command a wide range of other goods. It is monopolized whenever a single man or woman, a monarch in the world of value—or a group of men and women, oligarchs—successfully hold it against all rivals. Dominance describes a way of using social goods that isn't limited by their intrinsic meanings or that shapes those meanings in its own image. Monopoly describes a way of owning or controlling social goods in order to exploit their dominance. When goods are scarce and widely needed, like water in the desert, monopoly itself will make them dominant. Mostly, however, dominance is a more elaborate social creation, the work of many hands, mixing reality and symbol. Physical strength, familial reputation, religious or political office, landed wealth, capital, technical knowledge: each of these, in different historical periods, has been dominant; and each of them has been monopolized by some group of men and women. And then all good things come to those who have the one best thing. Possess that one, and the others come in train. Or, to change the metaphor, a dominant good is converted into another good, into many others, in accordance with what often appears to be a natural process but is in fact magical, a kind of social alchemy.

No social good ever entirely dominates the range of goods; no monopoly is ever perfect. I mean to describe tendencies only, but crucial tendencies. For we can characterize whole societies in terms of the patterns of conversion that are established within them. Some characterizations are simple: in a capitalist society, capital is dominant and readily converted into prestige and power; in a technocracy, technical knowledge plays the same part. But it isn't difficult to imagine, or to find, more complex social arrangements. Indeed, capitalism and technocracy are more complex than their names imply, even if the names do convey real information about the most important forms of sharing, dividing, and exchanging. Monopolistic control of a dominant good makes a ruling class, whose members stand atop the distributive system—much as philosophers, claiming to have the wisdom they love, might like to do. But since dominance is always incomplete and monopoly imperfect, the rule of every ruling class is unstable. It is continually challenged by other groups in the name of alternative patterns of conversion.

Distribution is what social conflict is all about. Marx's heavy emphasis on productive processes should not conceal from us the simple truth that the struggle for control of the means of production is a distributive struggle. Land and capital are at stake, and these are goods that can be shared, divided, exchanged, and endlessly converted. But land and capital are not the only dominant goods; it is possible (it has historically been possible) to come to them by way of other goods—military or political power, religious office and charisma, and so on. History reveals no single dominant good and no naturally dominant good, but only different kinds of magic and competing bands of magicians.

The claim to monopolize a dominant good—when worked up for public purposes—constitutes an ideology. Its standard form is to connect legitimate possession with some set of personal qualities through the medium of a philosophical principle. So aristocracy, or the rule of the best, is the principle of those who lay claim to breeding and intelligence: they are commonly the monopolists of landed wealth and familial reputation. Divine supremacy is the principle of those who claim to know the word of God: they are the monopolists of grace and office. Meritocracy, or the career open to talents, is the principle of those who claim to be talented: they are most often the monopolists of education. Free exchange is the principle of those who are ready, or who tell us they are ready, to put their money at risk: they are the monopolists of movable wealth. These groups—and others, too, similarly marked off by their principles and possessions—compete with one another, struggling for supremacy. One group wins, and then a different one; or coalitions are worked out, and supremacy is uneasily shared. There is no final victory, nor should there be. But that is not to say that the claims of the different groups are necessarily wrong, or that the principles they invoke are of no value as distributive criteria; the principles are often exactly right within the limits of a particular sphere. Ideologies are readily corrupted, but their corruption is not the most interesting thing about them.

It is in the study of these struggles that I have sought the guiding thread of my own argument. The struggles have, I think, a paradigmatic form. Some group of men and women—class, caste, strata, estate, alliance, or social formation—comes to enjoy a monopoly or a near monopoly of some dominant good; or, a coalition of groups comes to enjoy, and so on. This dominant good is more or less systematically converted into all sorts of other things—opportunities, powers, and reputations. So wealth is seized by the strong, honor by the wellborn, office by the well educated. Perhaps the ideology that justifies the seizure is widely believed to be true. But resentment and resistance are (almost) as pervasive as belief. There are always some people, and after a time there are a great many, who think the seizure is not justice but usurpation. The ruling group does not possess, or does not uniquely possess, the qualities it claims; the conversion process violates the common understanding of the goods at stake. Social conflict is intermittent, or it is endemic; at some point, counterclaims are put forward. Though these are of many different sorts, three general sorts are especially important:

1. The claim that the dominant good, whatever it is, should be redistributed so that it can be equally or at least more widely shared: this amounts to saying that monopoly is unjust.
2. The claim that the way should be opened for the autonomous distribution of all social goods: this amounts to saying that dominance is unjust.
3. The claim that some new good, monopolized by some new group, should replace the currently dominant good: this amounts to saying that the existing pattern of dominance and monopoly is unjust.

The third claim is, in Marx's view, the model of every revolutionary ideology—except, perhaps, the proletarian or last ideology. Thus, the French Revolution in Marxist theory: the dominance of noble birth and blood and of feudal landholding is ended, and bourgeois wealth is established in its stead. The original situation is reproduced with different subjects and objects (this is never unimportant), and then the class war is immediately renewed. It is not my purpose here to endorse or to criticize Marx's view. I suspect, in fact, that there is something of all three claims in every revolutionary ideology, but that, too, is not a position that I shall try to defend here. Whatever its sociological significance, the third claim is not philosophically interesting—unless one believes that there is a naturally dominant good, such that its possessors could legitimately claim to rule the rest of us. In a sense, Marx believed exactly that. The means of production is the dominant good throughout history, and Marxism is a historicist doctrine insofar as it suggests that whoever controls the prevailing means legitimately rules. After the communist revolution, we shall all control the means of production: at that point, the third claim collapses into the first. Meanwhile, Marx's model is a program for ongoing distributive struggle. It will matter, of course, who wins at this or that moment, but we won't know why or how it matters if we attend only to the successive assertions of dominance and monopoly.

SIMPLE EQUALITY

It is with the first two claims that I shall be concerned, and ultimately with the second alone, for that one seems to me to capture best the plurality of social meanings and the real complexity of distributive systems. But the first is the more common among philosophers; it matches their own search for unity and singularity; and I shall need to explain its difficulties at some length.

Men and women who make the first claim challenge the monopoly but not the dominance of a particular social good. This is also a challenge to monopoly in general; for if wealth, for example, is dominant and widely shared, no other good can possibly be monopolized. Imagine a society in which everything is up for sale and every citizen has as much money as every other. I shall call this the "regime of simple equality." Equality is multiplied through the conversion process, until it extends across the full range of social goods. The regime of simple equality won't last for long, because the further progress of conversion, free exchange in the market, is certain to bring inequalities in its train. If one wanted to sustain simple equality over time, one would require a "monetary law" like the agrarian laws of ancient times or the Hebrew sabbatical, providing for a periodic return to the original condition. Only a centralized and activist state would be strong enough to force such a return; and it isn't clear that state officials would actually be able or willing to do that, if money were the dominant good. In any case, the original condition is unstable in another way. It's not only that monopoly will reappear, but also that dominance will disappear.

In practice, breaking the monopoly of money neutralizes its dominance. Other goods come into play, and inequality takes on new forms. Consider again the regime of simple equality.

Everything is up for sale, and everyone has the same amount of money. So everyone has, say, an equal ability to buy an education for his children. Some do that, and others don't. It turns out to be a good investment: other social goods are, increasingly, offered for sale only to people with educational certificates. Soon everyone invests in education; or, more likely, the purchase is universalized through the tax system. But then the school is turned into a competitive world within which money is no longer dominant. Natural talent or family upbringing or skill in writing examinations is dominant instead, and educational success and certification are monopolized by some new group. Let's call them (what they call themselves) the "group of the talented." Eventually the members of this group claim that the good they control should be dominant outside the school: offices, titles, prerogatives, wealth too, should all be possessed by themselves. This is the career open to talents, equal opportunity, and so on. This is what fairness requires; talent will out; and in any case, talented men and women will enlarge the resources available to everyone else. So Michael Young's meritocracy is born, with all its attendent inequalities.

What should we do now? It is possible to set limits to the new conversion patterns, to recognize but constrain the monopoly power of the talented. I take this to be the purpose of John Rawls's difference principle, according to which inequalities are justified only if they are designed to bring, and actually do bring, the greatest possible benefit to the least advantaged social class. More specifically, the difference principle is a constraint imposed on talented men and women, once the monopoly of wealth has been broken. It works in this way: Imagine a surgeon who claims more than his equal share of wealth on the basis of the skills he has learned and the certificates he has won in the harsh competitive struggles of college and medical school. We will grant the claim if, and only if, granting it is beneficial in the stipulated ways. At the same time, we will act to limit and regulate the sale of surgery—that is, the direct conversion of surgical skill into wealth.

This regulation will necessarily be the work of the state, just as monetary laws and agrarian laws are the work of the state. Simple equality would require continual state intervention to break up or constrain incipient monopolies and to repress new forms of dominance. But then state power itself will become the central object of competitive struggles. Groups of men and women will seek to monopolize and then to use the state in order to consolidate their control of other social goods. Or, the state will be monopolized by its own agents in accordance with the iron law of oligarchy. Politics is always the most direct path to dominance, and political power (rather than the means of production) is probably the most important, and certainly the most dangerous, good in human history. Hence the need to constrain the agents of constraint, to establish constitutional checks and balances. These are limits imposed on political monopoly, and they are all the more important once the various social and economic monopolies have been broken.

One way of limiting political power is to distribute it widely. This may not work, given the well-canvassed dangers of majority tyranny; but these dangers are probably less acute than they are often made out to be. The greater danger of democratic government is that it will be too weak to cope with re-emerging monopolies in society at large, with the social strength of plutocrats, bureaucrats, technocrats, meritocrats, and so on. In theory, political power is the dominant good in a democracy, and it is convertible in any way the citizens choose. But in practice, again, breaking the monopoly of power neutralizes its dominance. Political power cannot be widely shared without being subjected to the pull of all the other goods that the citizens already have or hope to have. Hence democracy is, as Marx recognized, essentially a reflective system, mirroring the prevailing and emerging distribution of social goods. Democratic decision making will be shaped by the cultural conceptions that determine or underwrite the new monopolies. To prevail against these monopolies, power will have to be centralized, perhaps itself monopolized. Once again, the state must be very powerful if it is to fulfill the purposes assigned to it by the difference principle or by any similarly interventionist rule.

Still, the regime of simple equality might work. One can imagine a more or less stable tension between emerging monopolies and political constraints, between the claim to privilege put forward by the talented, say, and the enforcement of the difference principle, and then between the agents of enforcement and the democratic constitution. But I suspect that difficulties will recur, and that at many points in time the only remedy for private privilege will be statism, and the only escape from statism will be private privilege. We will mobilize power to check monopoly, then look for some way of checking the power we have mobilized. But there is no way that doesn't open opportunities for strategically placed men and women to seize and exploit important social goods.

These problems derive from treating monopoly, and not dominance, as the central issue in distributive justice. It is not difficult, of course, to understand why philosophers (and political activists, too) have focused on monopoly. The distributive struggles of the modern age begin with a war against the aristocracy's singular hold on land, office, and honor. This seems an especially pernicious monopoly because it rests upon birth and blood, with which the individual has nothing to do, rather than upon wealth, or power, or education, all of which—at least in principle—can be earned. And when every man and woman becomes, as it were, a smallholder in the sphere of birth and blood, an important victory is indeed won. Birthright ceases to be a dominant good; henceforth, it purchases very little; wealth, power, and education come to the fore. With regard to these latter goods, however, simple equality cannot be sustained at all, or it can only be sustained subject to the vicissitudes I have just described. Within their own spheres, as they are currently understood, these three tend to generate natural monopolies that can be repressed only if state power is itself dominant and if it is monopolized by officials committed to the repression. But there is, I think, another path to another kind of equality.

TYRANNY AND COMPLEX EQUALITY

I want to argue that we should focus on the reduction of dominance—not, or not primarily, on the break-up or the constraint of monopoly.

We should consider what it might mean to narrow the range within which particular goods are convertible and to vindicate the autonomy of distributive spheres. But this line of argument, though it is not uncommon historically, has never fully emerged in philosophical writing. Philosophers have tended to criticize (or to justify) existing or emerging monopolies of wealth, power, and education. Or, they have criticized (or justified) particular conversions—of wealth into education or of office into wealth. And all this, most often, in the name of some radically simplified distributive system. The critique of dominance will suggest instead a way of reshaping and then living with the actual complexity of distributions.

Imagine now a society in which different social goods are monopolistically held—as they are in fact and always will be, barring continual state intervention—but in which no particular good is generally convertible. As I go along, I shall try to define the precise limits on convertibility, but for now the general description will suffice. This is a complex egalitarian society. Though there will be many small inequalities, inequality will not be multiplied through the conversion process. Nor will it be summed across different goods, because the autonomy of distributions will tend to produce a variety of local monopolies, held by different groups of men and women. I don't want to claim that complex equality would necessarily be more stable than simple equality, but I am inclined to think that it would open the way for more diffused and particularized forms of social conflict. And the resistance to convertibility would be maintained, in large degree, by ordinary men and women within their own spheres of competence and control, without large-scale state action.

This is, I think, an attractive picture, but I have not yet explained just why it is attractive. The argument for complex equality begins from our understanding—I mean, our actual concrete, positive, and particular understanding—of the various social goods. And then it moves on to an account of the way we relate to one another through these goods. Simple equality is a simple distributive condition, so that if I have fourteen hats and you have fourteen hats, we are equal. And it is all to the good if hats are dominant, for then our equality is extended through all the spheres of social life. On the view that I shall take here, however, we simply have the same number of hats, and it is unlikely that hats will be dominant for long. Equality is a complex relation of persons, mediated by the goods we make, share, and divide among ourselves; it is not an identity of possessions. It requires then, a diversity of distributive criteria that mirrors the diversity of social goods.

The argument for complex equality has been beautifully put by Pascal in one of his *Pensées*.

> The nature of tyranny is to desire power over the whole world and outside its own sphere.
>
> There are different companies—the strong, the handsome, the intelligent, the devout—and each man reigns in his own, not elsewhere. But sometimes they meet, and the strong and the handsome fight for mastery—foolishly, for their mastery is of different kinds. They misunderstand one another, and make the mistake of each aiming at universal dominion. Nothing can win this, not even strength, for it is powerless in the kingdom of the wise. . . .
>
> *Tyranny.* The following statements, therefore, are false and tyrannical "Because I am handsome, so I should command respect." "I am strong, therefore men should love me. . . ." "I am . . . et cetera."
>
> Tyranny is the wish to obtain by one means what can only be had by another. We owe different duties to different qualities: love is the proper response to charm, fear to strength, and belief to learning.

Marx made a similar statement in his early manuscripts; perhaps he had this *pensée* in mind:

> Let us assume man to be man, and his relation to the world to be a human one. Then love can only be exchanged for love, trust for trust, etc. If you wish to enjoy art you must be an artistically cultivated person; if you wish to influence other people, you must be a person who really has a stimulating and encouraging effect upon others. . . . If you love without evoking love in return, i.e., if you are not able, by the manifestation of yourself as a loving person, to make yourself a beloved person—then your love is impotent and a misfortune.

These are not easy arguments, and most of my book is simply an exposition of their meaning. But here I shall attempt something more simple and schematic: a translation of the arguments into the terms I have already been using.

The first claim of Pascal and Marx is that personal qualities and social goods have their own spheres of operation, where they work their effects freely, spontaneously, and legitimately. There are ready or natural conversions that follow from, and are intuitively plausible because of, the social meaning of particular goods. The appeal is to our ordinary understanding and, at the same time, against our common acquiescence in illegitimate conversion patterns. Or, it is an appeal from our acquiescence to our resentment. There is something wrong, Pascal suggests, with the conversion of strength into belief. In political terms, Pascal means that no ruler can rightly command my opinions merely because of the power he wields. Nor can he, Marx adds, rightly claim to influence my actions: if a ruler wants to do that, he must be persuasive, helpful, encouraging, and so on. These arguments depend for their force on some shared understanding of knowledge, influence, and power. Social goods have social meanings, and we find our way to distributive justice through an interpretation of those meanings. We search for principles internal to each distributive sphere.

The second claim is that the disregard of these principles is tyranny. To convert one good into another, when there is no intrinsic connection between the two, is to invade the sphere where another company of men and women properly rules. Monopoly is not inappropriate within the spheres. There is nothing wrong, for example, with the grip that persuasive and helpful men and women (politicians) establish on political power. But the use of political power to gain access to other goods is a tyrannical use. Thus, an old description of tyranny is generalized: princes become tyrants, according to medieval writers, when they seize the property or invade the family of their subjects. In political life—but more widely, too—the dominance of goods makes for the domination of people.

The regime of complex equality is the opposite of tyranny. It establishes a set of relationships such that domination is impossible. In formal terms, complex equality means that no citizen's standing in one sphere or with regard to one social good can be undercut by his standing in some other sphere, with regard to some other good. Thus, citizen X may be chosen over citizen Y for political office, and then the two of them will be unequal in the sphere of politics. But they will not be unequal generally so long as X's office gives him no advantages over Y in any other sphere—superior medical care, access to better schools for his children, entrepreneurial opportunities, and so on. So long as office is not a dominant good, is not generally convertible, office holders will stand, or at least can stand, in a relation of equality to the men and women they govern.

But what if dominance were eliminated, the autonomy of the spheres established—and the same people were successful in one sphere after another, triumphant in every company, piling up goods without the need for illegitimate conversions? This would certainly make for an inegalitarian society, but it would also suggest in the strongest way that a society of equals was not a lively possibility. I doubt that any egalitarian argument could survive in the face of such evidence. Here is a person whom we have freely chosen (without reference to his family ties or personal wealth) as our political representative. He is also a bold and inventive entrepreneur. When he was younger, he studied science, scored amazingly high grades in every exam, and made important discoveries. In war, he is surpassingly brave and wins the highest honors. Himself compassionate and compelling, he is loved by all who know him. Are there such people? Maybe so, but I have my doubts. We tell stories like the one I have just told, but the stories are fictions, the conversion of power or money or academic talent into legendary fame. In any case, there aren't enough such people to constitute a ruling class and dominate the rest of us. Nor can they be successful in every distributive sphere, for there are some spheres to which the idea of success doesn't pertain. Nor are their children likely, under conditions of complex equality, to inherit their success. By and large, the most accomplished politicians, entrepreneurs, scientists, soldiers, and lovers will be different people; and so long as the goods they possess don't bring other goods in train, we have no reason to fear their accomplishments.

The critique of dominance and domination points toward an open-ended distributive principle. *No social good* x *should be distributed to men and women who possess some other good* y *merely because they possess* y *and without regard to the meaning of* x. This is a principle that has probably been reiterated, at one time or another, for every y that has ever been dominant. But it has not often been stated in general terms. Pascal and Marx have suggested the application of the principle against all possible y's, and I shall attempt to work out that application. I shall be looking, then, not at the members of Pascal's companies—the strong or the weak, the handsome or the plain—but at the goods they share and divide. The purpose of the principle is to focus our attention; it doesn't determine the shares or the division. The principle directs us to study the meaning of social goods, to examine the different distributive spheres from the inside.

THREE DISTRIBUTIVE PRINCIPLES

The theory that results is unlikely to be elegant. No account of the meaning of a social good, or of the boundaries of the sphere within which it legitimately operates, will be uncontroversial. Nor is there any neat procedure for generating or testing different accounts. At best, the arguments will be rough, reflecting the diverse and conflict-ridden character of the social life that we seek simultaneously to understand and to regulate—but not to regulate until we understand. I shall set aside, then, all claims made on behalf of any single distributive criterion, for no such criterion can possibly match the diversity of social goods. Three criteria, however, appear to meet the requirements of the open-ended principle and have often been defended as the beginning and end of distributive justice, so I must say something about each of them. Free exchange, desert, and need: all three have real force, but none of them has force across the range of distributions. They are part of the story, not the whole of it.

Free Exchange

Free exchange is obviously open-ended; it guarantees no particular distributive outcome. At no point in any exchange process plausibly called "free" will it be possible to predict the particular division of social goods that will obtain at some later point. (It may be possible, however, to predict the general structure of the division.) In theory at least, free exchange creates a market within which all goods are convertible into all other goods through the neutral medium of money. There are no dominant goods and no monopolies. Hence the successive divisions that obtain will directly reflect the social meanings of the goods that are divided. For each bargain, trade, sale, and purchase will have been agreed to voluntarily by men and women who know what that meaning is, who are indeed its makers. Every exchange is a revelation of social meaning. By definition, then, no x will ever fall into the hands of someone who possesses y, merely because he possesses y and without regard to what x actually means to some other member of society. The market is radically pluralistic in its operations and its outcomes, infinitely sensitive to the meanings that individuals attach to goods. What possible restraints can be imposed on free exchange, then, in the name of pluralism?

But everyday life in the market, the actual experience of free exchange, is very different from what the theory suggests. Money, supposedly the neutral medium, is in practice a dominant good, and it is monopolized by people who possess a special talent for bargaining and trading—the green thumb of bourgeois society. Then other people demand a redistribution of money and the establishment of the regime of simple equality, and the search begins for some way to sustain that regime. But even if we focus on the first untroubled moment of simple equality—free exchange on the basis of equal shares—we will still need to set limits on what can be exchanged for what. For free exchange leaves distributions entirely in the hands of individuals, and social meanings are not subject, or are not always subject, to the interpretative decisions of individual men and women.

Consider an easy example, the case of political power. We can conceive of political power as a set of goods of varying value, votes, influence, offices, and so on. Any of these can be traded on the market and accumulated by individuals willing to sacrifice other goods. Even if the sacrifices are real, however, the result is a form of tyranny—petty tyranny, given the conditions of simple equality. Because I am willing to do without my hat, I shall vote twice; and you who value the vote less than you value my hat, will not vote at all. I suspect that the result is tyrannical even with regard to the two of us, who have reached a voluntary agreement. It is certainly tyrannical with regard to all the other citizens who must now submit to my disproportionate power. It is not the case that votes can't be bargained for; on one interpretation, that's what democratic politics is all about. And democratic politicians have certainly been known to buy votes, or to try to buy them, by promising public expenditures that benefit particular groups of voters. But this is done in public, with public funds, and subject to public approval. Private trading is ruled out by virtue of what politics, or democratic politics, is—that is, by virtue of what we did when we constituted the political community and of what we still think about what we did.

Free exchange is not a general criterion, but we will be able to specify the boundaries within which it operates only through a careful analysis of particular social goods. And having worked through such an analysis, we will come up at best with a philosophically authoritative set of boundaries and not necessarily with the set that ought to be politically authoritative. For money seeps across all boundaries—this is the primary form of illegal immigration; and just where one ought to try to stop it is a question of expediency as well as of principle. Failure to stop it at some reasonable point has consequences throughout the range of distributions, but consideration of these belongs in a later chapter.

Desert

Like free exchange, desert seems both open-ended and pluralistic. One might imagine a single neutral agency dispensing rewards and punishments, infinitely sensitive to all the forms of individual desert. Then the distributive process would indeed be centralized, but the results would still be unpredictable and various. There would be no dominant good. No x would ever be distributed without regard to its social meaning; for, without attention to what x is, it is conceptually impossible to say that x is deserved. All the different companies of men and women would receive their appropriate reward. How this would work in practice, however, is not easy to figure out. It might make sense to say of this charming man, for example, that he deserves to be loved. It makes no sense to say that he deserves to be loved by this (or any) particular woman. If he loves her while she remains impervious to his (real) charms, that is his misfortune. I doubt that we would want the situation corrected by some outside agency. The love of particular men and women, on our understanding of it, can only be distributed by themselves, and they are rarely guided in these matters by considerations of desert.

The case is exactly the same with influence. Here, let's say, is a woman widely thought to be stimulating and encouraging to others. Perhaps she deserves to be an influential member of our community. But she doesn't deserve that I be influenced by her or that I follow her lead. Nor would we want my followership, as it were, assigned to her by any agency capable of making such assignments. She may go to great lengths to stimulate and encourage me, and do all the things that are commonly called stimulating or encouraging. But if I (perversely) refuse to be stimulated or encouraged, I am not denying her anything that she deserves. The same argument holds by extension for politicians and ordinary citizens. Citizens can't trade their votes for hats; they can't individually decide to cross the boundary that separates the sphere of politics from the marketplace. But within the sphere of politics, they do make individual decisions; and they are rarely guided, again, by considerations of desert. It's not clear that offices can be deserved—another issue that I must postpone; but even if they can be, it would violate our understanding of democratic politics were they simply distributed to deserving men and women by some central agency.

Similarly, however we draw the boundaries of the sphere within which free exchange operates, desert will play no role within those boundaries. I am skillful at bargaining and trading, let's say, and so accumulate a large number of beautiful pictures. If we assume, as painters mostly do, that pictures are appropriately traded in the market, then there is nothing wrong with my having the pictures. My title is legitimate. But it would be odd to say that I deserve to have them simply because I am good at bargaining and trading. Desert seems to require an especially close connection between particular goods and particular persons, whereas justice only sometimes requires a connection of that sort. Still, we might insist that only artistically cultivated people, who deserve to have pictures, should actually have them. It's not difficult to imagine a distributive mechanism. The state could buy all the pictures that were offered for sale (but artists would have to be licensed, so that there wouldn't be an endless number of pictures), evaluate them, and then distribute them to artistically cultivated men and women, the better pictures to the more cultivated. The state does something like this, sometimes, with regard to things that people need—medical care, for example—but not with regard to things that people deserve. There are practical difficulties here, but I suspect a deeper reason for this difference. Desert does not have the urgency of need, and it does not involve having (owning and consuming) in the same way. Hence, we are willing to tolerate the separation of owners of paintings and artistically cultivated people, or we are unwilling to require the kinds of interference in the market that would be necessary to end the separation. Of course, public provision is always possible alongside the market, and so we might argue that artistically cultivated people deserve not pictures but museums. Perhaps they do, but they don't deserve that the rest of us contribute money or appropriate public funds for the purchase of pictures and the construction of buildings. They will have to persuade us that art is worth the money; they will have to stimulate and encourage our own artistic cultivation. And if they fail to do that, their own love of art may well turn out to be "impotent and a misfortune."

Even if we were to assign the distribution of love, influence, offices, works of art, and so on, to some omnipotent arbiters of desert, how would we select them? How could anyone deserve such a position? Only God, who knows what secrets lurk in the hearts of men, would be able to make the necessary distributions. If human beings had to do the work, the distributive mechanism would be seized early on by some band of aristocrats (so they would call themselves) with a fixed conception of what is best and most deserving, and insensitive to the diverse excellences of their fellow citizens. And then desert would cease to be a pluralist criterion; we would find ourselves face to face with a new set (of an old sort) of tyrants. We do, of course, choose people as arbiters of desert—to serve on juries, for example, or to award prizes; it will be worth considering later what the prerogatives of a juror are. But it is important to stress here that he operates within a narrow range. Desert is a strong claim, but it calls for difficult judgments; and only under very special conditions does it yield specific distributions.

Need

Finally, the criterion of need. "To each according to his needs" is generally taken as the distributive half of Marx's famous maxim: we are to distribute the wealth of the community so as to meet the necessities of its members. A plausible proposal, but a radically incomplete one. In fact, the first half of the maxim is also a distributive proposal, and it doesn't fit the rule of the second half. "From each according to his ability" suggests that jobs should be distributed (or that men and women should be conscripted to work) on the basis of individual qualifications. But individuals don't in any obvious sense need the jobs for which they are qualified. Perhaps such jobs are scarce, and there are a large number of qualified candidates: which candidates need them most? If their material needs are already taken care of, perhaps they don't need to work at all. Or if, in some nonmaterial sense, they all need to work, then that need won't distinguish among them, at least not to the naked eye. It would in any case be odd to ask a search committee looking, say, for a hospital director to make its choice on the basis of the needs of the candidates rather than on those of the staff and the patients of the hospital. But the latter set of needs, even if it isn't the subject of political disagreement, won't yield a single distributive decision.

Nor will need work for many other goods. Marx's maxim doesn't help at all with regard to the distribution of political power, honor and fame, sailboats, rare books, beautiful objects of every sort. These are not things that anyone, strictly speaking, needs. Even if we take a loose view and define the verb to *need* the way children do, as the strongest form of the verb to *want*, we still won't have an adequate distributive criterion. The sorts of things that I have listed cannot be distributed equally to those with equal wants because some of them are generally, and some of them are necessarily, scarce, and some of them can't be possessed at all unless other people, for reasons of their own, agree on who is to possess them.

Need generates a particular distributive sphere, within which it is itself the appropriate distributive principle. In a poor society, a high proportion of social wealth will be drawn into this sphere. But given the great variety of goods that arises out of any common life, even when it is lived at a very low material level, other distributive criteria will always be operating alongside of need, and it will always be necessary to worry about the boundaries that mark them off from one another. Within its sphere, certainly, need meets the general distributive rule about x and y. Needed goods distributed to needy people in proportion to their neediness are obviously not dominated by any other goods. It's not having y, but only lacking x that is relevant. But we can now see, I think, that every criterion that has any force at all meets the general rule within its own sphere, and not elsewhere. This is the effect of the rule: different goods to different companies of men and women for different reasons and in accordance with different procedures. And to get all this right, or to get it roughly right, is to map out the entire social world.

HIERARCHIES AND CASTE SOCIETIES

Or, rather, it is to map out a particular social world. For the analysis that I propose is imminent and phenomenological in character. It will yield not an ideal map or a master plan but, rather, a map and a plan appropriate to the people for whom it is drawn, whose common life it reflects. The goal, of course, is a reflection of a special kind, which picks up those deeper understandings of social goods which are not necessarily mirrored in the everyday practice of dominance and monopoly. But what if there are no such understandings? I have been assuming all along that social meanings call for the autonomy, or the relative autonomy, of distributive spheres; and so they do much of the time. But it's not impossible to imagine a society where dominance and monopoly are not violations but enactments of meaning, where social goods are conceived in hierarchical terms. In feudal Europe, for example, clothing was not a commodity (as it is today) but a badge of rank. Rank dominated dress. The meaning of clothing was shaped in the image of the feudal order. Dressing in finery to which one wasn't entitled was a kind of lie; it made a false statement about who one was. When a king or a prime minister dressed as a commoner in order to learn something about the opinions of his subjects, this was a kind of politic deceit. On the other hand, the difficulties of enforcing the clothing code (the sumptuary laws) suggests that there was all along an alternative sense of what clothing meant. At some point, at least, one can begin to recognize the boundaries of a distinct sphere within which people dress in accordance with what they can afford or what they are willing to spend or how they want to look. The sumptuary laws may still be enforced, but now one can make—and ordinary men and women do, in fact, make—egalitarian arguments against them.

Can we imagine a society in which all goods are hierarchically conceived? Perhaps the caste system of ancient India had this form (though that is a far-reaching claim, and it would be prudent to doubt its truth: for one thing, political power seems always to have escaped the laws of caste). We think of castes as rigidly segregated groups, of the caste system as a "plural society," a world of boundaries. But the system is constituted by an extraordinary integration of meanings. Prestige, wealth, knowledge, office, occupation, food, clothing, even the social good of conversation: all are subject to the intellectual as well as to the physical discipline of hierarchy. And the hierarchy is itself determined by the single value of ritual purity. A certain kind of collective mobility is possible, for castes or subcastes can cultivate the outward marks of purity and (within severe limits) raise their position in the social scale. And the system as a whole rests upon a religious doctrine that promises equality of opportunity, not in this life but across the lives of the soul. The individual's status here and now "is the result of his conduct in his last incarnation . . . and if unsatisfactory can be remedied by acquiring merit in his present life which will raise his status in the next." We should not assume that men and women are ever entirely content with radical inequality. Nevertheless, distributions here and now are part of a single system, largely unchallenged, in which purity is dominant over other goods—and birth and blood are dominant over purity. Social meanings overlap and cohere.

The more perfect the coherence, the less possible it is even to think about complex equality. All goods are like crowns and thrones in a hereditary monarchy. There is no room, and there are no criteria, for autonomous distributions. In fact, however, even hereditary monarchies are rarely so simply constructed. The social understanding of royal power commonly involves some notion of divine grace, or magical gift, or human insight; and these criteria for office holding are potentially independent of birth and blood. So it is for most social goods: they are only imperfectly integrated into larger systems; they are understood, at least sometimes, in their own terms. The theory of goods explicates understandings of this sort (where they exist), and the theory of complex equality exploits them. We say, for example, that it is tyrannical for a man without grace or gift or insight to sit upon the throne. And this is only the first and most obvious kind of tyranny. We can search for many other kinds.

Tyranny is always specific in character: a particular boundary crossing, a particular violation of social meaning. Complex equality requires the defense of boundaries; it works by differentiating goods just as hierarchy works by differentiating people. But we can only talk of a *regime* of complex equality when there are many boundaries to defend; and what the right number is cannot be specified. There is no right number. Simple equality is easier: one dominant good widely distributed makes an egalitarian society. But complexity is hard: how many goods must be autonomously conceived before the relations they mediate can become the relations of equal men and women? There is no certain answer and hence no ideal regime. But as soon as we start to distinguish meanings and mark out distributive spheres, we are launched on an egalitarian enterprise.

APPENDIX

APPENDIX

Harrison Bergeron
KURT VONNEGUT, JR.

The year was 2081, and everybody was finally equal. They weren't only equal before God and the law. They were equal every which way. Nobody was smarter than anybody else. Nobody was better looking than anybody else. Nobody was stronger or quicker than anybody else. All this equality was due to the 211th, 212th, and 213th Amendments to the Constitution, and to the unceasing vigilance of agents of the United States Handicapper General.

Some things about living still weren't quite right, though. April, for instance, still drove people crazy by not being springtime. And it was in that clammy month that the H-G men took George and Hazel Bergeron's fourteen-year-old son, Harrison, away.

It was tragic, all right, but George and Hazel couldn't think about it very hard. Hazel had a perfectly average intelligence, which meant she couldn't think about anything except in short bursts. And George, while his intelligence was way above normal, had a little mental handicap radio in his ear. He was required by law to wear it at all times. It was tuned to a government transmitter. Every twenty seconds or so, the transmitter would send out some sharp noise to keep people like George from taking unfair advantage of their brains.

George and Hazel were watching television. There were tears on Hazel's cheeks, but she'd forgotten for the moment what they were about.

On the television screen were ballerinas.

A buzzer sounded in George's head. His thoughts fled in panic, like bandits from a burglar alarm.

"That was a real pretty dance, that dance they just did," said Hazel.

"Huh?" said George.

"The dance—it was nice," said Hazel.

"Yup," said George. He tried to think a little about the ballerinas. They weren't really very good—no better than anybody else would have been, anyway. They were burdened with sash-weights and bags of birdshot, and their faces were masked, so that no one, seeing a free and graceful gesture or a pretty face, would feel like something the cat drug in. George was toying with the vague notion that maybe dancers shouldn't be handicapped. But he didn't get very far with it before another noise in his ear radio scattered his thoughts.

George winced. So did two out of the eight ballerinas.

Hazel saw him wince. Having no mental handicap herself, she had to ask George what the latest sound had been.

"Sounded like someone hitting a milk bottle with a ball peen hammer," said George.

"I'd think it would be real interesting, hearing all the different sounds," said Hazel, a little envious. "All the things they think up."

"Um," said George.

"Only, if I was Handicapper General, you know what I would do?" said Hazel. Hazel, as a matter of fact, bore a strong resemblance to the Handicapper General, a woman named Diana Moon Glampers. "If I was Diana Moon Glampers," said Hazel, "I'd have chimes on

Sunday—just chimes. Kind of in honor of religion."

"I could think, if it was just chimes," said George.

"Well—maybe make 'em real loud," said Hazel. "I think I'd make a good Handicapper General."

"Good as anybody else," said George.

"Who knows better'n I do what normal is?" said Hazel.

"Right," said George. He began to think glimmeringly about his abnormal son who was now in jail, about Harrison, but a twenty-one-gun salute in his head stopped that.

"Boy!" said Hazel, "that was a doozy, wasn't it?"

It was such a doozy that George was white and trembling, and tears stood on the rims of his red eyes. Two of the eight ballerinas had collapsed to the studio floor, were holding their temples.

"All of a sudden you look so tired," said Hazel. "Why don't you stretch out on the sofa, so's you can rest your handicap bag on the pillows, honeybunch." She was referring to the forty-seven pounds of birdshot in a canvas bag, which was padlocked around George's neck. "Go on and rest the bag for a little while," she said. "I don't care if you're not equal to me for a while."

George weighed the bag with his hands. "I don't mind it," he said." I don't notice it any more. It's just a part of me."

"You've been so tired lately—kind of wore out," said Hazel. "If there was just some way we could make a little hole in the bottom of the bag, and just take out a few of them lead balls. Just a few."

"Two years in prison and two thousand dollars fine for every ball I took out," said George. "I don't call that a bargain."

"If you could just take a few out when you came home from work," said Hazel. "I mean—you don't compete with anybody around here. You just sit around."

"If I tried to get away with it," said George, "then other people'd get away with it—and pretty soon we'd be right back to the dark ages again, with everybody competing against everybody else. You wouldn't like that, would you?"

"I'd hate it," said Hazel.

"There you are," said George. "The minute people start cheating on laws, what do you think happens to society?"

If Hazel hadn't been able to come up with an answer to this question, George couldn't have supplied one. A siren was going off in his head.

"Reckon it'd fall all apart," said Hazel.

"What would?" said George blankly.

"Society," said Hazel uncertainly. "Wasn't that what you just said?"

"Who knows?" said George.

The television program was suddenly interrupted for a news bulletin. It wasn't clear at first as to what the bulletin was about, since the announcer, like all announcers, had a serious speech impediment. For about half a minute, and in a state of high excitement, the announcer tried to say, "Ladies and gentlemen—"

He finally gave up, handed the bulletin to a ballerina to read.

"That's all right—" Hazel said of the announcer, "he tried. That's the big thing. He tried to do the best he could with what God gave him. He should get a nice raise for trying so hard."

"Ladies and gentlemen—" said the ballerina, reading the bulletin. She must have been extraordinarily beautiful, because the mask she wore was hideous. And it was easy to see that she was the strongest and most graceful of the dancers, for her handicap bags were as big as those worn by two-hundred-pound men.

And she had to apologize at once for her voice, which was a very unfair voice for a woman to use. Her voice was a warm, luminous, timeless melody. "Excuse me—" she said, and she began again, making her voice absolutely uncompetitive.

"Harrison Bergeron, age fourteen," she said in a grackle squawk, "has just escaped from jail, where he was held on suspicion of plotting to overthrow the government. He is a genius and an athlete, is under-handicapped, and should be regarded as extremely dangerous."

A police photograph of Harrison Bergeron was flashed on the screen—upside down, then sideways, upside down again, then right side up. The picture showed the full length of Harrison against a background calibrated in feet and inches. He was exactly seven feet tall.

The rest of Harrison's appearance was Halloween and hardware. Nobody had ever borne heavier handicaps. He had outgrown hindrances faster than the H-G men could think them up. Instead of a little ear radio for a mental handicap, he wore a tremendous pair of earphones, and spectacles with thick wavy lenses. The spectacles were intended to make him not only half blind, but to give him whanging headaches besides.

Scrap metal was hung all over him. Ordinarily, there was a certain symmetry, a military neatness to the handicaps issued to strong people, but Harrison looked like a walking junkyard. In the race of life, Harrison carried three hundred pounds.

And to offset his good looks, the H-G men required that he wear at all times a red rubber ball for a nose, keep his eyebrows shaved off, and cover his even white teeth with black caps at snaggle-tooth random.

"If you see this boy," said the ballerina, "do not—repeat, do not—try to reason with him."

There was the shriek of a door being torn from its hinges.

Screams and barking cries of consternation came from the television set. The photograph of Harrison Bergeron on the screen jumped again and again, as though dancing to the tune of an earthquake.

George Bergeron correctly identified the earthquake, and well he might have—for many was the time his own home had danced to the same crashing tune. "My God—" said George, "that must be Harrison!"

The realization was blasted from his mind instantly by the sound of an automobile collision in his head.

When George could open his eyes again, the photograph of Harrison was gone. A living, breathing Harrison filled the screen.

Clanking, clownish, and huge, Harrison stood in the center of the studio. The knob of the uprooted studio door was still in his hand. Ballerinas, technicians, musicians, and announcers cowered on their knees before him, expecting to die.

"I am the Emperor!" cried Harrison. "Do you hear? I am the Emperor! Everybody must do what I say at once!" He stamped his foot and the studio shook.

"Even as I stand here—" he bellowed, "crippled, hobbled, sickened—I am a greater ruler than any man who ever lived! Now watch me become what I *can* become!"

Harrison tore the straps of his handicap harness like wet tissue paper, tore straps guaranteed to support five thousand pounds.

Harrison's scrap-iron handicaps crashed to the floor.

Harrison thrust his thumbs under the bar of the padlock that secured his head harness. The bar snapped like celery. Harrison smashed his headphones and spectacles against the wall.

He flung away his rubber-ball nose, revealed a man that would have awed Thor, the god of thunder.

"I shall now select my Empress!" he said, looking down on the cowering people. "Let the first woman who dares rise to her feet claim her mate and her throne!"

A moment passed, and then a ballerina arose, swaying like a willow.

Harrison plucked the mental handicap from her ear, snapped off her physical handicaps with marvelous delicacy. Last of all, he removed her mask.

She was blindingly beautiful.

"Now—" said Harrison, taking her hand, "shall we show the people the meaning of the word dance? Music!" he commanded.

The musicians scrambled back into their chairs, and Harrison stripped them of their handicaps, too. "Play your best," he told them, "and I'll make you barons and dukes and earls."

The music began. It was normal at first—cheap, silly, false. But Harrison snatched two musicians from their chairs, waved them like batons as he sang the music as he wanted it played. He slammed them back into their chairs.

The music began again and was much improved.

Harrison and his Empress merely listened to the music for a while—listened gravely, as though synchronizing their heartbeats with it.

They shifted their weights to their toes.

Harrison placed his big hands on the girl's tiny waist, letting her sense the weightlessness that would soon be hers.

And then, in an explosion of joy and grace, into the air they sprang!

Not only were the laws of the land abandoned, but the law of gravity and the laws of motion as well.

They reeled, whirled, swiveled, flounced, capered, gamboled, and spun.

They leaped like deer on the moon.

The studio ceiling was thirty feet high, but each leap brought the dancers nearer to it.

It became their obvious intention to kiss the ceiling.

They kissed it.

And then, neutralizing gravity with love and pure will, they remained suspended in air inches below the ceiling, and they kissed each other for a long, long time.

It was then that Diana Moon Glampers, the Handicapper General, came into the studio with a double-barreled ten-gauge shotgun. She fired twice, and the Emperor and the Empress were dead before they hit the floor.

Diana Moon Glampers loaded the gun again. She aimed it at the musicians and told them they had ten seconds to get their handicaps back on.

It was then that the Bergeron's television tube burned out.

Hazel turned to comment about the blackout to George. But George had gone out into the kitchen for a can of beer.

George came back in with the beer, paused while a handicap signal shook him up. And then he sat down again. "You been crying?" he said to Hazel.

"Yup," she said.

"What about?" he said.

"I forget," she said. "Something real sad on television."

"What was it?" he said.

"It's all kind of mixed up in my mind," said Hazel.

"Forget sad things," said George.

"I always do," said Hazel.

"That's my girl," said George. He winced. There was the sound of a rivetting gun in his head.

"Gee—I could tell that one was a doozy," said Hazel.

"You can say that again," said George.

"Gee—" said Hazel, "I could tell that one was a doozy."

Bibliography

Abernethy, G. L., ed. *The Idea of Equality: An Anthology*. Richmond, Va., 1959.

Ackerman, Bruce. *Social Justice in the Liberal State*. New Haven: Yale University Press, 1980.

Alexander, Larry, and Maimon Schwarzchild. "Liberalism, Neutrality, and Equality of Welfare vs Equality of Resource," *Philosophy and Public Affairs* 16:1 (Winter 1987): 85–110.

Arneson, Richard J. "Against Complex Equality," *Public Affairs Quarterly*, vol. 4.2, April 1990.

———. "Equality." *A Companion to Contemporary Political Philosophy*, edited by Robert Goodin and Philip Pettit (Basil Blackwell, 1993).

———. "Equality and Equal Opportunity for Welfare," *Philosophical Studies*, 1989, pp. 77–93.

———. "Liberalism, Distributive Subjectivism, and Equal Opportunity for Welfare," *Philosophy and Public Affairs* 19:2 (Spring 1992): 158–194.

Beardsley, Monroe. "Equality and Obedience to Law," *The Concept of Equality*, edited by W. T. Blackstone (Burgess, 1960).

Bedau, Hugo Adam. "Egalitarianism and the Idea of Equality." *Nomos IX Equality*, edited by J. Roland Pennock and John W. Chapman, (New York: Atherton Press, 1967), pp. 3–27.

Benn, Stanley I. "Egalitarianism and the Equal Consideration of Interests," *Nomos IX: Equality*, edited by J. Roland Pennock and John W. Chapman (New York: Atherton Press, 1967) pp. 38–60.

———. "Equality, Moral and Social," *Encyclopedia of Philosophy*. New York: Macmillan and Free Press, 1967; vol. 3, pp. 38–41.

Berlin, Isaiah. "Equality as an Ideal," *Justice and Social Policy*, edited by Frederick A. Olafson (Englewood Cliffs, N.J.: Prentice-Hall, 1961), pp. 128–150.

Bowie, Norman, ed. *Equal Opportunity*. Boulder, Colo.: Westview, 1988.

Carrit, E. F. "Liberty and Equality," *Law Quarterly Review* 56 (1940): 61–74. Reprinted in Anthony Quinton, ed. *Political Philosophy*. Oxford: Oxford University Press, 1967.

Charvet, John. "The Idea of Equality as a Substantive Principle in Society," *Political Studies* 17 (March 1969): 1–13.

Cohen, G. A. "Self-Ownership, World-Ownership, and Equality," in *Justice and Equality Here and Now*, edited by F. Lucash (Ithaca: Cornell University Press, 1986).

———. "On the Currency of Egalitarian Justice," *Ethics* 99 (1989): 906–944.

Dworkin, Ronald. *A Matter of Principle*. Harvard University Press, 1985.

———. "What is Equality?" "Part 1, Equality of Welfare," and "Part 2, Equality of Resources." *Philosophy and Public Affairs* 10: 3, 4 (Summer and Fall, 1981): 185–246, 283–345.

———. "Comments on Narveson: In Defense of Equality," *Social Philosophy and Policy* 1 (1983): 24–40.

———. "Why Liberals Should Care About Equality," *The New York Review of Books*, February 3, 1983. Reprinted in Ronald Dworkin, *A Matter of Principle* (Harvard University Press, 1983).

Fishkin, James. *Justice, Equal Opportunity and the Family*. Yale University Press, 1983.

———. "Liberty versus Equal Opportunity," *Social Philosophy and Policy*, 5.1 (Autumn 1987): 32–48.

Flathman, Richard. "Equality and Generalization, a Formal Analysis," *Nomos*, op. cit., pp. 38–60.

Flew, Antony. *The Politics of Procrustes: Contradictions of Enforced Equality*. Buffalo, N.Y.: Prometheus Books, 1981.

Frankfurt, Harry. "Equality as a Moral Ideal," *Ethics* 98 (1987): 21–43.

Gellner, Ernest. "The Social Roots of Egalitarianism," in *Culture, Identity and Politics*. Cambridge University Press, 1987.

Green, S. J. D. "Competitive Equality of

Opportunity: A Defense," *Ethics* 100 (1989): 5–32.

Gutmann, Amy. *Liberal Equality*. Cambridge University Press, 1980.

Hare, R. M. "Justice and Equality," *Justice and Economic Distribution*, edited by John Arthur and William H. Shaw (Englewood Cliffs, N.J.: Prentice-Hall, 1978).

Jencks, Christopher et al. *Inequality: A Reassessment of the Effect of Family and Schooling in America*. New York: Basic Books, 1972.

Kristol, Irving. "About Equality," Commentary 54 (November 1972): 41–47.

Kymlicka, Will. *Liberalism, Community and Culture*. Oxford University Press, 1989.

———. *Contemporary Political Philosophy*. Oxford University Press, 1990.

Landesman, Bruce. "Egalitarianism," *Canadian Journal of Philosophy* 8.1 (March 1983).

Lakoff, Sanford. *Equality in Political Philosophy*. Boston: Beacon Press, 1964.

Letwin, William, ed. *Against Equality*. London: Macmillan, 1983.

Levin, Michael E. "Equality of Opportunity," *Philosophical Quarterly* 31: 123 (April 1981): 110–125.

Lucas, J. R. "Against Equality," *Philosophy* 40 (1965): 296–307.

———. "Against Equality Again," in *Against Equality*, edited by William Letwin (London: Macmillan, 1983).

Mora, Gonzolo Fernandez. *Egalitarian Envy: The Political Foundations of Social Justice*, translated by Antonio T. de Nicolas (New York: Paragon House, 1987).

Margolis, Joseph. " 'That All Men Are Created Equal' " *Journal of Philosophy*, 52, no. 13 (1955): 337–346.

McKerlie, Dennis. "Equality and Time," *Ethics* 99 (1989): 475–491.

Nagel, Thomas. *Mortal Questions*. Cambridge University Press, 1979.

———. *Equality and Partiality*. Oxford University Press, 1991.

Narveson, Jan. "On Dworkinian Equality," *Social Philosophy and Policy* 1 (1983): 1–23.

Nielsen, Kai. *Equality and Liberty: A Defense of Radical Egalitarianism*. Totowa, N.J.: Rowman and Allanheld, 1985.

Norman, Richard. *Free and Equal: A Philosophical Examination of Political Values*. Oxford: Clarendon Press, 1987.

———. "Equality Is Compatible with Liberty," in *Contemporary Political Philosophy*, edited by Keith Graham (Cambridge University Press, 1982).

Nussbaum, Martha, and Amartya Sen, eds. *The Quality of Life*. Oxford: Clarendon Press, 1993.

Oppenheim, Felix E. "Egalitarianism as a Descriptive Concept," *American Philosophical Quarterly* 7 (1970): 143–152.

Phelps Brown, Henry. *Egalitarianism and the Generation of Inequality*. Oxford University Press, 1988.

Pogge, Thomas W. "An Egalitarian Law of Peoples," *Philosophy and Public Affairs*, 23:3 (Summer 1994): 195–224.

Pole, J. R. *The Pursuit of Equality in American History*. Cambridge University Press, 1978.

Pojman, Louis. "A Critique of Contemporary Egalitarianism: A Christian Perspective," *Faith and Philosophy* 8:4 (October 1991): 481–504.

———. "Are Equal Rights Founded on Equal Human Worth?" *Philosophy and Phenomenological Research* (October 1992).

———. "Co-operation and Equality," *Philosophy* (January, 1996).

———. "Theories of Equality: A Critical Analysis," *Behavior and Philosophy* (Summer, 1995).

Rae, Douglas. *Equalities*. Cambridge: Harvard University Press, 1981.

Rakowski, Eric. *Equal Justice*. Oxford University Press, 1992.

Rawls, John. *A Theory of Justice*. Harvard University Press, 1971.

———. "A Kantian Conception of Equality," *Cambridge Review* 96, 2225 (February 1975).

Raz, Joseph. "Principles of Equality," *Mind* 87 (1978): 321–342.

Rees, John. *Equality*. New York: Praeger, 1971.

Roemer, John E. "Equality of Talent," *Economics and Philosophy*: 1 (1985): 151–187.

Rosenberg, Alexander. "The Political Philosophy of Biological Endowments: Some Considerations," *Social Philosophy and Policy*, 5.1 (Autumn 1987): 1–31.

Rousseau, Jean-Jacques. *The Social Contract*. 1762.

———. *Discourse on the Origin of Inequality among Men*. 1755.

Schaar, John. "Equality of Opportunity and Beyond," *Nomos IX: Equality*, edited by R. Pennock and J. Chapman (New York: Atherton Press, 1967), pp. 228–249.

Sen, Amartya. *On Economic Equality*. New York:

Norton, 1973.

———. "Equality of What?" *The Tanner Lectures on Human Values*, vol. 1, The University of Utah, 1980.

———. *Inequality Reexamined*. Oxford: Clarendon Press, 1992.

Sikora, R. I. "Six Viewpoints for Assessing Egalitarian Distribution Schemes," *Ethics* 99 (1989): 492–502.

Spiegelberg, Herbert. "A Defence of Human Equality," *Philosophical Review*, 53, no. 2 (1944): 101–124.

Steiner, Hillel. "Capitalism, Justice and Equal Starts," *Social Philosophy and Policy*, 5.1 (Autumn 1987), 49–72.

Temkin, Larry S. "Inequality," *Philosophy and Public Affairs* 15 (1986): 99–121.

———. *Inequality*. Oxford University Press, 1993.

Thomas, D. A. Lloyd. "Competitive Equality of Opportunity," *Mind* 86:343 (July 1977):388–404.

———. "Equality within the Limits of Reason Alone," *Mind* 88:352 (October 1979): 538–553.

Thomson, David. *The Babeuf Plot*. London: Kegan Paul, 1947.

———. *Equality*. Cambridge: Cambridge University Press, 1949.

Tocqueville, Alexis de. *Democracy in America*, translated by T. Lawrence and edited by J. P. Mayer (New York: HarperCollins, 1988).

Vlastos, Gregory. "Justice and Equality," in *Social Justice*, edited by Richard B. Brandt (Englewood Cliffs, N.J. Prentice-Hall, 1962), pp. 31–72.

Walzer, Michael. *Spheres of Justice: A Defense of Pluralism and Equality*. Basic Books, 1983.

———. "In Defense of Equality," *Dissent* (Fall 1973): 399–408.

Westen, Peter. *Speaking of Equality*. Princeton: Princeton University Press, 1990.

———. "The Concept of Equal Opportunity," *Ethics* 95 (July 1985).

———. "The Empty Idea of Equality," *Harvard Law Review* 95.1 (1982): 537–596.

Westmoreland, Robert. "The Hobbesian Roots of Contemporary Liberalism," *Faith and Philosophy* 8.4 (October 1991).

Wildavsky, Aaron. *The Rise of Radical Egalitarianism*. Washington, D.C.: The American University Press, 1991.

Young, Michael. "Is Equality a Dream?" *Dissent* (Fall 1973): 415–422.

Wilson, John. *Equality*. London: Hutchinson, 1966.

Index

Ackerman, Bruce, 171
Affirmative Action, 1, 12, 154, 201f
Aristotle, 2, 3, 6, 7, 12, 13, 17–26, 56–60, 64, 94, 97, 121, 127, 219–223, 283, 286, 289
Arneson, Richard J., 3, 11–13, 229–41, 245–49, 299
Arthur, John, 13
Audi, Robert, 299

Babeuf, Francois-Noel, 3, 6, 13, 49–52
Barry, Brian, 240
Beardsley, Monroe, 64, 283
Benn, Stanley, 3, 7, 112–120, 283
Bentham, Jeremy, 10, 221, 288, 291
Berlin, Isaiah, 3, 57, 64
Blackeley, Donald, 299
Blackstone, W. T., 59, 64

Campbell, T.A., 159, 167
Carrit, E. F., 283
Cohen, G. A., 13
Conservative, 4, 138, 170, 208

Daniels, Norman, 213, 289
Davies, J. C., 116, 120
DeMarco, Joseph, 13
Democracy, 5, 6, 24, 49, 55, 121, 141–44, 185, 206, 296
Desert, 4, 12, 58, 59, 215, 223, 300, 308–9 (See also Merit)
Difference Principle, 9, 185–9, 202, 211–12, 270, 292
Diminishing Marginal Utility, 11, 223–27, 264–8, 288–9
Dworkin, Ronald, 1, 9–12, 65, 74, 171, 203, 212, 229, 234–5, 237, 268–69, 279–85, 296–299

Egalitarian, 1, 4, 9, 13, 55–65, 71–74, 80, 105–120, 204–217, 229–35, 242–47, 253, 256–63, 266–71, 274, 279, 282–290, 292–299, 311
  Radical Egalitarianism, 204–17, 285
Engels, Friedrich, 4, 13

Envy, 5–6, 226–27
Equal Opportunity, 1, 7–8, 11, 12, 57, 62–63, 100, 137–179
Equal Opportunity for Welfare, 11, 299–41, 244–45
Equal Outcomes, 12
Equal Respect, 7
Equality
  Absolute, 49–52, 101
  Complex, 11, 304–7, 311
  (of) Condition, 205
  Defined, 55–65
  Economic, 4, 261–73
  Equal Consideration, 2, 112
  Equal Worth, 1, 9, 11, 12, 120–133, 282–299
  Formal, 2, 3, 6, 12, 105
  Legal, 4, 105–108, 121, 205
  Manifesto of, 6, 49–52
  Natural, 30
  Percentage, 60
  Political, 4, 205
  Procedural, 60
  Proportionate, 57–58
  Rhetoric (of), 8, 142
  Resource, 5, 9, 207, 229–32, 235f, 274–81
  Simple, 11, 303f
  Social, 4, 132
  Substantive, 2, 3, 12, 222
  (of) Treatment, 56
  (of) Wealth, 62
  Welfare, 2, 5, 9–10, 75–76, 204–17, 232–3, 242–50

Family, 8, 9, 151–58
Feinberg, Joel, 191, 203, 287–288
Fishkin, James S., 8, 148–58, 167
Frankena, William, 64, 127, 132
Frankfurt, Harry, 11, 261–75, 281, 289, 293, 298
Fraternity, 104–111, 188
Freedom. *See* Liberty
Fried, Charles, 119–120
Friedman, Milton, 202–4

Galston, William, 8, 170–9
Gauthier, David, 286, 298

Gender, 8, 105, 163–4
Gewirth, Alan, 290–292, 298
Ginsberg, Morris, 64
God, 2, 36, 94, 105, 282, 292–297
Goodman, Evan, 299
Green, Ronald, 282, 297

Happiness, 10
Hare, R. M., 4, 5, 9, 10, 218–229, 283, 288
Hayek, F. A., 204
Hobbes, Thomas, 6, 26–36, 55, 64, 122, 195, 283
Hospers, John, 65
Human Worth, 1, 9–12, 27, 120–133, 282–99
Hume, David, 2, 6, 13, 46–49, 122

Inegalitarian. See Inequality
Inequality, 1, 5, 6, 37–45, 65–88, 137, 261–73,
    282–299
Injustice, 1, 2, 18, 19, 46, 87, 115, 132, 151, 193,
    245

Jefferson, Thomas, 1, 122
Jencks, Christopher, 5, 13
Justice, 2–4, 7–12, 80, 102–104, 107, 112–115,
    117–122, 130–33, 167, 170–173, 179,
    183–193, 195–197, 199–228, 248–49, 253,
    255–56, 274–75, 279–81, 293–95, 297,
    299–303
  In Aristotle, 17–26
  In Hume, 46–49
  Distributive, 17
  (as) Fairness, 183–190
  Rectificatory, 17, 20, 25

Kant, Immanuel, 12, 94, 127, 183, 217, 254–8,
    282, 293
Kymlicka, Will, 1, 2, 13, 282

LaFollette, Hugh, 13
Law, 3, 32–33, 104
Lawrence, D. H., 147
Levin, Michael, 167, 299
Liberal (Liberalism), 4, 9, 141, 148–58, 170–9, 202
Libertarianism, 204, 282, 285–6
Liberty (and Freedom), 1, 9, 12, 32, 37, 55,
    104–111, 127, 133, 174–175, 206, 210, 227
Locke, John, 9, 106, 122–23, 148–49, 183, 195,
    202, 298
Lockean, 9, 148–49
Lucas, J. R., 3, 7, 60, 64, 104–115, 204

Machan, Tibor, 285–286
Mackie, J. L., 282

Marechal, Sylvan, 3, 6, 49–52
Maritan, Jacques, 282
Marx, Karl, 4, 12, 50, 58, 64, 301, 305–7
Marxist, 10, 282, 290
Matson, Wallace, 9, 191–203
McKerlie, Dennis, 6, 65–75
Merit (meritocracy), 7, 9, 12, 63–64, 95, 121–25,
    130–31, 148–58, 177, 216, 302f
Miller, David, 217

Napoleon, 7
Nagel, Thomas, 4, 1, 13, 203, 250–61, 269–71,
    290–92
Need, 63, 122–4, 261–73, 283, 309–10
Nielsen, Kai, 3, 4, 9, 10, 14, 204–217, 284–5,
    289–90, 298
Nietzsche, Friedrich, 199, 217, 285
Norman, Richard, 4
Nozick, Robert, 7–8, 87, 102–104, 148–49, 167–9,
    178–79, 204, 208, 221–22, 285

O'Neill, Onora, 7, 14, 167
Oppenheim, Felix, 6, 55–65

Pareto Principle, 294
Parfit, Derek, 67, 74, 87
Pascal, Blaise, 305–7
Personal and Impersonal Standpoint, 250–6, 290
Peters, R. S., 283
Plantinga, Alvin, 284
Plato, 7, 17, 58, 121–22, 127–28, 225, 254, 283,
    288, 296
Pojman, Louis, 11, 282–299
Presumption of Equality, 283–84

Rainborough, Maj. William, 5
Race, 4, 57–59, 92, 126, 154, 158, 163–64, 189
Rachels, James, 284
Rakowski, Eric, 3, 9–13, 242–50, 274–81
Rawls, John, 3, 8–9, 12, 74, 75, 87, 117–120, 158,
    171, 179, 183–191, 200–2, 208–17, 219–22,
    229, 235–8, 253, 256–61, 274–89, 291–98
Respect, 94–95, 105–111, 190–91, 211–12, 293
Richards, David, 219
Richmond, Samuel A., 13
Rights, 1, 32, 33, 49–52, 56, 104, 121–133,
    160–61, 168–69, 207, 224–25, 276, 282f, 288,
    294
Rousseau, Jean-Jacques, 4, 6, 12, 36–45, 183
Rowe, William, 299

Sandel, Michael, 292
Scanlon, Thomas, 10, 14, 231, 238, 261
Schaar, John, 7–8, 64–65, 137–47, 178–79

Sen, Amartya, 236–8
Sidgwick, Henry, 75
Singer, Peter, 282, 288–89
Socrates, 292
State of Nature, 37
Stoicism, 296

Tawney, R. H., 158, 167
Temkin, Larry, 6, 75–88
Time, 6, 65–75
Tocqueville, Alex de, 5, 13, 14, 141, 147

Utilitarian, 10, 64, 66, 70, 74, 82, 200, 216, 242–43, 288–89

Vlastos, Gregory, 7, 12, 120–133, 286–288, 294, 298
Von Leydon, W., 64
Vonnegut, Kurt, 5, 11, 315–318

Walzer, Michael, 11, 12, 299–311
Wasserstrom, Richard, 203
Watson, Richard, 5, 13
Westen, Peter, 8, 158–67
Westmoreland, Robert, 299
Williams, Bernard, 3, 7, 59, 64, 91–104, 179

Young, Michael, 139, 147, 303